THE HOWARD MARKS
BOOK OF DOPE STORIES

Born in 1945 in Kenfig Hill, a small Welsh coal-mining village near Bridgend, Howard Marks rose through Oxford University and the British Secret Service to become 'the most sophisticated drugs baron of all time' (*Daily Mirror*). In 1996 Howard wrote his auto-biography, *Mr Nice*, which remains an international bestseller in several languages.

In 1997, Howard performed his first live shows which received excellent reviews throughout the national press, and his now legendary one-man comedy show, An Audience with Mr Nice, continues to sell-out at venues throughout Britain.

Howard Marks has his own hugely popular website (www.mrnice.net), record label (Bothered), and cannabis seed company (Mr Nice Seed Bank). He writes a monthly column for *Loaded* and has written features for the *Observer*, *Evening Standard*, *Time Out*, *GQ*, and the *Guardian*, campaigning vigorously for the legalisation of recreational drugs.

ALSO BY HOWARD MARKS
Mr Nice

THE HOWARD MARKS BOOK OF DOPE STORIES

EDITED BY
Howard Marks

VINTAGE

Published by Vintage 2001

6 8 10 9 7 5

Selection, selected writing and introduction copyright © Howard Marks 2001
For contributors' copyright see p. 539

First published in Great Britain in 2001 by Vintage

A VINTAGE ORIGINAL

Vintage
Random House, 20 Vauxhall Bridge Road,
London SW1V 2SA

Random House Australia (Pty) Limited
20 Alfred Street, Milsons Point, Sydney,
New South Wales 2061, Australia

Random House New Zealand Limited
18 Poland Road, Glenfield,
Auckland 10, New Zealand

Random House (Pty) Limited
Endulini, 5A Jubilee Road, Parktown 2193, South Africa

The Random House Group Limited Reg. No. 954009
www.randomhouse.co.uk

A CIP catalogue record for this book is available from the British Library

ISBN 0 09 942855 5

Papers used by Random House are natural, recyclable products made from
wood ground in sustainable forests. The manufacturing processes conform to
the environmental regulations of the country of origin

Typeset by SX Composing DTP, Rayleigh, Essex
Printed and bound in Great Britain by
Bookmarque Ltd, Croydon, Surrey

This book is dedicated to the memory of my father,
Dennis Marks.

CONTENTS

Dope:
Information about a subject, especially if not generally
  known
An additive producing a desired characteristic
A substance added to increase effectiveness and improve
  properties
A chemical substance taken for the pleasant effects it
  produces

Dictionary Definitions

INTRODUCTION

When I wrote *Mr Nice*, I did so with fellow elderly hippies in mind as potential readers. I was, therefore, truly astonished to discover that its unexpected best-seller status was primarily due to its popularity among people several decades younger than I was. Through a plethora of media interviews and several public book readings, it became clear that the predominant reason why so many adolescents and university students read and enjoyed *Mr Nice* was their frustration with the law prohibiting cannabis consumption and trade. Until then, I had no idea of the extraordinary extent of cannabis use by young people today.

Despite having made enormous amounts of money through illegally trading cannabis, I have never been able to begin to see this as a justification for condoning any prolonging of its prohibition and have always supported its legalisation. In the past, I had to do this clandestinely or anonymously: it would have been unforgivably unprofessional to do otherwise. After the publication of *Mr Nice*, I found myself swamped by the spotlight of media attention. I determined to use my sky-rocketing notoriety in as responsible a way as possible and to do whatever I could to hasten the day that cannabis would be relegalised.

My first high-profile attempt to move towards cannabis relegalisation was to smoke a joint at a London police station and offer myself as available for immediate arrest and imprisonment. The police declined. It occurred to me then (perhaps for the first time) that the police were not the enemy. Most policemen choose that profession for completely honourable reasons, such as protecting the society they love: they did not join up to imprison people for smoking herbs. Policemen have walked the streets far more than the rest of us and know what the problems are and what causes them. The ones that I've talked with, almost without exception, do not see the consumption of cannabis as problematic, but they do see the law prohibiting it to be so. I cannot think of any law that has done more damage in terms of social upheaval, parent-child alienation and police-public hostility.

Although it's hard for me to imagine anyone deciding to favour the prohibition of drugs after reading this book, its purpose is not an appeal for legalisation. The drug stories and extracts herein are chosen on the basis of their interest, rarity, amusement and provocation.

I suspect that all anthology compilers are plagued by which criteria to adopt for ordering the chosen extracts. I certainly was and longed for the sudden acquisition of an undefinable skill, somewhere between that of a hard-working house DJ and that of a full-time bibliographer. Do I do it by drug, by mood, by content, or by time? Eventually, I decided to let the order reflect my and many others' journeys through the world of drugs: a period of wonderfully gentle and civilised discovery followed by a smattering of learning, a far more intense and raw discovery phase ending with extreme frustration with the social taboos surrounding drugs, then a long but finite period of living from drugs, and finally an eternal time of living with them.

CHAPTER ONE

INTO IT

Mordecai Cooke
The Seven Sisters of Sleep

Author's Dedication

To all lovers of tobacco, in all parts of the world,
juvenile and senile, masculine and feminine;
and to all abstainers, voluntary and involuntary.

To all opiophagi, at home and abroad,
whether experiencing the pleasures, or pains
of the seductive drug.

To all haschischans, east and west, in whatever form they
choose to woo the spirit of dreams.

To all buyeros, Malayan or Chinese,
whether their siri-boxes are full, or empty.

To all coqueros, white or swarthy,
from the base to the summit of the mighty cordilleras.

To all votaries of stramonium and henbane,
highlander, or lowlander.

And to all swallowers of amanita, either in Siberia or
  elsewhere
these pages come greeting with the best wishes
of their obedient servant.

Published in 1860 by James Blackwood, London

James Grey Jackson
An Account of the Empire of Marocco

THE PLANT CALLED hashisha is the African hemp plant; it grows in all the gardens; and is reared in the plains at Marocco, for the manufacture of twine; but in most parts of the country it is cultivated for the extraordinary and pleasing voluptuous vacuity of mind which it produces in those who smoke it: unlike the intoxication from wine, a fascinating stupor pervades the mind, and the dreams are agreeable. The kief, which is the flower and seeds of the plant, is the strongest, and a pipe of it half the size of a common English tobacco pipe, is sufficient to intoxicate. The infatuation of those who use it is such that they cannot exist without it. The kief is pounded, and mixed with *el majune*, an invigorating confection, which is sold at an enormous price; a piece of this as big as a walnut will for a time entirely deprive a man of all reason and intellect; they prefer it to opium, from the voluptuous sensations which it never fails to produce. Wine or brandy, they say, does not stand in competition with it. The hashisha, or leaves of the plant, are dried and cut like tobacco, with which they are smoked, in very small pipes; but when the person wishes to indulge in the sensual stupor it occasions, he smokes the hashisha pure, and in less than half an hour it operates; the person under its influence is said to experience pleasing images: he fancies himself in company with beautiful women; he dreams that he is an emperor, or a bashaw, and that the world is at his nod.

An Account of the Empire Marocco, 1968

Howard Marks
Morocco

As I APPROACHED, a blanket of mist that had covered both of the old cities of Fes el Jedid (New Fes) and Fes el Bali (Old Fes) gradually lifted and revealed an underblanket of several hundred thousand satellite dishes covering an enormous basin of ten thousand tiny streets of medieval mayhem, the *medina*. I entered through one of the *medina*'s many imposing gates through which no cars were allowed to pass. The passages quickly become narrow and steep, with right of way given to weighted donkeys. Craftsmen were beginning to ply their trades in leather, carpets, wood, jewellery and spices. Aromatic whiffs of herbs, spices, succulent kebabs, fresh honey cakes and bread made everyone's mouth water. Dazzling coloured hanks of yarn, kettles, cassette players and shoes were suspended wherever there was space. Losing myself hopelessly in this labyrinth, I headed down bustling, twisting alleys lined with tiny shops selling multicoloured garments, sequinned slippers, brassware, tooth-cleaning twigs, spices and baked goods. All purchases, expensive and cheap, were tied up in black plastic bags. Deeper down still, pharmacies and herbalists displayed dried skins of lizards and snakes, leeches, scorpions, live hedgehogs and terrapins. These alleyways, I knew, hid magnificent homes and gardens behind their blank uncompromising walls. Unlike that of Europe, Islamic architecture aims to enclose space, to create a sheltered garden from a wilderness, relating to the deep-felt need to turn away from the outside world and look in upon a personal oasis. The Muslim concept of paradise is a place of abundant cool water and shade.

But at 3 p.m., the whole of the *medina* seemed dry, hot and sunny. Wandering around in an obviously futile attempt to find my bearings, encountering one dead end after another, I was quickly approached by a succession of people offering to be my guide, to lead me to my hotel, to show me the mosques and museums, to take me to the merchants who sell goods at the cheapest possible prices. I am always glad to have some sort of guide in foreign parts and am often amused by needlessly aggressive tourists cold-shouldering potential helpers and then consulting, with confusion and puzzlement, their imported obsolete maps and anecdotal guidebooks. It is a ridiculous but revealing insight into Western attitudes. Obviously some guides are rogues, but just look into their eyes and hire the nicest. (Forget anyone wearing dark glasses.) I settled on one named Rachid.

'Can you get me out of here?'

'Of course, sir.'

I followed Rachid down a few ancient passageways, liked his gentle company and arranged to meet him after dusk the following night. I would use him to find out the city's secrets and keep an eye on my back.

Just over twenty-four hours later, walls emerged from the dark night. Rachid emerged from the walls.

'What would you like to do, sir? Go to a museum or eat something?'

'Is there a restaurant with music?'

Among the countries of North Africa, Morocco offers the richest, most vibrant and diversified musical tradition and the most articulated contemporary documentation of the many stylistic cultural roots of so-called white African culture. The character of the music heard today in Morocco is a result of the many complex historical vicissitudes of the country, of its ethnic make-up and geographical location.

'You want belly dancer, sir?'

'Not really. Do you know Jajouka music, Rachid?'

'Yes, sir, but there is none here tonight in Fes.'

Jajouka is pagan ritual music that invokes the gods of fecundity, much like the ancient rites of Pan. The Jajouka revere hashish and are known for their 1969 recordings with Rolling Stone Brian Jones.

'Any other music about hashish?'

'There is Heddaoua, sir, playing in a restaurant I know.'

The Heddaoua are storytellers of an errant religious sect who normally perform in the squares and market places of small Moroccan towns and villages rather than city restaurants. They recite poems, maxims and proverbs in a strange, allusive and magical language and with a particular style of rhythmic diction. The ultimate scope of their message is an invitation to gives one's self up to hashish, as a source of freedom and an aid to meditation.

The restaurant was the standard sumptuous *medina* palace.

The Heddaoua appeared carrying weird lanterns, crouched on a rug spread out in front of rows of empty bottles and vases of artificial flowers, symbolising a blossomed, magical garden. Live doves rested on the shoulders and heads of the performers. They work in couples, and their form of recitation consists of questions and answers. The recurrent theme is an invitation to smoke. I asked Rachid to translate.

Light your pipe
Smoke your pipe
The Almighty will give you peace
Smoke and drink small sips of tea
The Almighty will set you free
From your tribulations
Smoke and breathe deeply
He who is jealous will know misery.

The message was fairly clear, and I was aching for a smoke.

Rachid placed a mixture of kif and hashish in a small clay bowl, which he gently placed at the end of an exquisite cedar-wood pipe, handed to me and lit. It was as good as any I'd had for the last twenty years. Perhaps I could squeeze some time for a visit to the hash fields, if only for old times' sake.

The mellow silence following the departure of the Heddaoua was suddenly punctured by ear-shattering clashes of heavy metal. In walked four males, each wearing a fez with its tassel spinning in time to the rhythm and each pounding enormous iron castanets. Instant frenzy spread through the restaurant. The Gnaoua is a spiritual brotherhood of Sudanese Negroes who, like the Heddaoua, normally perform as musicians and acrobatic dancers in the market places of southern Morocco. They use percussive instruments only. The music is closely related to Mali and Senegalese and is used to exorcise evil spirits. Heads are banged on stone flags, as the musicians eat glass and cut themselves with knives. This was wonderfully mad and made me more determined than ever to revisit the hash plantations.

What is a weed? A plant whose virtues have not yet been discovered

Ralph Waldo Emerson

Isabelle Eberhardt
The Oblivion Seekers

IN THIS *KSAR*, where the people have no place to meet but the public square or the earthen benches along the foot of the ramparts on the road to Bechar, here where there is not even a café, I have discovered a kif den. It is in a partially ruined house behind the Mellah, a long hall lighted by a single eye in the ceiling of twisted and smoke-blackened beams. The walls are black, ribbed with lighter colored cracks that look like open wounds. The floor has been made by pounding the earth, but it is soft and dusty. Seldom swept, it is covered with pomegranate rinds and assorted refuse. The place serves as a shelter for Moroccan vagabonds, for nomads, and for every sort of person of dubious intent and questionable appearance. The house seems to belong to no one; as at a disreputable hotel, you spend a few badly advised nights there and go on. It is a natural setting for picturesque and theatrical events, like the antechamber of the room where the crime was committed. In one corner lies a clean red mat, with some cushions from Fez in embroidered leather. On the mat, a large decorated chest which serves as a table. A rosebush with little pale pink blooms, surrounded by a bouquet of garden herbs, all standing in water inside one of those wide earthen jars from the Tell. Further on, a copper kettle on a tripod, two or three teapots, a large basket of dried Indian hemp. The little group of kif smokers requires no other decoration, no other *mise en scène*. They are people who like their pleasure. On a rude perch of palm branches, a captive falcon, tied by one leg.

The strangers, the wanderers who haunt this retreat, sometimes mix with the kif smokers, notwithstanding the fact that the latter are a very closed little community, into which entry is made difficult. But the smokers themselves are travellers who carry their dreams with them across the countries of Islam, worshippers of the hallucinating smoke. The men who happen to meet here at Kenadsa are among the most highly educated in the land.

Hadj Idriss, a tall thin Filali, deeply sunburned, with a sweet face that lights up from within, is one of these rootless ones without family or specific trade, so common in the Moslem world. For twenty-five years he has been wandering from city to city, working or begging, depending on the situation. He plays the *guinbri*, with its carved wooden neck and its two thick strings fastened to the shell of a tortoise. Hadj Idriss has a deep clear voice, ideal for singing the old Andaluz ballads, so full of tender melancholy. Si Mohammed Behaouri, a Moroccan from Meknes, pale-complexioned and with caressing eyes, is a young poet wandering across Morocco and southern Algeria in search of native legends and literature. To keep alive, he composes and recites verse on the delights and horrors of love. Another is from the Djebel Zerhoun, a doctor and witch doctor, small, dry, muscular, his skin tanned by the Sudanese sun under which he has journeyed for many years following caravans to and fro, from the coast of Senegal to Timbuctoo. All day long he keeps busy, slowly pouring out medicine and thumbing through old Moghrebi books of magic. Chance brought them here to Kenadsa. Soon they will set out again, in different directions and on different trails, moving unconcernedly toward the fulfilment of their separate destinies. But it was community of taste that gathered them together in this smoky refuge, where they pass the slow hours of a life without cares.

At the end of the afternoon, a slanting pink ray of light falls from the eye in the ceiling into the darkness of the room. The kif smokers move in and form groups. Each wears a sprig of sweet basil in his turban. Squatting along the wall on the mat, they smoke their little pipes of baked red earth, filled with Indian hemp and powdered Moroccan tobacco. Hadj Idriss stuffs the bowls and distributes them, after having carefully wiped the mouthpiece on his cheek as a gesture of politeness. When his own pipe is empty, he picks out the little red ball of ash and puts it into his mouth – he does not feel it burning him

– then, once his pipe is refilled, he uses the still-red-hot cinder to relight the little fire. For hours at a time he does not once let it go out. He has a keen and penetrating intelligence, softened by being constantly in a state of semi-exaltation; his dreams are nourished on the narcotic smoke.

The seekers of oblivion sing and clap their hands lazily; their dream-voices ring out late into the night, in the dim light of the mica-paned lantern. Then little by little the voices fall, grow muffled, the words are slower. Finally the smokers are quiet, and merely stare at the flowers in ecstasy. They are epicureans, voluptuaries; perhaps they are sages. Even in the darkest purlieu of Morocco's underworld such men can reach the magic horizon where they are free to build their dream-palaces of delight.

Circa 1925–27. From: *Shaman Woman, Mainline Lady: Women's Writings on the Drug Experience*, eds Cynthia Palmer and Michael Horowitz, 1982

I do hold it, and will affirm it before any prince in Europe, to be the most sovereign and precious weed that ever the earth rendered to the use of man

Ben Johnson

Charles Baudelaire
The Playground of the Seraphim

WHAT DOES ONE experience? What does one see? Marvellous things, is it not so? Wonderful sights? Is it very beautiful? Such are the usual questions which, with a curiosity mingled with fear, those ignorant of hashish address to its adepts. It is, as it were, the childish impatience to know, resembling that of those people never quitted their firesides when they meet a man who returns from distant and unknown countries. They imagine hashish drunkenness to themselves as a prodigious vast theatre of sleight of hand and of juggling, where all is miraculous, all unforeseen. That is a prejudice, a complete mistake. And since for the ordinary run of readers and of questioners the word 'hashish' connotes the idea of a strange and topsy-turvy world, the expectation of prodigious dreams (it would be better to say hallucinations, which are, by the way, less frequent than people suppose), I will at once remark upon the important difference which separates the effects of hashish from the phenomena of dream. In dream, that adventurous voyage which we undertake every night, there is something positively miraculous. It is a miracle whose punctual occurrence has blunted its mystery. The dreams of man are of two classes. Some, full of his ordinary life, of his preoccupations, of his desires, of his vices, combine themselves in a manner more or less bizarre with the objects which he has met in his day's work, which have carelessly fixed themselves upon the vast canvas of his memory. That is the natural dream; it is the man himself. But the other kind of dream, the dream absurd and unforeseen, without meaning or connection with the character, the life and the passions of the sleeper: this dream, which I shall call hieroglyphic, evidently represents the supernatural side of life, and it is exactly because it is absurd that the ancients believed it to be divine. As it is inexplicable by natural causes, they attributed to it a cause external to man, and even to-day, leaving out of account oneiromancers and the fooleries of a philosophical school which sees in dreams of this type sometimes a reproach, sometimes a warning; in short, a symbolic and moral picture begotten in the spirit itself of the sleeper. It is a dictionary which one must study; a language of which sages may obtain the key.

In the intoxication of hashish there is nothing like this. We shall not go outside the class of natural dream. The drunkenness, throughout its duration, it is true, will be nothing but an immense dream, thanks to the intensity of its colours and the rapidity of its conceptions. But it will always keep the idiosyncrasy of the individual. The man has desired to dream; the dream will govern the man. But this dream will be truly the son of its father. The idle man has taxed his ingenuity to introduce artificially the supernatural into his life and into his thought; but, after all, and despite the accidental energy of his experiences, he is nothing but the same man magnified, the same number raised to a very high power. He is brought into subjection, but, unhappily for him, it is not by himself which is already dominant. 'He would be an angel; he becomes a beast.' Momentarily very powerful, if, indeed, one can give the name of power of what is merely excessive sensibility without the control which might moderate or make use of it.

Let it be well understood then, by worldly and ignorant folk, curious of acquaintance with exceptional joys, that they will find in hashish nothing miraculous, absolutely nothing, but the natural in a superabundant degree. The brain and the organism upon which hashish operates will only give their ordinary and individual phenomena, magnified, it is true, both in quantity and quality, but always faithful to their origin. Man cannot escape the fatality of his moral and physical temperament. Hashish will be, indeed, for the impressions and familiar thoughts of the man, a mirror which magnifies, yet no more than a mirror.

Here is the drug before your eyes: a little green sweetmeat, about as big as a nut, with a strange smell; so strange that it arouses a certain revulsion, and inclinations to nausea – as, indeed, any fine and even agreeable scent, exalted to its maximum strength and (so to say) density, would do.

Allow me to remark in passing that this proposition can be inverted, and that the most disgusting and revolting perfume would become perhaps a pleasure to inhale if it were reduced to its minimum quantity and intensity.

There! There is happiness; heaven in a teaspoon: happiness, with all its intoxication, all its folly, all its childishness. You can swallow it without fear; it is not fatal; it will in nowise injure your physical organs. Perhaps (later on) too frequent an employment of the sorcery will diminish the strength of your will; perhaps you will be less a man than you are today; but retribution is so far off, and the nature of the eventual disaster so difficult to define! What is it that you risk? A little nervous fatigue tomorrow – no more. Do you not every day risk greater punishment for less reward? Very good then; you have, even, to make it act more quickly and vigorously, imbibed your dose of *extrait gras* in a cup of black coffee. You have taken care to have the stomach empty, postponing dinner till nine or ten o'clock, to give full liberty of action to the poison. At the very most you will take a little soup in an hour's time. You are now sufficiently provisioned for a long and strange journey; the steamer has whistled, the sails are trimmed; and you have this curious advantage over ordinary travellers that you have no idea where you are going. You have made your choice; here's to luck.

I presume that you have taken the precaution to choose carefully your moment for setting out on this adventure. For every perfect debauch demands perfect leisure. You know, moreover, that hashish exaggerates not only the individual, but also circumstances and environment. You have no duties to fulfil which require punctuality or exactitude. No domestic worries – no lover's sorrows. One must be careful on such points. Such a disappointment, an anxiety, an interior monition of a duty which demands your will and your attention, at some determinate moment, would ring like a funeral bell across your intoxication and poison your pleasure. Anxiety would become anguish, and disappointment torture. But if, having observed all these preliminary conditions the weather is fine; if you are situated in favourable surroundings, such as a picturesque landscape or a room beautifully decorated; and if in particular you have at command a little music, then all is for the best.

1910. From: *Hashish: The Herb Superb,* vol. II of *The Herb Dangerous: High Historical Writings for the Modern Haschischin*, ed. David Hoye, 1973

Johnny Edgecombe
Calypso Train

JAKE WAS REFLECTING on the first time he met Skyman. It was on his eighteenth birthday. His dad had bought him a new bike. He had forbidden Jake to hang around the waterfront with thieves and fornicators – the riff-raff. He reminded Jake that he had spent a lot of money on his education. Jake knew what he was going to say next.

'The wages of sin.'

Jake came from a long line of Preachers, as far back as way back. His old man had been trying to convince him to become a Preacher too. Jake often wondered if his father really believed all that shit he laid on his congregation. But he assured him he wasn't going near the waterfront. He was just taking his bike for a spin.

Jake took his bathing trunks off the clothes line, tied them on to the handlebar of his bike and started to ride out of Kingston, on the coast road. He was feeling good as he rode along the coast taking in the scenery.

He rode for about fifteen to twenty miles out of Kingston. He came to a nice cove with a sandy beach and decided that it was a good place to stop for a dip. There was only one boat in the bay and apart from a Rasterman painting his dinghy on the beach, there wasn't anyone else around. There was a groovy little shack in the right-hand corner of the cove. Whoever made it had done a good job.

Jake felt a wave of admiration for the Rasterman, who was among his father's categories of riff-raffs, ganja smokers and layabouts, as he watched him painting his dinghy like an artist. He stood there for a while, enjoying the Rasterman paint, seeing him stop from time to time to take a toke on his pipe.

Eventually he walked over, towing his bike and smiling.

'Hello, Raster, what's happening?'

The Rasterman didn't reply right off. He looked at Jake for a while. His eyes aloof – the shutters almost half closed. Skyman knew that apart from the authorities, no one else was aware that he was back in Jamaica; if anyone was, he was reasonably sure that they wouldn't recognise him. Just the same he didn't talk to many people.

He guessed that the young guy was from Kingston, he seemed a nice enough guy.

'What's your name?'

12

'Jake! What's yours?'

'Just call me Raster, for the time being.'

Jake knew, right off, that Raster – or whatever his name was – wasn't a real Rasterman, but you wouldn't know that by looking. His dreadlocks were very impressive and he had a full long beard, streaked with grey hairs. Jake was intrigued.

'Can you paint?' asked Raster.

Jake smiled. 'Yes, but not as good as you.'

'Well, grab a brush anyway.'

Jake was elated. They painted in silence for a while, Jake looking at Skyman from time to time. Every now and then Skyman stopped painting to reload his pipe. He picked up his corn-husk pipe from a makeshift workbench. First he would clean it carefully with a pipe-cleaner, testing it a few times, until he was satisfied. Then he fished into the small pocket on the front of his white T-shirt and brought out a white draw and extracted a fat bud before replacing the bag like it was a prized possession.

Jake noted the pungent smell of the herbs as it mingled with the paint in his nostrils, as Skyman crumbled the bud. Then the Rasterman took a king-size box of matches from the bench and started to light his pipe. He circled the bowl with the fire about four times, puffing gently each time, to effect an even light. Satisfied that the light was good and the pipe was drawing freely, he dragged hard and deep, the bowl glowing, as if about to catch light as he filled his lungs. He held the smoke for about a minute before reluctantly letting it go and automatically moving to pass the pipe to Jake. Hesitating a moment, he looked at Jake.

'Hey, man! You smoke?'

Jake wasn't really lying when he answered that he did. He had burned a few joints on several occasions with some of the guys from his school and dug it. But he had not indulged too much because he was aware that the worst thing that could happen to him was for the Preacher to hear that he had even tried the 'Devil's Weed'. But this was different.

Jake took the pipe without any hesitation and started to puff gently the way Skyman had done. Realising after the first puff that the pipe was ready, he hit it and tried to hold the smoke like Skyman but he felt that his head would explode if he didn't let go. He opened up all his valves and for all he knew, when he started to cough and he felt like his head was going to come off, smoke might have been even coming out of his ears! Skyman took the pipe from Jake and gave him some coconut water. Jake had drunk a lot of coconut water but now he felt like he was tasting it for the first time. The taste was so lucid he even thought he could see it.

Within minutes hot beads of perspiration gathered on his forehead. His mind was scrambled but he was acutely conscious of himself, as if he was filming everything he did. He felt that the sun was getting hotter and he had to get out of it. He wanted to tell Skyman that he was going over by a tree to sit in the shade for a while, but he couldn't string the words together. He saw himself gesturing, pointing at a tree. He realised he was still holding the empty coconut. In other circumstances he would've scooped out the jelly and enjoyed it before discarding it, but right now he couldn't think what the hell to do with the thing. He was relieved when Skyman took it from him in slow motion and told him he could use the hut.

Jake looked at the hut, sure that it had been much closer a while ago. He wondered about his legs, he knew that they were there because he was still standing, but he couldn't feel them. He looked down at his feet to make sure that they were facing the right way. He started to walk but his legs wouldn't move. He had to get out of the sun. His underclothes were already sticking to his body. He almost fell over with the first step. His legs were so heavy he had to lift his foot very high to compensate for the weight. He was doing a kind of knees-up walk on his way to the hut, mindful of each step as his feet seemed to stick in the sand every time he put them down.

By the time he got to the hut, Jake was exhausted. All he wanted to do now was flop out. He made straight for the bunk bed, which seemed to come up to him, as he flopped down on it. Now he was floating up there in the ceiling, looking down on his helpless carriage. He became aware that it was he, I and I, and not his mother or the Preacher that was in charge of his carriage. He saw a new dimension and knew there wasn't any way back.

He was counselling himself about some immediate changes

he had to make, when he fell off the ceiling and the bunk began to spin and rock as if he was on a boat. He eventually fell off the bunk. Back in himself, laying there on the floor Jake had decided he wasn't going back to bed when the floor started to perform as well. He couldn't decide which was worse – the floor or the bed, but in the end he opted for the floor because he figured he couldn't fall any further.

The floor was spinning faster and faster as if it was about to take off. He held on as long as he could, but the experience had wasted him. He let go and flew around the universe a few times before he fell into a deep sleep.

It was not only deep, but long. The sun brought him back among the living the next morning, with the sound of the sea, as it gently washes the sand. It was a nice way to wake up. Jake was feeling fresh and new until he realised that the sound of the sea washing the sand wasn't a familiar sound first thing in the morning. And he wasn't in his own room, on his floor. Then it all came back to him in a flash, so vivid that it was hard to decipher what was real, fantasy or dream.

Jake got up from the floor without giving a second thought to his legs. He had an urgent need for a piss. He looked for the door. There were two. He hurried for the nearest one, almost tripping over his bike. He was smiling as he relieved himself, thinking this was the best piss he had ever had.

He had wanted to piss since last night but the floor was spinning so fast he couldn't get off and when he dreamed that he had found a place to piss he couldn't find his cock. Jake went back into the hut; he had never felt better. He didn't see much of the hut yesterday apart from the bunk but now he noticed that there was a table with a hurricane lamp on it, two chairs and an open cupboard with fifteen suits hanging in it. Each suit carrying a silk shirt. Jake moved nearer to the cupboard for a closer look. Now he was really knocked out, these suits were a collection of the finest rags he had ever seen. You know, the stuff only the rich Americans can afford; sharkskin, silk and cashmere. On the floor were seven pairs of shoes made of snake, croc and calfskin. Three matching belts hung in a corner. Jake tried to visualise Skyman all done up, without his dreadlocks.

His perceptions were of a guy who looked like a million. Top drawer. Plenty of class and a lot of style. Jake had found a hero.

Jake undressed and got his swimming trunks from his bike, put them on and went looking for Skyman. He walked back towards the spot where they were painting the dinghy. It was no longer there. He looked out to sea, the boat was still there with the dinghy tied up astern. Skyman came up from below with a broom and bucket. He made out the name of the boat – *Seafree*. Jake waved. Skyman put down his bucket and waved back. Jake took a long run to the water and dived in and started swimming towards the boat. He thought about his parents, it was the first time he had ever stayed away from home under such circumstances and was amazed at himself that he felt no anxiety, it was more an obligation to phone and let his folks know that he was okay. He made a mental note to do that and went back to the task of swimming all the way out to *Seafree*. It was a tidy swim by most standards but he was a fit young guy and he made it easy.

Skyman tossed a ladder over the side for Jake and invited him to come aboard. As Jake got on board and sat on the rails to give his heart time to adjust its beat, he noticed the sound of jazz and that familiar smell of ganja coming from below. Skyman came over and extended his hand.

'Hey, man! How you feeling today?'

Jake smiled, full of confidence with his new being.

'Great! But I wasn't doing so good yesterday! I only just made it to the hut.'

Skyman smiled back.

'Welcome to the club.'

Calypso Train, 2001

O thou weed!
Who are so lovely fair and smell'st so sweet
That the sense aches at thee, wouldst thou hadst ne'er been
born

William Shakespeare

H. H. Kane
A Hashish-House in New York:
The Curious Adventures of an Individual Who Indulged in a Few Pipefuls of the Narcotic Hemp

'AND SO YOU think that opium-smoking as seen in the foul cellars of Mott Street and elsewhere is the only form of narcotic indulgence of any consequence in this city, and that hashish, if used at all, is only smoked occasionally and experimentally by a few scattered individuals?'

'This is certainly my opinion, and I consider myself fairly well informed.'

'Well, you are far from right, as I can prove to you if you care to inform yourself more fully on the subject. There is a large community of hashish smokers in this city, who are daily forced to indulge their morbid appetites, and I can take you to a house uptown where hemp is used in every conceivable form, and where the lights, sounds, odors, and surroundings are all arranged so as to intensify and enhance the effects of this wonderful narcotic.'

'I must confess that I am still incredulous.'

'Well, if it is agreeable to you, meet me at the Hoffman House reading-room tomorrow night at ten o'clock, and I think I shall be able to convince you.'

The above is the substance of a conversation that took place in the lobby of a downtown hotel between the writer of these lines and a young man about thirty-eight years of age, known to me for some years past as an opium smoker. It was through his kindness that I had first gained access to and had been able to study up the subject of opium-smoking. Hence I really anticipated seeing some interesting phases of hemp indulgence, and was not disappointed. The following evening at precisely ten o'clock I met the young man at the Hoffman House, and together we took a Broadway car uptown, left it at Forty-second Street, and walked rapidly toward the North River, talking as we went.

'You will be probably be greatly surprised at many things you will see tonight,' he said, 'just as I was when I was first introduced to the place by a friend. I have traveled over most of Europe, and have smoked opium in every *joint* in America, but never saw anything so curious as this, nor experienced any intoxication so fascinating yet so terrible as that of hashish.'

'Are the habitués of this place of the same class as those who frequent the opium-smoking dives?'

'By no means. They are about evenly divided between Americans and foreigners; indeed, the place is kept by a Greek, who has invested a great deal of money in it. All the visitors, both male and female, are of the better classes, and absolute secrecy is the rule. The house has been opened about two years, I believe, and the number of regular habitués is daily on the increase.'

'Are you one of the number?'

'I am, and find the intoxication far pleasanter and less hurtful than that of opium. Ah! Here we are.'

We paused before a gloomy-looking house, entered the gate and passed up the steps. The windows were absolutely dark, and the entranceway looked dirty and desolate. Four pulls at the bell, a pause and one more pull were followed by a few moments' silence, broken suddenly by the sound of falling chain, rasping bolt and the grinding of a key in the lock. The outer door was cautiously opened and at a word from my companion we passed into the vestibule. The outer door was carefully closed by someone whom I could not distinguish in the utter darkness. A moment later the inner door was opened and never shall I forget the impression produced by the sudden change from total darkness to the strange scene that met my eyes. The dark vestibule was the boundary line separating the cold, dreary streets and the ordinary world from a scene of Oriental magnificence.

A volume of heavily scented air, close upon the heels of which came a deadly sickening odor, wholly unlike anything I had ever smelled, greeted my nostrils. A hall lamp of grotesque shape flooded the hall with a subdued violet light that filtered through crenated disks of some violet fabric hung below it. The walls and ceilings, if ever modern, were no longer so, for they were shut in and hung by festoons and plaits of heavy cloth fresh from Eastern looms. Tassels of blue, green, yellow, red, and tinsel here and there peeped forth, matching the curious edging of variously colored beadwork that bordered each fold of drapery like a huge procession of luminous ants, and seemed to flow into little phosphorescent pools wherever the cloth was caught up. Queer figures and strange lettering, in the same work, were here and there disclosed upon the ceiling cloth.

Along one side of the hall, between two doors, were ranged huge tubs and pots of majolica-like ware and blue-necked Japanese vases, in which were plants, shrubs, and flowers of the most exquisite color and odor. Green vines clambered up the walls and across the ceiling, and catching their tendrils in the balustrades of the stairs (which were also of curious design), threw down long sprays and heavy festoons of verdure.

As my companion, who had paused a moment to give me time to look about me, walked toward the far end of the hall, I followed him, and passed into a small room on the right, where, with the assistance of a colored servant, we exchanged our coats, hats and shoes for others more in keeping with our surroundings. First a long plush gown, quilted with silk down the front and irregularly ornamented in bead and braid with designs of serpents, flowers, crescents, and stars, was slipped on over the head. Next a tasseled smoking-cap was donned, and the feet encased in noiseless list slippers. In any other place or under any other circumstances I should have felt ridiculous in this costume, but so in keeping was it with all I had seen, and so thoroughly had I seemed to have left my everyday self in the dark vestibule, that I felt perfectly at home in my strange dress. We next crossed the hall to a smaller room, where a young man, apparently a Frenchman, furnished us, on the payment of two dollars each, with two small pipes and a small covered bronze cup, or urn, filled with a dry green shrub, which I subsequently learned was *gunjeh* (the dried tops and leaves of the hemp plant), for smoking. My friend, on the payment of a further sum, obtained a curious little box which contained some small black lozenges, consisting of the resin of hemp, henbane, crushed datura

19

seeds, butter and honey, and known in India as *majoon*, among the Moors as *el mogen*.

Passing from this room we ascended the richly carpeted stairs, enarbored by vines, and paused upon a landing from which three doors opened. Upon one, a pink card bore Dryden's line, 'Take the good the gods provide thee.' The knob turned by my friend's hand allowed the door to swing open, and, welcomed by a spice breeze from India, we were truly in paradise.

'This,' he said, in a whisper, 'is the public room, where anyone having pipe or lozenge, and properly attired, may enter and indulge – eat, smoke, or dream, as best suits him.'

Wonder, amazement, admiration, but faintly portray my mental condition. Prepared by what I had already seen and experienced for something odd and Oriental, still the magnificence of what now met my gaze far surpassed anything I had ever dreamed of, and brought to my mind the scenes of the *Arabian Nights*, forgotten since boyhood until now. My every sense was irresistibly taken captive, and it was some moments before I could realise that I really was not the victim of some dream, for I seemed to have wholly severed my connection with the world of today, and to have stepped back several centuries into the times of genii, fairies and fountains – into the very heart of Persia or Arabia. Not an inharmonious detail marred the symmetry of the whole. Beneath, my feet sank almost ankle-deep into a velvet carpet – a sea of subdued colors. Looked at closely, I found that the design was that of a garden: beds of luxurious flowers, stars and crescents, squares and diamond-shaped plots, made up of thousands of rare exotics and richly colored leaves. Here a brook, edged with damp verdure, from beneath which peeped coy violets and tiny bluebells; there a serpentine graveled walk that wound in and out amongst the exquisite plants, and everywhere a thousand shrubs in bloom or bud. Above, a magnificent chandelier, consisting of six dragons of beaten gold, from whose eyes and throats sprang flames, the light from which, striking against a series of curiously set prisms, fell shattered and scintillating into a thousand glancing beams that illuminated every corner of the room. The rows of prisms being of clear and variously colored glass, and the dragons slowly revolving, a weird and ever-changing hue was given to every object in the room.

All about the side of the spacious apartment, upon the floor, were mattresses covered with different-colored cloth, and edged with heavy golden fringe. Upon them were carelessly strewn rugs and mats of Persian and Turkish handicraft, and soft pillows in heaps. Above the level of these divans there ran, all about the room, a series of huge mirrors framed with gilded serpents intercoiled, effectually shutting off the windows. The effect was magnificent. There seemed to be twenty rooms instead of one, and everywhere could be seen the flame-tongued and fiery-eyed dragons slowly revolving, giving to all the appearance of a magnificent kaleidoscope in which the harmonious colors were ever-blending and constantly presenting new combinations.

Just as I had got thus far in my observations I caught sight of my friend standing at the foot of one of the divans and beckoning to me. At the same moment I also observed that several of the occupants of other divans were eying me suspiciously. I crossed to where he was, esteeming it a desecration to walk on such a carpet, and, despite my knowledge to the contrary, fearing every moment to crush some beautiful rose or lily beneath my feet. Following my friend's example, I slipped off my list foot gear, and half reclined beside him on the divan and pillows, that seemed to reach up and embrace us. Pulling a tasseled cord that hung above our heads, my friend spoke a few words to a gaudily turbaned colored servant who came noiselessly into the room in answer to his summons, disappeared again, and in a moment returned bearing a tray, which he placed between us. Upon it was a small lamp of silver filigree-work, two globelike bowls, of silver also, from which protruded a long silver tube and a spoonlike instrument. The latter, I soon learned, was to clean and fill the pipes. Placing the bronze jar of hashish on the tray, my friend bade me lay my pipe beside it, and suck up the fluid in the silver cup through the long tube. I did so, and found it delicious.

'That,' he said, 'is tea made from the genuine coca leaf. The cup is the real *mate* and the tube a real *bombilla* from Peru. Now let us smoke. The dried shrub here is known as *gunjeh*, and is the dried tops of the hemp plant. Take a little tobacco from that jar and mix with it, else it will be found difficult to keep it alight. These lozenges here are made from the finest Nepal resin of the hemp, mixed with butter, sugar, honey, flour, pounded datura seeds, some opium and a little henbane, or hyoscyamus. I prefer taking these to smoking, but, to keep you company, I will also smoke tonight. Have no fear. Smoke four or five pipefuls of the *gunjeh*, and enjoy the effect. I will see that no harm befalls you.'

Swallowing two of the lozenges, my guide filled our pipes, and we proceeded to smoke and watch the others. These pipes, the stems of which were about eighteen inches in length, were incrusted with designs in varicolored beads, strung on gold wire over a ground of some light spirally twisted tinsel, marked off into diamond-shaped spaces by thin red lines. From the stem two green and yellow silken tassels depended. A small bell-shaped piece of clouded amber formed the mouthpiece, while at the other end was a small bowl of red clay scarcely larger than a thimble. As I smoked I noticed that about two-thirds of the divans were occupied by persons of both sexes, some of them masked, who were dressed in the same manner as ourselves. Some were smoking, some reclining listlessly upon the pillows, following the tangled thread of a hashish reverie or dream. A middle-aged woman sat bolt upright, gesticulating and laughing quietly to herself; another, with lackluster eyes and dropped jaw, was swaying her head monotonously from side to side. A young man of about eighteen was on his knees, praying inaudibly; and another man, masked, paced rapidly and noiselessly up and down the room, until led away somewhere by the turbaned servant.

As I smoked, the secret of that heavy, sickening odor was made clear to me. It was the smell of burning hashish. Strangely enough, it did not seem to be unpleasant any longer, for, although it rather rasped my throat at first, I drew large volumes of it into my lungs. Lost in lazy reverie and comfort,

I tried to discover whence came the soft, undulating strains of music that had greeted me on entering, and which still continued. They were just perceptible above the silvery notes of a crystal fountain in the centre of the room, the falling spray from which plashed and tinkled musically as it fell from serpents' mouths into a series of the very thinnest huge pink shells held aloft by timid hares. The music seemed to creep up through the heavy carpet, to ooze from the walls, to flurry, like snowflakes, from the ceiling, rising and falling in measured cadences unlike any music I had ever heard. It seemed to steal, now softly, now merrily, on tiptoe into the room to see whether we were awake or asleep, to brush away a tear, if tear there was, or gambol airily and merrily, if such was our humor, and then as softly, sometimes sadly, to steal out again and lose itself in the distance. It was just such music as a boatful of fairies sailing about in the clear water of the fountain might have made, or that with which an angel mother and would sing its angel babe to sleep. It seemed to enter every fiber of the body, and satisfy a music-hunger that had never before been satisfied. I silently filled my second pipe, and was about to lapse again into a reverie that had become delightfully full of perfect rest and comfort, when my companion, leaning toward me, said:

'I see that you are fast approaching Hashishdom. Is there not a sense of perfect rest and strange, quiet happiness produced by it?'

'There certainly is. I feel supremely happy, at peace with myself and all the world, and all that I ask is to be let alone. But why is everything so magnificent here? Is it a whim of the proprietor, or an attempt to reproduce some such place in the East?' I asked.

'Possibly the latter; but there is another reason that you may understand better later. It is this: the color and peculiar phases of a hashish dream are materially affected by one's surroundings just prior to the sleep. The impressions that we have been receiving ever since we entered, the lights, odors, sounds and colors, are the strands which the deft fingers of imagination will weave into the hemp reveries and dreams, which seem as real as those of everyday life, and always more grand. Hashish eaters and smokers in the East recognized this fact, and always, prior to indulging in the drug, surrounded themselves with the most pleasant sounds, faces, forms, etcetera.'

'I see,' I answered, dreamily. 'But what is there behind those curtains that I see moving now and again?' The heavy curtains just opposite where we lay seemed to shut in an alcove.

'There are several small rooms there,' said my companion, 'shut off from this room by the curtains you see move. Each is magnificently fitted up, I am told. They are reserved for persons, chiefly ladies, who wish to avoid every possibility of detection, and at the same time enjoy their hashish and watch the inmates of this room.'

'Are there many ladies of good social standing who come here?'

'Very many. Not the cream of the *demi-monde*, understand me, but *ladies*. Why, there must be at least six hundred in this city alone who are *habituées*. Smokers from different cities, Boston, Philadelphia, Chicago, and especially New Orleans, tell me that each city has its hemp retreat, but none so elegant as this.'

And my companion swallowed another lozenge and relapsed into dreamy silence. I too lay back listlessly, and was soon lost in reverie, intense and pleasant. Gradually the room and its inmates faded from view; the revolving dragons went swifter and more swiftly, until the flaming tongues and eyes were merged into a huge ball of flame, that, suddenly detaching itself with a sharp sound from its pivot, went whirling and streaming off into the air until lost to sight in the skies. Then a sudden silence, during which I heard the huge waves of an angry sea breaking with fierce monotony in my head. Then I heard the fountain; the musical tinkle of the spray as it struck upon the glass grew louder and louder, and the notes longer and longer, until they merged into one clear, musical bugle note that woke the echoes of a spring morning, and broke sharp and clear over hill and valley, meadowland and marsh, hilltop and forest. A gaily caparisoned horseman, bugle in hand, suddenly appeared above a hillcrest. Closely following, a straggling group of horsemen riding madly. Before them a pack of hounds came dashing down the hillside, baying deeply. Before them I, the fox, was running with the speed of desperation, straining every nerve to distance or elude them. Thus for miles and miles I ran on until at last, almost dead with fright and fatigue, I fell panting in the forest. A moment more and the cruel hounds would have had me, when suddenly a little field mouse appeared, caught me by the paw, and dragged me through the narrow entrance to her nest. My body lengthened and narrowed until I found myself a serpent, and in me rose the desire to devour my little preserver, when, as I was about to strike her with my fangs, she changed into a beautiful little fairy, tapped my ugly black flat head with her wand, and as my fangs fell to earth I resumed my human shape. With the parting words, 'Never seek to injure those who endeavour to serve you,' she disappeared.

Looking about, I found myself in a huge cave, dark and noisome. Serpents hissed and glared at me from every side, and huge lizards and ugly shapes scrambled over the wet floor. In the far corner of the cave I saw piles of precious stones of wondrous value that glanced and sparkled in the dim light. Despite the horrid shapes about me, I resolved to secure some, at least, of these precious gems. I began to walk toward them, but found that I could get no nearer – just as fast as I advanced, so fast did they seem to recede. At last, after what seemed a year's weary journey, I suddenly found myself beside them and, falling on my knees, began to fill my pockets, bosom, even my hat. Then I tried to rise, but could not: the jewels weighed me down. Mortified and disappointed, I replaced all but three, weeping bitterly. As I rose to my feet it suddenly occurred to me that this was in no way real – only a hashish dream. And, laughing, I said, 'You fool, this is all nonsense. These are not real jewels; they exist only in your imagination.' My real self arguing thus with my hashish self, which I could see, tired, ragged and weeping, set me to laughing still harder, and then we laughed together –

my two selves. Suddenly my real self faded away, and a cloud of sadness and misery settled upon me, and I wept again, throwing myself hysterically upon the damp floor of the cave.

Just then I heard a voice addressing me by name, and looking up, I saw an old man with an enormous nose bending over me. His nose seemed almost as large as his whole body. 'Why do you weep, my son?' he said. 'Are you sad because you cannot have all these riches? Don't, then, for some day you will learn whoso hath more wealth than is needed to minister to his wants must suffer for it. Every farthing above a certain reasonable sum will surely bring some worry, care, anxiety or trouble. Three diamonds are your share; be content with them. But, dear me, here I am again neglecting my work! Here it is March, and I'm not half through yet!'

'Pray, what is your work, venerable patriarch?' I asked. 'And why has the Lord given you such a huge proboscis?'

'Ah! I see that you don't know me,' he replied. 'I am the chemist of the earth's bowels, and it is my duty to prepare all the sweet and delicate odors that the flowers have. I am busy all winter making them, and early in the spring my nymphs and apprentices deliver them to the Queen of the Flowers, who in turn gives them to her subjects. My nose is a little large because I have to do so much smelling. Come and see my laboratory.'

His nose a little large! I laughed until I almost cried at this, while following him.

He opened a door, and, entering, my nostrils met the oddest medley of odors I had ever smelled. Everywhere workmen with huge noses were busy mixing, filtering, distilling and the like.

'Here,' said the old man, 'is a batch of odor that has been spoiled. Mistakes are frequent, but I find use for even such as that. The Queen of the Flowers gives it to disobedient plants or flowers. You mortals call it asafoetida. Come in here and see my organ,' and he led the way into a large rocky room, at one end of which was a huge organ of curious construction. Mounting to the seat, he arranged the stops and began to play.

Not a sound could be heard, but a succession of odors swept past me, some slowly, some rapidly. I understood the grand idea in a moment. Here was music to which that of sound was coarse and earthly. Here was a harmony, a symphony, of odors! Clear and sharp, intense and less intense, sweet, less sweet, and again still sweeter, heavy and light, fast and slow, deep and narcotic, the odors, all in perfect harmony, rose and fell and swept by me, to be succeeded by others.

Irresistibly, I began to weep, and fast and thick fell the tears, until I found myself a little stream of water, that, rising in the rocky caverns of the mountain, dashed down its side into the plain below. Fiercely the hot sun beat upon my scanty waters, and like a thin gray mist I found myself rising slowly into the skies, no longer a stream. With other clouds I was swept away by the strong and rapid wind far across the Atlantic, over the burning sand wastes of Africa, dipping toward the Arabian Sea, and suddenly falling in huge raindrops into the very heart of India, blossoming with poppies. As the ground greedily sucked up the refreshing drops I again assumed my form. Suddenly the earth was rent apart and, falling upon the edge of a deep cavern, I saw far below me a molten, hissing sea of fire, above which a dense vapor hung. Issuing from this mist, a thousand anguished faces rose toward me on scorched and broken wings, shrieking and moaning as they came.

'Who in Heaven's name are these poor things?'

'These,' said a voice at my side, 'are the spirits, still incarnate, of individuals who, during life, sought happiness in the various narcotics. Here, after death, far beneath, they live a life of torture most exquisite, for it is their fate, ever suffering for want of moisture, to be obliged to yield day by day their life-blood to form the juice of the poppy and resin of hemp in order that their dream, joys, hopes, pleasures, pains, and anguish of past and present may again be tasted by mortals.'

As he said this I turned to see who he was, but he had disappeared. Suddenly I heard a fierce clamor, felt the scrawny arms of these foul spirits wound about my neck, in my hair, on my limbs, pulling me over into the horrible chasm, into the heart of hell, crying shrilly, 'Come! thou are one of us. Come! come! come!' I struggled fiercely, shrieked out in my agony, and suddenly awoke, with the cold sweat thick upon me.

'Are you, then, so fond of it that nothing can awaken you? Here have I been shaking and pulling you for the past five minutes. Come, rouse yourself; your dreams seem to be unpleasant.'

Gradually my senses became clearer. The odors of the room, the melodies of early evening, the pipe that had fallen from my hand, the faces and forms of the hemp smokers, were once more recognized.

My companion wished me to stay, assuring me that I would see many queer sights before morning, but I declined, and after taking, by his advice, a cup of Paraguay tea (coca leaf), and then a cup of sour lemonade, I passed downstairs, exchanged my present for my former dress, returned my pipe, and left the house.

The dirty streets, the tinkling car-horse bell, the deafening 'Here you are! Twenty sweet oranges for a quarter!' and the drizzling rain were more grateful by far than the odors, sounds, sights, sweet though they were, that I had just left. Truly it was the cradle of dreams rocking placidly in the very heart of a great city, translated from Baghdad to Gotham.

1888. From: *Fitz Hugh Ludlow Memorial Library Hypertext Collection*

Mrs Frank Leslie
California: A Pleasure Trip from Gotham to the Golden Gate

FROM THE THEATRE we were taken to visit an Opium Den, as we of the East are prone to call the *tabazies*, where the Celestial seeks respite from toil and privation and home-sickness in the indulgence of a habit not so horrible after all as drunkenness of another nature; since the opium smoker injures only himself, and the man crazed by liquor is dangerous to his family and the community at large!

Passing through an alley-way, we entered a perfectly dark court where nothing was to be seen but so much to be smelled that the imagination became more painful than the reality could have been. A light twinkled from some windows on a level with the sidewalk, and our guide, unceremoniously pushing open the door, led us into a small, close, but apparently clean room, filled with the fumes of burning opium – resembling those of roasting groundnuts, and not disagreeable. A table stood in the center, and around three sides ran a double tier of shelves and bunks, covered with matting and with round logs of wood with a space hollowed out, cushioned or bare, for pillows. Nearly all of these were filled with Chinamen, many of them containing two, with a little tray between them, holding a lamp and a horn box filled with the black, semi-liquid opium paste. But although everyone was smoking, it was so early in the evening that the drug had not as yet wrought its full effect, and all were wide awake, talking, laughing, and apparently enjoying themselves hugely. The largest of the Chinamen was lying upon the shelf nearest the door, preparing his first pipe. He looked up and nodded as we crowded around him, and then calmly continued his occupation, we watching the *modus operandi* with considerable interest. The pipe was a little stone bowl, no larger than a baby's thimble, with an orifice in the bottom the size of a pin's head. This bowl is screwed on to the side of a long bamboo stem, and the smoker, taking up a mass of the opium paste upon the end of a wire, holds it to the flame of the lamp until it is slightly hardened, and then works it into the pipe, inhaling strongly as he does so, and drawing the smoke deep into his lungs, where it remains for a moment and then is ejected through the nostrils, leaving its fatal residuum behind; for opium is an accumulative poison, and when once the system becomes saturated with it, there is no release from the misery it entails but death. The tiny 'charge' constituting one pipe-full is soon exhausted, and holding the last whiff as long as possible, the smoker prepares another, and another and yet another, as long as he can control his muscles, until, at last, the nerveless hand falls beside him, the pipe drops from his fingers, and his head falls back in heavy stupor, the face ghastly white, the eyes glazed and lifeless, the breathing stenorous, the mind wandering away in visions like those De Quincey has given to the world in the *Confessions of an English Opium Eater*. Looking at the stalwart Chinaman, with his intelligent face and fresh, clean costume, we tried to fancy this loathsome change passing upon him and felt quite guilty as he looked up with a twinkling smile and offering us the lighted pipe said: 'Havee Smokee?' and when we declined, held out the wire with the little ball on the end for us to smell. As we talked to this man, we were startled by perceiving two persons curled up in the bunk below his shelf, both smoking and watching us with their narrow slits of eyes like crouching wild beasts. They did not speak, but our friend above answered all our questions in a cool, matter-of-fact sort of a way, and with an amiable superciliousness of manner we bade him good-by and went out, his eyes following us with a look and a laugh strangely resembling a sneer. Perhaps, carrying out the proverb *in vino veritas*, there is something about the first stages of opium intoxication dispelling to customary caution and disguise, for in that sneering look and laugh we seemed at last to get the true expression of feeling which forever haunts the writer as the real meaning underlying the bland, smiling or inane exterior, presented to us by these Celestials.

We looked into another room in the same court, much smaller but better furnished, the bunks neatly fitted up with mattresses and each containing its little tray with the lamp, pipe and opium all ready for the smokers not yet arrived. Our guide informed us in a mysterious tone that there are yet other opium dens to which access is impossible except to the initiated, where may be found at a later hour of the night young men and women as 'white as you are' as he said, and with no drop of Mongolian blood to excuse their participation in this imported vice.

'Not respectable Americans?' asked someone incredulously, and the detective, with a glance inscrutable as the Sphinx, replied:

'That's according to what you call respectable. The women I don't suppose are generally received in your society, but as for the men – well, a lady would be surprised, sometimes, if she knew just how the gentleman she has danced with all the evening spends the rest of the night!'

'If Asmodeus could visit San Francisco and take us on one of his flying trips over the tops of these houses with the power of unroofing them as we passed, we should see some strange scenes,' thoughtfully murmured the poet of the party, and Officer MacKenzie, with one of his keen glances, replied:

'I don't know much about flying through the air, but I reckon I can show you as strange and tough a sight if you want to see, if you like to risk it, for the ladies.'

April, May, June 1877. From: *Fitz Hugh Ludlow Memorial Library, Hypertext Collection*

Victor Bockris
With William Burroughs

At BURROUGHS' *apartment,* TER *emptied the bag of drug samples on to* BILL's *big parlor table, and as I turned on the tape and fired up the bomber,* BILL *motioned us to fix our drinks, donned his reading glasses, and settled in for a good scrutiny of the dope labels, using a magnifying glass like a jeweler examining precious stones.*

BURROUGHS: Now then, what is all this shit, Terry?

TERRY SOUTHERN: Bill, these are pharmaceutical samples, sent by the drug companies to Big Ed Fales, the friendly druggist, and to Doc Tom Adams, the writing croak. Anything that won't cook up, we'll eat. Give them good scrutiny, Bill.

BURROUGHS: Indeed I shall. Pain – I'm on the alert for the word pain . . . (murmuring, as he examines the label]: Hmm . . . yes . . . yes . . . yes, indeed . . . "Fluid-control that can make life liveable." Well, that could apply to blood, water . . .

SOUTHERN: All our precious bodily fluids!

BURROUGHS: I'll just go through these methodically. Anything of interest I'll put to one side . . .

SOUTHERN [getting a paper bag]: We'll put rejects in here. [picks up a bottle and reads]: "For pimples and acne" [throws it aside in disgust]. Now here . . . "Icktazinga" [handing it to Bill]: Ring a bell?

BURROUGHS [examining it]: "Chewable." I'm not much interested in anything chewable . . . [makes a wry face].

SOUTHERN: But they're saying, "Chew one at a time," and I'm saying, "Cook up eight!" If One Will Chew, Eight Will Cook Up! There's a title for you!

BOCKRIS: Here's a diuretic.

SOUTHERN: A diuretic may contain paregoric – and you know what that means!

BURROUGHS: No, no . . .

SOUTHERN: I say a diuretic is chock-a-block full of a spasm-relieving nerve-killer . . . definitely a coke-based medication!

BURROUGHS: A diuretic . . .

SOUTHERN: It'll cook right up, Bill.

BURROUGHS: . . . is something to induce urination, my dear – that's all that it is.

SOUTHERN: Is that all a diuretic does? Induce urine?

BURROUGHS: Yes.

SOUTHERN [gravely]: Well, Doctor, I suppose we're in for another damnable stint of trial-and-error.

BURROUGHS: Yes, I'm afraid so. Such are the tribulations of the legitimate drug industry. A codeine-based cough syrup sold over the counter a few years ago.

BOCKRIS: Nicotinic acid! What's that like?

BURROUGHS: That's vitamins, my dear.

SOUTHERN: Hold on, Doctor, it could be some sort of synthetic speed!

BOCKRIS: Yes, it says, "For prolonged action."

BURROUGHS [scrutinizing yet another label]: Pain! – look for the word "pain" . . . that's the key.

SOUTHERN: Let "pain" be our watchword!

BURROUGHS: Here we are, this could be it. [He inspects an ancient looking bottle with dark green label on it.] Yes, this is the stuff. It's got a little codeine in it.

SOUTHERN: We'll have to savor it . . . . But, Bill, I hope you're not underestimating these synthetic painkillers, just because they're not labeled heroin or morphine . . .

BURROUGHS [impatiently]: Man, I know every synthetic . . .

BOCKRIS: Now here's one for hypertension – so it's a down, right?

BURROUGHS: No, hypertension is merely indicative of high blood pressure . . .

SOUTHERN: But surely it's a down, man, if it's antihypertension it must be a down . . .

BURROUGHS: NO, it isn't.

BOCKRIS [with another]: Now this one could be speed. "Prolonged activity" it says.

SOUTHERN: Good!

BURROUGHS: What kind of activity? I'm not sure I want any more activity.

BOCKRIS [reading]: "Niacin!"

BURROUGHS: Man, don't you know what niacin is?

SOUTHERN: Down the hatch for heavy action, Bill!

BURROUGHS: You know what niacin is, don't you? It's a vitamin-B complex! . . . Now, this is the one thing we got – it contains half a grain of codeine sulfate – hardly any, but if you drank one of these bottles you might get a little buzz.

SOUTHERN: Down the gullet, Bill!

BOCKRIS: What we should do is take William out to dinner.

BURROUGHS [ignoring this]: You can get all the codeine you want right across the counter in France or Switzerland, but you can't get it here. [He picks up a bottle and reads]: "Confused, forgetful, cranky, unkempt, suspicious personality . . . Transient cerebral ischemia, inimical psychological condition for the second day in a row and they deal with underlying circulatory . . ."

BOCKRIS: I want to get straightened out. "Unkempt." I'll take one of those.

BURROUGHS: Each to his taste, as the French say, but I advise against it. [crumbling]: Now here's something that goes straight in the wastepaper basket – "non-narcotic"! . . . I don't want anything non-narcotic on these premises! Heh-heh-heh.

SOUTHERN: Listen, they can say "non-narcotic," but they may

have some really weird definition of narcotic, like something out of Dracula . . . I mean, think of the fantastic competition that must be going on between the headache-remedy people – trying to cure headaches and make you feel good.

BURROUGHS [reading another label and tossing the bottle aside]: Well, we don't need any inflammatory agents for ancient arthritic conditions.

SOUTHERN: Wait! That's a painkiller! "Arthritis" is the word they use now for "pain," and that means heavy codeine, Bill!

BOCKRIS: This potion is well known to me – it's merely your friendly cough syrup with all the regular ingredients.

SOUTHERN: But it might cook up into something really sensational! You cook it up until everything disappears except the essence, which would be dynamite in terms of sense derangement . . .

BOCKRIS: We need an isolizer to isolize it.

SOUTHERN: No. Trial and error, trial and error . . .

BURROUGHS: We'll not go the trial-and-error route on these premises.

BOCKRIS: Shall we smoke another joint before we go out?

SOUTHERN [opening a small metal can]: Now this is from the Republic of Columbia-dynamo-dynamite. I'll just twist one up [takes out pink papers] using these clitoral pinks to give it zest.

BOCKRIS: Why don't you twist up another one? It looks like Bill might smoke that one up himself. [Burroughs has picked up a series of newspaper clippings about murders and is acting out the various parts on the other side of the room, Terry's first joint in one hand.] Bill, was there a lot of cocaine in Paris during Hemingway and Fitzgerald's time?

BURROUGHS: Man, there was plenty of cocaine and heroin. In the late 1920s it was all over the place in Europe, if you knew how to go about getting it. It was about 1/100th the price it is now.

SOUTHERN: Hemingway and Fitzgerald never mentioned it – no reference to dope . . . in their "entire collective oeuvre," so to speak. They were both heavily into the juice.

BOCKRIS: What I'm asking is, were Picasso and Gertrude Stein and Hemingway snorting coke?

SOUTHERN: No, but in Paris, where you have a large Arab population, you can turn on with hash quite openly – in the Arab cafes near the Hotel de Ville. They have the strongest hash you can get, so they had that thing in the Gide, Baudelaire tradition . . .

BURROUGHS: You are confounding your times in this message. You got Gide and Baudelaire at the same fucking table sniffing cocaine. Why don't you throw in Villon, for Christsake! They all had a sniff of cocaine together! I think you're sniffing time-travel, baby!

SOUTHERN [with a show of indignation]: Doctor! I am referring to the sustained tradition of sense-derangement among decadent frogs of the so-called Quality-Lit crowd! Baudelaire! Rimbaud! Verlaine! And the late great Andy Gide!

BURROUGHS [adamant]: Time-travel!

SOUTHERN: Bill's threshold of tolerance is about the width of a thai stick.

BOCKRIS: I hate Quaaludes.

BURROUGHS: You really feel logy in the morning. It's terrible stuff. I don't like them at all.

BOCKRIS: I hate that stuff – and Mandrax.

SOUTHERN: The great Mandrax! Is that the same as quay?

BOCKRIS: Stronger than quay. The English equivalent, but stronger. They use it a lot for seduction.

SOUTHERN: That's the thing about Quaaludes – chicks love Quaaludes – makes them less self-conscious, I suppose, about fucking. The druggist says it's a great favorite with hookers. With students and hookers. They must have something in common.

BURROUGHS: Intense pain.

SOUTHERN: They call them "floaters" – I guess they float above the pain.

BURROUGHS: On it, more likely – floating on a sea of pain!

We go over to Mickey Ruskin's restaurant at One University

Place for dinner.

BURROUGHS: I've reached the age where I can get a drink in Chicago without showing my ID. God man, listen to this, we walk into this bar and they demand IDs. The waitress looked at me coldly and said, "I guess you're all right." Were you along on that? Did you get a drink, Terry? Were you "all right"? If anyone asks for my ID I should be deeply flattered.

The cab arrives outside the restaurant. As we walk toward the door BURROUGHS *growls, gangster style, "I'll get you boys in, I swear." Inside, Roy Orbison is beginning to sing "Pretty Woman." The music washes over us as we take a table . . .*

BOCKRIS: Doesn't it seem obvious that the most salable drug of all would turn out to be the drug that would make sex better? Imagine if you could advertise and say this drug makes sex better. That's the drug that's going to sell the most, right?

BURROUGHS [emphatically]: No, I don't think so at all . . . Because the drug that's always sold the most on any market, and which will eventually replace any drug that makes sex more possible, is the drug that makes sex unnecessary, namely heroin. On an open market heroin would push marijuana right off the market, which is a fairly good sex drug. See, most people don't like sex – they want to be rid of sex. Their sex life is terrifically unsatisfactory. They have a wife who they were attracted to forty years ago, it's terrible, what do they want their sex life stimulated for? Their sex life is horrible. So heroin enables them to get rid of that drive, and that's what they really want.

SOUTHERN: Which drugs are sexually stimulating?

BURROUGHS: Marijuana.

BOCKRIS: A good mixture of coke and marijuana can sometimes work, depending on the catalyst, I guess.

BURROUGHS: I don't like coke.

BOCKRIS: No, but a small amount of it can help.

BURROUGHS: Get high on marijuana and then a couple of poppers.

BOCKRIS: Do you keep poppers next to the bed?

BURROUGHS: Well naturally, you see, all the young people do.

They say the stink of amyl nitrate fills the halls of the hotels up at Bellows Falls.

BOCKRIS: Terry, which drug would you most like to have for yourself?

SOUTHERN: Cocaine is the most enjoyable drug for me – in moderation, natch, due to its price.

With William Burroughs, 1997

Antonil
Thunder Over the Coca Fields

'. . . IT IS NOT for the anthropologist to attempt to usurp the role of the gods whose worship he studies.' A quote from a standard textbook on the sociology of shamanism.

The path seems to wind uphill for ever, a thin drizzle laying its damp hand across your shoulders, as you stagger uncertainly over yet another bank of eroded clay, slipping into a dark grove of sodden banana plants. The surface of the path turns from a hard, compacted orange subsoil to a thick black mire mixed with jagged pebbles and rotting leaves, churned by the hooves of a thousand stamping horses which have passed this way before. You cast off your shoes and plunge knee-deep into the ooze, the *barrial*, toes squirming as you are sucked down to a narrow stream and through the flow of its icy waters – your body one transient slick of mud and sweat driving relentlessly through a slipping universe. Shooting star or retinal flare, after-image fading . . .

Slime-climb the next rise, grabbing hold of roots which slack and slap back, your butt-end falling through endless space to a single, solid curse: 'What the *fuck* am I doing *here*?' The gods thunder without lightning. Clouds sunder, yielding shaft-rays of luminous afternoon sun, pouring gold across the open valley. Flame sparkles on the leaves, tanager birds come out to strut, prance across and twitter, pearls of water casting reflections from their yellow feathers. The scent of sodden leaves, a curtain pierced as you break out across the open hillside, long grass itching, pricking, as it wipes blood and blister from your feet, shirt heaving in a cloud of steam.

And then – you hit that picture of a house, the first one since five miles back, since before the rain began. Brown mud walls, thatched roof, small outhouses made of split bamboo and rushes. A wooden mill, the sugar-cane crusher, set in the middle of a patch of horse-shit and vegetable debris. Dog barks, hens cackle. A couple of kids' faces, covered with soot, loom out from the darkness at the door. Alarm. Man appears, leans against the wooden door frame, feigning nonchalance. He greets you with a suspicious smile. *Eucha*, you reply, careful to put the stress on the first syllable. You enquire as to the state of the path further on, you mention the names of some mutual friends. *Esh gueninga?* You offer some coca leaves, a little tobacco. You are asked indoors.

Enter one large square room with an open wood fire set on the floor over to one side. The smoke makes your eyes water. It has long covered all the rafters with a thick layer of the blackest grime, but you can make out a few net bags hanging above the fire, preserving dead meats, suspending cobs of red, black and yellow-speckled corn beyond the reach of hungry rodents. Beaten earth floor covered with cowhides, large dented pans and the occasional bundle of tattered woollen blankets. Maybe a half-dozen stools placed around the hearth, small blocks of wood a foot long by half across, carved anatomically to hold the body in a squatting pose, no more than three or four inches from the ground.

You sit – women and children retire to the other side of the fire and eye you with amazement. You are presented with an enamel bowl filled with about a pint of steaming soup – *mote* – containing maize and beans and cabbage, tasting strangely of a light wood ash used to dehusk the grains of corn, the whole effect somehow rotten and fermented, as if the vegetables have been sitting in water for a few days. Then, the inevitable questions: Where from? And what for? But most of all, why here?

Why, indeed. Hardly the right time to trundle out a string

of platitudes about scientific models and methodologies, about the need for an abstract Mama Coca as a prop to structure your research.

Your answer, therefore, comes out direct and to the point, measured with a blade of tempered absence: 'To learn how to chew coca . . .'

Your words are greeted with a smile. A knowing smile. A friendly smile, even. And yet an edge of doubt, of disbelief suspended only through cunning, a flash of mockery in the Indian's eyes.

You spring forward – metaphorically baring your chest – preferring some direct, explicit repudiation to the dead weight of misunderstanding, hoping that some final encounter will at last shake off that ghostly academic identity carried with you like a shield, *muy estimado, Doctor*, allowing the field of enquiry to strike back and finally gobble you entire. Phrases like: 'No more trying to become something while maintaining a critical distance from the process of becoming . . .' – or even, curse the thought, 'A rich confrontation between the thing itself and one's own awareness of it . . .' *Logico, hermano, ni hablar . . .*

Personal bees in your bonnet swatted, brought down by sudden hits of the specific. The next morning you may awake with a terrible rash spreading up your arm from the fingers to the elbow. You could rush out to smother the fact with some timely explanation, only to find that the tools of such a deliverance are no longer in your own hands – that in Tierradentro it is the Paez *te'ue* who call the shots. Rash on the right arm; that is a sign of something coming in. On the hand, notice, meaning that you have touched on things you would have done well to leave alone. Things like *sena*-magic? The coke business?

Or, wait a minute – the horror, the thrill, the dawning realisation – could not these trips be entirely tame in comparison to the overbearing Pride, the sheer aggressive witchcraft, underlying your belief in the scientific endeavour itself? The evidence is conclusive – so take it, your itch and show it to Eliozondo:

'A *caspi* rash. An *ech* attack. Either you must leave Tierrandentro for ever, or . . .'

Accept that the persona of the mere rational scientist is dead – yes, dead, deaded, dead.

Eliozondo sits in a menacing huddle in the dark, moonless night, the thousand muscles of his body in *sena*-communication with the spirit legions of the rainbows, riverbeds, the springs and caves. Maybe he sees them in the flesh, hairy bodies moving in and out through the lace outlines of the undergrowth, their presence in his vision sending a cackle of reciprocal machine gun *senas* echoing through your body. Your I dissipates into a twinkling of an eye to eye. The earth, the sky no longer simply up and down, but curling over the edges, a drunken swirling around the dead point you call observation.

A rush of cold fear and nausea breaks across you like a wave. You take a long, hard suck on your wad of coca leaves – but you get no freeze this time, no substance, no hard edge with which to draw the line. Coca dissolves into a vortex of spinning head and swoon – a clammy sweat on the body, a final panic of bubbles as you go down and out – your choking voice from offstage blurting out a desperate 'Hey, wait a minute . . .' The axis of your sense perception spiralling down, telescoped into an empty hole – black, still, a vacuum . . .

You wake up to the perfect stillness of the dead. All is a play of light on darkness, everywhere a timeless sleep. A long, hollow roll of thunder. In front of you an old man with half a dozen coca bags slung around his neck.

You croak. 'Are you?'

A green smile. Ground shudders, trees bend without any wind. Feel the tongue, frozen, speechless . . .

Awe and wonder as you are forced to recognise.

Mama Coca, 1978

M. Ageyev
Novel with Cocaine

DURING THE LONG nights and long days I spent under the influence of cocaine in Yag's room I came to see that what counts in life is not the events that surround one but the reflection of those events in one's consciousness. Events may change, but insofar as the changes are not reflected in one's consciousness their result is nil. Thus, for example, a man basking in the aura of his riches will continue to feel himself a millionaire so long as he is unaware that the bank where he keeps his capital has gone under; a man basking in the aura of his offspring will continue to feel himself a father until he learns that his child has been run over. Man lives not by the events surrounding him, therefore, but by the reflection of those events in his consciousness.

All of a man's life – his work, his deeds, his will, his physical and mental prowess – is completely and utterly devoted to, fixed on bringing about, one or another event in the external world, though not so much to experience the event in itself as to experience the reflection of the event on his consciousness. And if, to take it all a step further, everything a man does he does to bring about only those events which, when reflected in his consciousness, will make him feel happiness and joy, then what he spontaneously reveals thereby is nothing less than the basic mechanism behind his life and the life of every man, evil and cruel or good and kind.

One man does everything in his power to overthrow the tsar, another to overthrow the revolutionary junta; one man wishes to strike it rich, another gives his fortune to the poor. Yet what do these contrasts show but the diversity of human activity, which serves at best (and not in every case) as a kind of individual personality index. The reason behind human activity, as diverse as that activity may be, is always one: man's need to bring about events in the external world which, when reflected in his consciousness, will make him feel happiness.

So it was in my insignificant life as well. The road to the external event was well marked: I wished to become a rich and famous lawyer. It would seem I had only to take the road and follow it to the end, especially since I had much to recommend me (or so I tried to convince myself). But oddly enough, the more time I spent making my way towards the cherished goal, the more often I would stretch out on the couch in my dark room and imagine I was what I intended to become, my penchant for sloth and reverie persuading me that there was no point in laying out so great an expenditure of time and energy to bring the external events to fruition when my happiness would be all the stronger if the events leading up to it came about rapidly and unexpectedly.

But such was the force of habit that even in my dreams of happiness I thought chiefly of the event rather than the feeling of happiness, certain that the event (should it but occur) would lead to the happiness I desired. I was incapable of divorcing the two. The problem was that before I first came in contact with cocaine I assumed that happiness was an entity, while in fact all human happiness consists of a clever fusion of two elements: 1) the physical feeling of happiness, and 2) the external event providing the psychic impetus for that feeling. Not until I first tried cocaine did I see the light; not until then did I see that the external event I had dreamed of bringing about – the result I had been slaving day and night for and yet might never manage to achieve – the external event was essential only insofar as I needed its reflection to make me feel happy. What if, as I was convinced, a tiny speck of cocaine could provide my organism with instantaneous happiness on a scale I had never dreamed of before. Then the need for any event whatever disappeared and, with it, the need for expending great amounts of work, time and energy to bring it about.

Therein lay the power of cocaine – in its ability to produce a feeling of physical happiness psychically independent of all external events, even when the reflection of the events in my consciousness would otherwise have produced feelings of grief, depression and despair. And it was that property of the drug that exerted so terribly strong an attraction on me that I neither could nor would oppose or resist it. The only way I could have done so was if the feeling of happiness had come less from bringing about the external event than from the work, the effort, the energy invested in bringing it about. But that was a kind of happiness I had never known.

Novel with Cocaine, 1936

Nelson Algren
The Man with the Golden Arm

THE CLOCK IN the room above the Safari told only Junkie Time. For every hour here was Old Junkie's Hour and the walls were the color of old junkies' dreams: the hue of diluted morphine in the moment before the needle draws the suffering blood.

Walls that went up and up like walls in a troubled dream. Walls like water where no legend could be written and no hand grasp metal or wood. Nor Nifty Louie paid the rent and Frankie knew too well who the landlord was.

He had met him before, that certain down-at-heel vet growing stooped from carrying a thirty-five-pound monkey on his back. Frankie remembered that face, ravaged by love of its own suffering as by some endless all-night orgy. A face forged out of his own wound fever in a windy ward tent on the narrow Meuse. He had met Private McGantic before: both had served their country well. This was the fellow who looked somehow a little like everyone else in the world and was more real to a junkie than any real man could be. The projected image of one's own pain when that pain has become too great to be borne. The image of one hooked so hopelessly on morphine that there would be no getting the monkey off without another's help. There are so few ways to help old sad frayed and weary West Side junkies.

Frankie felt no pity for himself, yet felt compassion for this McGantic. He worried, as the sickness rose in himself, about what in God's name McGantic would do tomorrow when the money and the morphine both gave out. Where then, in that terrible hour, would Private M find the strength to carry the monkey through one more endless day?

By the time Frankie got inside the room he was so weak Louie had to help him on to the army cot beside the oil stove. He lay on his back with one arm flung across his eyes as if in shame; and his lips were blue with cold. The pain had hit him with an icy fist in the groin's very pit, momentarily tapering off to a single probing finger touching the genitals to get the maximum of pain. He tried twisting to get away from the finger: the finger was worse than the fist. His throat was so dry that, though he spoke, the lips moved and made no sound. But Fomorowski read such lips well.

'Fix me. Make it stop. Fix me.'

'I'll fix you, Dealer,' Louie assured him softly.

Louie had his own bedside manner. He perched on the red leather and chrome bar stool borrowed from the Safari, with the amber toes of his two-tone shoes catching the light and the polo ponies galloping down his shirt. This was Nifty Louie's Hour. The time when he did the dealing and the dealer had to take what Louie chose to toss him in Louie's own good time.

He lit a match with his fingertip and held it away from the bottom of the tiny glass tube containing the fuzzy white cap of morphine, holding it just far enough away to keep the cap from being melted by the flame. There was time and time and lots of time for that. Let the dealer do a bit of melting first; the longer it took the higher the price. 'You can pay me off when Zero pays you,' he assured Frankie. There was no hurry. 'You're good with me any time, Dealer.'

Frankie moaned like an animal that cannot understand its own pain. His shirt had soaked through and the pain had frozen so deep in his bones nothing could make him warm again.

'Hit me, Fixer. Hit me.'

A sievelike smile drained through Louie's teeth. This was his hour and this hour didn't come every day. He snuffed out the match's flame as it touched his fingers and snapped the head of another match into flame with his nail, letting its glow flicker one moment over that sievelike smile; then brought the tube down cautiously and watched it dissolve at the flame's fierce touch. When the stuff had melted he held both needle and tube in one hand, took the dealer's loose-hanging arm firmly with the other and pumped it in a long, loose arc. Frankie let him swing it as if it were attached to someone else. The cold was coming up from within now, a colorless cold spreading through stomach and liver and breathing across the heart like an odorless gas. To make the very brain tighten and congeal under its icy touch.

'Warm. Make me warm.'

And still there was no rush, no hurry at all. Louie pressed the hypo down to the cotton; the stuff came too high these days to lose the fraction of a drop. 'Don't vomit, student,' he taunted Frankie to remind him of the first fix he'd had after his discharge but he was too cold to answer. He was falling between glacial walls, he didn't know how anyone could fall so far away from everyone else in the world. So far to fall, so cold all the way, so steep and dark between those morphine-colored walls of Private McGantic's terrible pit.

He couldn't feel Louie probing into the dark red knot above his elbow at all. Nor see the way the first blood sprayed faintly up into the delicate hypo to tinge the melted morphine with blood as warm as the needle's heated point.

When Louie sensed the vein he pressed it down with the certainty of a good doctor's touch, let it linger a moment in the vein to give the heart what it needed and withdrew gently, daubed the blood with a piece of cotton, tenderly, and waited.

Louie waited. Waited to see it hit.

Louie liked to see the stuff hit. It meant a lot to Louie, seeing it hit.

'Sure I like to watch,' he was ready to acknowledge any time. 'Man, their *eyes* when that big drive hits 'n' goes tingling down to the toes. They retch, they sweat, they itch – then the big drive hits 'n' here they come out of it cryin' like a baby 'r laughin' like a loon. *Sure I* like to watch. *Sure I* like to see it hit. Heroin got the drive awright – but there's not a tingle to a ton – you got to get M to get that tingle-tingle.'

It hit all right. It hit the heart like a runaway locomotive, it hit like a falling wall. Frankie's whole body lifted with that smashing surge, the very heart seemed to lift up-up-up – then rolled over and he slipped into a long warm bath with one long orgasmic sigh of relief. Frankie opened his eyes.

The Man with the Golden Arm, 1949

Christopher Mayhew MP
An Excursion out of Time

WHAT HAPPENED TO me between 12.30 and four o'clock on Friday, 2 December 1955? After brooding about it for several months, I still think my first, astonishing conviction was right – that on many occasions that afternoon I existed outside time.

I don't mean this metaphorically, but literally. I mean that the essential part of me (the part that thinks to itself 'This is me') had an existence, quite conscious of itself, enjoying itself, reflecting on its strange experience, in a timeless order of reality outside the world as we know it.

And I believe this in spite of the fact that the experience was induced by a drug, the much-discussed mescaline.

People who are drugged, of course, often suffer from delusions; and the common-sense explanation of my experience is simply that I took an hallucinogen and had an hallucination. And if I dispute this now, when I am undrugged, there is, says common sense, nothing strange about that either. People who have hallucinations often cannot believe that they are hallucinations.

This common-sense attitude is persuasive, but I don't think it is wrong; and at the risk of making a complete fool of myself, I would like to put forward an alternative explanation. At least this may stir up some controversy, and perhaps even encourage some research along what seems an extremely promising line of scientific inquiry.

Let me first explain how I came to take the drug. I am an old school friend of Dr Humphrey Osmond, who is the Medical

Superintendent of a mental hospital in Saskatchewan. In his search for a cure for his schizophrenic patients, Dr Osmond has for some years past been experimenting with a particular range of drugs known as 'psychotomimetics', which produce in those who take them some of the symptoms of insanity. It was Dr Osmond who administered one of these drugs – mescaline – to Mr Aldous Huxley in the fascinating experiment described in Huxley's *The Doors of Perception*.

For years I had been in desultory correspondence with Dr Osmond, and in the course of this he had told me about his research work and expounded the exciting theory that certain drugs can, by inhibiting parts of our brain which act as a 'filter', enable us to receive a wider, more representative range of signals from the outside world – i.e. to experience the outside world more nearly as it 'really' is, before our minds impose their pattern on it.

Last autumn, in anticipation of a visit to Britain, Dr Osmond asked me to approach the BBC about the possibility of his doing some broadcasts on his work. I replied by suggesting that we should make a television film together about mescaline, in the course of which he would give me the drug and I would describe my reactions.

Dr Osmond liked this idea, and so did the BBC. So on 2 December, a BBC producer and film team – old colleagues of mine – arrived at our home in surrey, converted our drawing-room into a studio, and at 12.05 p.m., filmed me drinking down 400mg of mescaline hydrochloride.

For half an hour nothing happened. Then I began feeling sick, and various nerves and muscles started twitching unpleasantly. Then, as this wore off, my body became more or less anaesthetised, and I became 'de-personalised', i.e. I felt completely detached from my body and the world, and was aware of my eyes seeing, my ears hearing and my mouth speaking as though at some distance below me.

By 1.15 I was in the full flood of the extraordinary visual phenomena described in *The Doors of Perception*. I will not describe these fully, as Huxley has done it so well already. Perspectives and colours everywhere had an astonishing, mysterious beauty. The red curtains of our drawing room took on a dozen ethereal shades of mauve and purple.

This experience alone would have fully justified the entire experiment for me (e.g. I think I shall always be more sensitive in future to certain kinds of painting), but at about 1.30 all interest in these visual phenomena was abruptly swept aside when I found that time was behaving even more strangely than colour. Though perfectly rational and wide awake (Dr Osmond gave me tests throughout the experiment which showed no significant falling-off in intelligence), I was not experiencing events in the normal sequence of time. I was experiencing the events of 3.30 before the events of 3.00; the events of 2.00 after the events of 2.45, and so on. Several events I experienced with an equal degree of reality more than once.

I am not suggesting, of course, that the events of 3.30 happened before the events of 3.00, or that any events happened more than once. All I am saying is that I experienced them, not in the familiar sequence of clock time, but in a different, apparently capricious sequence which was outside my control.

By 'I' in this context I mean, of course, my disembodied self, and by 'experienced' I mean learned by a special kind of awareness which seemed to comprehend yet be different from, seeing, hearing, etc.

In films, 'flash-backs' transpose us backwards and forwards in time. We find events of 1956 being suddenly interrupted by events of 1939. In the same way I found later events in our drawing-room – events in which I myself was participating at the bodily level – being interrupted by earlier events and vice versa.

I count this experience, which occurred when, as I say, I was wide awake and intelligent, sitting in my own armchair at home, as the most astounding and thought-provoking of my life. The experience lasted about two and a half hours, when the drug began wearing off. An amusing by-product was that I never knew whether or when the experiment was ending. True, I could, and constantly did, consult my watch;

and would be aware of my eyes registering, say, three o'clock; but this information would be of no value to me myself, in my strange detachment, since I knew I might soon be transported to some earlier part of the experiment, when I would be aware of my eyes registering, say, 2.30.

However, as the drug wore off, I managed to work out a way of telling that the experiment was ending. I noticed that I was experiencing events of a particular type with increasing frequency and regularity. These were events associated with our tea trolley (which was brought in at the end of the experiment). Their increasing frequency of recurrence gave them a special importance and significance. After a time, they held the field, and were no longer interrupted by earlier events. The tea trolley stayed there all the time, and I judged from this (it was my only clue) that I was back in the normal world of time.

Observer, 28 October 1956

Harry Asher
They Split My Personality

I SHOULD HAVE had the sense not to volunteer for this experiment. But one so seldom does the sensible thing and I did agree, on request, to act as one of the subjects in a test of the new drug, lysergic acid, sometimes known as LSD.

This drug has exciting possibilities because it produces in some subjects symptoms which resemble those of schizophrenia. Since the composition of the drug is known, there is the hope that antidotes to it may in turn be developed, and that either these antidotes or compounds related to them may be a cure for schizophrenia itself.

One of the early steps in the research was to make a careful study of the symptoms that the drug produces. It was in this early stage that I was involved.

The day came when I sat in a chair in a laboratory, and a man in a white overall handed me a beaker containing thirty-millionths of a gram of lysergic acid.

49

Effects were expected to develop after about half an hour. 'Any symptoms?' I was asked at the end of that time.

'No. Sorry. Nothing at all.'

Later the question was repeated.

'No. Sorry. Nothing at all.'

'Don't you feel sick?'

'Good Lord, yes. Perfectly horrible. I never thought of reporting that. It's your stuff, is it? All right, record a considerable nausea.'

After about an hour with nothing but nausea, I said, 'Look. You've got to observe me for the next four hours. We might as well enjoy ourselves. It's a lovely day. Let's break out from this stuffy building and walk for miles and miles in the country.'

Looking back now and remembering that I seldom go for walks, it is clear that the drug was beginning to act. However, I did not realise it then.

'Any change in the way things look?' I was asked.

'No. No change.'

'Don't you see anything at the edges of the buildings, for instance?'

'Good Lord, yes! That factory chimney has got a spectrum down the edge! Just as though it was seen through a prism.'

The drug has certainly started to work, and we returned to the laboratory, where more accurate observations could be recorded.

The early experiences were wholly delightful. There was a feeling of exhilaration and self-confidence, such as is rarely experienced, and an exaggerated tendency to laugh at anything at all. The failure of anyone else to understand what the joke was became in itself irrepressibly funny. The laughter became difficult to control. Things got funnier and funnier, and I laughed until I was in a condition of painful spasm, with tears running down my cheeks. Then the visual distortions began. I noticed a patch of sunlight on the floor. Because its brightness appeared to be fluctuating I enquired if clouds were crossing the sky. No, the light was really steady. I dictated into the tape recorder a running commentary on the apparent changes of intensity of this steady patch of sunlight.

At about this time, distortions of depth also began to occur. The object that made the greatest impression on me was a pair of spectacles worn by one of the assistants. They stood out in front of his face, which itself was increased in depth.

'You've no idea how funny you look,' I said to the man.

He looked puzzled. In some curious way the fact that he was, as it were, at the same time both in the experiment looking distorted and outside the experiment looking puzzled, with the puzzled look showing in the distorted face with the protruding spectacles, struck me very forcibly.

Then the nausea increased, the depth distortions became greater, and colour changes were more noticeable. Earlier, it had been fun but now I was ill.

At their height, the depth distortions alternated. At one moment the feet would seem to be far away and small, just exactly as they do when opera glasses are used the wrong way round. Then the effect would reverse, and the legs and body would look very short. The feet appeared to be about eighteen inches below my eyes, and it seemed that they had come up rather than that I had gone down. The illusion reversed direction several times per minute.

Having played the game of trying to walk along a line while looking down binoculars the wrong way, and remembering that equilibrium is then upset, I set out very, very gingerly on a visit down the corridor to the toilet, expecting to fall over. The corridor, which really is long, kept changing in length. If I looked down, my feet might be far or near according to what 'phase' they happened to be in. But, despite the alternate stretching of the corridor to perhaps two or three times its normal length followed by compression to one-half or one-third its length, accompanied by the apparent alteration in my own height, there was no difficulty in walking. There was, perhaps, a slight feeling of dissociation, which was to become more apparent later. The walking was done by a walking man, and on top of him was a pair of eyes which saw things distorted but these eyes were not in control of the motion.

On coming out into the corridor, I met the Deputy Vice-Chancellor of the university. If I had not been fully conscious of his status, I would surely have bitten him in the waistcoat. Of all the places to bite a man, the waistcoat is the least profitable, but it was only there that I wanted to bite him.

The wish came in the form of a visual change. My false teeth were snapping away in the air, rather as a barber snips the air with his scissors between cuts of the hair.

All that the Deputy Vice-Chancellor saw was two men walking, my observer and myself, one looking at him very fixedly and walking slowly and with elaborate care.

At times on the way back from the toilet I would make a running commentary, like this: 'Steady now. Someone's coming. Corridor's long. Can we get past? Good Lord, yes. Lots of room. Dead easy after all.'

Soon we were back in the lab, and they were showing me a flickering light made by an electronic flash lamp which consisted of a concave mirror, maybe eighteen inches in diameter, with a small bent hollow glass tube in the centre. The tube contained gas under low pressure, and gave a flash each time a condenser discharged through it. In this way the rate of flashing could be controlled very simply. The flash was bright enough to be irritating, but not painful. They set the lamp flashing at a fairly rapid rate and asked me to report what I saw. There was quite a complex pattern of light in the mirror, and it was easy to see many pictures in this pattern, just as one can by looking into a fire. The most striking thing was a set of teeth quite near the middle of the lamp. They were about one-third normal size, and absolutely distinct. I think, too, there was an eye.

In giving a description of what I saw, I was so slow, and insisted in describing each in order, going round clockwise, that I never got as far as describing the teeth. It was only after I was told that people often see teeth that I mentioned this neat little set which I had seen.

The next treatment was to lie down and close the eyes, while the light was flashed on the closed lids at various frequencies.

A lady psychiatrist sat by the side of the couch with a notebook in her hand. She could control the frequency of the flashes by turning a knob. She asked me to indicate into the tape recorder a commentary on the experience which would follow.

At the lower frequencies of flashing, nothing especially striking was seen. But at higher frequencies an illusion began to build up. I think it was at a frequency of twenty-three flashes per second that the picture became most vivid.

I was by the seaside lying on my back on the yellow sand, with the blue sea on my left. I had no desire to turn my head to look at the sea or sand, so that in a certain sense I could not actually see them. Normally, if a person lies on his back, little more than the sky is visible. Yet my appreciation of the sand and sky was certainly visual. It is hard to convey these illusions. If you lie on your back you can picture to yourself the sand and sea without looking at them; it was like that, only the picturing was as vivid as seeing them.

It was a bright day at the seaside. The sky was blue, and the sun was down straight into my eyes. I tried to close them and found them shut already.

I was not alone on the beach. Just out of sight, to my right, were three women. They were exceedingly lovely women, and again I could see them only in a certain sense. Suppose I were to meet one of these women, I would not be able to recognise her. All the same, I knew a lot about them because I could appreciate their presence so vividly. Their womanliness was most intensely felt.

This was not an ordinary erotic dream where one experiences certain sensations and even emotions more vividly than in the waking condition. It was along those lines, but much more impressive.

It was not just that I liked or loved these women very, very much. Rather, it was that I felt a wonder that was really there, really there in the illusion, if you follow me; it just cannot be described in words.

What a pity the sun was so dazzling. I wanted to lie back and enjoy the feeling of the presence of these women. They were so very kind.

When the frequency of the flashing light was twenty-three, everything was just right. When it went higher than that, the dream deteriorated. So, when we had covered the frequency range, I asked the lady psychiatrist who was turning the control knob if I could have twenty-three again. She put the frequency back to twenty-three, but this time it wasn't so good. Also, I had the greatest trouble in understanding that she had given me twenty-three, although she repeated 'This is twenty-three' many times quite clearly.

Then the flashing light was turned off and I 'came to' or 'woke up'. It is not clear how to describe it. I was extremely surprised to find that there were only the lady psychiatrist and myself in the inner room of the laboratory.

'Only you and me? Oh well, just you and me. It's all quite friendly, isn't it?' I remember saying, rather foolishly.

When the lady had finished her research, a man came in to record the electro-encephalogram. 'For goodness' sake, try and keep still just half a minute. I can't get a decent recording,' he said.

This puzzled me. I was keeping still. I was lying on the couch and was not making any muscular movements. I was apparently floating about in space, but clearly that would not affect him or his instrument – that only affected me.

'You don't mind me floating about, do you? That doesn't affect your instrument, does it?'

'You're wriggling,' he said.

'I'm just getting comfortable. I'll be still for a quarter of an hour.' I lay still for what seemed about a quarter of an hour, floating for much of the time.

'There you are,' I said. 'I hope you got a good record.'

'You were still for about a minute,' he said.

The thought occurred to me that since time seemed to pass so slowly, and since my speech seemed at this particular period to be of normal speed, it would seem to follow that I would be able to utter many more words in a given time than would normally be possible.

Accordingly the attempt was made, at my suggestion, to count up to as high a number as possible in five seconds. I seemed to count very rapidly for a long time, but I only got as far as thirty.

The experiment had started at 10.15 a.m. and it was now 4 p.m. We had had sandwiches and coffee for lunch. It was thought to be safe to take me along for a cup of tea in the common room. The custom is to take afternoon tea so that now, at 4 p.m., only one person remained, a pharmacologist who was a good friend of mine. He knew all about LSD and looked at me pityingly. I began talking to him with the boring, monotonous half-nonsense speech I was compelled to turn out.

'Now then, Bobby, I know I am boring you, you see I can't stop talking. I am cut off from reality, but one thing is very real and that is the terrible look of boredom in your eye. So please don't go on listening.'

Back we went to the laboratory. It was about that time I first felt that I was split into two people. The following report is made with particular care:

There were two of me walking down the corridor. The two people were not very accurately localised in space, but the main one corresponded to the position where I would have been had there been only one of me. The shadowy or more tenuous individual, the naughty one, was slightly to the left. We could talk to each other, exchanging verbal thoughts, but not talking aloud.

The main person was really me, but in an improved form. He was a very strong character. He had an effortless strength that I never knew before that I possessed. The other individual on the left was much less well known to me.

'Why not jump out of a window?' he said to me.

The invitation had a compulsive quality which was difficult to resist. But just as I was considering it, the main person answered for me, speaking with effortless strength.

'Of course not. Don't be such a bloody fool!'

I was delighted with this man, with myself, that is. I thought, 'I had no idea what strength of character I had.'

Those in charge were beginning to get a bit worried as to what was to be done with me. The effects which would normally have worn off by now were lasting for an unexpectedly long time.

They asked me whether I thought it was safe for me to go home.

'Take me home,' I said abruptly.

I was a little worried that I might want to jump out of the window when I got home, but decided to rely on my super-self to look after the naughty one. I never told the experimenters that I was at times double.

The lady psychiatrist was to take me home, so she asked me to tell her the way.

'Hell, it's up to *you* to get me home' was the thought that was in my mind. What I said was 'Drive round this roundabout for about a quarter of an hour and then turn off to the left. I'll tell you when we come to it.'

It cannot have taken much more time than was used in uttering that sentence to have driven a quarter of the way around the roundabout. But it seemed that that remark took the usual time and yet occupied only an inconsiderable proportion of the long time which appeared to elapse in going round the roundabout.

The psychiatrist seemed worried.

'Is this the turning?' she asked.

'You've been driving quite some time now. Yes, I should think this is it. Try it, anyway,' I replied.

The road we were on was not recognisable, but I had ceased to bother. The day's work was over, and I relaxed. Actually, as the map showed, we had gone 180 degrees around. I was prepared for the journey home, which is one mile precisely, to seem very long in the car. So I settled down to endure it.

'Bristol Road,' I said. 'When you come to Bristol Road you turn right, then left down Bournbrook Road.'

She did a right turn down Bristol Road but, being wrong already, the turn took her farther wrong.

It was really surprising how much the psychiatrist relied on me to direct her to my home. I must have failed entirely to convey to her my inability to interpret the changing world around me. I could, however, feel her anxiety and worry, and could see that she had her family on her mind. But one of the final symptoms of LSD was beginning to develop in me, and that was lassitude and complete selfishness. I did not care if her children were waiting for her, or if she had a party. If her house had been on fire, that would have been entirely her problem.

'We may be wrong. We may be right. Drive what way you will,' I said.

She stopped to ask a policeman the way. And, after what I believe now was a real half-hour's car drive, we arrived home.

The psychiatrist explained the situation to my wife. 'He can't help talking,' she said, gave a brief résumé of the case, and then drove off.

'No, thank you, darling, I think I won't come in just now,' I said to my wife. 'I will go for a walk. Keep the children away from me, will you please?'

I had a compulsive urge to do violence to my children and did not like to tell her about it.

'Are you safe? Can you get back?' she asked. For her, the situation must have been extremely distressing.

'I haven't a hope of crossing a road with traffic on it. How can I possibly judge speed?' I replied. 'But I can go round the block. I will always turn left. It is about half a mile round, so you will see me going past from time to time!'

And I set off.

Although the nausea was still present, the muscular system felt in order, and the exercise was more pleasing than usual. Also, the concertina effect added interest. I had a feeling, too, that the exercise would help work off the effects of the drug. There was no difficulty in recognising the different streets, and no question of becoming lost.

I must have gone around a great many times. I remember passing some people to whom my wife and I had previously made a friendly approach, but who had snubbed us decisively. Should I now, with the licence, as it were, of being able to blame any peculiarity of behaviour on the drug, go and tell them what I thought of them? But no, I did not. The ordinary natural human reserve prevented it. I noticed this myself and regarded it as a most excellent sign that the drug action was abating.

I still could not stop talking to myself on the way round. But I could not sense when I was really talking and when I was merely having verbal thoughts. To find out, I would place a hand to my lips. I could then tell from the movement felt whether I was talking or not. Whenever the test was made, I was talking, but could not stop.

I got into conversation with one gentlemen who was cutting his hedge. For an Englishman to speak to a near neighbour after passing him six times during an evening since there was no one to introduce us, suggests a certain lack of reserve, but the fact that the conversation did not start until the sixth encounter was an indication that recovery had started.

After walking around the block, at a brisk pace, for about an hour to an hour and a half, I went into my own garden.

'Keep the children away from me, please!' I said to my wife. I could not convey to her how important it was that she should do this, nor do I know myself to this day how great the gap was between the violent thoughts in my mind and their possible execution.

Most fortunately, the children were both in a blessedly and amenably happy mood. When Patricia called they ran into the drawing-room, settled around her, and she began to read to them, having explained that Father was not well and that he wanted to sit undisturbed in the garden. I settled down in a deckchair, bathed in the evening sunlight, and looked at the happy little group in the drawing-room which I could see through the French windows. The children could see one looking at them, and waved to me.

That scene made a big impression. I felt that I was a long way off, and that no effort of mine could bring me any nearer. But I knew it would be all right if I waited; so I waved back to them, and settled down to wait.

The nausea wore off and other effects of the LSD seemed to be abating. So after a while I agreed to read to the elder child, Robert, in bed. The reading was a failure from his point of view. His father seemed inattentive, and to be reading so poorly and slurring his speech so badly that the story was barely intelligible. From my point of view, the concertina and stretching effects were troublesome again. The boy seemed to have such peculiar limbs. While I was reading to Robert, Patricia was ringing up some friends, both doctors, who had invited us to have dinner with them that evening.

'I would much rather bring him along that leave him at home with the "sitter-in" and the children,' she explained, 'if you don't mind.'

So off we went to dinner.

Over coffee, in my slow and boring way, I began to address my host on the subject of fireplaces, and the theory of heating dwellings.

'There is a little man on the roof,' I said, and paused, confident that I could resume without being interrupted. There are few who dare pause in a conversation. Most of us have to scurry on desperately, fully conscious that if the flow weakens someone else will nip in. It is rare to manage the pause. Two very effective constituents of the technique are, firstly, to get your audience to lose the thread of the conversation, and that had been ensured with my opening remark, and, secondly, to have the confidence not to mind boring the audience. This I had to the full.

'He has a thermometer in his hand,' I continued. 'He measures the temperature of the smoke. "Bad," he says. "Too hot." Now, with any convenient apparatus he measures the mass of smoke and of hot air, i.e. the mass of all that comes up the chimney. Knowing the mass and the temperature change he calculates the amount of heat entering the sky.'

My host politely adjusted his features to simulate interest but his distress was apparent. Furthermore I knew he had got me quite wrong. He thought that I thought there was a little man on the roof with a thermometer and a telephone. I knew perfectly well there was not. My mental processes, with respect to thinking of the little man, were approximately normal. That is the way that I, and probably many others, would normally consider the question of heat waste in fires.

The only abnormal aspect was reporting the mental processes directly, instead of transposing them as one normally would by saying, 'The heat loss to the sky is equal to that absorbed by raising the temperature of the waste gases from the temperature of the room to that in the chimney.'

'He phones down,' I went on. 'He says "How much fuel have you burnt?" You tell him. "Your efficiency is only five per cent," he replies. Don't you see? The only thing he needs to know is how much fuel has been used, and how much heat has gone into the sky. Then he knows what the efficiency is.'

We went home, Patricia driving of course, and so to bed. I did not take the barbiturate sleeping tablet I had been given. I had had enough drugs for one day.

The night was very wakeful, but it did not seem too long. An eye was seen very clearly from time to time in the darkness. This was neither distressing nor particularly interesting. Just an eye – rather diagrammatic.

Next day, unfortunately, I still was not right. There was no question of getting out of bed. I just lay there talking, babbling rather, mostly about my past. Often I cried, which was very distressing for my wife, who naturally thought it represented a condition of deep grief. As far as I can remember it did not. It was as though my body were crying and I was outside it, admittedly feeling rather hopeless, but not moved to tears.

The colour distortion was still there. The psychiatrist and others from the laboratory came to see me, looking very worried – and green. All their faces had that unpleasant green tinge. I still wanted to jump out of the window, but had no feeling of wanting to commit suicide. It was an absolutely specific compulsion to jump out of one particular window in the bedroom. I was no longer split into two, and the very strong character who had been so easily able to resist the temptation before had gone. The temptation was vaguely associated with the naughty character but he was not very distinct from me now. It was more as if I myself wanted, in a purely irresponsible way, to jump out of the window.

I was in bed for a few days and when not babbling or

crying, I lay very limp and completely apathetic. I must try to convey why I made no attempt to get up and generally pull myself together, because the reason was interesting and important. I saw my own mind divided somewhat in the way that Freud sees it, divided into parts having different functions at different levels. As in his scheme, the different functions and different levels were represented as having different positions in the diagram. In this case the diagram was not drawn, but was thought of as being in the head. Now one part of this diagram sees 'will power'. It was rather low down, and lines went vaguely from it to other parts of the brain which represented different channels through which the will power could exert its effects.

I could see quite clearly in the diagram that this drug had paralysed the 'will power' section. I can remember saying, 'I'm prepared to do battle against the ordinary afflictions but hell – I've nothing left to do battle with. This drug has cut me off at the source. It's completely knocked out the will power.'

After a fortnight I was still very jumpy and susceptible to illusions. In the bathroom, I could see pictures made from the irregular condensation of steam on the walls. The pictures in steam were noble, and reminded me of the strange sweetness of the women by the seaside.

Then there was the insect.

One morning, on looking into the sink, I saw this enormous creature, standing at one edge. It looked so real that I frankly did not know what sort of action to take. Rather feebly I blew on it, and to my horror it made grotesque movements, impossible for any normal insect to achieve; and with these movements it fluttered around the sink. The illusion of the movement lasted only about one second. But one second can be a long time and the sensation in the solar plexus was felt very strongly indeed. Then, with immense relief, I could see it was only the black charred remains of a piece of paper.

The most striking illusion of all was the Christmas card on the mantelpiece of the nursery at home. One day, coming down to the nursery stove before breakfast I saw a horrific face looking out of the card. Again, there was that shock of fear. I braced myself to look this damned face straight in the eyes. It would not change into any other kind of picture. I walked up closer, and then I could see it was really nothing but a little drawing of a cottage. I took a step back and again the horrific-face interpretation reappeared. At a certain critical distance the two pictures alternated just exactly in the same way as the cubes commonly shown on inlay patterns will alter suddenly and independently of any effort of the will. I began to practise obtaining the cottage and repressing the face. I used to do these exercises for perhaps one minute every morning, to try to learn to suppress the horrific images. It would make a nice story to say how I thus became master of my fate, and cured myself by my own determined efforts. But things didn't happen that way.

For several months I was dependent on barbiturates in order to get a reasonable amount of sleep. After that, I could manage to sleep from 12 midnight until about 4 a.m. most nights without any drug. From then on the time passed pleasantly enough, and the insomnia was not a thing which mattered much. Normally I was a very heavy sleeper, and it was surprising to me to realise how much time is wasted in bed. One morning, to reduce this waste, I got up at 5 a.m. and spent three hours breaking up old bricks in the garden before breakfast. Whether it was the bricks or a coincidence will never be known, but that day marked the end of the insomnia. A great sleepiness overwhelmed me by 8 p.m. the next evening. For the first time in months a full night's sleep was obtained, and a normal sleep rhythm was established very shortly afterwards.

The only definite permanent effect which has been observed to follow my taking thirty-millionths of a gram of lysergic acid is that after-images are now always seen more vividly than they ever were before. But if the condition I had been in was schizophrenia, my sympathy for those so afflicted has been increased many times.

Saturday Review, 1 June 1963
From: *Mindscapes: An Anthology of Drug Writings*, ed. Antonio Melechi, 1998

Howard Marks
The Origins of Smoking

PRECIOUS FEW ATTRIBUTES distinguish humans from animals. Sheep shag, monkeys wank, pigs snort, wolves piss, dolphins talk, tigers fart, dogs throw up, skunks drink, elephants sniff, horses count and leeches suck. But no animals smoke. It's not merely because they can't skin up. Animals, other than reindeer and dragons, are terrified of flames and smoke and stay away from chimneys and tobacconists. I began to research the origins of smoking.

There were two main theories, the first scientific, the second religious.

In the scientific theory, the Welsh Wizard Merlin was the first human to smoke in the western hemisphere. Merlin shagged witches, used broomsticks as dildos, shat toadstools, and guzzled a mixture of liquid psychoactives from his Holy Grail. Merlin time-travelled to twenty-first-century Cardiff and smuggled in a catatonic leek, a stereophonic spliff, a zygotic monkey, a slice of Caerphilly, a bag of magic mushrooms, a manic street preacher, two super furry animals, and a sixty-foot blow-up doll. Back at King Arthur's Round Table, one super furry animal got dizzy and started doing things backwards. Smoke poured out of his nostrils, the spliff went away from his mouth and he roared, 'Drag On.' The other super furry animal grew horns, had a huge piss and fucked off to the North Pole shouting, 'Reign Deer, I'm a leek.' Since then the Welsh haven't stopped drinking and smoking and producing things vaguely connected, like coal, reservoirs, crematoriums and sheep-shagging. They honour the smoking dragon and a leek after a good skinful.

Smoking wasn't exported from Wales until the twelfth century, when Prince 'Mad Dog' Madog ran aground in America long before Big Chief Lying Bullshit had thought of an Oval Orifice. Mad Dog's stash hadn't run out, so he offered a pipe of peace. Six weeks later, Mad Dog was back in Florida with a load of seeds, and all the Red Indians spent several centuries having squaws rather than wars, bongs rather than bombs, and perfecting the art of communicating and signalling over vast distance by smoking enormous spliffs and emitting an ordered series of smoke rings.

Due to the treachery of Big Chief Lying Bullshit, foreign tribes of Puritans, Prohibitionists and other Pricks were allowed to invade and gain control. Most ganja and ganja smokers were completely wiped out. Lucky ones (the Arawaks) fled to Jamaica and set up their culture over there. The Arawaks played ball games, sang, feasted, danced, shagged, drank maize alcohol to get pissed, smoked dried leaves to get stoned, and snorted white powders through inverted Y-shaped tubes to get completely trolleyed. They wore sexy short skirts, tattoos, ornaments, necklaces and feathers. They had no wheels (hadn't even thought of them) and no written language. They had a few words, including *canoe* (enabling transport) and *hurricane* (fucking up transport). *Barbecue* is also an Arawak word. So is *hammock*. So is *tobacco*. A typical Arawak day was up at any time, have a smoke, lie in the hammock and wait for some barbecue red snapper. Sorted.

Welshman Henry Morgan, through the devious route of rum, piracy, slavery and trade, managed to stock the island with weed-smoking Africans and hash-smoking shopkeepers from the Indian subcontinent, thereby ensuring a permanent ganja culture. St Bob Marley did the rest.

It is quite a three pipe problem

Arthur Conan Doyle

R. Raffauf and R.E. Schultes
Vine of the Soul

THERE ARE FEW plants more important in South American shamanism, whether as medicines or in mythology, than tobacco: *Nicotiana tabacum* of the Solanaceae or Nightshade family. It is native to the Andes. South American Indians had long ago discovered every way of utilizing it: smoked, as a snuff, chewed, licked, as a syrup applied to the gums, and in the form of an enema. In many tribes, *payes* use tobacco smoke blown over a sick patient, especially on the area theoretically affected, with appropriate incantations, in the belief that this practice can cure of itself or at least serve as a prelude to other treatments.

Tobacco is essential in the training of young men wishing to be *payes*. This aspect of their training is present in virtually every tribe in the Colombian Amazonia.

Amongst the Yukunas, for example, students must snuff tobacco in large amounts. It may take several years of this training before they master the knowledge of the *paye* and before they satisfy him of their proficiency.

The tobacco plant and the methods of its use among New World Indians never ceased to astonish the earliest European 'explorers.' It was unknown, of course, in the Old World before 1492, and snuffing was unknown in the Eastern Hemisphere before that time.

Vine of the Soul, 1992

You abuse snuff! Perhaps it is the final cause of the human nose

Samuel Taylor Coleridge

Jeremy Narby
The Cosmic Serpent

THE ASHANINCA SAY that by ingesting ayahuasca or tobacco, it is possible to see the normally invisible and hidden Maninkari spirits. Carlos Perez Shuma had told me that tobacco attracted the Maninkari. Amazonian shamans in general consider tobacco a food for the spirits, who crave it 'since they no longer possess fire as human beings do.'

The idea that the Maninkari liked tobacco had always seemed

funny to me. I considered 'spirits' to be imaginary characters who could not really enjoy material substances. I also considered smoking to be a bad habit, and it seemed improbable that spirits (inasmuch as they existed) would suffer from the same kinds of addictive behaviors as human beings. Nevertheless, I had resolved to stop letting myself be held up by such doubts and to pay attention to the literal meaning of the shamans' words, and the shamans were categorical in saying that spirits had an almost insatiable hunger for tobacco.

There are, however, fundamental differences between the shamanic use of tobacco and the consumption of industrial cigarettes. The botanical variety used in the Amazon contains up to eighteen times *more* nicotine than the plants used in Virginia type cigarettes. Amazonian tobacco is grown without chemical fertilizers or pesticides and contains none of the ingredients added to cigarettes, such as aluminum oxide, potassium nitrate, ammonium phosphate, polyvinyl acetate, and a hundred or so others, which make up approximately 10 percent of the smokable matters. During combustion, a cigarette emits some 4,000 substances, most of which are toxic. Some of these substances are even radioactive, making cigarettes the largest single source of radiation in the daily life of an average smoker. According to one study, the average smoker absorbs the equivalent of the radiation dosages from 250 chest X-rays per year. Cigarette smoke is directly implicated in more than 25 serious illnesses, including 17 forms of cancers. In the Amazon, on the other hand, tobacco is considered a *remedy*. The Ashaninca word for 'healer,' or 'shaman,' is sheripiari – literally, 'the person who uses tobacco.' The oldest Ashaninca men I knew were all sheripiari. They were so old that they did not know their own age, which only their deeply wrinkled skin suggested, and they were remarkably alert and healthy.

Intrigued by these disparities, I looked through data banks for comparative studies between the toxicity of the Amazonian variety *(Nicotiana rustica)* and the variety used by the manufacturers of cigarettes, cigars, rolling tobacco, and pipe tobacco *(Nicotiana tabacum)*. *I* found nothing. The question, it seemed, had not been asked. I also looked for studies on the cancer rate among shamans who use massive and regular doses of nicotine: again, nothing. So I decided to write to the main authority on the matter, Johannes Wilbert, author of the book *Tobacco and Shamanism in South America,* to put my questions to him. He replied: 'There is certainly evidence that Western tobacco products contain many different harmful agents which are probably not present in organically grown plants. I have not heard of shamans developing cancers but that may, of course, be a function of several things like lack of Western diagnosis, natural life span of indigenous people, magico-religious restriction of tobacco use in tribal societies, etc.'

In any case, scientists have never really considered tobacco as a hallucinogen, because Westerners have never smoked large enough doses to reach the hallucinatory state.

The Cosmic Serpent, 1998

Alexandre Dumas
The Count of Monte Cristo

MEANWHILE, THE SUPPER went ahead, and appeared to have been supplied solely for Franz, for the unknown man scarcely touched one or two dishes of the splendid feast to which his unexpected guest did such ample justice. Then Ali brought on the dessert, or rather took the baskets from the statues' heads and placed them on the table. Between the two baskets he placed a small vermeil cup, closed with a lid of the same metal. The respect with which Ali had carried this cup piqued Franz's curiosity. He raised the lid and saw a kind of greenish paste that looked like preserved angelica, but which was entirely unknown to him. He replaced the lid, as ignorant of what the cup contained as he was before he had lifted it, and then, glancing at his host, he saw him smile at his disappointment.

'You cannot guess what sort of eatable is contained in that little vase, and that intrigues you, doesn't it?'

'I confess it does.'

'Well, then, those green preserves are nothing less than the ambrosia that Hebe served at the table of Jupiter.'

'But,' replied Franz, 'this ambrosia, in passing through human hands, has no doubt lost its heavenly name to assume a human one.

'In vulgar language, what do you call this thing – for which, in any case, I do not feel any great desire?'

'Ah, thus is our material origin truly revealed!' cried Sinbad. 'We frequently pass so near to happiness without seeing it, without really looking at it; or even if we do, we still do not recognize it. Are you a practical man, and is gold your god? Then taste this, and the mines of Peru, Gujarat, and Golconda are open to you. Are you a man of imagination, a poet? Then taste this, and the boundaries of possibility disappear, the fields of infinite space will be open to you: you will walk about, free in heart and mind, into the boundless realms of reverie. Are you ambitious, do you run after the grandeur of the earth? Only taste this, and in an hour you will be a king, not of some petty kingdom hidden in a corner of Europe, like France, Spain, or England, but a king of the world, of the universe, of creation. Your throne will be established on that mountain to which Jesus was taken by Satan, and without being obliged to do homage to the devil, without having to kiss his claw, you will be sovereign master of all the kingdoms of the earth. Is it not tempting, what I offer you? And is it not an easy thing, since it is only to do thus? Look!' With these words he uncovered the little vermeil cup containing the substance so highly praised, took a teaspoonful of the magic preserves, raised it to his lips, and savoured it slowly, with his eyes half shut and his head bent backward. Franz did not disturb him while he ate his favourite dish, but when he had finished, he inquired:

'What, then, is this precious preparation?'

'Did you ever hear,' asked his host, 'of the Old Man of the Mountain, who attempted to assassinate Philip Augustus?'

'Of course I have.'

'Well, you know he reigned over a rich valley dominated by the mountain from which he derived his picturesque name. In this valley were magnificent gardens planted by Hasan-ben-Sabah, and in these gardens were isolated pavilions. Into these pavilions he admitted his chosen ones, and there, says Marco Polo, he had them eat a certain herb, which transported them to Paradise to the midst of ever-blooming shrubs, ever-ripe fruit, and ever-fresh virgins. Now, what these happy young men took for reality was only a dream, but it was a dream so soft, voluptuous, and enthralling, that they sold themselves body and soul to him who gave it to them, and obeyed his orders as if they were God's own. They went to the ends of the earth to strike down their destined victims, and would die under torture without a word, believing that the death they suffered was only a transition to that life of delights of which the holy herb, now served before you, had given them a foretaste.'

'Then,' cried Franz, 'it is hashish! I know it, by name at least.'

1855. From: *Tales of Hashish* by Andrew C. Kimmens, 1976

George Lane
The Mongols and the Advent of Hashish in Western Asia

LEGENDS MAINTAIN THAT Ḥasan-i Ṣabbāh kidnapped peasant boys while they were in a hashish-drugged sleep, then woke them in an artificial paradise of lithe, dancing *horis* (Islamic angels), fragrant wine and more slumber-inducing hashish. They would then be thrust back into the harsh reality of their poverty-stricken life with the option of a return to paradise, proffered through murderous service of the Master and martyrdom. This and other legends of Alamūt and the gardens of paradise and of Ḥasan-i Ṣabbāh and his hashish-crazed followers are the result of medieval disinformation, rumour-mongering, and over-reliance on limited early source material.

The followers of Ḥasan-i Ṣabbāh, or more correctly the Nīzārī Ismāᶜīlīs (1009–1256 CE) of Iran and Syria, were, indeed, given the name *Hashīshīn*. This appellation was picked up by the Crusaders and transmuted into 'assassin', a term found in many languages today. However, it is the second label 'assassin' which bears closer association with the reality than the first.

The rulers of the Nīzārī Ismāᶜīlīs were unassailable in their mountain retreats. Their fanatical followers who were promised their rewards in the afterlife used political assassination and subterfuge rather than heroics on the battlefield as their *modus operandi*. Although small in number, their fingers stretched far, and the kings and rulers of the medieval Islamic world slept uneasily in fear of these Islamic terrorists from Iran. Hence their infamy, and hence the stories of their exploits reaching the ears of both Marco Polo, who introduced to Europe the stories of the fabulous gardens and drugs, and the Crusaders, who carried back tales of the Assassins' killing and terror.

The connection between a group of religious fanatics and indolent drug use is not so obvious, for the Ismāᶜīlīs were strict in many of their religious observances. The explanation is the use of the term *hashīshīn* or *hashīshiyya*, meaning literally a user of hashish but also used as a general term of abuse for any disreputable person or group – similar to the meaning of 'vagabond'. The Ismāᶜīlīs were secretive, feared, and rumours of their beliefs and practices abounded but were not widely known. They were hated, and they terrified the Sunni establishment and its leaders. A grave insult at the time was to denounce them as hashish users, though in reality nothing could have been further from the truth. They were devout adherents of an Islamic doctrine who believed that their leader was the reincarnation of God. Religion and their moral code were of overriding importance and there was no room for drug-induced indulgence in their world.

Hashish, although not as widespread as alcohol, which was explicitly prohibited under Islamic law, was certainly known in the medieval period, and its properties were recognised as hardly violence-inducing. However, the ʿulemā, or religious classes, other than some dubious Sufi or Qalandar groups, rarely endorsed the use of cannabis in any of its forms.

Qalandars and their strange practices, in which hashish figures prominently, have been the source of many of the associations wrongly made between Sufism and the use of drugs. The Sufis believed in the quest for mystical experience and of the possibility of personal knowledge of God through a spirituality independent of the traditional religious schools (maḍhab). However, for the most part the Sufi lodges and the leading Sufi shaykhs were upholders of the establishment and supporters of traditional Islamic teachings and practices. They, as much as the most conservative of the traditional ʿulemā, disapproved strongly of the activities and the reputation of the Qalandars.

The Qalandars were a very distinctive group seen on the medieval landscape and they became particularly prominent in the later thirteenth century in the Ilkhanate. They affected a characteristic coiffure (the so-called 'four blows', chahār żarb) by shaving head, beard, moustache and eyebrows, although such groups as the H̤aydarīs grew their moustaches excessively long. Their dress was sometimes completely absent, sometimes restricted to a simple loincloth, but more often a traditional Sufi garb: the woollen or felt cloak, but coloured black or white rather than the usual Sufi colour, blue. Others wore simple sacks. When they wore headgear it was invariably distinctive. Qalandars went barefoot. Qalandars were recognised by their strange appearance and the paraphernalia they carried. The traditional black begging bowl and wooden club were ever-present, as was other distinctive equipment such as iron rings, collars, bracelets, collars, belts, anklets, chains, hatchets, ankle-bones, leather pouches and large wooden spoons. Most noticeable maybe were the rings, which were sometimes pierced through the penis to enforce sexual abstinence. This deliberately provocative external appearance was further exaggerated by their eccentric and scandalous behaviour which itself was discouraged by their well-attested use of intoxicants and hallucinogenic drugs, cannabis in particular.

The Qalandars justified their outrageous behaviour with clever and, no doubt, hashish-strengthened logic, as they defiantly maintained their adherence to Islam and the teachings of the Prophet. They were, they would earnestly insist, engaged on the quest for God and enlightenment, and this, of course, entailed the suppression of 'self' and 'selfishness'. Too many, they claimed, were the Sufis who trod the path of self-denial and asceticism and yet who were ultimately defeated and seduced by the demon of self-aggrandisement. Too often these same ascetics took secret satisfaction and pleasure from the acclaim and admiration they elicited from their disciples and admirers and relished the fame that their hardship engendered. Their egos increased in proportion to the miseries they endured, and their public acclaim defeated the worldly self-denial they cultivated. The Qalandars rejected such courting of public esteem and considered false this publicly paraded saintliness and piety. For them such public honour would undermine their attempts at self-abasement and true denial. It was therefore to avoid the pitfalls of public respect that they sought the opposite, namely public contempt and disgrace. They actively sought disapproval not only from the establishment but also from the public in general, and in this way they considered themselves freer to follow their spiritual path towards truth.

It was with this aim that the Qalandars adopted their distinctive dress and practices, and it was with this as their justification that they took up with relish the consumption of hashish. Alcohol, music and various forms of less common sexual practices, however, were also indulged in for the same pure reasons as mentioned above. The Qalandars were indulging in these excesses of sex, drugs and trance-inducing music merely to throw people off their trail, and to avoid the sin of vanity. They were not really hedonistic libertines but closet ascetics willing to endure public scorn and disgrace in the service of true humility.

Early Mongol Rule in 13th-Century Iran:
a Persian Renaissance, 2001

Hassan Mohammed ibn-Chirazi
How Hashish Was Discovered

THE YEAR 658 [AD 1260], being at Tuster, I asked Sheik Hirazi, monk of the order of Haidar, on what occasion they discovered the properties of the herb of the devotees, and how, after being adopted by the devotees in particular, it had afterward come into general usage. Here is what he told me.

Haidar, chief of all the sheiks, practiced many exercises of devotion and mortification: he took but little nourishment, carried to a surprising extent the detachment from all worldly things, and was of an extraordinary piety. He was born at Nichapur, a city of Khorasan, and he made his home on a neighboring mountain. There he established a convent, and a great number of devotees came together around him. He lived alone in a corner of this convent, and spent more than ten years in this manner, never going out, and never seeing anyone at all except me, when I was acting as his servant. One day when it was very hot, at the hour of the very greatest heat, the sheik walked out alone into the countryside, and when he later returned to the convent, we saw on his face an expression of joy and gaiety very different from what we were accustomed to see there: he allowed his fellow devotees to come and visit him and began to converse with them. When we saw the sheik so humanized and conversing familiarly with us, after being for so long in an absolute retreat without any communication with men, we asked him the cause of this surprising effect.

'While I was in my retreat,' he replied, 'it occurred to my spirit to go out alone into the countryside. When I had done so I noticed that all the plants were in a perfect calm, not experiencing the least agitation, because of the extreme heat untempered by the slightest breath of wind. But passing by a certain plant covered with foliage I observed that, in that air, it was moving softly from side to side with a soft light movement, like a man dizzied by fumes of wine. I began to gather the leaves of this plant and to eat them, and they have

73

produced in me the gaiety that you witness. Come with me, then, that I may teach you to know it.'

So we followed him into the countryside, and he showed us that plant. We told him, on seeing it, that it was the plant they call hemp. On his orders, we took the leaves of this plant and ate them, and once back in the convent experienced in ourselves the same gay, joyous disposition that he had found impossible to hide from us. When the sheik saw us in that state, he charged us to keep secret the discovery that we had just made of the plant's virtues and made us promise on oath never to reveal it to ordinary men and never to hide it from religious men.

'God almighty,' he told us, 'has granted you, as a special favor, an awareness of the virtues of this leaf, so that your use of it will dissipate the cares that obscure your souls and free your spirits from everything that might hamper them. Keep carefully, then, the deposit he has confided in you, and be faithful in hiding the precious secret he has committed to you.'

Sheik Haidar thus made known to us this secret during his life, and ordered me to sow the plant around his tomb after his death, so I cultivated it in the convent. The sheik lived for ten more years after this event; during all the time I remained in his service not a day went by that he did not use this leaf, and he recommended to us to eat little food and to take the herb instead. Sheik Haidar died in the convent in the mountain in the year 618 [AD 1221]. They erected over his tomb a great chapel, and the inhabitants of Khorasan, full of veneration for his memory, came there on pilgrimage, bringing many presents to fulfil their vows and developing a great respect for his disciples. Before his death he had recommended to his companions to tell their secret to the most distinguished people of the province, and by instructing them in the virtues of the plant they adopted its use. Thus hashish spread rapidly in Khorasan and in the various departments of Fars province, but they knew nothing about its use in Iraq until the year 628 [AD 1231], in the reign of Calif Mustansir. At that time, two princes, whose states were among the maritime countries situated on the Persian Gulf, the Sovereign of Ormuz and the Prince of Bahrein, having come into Iraq, men of their retinue brought with them some hashish and taught the Iraqis to eat it. The drug spread in Iraq, and the people of Syria, Egypt and the lands of Rum, having heard tell of it, took up the use of it.

From: *A Treatise on Hemp*, 1300

Carl Kerenyi
Dionysos

IT SEEMS PROBABLE that the Great Mother Goddess, who bore the names Rhea and Demeter, brought the poppy with her from her Cretan cult to Eleusis, and it is certain that in the Cretan cult sphere, opium was prepared from poppies.

The making of opium from poppies requires a special procedure. A pharmacobotanist discovered that 'the poppies on the lead of the goddess figurine found in Gazi reveal incisions which the artist colored more deeply than the rest of the flower to make them plainly visible'. This is a most significant discovery, because opium is obtained through such incisions. The coloring of the incisions was a way of displaying one of the goddess's gifts to her worshipers. They were reminded of experiences that they owed to her. This is concrete evidence that should not be blurred by vague reference to 'medicines' (*pharmaha*) or to an unspecified ecstasy connected with the gifts of this goddess. What she bestowed through opium cannot have been essentially different in the late Minoan period from today. What was it?

We may turn to the modern classics on opium, from which I shall cite a few of the passages least conditioned by our own culture and closest to the atmosphere of Minoan art. 'The ocean with its eternal breathing, on which, however, a great stillness brooded, symbolized my mind and the mood that then governed it . . . a festive peace. Here . . . all unrest gave way to a halcyon serenity.'

These are De Quincey's words, quoted by Baudelaire. Baudelaire himself, in 'Le Poison' (*Les Fleurs de Mal*), speaks of extending, not shattering, the limits of nature:

> *Opium enlarges the boundless,*
> *Extends the unlimited,*
> *Gives greater depth to time . . .*

Others, however, have spoken of a 'world in which "one can hear the walk of an insect on the ground, the bruising of a flower." ' According to Cocteau, 'opium is the only vegetable substance that communicates the vegetable state to us.'

It may be presumed that toward the end of the late Minoan period, opium stimulated the visionary faculty and aroused visions which had earlier been obtained without opium. For a time, an artificially induced experience of transcendence in nature was able to replace the original experience. In the history of religions, periods of 'strong medicine' usually occur when the simpler methods no longer suffice. This development may be observed among the North American Indians. Originally mere fasting sufficed to induce visions. It was only in the decadent period of Indian culture that recourse was taken to peyote, or mescaline. Earlier it was unnecessary. This powerful drug had not always been an element in the style of Indian life, but it helped to maintain this style consonant with the style of Minoan culture and helped to preserve it.

When Minoan culture came to an end, the use of opium died out. This culture was characterized by an atmosphere which in the end required such 'strong medicine.' The style of Minoan *bios* is discernible in what I have called the 'spirit' of Minoan art. This spirit is perfectly conceivable without opium.

Dionysos, 1976

Opium teaches only one thing, which is that aside from physical suffering, there is nothing real

Andre Malraux

Charles Dickens
The Mystery of Edwin Drood

AN ANCIENT ENGLISH Cathedral Tower? How can the ancient English Cathedral Tower be here? The well-known massive grey square tower of its old Cathedral? How can that be here! There is no spike of rusty iron in the air, between the eye and it, from any point of the real prospect. What is the spike that intervenes, and who has set it up? Maybe it is set up by the Sultan's orders for the impaling of a horde of Turkish robbers, one by one. It is so, for cymbals clash, and the Sultan goes by to his palace in long procession. Ten thousand scimitars flash in the sunlight, and thrice ten thousand dancing-girls strew flowers. Then, follow white elephants caparisoned in countless gorgeous colours, and infinite in number and attendants. Still the Cathedral Tower rises in the background, where it cannot be, and still no writhing figure is on the grim spike. Stay! Is the spike so low a thing as the rusty spike on the top of a post of an old bedstead that has tumbled all awry? Some vague period of drowsy laughter must be devoted to the consideration of this possibility.

Shaking from head to foot, the man whose scattered consciousness has thus fantastically pieced itself together, at length rises, supports his trembling frame upon his arms, and looks around. He is in the meanest and closest of small rooms. Through the ragged window-curtain, the light of early day steals in from a miserable court. He lies, dressed, across a large unseemly bed, upon a bedstead that has indeed given way under the weight upon it. Lying, also dressed and also across the bed, not longwise, are a Chinaman, a Lascar, and a haggard woman. The two first are in a sleep or stupor; the last is blowing at a kind of pipe, to kindle it. And as she blows, and shading it with her lean hand, concentrates its red spark of light, it serves in the dim morning as a lamp to show him what he sees of her.

'Another?' says this woman, in a querulous, rattling whisper. 'Have another?'

He looks about him, with his hand to his forehead.

'Ye've smoked as many as five since ye come in at midnight,' the woman goes on, as she chronically complains. 'Poor me, poor me, my head is so bad. Them two come in after ye. Ah, poor me, the business is slack, is slack! Few Chinamen about the Docks, and fewer Lascars, and no ships coming in, these say! Here's another ready for you, deary. Ye'll remember like a good soul, won't ye, that the market price is dreffle high just now? More nor three shillings and sixpence for a thimbleful! And ye'll remember than nobody but me (and Jack Chinaman t'other side the court; but he can't do it as well as me) has the true secret of mixing it? Ye'll pay up accordingly, deary, won't ye?'

She blows at the pipe as she speaks, and, occasionally bubbling at it, inhales much of its contents. 'O me, O me, my lungs is weak, my lungs is bad! It's nearly ready for ye, deary. Ah, poor me, poor me, my poor hand shakes like to drop off! I see ye coming-to, and I ses to my poor self, "I'll have another ready for him, and he'll bear in mind the market price of opium, and pay according." O my poor head! I makes my pipes of old penny ink-bottles, ye see, deary – this is one – and I fits-in a mouthpiece, this way, and I takes my mixter out of this thimble with this little horn spoon; and so I fills, deary. Ah, my poor nerves! I got Heavens-hard drunk for sixteen year afore I took to this; but this don't hurt me, not to speak of. And it takes away the hunger as well as wittles, deary.'

She hands him the nearly-emptied pipe, and sinks back, turning over on her face.

He rises unsteadily from the bed, lays the pipe upon the hearthstone, draws back the ragged curtain, and looks with repugnance at his three companions. He notices that the woman has opium-smoked herself into a strange likeness of the Chinaman. His form of cheek, eye, and temple, and his colour, are repeated in her. Said Chinaman convulsively wrestles with one of his many Gods or Devils, perhaps, and snarls horribly. The Lascar laughs and dribbles at the mouth. The hostess is still. 'What visions can SHE have?' the waking man muses, as he turns her face towards him, and stands looking down at it. 'Visions of many butchers' shops, and public-houses, and much credit? Of an increase of hideous customers, and this horrible bedstead set upright again, and this horrible court swept clean? What can she rise to, under any quantity of opium, higher than that! – eh?'

The Mystery of Edwin Drood, 1870

Opium is the only vegetable substance that communicates the vegetable state to us. Through it we get an idea of that other speed of plants

Jean Cocteau

Jack Beeching
The Chinese Opium Wars

THE LINKAGE THAT comes at once to mind between the word *Chinese* and the word *opium* might make one suppose that the Chinese had been drugging themselves with the stuff for thousands of years. In fact the Chinese took to opium a long while after Europeans first started drinking coffee or smoking tobacco. The opium poppy travelled from Asia Minor along Arab routes into Persia, reaching India only with the Mongols, and China even later.

When, in the mid-eighteenth century, they conquered Bengal, the soldier-merchant-administrators of Britain's Honourable East India Company inherited, along with much else worth having, the Moghul Emperor's monopoly of selling Patna opium, which came in 1778 under the direct control of the Bengal government. Into their hands had accidentally fallen abundant supplies of a product which any keen merchant might be forgiven for regarding as the answer to his dream – an article which sold itself, since any purchaser who has acquired a taste for opium always comes back anxiously for more, cash in hand.

As well as being a painkiller, opium is a specific against

dysentery, and the word then current in China for opium was *a-fu-jung*, derived from Arabic, and signifying *foreign medicine*. In 1678 the Chinese had put a duty on the small quantity of opium they imported for medical needs, and for the next seventy-seven years the annual import of the drug was fairly steady, never rising above 200 chests a year. As a medicine, opium was swallowed raw. Meanwhile, the remotest western provinces of inland China were becoming familiar with opium as a drug of addiction, the poppy having reached them by overland trade routes through Tibet and Burma. The ban on opium-smoking was apparently not complete. By 1767 the Chinese were importing 1,000 chests of opium a year.

Opium-smoking was, however, strongly condemned in China, since according to Confucian morality the smoker's body was not his own, to demolish exactly as he chose, but had been entrusted to him by his ancestors as their link with his descendants. Since using the drug habitually led to this gross offence against filial piety, the Imperial decree against opium-smoking was supported by public opinion . . .

In 1799 a new and more thoroughgoing Imperial decree condemned a growing traffic in opium. Observing that opium-smoking was now beginning to spread inland from the coastal provinces of Kwangtung and Fukien, the Emperor's Edict prohibited both the smoking of the drug and its importation. Opium alone was to be exempted from the 'free interchange of commodities' permitted with the foreign nations at Canton. 'Foreigners obviously derive the most solid profits and advantages,' said the decree of the opium trade, '. . . but that our countrymen should pursue this destructive and ensnaring vice . . . is indeed odious and deplorable.'

During ten days of its annual life cycle, the seed-box of the white poppy exudes a milky juice of extraordinary chemical complexity, not yet fully understood, and from this is derived a bitter, brown, granular powder: commercial opium.

The white poppy had been grown as a crop in antiquity in Egyptian Thebes. Later, opium and poppy seeds were carried in the caravans of Arab traders all through Asia. Some time before 1750 the white poppy was being grown as a crop in Szechwan, a remote Chinese province on the borders of Tibet, but the opium habit remained local there. What encouraged the spread of the drug on the sea coast of China was the new technique of opium-smoking. The taste of raw opium in the mouth was somewhat repugnant and its absorption into the body slow; smoking overcame both these disadvantages. The smoker dipped a needle into his prepared extract, dried it over a flame, and put the bead of flame-dried opium into a tiny pipe-bowl of tobacco. The smoke reached the bloodstream through the lungs, giving a quick narcotic effect.

A drug culture can spread fast, and not least in such times of social unease as no doubt existed when the Manchu emperors were beginning to fail at their job.

Sensing that their ancient culture – which had surrounded them comfortingly from cradle to grave – might be entering the agony of breakdown, some Chinese must have sought a similar consolation to that found by the opium-eating romantic writers of Europe in their escape from the early horrors of urban industrialism. The use of opium in China was not simply a question of economics, though supplies may have been pumped in under an urgent economic pressure.

A few grains of opium give the novice a feeling of euphoria. His first pipe is the future addict's honeymoon; but afterwards comes a wearisome listlessness. To face life once more he must decide either to leave opium alone, or to go on repeating and, usually, increasing his dose. The Chinese formed from experience the view that one pipe smoked daily for a week or ten days would leave a man in the grip of addiction thereafter.

He would soon work up to three pipes a day, and at this point one day without opium would bring on acute withdrawal symptoms: giddiness, watering of the eyes, prostration, torpor. A three-pipe addict, denied his drug for longer than one day, might expect to go through hell: a chill over the whole body, an ache in all his limbs to the very bone, diarrhoea, and agonising psychic misery. To break the habit by an act of will was somewhat rare.

A smoker well able to afford his daily dose, if by some lucky chance of body chemistry he was under no compulsion to increase it, might hope to reach equilibrium – as with the present-day heroin 'user', so-called. This was the lucky man the professional apologists for the opium trade were later fond of pointing to – the addict who lived to be *eighty*. A prosperous Chinese official might well manage his life like this, but the money income of an ordinary Chinese who began smoking opium was liable to be so small that he could afford his drug only by neglecting his family, which would eventually exile him from Chinese society, and make of him a social pariah.

Intelligent Chinese saw opium in extreme terms – as a social poison introduced by foreign enemies. To their country's two armed conflicts between 1838 and 1860 with Britain (later allied with France) – periods of open warfare linked by a turbulent armed truce – they have, reasonably enough, given the name, the Opium Wars.

The Chinese Opium Wars, 1977

So then Oxford Street, stony-hearted stepmother, thou that listenest to the sighs of orpans, and drinkest the tears of children, at length I was dismissed from thee

Thomas De Quincey

R.K. Newman
Opium-Smoking in Late Imperial China: A Reconsideration

A SOCIAL PROBLEM in one country may often be held up as an example to others, but it is rare for it to bring forth an internationally coordinated response with a world-wide application. One of these rarities is the campaign against 'hard' drugs. While liquor laws differ widely from country to country, the modern system of laws against cocaine and the opiates have been established by international convention. These arrangements evolved out of the measures taken to help imperial China with its opium problem, which was regarded, at least in part, as a foreign responsibility arising out of the vast quantities of Indian opium which had been imported by foreigners into China throughout the nineteenth century, often in questionable circumstances. The behaviour of the opium merchants and their governments seemed all the more reprehensible because of the encouragement which it gave to the Chinese to break their own government's laws against opium-smoking and poppy cultivation. The first International Opium Commission met in Shanghai in 1909 and passed a number of resolutions to help China; it also laid down principles of cooperation between producing and consuming countries which tended logically to expand in scope and force, leading to a global system of control of all narcotic substances, and to the institutionalisation of these arrangements under the United Nations.

China has also been a major influence on the world's understanding of the 'opium evil'. Unfortunately much of the information about China was tendentious from the start as missionary and philanthropic organisations tried to mobilise public opinion against opium and exert political leverage against the trade. The classic depiction of the Chinese opium smoker – a pathetic and degenerate creature with 'lank and shrivelled limbs, tottering gait, sallow visage, feeble voice and death-boding glance of eye' – became established as a stereotype and was reinforced by literary and journalistic depictions of opium dens, xenophobic reactions to Chinese communities abroad and late-nineteenth-century intellectual movements such as progressive and social Darwinism. The depiction of the Chinese opium smoker now finds its echo in the popular image of the modern junkie, 'screwed up' by heroin into an emaciated human wreck. These mental images seem to be ineradicable, despite the fact that many chronic opiate users are indistinguishable in everyday life from their fellow citizens and despite the scientific studies which have uncovered 'either only minor injurious effects or none at all that can be traced directly to the drug'.

This last point needs to be stressed because the physiological dangers of opium consumption were greatly exaggerated in the late nineteenth century and these exaggerations have shaped our assumptions about the drug ever since; in addition, our anxieties about opium have been reinforced in modern times by the activities of the underworld drug pusher, with his heavily adulterated heroin and his financial interest in maximising the damage to his clients. The Chinese smoker consumed *chandul*, a purified and concentrated solution of poppy sap and water. Medical experiments with this form of the drug and with pure samples of its derivatives, heroin and morphine, have shown few if any harmful effects upon the human body.

Historians have done little to clarify these aspects of the subject. Some have found it useful to repeat the condemnations of opium, since these provide evidence of the social damage done by British imperialism. Others have treated the subject more dispassionately but without breaking away from the assumptions that the missionaries so vigorously promoted: that all opium use is harmful and that it leads to addiction and therefore to physical ruin.

If we are to understand the true effect of opium on the health of individual Chinese, and cumulatively on Chinese society, we must distinguish carefully between those who were addicted, those who were damaged in some way by the addiction, and the many millions of light and moderate consumers who were not addicted at all.

[D]ens did not necessarily promote immoderate use: 'I have been in no place in China,' wrote the British consul in Chefoo, 'where fewer signs of opium-smoking are brought to one's notice.' In spite of their evil reputation in the West, most Chinese opium dens were no more dingy and disgusting than other public places, such as inns. It is true that some were disreputable, though that was due more to the gambling that went on in them than to the opium that was consumed there. Many others, however, were clean and homely, their customers quiet and self-absorbed. The more fashionable dens in the cities were positively opulent. One of the largest in Shanghai was built around a courtyard which was laid out with shrubs and rockeries. Inside was a succession of public and private rooms with carved and gilded ceilings, furnished with couches and tables and provided with finely crafted pipes, lamps and tea sets, 'an excellent example of sensual oriental luxury'. It reminded the Western visitor of the best coffee shops in Paris, London and Vienna: 'there was no crowding, no loud talking; the guests lingered over their tea and lamp from three-quarters of an hour to an hour, then went away as unhurriedly and self-possessed as they had entered'.

Another advantage of reconsidering the history of opium in a way that removes the usual moralistic and anti-foreign biases is that it focuses attention on opium as an economic and political phenomenon in China itself. An important and little-studied aspect, and one where modern parallels abound, is the spread of opium production within the Chinese empire; it is clear that the techniques of poppy cultivation and juice extraction were known long before the import trade began in Canton. Some provinces had substantial Muslim minorities and these may have been the agents in transplanting the poppy from older and more developed centres of Islamic culture, in one case along the central-Asian trade routes from the Middle East and in the other from Mughal India through Burma. Perhaps we should see the poppy's presence in China as part of the geographical diffusion of a useful crop, and possibly as an element in the diffusion of central-Asian cultures, rather than as a curse visited by imperialists on a weaker nation.

The history of opium in China should focus more on the native variety of the drug, the conditions of production and the social controls over consumption and concern itself less with foreign opium and the problems of addiction. Our view of the subject has been distorted for too long by the myth of the addict, with his wasted frame and 'death-boding glance of eye'.

Opium-smoking undoubtedly produced some addicts, and some of those addicts were reduced to a pitiable condition, but it is not their image that should be foremost in the mind; we should also remember the peasants carrying their lumps of poppy juice to market, the boatmen wrapped in their blankets passing round an opium pipe in the twilight, and the Chinese gentleman smoking peaceably at home with his friends. It is not the existence of addiction that requires explanation so much as the fact that, in a society in which opium was cheap and widely available, so many people smoked lightly or not at all. The production and consumption of opium were, for most people, normal rather than deviant activities and it is the implications of this normality which ought to be explored, both for the sake of China's history and for the sake of their relevance to modern societies learning to live with drugs.

From: *Modern Asian Studies 29*, 4, 1995

Aleister Crowley
Diary of a Drug Fiend

WHEN ONE IS on one's cocaine honeymoon, one is really, to a certain extent, superior to one's fellows. One attacks every problem with perfect confidence. It is a combination of what the French call *élan* and what they call *insouciance*.

The British Empire is due to this spirit. Our young men went out to India and all sorts of places, and walked all over everybody because they were too ignorant to realise the difficulties in their way. They were taught that if one had good blood in one's veins, and a public-school and university training to habituate one to being a lord of creation, and to the feeling that it was impossible to fail, and not to knowing enough to know when one was beaten, nothing could ever go wrong.

We are losing the Empire because we have become 'sicklied o'er with the pale cast of thought'. The intellectuals have made us like the 'the poor cat i' the adage'. The spirit of Hamlet has replaced that of Macbeth. Macbeth only went wrong because the heart was taken out of him by Macduff's interpretation of what the witches had said. Coriolanus only failed when he stopped to think. As the poet says, 'The love of knowledge is the hate of life.'

Cocaine removes all hesitation. But our forefathers owed their freedom of spirit to the real liberty which they had won; and cocaine is merely Dutch courage. However, while it lasts, it's all right.

Diary of a Drug Fiend, 1970

I have measured out my life in coffee spoons

T. S. Eliot

Stewart Lee Allen
The Revolution

I STARTED THIS coffeecentric history of humanity in jest.

After all, people have made similar charts based on the rise and fall of the hemline, and it would be absurd, even for me, to fail to acknowledge that historic events are spawned by a myriad of circumstances. But the coincidences at times seem overwhelming. When coffee was the sole provenance of the Arabs, their civilization flourished beyond all others. Once the Ottomans got hold of the bean, they became the most powerful and tolerant nation on the planet. Its early appearance in Great Britain helped jump-start that nation's drive for world dominance. It was in the cafés of Paris that the French Revolution was born.

Napoleon, a coffee lover equal to any, then led his countrymen to the domination of Europe, only to fall almost immediately after foolishly banning Paris's beloved *petit noir*;

he repented, and his dying request was for a cup of St Helena's espresso. As colonists, the Americans actually made tea illegal. They replaced it with joe (coffee), causing an inevitable power shift that continues today, with Japan, traditionally tea-consuming, now doting on the finest Jamaican Blue Mountain.

Only three times has the West voluntarily dosed itself with mind-altering agents: alcohol starting at an unknown date, caffeine in the seventeenth century and psychedelics in the late twentieth. How alcohol affected early society is impossible to measure, and the jury is still out on psychedelics. But it's worth noting that coffee (or caffeine) and psychedelics have been associated with strikingly similar cultural revolutions. Richard Steele drinking coffee and talking about reforming the monarchy is the same person as Abbie Hoffman smoking a joint and plotting how to resist the Vietnam War. Voltaire's caffeinated cynicism was as symptomatic of his era's favorite buzz as Ginsberg's was of his. Politically, the human-rights movement of the 1700s (antimonarchical) and the 1900s (civil rights) both came to fruition as their associated pharmacies entered the mainstream. The coffee-crazed mobs of the French Revolution bear a certain resemblance to the pot-addled Vietnam War protesters of the 1960s. All this, by the way, is why American pundits should find consolation in the popularity of drugs like caffeine: despite their negative effects, it indicates Yanks still view getting wired as the preferred state of being. They should reserve their wails for the day when heroin and hot milk become the drugs of choice.

The Devil's Cup, 2000

Coffee, which makes the politician wise
And see through all things with his half shut eyes
Alexander Pope

Philip Jenkins
Synthetic Panics:
The Symbolic Politics of Designer Drugs – 1

THE CONCEPT OF synthetic drugs is itself problematic, and the term 'designer drug' has no precise scientific or sociological meaning. Generally, it refers to a substance synthesized in a laboratory, usually in an attempt to imitate some better-known chemical, to create an analog; the imitation might be undertaken to make the drug cheaper, safer, more effective, or more readily available to a mass public, and the designer phrase is often used to refer to quite legal pharmaceuticals. The popular science press regularly refers to the promise of new designer hormones, designer estrogens, designer genes, and so on. A large portion of modern industry owes its origin to a botched quest for a designer drug, when in 1856, William H. Perkin unsuccessfully attempted to synthesize quinine. He accidentally discovered a mysterious, brightly colored substance, the first of the synthetic aniline dyes that became the basis for the subsequent development of industrial chemistry worldwide; it also made Perkin very rich. In view of the modern stereotype of clandestine drug laboratories run by irresponsible teenagers, it is ironic that this epoch-making innovation was the work of an eighteen-year-old, amateur chemist undertaking an unauthorized experiment.

The discovery of synthetic chemicals marks a turning point in the history of science. Through the first half of the nineteenth century, scientists isolated valuable drugs from various plants, often from ones encountered during European explorations of distant lands. These new substances included morphine, strychnine, quinine, caffeine and codeine, and cocaine itself was isolated in 1844. From the 1860s onwards, a whole pharmacopoeia of revolutionary new synthetic drugs appeared as chemists sought to improve upon these naturally derived substances, as for example when the anesthetic procaine (Novocaine) was created to provide the beneficial effects of cocaine without its drawbacks. In 1898 a new synthetic derivative was claimed to offer the benevolent effects of morphine without the addictive side effects: this was diacetylmorphine, marketed under the trade name of Heroin. And in 1903, the first of the barbiturate drugs became commercially available as a sedative and hypnotic, replacing the alcoholic drinks previously recommended as the best means of calming nerves and sleeping soundly. All of these substances are synthetic or designer drugs, as are twentieth-century products such as LSD and the whole amphetamine group: all were made not by black-market chemists, but by European pharmaceutical corporations such as Merck, Bayer, Hoechst and Sandoz. The impact of the new drugs was vastly enhanced by the introduction in 1853 of the hypodermic syringe, which permitted substances to be injected directly into the bloodstream.

Though the concept of designer drugs has deep roots, the term is of much more recent origin: it appeared around 1980, after the appearance of the term 'designer jeans,' and was initially applied to outré analog substances created and marketed as a kind of synthetic heroin. After this usage was publicized during congressional hearings in 1985, the term was more widely – and unsystematically – applied to other synthetic drugs that came into vogue over the next decade, including MDMA (Ecstasy), fentanyl, methcathinone, GHB and ketamine. Applying the designer label to newer synthetics carried the implication that these substances were ipso facto as lethal as the most notorious synthetic heroins of the early eighties, which incontestably had caused brain damage and even death.

Synthetic Panics: The Symbolic Politics of Designer Drugs, 1999

Antonio Escohotado
New Drugs

AN EXTRAORDINARY DISCOVERY, commercialized during the thirties, was that of certain amines (amphetamine, dex-amphetamine, methamphetamine) appearing as products freely sold in pharmacies for nasal congestion, dizziness, obesity, depression, and the treatment of sedative overdoses. They were really stimulants of the nervous system, ten or twenty times more active than cocaine, much cheaper, and capable of not only improving endurance but of considerably improving scores in certain tests such as the intelligence quotient (IQ).

Their powerful euphoric effect led to their being sold to treat all discomforts related to depression, and they were given in sometimes formidable amounts to soldiers in the Second World War. They would reduce appetite sometimes for days, as well as sleep, nausea, exhaustion and discouragement – something too tempting for military hierarchies, which began using them in the Spanish Civil War and launched full methamphetamine use with highly stressed troops from 1939 to 1945. The Germans, British, Italians and Japanese, especially, distributed hundreds of millions of annual doses as a supplement to war rations, even though plenty of lethal intoxications occurred. Japan, for example, increased the production of this stimulant to the maximum during the war.

Upon surrender, the warehoused excess disappeared, producing a flooding of the streets with those drugs, which in 1950 supplied one million delirious users and several other million who were less suicidal, the perpetrators of over half of the murders and self-inflicted permanent cerebral lesions, and being admitted by the hundreds into hospitals, with a diagnosis of furious schizophrenia. In England, the greater part of amphetamines ended up in Montgomery's army and the Royal Air Force, and in 1941 a newspaper from the capital carried the headline METHEDRINE WINS THE BATTLE OF LONDON.

The postwar period modified user patterns, shifting the use of these amines to older persons, housewives and students: groups subject to boredom and lack of motivation or to the stress of having to face examinations. The free-sales regime alternated with advertisements such as 'Two pills are better than one month's vacation', and soon there were moderate and immoderate users all over the planet. In 1950 the United

States produced about one thousand tons yearly – eighty doses per capita, children included – a rate equaled by other nations. Amphetamine and dexamphetamine inhalers were considered medicines comparable to methol lozenges and soothing ointments, and their use in sports led to doping. Toward the end of the fifties, a world-champion cyclist died during an ascent aided by Maxiton, a methamphetamine. Shortly thereafter, twenty-three participants of the European Tour fell sick upon leaving Luchon, with symptoms described by the race doctor as caused by acute amphetamine intoxication. Two rounds later, a newspaper related that 'it was necessary to put one of the contestants in a strait-jacket because he suffered an insanity crisis' after ingesting one hundred pills of Tenedron, another amphetamine.

Barbiturates enjoyed popularity comparable to that of the stimulants. If the word *narcotic* is taken literally – as something that produces numbness in the user – one could say that barbiturates, among known drugs, are the ones with the highest capacity to produce numbness, were it not for the appearance in the end of the fifties of the neuroleptics, or major tranquilizers: compounds able to compete with barbiturates for that dubious honor. But numbness became useful, especially in the absence of opiates – more so if alcohol was banned, as was the case in North America when massive sales of them started. Contrary to stimulants, barbiturates incline to extroversion and disinhibition; their effect is to produce a state between alcoholic inebriation and sleep, providing numbness as a release for those pursued by their conscience, and satisfaction obtained by the timid when they are able to access their nerve. We must add to those qualities the almost inevitable ability to kill in high doses: a detail that converted these drugs into the most common means of committing suicide.

But the fact that they were not 'narcotics' under the law, and their free sales without prescription throughout the world, with an honourable description as 'sedatives, not opiates,' led many people to have a container of barbiturates in their night tables, with foreseeable results. By 1965 about 135,000 British subjects were dependent on these drugs, and in Scandinavia, by 1960, 73 percent of addicts were users of barbiturates. In 1962 a doctor stated before a special committee created by President Kennedy that there might be 250,000 American addicts ('and they are addicts who ignore their status,' he added – not an inflated number, considering that by then the nation manufactured some thirty tablets per capita annually. In narcotic power, this production was equivalent to 4,000 tons of crude opium, and we must remember that the first voices of alarm on account of the 'narcotic problem' were raised in the United States when imports amounted to 200 tons annually.

Otherwise, any competent doctor had known since the twenties that there is no worse dependency that is more destructive to personality. Studies made within the American prison population from 1945 to 1948 showed that 'the same convicts subjected to doses of morphine and heroin were sensate, prudent, able and scarcely affected sexually, while under the effects of barbiturates they became obstinate, aggressive, capable of masturbation in public, repeating idle excuses for the stumbling gait and mumbling speech.' The catastrophic withdrawal syndromes were also well known, much more prolonged than that of heroin and with greater risks of death, both in the convulsive phase and in the later protracted delirium.

Last, there existed the possibilities of accidental overdose; this occurred when people ingested pills when inebriated, or else took some, forgot they had done so, and took them again, as probably happened to Marilyn Monroe.

There was no legal recourse regarding 'functional disturbances and insomnia,' one of the main reasons to visit a doctor until different hypnotics and sedatives were introduced, and combinations of barbiturates and amphetamines were the rage in medical offices, since they avoided extensive testing of patients. Despite their ability to serve as a comfortable remedy for nerves – available, inexpensive and pure – during the space of almost fifty years, only some few million people became addicted to these drugs and had to travel that miserable road. The great majority had the same bottle of

Veronal or Luminal in their night tables for months or years and used it with moderation. As was the case with stimulant amines, barbiturates were never linked to social or ethnic minorities, and the absence of stigma protected them from the passion for the forbidden.

Among the drugs discovered during the period between the two world wars, we must mention several dozen synthetic opiates. The preparations for a second world conflict induced armies to search for anesthetics that were independent of the poppy, synthethized from coal tar and heavy oils, and they were introduced around 1945.

One of the common ones was pethidine, commercialized as Dolantin by Hoechst, and introduced as a non-addictive analgesic. In 1952 some 500 people addicted to the drug were admitted to American hospitals, unable to suppress a habit induced by their own doctors in 81 percent of the cases. By 1967 the American production of pethidine reached nineteen tons, sold under more than eighty different names.

Methadone turned out to be seven times more active; it was discovered by German army chemists and originally christened Dolofin by Adolf Hitler, although it was considered to be too addictive and toxic, and was never given to German troops. In 1964, under several names, some ten tons were consumed in the United States.

But the success of synthetic narcotics amounted to nothing compared with that of other drugs introduced during the fifties. Described as remedies for 'the rhythm of modern life,' their effect in small and medium doses is that of muscle relaxants, which instead of producing the emotional analgesia of opium (with its rich currents of dreamlike visions) give rise to an intellectual analgesia, characterized by logic and esthetic indifference.

Meprobamate, another petroleum derivative, was introduced in 1955 under hundreds of different names, with an unprecedented publicity barrage, as a 'happy pill, granting moral tranquillity with addiction,' even though three years later several experiments showed that its spectacular withdrawal syndrome closely resembled that of alcohol/barbiturates.

Nevertheless, 600 tons of this drug were consumed in the United States in 1965, and several thousand in the rest of the world; in that same year, for example, India notified the United States that this 'happy pill' was creating many cases of imbecility and dependence among the middle and upper classes of that country, who lined up behind the cause of substituting traditional opium for scientific medicines.

The kilos of meprobamate were soon to be exceeded – and later tripled – by the benzodiazepines, which arrived as anxiolytics ('dissolvers of anxiety') and hypnotics, free of addictive properties. Studies published in 1961 showed that the withdrawal syndromes of the benzodiazepines (Valium, diazepam, Aneural, Orfidal, Rohypnol, Dormodor, etc.) included trembling, nausea, muscular fibrillation, anorexia, insomnia, depression, and convulsive crises lasting several days.

Several thousand tons of many other hypnotics and sedatives were sold. The one with the bitterest memory was softenon, or thalidomide, commercialized in 1957 as a 'harmless sleeping pill, ideal for pregnant women.' Two years later, the birth of deformed babies began, rising to more than 3,000 and producing a wave of abortions in Europe as well as a famous euthanasia trial in Liège, where one doctor and four relatives were absolved.

A Brief History of Drugs, 1999

Philip Jenkins
Synthetic Panics:
The Symbolic Politics of Designer Drugs – 2

IN THE BEGINNING was the amphetamine. The amphetamine drugs are a chemical family initially synthesized in the late nineteenth century in order to mimic the effects of natural and herbal substances like ephedrine: they are archetypal designer drugs. Benzedrine (racemic or dextro-levo-amphetamine) was first synthesized in 1887, but its uses were not widely recognized until the 1920s, when its 'right-handed' isomer, dextro-amphetamine, or Dexedrine, also came into use. Also synthesized at about this time was d-phenyl-isopropyl-methylamine hydrochloride, better known as methamphetamine, which was marketed under the brand names Methedrine and Desoxyn. By 1970, over thirty amphetamine preparations were being distributed by fifteen pharmaceutical companies. The reason these drugs are so powerful has only become apparent with the investigation of the brain's neurotransmitters in recent decades.

Amphetamines, we now know, have a close chemical relationship to naturally occurring catecholamines like dopemine, epinephrine and norepinephrine, which help regulate cardiovascular functions and the central nervous system. As sympathomimetic drugs, the amphetamines mimic naturally occurring neurotransmitters and help trigger the release of additional natural chemicals. Amphetamines thus cause the nervous system to become intensely aroused, mimicking the effects of extreme external stimuli.

From 1932, amphetamines were widely used in the legal form of Benzedrine inhalers, marketed by the Smith Mine French corporation, and from 1936 tablets became available, ostensibly to treat the rare condition of narcolepsy. Through the mid-twentieth century, the amphetamine group was so widely prescribed for a variety of physical and emotional conditions as to make it seem an authentic wonder drug; coincidentally or not, 1932 was also the year in which Aldous Huxley described his fictional Soma. Amphetamines were associated with endurance, wakefulness, and the capacity to undertake long and demanding tasks of manual labor. As such, they were particularly favored by truck drivers. The stimulant was a godsend for workers in heavy industrial plants operating under the shift system, which paid so little regard to normal biorhythms. The drug had military applications as well: during the Second World War and afterwards, the United States and other nations issued amphetamine products (mainly Benzedrine) to soldiers facing long periods without sleep. Illicit supplies were available to almost anyone living in proximity to a military base, an industrial plant or a major trucking center.

The appeal of amphetamine was many-sided. Women were likely to encounter amphetamine in its role as appetite suppressant. In middle-class circles, the drug found its main users among college and high-school students studying desperately for exams. According to Harvey Cohen, '[a]mphetamine is very much an over-achiever's type of chemical,' and as such it had a following among business people and executives. It also had a large surreptitious market in college and professional sports, as speed promoted desirable qualities of aggression and toughness; the habit was probably introduced by servicemen returning after the Second World War. In schools, amphetamine analogs such as Ritalin (methylphenidate) were prescribed for schoolchildren diagnosed, rightly or wrongly, as hyperactive. The amphetamine business became a vast and profitable economic enterprise: by 1958, some eight billion pills and tablets were produced legally each year in the United States, in addition to the sizable illegal market and clandestine imports from Mexico; by 1971 legal production had risen to twelve billion pills. Just the amount produced within the law had the potential 'to provide a month's supply to every man, woman and child in the country.'

Synthetic Panics: The Symbolic Politics of Designer Drugs, 1999

To fathom hell or soar angelic
Just take a pinch of psychedelic

Humphrey Osmond

Michael Hollingshead
The Man Who Turned on the World

IN THE BEGINNING, more exactly, in 1943, Albert Hoffman, a Swiss biochemist working at the Sandoz Pharmaceutical Laboratories in Basel, discovered – by accident, of course; one

97

does not deliberately create such a situation – a new drug which had some very remarkable effects on the human consciousness. The name of this drug was d-Lysergic Acid Diethylamide Tartrate-25, a semi-synthetic compound, the lysergic-acid portion of which is a natural product of the ergot fungus *Claviceps pupurea*, which grows on rye and other grains. Its most striking pharmacological characteristic is its extreme potency – it is effective at doses as little as ten-millionths of a gram, which makes it 5,000 times more potent than mescaline.

It was during the synthesis of d-LSD-25 that chance intervened when Dr Hoffman inhaled some of the whitish-brown powder and discovered that it produced some strange effects on his mind . . . 'Objects, as well as the shape of my associates in the laboratory, appeared to undergo optical change . . . fantastic pictures of extraordinary plasticity and intensive colour seemed to surge towards me.'

New York City, 1960, seventeen years later . . . a small package from Switzerland arrived in my mail one morning containing one gram of Dr Hoffman's acid, which I had arranged to be sent to me. There was also a bill for $285. I had first heard of LSD from Aldous Huxley, when I had telephoned him at his home in Los Angeles to enquire about obtaining some mescaline, which he had recently been using. His information also included the name of Dr Albert Hoffman and a caution, subsequently unheeded, to take great care if ever I should take any of the stuff:

'It is much more potent than mescaline, though Gerald [Heard] and I have used it with some quite astonishing results really.'

There had been no difficulty obtaining even one gram of LSD. I simply asked an English doctor friend of mine to write the order on a sheet of New York hospital letterhead saying that I needed this ergot-derivative as a 'control' drug for a series of bone-marrow experiments. Eagerly I unwrapped the package. The acid was in a small dark jar marked 'Lot Number H-00047', and in appearance looked a bit like malted milk powder. My problem was how to convert the loose powder into a more manageable form. One gram would make 5,000 individual doses and I was obviously going to need to measure it out in some way. I decided to randomise it by mixing it into a stiff paste made from icing sugar.

I cleared the kitchen table and set to work. First I poured some distilled water into a bowl, and then mixed in the LSD. When all the acid had dissolved I added confectioner's sugar until the mixture was thick paste. Then I transferred my 'divine confection', spoon by laborious spoon, into a sixteen-ounce mayonnaise jar, and, by what magical alchemic process, the stuff measured exactly 5,000 spoonfuls! In other words, one teaspoon of the stuff ought to contain 200 gamma (millionths of a gram), which would be sufficient for an eight- to ten-hour session, and a pretty intense one at that.

I should add at this point that I had, like all good chefs, been tasting the preparation during its making with my finger, and must have absorbed about the equivalent of five heavy doses before I finally screwed the lid on the mayonnaise jar, which left me somewhat unprepared for what was to follow.

It was a very strange first trip indeed, and it was of many hours' duration, perhaps fifteen. What I had experienced was the equivalent of death's abolition of the body. I had literally 'stepped forth' out of the shell of my body, into some other strange land of unlikeliness, which can only be grasped in terms of astonishment and mystery, as an *état de l'absurde*, ecstatic nirvana. I could now 'understand' why death could produce the sort of confusion I was experiencing. In life we are anchored through the body to such inescapable cosmic facts as space, gravity, electro-magnetic vibrations and so forth. But when the body is lost, the psychic factor which survives is free to behave with uninhibited extravagance.

Once back in the present, when the 'mountains were again the mountains, and the lakes again the lakes', I felt a degree of apprehension about the acid I had by now stashed away in my study. It was pretty volatile stuff. How on earth could the energy of this strange atom be utilised; how could man adapt it to his needs? LSD was a bundle of solutions looking for a problem, the problem being how to undertake a work of integration on a massive scale. Modern man had fallen victim to the merciless vision of his own sceptical intelligence. Caught up in a wilderness of externals, he was a stranger to himself.

Accordingly, I telephoned Aldous Huxley at his home; he might at least advise me about what was happening with regard to LSD. Huxley had used both mescaline and LSD and had found in them, perhaps, the visions he had so long sought. On the phone, he was very sympathetic. No, there was still no one in a position to say what was happening in relation to visionary experience via LSD, though it seemed to excite a great curiosity in the minds of many he had discussed it with.

Huxley called me back a few days later, having thought over my problem, and suggested that I go to Harvard to meet a Dr Timothy Leary, a professor there, whom he'd met earlier that year in Copenhagen, when he had presented a paper on induced visionary experience before the Fourteenth International Congress of Applied Psychology. Leary had also read a paper on 'How to Change Behaviour', describing the induction of visionary mental states by psilocybin, the synthetic of the sacred mushroom of Mexico. He spoke very warmly of Leary as a scientist but also as a man, whom he described as 'a splendid fellow'. Leary had also written three classic monographs on personality and psychotherapy.

'If there is any one single investigator in America worth seeing,' Huxley assured me, 'it is Dr Leary.'

There had been quite a bit of free-floating acid around Greenwich Village that winter, but mostly restricted to the 'beats' of the East Village and a few wealthy Manhattan cats to whom they sold it. It was legal, of course, in those days, and this considerably reduced the paranoia level. 'Taking acid' had not yet become the popular pastime of a turned-on youth, for such didn't exist. The world of the late fifties and early sixties was unimaginably drab and dreary. It was still a tight little conformist world of roles and rules and rituals. Our culture had drowned itself in a sea of contradictory and conflicting

100

voices. And, politically, Dulles & Co. had tied the Cold War noose around all our throats. We had finally conned ourselves into submission to some nameless fear. Western civilization lived under the paranoia of the mushroom cloud. Liberal and religious values had eroded to the point of insignificance. Twentieth-century mass society showed the political inhumanity inherent in technological life-worlds. And it was perhaps inevitable that some of us took to acid (and later to myths and ancient stories) to seek a formula that would turn the surrounding world to dust and reveal the portals of paradise.

But I think that for perhaps the majority of the avant-garde, in this very early period, LSD was still something of an 'exotic', whose effects could not be taken for granted. LSD involved risk. It was anarchistic; it upset our apple carts, torpedoed our cherished illusions, sabotaged our beliefs. It was something you had to guard against, or you might explode. It was a difficult experience to assimilate. It was impossible to integrate with the ordinary world. And so on and so forth.

'Turning on' had not yet become a natural part of our existence, a symbol of certain lifestyles, or philosophy, or religion, or personal liberation. Yet there were some, of my circle, who, with Rimbaud, could say, 'I dreamed of crusades, senseless voyages of discovery, republics without a history, moral revolution, displacement of races and continents: I believed in all the magics.'

And our Crusade was to launch LSD on the world! While other artists/visionaries/seers had been content to observe the world, the New Message was simple: if things are not right, then change them!

We would make the dynamic life-giving adventure exploring Inner Space the New Romance! We would set off an explosion that would sweep through our culture and give birth to a New Radicalism!

We would even found a drug-based religion, whose message would be 'Turn On, Tune In, Drop Out!' We would proclaim the Reign of the Happily Integrated Modern Soul!

The Man Who Turned on the World, 1973

Stuart Walton
Out of It – 1

LEARY WAS A Harvard psychology lecturer who, during a visit to Mexico in 1960, took psilocybin mushrooms and declared he had had a religious epiphany. In 1961, in the atmosphere of feverish curiosity fomented by Hubbard, he took LSD and had another spiritual experience. He, too, now began insisting that everybody should take it, much to the disquiet of his employers. Leary got away with this increasingly obsessive campaign for two years before Harvard, fearful that its psychology department was being brought into disrepute, finally dismissed him.

Wondering just what had taken them so long, he embarked on his self-styled career as the High Priest of LSD, enjoying to the utmost the role of dropout academic consultant to the hippie movement. His literary output during this period is now of no consequence whatsoever, for the reason that he himself later recanted the acid faith, disowning virtually all the subversive pronouncements of his post-Harvard career (the most famous of which – 'Turn on, tune in and drop out' – was the 'Come on in, the water's lovely' of its day). He is reliably reputed to have grassed on several former associates, and happily provided information that led to the arrest of those who had helped him escape from prison while serving a term for possession of cannabis. When he died in 1997, having written a final book on the subject of dying, his last wish was for his ashes to be sent into extraterrestrial orbit. Leary was no guru, but a man of strikingly mediocre intellect whose career stands as a salutary caution against the fake appropriation of tribal cosmology in societies long grown out of it, and who – to borrow Lenin's famous sneer at the bourgeois Western Marxist – was more likely viewed by the mud-caked crowds at Woodstock as a 'useful idiot'.

Out of It, 2001

Howard Marks
Nazi Narcotics

I WENT TO Heidelberg.

I passed by Weinheim, the home where my old mate Werner Piper used to live. Werner devotes himself to archiving dope music and literature, wearing dreadlocks provided by Frankfurt's Korean Institute of Plastic Hair, and systematic psychedelic adventuring. He was the Pink Floyd's Piper at the Gates of Dawn. I called him.

'Werner, are the Nazis still in charge?'

'Absolutely, Howard. But instead of coming from Frankfurt and Hamburg and eating boys, they come from Boise and eat hamburgers and frankfurters. Heidelberg serves as headquarters for the United States Europe and Seventh Army (HQ USAAREUR/7A), the Central Army Group (CENTAG), and the Fourth Allied Tactical Air Force (4ATAF).'

'What exactly do these American Nazis run, Werner?'

'Drugs, basically. The agenda is slightly more sophisticated: control the minds of the people through dope and misinformation. If it doesn't work, kill them. That's why the German and American Nazis are always fighting wars.'

'Hold on, Werner. The Brits like war, too. And we ain't Nazis.'

'You Brits were Nazis, right at the very top. England and Scotland's first king was James I. His daughter, Elizabeth Stuart, came to Heidelberg, where she shagged and married out King Frederick V. Since then, you Brits have been controlled by Nazis – House of Hanover and all that. Britannia might have ruled the waves, but Nazis ruled Britannia. Even Queen Victoria was educated here in Heidelberg. The British Empire was a totally Nazi trip. Look at the Opium Wars. Look at the countries the Brits colonised: India, Burma, Jamaica, Nigeria: all major dope producers. Look at Bermuda, Hong Kong, Cayman Islands: all major money launderers.'

'So why did we fight two world wars against each other if we're the same side?'

'To get rid of our arseholes, Howard. Every country has them.'

'But how do the Nazis control dope? I thought we dope dealers were in charge of that.'

'That's why there's a war on drugs. The Nazis' main problem was being unable to discover a drug that turned individuals into unthinking and aggressive murderers. Every drug just seemed to turn people on and chill them right out. The only partial exceptions were American cigarettes and European shite lager. So that's why Heidelberg has been the centre of booze for several centuries, since 1600, in fact. And that's why Heidelberg has been Germany's tobacco centre since 1945, when the US Army took over Heidelberg's tobacco factory, Landfried House, next to the railway station. The Yanks cut off the excellent quality Turkish and local tobacco supplies, and got us hooked on Virginian rubbish. But far more interesting for you, I would have thought, is the German Pharmacy Museum. It's in Heidelberg Castle.'

Werner was right. The fixtures and fittings inside Apothecary Tower were most accommodating: prescription counters, bowls for bloodletting and medicine chests. I gazed at dope manufacturers' Aladdin's Caves of distillation heads, glass retorts, percolators, crucibles, blowpipes, pipettes, siphons, pestles, mortars, scales, stone ball weights, powder mixers, liquorice graters, pill machines, troughs and boards for cutting chopping and crushing, sifters, medicine spoons, tincture squeezers, sieves, ointment mills, measuring containers, tab dividers, pastille presses, urine glasses, breast pumps and pewter enema syringes. Glass cabinets were crammed full of the greatest varieties of dope I'd ever witnessed in my life: thousands of brain-tickling chemicals: friendly plant stuff like opium, morphine and hash; unfriendly plant stuff like curare (South American arrow poison) and a really mind-blowing collection of drugs of animal origin, including powdered toads, ground lizards and parts of human mummies. An aphrodisiac subdivision yielded the once-prized castor, secreted from the anal glands of beavers. (Imagine having to suck a beaver's arse just to get a hard-on.)

We entered a shrine full of offerings, largely toads, for the gods of convalescence. It was explained that toads symbolised female genitals.

Covering the walls were paintings of St Sebastian, St Rosalia, St Vitus and St Rochus, the patron saints of the plague; St Damien, the patron saint of pharmacists; and, holding a urine glass in his right hand, St Cosmas, the patron saint of piss-testing physicians. Dominating the paintings was one with a background of jars of dope and a foreground of a guy with a halo holding up a pair of dope scales. It was the man himself: Jesus Christ, the highest dope dealer of them all.

Before we left, I noticed that a spotlighted offering was of a mixture of unicorn-horn powder, aloe wrapped in ape skin and bezoar stone (calcifications found in the entrails of Persian goats). A company calling themselves Merck AG (Darmstadt) had donated it, along with the most impressive chunk of the dope display we'd seen. These guys must have been really hardcore. Got to get to the bottom of this one.

I went to Darmstadt.

During the middle of the seventeenth century, Friedrich Jacob Merck was born and bred in a place called Pig Castle (Schweinfurt). He was such a dedicated worshipper of drugs that he set up a dope-manufacturing company called Angel Pharmacy. Merck decided to house the Angel Pharmacy in Darmstadt, which is German for 'City of Entrails'. (Back to the goats.) The company has been in the possession of the family ever since.

By the turn of the century, Merck's 1,000 employees were busily manufacturing a wide variety of different chemical products. The Pharmacy of Angels survived World War I remarkably well, but was occupied by the American Army immediately World War II ended. Within a month, the Pharmaceutical Angels were manufacturing dope again, with the Yanks in charge. Merck's product range now comprises over 20,000 different items and has product facilities in over twenty-five countries. In addition, 170 companies operate on behalf of Merck in a further forty-six countries. Merck's propaganda omits to mention that in 1912 the

Pharmaceutical Angels of Darmstadt, the City of Entrails, discovered and synthesised Ecstasy. A patent for manufacturing MDMA was granted in 1914. Merck's official blurb also fails to disclose that for several decades Merck has sold far more cocaine hydrochloride than all the Colombian cartels put together.

Furthermore, Europe's answer to NASA is the European Space Agency (ESA) and is controlled by the European Space Operations Centre (ESOC), Darmstadt, the City of Entrails. Germans like dicks. Psychedelic mushrooms and space rockets both look like dicks. Germans discovered LSD, MDMA, etc. It was a German, Herman Gainswindt, who, in 1891, first conceived of a space rocket, a giant dick with a little man in it being thrust into the moon, the mother symbol. V-2s were unmanned rocket bombs, guided missiles, successfully aimed at London during the last war. They were pioneered at Darmstadt, City of Entrails. Now, every condom manufactured in Germany is tested in Darmstadt, City of Entrails. Until 1945, Wernher von Braun headed the Nazi V-2 programme. Since then, von Braun and his mates have changed their diet from wurst to apple pie. Otherwise, nothing's changed.

Nazi Narcotics, 2001

Dominic Streatfield
Cocaine

WHILE THE PRICE of cocaine is high for consumers, it is considerably higher for producers. Here in South America the dangers of the drug are a lot more scary than the occasional perforated nasal septum. The unfeasible amounts of hard currency generated by the drug ricochet around this continent, creating casualties wherever they go. In the last twenty-five years alone, cocaine-generated cash has been responsible for *coups d'état* in Bolivia and Honduras; has infiltrated the governments of the Bahamas, Turks and

Caicos, Haiti, Cuba, and every single Latin American country without exception; has helped to fund a guerrilla war in Nicaragua (creating one of the most embarrassing scandals in the CIA's history); and has prompted the US invasion of Panama. In the late 1980s, traffickers in Peru and Bolivia were so wealthy that they offered to pay off their countries' national debts; meanwhile, Cololmbia's traffickers were so powerful that they declared war on their own country – and brought it to its knees. At the time of writing, the cocaine industry is creating riots in Peru, policemen are being kidnapped and tortured to death because of it in Bolivia and, if I was a betting man, I would put money on the cocaine industry cranking Colombia's ongoing civil war to its highest levels for the last thirty-six years within the next six months. At this very moment the governments of Peru, Ecuador and Venezuela are stationing troops on their Colombian borders to handle the expected influx of refugees.

All this trouble, just because of cocaine? The drug you take on special occasions, in the lavatory with your mates, when out clubbing? The drug you take because it's a laugh? Crazy, isn't it?

Cocaine, 2001

Elizabeth Wurtzel
Prozac Nation

NOT TOO LONG ago, my friend Olivia brought her cat to the veterinarian because she was chewing clumps of fur off her back and vomiting all the time. The doctor looked at Isabella and immediately diagnosed the animal with something called excessive grooming disorder, which meant that the cat had grown depressed and self-absorbed, perhaps because Olivia's boyfriend had moved out of the apartment, perhaps because Olivia was traveling so much. At any rate, the vet explained, this was an obsessive-compulsive disorder. Isabella couldn't stop cleaning herself just as certain people can't stop vacuuming their apartments, or washing their hands all the time like Lady Macbeth. The vet recommended treating the cat with Prozac, which had proved extremely effective in curing this condition in humans. A feline-size prescription was administered.

Now, you have to understand that Olivia had been on and off Prozac and its chemical variants for a couple of years herself, hoping to find a way to cope with her constant bouts of depression. Olivia had also recently insisted that her boyfriend either go on Prozac or take a hike because his sluggishness and foul moods were destroying their relationship. And I had, or course, been on Prozac for more than six years at that point. So when she called to tell me that now Isabella was on it too, we laughed. 'Maybe that's what my cat needs,' I joked. 'I mean, he's been under the weather lately.'

There was a nervous edge to our giggling.

'I think this Prozac thing has gone too far,' Olivia said.

'Yes.' I sighed. 'Yes, I think it has.'

I never thought that depression could seem funny, never thought there'd be a time when I could be amused thinking that of the $1.3 billion spent on prescriptions for Prozac last year (up about 30 percent since 1992), some of them might even be for our household pets, who are apparently as susceptible to mental trauma as the rest of us. I never thought I would amazedly read about Wenatchee, Washington, a town known as 'the Apple Capital of the World,' a place where 600 out of its 21,000 residents are all on Prozac, and where one psychologist has come to be known as 'the Pied Piper of Prozac.' I never thought that the New York Times, reporting on the eleven million people who have taken Prozac – six million in the United States alone – would declare on its front page that this constituted a 'legal drug culture.' I never thought there would be so many cartoons with Prozac themes in the New Yorker, illustrating, among other things, a serotonin-happy Karl Marx declaring, 'Sure! Capitalism can work out its kinks!' I never thought that in the same week I would stare down at both a Newsweek cover with a large, missile-like capsule beneath the caption 'Beyond Prozac' and a *New Republic* cover of some shiny, happy people enjoying their sunny lives above the headline 'That Prozac Moment!'

I never thought that this antidote to a disease as serious as depression – a malady that easily could have ended my life – would become a national joke.

Prozac Nation, 1996

CHAPTER TWO

OUT OF IT

Howard Marks
Over-the-Counter Highs

MARKETED AS MANDRAX in the United Kingdom and easily obtained on prescription, methaqualone became the 1960s London substance of sexual preference. A fair percentage of thirty-year-old readers were probably conceived as a direct result of Britain's nocturnal drug of choice shifting from Horlicks to Mandrax. Being stoned qualified as a British domestic comfort: safe and exciting. Notting Hill Gate stoners heard tales of globe-trotting hippies sleeping into corpses as they drove off Greek island roads keeping their eyes on the dawn. Foreign hospitals weren't too much fun. Neither were foreign jails, even before *Midnight Express*. The music was better at home. European rock was absolute shite. There was no need to travel.

However, during 1967, Mick Jagger was busted and jailed in England for being in possession of legally obtained Italian speed. Although the appeal-court judges eventually cut him loose, the incident convinced pursuers of altered mind states that being a bombed-out tourist abroad was considerably safer than staying at home minding one's business. Even worse, the authorities made the worrying discovery that Mandrax took the fun out of television ratings. They stopped doctors prescribing it. Gee's Linctus is not much of an

111

aphrodisiac, and the hallucinations on Feminax are well overrated. So, the heads took to travel.

Nowadays, travellers to foreign lands tend to indulge themselves with New Age worries such as catching a strong dose of clap or the cost of mobile-phone diversions from one's unattended office. I remember so well the days when foreign travel fulfilled with remarkable efficiency my desires to get off my face. It was so easy in the sixties and seventies: catch a cheap flight to Ibiza, walk from the Farmacia airport to a beach full of sex, lie on the tidemark, drop a Dormidina, let my wet dreams ooze into reality, have a happy night, and be woken at dawn by Guardia Civil attacking me with pointed sticks. It was what going abroad was all about. Spain for downers, Italy for uppers, South America for cactus and coca preparations, Morocco for marijuana tea, and up the Khyber for edible, drinkable and smokable hash suppositories.

Foreign chemists always seemed to do a good job catering for sufferers of diarrhoea and hypochondria. Furthermore, the happy Mediterranean pharmacist did not seem troubled that the customer might experience effects over and above mere cure and soon beg for more. British high-street chemists, on the other hand, were nothing more than drug-squad officers dressed in white. One had to be ill to get high. But many medicines continued to be purchased for reasons other than the usual ones of rectifying the irregularity of the discharge of bodily fluids and easing pain. Acetaminophen is the active ingredient in Panadol, Anacin-3, Datril and Tylenol, all of which were manufactured initially for headache relief but are now often acquired for use as sedatives and, more puzzlingly, for neutralising the quite pleasant comedown effects known as jet lag. Mix acetaminophen with codeine, and one might be lucky enough to get a small rush of euphoric bliss. Ready mixes of these two narcotics could be found in Tylenol #3 and Phenephen #3. Ibuprofen, found in Advil, Midol, Motrin, Panprin, Rufen and other mild painkillers, was discovered to have the additional qualities of relaxing muscles and producing mild visual distractions. Some fortunates even hallucinate when taking the decongestant pseudoephedrine hydrochloride, found in everything from Vick to Children's Sudafed.

Need a lift? Catch a flight to Malta, go straight to Valetta's Freedom Square, which has long housed the inviting shelves of Chemimart. Buy some Stilnox, the crème de la crème of sleeping draughts, very similar to Mandrax. Then go to Paris. At the Champs Élysées and avenue Matignon are real drug-stores called 'Drugstores', where one can by very sexy sleepers (Dornomyl). From Paris go to Milan, where the Farmacia Bracco will sell you Novalhina, which will kill any pain as it smoothly knocks you out. Then go to Spain where you can still neck a Dormidina for siesta and pop Prozac for pleasure.

But it still requires a visit to the Third World to get serious about chemistry shopping. Sample South-East Asia, where benzodiazepine medications, for example Valium and Librium, are widely used tranquillisers that definitely require prescription in most parts of the world. Not so in Thailand, where the authorities react quizzically to concern about its widely documented potential for use as a recreational drug. A regular Bangkok chemist will happily supplement your Valium supplies with some Rohypnol, ten times stronger and rapidly gaining street cred as a date-rape drug.

Psychedelically, Britain is far behind the Third World, quite a way behind Europe, and wrestling with America for last place. In fact, Britain is even worse than America, where many over-the-counter medications with reputations of inducing euphoria and a good night's kip as side effects are, unlike here, available without prescription. These include Aleve, Naprosyn and Novonaprox, preparations containing naproxen, an anti-inflammatory non-steroid, which took me quite a long and relieving way from pain. A mate of mine had bought them for me at a Manhattan chain store called S & M Pharmacy. He'd also legally scored far more interesting dope called secbarbital and sold as 'Big Reds'. These actually produced a slice of long-lasting silent giggles.

The United States even outclasses European countries when it comes to the availability of some particular over-the-counter drugs. Melatonin is the best example. It can be bought in Boise, Idaho, but not in Amsterdam, Paris or Madrid. The presence of adequate melatonin, a hormone secreted by the pineal gland, induces sleep and reverses the ravages of time. Benefits supposedly range from its gentle effective sleeping aid to an extremely powerful free radical. (Free radicals are molecules that are highly corrosive to the cells of the body and are believed to be one of the major contributors to the ageing process. They are formed as a by-product of the body's normal chemical processes, particularly of the reaction between oxygen and fat.) Melatonin is also claimed to be an immune-system enhancer, as well as a confirmed inhibitor of jet lag.

If not allowed to breeze into Miami, do not despair; hop on a plane to Johannesburg and buy some melatonin at any high-street chemist. While there, stock up on Syndol, a strong soporific spiked with codeine.

So, if you want to keep stoned, keep rolling or keep moving.

Julian Keeling
Drugstore Cowboy

FOR OTHER CHILDREN it was entering a sweetshop that made them feel like a kid in a sweetshop, but it was a trip to the local chemist that invariably aroused the finer feeling in me . . . It was the pills and powders and preparations, the tinctures and mixtures and linctuses. It was the bank of square, dark wood drawers with exotic abbreviations like 'sticta. pul.' or 'sur. papav.' that stimulated my nameless longings.

Worryingly, my appreciation was not just an aesthetic one, for, even when I was only label-high to a bottle of codeine linctus, I had come to understand the benefits of a slight chemical shift. At the age of seven I was already faking stomach aches in return for a generous dose of Kaolin & Morphine, a mixture that would spread warmth throughout my body.

At boarding school my quest continued. Throughout the winter I would line up after breakfast in the hope of being doled out a sweet spoonful of Gee's Linctus for my perpetual cough. It seemed to have pretty much the same effect as the tummy-ache medicine and I was not surprised to discover later that anhydrous morphine was again the active ingredient in this opiate squill mixture. Also, thanks to some advice from my older brother, I experimented with some tablets called Do-Do. Each pill contained 18.31mg of ephedrine, the same variety of speed that precipitated the downfall of the footballer Maradona during the 1994 World Cup finals. I found that the drug worked extremely well with alcohol, enabling you to carry on drinking long after you were too drunk to drink any more. The downside was the strain it placed on the heart muscles and the tendency to produce bizarre hallucinations at inconvenient times. It was hard to get my homework done when, for instance, my housemaster – in bondage outfit, but with the tail of a mermaid – would make unscheduled visits from the electrical socket.

Over-the-counter drugs are cheap, they're easy to get hold of (provided your pharmacist isn't some bitter old fuck with a chip on their shoulder because they failed to get into medical school), and there's a wide range of pleasures available. My staple diet is opiates, which come in a bewildering array of pills and sticky liquids. The king of these pills is Paramol. They come in a sinister black packet with a partially eclipsed blue sun, so similar to a pinned-out eye that you wonder if their real market might actually be the recreational users.

Other opiates are on the market in bottles, each one strong enough to get you into a fairly nice nod, or at least make things comfortably blurred around the edges. They will also soothe your nerves after an E too many or a night on the nose – at least that's what my friends tell me. I've given up all those class-A drugs. They're illegal; they're expensive; you have to buy them off dodgy people; the doses are hard to predict and, worst of all, they've become socially acceptable. Raving the night away on MDMA or spending hours in the locked toilet cubicle of a fashionable nightspot now makes you feel like a regular pillar of society.

But spending my days on a grand tour of west London's better-stocked chemists, faking the symptoms of a bizarre range of ailments and telling outrageous fibs to a mistrustful pharmacist, makes me feel subversive, delinquent and different.

And it makes me feel young again.

Drugstore Cowboy, 1996

Jim Hogshire
The Test

I DRANK ABOUT eight ounces of DM cough syrup. I was feeling kind of achy and wanted to see if it would kill pain. Previous smaller-dose experiments had shown me that the stuff could cause confusion and restlessness, but I couldn't remember how much I'd taken.

Soon enough, pain went away, and I went to bed a couple of hours later. It was midnight. I felt neither awake nor asleep, sort of like a typical narcotic high, but no great shakes. Mildly content, kind of nodding – just not as pleasant.

At four o'clock in the morning I woke up suddenly and remembered that I had to go to Kinko's copy shop and shave a week's worth of stubble from my face. These ideas seemed very clear to me.

That seems normal enough, except I HAD A REPTILIAN BRAIN. My whole way of thinking and perceiving. It was like I was operating with a medulla only.

I had full control over motor functions, but still had the impression that I was ungainly. That's because I felt detached from my body, as if I was inhaling nitrous oxide. I got in the shower and shaved. For all I knew I was hacking my face to pieces – or maybe not. Since I didn't see any blood or feel any pain, I had no worries about it. In fact, 'feelings' were so shallow or nonexistent that I probably couldn't have felt anything like anxiety. I lost any sense of time.

I knew I was capable of performing various actions, but could not conceive of any consequences to those actions. Had I looked down and seen another limb, I wouldn't have been surprised at all. It was very much like being a passenger inside my own body.

During this experience I gained the sort of insight associated with acid or dreams. Like a dream, you aren't surprised by the absurd (an extra limb) and, like an LSD trip, you realize the absurdity of it all. But without hallucinations.

The world became a binary place of dark and light, on/off, safety/danger. When I felt a need, I determined it was hunger, and ate almonds until I didn't feel the need any more. Same thing with water. It was like playing a game. Staying alive, but with no fear at all. I sat down at my desk and tried to write down how this felt so I could look at it later. I was very aware that I was stupid. I wrote down the word 'Cro-Magnon.'

I thought I would have trouble driving but I had none. I felt 'unsafe' confronting the dark street but then this feeling disappeared when I crawled into the 'safe' car. Luckily there were only a couple of people in Kinko's and one of them was a friend. She confirmed that my pupils were of different sizes.

I was fucked up.

There was no way I could make any subjective decisions or know if I was correctly adhering to social custom. I didn't even know how to modulate my voice. Was this too loud? Do I look like a normal human? Outside, my friend shivered, so I asked her if it was cold, because for me there were only two temperatures – tolerable/intolerable (I found that out in the shower). I guess I wasn't cold since I had no urge to change locations.

I understood that I was an entity in the big contraption called civilization and that certain things were expected of me – but I could not comprehend what the hell they might be.

All the words that came out of my mouth seemed equivalent in meaning. Instead of saying 'Reduce it about 90 percent,' I could have said 'Two eggs and some toast, please,' and these two phrases would have been the same. The whole world broke down into elemental parts, each of equal 'value' to the whole, which is to say, of no value at all.

I sat at a table and read a newspaper. It was the most absurd thing I had ever seen! Each story purported to describe a thing or event, or was supposed to convey 'news' of a reality of some other location. This seemed stupid. An article on a war in Burma was described as 'the war the West forgot.' It had an 'at-a-glance' chart that said Burma was three times the size of the state of Washington.

This was meaningless, and I knew it. The story did not even begin to describe the tiniest fragment of the reality of that place. From a vague recollection of my pre-reptilian days, I knew of things called 'complicated.' But the paper's pitiful attempt to categorize individuals as 'rebels' or 'insurgents' or to describe the reasons for the agony was literally ridiculous. I laughed out loud.

I found being a reptile kind of pleasant. I was content to sit and monitor my surroundings. I was alert, but not anxious. If someone had come at me with an axe, I would have acted appropriately. Fight or flight. Every now and then I would do a 'reality check' to make sure I wasn't masturbating or strangling someone, due to a vague awareness of non-reptilian expectations. At one point, I ventured across the street to a hamburger place to get something to eat. It was locked up and yet there were workers inside. This truly confused me, and I considered trying to break in, and make off with food. Luckily, the store opened (now that it was six a.m.) and I entered the front door like a normal customer.

It was difficult to remember how to do a money-for-merchandise transaction and even more difficult to put words into action, but I finally succeeded at the task. I ate bite by bite until I was full. If I had become full before finishing the hamburger, I think I would have simply let it fall from my hand.

The life of a reptile may seem boring to us, but boredom has no place in a reptilian brain. If, as a reptile, something started to hurt, I took steps to get away from it. If it felt better over here, that's where I went. Writing this, twenty-four hours after becoming a reptile, it seems that my neocortex is reconnecting. Soon, I hope to be human again.

As a reptile I still believed in God. I didn't feel like praying (which seemed ludicrous), but there was no diminishing of my belief. Why? Is a purely human question. As a reptile, questioning my existence was none of my business. I just didn't care. Become a reptile for a while; it straightens out a thing or two.

From: *Pills-A-Go-Go: A Fiendish Investigation into Pill Marketing, Art, History & Consumption*, 1999

Medlar Lucan and Durian Gray
The Decadent Gardener

A FEW YEARS ago, Durian, Heinrich and I took a house in Slovenia with no intention other than idling away the summer. It was a peasant house with a small garden and along one side of the house there grew in abundance a plant which I recognised as henbane, *Hyoscyamus Niger*. I watched the plant with an interest bordering on obsession throughout the summer, as I waited for its seeds to ripen. When this occurred I collected a quantity and set about preparing them.

I discovered that there are two ways of experiencing henbane. One is to make a sort of paste from the seeds and to rub it into an area of the chest close to the heart. The other is to roast the seeds and inhale the fumes. Feeling unconvinced about the first method, I decided to start with the second. I took a handful of the flat, greyish seeds and placing them on a metal plate, I heated them slowly from below using a spirit stove. I watched with anticipation and unease as the seeds began to swell. Shortly after, their shells burst and the fumes began to rise. I inhaled deeply. . .

It was not long (although I cannot say how long) before it became clear that the fumes were beginning to penetrate my consciousness. The first effects were physical and I began to feel very unsteady on my feet. My head was aching and I experienced a sickening dizziness. Also my mouth and throat became parched, to the point where I could barely swallow, let alone speak. I began to feel frightened. One might have thought that this was related to having taken the henbane, that it was a fear of poisoning or death. But it could not have been, as I no longer had any idea how I had got into this state. No, it was just a vague, unspecific terror. I remember looking in a mirror and this increased my anxiety. My face had swollen and become livid. The flesh on my head had grown much heavier and I could feel the bulk of it weighing about my cheeks, distorting the shape of my face. My eyes stared out at me, enlarged and black. I had trouble fixing my gaze on the mirror as it kept moving back and forth. Soon not just the mirror but the entire room was on the move. I had to clutch hold of something to stop myself from sliding rapidly first to the left then to the right. My senses were diminishing. Sounds began to fade and the objects in the room began to darken. My peripheral vision became lost in a grey fog, I was drenched in perspiration by now and as the darkness deepened, sight was replaced by a series of terrifying hallucinations. A thin stone column with an elaborately carved capital suddenly presented itself to my sight. It stood in front of me and was looking at me. I tried to move my head to avoid its gaze but found I was unable to. My body no longer responded to my wishes. I was paralysed. The gaze of the column became unbearable. I was overcome with a terrible sense of shame and terror towards this. My whole body seemed to be shaking uncontrollably. As I stood there, unable to move, the column slowly dissolved and reformed in the shape of a grotesque infant. Its face was hideously contorted in a silent scream. It appeared to be in great pain, but I felt no sorrow or pity for it. I knew that it bore me ill-will, and I desperately wanted to escape its malevolence. There was something deeply violent and almost satanic about it. At this point, a whole host of images crowded around me – weird animals, talking plants, a cloud of tiny black insects, demented voices whispering urgently to me, as if semi-human creatures were trying to crawl inside my ears. It was as if I was inhabiting the world of a medieval text, a bestiary of madness. All the time I was trying to move, to escape, but my legs refused to respond. A wave of sickness rose up in me, to the point where I was sure I would collapse, although at the same time I knew that this would not bring me unconsciousness. The grotesque visions would continue to haunt me.

The next stage which I remember was both the most horrifying and also the most exultant. Between the waves of nausea, I experienced moments of profound well-being. These were accompanied by a feeling of bodily disintegration. Although I was paralysed, it appeared that parts of my body were beginning to detach themselves and take on a separate existence. My head was stretching upwards and at any moment would be parted from my body. Simultaneously, a sensation of flight began to take hold of me. With this came a relaxation. As I experienced the terror of my dissolving body, I abandoned myself to my hallucinations and I was soon at one with them, drifting through a gloomy sky and over a strange, crepuscular landscape. This was little short of euphoric. The terror had lifted and I accepted the horror of the images which presented themselves as a matter of course.

When I returned to consciousness, I was totally disoriented. Durian and Heinrich must have carried me to my bed, where I lay for some days languishing in deep gloom. My body was racked with discomfort and the nausea remained with me. Even several days later I was still unsteady and found it difficult to walk or take hold of objects.

This account is inevitably sketchy and incoherent. One consequence of henbane narcosis is memory failure, so all that I was left with are one or two particular hallucinations and a general sense of the physical effects. This may be for the best. I shudder to think what nightmarish images I have forgotten.

The Decadent Gardener, 1998

Hunter S. Thompson
Drug Frenzy at the Circus-Circus

HE CAME BACK with the ether bottle, uncapped it, then poured some into a Kleenex and mashed it under his nose, breathing heavily. I soaked another Kleenex and fouled my own nose. The smell was overwhelming, even with the top down. Soon we were staggering up the stairs towards the entrance, laughing stupidly and dragging each other along, like drunks.

This is the main advantage of ether: it makes you behave like the village drunkard in some early Irish novel . . . total loss of all basic motor skills: blurred vision, no balance, numb tongue – severance of all connection between the body and the brain. Which is interesting, because the brain continues to function more or less normally . . . you can actually watch yourself behaving in this terrible way, but you can't control it.

You approach the turnstiles leading into the Circus-Circus and you know that when you get there, you have to give the man two dollars or he won't let you inside . . . but when you get there, everything goes wrong: you misjudge the distance to the turnstile and slam against it, bounce off and grab hold of an old woman to keep from falling, some angry Rotarian shoves you and you think: What's happening here? What's going on? Then you hear yourself mumbling: 'Dogs fucked the Pope, no fault of mine. Watch out! . . . Why money? My name is Brinks; I was born . . . born? Get sheep over side . . . women and children to armored car . . . orders from Captain Zeep.'

Ah, devil ether – a total body drug. The mind recoils in horror, unable to communicate with the spinal column. The hands flap crazily, unable to get money out of the pocket . . . garbled laughter and hissing from the mouth . . . always smiling.

Ether is the perfect drug for Las Vegas. In this town they love a drunk. Fresh meat. So they put us through the turnstiles and turned us loose inside.

Fear and Loathing in Las Vegas, 1972

Human kind cannot bear very much reality

T. S. Eliot

Alexander and Ann Shulgin
The Chemistry Continues

QUALITATIVE COMMENTS: DMT

(with 150mg, orally) 'No observable psychic or vegetative effects.'

(with 250mg, orally) 'It was inactive.'

(with 350mg, orally) 'Completely without effect either physiological or psychological.'

(with 100mg, via the buccal mucosa) 'Numbness at the site, but no central effects.'

(with 20mg, intramuscularly) 'I began to see patterns on the wall that were continuously moving. They were transparent, and were not colored. After a short period these patterns became the heads of animals, a fox, a snake, a dragon. Then kaleidoscopic images appeared to me in my inner eye, fantastically beautiful and colored.'

(with 30mg, intramuscularly) 'There was eye dilation and, subjectively, some perception disturbances.'

(with 50mg, intramuscularly) 'I feel strange, everything is blurry. I want my mother, I am afraid of fainting, I can't breathe.'

(with 60mg, intramuscularly) 'I don't like this feeling – I am not myself. I saw such strange dreams a while ago. Strange creatures, dwarfs or something; they were black and moved about. Now I feel as if I am not alive. My left hand is numb. As if my heart would not beat, as if I had no body, no nothing. All I feel are my left hand and stomach. I don't like to be without thoughts.'

(with 75mg, intramuscularly) 'The third or fourth minute

after the injection vegetative symptoms appeared, such as tingling sensation, trembling, slight nausea, mydriasis, elevation of the blood pressure and increase of the pulse rate. At the same time, eidetic phenomena, optical illusions, pseudo-hallucinations, and later real hallucinations, appeared. The hallucinations consisted of moving, brilliantly colored oriental motifs, and later I saw wonderful scenes altering very rapidly. The faces of people seemed to be masks. My emotional state was elevated sometimes up to euphoria. At the highest point I had compulsive athetoid movements in my left hand. My consciousness was completely filled by hallucinations, and my attention was firmly bound to them; therefore I could not give an account of the events happening to me. After three-quarters to one hour the symptoms disappeared, and I was able to describe what had happened.

(with 80mg, intramuscularly) 'My perceptual distortions were visual in nature and with my eyes closed I could see colored patterns, primarily geometrical patterns moving very fast, having sometimes very deep emotional content and connotation. My blood pressure went up and my pupils were dilated.'

(with 30mg, smoked) 'I spread it evenly on a joint of *Tanacetum vulgare* and melted it with a heat lamp. In about thirty seconds a strong light-headedness started, with a feeling of temporal pressure. Some yellowing of the visual field. There was nothing for me to do because I had to turn complete control over to the drug. Off the plateau in three to four minutes and the fact that the radio was on became apparent. I was out in a few more minutes.'

(with 60mg, smoked) 'We did it together. Swift entry – head overwhelmed – elaborate and exotic. Slightly threatening patterns – no insight slight sense of cruelty and sharpness between us, but enjoying. His face, as before with MDA, demonic but pleasantly so. He said he saw my face as a mask. He asked me to let him see my teeth. I laughed – aware that laughter was slightly not-funny. Heavy, massive intoxication.

Time extension extraordinary. What seemed like two hours was about thirty minutes.'

(with 60mg, smoked) 'Rapid onset, and in a completely stoned isolation in about a minute for about three minutes. Slow return but continued afterglow (pleasant) for thirty minutes. Repeated three times, with no apparent tolerance or change in chronology. Easily handled. The intoxication is of limited usefulness but the residues are completely relaxing.'

(with 100mg, smoked) 'As I exhaled I became terribly afraid, my heart very rapid and strong, palms sweating. A terrible sense of dread and doom filled me – I knew what was happening, I knew I couldn't stop it, but it was so devastating; I was being destroyed – all that was familiar, all reference points, all identity all viciously shattered in a few seconds. I couldn't even mourn the loss – there was no one left to do the mourning. Up, up, out, out, eyes closed, I am at the speed of light, expanding, expanding, expanding, faster and faster until I have become so large that I no longer exist – my speed is so great that everything has come to a stop – here I gaze upon the entire universe.'

(with 15mg, intravenously) 'An almost instantaneous rush began in the head and I was quickly scattered. Rapidly moving and intensely colored visuals were there, and I got into some complex scenes. There were few sounds, and those that were there were not of anyone talking. I was able to continue to think clearly.'

(with 30mg, intravenously) 'I was hit harder than I had ever been when smoking the stuff. The onset was similar, but the euphoria was less.'

Tryptamines I Have Known and Loved: The Continuation, 1997

William Burroughs
Junky – 1

PEYOTE IS A small cactus and only the top part that appears above the ground is eaten. This is called a button. The buttons are prepared by peeling off the bark and fuzz and running the button through a grater until it looks like avocado salad. Four buttons is the average dose for a beginner.

We washed down the peyote with tea. I came near gagging on it several times. Finally I got it all down and sat there waiting for something to happen. The herb dealer brought out some bark he claimed was like opium. Johnny rolled a cigarette of the stuff and passed it around. Pete and Johnny said, 'Crazy! This is the greatest.'

I smoked some and felt a little dizzy and my throat hurt. But Johnny bought some of that awful-smelling bark with the intention of selling it to desperate hipsters in the US.

After ten minutes I began to feel sick from the peyote. Everyone told me, 'Keep it down, man.' I held out ten minutes more, then headed for the WC ready to thrown in the towel, but I couldn't vomit. My whole body contracted in a convulsive spasm, but the peyote wouldn't come up. It wouldn't stay down either.

Finally, the peyote came up solid like a ball of hair, solid all the way up, clogging my throat. As horrible a sensation as I ever stood still for. After that, the high came on slow. Peyote high is something like Benzedrine high. You can't sleep and your pupils are dilated. Everything looks like a peyote plant. I was driving in the car with the Whites and Cash and Pete. We were going out to Cash's place in the Lomas. Johnny said, 'Look at the bank along the road. It looks like a peyote plant.'

I turned around to look, and was thinking, 'What a damn silly idea. People can talk themselves into anything.' But it did look like a peyote plant. Everything I saw looked like a peyote plant.

Our faces swelled under the eyes and our lips got thicker through some glandular action of the drug. We actually looked like Indians. The others claimed they felt primitive and were laying around on the grass and acting the way they figured Indians act. I didn't feel any different from ordinary except high like on benny.

We sat up all night talking and listening to Cash's records. Cash told me about several cats from 'Frisco who had kicked junk habits with peyote. 'It seems like they didn't want junk when they started using peyote.' One of these junkies came down to Mexico and started taking peyote with Indians. He was using it all the time in large quantities: up to twelve buttons in one dose. He died of a condition that was diagnosed as polio. I understand, however, that the symptoms of peyote poisoning and polio are identical.

I couldn't sleep until the next morning at dawn, and then I had a nightmare every time I dozed off. In one dream, I was coming down with rabies. I looked in the mirror and my face changed and I began howling. In another dream, I had a chlorophyll habit. Me and about five other chlorophyll addicts are waiting to score on the landing of a cheap Mexican hotel. We turn green and no one can kick a chlorophyll habit. One shot and you're hung for life. We are turning into plants.

Junky, 1977

John Symonds
Chloroform

I JUST NOW quoted J. A. Symonds. [He] also records a mystical experience with chloroform, as follows:

'After the choking and stifling had passed away, I seemed at first in a state of utter blankness; then came flashes of intense light, alternating with blackness, and with a keen vision of what was going on in the room around me, but no sensation of touch. I thought that I was near death; when, suddenly, my soul became aware of God, who was manifestly dealing with me, handling me, so to speak, in an intense personal present reality. I felt him streaming in like light upon me . . . I cannot describe the ecstasy I felt. Then, as I gradually awoke from the influence of the anesthetics, the old sense of my relation to the world began to return, the new sense of my relation to God began to fade. I suddenly leapt to my feet on the chair where I was sitting, and shrieked out, "It is too horrible, it is too horrible, it is too horrible," meaning that I could not bear this disillusionment.

'Then I flung myself on the ground, and at last awoke covered with blood, calling to the two surgeons (who were frightened), "Why did you not kill me? Why would you not let me die?" Only think of it. To have felt for that long dateless ecstasy of vision the very God, in all purity and tenderness and truth and absolute love, and then to find that I had after all had no revelation, but that I had been tricked by the abnormal excitement of my brain.

'Yet, this question remains, is it possible that the inner sense of reality which succeeded, when my flesh was dead to impressions from without, to the ordinary sense of physical relations, was not a delusion but an actual experience? Is it possible that I, in that moment, felt what some of the saints have said they always felt, the indemonstrable but irrefragable certainty of God ?'

From: *The Varieties of Religious Experience: A Study in Human Nature* by William James, 1902

Mike Jay
Blue Tide – 1

LOUISE AND I buy some isopropyl alcohol, borrow a friend's coffee grinder and set to work.

First, we roast the seeds slowly in a pan. Above a certain temperature, the harmaline will break down, but a gentle application of heat evaporates some of the dyes and makes the seeds blister and spit like popcorn. Then we put the roasted seeds in the coffee grinder and produce a reddish-brown powder. This looks like ground coffee and smells surprisingly delicious, roasted, nutty and slightly spicy. It looks as if it might smoke well with tobacco, so we try it. It burns rather hot, tending to congeal into little burning coals, but it tastes very pleasant, rather like the incense. It's a little rough on the throat, but the main problem with this method is that you'd have to smoke an unfeasibly large quantity of it to approach the 300mg or so which constitutes an active dose. We need to work further with an oral preparation.

We fill a coffee filter with roasted harmal grounds and drip isopropyl through it slowly. The liquid which emerges at the other end is a dark ruby red, an interesting echo of the Avestan description of haoma juice as reddish-brown: clearly this method is bringing the red dye out with it too. We wait for the alcohol to evaporate and are left with a red, sticky oil. This presumably contains all the alcohol-soluble alkaloids in the plant and none of the inert plant material.

We christen this ruby oil 'red mercury'. It certainly has a higher concentration of harmaline than the seeds: probably approaching about 50 per cent by weight. It can be smoked in a glass pipe, heating it gently from the outside so as not to break too much of the harmaline down. It can also be put into gel-caps and swallowed, making ingestion far easier. But the nausea and the effects remain largely inseparable. An active dose is always accompanied by the smell of harmaline on the skin, in the pores of the fingers, and the churning stomach which soon becomes numb, distant and is forgotten.

I make some enquiries on the Internet while I'm engaged in this, offering my work-in-progress suggestions and casting around for anyone who can answer my questions. Eventually I'm referred to someone else who's engaged in similarly arcane practices. He's making a drink he calls 'rue brew' from Syrian rue seeds, and is having an interesting time working with it. Eventually we speak on the phone. He's called Greg, he lives in north London and he invites me to dinner.

I set out for the evening an hour or so before a partial eclipse of the sun. Up Ladbroke Grove, the roofs are crammed with people wearing shades and waving pinhole squares of cardboard. The effect is somehow apocalyptic, like an H.G. Wells fantasy about an approaching comet. It's high summer, and the sun beats down with a force which seems all the stronger for its unwonted human scrutiny.

I arrive at Greg's just as the eclipse is approaching. We sit out in the street to watch it. While everyone else is fiddling with smoked glass and mirrors, Greg has a better idea. He disappears into the house and reappears with a multifaceted quartz crystal. Tilting it towards the sun, we see the eclipse reduplicated across the crystal's face in dozens of perfect miniatures.

Greg turns out to be a trader and marketer of natural Third World foodstuffs, responsible for bringing items like mung beans into the health-food shops and subsequently into the supermarkets. He's very excited about harmal, reckons somebody should get in there now, start planting and buying futures. He thinks it has the potential to produce a natural, organic, mildly psychoactive coffee substitute with a huge global market.

We sample his 'rue brew', which is basically the roasted, ground seeds drunk black with honey or sugar. It's not unpleasant, but the bitterness of the harmaline still seeps through the sweetening. He drank it on a daily basis for several weeks, and found that it produced a mild but pervasive dreaminess, unobtrusive in normal life but noticeable whenever he shut his eyes to dream or meditate. He found himself in a state where he could function perfectly normally, but whenever he chose to he could drift off on the blue tide of dreams. After a few weeks, though, he began to notice his urine becoming greenish-yellow, and stopped drinking it out of concern that its constant presence was impairing his kidney functions. He thinks this was probably to do the presence of cheese, yoghurt and other tyramine-containing foods in his diet, which is of course a potential problem with any food or drink which is also an MAOI. But he too is fascinated by the harmal visions, and has continued using it on an irregular basis with no ill effects.

Another person who's been using it on a daily basis is Skip, who's waiting for a hip-replacement operation and spending most of his time bedridden on various heavy pain medications. He gets into the habit of drinking a cup of it before going to bed, and spending his previously uncomfortable and semi-conscious nights floating off into its world of visions. He reports that, in several half-waking states, he's found himself returning to the same visionary worlds, corridors and cities peopled by entities whose presence he feels rather than sees. Many are pleasant, but some are not: he reports visiting one particular 'Lovecrattian space' where he finds himself in partial sleep paralysis, moving involuntarily through icy blue caverns and corridors with people frozen into the walls, knowing that if he stops moving he'll freeze too. This space seems to be occupied by entities which he calls 'the Daa', and the '*daa daa*' sound which always seems to echo round the caverns.

Thanks to the pioneering efforts of Greg and Skip, a pattern is beginning to form around the effects of constant, low-level doses of harmal. But the other question which interests me is the effect of a high-level dose, two or three times more than I've been taking. I haven't done this, partly because the effects would undoubtedly include high levels of nausea, but also because I'm unaware of the ceiling of physical safety. With most traditional psychedelics, toxic doses are many orders of magnitude greater than effective doses, and a high dose produces nothing more than a more intense mental bombardment; with harmaline, between three and five times the effective dose produces significant levels of toxicity.

Fortunately someone else does this experiment for me. I gave a bag of seeds to Charlie before he moved to Australia; a few weeks later, I receive his account by e-mail:

We took a trip up the coast a few hours' drive to this beautiful lake/lagoon spot where we camped. Gorgeous sunsets and creature/bird noises. Mark saw a kangaroo and so was a happy man. We brewed up a big batch of harmaline in some milk Milo. We'd ground up about half a packet of seeds before we went. Some very gung-ho sub-personality must have taken me over, as I directed Shelley to bung it all in the brew (even though I had no idea of sensible doses). It was truly disgusting – as you know – bitter and gritty. Mark and I had full cups and Shell had very little, her stomach flatly refusing to ingest such stuff in quantity. Then a little later half a teaspoon of 'shrooms to catalyse. Nothing much happened, and then the tell-tale flashing things at the edge of the field of vision started happening. The stars were intense (in reality) and it was as though there were shooting stars everywhere. Physical coordination started to go very haywire – like drunk, only more disorienting and made worse by movement, so we started to subside. I gamely went for half a cup more brew, which was rash because we were still on the way up.

Nausea started to get pretty intense and I had a long phase of vomiting and felt pretty lousy. Stumbling about vomiting and complaining. Shelley said I was quite impossible. Looked into the car boot for something and – Oh my God – weird visual light-show.

Streamers of light everywhere, flashing and zipping across the visual field.

But standing up and moving about was becoming awful so we gradually collapsed into lying-down mode. I was really rather panicked. I don't know why but I didn't make the connection that this was a plant hallucinogen, and that therefore some unwanted physical effects were probably par for the course. I just remember thinking – shit what if I've really had loads too much.

Then started what I believe is one of the most characteristic effects of harmal. Mark and I both noticed it. Not hallucinations but the ability to be able to conjure up amazing visual scenes in the mind's eye – in full detail and 24-bit colour. You thought of it, and it was there, and you could examine it or go into it or embroider it with no effort at all. I think harmal is an imagination-enhancer, rather than a true hallucinogen.

I also imagined a lot of things (eyes open) and then they turned out to be something else entirely. I guess this is kind of hallucinogenic.

Another effect was some amazing flashbacks. Links between things became obvious. I remember recalling with astonishing clarity something you said to me, Mike (I forget what now), but it seemed very important at the time and very wise too.

Of course this went on and on and on. We had no idea how much we had taken compared to a notional recommended dose, but a lot and I kind of wondered when it would stop.

I guess this was after about 6 hours and things had quietened down a mite, but I was still nauseous, stumbling and totally off on one. I remember thinking that it might go on the next day. And so at 3.00 a.m. to bed. And kind of a trance, rather than sleep. Immobile, semi-conscious, mind and imagination wandering.

Of course by 11.00 a.m. things were back to normal again. But quite a roller-coaster.

Even allowing for the small handful of mushrooms, this demonstrates that harmaline does indeed have a powerful psychedelic action. I was to reach this kind of effect eventually, though without a noticeable increase in dose.

Blue Tide, 2000

William Barton
A Dissertation on the Chymical Properties and Exhilarating Effects of Nitrous Oxide Gas

JANUARY 1807, I first inhaled pure nitrous oxide. I breathed six quarts of it from a bladder. The first inspiration, by which I took about a quart of air into my lungs, produced no unusual effects on them, owing, I suppose, to its union with air contained therein.

The second by which I inhaled the whole volume of air contained in the breathing bag, was attended with slight giddiness, and a kind of tranquil, pleasurable sensation, accompanied with an impatient eagerness to expel the air from my lungs that I might again experience the same feelings by a new inspiration; this eagerness I manifested by a violent expiration, 'that seemed', to use the emphatick words of a by-stander, 'as if it would have blown the bladder through'. During both these inspirations I was perfectly sensible of my situation, and of my object in breathing from the bladder.

When I inhaled the gas a third time it imparted a saccharine taste like that of fine cider; my vision became suddenly obscured, so that I had not a distinct perception of the nearest objects. I again felt the same pleasant sensation, previously experienced, the difference of its being less tranquil. This continued till it produced a pleasurable elixity I never before experienced, and of which no words can convey just idea; but, like all original sensations, it must be experienced to be known. I was affected with a *tinnitus aurium*, which I well recollect to have continued as long as I was sensible of my situation. A glow was diffused throughout my lungs, and at the same time they were affected with a thrilling or titillating sensation which afterwards extended itself through every part of my frame; but dwelt longest on the extremities. This sensation, as it respects its effects on the lungs, very much resembles the thrilling or actual vibration induced by the loud blowing of a mail stage horn, in the lungs of a passenger in the close carriage. My lungs felt as if they were dilating, and continued to impart this sensation of enlargement till I suppose they occupied the whole laboratory with their immensity. I now became totally insensible to the impressions of external things, and the rapturous delight which then entranced my faculties mars my feeble essay towards its description. This indescribable ecstasy must be what angels feel; and well might the poetick Southey exclaim upon experiencing it, that 'the atmosphere of the highest of all possible heavens must be composed of this gas'.

From these extatical sensations of joy, I was aroused by Dr. Woodhouse, who now endeavoured to take the breathing bladder from my mouth. This I obstinately and violently resisted, holding the pipe with great force between my teeth, and directly began to strike him with frequent blows, which were reiterated with energetick strength, as I was afterwards informed, though I was totally unconscious of anything that happened during this delirious paroxysm, nor did I recollect it when it was over. The resistance I made was prompted, I suppose, by a sensation I well recollect with experience, of some intruding power attempting to remove the cause of my pleasurable inebriety. All my muscles seemed to vibrate, and I felt strong enough to root out mountains and demolish worlds, and, like the spirit of Milton, was 'vital in every part'. At length I suffered the bag to be taken from me; and as soon as it was removed, felt ten times lighter than the surrounding atmosphere, which prompted a strong and almost irresistible disposition to mount in the air, which I discovered to the spectators by repeatedly jumping from the floor with great and uncommon agility. My sensations were just as I should imagine would be produced by flying. I experienced an unrestrainable inclination to muscular motion, opposing much and powerful resistance to all those who endeavoured to restrain me. I resembled those varlets, who, as Ariel tells Prospero, in *The Tempest*,

> were red hot with drinking;
> So full of valour, that they smote the air
> For breathing in their faces; beat the ground
> The kissing of their feet . . .

And feeling like the presiding genius of all I beheld, beat with indignant resentment every person that attempted, vainly, to impede my progress. This superiority that I fancied I possessed over all around me was so ably seconded by my increased muscular strength, that some of the gentlemen who received my blows told me that they were applied with wonderful and disagreeable force. I seemed to be placed on an immense height, and the noise occasioned by the reiterated shouts of laughter and hallooing of the by-standers appeared to be far below me, and resembled the hum or buz which aeronauts describe as issuing from a large city, when they have ascended to a considerable height above it. I had a sense of great fulness and distension in my head, and my thoughts and perceptions, as well as I can recollect, were rapid and confused, but very unlike any I had ever experienced. By a sensation as sudden as,

> with quick impulse through all nature's frame,
> Shoots the electrick air, in subtle flame . . .

I seemed to descend from the immense height to which I had flown, and by a quick, but complete prostration of muscular energy, fell into a kind of trance-like state. During the short continuance of this trance my feelings were placidly delicious, and extremely analogous to those I have often experienced in that state of voluptuous delight vibrating between a waking consciousness and the torpor of sleep, so elegantly, so feelingly delineated by Rousseau in these words,

> Thus lifeless yet with life, how sweet to lie!
> Thus without dying oh how sweet to die!

To this state syncope succeeded, and I was carried into an adjoining room and placed on a table near an open window. Here I experienced a slight return of the agreeable feelings I have before described, but only of instantaneous duration. The first idea that occurred to me upon my partial revival, was a confused one of nitrous oxide, which words I vociferated as I jumped the table with great vehemence, as I was afterwards informed. I felt much indignation and pride towards the persons around me, and entertained the momentary contempt for everything that excited an idea in my still chaotick brain. I felt as if I was an inhabitant of the Elysium of Rousseau, or the island of Calypso, of Fenelon, blown by a rudely malicious blast into a world of reptiles, where the atmosphere like the pestiferous samiel of the deserts of Arabia, was pregnant with destruction, and threatened inevitable annihilation to all those who inhaled its morbid breath. I now, however, as quick as thought, completely revived, and made the mortifying discovery, that the aerial world through which I had been roving with footsteps as light as air, was but the fascination of an inebrieting elixity, whose siren spell of pleasure wrapped me in delight.

A profuse diaphoresis appeared all over me, but was particularly abundant on my forehead and cheeks; and the temporal arteries both during the experiment and after it was over, seemed ready to burst with fulness.

The next time I breathed the gas, my feelings were, as well as I can recollect, nearly similar to those just described. In this experiment, however, I experienced one sensation, I did not feel in the first, viz. a kind of titillation of the eyes as if water had been dropping between the ball of the eye and its palpebrae.

I must not omit to mention here, that I also experienced in this experiment, and in every other that I made except the one just detailed, a sensation extremely singular. It consisted in a kind of semi-consciousness of my situation, yet unattended by perfect volition. Thus I became engaged as in the preceding experiment, at the vain presumption, as I deemed at it, at those who dared to oppose my motions, supposing them my antagonists; at the same time I seemed sensible they were not so, and could see myself under the influence of some incomprehensible hallucination, the effect of which, however, I was unable to resist, and of consequence combated with them against my will. I seemed as it were to have two types of consequence, the one persuading me that I was actually opposed by enemies, the other rendering me sensible, that this was entirely a misconception of the obvious reality, which was that my enemies were indeed no other than friendly spectators and that their actions, which were ostensibly inoffensive, I had misconstrued into the exertion of violence and power against me. Volition, however, was wholly inactive, or, if I may be allowed the expression paralized; of consequence I derived no benefit from the effect of its operations. I may perhaps illustrate this semi-conscious, semi-delusive of which, not withstanding my efforts to describe it,

I feel unable to convey a just conception, by the following description of an analogous situation, by the celebrated Kotzebue. It occurred to him during the night after his arrival at Tobolsk, after a fatiguing, an anxious, and distressing journey; he had been, perhaps, affected with a disordered state of his mind, induced by the contemplation of a melancholy exile in the chills of Siberia, separated from his beloved family. 'In the course of the night,' says he,

> a remarkable circumstance took place, the explanation of which I must leave to my good friends Dr. Gall and Dr. Hufeland. I had fallen asleep; towards 12 o'clock I awoke and fancied myself on board a ship. Not only felt the rocking motion of the vessel, but heard the flapping of the sails, and the noise and bustle of the crew. As I lay on the floor I could see no objects through the window, except the sky, and this circumstance added to the force of the illusion. I was sensible it was such, and endeavoured to overcome it. I felt myself, as it were, furnished with two separate minds, the one confirmed what I fancied, the other convinced me that it was all imaginary. I staggered about the room, thought I saw the counsellor, and everything that surrounded me the evening before, remaining in the same place. I went to the window; the wooden houses in the streets I thought were ships, and in every direction I perceived the open sea. Whither am I going? seemed to say one mind. Nowhere, replied the other; you are still in your own house. This singular sensation which I cannot well describe, continued for half an hour; by degrees it became less powerful, and at length entirely quitted me. A violent palpitation of the heart, and a quick convulsive pulse succeeded. Yet I was not feverish, nor did I feel any headache. My own opinion and conviction is, that the whole must have been the commencement of a species of insanity.

1808. From: *Mindscapes: An Anthology of Drug Writings*, ed. Antonio Melechi, 1998

I mount! I fly!
O grave! Where is thy victory?
O death! Where is thy sting?

Alexander Pope

Unknown
The African Fang Legends

ZAME YE MEBEGE (the last of the creator gods) gave us *eboka*.
He saw the misery in which blackman was living. He thought
how to help him. One day he looked down and saw a blackman, the Pygmy Bitumu, high in an Atanga tree, gathering its
fruit. He made him fall. He died and Zame brought his spirit
to him. Zame cut off the little fingers and the little toes of the
cadaver of the Pygmy and planted them in various parts of the
forest. They grew into the *eboka* bush.

THE VISION (*NDEM EBOKA*) OF NDONG ASSEKO (*AGE 22;
CLAN ESSABAM; UNMARRIED*)

When I ate *eboka*, I found myself taken by it up a long road in
a deep forest until I came to a barrier of black iron. At that
barrier, unable to pass, I saw a crowd of black persons also
unable to pass. In the distance beyond the barrier it was very
bright. I could see many colors in the air but the crowd of black
people could not pass. Suddenly my father descended from
above in the form of a bird. He gave me then my *eboka* name,
Onwan Misengue, and enabled me to fly up after him over the
barrier of iron. As we proceeded the bird, who was my father,
changed from black to white – first his tail feathers, then all his
plumage. We came then to a river the color of blood in the
midst of which was a great snake of three colors – blue, black,
and red. It closed its gaping mouth so that we were able to pass
over it. On the other side there was a crowd of people all in
white. We passed through them and they shouted at us words
of recognition until we arrived at another river – all white. This
we crossed by means of a giant chain of gold. On the other side
there were no trees but only a grassy upland. On the top of the

139

hill was a round house made entirely of glass and built upon one post only. Within I saw a man, the hair on his head piled up in the form of a Bishop's hat. He had a star on his breast but on coming closer I saw that it was his heart in his chest beating. We moved around him and on the back of his neck there was a red cross tattooed. He had a long beard. Just then I looked up and saw a woman in the moon – a bayonet was piercing her heart from which a bright white fire was pouring forth. Then I felt a pain on my shoulder. My father told me to return to earth. I had gone far enough. If I went further I would not return.

THE VISION OF EMAN ELA (*AGE 30; CLAN ESSAMENYANG; MARRIED WITH ONE WIFE*)

When I ate *eboka* very quickly my grandfather came to me. First he had black skin. Then he returned and he had white skin. It was he that gave me my *eboka* name. My grandmother then appeared in the same way. Because my grandfather was dead before I was born he asked me if I knew how I recognized him. It was through *eboka*. He then seized me by the hand and we found ourselves embarked on a grand route. I didn't have the sense of walking but just of floating along. We came to a table in that road. There we sat and my grandfather asked me all the reasons I had eaten *eboka*. He gave me others. Then my grandfather disappeared and suddenly a white spirit appeared before me. He grasped me by the arm and we floated along. Then we came to a crossroads. The road on which we were traveling was red. The other two routes were black and white. We passed over. Finally we arrived at a large house on a hill. It was built off one post. Within I found the wife of my mother's father. She gave me my *eboka* name a second time and also gave me the talent to play the *ngomi* harp. We passed on and finally arrived after passing over more crossroads at a great desert.

Then I saw descend from the sky – from the moon – a giant circle which came down and encircled the earth, as a rainbow of three colors – blue, red, and white. I began playing the *ngombi* under the rainbow and I heard the applause of men. I returned. All the *banzie* thought I had gone too far and was dead.

Since then I have seen nothing in *eboka*. But each time I

take it I hear the spirits who give the power to play the *ngombi*. I play what I hear from them. Only if I come into the chapel in a bad heart does *eboka* fail me.

1982. From: *White Rabbit: A Psychedelic Reader*,
eds, John Miller and Randall Koral, 1995

And the leaves of the trees were for the healing of the nations
Revelations

Dawn F. Rooney
Betel-Chewing Traditions in South-East Asia

FEW TRADITIONS IN South-East Asia have the antiquity and universal acceptance of betel-chewing. The custom is over 2,000 years old and has survived from ancient times into the twentieth century. Its use cuts across class, sex, or age. Its devotees include farmers, priests and kings; men, women, and children. The homeliness of the name belies its importance.

Three ingredients – an areca nut, a leaf of the betel pepper, and lime – are essential for betel-chewing; others may be added depending on availability and preference. The leaf is first daubed with lime paste and topped with thin slices of the nut, then it is folded or rolled into a bite-size quid. The interaction of the ingredients during chewing produces a red-coloured saliva. Most of the betel juice is spat out. The tell-tale residue looks like splotches of dried blood. Indeed, the resemblance is so close that some early European visitors thought many Asians had tuberculosis. The splotches of betel spittle are spaced consistently enough for use as measurements of time and distance in rural areas. A short time is 'about a betel chew' and the distance between two villages, for example, may be 'about three chews'.

Besides being chewed, the betel quid and the individual ingredients are widely used for medicinal, magical and symbolical purposes. It is administered as a curative for a plethora of ills, including indigestion and worms. It is believed to facilitate contact with supernatural forces and is often used to exorcise spirits, particularly those associated with illness. In its symbolical role, it is present at nearly all religious ceremonies and festivals of the lunar calendar. Betel fosters relationships and thus serves as an avenue of communication between relatives, lovers, friends and strangers. It figures in male–female alliances and its potency in this area is especially telling. Because of its power in bonding relationships, betel is used symbolically to solidify acts of justice such as oaths of allegiance and the settlement of lawsuits. Betel is a surrogate for money in payment to midwives and surgeons for services rendered.

A key to the unconditional patronage of betel is its use on four levels – as a food and medicine, and for magical and symbolical purposes. As such, this single tradition is an integral part of the art, ceremonies and social intercourse of daily life.

Why do people chew betel? The multi-purpose benefits are described explicitly in Indian literature as early as the sixth century. 'Betel stimulates passion, brings out the physical charm, conduces to good luck, lends aroma to the mouth, strengthens the body and dispels diseases arising from the phlegm. It also bestows many other benefits.' According to a sixth-century Indian text, betel is one of the nine enjoyments of life – along with unguents, incense, women, garments, music, beds, food and flowers named in a Sanskrit verse of the twelfth century.

The main reason for chewing betel seems to lie in the social affability produced by sharing a quid with friends. This enjoyment can be seen on the faces of a group of elderly men squatting around a betel box, or heard in the laughter of women relaxing in a rice field with a betel basket. Offering a quid to someone is a mark of hospitality.

From: *Artificial Paradises: A Drugs Reader*, ed. Mike Jay, 1999

Stewart Lee Allen
Ethiopian Prayer

> *Me buna nagay nuuklen*
> *Me buna iijolen haagudatu*
> *hoormati haagudatu*
> *waan haamtu nuum dow*
> *bokai magr nuken.*
> — Garri/Oromo prayer

The coffee bean has long been a symbol of power in Harrar. The caste of growers, the Harash, not only bore the city's name but were forbidden to go beyond its walls lest the art of cultivation be lost. The head of the emir's bodyguard was allowed a small private garden as a sign of his rank. And of course, natives worshiped their coffeepots, as in the prayer above, which translates:

> Coffeepot give us peace
> coffeepot let children grow
> let our wealth swell
> please protect us from evils
> give us rain and grass.

I think we all pray to the first cup of the day. It's a silent prayer, sung while the mind is still foggy and blue. 'O Magic Cup,' it might go, 'carry me above the traffic jam. Keep me civil in the subway. And forgive my employer, as you forgive me. Amen.'

But the prayer from the Garri/Oromo tribe is more serious, part of a ritual called *bun-qalle* that celebrates sex and death, and in which the coffee bean replaces the fatted ox in a sacrifice to the gods. Among the Garri the husking of the coffee fruit symbolizes the slaughter, with the priests biting the heads off the sacrificial creatures. After this, the beans are cooked in butter and chewed by the elders. Their spiritual power thus enhanced, they pronounce a blessing on the proceedings and smear the holy coffee-scented butter on the participants' foreheads. The beans are then mixed with sweet milk, and everybody drinks the liquid while reciting the prayer.

If the whole affair seems vaguely familiar, it should. Who has gone to a business meeting where coffee is not offered? Its use as an intellectual lubricant, along with its ability to 'swell our wealth,' per the Garri prayer, has made having a pot ready for consumption an international business norm. Looked at this way, a modern business office is nothing more than a 'tribe' camped out about its own sacred pot, and the *bun-qalle* is nothing less than man's first coffee klatch, archetype of the world's most common social ritual.

Two things about the *bun-qalle* mark it as probably the earliest use of coffee as a mind-altering or magical drug. The first is that the beans are fried and then eaten, a practice clearly derived from the coffee balls chewed by Oromo warriors near Kefa. The Garri, who live a few hundred miles south of Harrar, are related to the Oromo and share their language. The second part of the ceremony, where the roasted beans are added to milk and imbibed, indicates it predates Islam (AD 600) because Islamic alchemists believed that mixing coffee and milk caused leprosy (a belief that lies at the root of the disdain many Europeans have for coffee with milk).

Further indication of the ceremony's extreme antiquity is the fact that the Garri associate *bun-qalle* with the sky god Waaq. His name may sound uncouth to us, but the worship of this sky god is thought to be among the world's first religions. Whether the eating of coffee beans was performed in the original Waaq ceremonies is beyond knowing. One can say, I think, that since the Garri were doubtless among the first to taste our favorite bean, and since primitive people who discover psychoactive drugs tend to worship them (a penchant today denigrated as mere substance abuse), it seems likely that consuming the beans was added to the Waaq ceremonies at a relatively early date.

In the Oromo culture of western Ethiopia, the coffee bean's resemblance to a woman's sexual organs has given birth to another *bun-qalle* ceremony with such heavy sexual significance that it is preceded by a night of abstinence, according to the work of anthropologist Lambert Bartel. Oromo elder Gammachu Magarsa told Bartel that 'we compare this biting open of the coffee fruits with the first sexual intercourse on the wedding day, when the man has to force the girl to open her thighs in order to get access to her vagina.'

After the beans are husked, they are stirred in the butter with a stick called *dannaba*, the word for penis. Some people replace the stick with bundles of living grass because a dead piece of wood cannot 'impart life' or impregnate the beans. As the beans are stirred, another prayer is recited until finally the coffee fruits burst open from the heat, making the sound *tass!* This bursting of the fruit is likened to both childbirth and the last cry of the dying man. The person stirring the beans now recites: 'Ashama, my coffee, burst open to bring peace there you opened your mouth please wish me peace keep far from me all evil tongues.'

In being eaten the coffee bean 'dies,' blessing new thought and life, a tradition the Oromo say goes back as far as anyone can remember. After the bean has spoken, the assembly moves on to the matter at hand, such as a circumcision, marriage, land dispute, or the undertaking of a dangerous journey.

One important point about the *bun-qalle*. The beans are simply added whole to the milk, not pulverized. True infusion, where crushed beans are added to a neutral liquid like water, thus completely releasing the bean's power, is reserved for the darker acts such as laying a curse or, as in tonight's ceremony, the exorcism of evil spirit.

The Devil's Cup, 2000

Howard Marks
A Dope Strategy for the Third Millennium

AS THE WAR against drug users increases in intensity, with weed being ripped out of wardrobes and pills pulled out of pockets by pillocks and police, one needs to seriously and tenaciously seek alternative ways to get hammered during this current millennium. One obvious solution is to venture forth into the remote countryside and grow more weed. Plough the fields and scatter skunk seeds everywhere. But a far more pioneering and vastly overlooked defence against the anti-caning brigade is the sensible use of animal products as psychoactive sources. Most outbuildings can be easily converted into zoos and menageries of supplies for getting stoned.

The first animal to acquire is, of course, a reindeer, a far more interesting pet than either a dog or cat: reindeer are attracted to smoke, eat mushrooms, go into psychedelic trances; and their piss gets you off your tits. The Chukchi people of eastern Siberia are rarely found without a couple of bags of reindeer piss by their side. And no country has yet made piss illegal.

Another valuable potential psychoactive pet is the good old giraffe. The Humr tribe of Baggara, Arabs who live in Kordofan, Sudan, are normally strict abstainers. But they kill giraffes and boil up their livers and bone marrow to make a drink called *umm nylokh*. After drinking *umm nylokh*, one sees hallucinations of giraffes everywhere, stretching their necks longer to get at the leaves and making a mockery of Darwin.

Admittedly, giraffes and reindeer are a bit on the large side and need a lot of land and sky for exercise. So unless one wishes to make a business out of it, start small: get an insect house, and stock insects that can get you spannered or make you want to shag all night. Such an aphrodisiac is Spanish fly, which is made from beetle wings and 'if anointed on the soles of the feet, testicles and *perineum* provokes and stirs up lust to a miracle in both sexes and invigorates the feeble instruments of generation'. It's not really like that, but it does cause itching sensations in the genitals that are excellent fun to be scratched.

Ants, tarantulas, ground-up scarab beetles and various other insect potions are also documented as able to either get one out of it or keep one's dick big and hard. So there's plenty of opportunity for experiment, and it's legal. Next to the insect house build an aviary, catch some South American birds called *pitohui* and eat them. You'll see heavenly visions of birds of paradise. Next to the aviary, build a small reptile house and tropical pond. Inside the reptile house, put a load of king and other cobras. Get some of their venom, crystallise it, mix it with a skunk bud, put it in a pipe and smoke it. Hear the music of the snake charmers.

For the slightly more adventurous and wealthy, I would suggest converting all swimming pools into aquariums and stocking them with puffer fish (key ingredient of the very hardcore zombie drug), certain species of mullet (be careful of mental paralysis and delirium), tang (the nightmare fish) and yellow stingray (stoning aphrodisiac).

If skint, then simply rely on ponds full of newts, salamanders, frogs and toads. I, along with countless others, have licked toads and got absolutely legally wasted. Not just any old toad will do, of course. Ideally, it has to be the Sonoran Desert toad (aka the Colorado River toad: *Bufo alvarius*) which is found in Mexico and the southern United States. Pus is extracted, dried and smoked. It contains tryptamine 5-MeO-DMT, which is at least four times stronger than regular DMT and mimics the death and dream experiences. Devotees of its consumption call their cult the 'Church of the Toad of Light'. So, fill the pond with these toads, and examine their shit for toadstools.

Squat like a toad, close at the ear of Eve

John Milton

Albert Most
The Psychedelic Toad

FRESH VENOM CAN easily be collected without harm to the toad. Use a flat glass plate or any other smooth, non-porous surface, at least twelve inches square. Hold the toad in front of the plate, which is fixed in a vertical position. In this manner, the venom can be collected on the glass plate, free of dirt, and liquid released when the toad is handled. When ready to begin, hold the toad firmly with one hand and, with the thumb and forefinger of the other hand, squeeze near the base of the gland until the venom squirts out of the pores and on to the glass plate. Use this method to systematically collect the venom from each of the toad's granular glands: those on the forearm, those on the tibia and femur of the hind leg, and, of course, the parotoids on the neck. Each gland can be squeezed a second time for an additional yield of venom if the toad is allowed a one-hour rest period. After this the glands are empty and require four to six weeks for regeneration. The venom is viscous and milky-white in color when first squeezed from the glands. It begins to dry within minutes and acquires the color and texture of rubber cement. Scrape the venom from the glass plate, dry it thoroughly and store it in an airtight container. Smoke it.

Eros and the Pineal: The Layman's Guide to Cerebral Solitaire,
1986

Sweet are the uses of adversity
Which like the toad, ugly and venomous
Wears yet a precious jewel in his head

William Shakespeare

Hunter S. Thompson
A Terrible Experience with Extremely Dangerous Drugs

'AS YOUR ATTORNEY,' he said, 'I advise you not worry.' He nodded toward the bathroom. 'Take a hit out of that little brown bottle in my shaving kit.'

'What is it?'

'Adrenochrome,' he said. 'You won't need much. Just a little *tiny* taste.'

I got the bottle and dipped the head of a paper match into it.

'That's about right,' he said. 'That stuff makes pure mescaline seem like ginger beer. You'll go completely crazy if you take too much.'

I licked the end of the match. 'Where'd you get *this*?' I asked. 'You can't buy it.'

'Never mind,' he said. 'It's absolutely pure.'

I shook my head sadly. 'Jesus! What kind of monster client have you picked up *this* time? There's only one source for this stuff . . .'

He nodded.

'The adrenalin glands from a *living* human body,' I said. 'It's no good if you get it out of a corpse.'

'I know,' he replied. 'But the guy didn't have any cash. He's one of these Satanism freaks. He offered me human blood – said it would make me higher than I'd ever been in my life,' he laughed. 'I thought he was kidding, so I told him I'd just as soon have an ounce or so of pure adrenochrome – or maybe just a fresh adrenalin gland to chew on.'

I could already feel the stuff working on me. The first wave felt like a combination of mescaline and methedrine. Maybe I should take a swim, I thought.

'Yeah,' my attorney was saying. 'They nailed this guy for child molesting, but he swears he didn't do it. "Why should I fuck with *children*?" he says. "They're too small!"' He shrugged. 'Christ, what could I say? Even a goddamn werewolf is entitled to legal counsel . . . I didn't *dare* turn the creep down. He might have picked up a letter opener and gone after my pineal gland.'

'Why not?' I said. 'He could probably get Melvin Belli for that.' I nodded, barely able to talk now. My body felt like I'd just been wired into a 220-volt socket. 'Shit, we should get us some of that stuff.' I muttered finally. 'Just eat a big handful and see what happens.'

'Some of what?'

'Extract of pineal.'

He stared at me. 'Sure,' he said. 'That's a *good* idea. One *whiff* of that shit would turn you into something out of a

149

goddamn medical encyclopedia! Man, your head would swell up like a watermelon, you'd probably gain about a hundred pounds in two hours . . . claws, bleeding warts, then you'd notice about six huge hairy tits swelling up on your back . . .' He shook his head emphatically. 'Man, I'll try just about anything; but I'd never in hell touch a pineal gland.

'Last Christmas somebody gave me a whole jimson weed, the root must have weighed two pounds; enough for a *year* but I ate the whole goddamn thing in about twenty minutes!'

I was leaning toward him, following his words intently.

The slightest hesitation made me want to grab him by the throat and force him to talk faster. 'Right!' I said eagerly. 'Jimson weed! What happened?'

'Luckily, I vomited most of it right back up,' he said. 'But even so, I went blind for three days. Christ I couldn't even walk! My whole body turned to wax. I was such a mess that they had to haul me back to the ranch house in a wheelbarrow . . . they said I was trying to talk, but I sounded like a raccoon.'

'Fantastic,' I said. But I could barely hear him. I was so wired that my hands were clawing uncontrollably at the bedspread, jerking it right out from under me while he talked. My heels were dug into the mattress, with both knees locked . . . I could feel my eyeballs swelling, about to pop out of the sockets.

'Finish the fucking story!' I snarled. 'What *happened*? What about the *glands*?'

He backed away, keeping an eye on me as he edged across the room. 'Maybe you need another drink,' he said nervously. 'Jesus, that stuff got right on top of you, didn't it?'

I tried to smile. 'Well . . . nothing worse . . . no, this is worse . . .' It was hard to move my jaws; my tongue felt like burning magnesium. 'No . . . nothing to worry about,' I hissed. 'Maybe if you could just . . . shove me into the pool, or something . . .'

'Goddamnit,' he said. 'You took too *much*. You're about to . . .'

I couldn't move. Total paralysis now. Every muscle in my body was contracted. I couldn't even move my eyeballs, much less turn my head or talk.

'It won't last long,' he said. 'The first rush is the worst. Just ride the bastard out. If I put you in the pool right now, you'd sink like a goddamn stone.'

Death. I was sure of it. Not even my lungs seemed to be functioning. I needed artificial respiration, but I couldn't open my mouth to say so. I was going to *die*. Just sitting there on the bed, unable to move . . . well, at least there's no pain.

Probably, I'll black out in a few seconds, and after that it won't matter.

My attorney had gone back to watching television. The news was on again. Nixon's face filled the screen, but his speech was hopelessly garbled. The only word I could make out was 'sacrifice'. Over and over again: 'Sacrifice . . . sacrifice . . . sacrifice . . .'

I could hear myself breathing heavily. My attorney seemed to notice. 'Just stay relaxed,' he said over his shoulder, without looking at me. 'Don't try to fight it, or you'll start getting brain bubbles . . . strokes, aneurisms . . . you'll just wither up and die.' His hand snaked out to change channels.

It was after midnight when I finally was able to talk and move around . . . but I was still not free of the drug; the voltage had merely been cranked down from 220 to 110. I was a babbling nervous wreck, flapping around the room like a wild animal, pouring sweat and unable to concentrate on any one thought for more than two or three seconds at a time.

My attorney put down the phone after making several calls. 'There's only one place where we can get fresh salmon,' he said, 'and it's closed on Sunday.'

'Of course,' I snapped. 'These goddamn Jesus freaks! They're multiplying like rats!'

He eyed me curiously.

'What about the Process?' I said. 'Don't they have a place here? Maybe a delicatessen or something? With a few tables in back? They have a fantastic menu in London. I ate there once; incredible food . . .'

'Get a grip on yourself,' he said. 'You don't want to even *mention* the Process in this town.'

'You're right,' I said. 'Call Inspector Bloor. He knows about food. I think he has a list.'

'Better to call room service,' he said. 'We can get the crab looey and a quart of Christian Brothers' muscatel for about twenty bucks.'

'No!' I said. 'We must get out of this place. I need air. Let's drive up to Reno and get a big tuna fish salad . . . hell, it won't take long. Only about four hundred miles; no traffic out there on the desert . . .'

'Forget it,' he said. 'That's Army territory. Bomb tests, nerve gas – we'd never make it.'

We wound up at a place called the Big Flip about halfway downtown. I had a 'New York steak' for $1.88. My attorney ordered the 'Coyote Bush Basket' for $2.09 . . . and after that we drank off a pot of watery 'Golden West' coffee and watched four boozed-up cowboy types kick a faggot half to death between the pinball machines.

'The action never stops in this town,' said my attorney as we shuffled out to the car. 'A man with the right contacts could probably pick up all the fresh adrenochrome he wanted, if he hung around here for a while.'

I agreed, but I wasn't quite up to it, right then. I hadn't slept for something like eighty hours, and that fearful ordeal with the drug had left me completely exhausted . . . tomorrow we would have to get serious. The drug conference was scheduled to kick off at noon . . . and we were still not sure how to handle it. So we drove back to the hotel and watched a British horror film on the late show.

Fear and Loathing in Las Vegas, 1972

Howard Marks
Spunk

> '*The last man in line at the multiple public copulation
> had the honor of sucking the accumulated semen from
> the lady's vagina.*'
>> N. E. Himes, *Medical History of Contraception*
>> (Gamut Press, New York, 1963)

IT USED TO be thought that women became pregnant through all kinds of ways: fire, wind, star formations, and even the Holy Ghost. The guys didn't think spunk was for reproduction: they just loved to drink the stuff, even if it was smelly, stale, or someone else's. Most of the world (until the sixteenth century) believed that a mixture of spunk and menstrual blood was all that was required to produce kids and tit milk. They believed, too, in the Incubi, a bunch of the Devil's gofers who stole spunk from guys while they were having wet dreams, made spunk cocktails, and rammed them up women to mix with the menstrual blood and make double monsters. It was also believed that spunk was a kind of distillate of the bodily fluids that kept men kicking. For this reason, wanking and shagging were frowned upon. Losing spunk was not cool. But if too much was lost, one could always reach for the spunk nightcap or suck a second-hand vagina.

Then the broomstick-wanking, toad-wart-pus-sucking witches took over and invented pox, homophobia, AIDS, and come-carrying condoms designed after the Holy Grail (which God slapped on his dick to stop him fucking virgins). That's why now it's largely women that drink spunk, usually when both are warm and fresh. The current popularity of blow jobs is clearly the result of a feminist conspiracy to suck out our vital forces.

Terence McKenna
Food of the Gods

ELECTRONIC DRUGS

In his science-fiction novel *The Man in the High Castle*, Philip K. Dick imagined an alternative world in which World War II had been won by the Japanese and the Third Reich. In Dick's fictional world, the Japanese occupation authorities introduced and legalized marijuana as one of their first moves at pacifying the population of California. Things are hardly less strange here in what conventional wisdom lightheartedly refers to as 'reality.' In 'this world,' too, the victors introduced an all-pervasive, ultra-powerful society-shaping drug. This drug was the first of a growing group of high-technology drugs that deliver the user into an alternative reality by acting directly on the user's sensorium, without chemicals being introduced into the nervous system. It was television. No epidemic or religious hysteria has ever moved faster or made as many converts in so short a time.

The nearest analogy to the addictive power of television and the transformation of values that is wrought in the life of the heavy user is probably heroin. Heroin flattens the image; with heroin, things are neither hot nor cold; the junkie looks out at the world certain that whatever it is, it does not matter. The illusion of knowing and of control that heroin engenders is analogous to the unconscious assumption of the television consumer that what is seen is 'real' somewhere in the world. In fact, what is seen are the cosmetically needed surfaces of products. Television, while chemically non-invasive, nevertheless is every bit as addictive and physiologically damaging as any other drug.

Not unlike drugs or alcohol, the television experience allows the participant to blot out the real world and enter into a pleasurable and passive mental state. The worries and anxieties of reality are as effectively deferred by becoming absorbed in a television program as by going on a 'trip' induced by drugs or alcohol. And just as alcoholics are only vaguely aware of their addiction, feeling that they control their drinking more than they really do . . . people similarly overestimate their control over television-watching . . . Finally it is the adverse effect of television viewing on the lives of so many people that defines it as a serious addiction. The television habit distorts the sense of time. It renders other experiences vague and curiously unreal while taking on a greater reality for itself. It weakens relationships by reducing and sometimes eliminating normal opportunities for talking, for communicating.

THE HIDDEN PERSUADER

Most unsettling of all is this: the content of television is not a vision but a manufactured data stream that can be sanitized to 'protect' or impose cultural values. Thus we are confronted with an addictive and all-pervasive drug that delivers an experience whose message is whatever those who deal the drug wish it to be. Could anything provide a more fertile ground for fostering fascism and totalitarianism than this? In the United States, there are many more televisions than households, the average television set is on six hours a day, and the average person watches more than five hours a day, nearly one-third their waking time. Aware as we all are of these simple facts, we seem unable to react to their implications. Serious study of the effects of television on health and culture only begun recently. Yet no drug in history has so quickly or completely isolated the entire culture of its users from contact with reality. And no drug in history has so completely succeeded in remaking in its own image the values of the culture that it has infected.

Television is by nature the dominator drug par excellence. Control of content, uniformity of content, repeatability of content make it inevitably a tool of coercion, brainwashing and manipulation. Television induces a trance state in the viewer that is the necessary precondition for brainwashing. As with all other drugs and technologies, television's basic character cannot be changed; television is no more reformable than is the technology that produces automatic assault rifles.

Food of the Gods, 1992

155

John Baptista Porta
Women are Made to Cast Off Their Clothes and Go Naked

TO LET NOTHING pass that Jugglers and Impostors counterfeit, They set a Lamp with Characters graved upon it, and filled with Hare's fat; then they mumble forth some words, and light it; when it burns in the middle of women's company, it constrains them all to cast off their clothes, and voluntarily to shew themselves naked unto men; they behold all their privities, that otherwise would be covered, and the women will never leave dancing so long as the Lamp burns: and this was related to me by men of credit. I believe this effect can come from nothing but the Hare's fat, the force whereof perhaps is venemous, and penetrating the brain, moves them to this madness. Homer saith, The Massagetae did the like, and that there are Trees whose fruit cast into the fire, will make all that are near to be drunk and foolish; for they will presently rise from their seats, and fall to leaping and dancing.

From: *Wildest Dreams: An Anthology of Drug-related Literature*,
ed. Richard Rudgley, 1999

Eye of newt and toe of frog
Wool of bat and tongue of dog

William Shakespeare

John G. Bourke
Scatological Rites of All Nations

THE MOST SINGULAR effect of the *amanita* is the influence it possesses over the urine. It is said that from time immemorial the inhabitants have known that the fungus imparts an intoxicating quality to that secretion, which continues for a considerable time after taking it. For instance, a man moderately intoxicated today will by the next morning have slept himself sober; but (as is the custom) by taking a cup of his urine he will be more powerfully intoxicated than he was the preceding day. It is therefore not uncommon for confirmed drunkards to preserve their urine as a precious liquor against a scarcity of the fungus.

The intoxicating property of the urine is capable of being propagated, for everyone who partakes of it has his urine similarly affected. Thus, with a very few *amanitae*, a party of drunkards may keep up their debauch for a week. Dr Langsdorff mentions that by means of the second person taking the urine of the first, the third of the second, and so on, intoxication may be propagated through five individuals.

In *Letters from a Citizen of the World*, Oliver Goldsmith speaks of 'a curious custom' among the Tartars of Koraki. The Russians who trade with them carry thither a kind of mushroom. These mushrooms the rich Tartars lay up in large quantities for the winter; and when a nobleman makes a mushroom feast all the neighbours around are invited. The mushrooms are prepared by boiling, by which the water acquires an intoxicating quality, and is a sort of drink which the Tartars prize beyond all other. When the nobility and the ladies are assembled, and the ceremonies usual between people of distinction over, the mushroom broth goes freely round, and they laugh, talk double entendres, grow fuddled, and become excellent company. The poorer sort, who love mushroom broth to distraction as well as the rich, but cannot afford it at first hand, post themselves on these occasions round the huts of the rich, and watch the opportunity of the ladies and gentlemen as they come down to pass the liquor, and holding a wooden bowl, catch the delicious fluid, very little altered by filtration, being still strongly tinctured with the intoxicating quality. Of this they drink with the utmost satisfaction, and thus they get as drunk and as jovial as their betters.

'Happy nobility!' cried my companion, 'who can fear no diminution of respect unless seized with strangury, and who when drunk are most useful! Though we have not this custom among us, I foresee that if it were introduced, we might have many a toad-eater in England ready to drink from the wooden bowl on these occasions, and to praise the flavour of his lordship's liquor. As we have different classes of gentry, who knows but we may see a lord holding the bowl to the minister, a knight holding it to his lordship, and a simple squire drinking it double distilled from the loins of knighthood?'

1981. From: *Artificial Paradises: A Drugs Reader*,
ed. Mike Jay, 1999

Monkeys, who very sensibly refrain from speech, lest they be set to earn their livings

Kenneth Grahame

Stewart Lee Allen
Monkey Droppings

CHATERJEE TOLD ME that he had once been in the coffee business down by a place called Shrevenoot.

'Excellent coffee. You know, of course, that Karnataka grows the best coffee beans in the world?'

'I'd heard,' I replied politely. 'I must say, though, I find the coffee here a little milky.'

'Well, milk is another matter entirely.'

I let it pass and asked instead about some of the stories I'd heard.

'Do you know anything about how Baba trained his tigers to milk cows?'

'That is just mythology.'

'Like the monkeys, I suppose.'

'I know no monkeys.'

'You haven't heard how he trained his monkeys to pick the beans for him?'

'More nonsense.' He took a sip of his tea. 'There are, of course, the coffee-picking monkeys of Shrevenoot.'

I laughed. 'Wait – so there are actually monkeys trained to pick coffee beans?'

'Of course not. They are not trained. It is a natural phenomenon. They pick the fruit off the tree and eat. That is how you get Monkey Coffee. Surely you have heard?'

Actually, I had read about this stuff. Monkey Coffee was something that had existed in the nineteenth century, supposedly the best brew in the world.

'So there really is such a thing?' I asked.

'It is a well-known fact. I have read it is a delicacy in some countries.'

'Yes, yes. I've read that too. They say it is because the monkeys will pick only the best, the ripest berries, right?'

'So some say. Others claim it is the chemical reaction within the bowels.'

'Bowels?'

'Yes. The monkeys eat the beans and then pass them through their digestive system. That is the Monkey Coffee.'

'You mean it's monkey, uh, feces?'

'As I have said, nobody drinks it here. They are unclean animals.' He wrinkled his nose. 'But it was a terrible problem in Shrevenoot. The monkeys ate all the best beans.'

I was never quite sure whether to believe all this until much later, back in the States, when I discovered that Monkey Coffee had recently become part of the gourmet coffee roster. It does not, however, come out of either a monkey or India, but a small Indonesian creature called the palm toddy cat, a nocturnal tree lover that lives on the naturally alcoholic tree sap used to make toddy (wine) and fresh coffee berries. Whether it's because the animal's intestinal juices impart some special flavor (perhaps because of its alcoholic diet) or merely because it eats only perfectly ripe berries, the toddy cat's droppings, cleaned, produce what many say is the world's finest coffee. Japan buys most of the stuff nowadays, but the US firm of ME Mountanos (800-229-1611) sells it under the name Kopi Luwak at about three hundred dollars a pound, making it the world's most expensive cup of joe. Another firm, called Raven's Brew Coffee (ravencup@ptialaska.net or 800-91-RAVEN), sells it by the quarter-pound for seventy-five dollars and, in that grand American tradition, throws in a free T-shirt showing the beast hard at work with a cup under its ass and the caption 'Good to the Last Dropping.'

The Devil's Cup, 2000

Howard Marks
A Personal Stash

I ARRIVED AT Heathrow's Terminal Two to be confronted by some stupid fucking leaflet portraying the customs channels as traffic lights (lights for traffickers: green for go, red for stop). Why has the orange become blue? While I was transferring my baggage from the carousel to a trolley, my dick suddenly experienced a warm soft pressure, nudging, stroking, licking and fondling. I looked down full of expectation and disappointingly discovered a dog's head sniffing away at my balls. The dog was attached to an officer of Her Majesty's Customs & Excise.

'Get this fucking dog away from me.'

'Your name and occupation, sir?'

'I used to be a dope smuggler and an MI6 agent. That pillock with headphones behind the two-way mirror knows exactly who I am.'

The pillock with headphones behind the two-way mirror joined his colleague.

'We'd like to search your luggage, Mr Marks.'

Although my suitcase contained enough subversive literature to convict your average lightweight narcoterrorist, enough porn to ruin a politician's career, and enough paraphernalia to open up a head shop, I knew there was no dope in there. I had rolled two spliffs in case the plane had been late on departure. These were still in my shirt. And I had a little lump up my arse. That's what that fucking mongrel had picked up on.

*

It had been a long time since I'd tried any new tricks on how to dodge Her Majesty's Customs & Excise. I thought of simply tearing through as fast as my legs, or wheels, could carry me. There weren't any 'Walk, Don't Run' notices and no speed limits. Even if there had been a speed limit, I'd had only one line (which I'd sniffed mistakenly believing it to be a cocktail of coke and MDMA), and that was wearing off.

Trolleying severely, I rushed to the trolley point, grabbed a trolley, pretended I was a trolley, and sped off like the clappers towards the Green Channel. Two overweight customs officers and twenty-five plain-clothes cops (who'd been ligging around the carousels making out they were badly behaved lads) tore after me. I let go the trolley and tripped over my shoelaces. 'In a bit of a rush, are we, sir?'

'No. It's worn off.'

'Well, you know what they say, sir. More paste, less speed.'

'I haven't got any speed, other than what might be stuck up my fucking nostril. And I prefer leaves to paste.'

A senior Customs & Excise Investigation Officer tapped me on the shoulder.

'Marks, isn't it? You think you're such a clever dick, don't you? I think me and the other officers used to like you more when you had the balls to actually smuggle sensible quantities of dope, not just a squidge up your arse.'

Some other plain-clothes customs approached.

'Mr Marks, you have just attempted to go through the Green Channel, thereby stating you have nothing to declare. Where have you been?'

'All kinds of places. Should I start alphabetically?'

'Get on with it, Marks.'

'Amsterdam . . .'

'So, what were you doing when you were in Amsterdam?'

'Shagging, from what I remember. Oh! And smoking dope in coffee shops. And drinking coffee in dope shops. In Amsterdam, it's okay to always be in possession of a cup of coffee and five grams of mind-blowing dope. So, when I got on the plane at Amsterdam airport, I wasn't bustable. I drank the coffee, but they wouldn't let me smoke a fag, let alone a

161

bong, on the plane, so I couldn't get rid of the dope. Presumably, these days you carry the appropriate forms?'

'Forms?'

'Well, thousands of people arrive in London every day from Amsterdam with no worries about the five grams of dope they're carrying until going through British Customs. Accordingly, I imagine there to be a procedure whereby the passengers deposit their five-gram lumps with HM Customs. You issue a receipt, so the passengers can pick up their dope when next leaving the country. I remember once going through a similar procedure when trying to take a blow-up doll looking like Mickey Mouse into America. You must have a load of dope here. And a load of forms.'

'Are you taking the piss, sir?'

'No.'

An even more senior Customs & Excise Investigation Officer approached.

'Where have you just flown in from, Mr Marks?'

'Oslo.'

'Oslo? My colleague just informed me otherwise.'

'He's a lying, evil, gutless wanker.'

'Mr Marks, we have everything tape-recorded. Why did you tell my colleague Amsterdam?'

'Because Amsterdam begins with A. I was trying to give an alphabetical list of where I'd been. Actually, I should have started with Aberavon. I drank several litres of wine on the flight, and I'm completely fucking pissed.'

'Why were you running?'

'I was busting for a piss.'

'Any other reason?'

'I'm pissed off with being busted.'

'Do you have anything to declare?'

'Yeah.'

'What?'

'Piss.'

'You'll just have to wait for a piss while my colleagues finish searching your bags. They've already found bottles of booze.'

'That's not booze,' I said.

'What is it?'

'Piss. Fresh reindeer piss from the north of Norway. It's not illegal. I would be well and truly pissed off to get busted for piss while I was busting for a piss.'

'Mr Marks, we know full well that you arrived on an Iberia flight from Palma.'

'Well, P comes after O which comes after A.'

'Why were you in Palma, Mr Marks?'

'I live there.'

'And why are you visiting England?'

'I live here.'

'And the nature of your current work, sir?'

'Crime.'

'It would make me happy, sir, if you provided me with honest and consistent answers.'

'Why the fuck should your happiness be my concern? Unless you smoke dope and you've run out.'

'I don't. Do you still smoke cannabis, Mr Marks?'

'Of course. As much as possible.'

The dog handler and the pillock with headphones that had been behind the two-way mirror were now joined in their luggage-frisking by a female member of Her Majesty's Customs & Excise. She had big tits. The dog handler leered at her. I leered at her. Not really sexy, but she was wearing a uniform.

'I want her to do my body search,' I cried, tugging at my belt. 'I always keep my dope under my foreskin.'

'Body search!' yelled the pillock. 'You'll be lucky. Pack up your cases and proceed to the arrivals hall. You've been cleared.'

I staggered from the arrivals hall into the carriage of a miserable-looking tube and slumped firmly on to the hard seat. Suddenly, searing pain shot right up my arse. I squealed, jumped up and looked for the offending rat, spring or rusty tin can. There weren't any. And the pain was gone. There's so much unused booze and other psychoactive juice swelling around in my lobes and lubricating my receptors that I tend to ignore inconsistencies between perceptions and sensations. I sat down again. Zap! The pain returned with increased severity. The inside of my rectum felt like it was being mainlined with chilli sauce by a crab. What was going on? Had I eaten a glass instead of drinking what was inside? Was it piles? Please no! It's bad enough having false teeth, smouldering lungs, red eyes, a pot belly. Spare me the haemorrhoidal trip.

Then I realised I still had the dope up my arse: about half an ounce of smokable, but sharp, Moroccan. I'd forgotten to go to the loo after dodging Her Majesty's Customs & Exiles. No problem. At least I knew what the score was. I could handle it. Come to think of it, the only sure criterion of good dope these days is whether or not it's been up someone's arse. No one is going to suffer that for a lump of mouldy soap-bar shite.

Opposite sat a guy and a dog in a box. They had just flown in together. The dog looked stoned and jet-lagged.

My arse stopped hurting. The sharp bits of the dope must have dissolved into my mucous membrane, anal-suppository style. Small wonder I was bonding mildly with the dog.

Next time, I'll buy a dog, stick some dope up its arse, ram some All Bran down its throat, put the fucker into a box and get on a plane. Even if at the other end the British Customs mongrel did sniff around my dog's arse, explanations other than canine couriering would certainly be forthcoming. Who ever heard of a dog being a mule? Better still, I could buy lots of dogs and ram lots of dope up their arses. I could use big dogs with big arses. I'll write a play and call it *1,001 Alsatians*. I'll take scenery, actors and dogs on the road up the Khyber Pass. I'll buy a rectal ton of the finest Afghan hashish and pretend the Siva shit is dogshit. Stick it right up them.

I wonder how much an elephant's arse could take.

I have nothing to declare except my genius

Oscar Wilde

The Equinox
Testing Cannabis on Dogs

THE METHOD OF assay, which has previously been called to the attention of this Society, is that which one of us (Houghton) devised and has employed for the past twelve years. This method consists essentially in the careful observation of the physiological effects produced upon dogs from the internal administration of the preparation of the drug under test. It is necessary in selecting the test animals to pick out those that are easily susceptible to the action of the Cannabis, since dogs as well as human beings vary considerably in their reaction to the drug. Also, preliminary tests should be made upon the animals before they are finally selected to test purposes, in order that we may know exactly how they behave under given conditions. After the animals have been finally selected and found to respond to the standard test does, 0.01 grams per kilo, they are set aside for this particular work, care being taken to have them well fed, well housed, and in every way kept under the best sanitary conditions. Usually we have found it desirable to keep two or more of the approved animals on hand at all times, so there may not be delay in testing samples as they come in.

In applying the test, the standard dose (in form of solid extract for convenience) is administered internally in a small capsule. The dog's tongue is drawn forward between the teeth with the left hand and the capsule placed on the back part of the tongue with the right hand. The tongue is then quickly released and the capsule is swallowed with ease. In order that the drug may be rapidly absorbed, food should be withheld for twenty-four hours before the test and an efficient cathartic given if needed.

Within a comparatively short time the dog begins to show the characteristic action of the drug. There are three typical effects to be noticed from active extracts on susceptible animals: first a stage of excitability, then a stage of inco-ordination, followed by a period of drowsiness. The first of these is so dependent on the characteristics of the dog used that it is of little value for judging the activity of the drug, while, with only a few exceptions, the second, or the stage of incoordination, invariably follows in one or two hours; the dog loses control of its legs and of the muscles supporting its head, so that when nothing occurs to attract its attention its head will droop, its body sway, and, when severely affected, the animal will stagger and fall, the intoxication being peculiarly suggestive and striking.

Experience is necessary on the part of the observer to determine just when the physiological effects of the drug begin to manifest themselves, since there is always, as in the case of many chemical tests, a personal factor to be guarded against. When an active extract is given to a susceptible animal, in the smallest dose that will produce any perceptible effect, one must watch closely for the slightest trace of inco-ordination, lack of attention, or drowsiness. It is particularly necessary for the animals to be confined in a room where nothing will excite them, since when their attention is drawn to anything of interest the typical effect of the drug may disappear.

The influence of the test dose of the unknown drug is carefully compared with that of the same dose of the standard preparation administered to another test dog at the same time and under the same conditions.

Finally, when the animals become drowsy, the observations are recorded and the animals are returned to their quarters.

The second day following, the observations upon the two dogs are reversed, i.e. the animal receiving the test dose of the unknown receives a test dose of the known, and *vice versa*, and a second observation is made. If one desires to make a very accurate quantitative determination, it is advisable to use, not two dogs, but four or five, and to study the effects of the test dose of the unknown specimen in comparison with the test dose of the known, making several observations on alternate days. If the unknown is below standard activity, the amount should be increased until the effect produced is the same as for the test dose of the standard. If the unknown is above strength, the test dose is diminished accordingly. From the dose of the unknown selected as producing the same action as the test dose of the standard, the amount of dilution or concentration necessary is determined. The degree of accuracy with which the test is carried out will depend largely upon the experience of the observer and the care he exercises.

Another point to be noted in the use of dogs for standardising Cannabis is that, although they never appear to lose their susceptibility, the same dogs cannot be used indefinitely for accurate testing. After a time they become so accustomed to the effects of the drug they refuse to stand on their feet, and so do not show the typical incoordination which is its most characteristic and constant action.

1905. From: *The Equinox: The Review of Scientific Illuminism*, vol. 1, no. 1, 1909

Ronald K. Siegel
Intoxication: Life in Pursuit of Artificial Paradise

Cats are attracted to catnip purely for reasons of chemical pleasure. Catnip (*Meseta cataria*) is a perennial herb with downy leaves and a strong mint odour. It is native to such diverse locales as Scandinavia, Kashmir, Canada and New Jersey. Today it is widely cultivated throughout the world. Surprisingly, there is no overlap in the distribution of the catnip plant and its namesake. Yet when placed near catnip, cats will seek the plant and return to it each day. The behaviour is illustrative of our own attraction to drugs that may be alien to our immediate environment but that, once introduced, evoke strong natural feelings. Unlike the birds seeking berries, the cats are exhibiting deliberate intoxications.

When cats encounter the plant, their first reaction is to sniff. To humans, fresh catnip has the odour of mint mixed with fresh-cut grass or alfalfa. In the dried plant, or in commercial cat toys, the alfalfa odour predominates. Upon reaching the plant source, the cat commences to lick and sometimes chew the leaves, in the second stage of the response. The chewing is often interrupted when the cat momentarily stares into space with a blank expression, then quickly shakes its head from side to side. In the third stage the cat will usually rub against the plant with its chin and cheek. Last, there is a 'head-over' roll with rubbing of the entire body. Extremely sensitive cats may also flip from side to side by rolling over on their backs. The four-stage reaction runs its fixed course in approximately ten minutes.

Biologists have referred to this intoxication as an example of animal addiction to pleasure behaviour. The nature of the pleasurable intoxication becomes increasingly evident when high doses of catnip in the form of concentrated extracts are offered to the animals. The subsequent reactions are intense: cats head-twitch violently, salivate profusely, and show other signs of central nervous system excitation. One sign is sexual stimulation. Males have spontaneous erections while females adopt mating stances, complete with vocalisation and 'love-biting' of any available object.

The similarity of the catnip response to the normal sexual behaviour of cats is striking. The presentation of catnip results in a rolling pattern of behaviour that is exhibited by oestrous females during the course of normal sexual displays. These displays have prompted naturalists to speculate that catnip once served the evolutionary function in the wild of preparing cats for sex, a natural springtime aphrodisiac.

Matatabi, which the Japanese call a pleasure plant, does the same trick for cats even better. This plant contains secondary compounds closely related in chemical structure and behavioural activity to nepetalactones. Concentrated *matatabi* chemicals, in doses unavailable to the cats in the natural plant, were placed on cotton balls and presented to the large cats at the Osaka Zoo. After an initial exposure, the cats became so eager for more that they would ignore whatever else they were doing – eating, drinking, or even having sexual intercourse – whenever the chemicals were made available.

They displayed a very intense 'catnip' response, then rolled on their backs where they stayed for some time 'in complete ecstasy'.

1989. From: *Artificial Paradises: A Drugs Reader*,
ed. Mike Jay, 1999

Robert Lund
Mikey's Tale

Zoë loved her rats dearly. At first there were just two, in a twenty-gallon fishtank. They had offspring, and became a close family. Soon, Z started letting one or two at a time out to play for a while each day, just to allow them to enjoy the absence of those glass walls. Soon it became harder and harder to put them back inside at night. After some time, the tank was left uncovered, and they were permitted to come and go as they pleased.

And come and go they did – mostly come. Over a period of months, their numbers multiplied steadily, to the point where upon entering the apartment one would encounter a veritable 'ratrug', made up of over a hundred little black-and-white bodies, with a few whites and tan-and-whites mixed in, eagerly greeting you. Of course, they weren't given free access to the entire seven-room apartment. Two of the three bedrooms were closed off to the little ones – leaving them more than enough space to roam.

Aside from our actual bedroom, the other ratless bedroom had been converted years earlier into something of an office. Atop a thick green wall-to-wall carpet sat a work table and an industrial equipment rack full of ancient minicomputers and peripherals. A bathroom was also accessed by going through this room, as well as a closet. Zoë and I used to throw all our empty dope bags into a thirty-gallon trash bag, kept in the office closet. We did this not only out of fear of someone coming across contraband trash in our garbage, but also because of the residue that came in handy on desperate days.

You can scrape up quite a healthy dose out of nearly thirty gallons of 'empty' dope bags.

Some rats were more exploratory in nature than others. Eventually, one enterprising young rat apparently found (or made?) a hole in the wall behind the piano in the living room, leading him to a space behind the bathtub, from which he wandered around to some loose tile behind the toilet. *Voilà*, he found himself in the cut-off bathroom, then making his way into the off-limits 'office.' We had no knowledge of his journey until one needy day, looking for bag-residue in the trash bag, we found a hole torn in the bottom of the trash bag, and many dope bags chewed to bits. Clearly the work of one of our little friends. We soon detected the means by which he must have gotten into the closet, but couldn't find him. On successive days, we found more and more bags chewed up, but never caught him in the act. But it was clear that we had a regular little user on our hands. Just like in the experiment they used to show us only the first half of on TV, where the rats placed in the cage with cocaine would gobble it up until they died, but the rats placed in the cage with heroin would take enough to feel straight, and level off their usage – so this little fella seemed to be using it regularly, but not gorging himself on the entire pile in any one day.

This went on for some time. We gave up on using our trash bag as an emergency supply, since Mikey seemed to be keeping well ahead of us, and evading detection. (He was called Mikey after the signal the lookouts at the 2nd Street dope spot used to shout when cops were approaching – 'Mikey! Mikey!' – scattering everyone on-line to the winds.) Finally, one day, I happened to open up one of the old PDP-11 computers mounted in the equipment rack. On the surface of an unused portion of the backplane, there was Mikey's nest. This little guy wasn't commuting from the living room anymore – having found happiness in the closet trash bag, he had settled in the office, alone. His little nest consisted of the basic rat essentials: a floor made up of chewed-up toilet paper; a pile of food pellets, collected from what we used to pour out onto the floor for the rat mob, who made a sound like that of hail on a tin roof while eating it up; a single bar of soap(?); assorted chewed-up bits of cardboard collected from around the house; and, most alarmingly, a neat stack of Monopoly money – totally untouched by rodential teeth, in pristine condition! He knew better than to chew up the cash.

I realized then that Mikey was indeed a self-sufficient fellow. Obviously, aware that the finite scrapings in the trash bag were diminishing faster than we were replenishing them, he gathered up a supply of cash for the day when he'd have to go out and cop on his own. Oh, the Great 'G of J' (God of Junk), as Zoë used to exclaim so often. He tends to all creatures great and small.

'Mikey's Tale', 1997

Bridget O'Connor
Heavy Petting

for Tiny and Twinkle

I COME FROM a long line of pet deaths. Bunny and Clyde . . . Tiny and Twinkle. Sid and Nancy. Mungo . . .

But it's Godfrey who haunts me.

At night, when the cistern gurgles, it's like he's back with a splash.

Majella hooped him at a fairground and brought him home, dangling from her thumb, gulping mist in a plastic bag. He wasn't expected to live for long. She plopped him in the dead terrapin's tank: watched him loop. Blessed his tank. Named him after her ex-fiancé, the paratrooper: the one who'd chucked her out on the street, howling. Godfrey.

Godfrey was like Godfrey: he was quick, ginger, flash, but he was never mean.

He was so *bright* in our dingy house. He blew air kisses all day, puffed out silvery smoke rings . . . link chains. A stray sunbeam hit his glossy water and he sparkled. Round and round, an endless U-ie . . . At first, Majella blew him kisses back, showered him with presents from the pet shop: bright coral-gravels, a pagoda, a stone-coloured hide'n'seek boot, as fluorescent pink plastic hanging garden . . . and sieved him out, with the tea strainer, for long transatlantic journeys in the bath – and then she *turned*. She turned to clubbing, drugging and a bloke called either Mr Ecstasy or Marv. Or both. Majella, my sister, went *rave* mad.

One day Majella was a laughter-line in a nightie, spitting on an iron, singeing a pleat down her navy work skirt, and next, she was this gum-snapping *stranger* pacing up our hall: wearing tight T-shirts with daisies on them, calling cabs at midnight; hipped out, with her belly button sticking out of flab. (Later, she had it pierced: it went septic. Septicaemia . . . She got gangrene. She had to go to hospital. It went the size of a yeasty currant bun. But that was *much* later.)

Majella really *loved* Godfrey but, after she hit the clubbing scene, got, as she called it, 'loved up', she hated him.

I didn't think pretty Godfrey could live for long.

'Mum?' I said. '*Look!*' I'd airlifted him out from the hellhole of Majella's bedroom: blown away his sky of talcum powder, reeled out a foot of Majella's tan-coloured, scummy tights, and set him down by the scummy cooker in the kitchen. Though he was thin, a red bone in a white sock – he was, I thought, *all the light in our house boiled down*.

In the hot kitchen Godfrey blinked his gold. 'Look, Mum,' I said, 'isn't he sweeeet?'

Mum looked down: her cheeks steamed, flushed like two rubbed spots. Her eyes, under her sweaty eyebrows, gleamed. I looked from her to the brown sudsy cooking pots, back to Godfrey, back to Mum.

I thought: Poor Godfrey, he won't last for long. Out of the fire, into the pan.

Mum had gone . . . funny in the head. That's what Majella yelled, tapping her temple: 'You're *funny-in-the-head*,' as though Mum's head had been stacked (when we weren't looking) with comic books, sitcoms . . . I couldn't think of a better explanation myself.

Outside, our other pets howled on the lawns, sang like

exiles, made a heady high white noise, scribbled their nibbled light-pink legs in the sheds, kicked up for dinner time. The toy poodles shook their pale dreadlocks. Our albino rabbits stretched their dirty jaws. Across the neighbourhood, strays joined in: cats caterwauled. Mum stirred away in the kitchen. She boomed a silent radar: her animal attraction. The pets on the lawns crackled, eared up and somersaulted back. Or they'd bounce and pose above the grassy gore, suspended for a moment, hunched like fridge magnets.

In his tank Godfrey (plumped up), beaming bright, would pause. He'd leap above the pagoda, hang out in the hanging garden. Dirty strobe light smacked his back. His tail thumped. He swam on.

We had to ring for takeaways. At night, when the cat songs got too much, I'd lob our leftover cartons of chicken tikka, the chewy rinds from our takeaway pizzas, salty chip rejects, up out and into the long splattered grass. Shrieks! A scrummage. A feral pet race. The air filled with clods of earth: back-kicked peas. Tree-high stalks shook. As I noted in my red notepads, only the very fast survived.

Doctor Trang upped Mum's medication. The side effects, he said (zombie-ism, intense communion with small dumb animals), were a small price to pay, believe him. I did. I'd already noted the symptoms: synchronicity: in the hot kitchen, when Mum paused, holding a ladle, Godfrey paused too; when one stirred, the other whizzed rapidly round.

In the kitchen Godfrey's light drew me to him. He surfed the surface; flayed gold . . . green . . . red. His tank bubbled like a miniature jacuzzi: full of air and spinning fat globes. He'd flip on his side, fin a zippy sidestroke, blow a little link kiss at Mum as she sipped, with deep concentration, at her wooden spoon. Mum looked down at Godfrey and blew him a crumb, a grape, a rubber fish face. They were one.

At least, I knew, with Mum around, Godfrey was safe.

At night, our other pets sat in line on the black grass: ruby-red-eyed. They were the lifers: all born to us, given to us, at a time when we must have seemed, no, we were *exactly* like a photograph happily framed: there was Mum in rose-tinted

C&A blouse; Dad, roastily tanned in his crisp blue cotton overalls; Majella and me in our steam-ironed bottle-green school uniforms (Majella's big hands on my little shoulders), showing our heavy-metal orthodontistry. Behind us surged a thunderous studio sky. Around us hopped the albino rabbits, the tortoise. The mongrels. The cats. Poodles . . . they all began to die.

Majella started clubbing it once a week, then twice . . . thrice . . . Mr Marv was a light voice on the line (a 'Yeah', a 'She in?'). He was a slice of shadow, a stripe of Adidas in the crack of a cab. Majella came home shiny, she sniffed, snapped her chewing gum at Godfrey. (Her luminous inks flowered first in the choke of the hall.) In the kitchen she drank tap water, spat green tubes of it through gaps in her teeth at me, at my homework; stared in at Godfrey as he flashed to and fro in his tank. Her face greyed, grew stone. She hovered over his tank, dribbled strands of her long beige hair in, eyes set wide apart: black-pooled, scary, like a shark's. Godfrey cowered in his hide'n'seek boot. I cowered too. 'Godfrey,' Majella chanted, 'I'm going to *get you*. What am I going to do Godfrey? *Get you*.' I didn't think Godfrey could survive for long.

Outside on the lawns, all the pets cried.

In my trainee notepads, I noted, sipping a Lemsip, 'We're all on medication now.' Mum had little white pills. Majella had her little white pills. Even Dad, who I was in love with, took massive painkillers. He had migraine. He'd come home from the railways like a train. Light stabbed him. Coffee killed him. Pineapple juice made him cry. He had migraine so bad he had to inject himself in the bathroom, using his leather belt as a tourniquet. (His injection kit was a toy briefcase, deadly black; inside, chrome cylinders, needles so think they made your skin lock.) He had blinders. He'd charge home honking noise, smoking rust, with one eye spinning like a shot blue marble, the other scrunching up his forehead, his bobble hat thick with dust. I don't think he noticed the litter under his boots, or chicken tikka again for tea. I stood in the kitchen sipping blackcurrant Lemsip, studying my books, peeping in at Godfrey as he swam round . . . round.

Godfrey swam. He swam in brackish oily water and then, it seemed, he was deep in soup. He paddled past florets of cauliflower, dived under broccoli bombs, breasted logs of carrots, stinking shreds of chicken and lamb. He moved not in water but in stuff he really had to fin through. Gazpacho. The air flowered with stock. Godfrey gave little shivery, fastidious leaps. Mum, stirring, leaped too. Leaning, trying to talk sense into Mum, one day, yelling above the radio blah-blah of LBC, I saw Godfrey take a leap at the edge. But the walls of the terrapin tank were too high. He leapt but a stray *calamaro* ringed his neck, winched it back, cut his arrow-like route to the floor. My heart flipped. Godfrey's battered, swollen, mottled, white-veined mouth glugged each time, sank to blank – down among the greasy olives, baggy purple prunes, hairy anchovies swishing by like unshaved legs: the assorted mucus beneath the murk. I'd mumble above his surface: 'Leeds . . . Aberystwyth . . . Godfrey, you hang on.' I changed Godfrey's water but Mum souped it straight back up. I tried putting Godfrey in my bedroom near my computer and neat stacks of homework but Mum kept bringing him down, sloshing, bashing his delicate lips brown. I tried to keep Godfrey on the up.

But I failed. I failed my mocks. An (unpredicted) D, D, E. When I told Godfrey he flickered away. I looked for him in the grey TV screen of his tank. 'I'm sorry, Godfrey,' I said. I turned to Mum. She stirred away.

I tried to stay focused, stay head-down, but . . .

I thought Majella was now heavily into the drug scene, was like a suburban drug queen, and I was worried.

I saw adverts in the papers for people to appear and confess personal family information on *Esther* or on *Vanessa* and I was thinking of appearing. I'd snitch Majella up for her own good. I'd get her into rehab. Write to her from my tidy room. I circled the adverts with red biro and left them on Majella's littered grey bed, as a warning, a hint for her to pull *herself together*. I tapped Mum's arm in the kitchen. 'Mum?' Godfrey paused. 'Godfrey?' I said. 'Newcastle Polytechnic? Brighton FE?' Godfrey swam away.

Majella started clubbing it four times a week, five. She'd come home at around four o'clock in the morning, with Mr Marv. (She'd sleep maybe two hours, then speed off to work. Her eyes were like slots.) I'd wait up, reassuring Godfrey there'd be no game-playing tonight whatsoever, watching as his sides bulged at the scrape of a key . . . Mr Marv swung in first: smirked, picked up a dirty fork, toyed with its crusty prong, slid it up his sleeve. Majella doubled behind him: they were thin, shiny, daisy-topped. They'd sloppy-kiss, edge to the tank; rub each other up, but I was on guard, stayed solid, watched for the sudden lunge, the stabbing fork. They'd kiss out. Then, without warning, double back, *crash* into the kitchen tooled up to play, in between licks and despite my protestations, the Get Godfrey Game. They forked but Godfrey dived under the blue pagoda. They stabbed but Godfrey ducked into the hide'n'seek boot. He whizzed rapidly around a roast spud. Watching his dive I *felt* the full surge of his life force: he'd leap back from a death wish; got firmly back *into* the swim; he swam away. Majella and Marv forked up sodden Cocoa-Pops, fried clumps of wire wool, crumbless stiff blue fingers of fish. Godfrey lived to flicker away. Godfrey survived all through Majella's Marv stage, her Darren & speed stage, her LSD-plus-E stage. His stroke became really butch, determined. His nose grew blunt from speeding U-ies against the glass. Majella went clubbing six times a week. She looked thin-skinned. I could see the blood network through her face. She'd come home haggard in her NatWest uniform looking forty years old and emerge from her room, hours later, remarkably refreshed; showing tight arse-cleavage, her cheeks sparkly like two just-peeled spuds, her hair with a wide road of centre-parting, looking *just* eleven years old. In a rare burst of sisterhood, once, she showed me the three moves I'd need should I ever give up being a 'snitchy-bitch' and take up clubbing instead:

1. You put your fingers in the air and stab as though you're telling someone to piss off a lot.
2. You dance like snakes would.

3. You maintain an ironic hipster pose at all times.

Our other pets went funny, *funnier*, in the head: showed acute symptoms of distress, neuroses, when they heard the squeal of a taxi. They bounced up and down on the grass, paced two steps forward, two steps back.

Summer was awful. I failed my A levels and then I failed my resits (Fs). Tiny died in the sheds (she was all loose inside, really awful, like a bag of curds), and then Twinkle got run over. The tortoise fell into a coma and died. Suzi developed some kind of tumour on her neck and started going for Dad as he stepped in through the door from work. Really for his neck. Like *flying* through the air, like hiding under the stairs or crouched in the airing cupboard like Patience on a stack of dank sheets . . . the vet said a tumour-removal operation would cost about forty pounds. One day I came in from signing on and Suzi wasn't there. Dad said she'd gone: 'Doggone.' He'd probably let her loose on the motorway, the bastard.

So we only had Godfrey left.

And Godfrey was getting bigger. He lived on juicy blue flies that fell from the ceiling and cod in butter sauce. He really liked chips. If you plopped a chip in the tank Godfrey gobbled it down in one, like a piranha. Godfrey was so fat now he could barely turn around in his tank. He swam on though. He only paused in his heavy front crawl to listen to Mum's long radio monologues or watch her manic hands chop the air. He still blew her kiss and kiss kiss. Mum gleamed. She poured old cups of sugary sun-warmed tea on his back to keep his water level up, pulled a few rubbery fish faces; flipped in chips. With each look-in Godfrey swam with extra verve; blew out kiss and . . . kiss and . . . kiss. Sometimes, Mum kissed back. As the kitchen boiled up, Godfrey's tank became just like another steaming bowl of soup: he smelt, sometimes, really tasty.

I wasn't so happy then. I tried to keep my spirits up by writing an epic novel slowly by computer in the morning and swimming slowly in the swimming pool down the road in the afternoon. I was quite good at breaststroke and, as I breasted the clear blue water, I thought about Godfrey: his immense powers of endurance, his selflessness. I admired the sheer *purity* of his direction. His staying power. I would, I told myself, now eschew all Lemsips and paracetamol. I would be as Godfrey, and simply *endure*.

Dad started coming home late, becalmed, with rust marks like vicious love bites on his neck. I noted his clothes no longer billowed their usual bluey-grey cloud of concrete dust. Had he shaken it elsewhere? I thought: Yes. (I imagined a bottle-blonde in a nylon cream cardigan donned like a cloak . . . I drew a picture of her in my notebook, stabbed big juicy blackheads into her chin.) His boots also had new bootlaces on them. I swam and listed clues like that. I was even more worried about Majella. I could smell her rotting flesh. It smelt light green. I'd be up guarding Godfrey, watching late-night Hindu films on the telly, waiting for dawn to crack light across the old chicken tikka cartons on the still black lawns: I'd wait for Majella to come home. Majella staggered from her cab. I'd smell her first: rot. She'd come up daisies in the hall, push straight through me, sneer, throw the drug literature I'd got from Dr Trang back in my face, push me off. Her forehead and temples were glossed with sweat; above her hipsters the belly button rose from its punctured hood like a lump of red, still-cooking, bread. 'Majella?' I called. I had Dettol on hand, TCP ready. Majella staggered past me, zigzagged up the stairs, shook the light fittings, and slammed a heavy screen of dust from her door frame.

Godfrey swam in his tank. Gulped, slowly, round.

Mum's medications went haywire. She was talking more or less out loud: answering all the voices chanting in her head. Under Dr Trang's direction she had to swallow his pills and lift her flabby grey tongue for his inspection. Mum swallowed. The muscles in her throat rippled. Dr Trang shook his head perplexed, and wrinkled his nose.

Mum talked back to LBC on the radio, nodded vigorously at whichever other airwave was tuning her in . . . fuzzing her out. A new pet-fan squeaked from the bread bin: a pet mouse. The mouse begged at her heels as she stirred the soup. Or it climbed on to the beige stubble plains of her worn-out carpet slippers, shiny pink mouse marigolds signing up supplications; squeak plaintive. Mum stirred the soup. The mouse scampered up her leg, her sleeve, her muscled arm, on to her shoulder, turned somersaults, squivelled, squeaked for attention, its cute black persistent eyes gleaming. Mum stirred on. The mouse cut a squeak through her airways. Godfrey, in his tank, splished up distraction: whacked up prawns, corn on the cob . . . splashed. The mouse tricked on. Wandering into the kitchen one hot afternoon, chewing my hand, I heard a different squeak. Human: 'A carrot is essential, mango chut . . .' The mouse was poised up on Mum's thumb, paws in beg mode, raised so its whiskers could tickle her own. Mum was squeaking, in a squeaky Nice-Aunty voice, the secret of her secret-recipe soups. She roared: '*Vanilla essence obviously, stupid mouse, ha, ha, ha, fluff! One cornflake, leather thong . . .*'

Godfrey broke surface. Red-eyed. Slowly dived. He no longer got a look-in.

Then one day I came home from a dole recall interview, chewing my lip. I thought I'd just look in on old Godfrey and start a really pure and positive Zen afternoon: Go on. Just *get* on. Chapter 200. Chapter 201 . . . I caught Mum leaning over Godfrey's tank. She was sly-faced, hugely pored. Her mouse-fan was boxing with excitement, shrieking squeaks from the bowl of her collarbone; it leapt at her stiff ponytailed head, climbed her ponytail scaffold. Wheeeeed round. The mouse grinned as Mum, gum frilled, tippled and dribbled the contents out of her brown pill bag.

The little white pills slid on a slide through Godfrey's murk, became, I noted, with their powdery star tails, like ultra-white planets in flux. I saw Godfrey buoyed up by half a cheese'n'viscous roll, by a boiled egg, pickled and embryonic like new baby skin – pause. The Plants glazed his right side-eye, shock-waved, rearranged. You . . . good Godfrey, I urged, ignore. Just swim on . . . Godfrey. You *swim* on! Godfrey swam on, swam and swam on, till, with a flash of tail rudder, a shiver, a final soup-thwacking U-ie he – gulped. His throat rippled and he gulped again.

I went into the garden and, lying out among the stale pizza crusts, with big raindrops splashing on my forehead, I began to cry.

Godfrey lay at the bottom of the tank, slowly burbling, like a miniature ginger whale.

Doctor Trang gave me pills. I had growing pains, he said. He patted my hand kindly and suggested I wash more. I smelt a bit fishy. I was a pretty little thing underneath all those eyebrows. I wandered the high streets, up and down, as the drugs made me march, and thought about a new novel I would write by hand, using pencil. No more computers. I'd get back into the raw.

In the kitchen, Mum shouted at the mouse-fan and the mouse-fan ran to fetch a friend. The two mice looked up and nervously conferred as Mum ranted and confused them, sent a pea-green football flying off her wooden spoon. They chased.

I bent my knees to the tank and looked, with my slow-motion blink rate, into the thunderous grey matter where something large and orange glowed. 'I forgive you, Godfrey,' I said, reaching for a fork. 'I'm . . .' I stabbed, stammering, 'o-out of it ta-too.' I smelt light green: saw, on my periphery, luminous daisies bloom. 'Godfrey,' I said, 'the ga-game is o-o-ver.' Godfrey bellied up. Beside me, I heard Majella sob.

From: *Intoxication: An Anthology of Stimulant-Based Writing*,
ed. Toni Davidson, 1998

Howard Marks
Israel

I WAS IN Israel for a few days promoting the Hebrew translation of my book, *Mr Nice; Every Jewish Mamma's Nightmare (But He's All Right Really)*, and had absolutely no desire to get bollocksed by any aspect of the Arab-Israeli dispute. It's all the same, all the time, everywhere, from Genesis to CNN, and it's got too boring. All right, some of the ancient history is quite intriguing: Jews being originally enslaved because they shagged too much; Solomon, the wise geezer, shagging Sheba, Queen of the Rastas, and letting her scarper to Ethiopia with the Ark of the Convenant. But the only bit I had ever found either funny or really interesting was the plethora of religious conflicts saturating the issue, and I'd sorted that lot out long ago. I did not want the top of my dick cut off, definitely wanted to get pissed on booze, liked miniskirts, got bored by Sabbaths, totally avoided any kind of truthful confessions, did not fancy any angels or virgins, loved bacon sandwiches, got turned on by adultery, didn't want to cover some women's faces, preferred hers to hymns, and only wanted to meet God if he could dance. I freely admit, however, that I like a few religious traditions like having four wives and a harem, covering some women's faces, and segregating menstruaters. Also, I enjoy eating turkey balls and falafel, really fancy Mary Magdalene, would like to know how to turn water into wine, approve of banning cheeseburgers and banning girls wearing sexless shorts, and wouldn't mind living for ever as long as I could take drugs, have sex and dance.

We were on the air.

'So what do you think of Israel, Mr Marks?'

'It's great. Fantastic weather, amazing women.'

'And of the Israeli character?'

This was an interview taking place in Tel Aviv, going out live on prime-time Israeli national television. I had to be careful. Sad Adam Hussein was still in the Garden of Eden, ready with his scuds and non-psychoactive chemicals. Armed ex-soldiers (every Israeli has been one) were surrounding me. The interviewer was terrified. He'd been told I was always stoned and more than capable of suddenly skinning up without any four-minute warning. And that I liked taking risks and tasting adrenalin.

'I think it's like mine,' I answered.

'Like a mine? You mean it can suddenly explode?'

'No. I mean like my character. I see similarities between my personal character and the national character of Israel. We're both outlaws.'

The adrenalin kicked in as the blood rushed from the interviewer's face into my head.

'Please explain, Mr Marks.'

'Outlaws control as much of their destiny as they can and put up with the consequences of their actions without whingeing. That's very much my motto: work out what you want to do, do it, don't give a fuck what anyone else says, and take any shit on your chin. Keep a stiff upper lip, even under E.'

They liked that and took me to a club.

Tel Aviv is a unique city and provides the only point of agreement between ultra-Orthodox Jew and fundamentalist Muslim. They both hate the fucking place. That makes it cool. Accompanied by a bunch of skunk lovers, I squeezed into the appropriately named Lemon on HaNagarim Street, an industrial wasteland in south Tel Aviv. There were no bouncers. Asi Kohak was DJ. It was happy house in a happy house, despite the rather weird Boy Scout jamboree-type spectacle of guys dancing with machine guns dangling between their legs (losing one means seven years in an army nick). Draft is at eighteen, so combats and fatigues are swiftly supplemented by mobiles and Ray-Bans; Uzis are clutched like teddy bears on comedowns; and M16 rifles have become crucial fashion accessories. I asked the barman for an Irish whiskey mixed with an energy drink.

'Energy drinks are illegal in Israel. But I know you, Mr Nice. Drink this.'

I think it was just alcohol, but it was strong. I went out for some air, smoked some strong grass with some kids, and tottered with them down the coast to Old Jaffa. In one of the old streets was a giant statue of a fish.

'What the fuck is that?'

'That's where Jonah came out of the whale.'

'Whaw, man! That's amazing,' I gasped. 'That happened here. I always figured it was on some other planet. But it really did happen where I am now. I can't believe it.'

'Howard, that drink has got to you.'

We got back to the club by dawn. People were leaving in droves to an after-party at the massive Ha Oman club in Jerusalem. I was up for it, but I had to ride for an hour on the back of a motor scooter. We pulled up outside a car-park sign stating: 'Drive Carefully. The Pathologist Awaits.' Jewish belief is that we eventually see God in our physical form, and it certainly wouldn't do to have your liver on your face and your lungs hanging out when you do. Thinking about it slows you down and makes you park and puke.

The club was first class and at sunset I headed towards the Mount of Olives, believed to be the location of the coming of the Messiah on the day of the Resurrection. Heavy shit. (There's a hell of a waiting list to get buried here. Robert Maxwell managed it, despite failing the walk-on-water test.) I reached the top, pulled out a spliff, and walked down smoking. Within seconds I found myself audibly reciting 'Mary had a little Lamb', and pretending I was the Lamb of God. A large stone whistled past my ear. I ducked pointlessly and hit my head on a warlike olive branch. A shepherd jumped out and swore at me. Which side did he think I was on? What side was he on? I mustn't look scared. I'll be a wise man.

I woke up in a hospital on the outskirts of Jerusalem, where hundreds of otherwise normal people are admitted and treated for what is known as the Jerusalem Syndrome. These individuals are usually tourists, who when visiting the places that Jesus, Mohammed, Elijah, Moses and that lot hung out, suddenly lose their identities and adopt ones from the Bible. The most popular new identity is John the Baptist, who despite being executed, got to shag Salome. I'd been badly hit by that flying rock on the Mount of Olives and had, apparently, been dragged from the Garden of Gethsemane into this ward screaming, 'I want to be a hippie and I want to get stoned.' I was immediately diagnosed, without examination, as suffering from the belief that I was St Stephen, the first Christian martyr, the first guy to get stoned to death. On the bed to my left lay an Egyptian wearing a crown of thorns thinking he was Christ. On the bed to my right lay a white Jamaican, Christ-A-Fairy, also wearing a crown of thorns and also thinking he was Christ. He smoked spliffs through the holes in his hands and feet. Despite each sharing roughly the same diet (loaves and fishes), each being able to get drunk on water, and each preaching love and peace, they hated each other, disagreeing violently on matters such as dope, each other's identity and divinity. I was getting really bored until the Egyptian Christ, Cheese-Us, offered me an intriguing-looking substance, which I assumed to be psychoactive.

'Please try, good saint.'

'What is it, Cheese-Us?'

'Verily, it is known by many names, good saint: man-dragora, morion, nam-tar, abul'ruh, lakshmana, mandrake.'

Although I'd never tried it, I knew the mandrake plant to be a hypnotic, aphrodisiac and hallucinogenic. I'm not sure if it's legal, and I don't give a fuck, but mandrake really is hardcore. The berries look like bollocks and were actually called 'Satan's Testicles' by the Coptic Church, the early Christians in Egypt. Before being so demonised by both Christians and Muslims, mandrake was worshipped as the lord of the spirit and master of the breath of life. Pythagoras thought the root to be a tiny human being. The sponge held up to Christ on the cross was soaked in mandrake wine. The Germans, who call it *Hexenkraut*, believe that the plant springs up from the semen ejaculated by a man when hanged. Voodoo priests, it is said, use it to turn people into zombies.

'Cheese-Us, I don't mind falling asleep or seeing a few hallucinations, but what's the point of getting randy? There's not even any *Carry On* nurses here. They're all nuns.'

'No Woman No Try,' agreed Christ-A-Fairy.

'They're not nuns, they're penguins,' yelled a Coventry DJ who thought he was St Francis, the patron saint of birds.

'When you take mandrake, she will make love with you,' said Cheese-Us.

'I've never fucked a plant, Cheese-Us, and I'm not going to fuck one now.'

'Even if she's a goddess, good saint? Mandrake was the first plant god.'

'A goddess or a god, Cheese-Us?'

'Most British females are plants, are they not? Rose, Violet, Daisy, Lily, Hazel.'

'So is a Pansy.'

'But mandrake will adapt to your every need, Saint Stephen. The Germans, who call the mandrake berries "Dragon Dolls", think she alone used to make love to dragons.'

'Okay, Cheese-Us, let me have some.'

Give me to drink mandragora

William Shakespeare

Niall Griffiths
Sheepshagger

SUDDENLY THEY LEAVE the forest they have been driving through for some moments and are in a muddied clearing in the trees with cars and vans and bikes and one old painted double-decker bus like a lone pike in a shoal of minnows parked chaotically and the shapes of people drifting between the vehicles and through the trees blue-tinged by the climbing moon towards and then above and past a fire burning in an oil drum illuminating the words THIS WAY in dripping black letters on a car bonnet propped up against a young pine. There are many people, scores of them, scrambling over auto-mobiles and ducking under tree branches and piggybacking each other some running some walking all towards the fire and the sign. Attenuated figures drifting through the trees like sprites or phantoms.

—This must be it, aye.

—I reckon so.

Marc squeezes the car between a Mini and a birch tree and turns the engine off and the music dies and in the relative quiet they can hear the noise of the people, the babble and the laughter, and the dull thump of distant techno coming over the mountain and through the trees.

—One for the road, ey, lads.

Griff takes a bag of powder out of his jacket pocket and dabs in it with a finger and licks it and rubs it around and over his gums, then passes the bag over the back seat to Danny.

—Good Christ, Griff, how much is in here? Fuckin' sherbert dip, mun. Where's the lollipop, like?

—Three ounces. Off Roger. Make a lot of dosh up yer, I can see. So if any of yew need to buy any more later, like, then I'm yer man. Yer's plenty to keep us going. And notice I said 'buy'.

The bag is passed from man to man and dabbed at by each one. Ianto uses two crooked fingers to scoop almost a gram of the powder into his mouth, grimacing at the vile taste then palpating his cheeks to stimulate saliva and mixing it around in his mouth then swallowing the foul and acrid paste in one huge gulp, suppressing the gag reflex with one hand clamped across his lower face and frantic swallowing.

—Pill time as well. Do em in now an we'll be well up by-a time we get yer.

Marc passes small white pills around to each person excluding Ianto, who holds his hand out expectant. Marc stares down at the open waiting palm.

—What's all that about then, Ianto? What the fuck are yew after?

—An E.

—Oh aye. Paid for one, av yew?

Ianto doesn't reply.

—Iant, these cost fuckin money. I asked the other day didn't I. I said, if anyone wants a pill for TalyBont then put up-a cash an I'll get it sorted. Yew were there. Didn't I say that?

Nods and murmurs.

—Yew gave no money so yew get no pill. Simple as fuckin that, mun.

Ianto drops his hand and Danny slings an arm around his shoulder. —Ah don't get upset Ianto, mun. Yew'll be able to get a pill up yer, like, in-a rave. Yer'll be hundreds floating about. An anyway, you've still got some whizz left, ant yer?

Ianto nods.

—Well, there yew are then.

Ianto nods again and then finds that he cannot stop nodding or indeed blinking because he has in fact ingested a large amount of amphetamine throughout the afternoon as well as various blends of alcohol and that scoop of Griff's speed he has just eaten has brought it all up to critical mass and as they leave the car and move through the trees and other parked cars and past the fire in the barrel and the sign and up and over the hill via the muddy track towards the music, growing louder, and the mad flashing lights in the sky, growing brighter, Ianto's heart begins to rattle and shake like a rock in a tumble-dryer and his hands and face are all twitchy and his scalp crawls and there is a lovely toothy tension in his mouth and to burn some of this wire-tight energy off he wants to run. Look for any lassitude within him and it will not be found, not now, not ever; never among the flame and light crackling through him, battling through him, although he knows it not. He just wants to run, and indeed he does run, roaring, reedy arms above his head towards the growing music and the brightening multi-coloured lights.

—G'wahn, Ianto!

—Get the fuckers, boy!

—Go for it, mun!

He runs up and over the hill splashing through mud ruts and past and through walking groups of people who look at him bemused or yell encouragement and he crests the hill and there below him in a natural bowl between an encircling rim of high hills is the main body of the rave with people swarming insectile and hive-like around tents and fires, strobes shredding the scene and the music rocking the thick-trunked old trees and the moon and the stars above it all and the ramshackle mansion up on the valley rise bursting blue then red from its windows, dancing silhouettes moving behind the glass, and from each of the throbbing marquees the beats of different musics merge and mix into one single

187

mad euphony and it is like a world separate yet within, host to another race different yet in some ways assimilated, gathered here via a wide network of recondite signals and codes comprehensible to its members alone to come and celebrate as they do their willed apartness secret and discrete. Like an alien species of nomenclature unknown among the world hiving then swarming to prove in a display of their twinned two navels that most others have only one. That their origins differ, that their conceptions oppose.

Ianto moves downslope towards the largest fire, across whose thrashing flames black shadows of humans and dogs leap and tumble. Groups stand in silhouette drinking from cans and bottles and passing around long spliffs, whose gleaming ends flit from face to face like luminous winged insects that feed on human spit. Glo-sticks dart and drift like angler fish and a member of the Eternal Om sits in the mud with his back against a tree dealing wraps from the deep pockets of his Diesel anorak. A long-bearded man in a top hat and sporting a silver-topped cane treads his foppish proud-backed way through a fallen galaxy of empty beer cans. A small skinny man hunched over in a green baseball cap and square green shades executes some sort of intent chopping dance with the blunt blades of his hands as he orbits a group of four squatting on the wet grass around an elaborate bong. Ianto waves to and grins at those who greet him, slapping backs and squeezing arms, and jerks into the large barn out of which the best music pulses and in here steam rises from the clustered dancing bodies up towards the high rafters, upon which their figures dance too, feet firmly planted on the thin beams, rhythmically swaying their arms and torsos and heads, and one girl hangs upside down with her knees hooked over the rafter pumping her arms madly, her long hair falling in a curtain groundwards, her T-shirt slipped down to reveal the pronounced and stretched muscles of her stomach and her breasts spilling out of the tight white lace of her bra. Some in here remain wallbound drinking or smoking and watching and some dance with a wide-eyed determined drive towards exhaustion and some dance atop others' shoulders and one walks on his hands and others merely stand resting or observe. Bright clothes abound like aposematic coloration, warning potential predators of poison, peril. The DJ is a hunched dark featureless shape in an elevated grotto of yellow light at the far end of the barn, hurling out these deep and fervent sounds which throb in the earth and pulse in the walls of this old stone structure, which sway these massed people now this way now that, now slowing them down to an almost stately pace then instantly smashing them together and up again with beats born in bloodrun and breathing, in the exaggerated pumping of sexuality and the stamp of danced sacrifice or entreaty enacted on the cones of the surrounding volcanoes when they still smouldered, or on the skyscraping crests and flanks of the encircling mountains when parts of them were still soft to the attentions of wind and of rain like faces creased by the wailing and weeping of the planet, or on the bog-soft banks of the lakes and rivers beseeching harvest and bounty in the only way they knew how and which worked, sometimes.

Ianto feels arms around his neck and turns to face Gwenno grinning up at him and moving her hips with the lights miniatured in her dark large eyes and bouncing back off her teeth and the bolt through her eyebrow and his heart accelerates still further. She yells something in his ear and he feels her breath warm and smells it minty with a faint metallic underwhiff of MDMA, and he can't make out her words so he leans closer and she yells it again but all he can make out is the one word 'fine' which is enough and he encircles her naked waist with his hands and she dances away again, punching the air with her arms above her head and her long hair bouncing, and he sees the span of her belly smooth and honey-hued between the cropped top and the belt of her faded jeans hanging low on her prominent hips, the wide legs almost entirely covering apart from the toes her mud-splattered black and white trainers. Ianto tries to move towards her, a need in him both to stoke and feed from her gorgeous delirium but she is lost in the crowd and he sees the upturned face of Margaret Jones between shoulders, lost in pleasure and surprise as she watches a small sparrow-sized bird flit into the barn through one entrance and whir through the lights and the steam above the rippling close-packed heads of the dancers and out through another entrance into the darkness again. Imagines that, that small slice of light and noisy activity between the two immensities of blackness.

Ianto is lost, spinning. A roaring ponytailed Irishman steams by with a small dark bottle of amyl pressed to his nostril, his shouting face bright red. A small blonde girl with a Welsh dragon flag draped across her back floats on by someone's shoulders, drifting above the swarming heads like a strange fakir proving the falseness of our corporeal claims. The speed in Ianto is rampant, jackhammering his heart and bulging the veins at his neck and temples and he dances madly, twitching like some young bird attempting take-off or a puppet in the hands of a mad master, bent slightly forwards at the waist with his arms hacking the clogged air and his teeth like his fists clenched, the very image of one swiftly sluicing the rage resultant from some terminal acceptance. He sees nothing but lights and shapes and he smells nothing but fresh sweat and ganja smoke and the sweetness of trampled grass and all his muscles are alive beneath the giant organ of his skin, atingle, grasped in the ecstasy of the moment and only that, the eternal present with its tremendous release and relief and the expression of the enraptured realisation which can demand or even indeed be satiated by not one other method.

This is all Ianto requires, here, this is all he could need, just this perennial thumping second, the movement gravewards halted, and the sweat and the booming and all the motion outside his spinning sphere and if Ianto could stretch and reach and rip the moon from its moorings then he assuredly would. He dances like some laggard seeking to supercede the world's fury, its insanity, he dances as if in fevered denial of those times he has danced alone in the cold and the darkness with no music playing, as if to disprove how difficult it is to do that. He dances among these reaching bodies in the polish and refinement of that first primal prowl and pounce, more than football, more than war. A bodily victory speech, frantic and static lap of honour circumscribing only the body's orbit. Simple praise of itself.

He dances until thirst overtakes him and he cannot swallow, his spit is wool, so he ceases his movement suddenly no winding down just split-second cessation, one second a blur the next a person and leaves the barn in search of fluid. Parked outside the building is a small car with its hatchback up like a spread carapace revealing slabs of canned beers and soft drinks. Ianto buys a can of Challenge lager for £1.50 and shakes his head in answer to the man who asks him if he needs anything else and drinks half the lager in one warm gulp and takes it to sit under a dripping tree at the side of the path rapidly becoming a quagmire, then moves as he catches a whiff of the Portaloos nearby and finds a place beneath the low branches of another tree at the bottom of the bottom field, the hills rising above. He leans back against the ridged bark among the moths falling silently like petals, like snow, to escape the sonic seeking of the hungry bats above the trees and stands sipping at the lager, feeling the moisture dry on his face, his clothes hanging in heavy wet folds from his thin frame, his prominent bones. He smokes a cigarette and watches balloons trail their strings like tadpoles or spermatozoa across the moon's pale face, feels the music throb in the soft earth beneath his feet, through the worn soles of his trainers. People are having sex somewhere in the bushes behind him; the almost-pained groans of the woman sound to him like the cries of a sea-bird unseen and heard across the estuarial sand flats at night-time, almost yearning, beseeching. Were he able to he would tumesce at these sounds alone, but the amphetamine has temporarily robbed his penis of all resilience and all blood and he knows from past experience the futility of kneading and palpation resulting only in a sore wrist and skin rubbed raw, although the desire is there heightened irrepressibly to grab flesh and thrust and slide, exacerbated by the sulphate, which sensuous accentuation of a need containing within it the frustration and hindrance to the satisfaction of that same need can be instanced as some summation of the war which burns in Ianto's skull and chest whenever consciousness itself returns to him with each new day, be it in cottage or squat or cave or copse or hovel. He is tempted to squirm his hand into his jeans and pull and tug at his prick anyway because of the way it simply tingles, but he doesn't. Then he does; he slides his hand between denim and flesh and with the fingertips of his first two fingers tweaks the end of his knob, feels it small and sulphate-shrivelled and lacking in all incipience of growth or expansion and he runs his thumbtip over the rough ridge of scar tissue and he caresses that almost tenderly then withdraws his hand and sniffs at his fingers and with that hand takes the wrap of amphetamine from the inner pocket of his jacket and dabs at it twice then tips the remainder into his lager, swishing the can around to assist dissolution and then takes rapid pecking sips at it like a bird at seed. He smokes another damp cigarette, his jaw working now like some piston-powered machine, and he notices that the pleasured sounds in the bushes behind him have ceased and there is rustling and then a boy emerges his top half swallowed in a big baggy fleece, leading, by the hand, a long-haired girl crop-topped and hipstered and Ianto catches the light reflected off her teeth as she smiles and the metal in her eyebrow and he also gets a glimpse of snub nose as she walks just-fucked, holding hands with the boy, up and into the vast mad body proper of the rave and was it Gwenno? Was it her? Ianto thinks with a lurch that it might have been Gwenno, Gwenno he heard groaning in the bushes only a few feet behind his back. Gwenno not a body's length behind him surrendering to some stranger thrusting, insistent and she smiling. Eyes closed and lips parted.

He drains the can and tosses it away, then strides up the softly sloping wet meadow, attempting to trace the route of the maybe-Gwenno and her partner. Danny dashes out of the crowd to embrace him and slap his back and bellow something in his ear and Ianto responds distracted and perfunctory then ducks into the nearest marquee, where he is instantly assaulted by the deafening drum and bass, the body-shocking jerks of the irregular spiralling drum and the whining sliding movement of the bass, so deep and loud as to vibrate in the spongy soles of his soaked shoes and rattle the bones of his ankles. It is dark in this tent, very dark; gangling shapes vault and gibber through what weak light there is and looming still figures clustered around the sturdy central pole pass around small pipes which they entirely envelop with their hands as they suck at them. Quick glimpses of heavy jewellery and sweat gleaming on bared skin. Ianto stands and stares for a minute or two, but there is nothing for his eye to lock on to; each focal point seems to burst and re-gather in a manner unacquainted with each sudden shift in the tempo of the music and no two tableaux the same or even akin excepting the main players involved, the only constant is extreme transformation second by second by second, in an eyeblink a leaping overcoated figure has moved to the back of the marquee twenty yards away, where the overcoat becomes a bomber jacket and a large woolly hat is donned and then there is a woman in the time it takes to blink an eye, which Ianto is doing very very rapidly now, several times per second in fact, as he buckles under yet another powerful sulphate rush and the immediate world is coming at him in shredded tendrils sundered and unconnected, so he leaves that tent in one fluid movement turn and dash and trips over a guyrope and falls headlong in the mud. Lying there still and face-down and blaming the planet, the way it spins for ever. How he can never feel its whirl. Quickly there are hands in his armpits lifting him upright.

—You all right, man?

A friendly black face looks concerned into his. Ianto nods and spits mud.

—Fuckin lethal them things are, aren't they? Went flying over one meself earlier. Should paint em white or tie ribbons on em or something so we can see. Sure yer all right now, yeh?

—Yeh.

—Good.

He pats Ianto's back and disappears into the drum and bass tent and Ianto rubs the mud off his hands on to his jeans and uses the hem of his shirt to wipe his face clean and crunches grit between his teeth and will not feel embarrassed. A passing man in a woolly hat sees Ianto spit and offers him a bottle of Volvic, which Ianto takes and drinks gratefully and greedily, then returns it and wipes his lips with the back of his hand which comes away dark-striped and he moves towards a squat stone outhouse-type building across the field outside which very young people, say mid-teens, are gathered looking almost terrified, white-skinned and stalk-eyed like the damned. Ianto moves through them stopping once to stare unabashed at a very young girl whose white and growing breasts are spilling out of the top of a pale blue Wonderbra and she thrusts these out at him, insulted and defiant hands on her hips, and Ianto grins loose-lipped at her and opens his mouth to say something, but is then bundled by a bouncing crowd of school-age people into the gabba and is in half a second battered and left jellylike by the insane thrashing ear-raping noise and the epileptic lights and the MC screaming in the voice of a demon. Ianto shakes his head and roars and plunges gleefully into this collective fit, sweat looping through the lights and the heat instantly resoaking his clothing and he has forgotten the maybe-Gwenno or remembers her only half-lit and vague and stumbled as he would perhaps a dream, but the hot fist still remains clenched in his breast goading him to leap and seethe along within this crazed demented noise and tempest, the people moving like smithereens each one random and uncontrolled and haphazard with no real purpose pre-mapped or pre-empted, none apart from the brief but vital destruction of all that lies beyond the encircling ring of lakes and mountains in the quiet houses under the falling drizzle and yellow sodium of the street lights. That's all. Some of these people here, sixteen maybe seventeen, sat down in this but hours ago as the amps and decks were being brought in and banged up on skag or temazepam or methadone or any other brain-hammering opiate derivative and they will remain here through the same unchanging hysterical shrieking frenzy without rest or respite until the dancers drift damaged and ghost-like away and the music winds down twenty, twenty-four hours ahead in the formless future. They sit there now nodding at the edges of the dance floor slick with liquid spilled, secreted, their backs propped up against the sweating stone walls, moving only to lean to the side and spew or slowly to lift their heavy slack unsteady heads and grin.

Ianto moves madly, bouncing and spinning and kicking and pumping his arms, injecting the chaos of this furnace place with the hot blast of his own fury, and he does this and does this and does this over and only ceases when the urge to piss is so great that his belly hurts and his thighs are damp with impatient pee and the need to drink scorches his throat. He can see blue morning sky through the open door of the hut. He leaves and stands there rocking in the daylight with the muscles in his legs screaming and his ears throbbing and a cliff-face of slag about to shift and slide in his humming head. The speed wars with the exhaustion within his body, the need to lie down, rest and sleep punched dumb by the amphetamine. He walks unsteady up the mud-swamp track to the Portaloos, one of which is engaged and the other of which is sizzling over with shit stinking so he pisses up against the side of it, groaning in relief, his knees trembling as his cloudy yellow urine meanders through the grass to join the wider and deeper tributary of the track.

—Aw Jesus. You dirty bastard.

A man has left the previously engaged toilet and is standing there in disapproval watching Ianto piss.

—Fucking disgusting that. Could you not have just waited? I was only a couple of minutes, man. Christ, have you no control? There're kiddies gonner be playing around here in a minute. God, have some respect for others, ey? Least you could've done is gone in the woods, like, if you were really desperate. Full view of everybody.

Ianto bites his lower lip and shakes off and shoves his dick back into his soaking jeans and walks over to the man, three strides, and punches him full in the face.

He feels the connection in his shoulder and neck and the impact explodes in his bunched knuckles and the man falls back flat in the running midden of mud and piss, his nose a flattened burst of rapidly spreading redness and his eyes rolled back, showing nothing but slightly yellowed whites fine-laced with bloodshot veins. Ianto pulls his foot back to kick and probably kick again, but there are faces watching him from inside a parked car so he simply steps over the man as he would any other small obstacle and follows the track down and around to the bottom of the site by the small birdless pond, where a low khaki tent emanates soft music tinkling like rain off forest leaves and a wooden crate by the entrance has been painted with the white words: CHILL OUT/FOOD/ FIRST AID. This is what Ianto needs.

And they have him, these days, these moments of misrule; possessed of them he is quick and entire in his thin, zinging skin, alive, real, on the planet. In them and of them he stirs on this earth, connected to others and himself also in a peril formed from his own forcing, spun from his zinging skin. Better this mess of a life than a life so pointless. Better this botch of a life than one so drab.

Sheepshagger, 2000

Charlie Hall
The Box

I COULD HAVE said some kind words before I went to sleep, but my travel anxiety was already bubbling and the coke kept me awake, so I smoked a spliff. As I got back into bed, she curved herself into me and it made me feel like I was made of crystal and I was afraid I'd shatter. Jesus, I'd only got back from the Complex buzzing a few hours before. I'd spliffed up with the boys and they'd gone and I was left with her, so I went to bed and lay listening to her wondering if she was awake, the tension throbbing in the air, words on my lips. I could have just said something. Her hot legs on mine, I was so jittery I wanted to punch her but the spliff calmed me down. I managed a half-hearted cuddle which made the words want to come out more. Just as I was drifting off, the alarm went.

We're all gazing up at the screens like obedient schoolkids. The flight number comes up and we race off with our trolleys. Like I've any confidence my boxes will come bursting joyously first in line on to the carousel! On the other side of the rubber curtains, I can hear the handlers chatting to each other as they sling the bags on to the belt like so many corpses. Here they come: battered suitcases; chirpy rucksacks; sleek executive walk-in wardrobes.

Just about everyone lunges forward at the luggage and then hesitates. 'No, wait a minute. In this light I'm not sure. I thought mine was bluer?' They glance around, harassed. The dilemma, 'If anyone grabs it then it's theirs, but if it's mine and I hesitate then it'll go back through the rubber curtains and the handlers will have carte blanche to tear it open, squirt toothpaste all over my underwear, nick my . . . Oh fuck it, it's mine, it's mine . . .'

I tough it out, trying to look unconcerned, just wanting a fag. If this was Italy we'd all be puffing away, leaning up on the 'No Smoking' sign, which is always situated by an overflowing ashtray. But this is Sweden where you get nicked for smoking in the street.

I hardly know her. Usual story – arrived at the club that night whenever it was (last week? last month?) and I saw her again. We'd sort of been on each other's case here and there. You know, a bit of back-room flirting in the Ministry; skinning up together as I waited for David Holmes to finish his set at Final Frontier; plenty of laughs out in the garden at the old Full Circle. We'd had our eye on each other, both thinking maybe we knew each other too well. I used to get home from a night out, lie in bed and she'd come to mind. I'd still be awake with the drugs slowly draining through my system, tweaking the last synapses and I'd want to call her. But I wanted to be good, didn't want to make it all just a wank. I wanted to be fair.

I had been on a roll the night we finally got together. High summer and for once London was kicking. You'd come out of a club and there'd be people standing about in the street messing around. The atmosphere was stupendous and everyone was there. Good times to be a DJ.

I had DJ bookings stretching through till October and I was as high as a fucking kite. That night I was playing for a mate in a sweaty gaff in the basement of a kebab shop on the

Edgware Road. The vibe was perfect: underground and mellow. The boys on the gate were super-chilled and you could puff if it was done discreetly.

I had a few beers and socialised a bit, trying to stay straight-headed. If I tuck into too much skunk or bugle before I get on the decks all sorts of chaos is likely to follow. It's a question of getting locked into the groove. The ideal night is one where the first mix goes right. There's a surge from the crowd as they sense new energy on the decks and you go with it. After that, you can stuff yourself with what you like – even done it tripping a few times, which is quite a challenge. I've heard a couple of DJs who brag that they play best on a trip. So do I, but it's a social one, tense with the anticipation, keeping an eye on my watch.

It was one of those nights you dream about, when everything falls into place. All the right records were at my fingertips as soon as I dug in the box. Then, halfway through my set, I saw her best mate giving it some shimmy. So she was bound to be here! My senses tightened and I concentrated on the set. The records kept on coming, the heat was building, the vinyl grew hazy with condensation as soon as it came out of the sleeve.

The heat was outrageous. I was throwing beers back. We had to cane all the charlie before it sweated up. People were starting to lose it, but they kept right on dancing. We were all locked in together, a rare and utterly fucking wondrous moment: pure ecstasy. More coke, more beer, more T-shirts pulled off, more skunk in the air, and when it seemed like there wasn't any further to go, the buzz just kept building, bodies sliding against each other to the music. It was so hot, so scary, everyone was laughing in amazement. They were shrieking, hollering and whistling when it seemed like there just wasn't any more air to even draw breath.

I play house. When I first heard it, I was into reggae and funk and a mate came back from America with a bag of tunes. We had already developed a boys' club – trainspotting Fred Wesley, Maceo, the deep dirty funk from America's East Coast and the crazy Latin boogie from Los Angeles.

Washington threw out mad go-go beats that had us all sweating our arses off, speeding things up. Then came dark, marijuana nights down in Melon Road, Peckham, with Jah Shaka giving us pumping acid dub. We'd stay out until the break of dawn, dancing all night, fuelled only by ganja and Red Stripe.

That was then. And with the help of a few little pills and a bit of understanding, THIS is now.

I play house. I keep it fat and I keep it funky. I want to convey that happy sexy vibe I got through funk, as well as the moody weird shit and the trippy frequencies of dub – like when you realise that you've been dancing for two or three hours just to a rhythm. I want people to feel what I feel. I want them to feel the simple joy of dancing, the release of losing the plot in a little room with a couple of hundred other people who want to do the same. Shit, I love dancing!

Then she was there and we hugged each other, bursting with a simple feeling of happiness and we held each other tight. I could feel her body pressing against mine in the heat. With sweat streaming down my face, I kissed her mouth and she kissed me back and at that moment I was the fucking king of everything and this was RIGHT.

We stayed up until Tuesday: hanging out in Full Circle, then round someone's house, then off to Strutt, then off to someone else's gaff. We were full of each other, in fucking LOVE, mate, buzzing, drugged-up with Es, spliff, charlie and more charlie . . .

Got me thinking about that coke. I should get rid of it before I hit customs. They might have a dog, like in Naples. I'm sure that dog isn't a drug dog, it snarls and lunges at everyone. You can see the handler making stupid secret noises and twitching the fucker's leash so he goes for me (it's the BOX). I was clean. They gave up when I was down to my Calvin's. So what to do? Go and do it now and risk my boxes getting raped by the handlers when they go back through the rubber curtains unclaimed . . .? Or wait and squeeze into that toilet over there with all my boxes and trolley . . .?

WHAM!!! Ah, that'll be my boxes, last as usual. There're

couple of nice Swedish girls watching me now, a bit of the old DJ mystique. They look furtive and almost interested but I can see they're not ravers, they're just curious in an anthropological way. My first box, a big steel fucker, has KO'd one of those sad anonymous blue Samsonite copies and scarred the corner and there's a sort of fluid seeping out on to the rubber. My boxes are hardly scratched (I'm always amazed they let these through with regular luggage, it's senseless violence!). The bag's owner, herself a bit of a dented old bag, looks at me with a beaten look on her face like she's used to it and my victory is diminished sizeably.

The toilet's great – typical Scandi hygiene. Loads of shiny, gleaming, sweet-smelling surfaces. Perfect. I'm scooping the gear out and as my eyes sweep the interior of the cubicle I notice a little flash of colour right down behind the toilet bowl.

Curiosity drives me and I bend down. I pick up a wrap and it's FULL. The powder twinkles, maybe a little too much, but it's got that right crystalline tweak to it, the overhead lighting glancing off it in wide beams. I take a dab. 'OOH! It's bitter-as-fuck. Yoinks!'

I start off with the rest of my gear, which perks me up and then I cut out a gleaming sexy curve of the new stuff. A quick double-check. It's not ketamin, smack or speed, and it's free. Greedy old me. 'If she wasn't sure it was me on the phone, then who did she think it was?' I think. A sharp lancing snap of suspicion in my belly and then gone.

The light outside has improved when I step out of the cubicle. It has a kind of twinkling property that I hadn't noticed before. It's a little bit stuffy but that's bound to be partly down to the drugs. It's weird, the muzak and people's voices blend and then jar slightly.

I look down to check my bags. All present and correct and they look fucking ace: gleaming steel boxes, tools of me trade, mate. I'm the Lone fucking Ranger, blown into your town so strap yourselves down 'cos I'm-a-comin' in! I'm the hired gun with his pistols packin' blazin' *HOUSE MUSIK!* Come one, let's have you!! I'm itching to play. I square my shoulders and stride on. Fuck me, this gear's the business.

The victim's wobbling ahead of me, the liquid still oozing out of her bag. It dribbles on to the (fantastically shiny, sort of like when you look at a deep pond and you can see the surface, but you can see the dark depths as well) brown linoleum floor. It looks like a beautiful glittering cord. Her feet splatter through it. We're going through customs. I'm cool and totally clean and buzzing like a bee. Just then the old woman notices the brook of gunk and starts squawking. I swerve round her, expert in my trolley-handling, but the incident has been enough to get some unformed twit out of his office. First thing he sees are my boxes.

'Pssst!' goes the official and nods in the direction of the counter. I follow him. His trousers are neat and pressed and halfway up the crack of his arse. His hair is cut neat, halfway up his red neck.

'Passport!' He holds out his hand. He looks at my passport photo and back at me, like I'm a wanted criminal, narrowing his eyes. He's either on a highly sophisticated wind-up or he's so fucking dumb he doesn't think I've seen all this before. Off comes the immaculate cap and he puts it on the steel counter and gently smoothes his pink hand over his blond hair.

'And what is your purpose for coming to Sweden, Mr . . . S . . . m . . . ithhh?' He fixes me with another of those killer looks. Well, now, with those record boxes, I wonder what I could possibly be doing, for fucksake?

'I'm over here to DJ . . . Mr . . .' I say and peer at his name tag, but the letters seem to be dancing around. 'Yeh . . . Mr.'

'Your bag?'

'Yes, they all are, mate.' I reply. I'm not going to pass it straight over to him. He's going all the way so I may as well go with him to see how long it is before he gets fucked off with it. He looks up sharply, now he knows it's 'Game On'.

'Your bags, please. Up here!' He slaps the counter. I move faster than I've ever moved before and in one gorgeous fluid movement I twist round in a kind of t'ai chi (crane gets angry at monkey picking nuts from tree) move and my heaviest box smashes with a crash on to the counter. A crash that's only partly softened by his cap taking the first hit. He's so gobsmacked at the speed of my move, he hasn't even noticed the cap.

'Open please.' I twist the box round, grinding his cap and smiling. 'There! My records! Help yourself!' He's a bit confused. There're almost two hundred tunes there. Is he going to go the whole hog? Go on, I dare you! I think. If he does he has won, because he doesn't actually have to put them back. This is one chance to wind me up.

I got into this business through house music, which is all about understanding and togetherness. OK, so we all took drugs too and people have got fucked up, but on any journey there're casualties. The upside of the house movement was amazing, but now commercial interests have elbowed their way in: big-time drug lords, crap clubs, stupid records. More people go to clubs now and with the growing market the quality of drugs is lowered, so more people get sick and the witch-hunt begins. And who is it who gets it in the neck? The most visible members of the movement: those of us marked out by our metal boxes. It's like we're the drug dealers.

If I was going to be smuggling drugs I'd scarcely be doing it with a couple of record boxes. I bet that old lady had half a kee of coke in her doffed-up suitcase. It's a battle that I'm used to. It's like the border guards used to be like when you were travelling abroad for the football. One false move and you'd be straight back home, so you had to bite your lip while they treated you like vermin.

He puts his fingers on the records, where to start? I'm just looking at him in a totally unthreatening manner, which will make it worse for him. He's hesitating. I can feel his mind clicking away. Shit, I can feel it, it's a kind of rapid tremble like a small dog shakes when it wants to do something but is held back. He looks up at me, his eyes have still got some fight in them.

'Come on, mate!' So he goes to my holdall, rips it open, throws all my clothes around in a frenzy, thrusts and pokes his thick, clean fingers in corners, but he's moving slowly and missing loads. He goes back to the box and scoops about thirty records out. I notice the beads of sweat on his head. He looks through those records, quite thoroughly, bless him.

He takes my ticket and passport and goes into a back room. Oooh, he's shaken me up a bit. I suck in some air right down into my lungs, charging through bronchial tubes, swelling those little aureoles down there, squeezing the oxygen into my bloodstream, powering me up. I let the air hiss back through my teeth. I mustn't grind them. Jesus, they're clenched so tight . . .

Then he comes out again. 'Put your bags back on the trolley.' I'm free! Then his clean young face crumples up when he sees the ruined cap. He points! In the back of the net!

'Follow me!' The Search Scenario. Here we go, Round Two.

'Can I have your clothes?'

So I strip off in a flash. I feel like my body's in perfect nick, honed down by careful years of drug use and the good life. I flex my muscles gently and stare into his face, still with that nutter's friendly look.

'I see you are used to this,' he sneers.

'It's the Box isn't it? That's why you're doing this,' I say.

'Ah, you know it is my job. You know what I'm looking for.' He's on his trip now, the justification (you're sick with your acid house and children dying in the clubs).

He gives up. I've kept my cool and I'm clean, although a urine test might tell another story. I pick my passport and ticket up and fuck off to the bar on the other side of customs. The ice-cold lager tastes so fucking sweet I feel like eating the glass, so I order four more and tip them down my throat. As the last one goes down I catch a glimpse of myself in the bar mirror. My face is streaked with sweat, there's beer foam round my chops and my eyes are bulging out on bleedin' stalks. What was in that wrap I found? I guess it must have been PCP.

But Sweden made me feel kind of cheap. The punters have to pay over the odds to get me in their club – wouldn't they be just as happy with one of their homegrown DJs? Isn't this all part of the cheapening of the scene? It makes me yearn for the simple underground. I just want to play house.

From: *Disco Biscuits*, ed. Sarah Champion, 1997

He did not see any reason why the devil should have all the good tunes

Rowland Hill

Howard Marks
My First Ecstasy

I WENT TO the Reading Festival. The Super Furry Animals had promised me I could drive their tank, which had been converted to a giant technoblaster with a gun barrel modified to fire sliced bread into famine stricken pockets of the festival crowd.

'Creation Records won't let you drive the tank, Howard. They won't let any of us drive it,' said Daf, the Furries' drummer.

'Why the fuck not?'

'Something about it not being insured, I think. Anyway, we're thinking of getting a Spitfire once Creation get shot of our tank.'

'Why are they getting rid of it?' I asked.

'Economics, I expect, Howard. You know what these record companies are like. Nobody we know can actually drive it, it's too big for most roads, a transporter has to carry it with a special police escort, parking fees are bad, and we never charge for anyone to listen to it.'

'So this is our last chance to drive it.'

Someone interrupted.

'Howard, have you taken Ecstasy yet?'

It was a guy I'd met some weeks earlier at the Bar Lorca in Stoke Newington. We'd got drunk and stoned for most of one night, and I'd talked about how I'd been busted in the eighties, had just got out of nick, and had missed the whole rave culture: the music and the psychoactives.

'No, I haven't. I'm still funny about pills. I have to be sure what I'm taking. I can do that with weed and hash, but not with pills.'

'What if I guaranteed you with my honour that this tab is pure unadulterated Ecstasy.'

I looked into his eyes. I trusted him totally.

Half an hour later, I was gazing at the tank. Its name was Think. DJs were inside its body, letting loose tidal waves of hammering, honking and hoofing techno. Frenetic, serious and beautiful humans were dancing on its roof and all around. The tank pulsed to the lowest bpm, focused, and began heavily bonding with me. Think had had a pretty shite life lumbering through Northern Ireland, the Falklands and Bosnia. Think must have witnessed immeasurable misery, death and sadness. Think had been stuck in trenches, overturned in bloody mud, covered in muddy blood, shot at, given headaches by hand grenades, impounded and busted. Now God had given it a heart transplant. Gone were the arteries of artillery. This was a different kind of smoke that filled its lungs. Joy boom boom boom-boom-boomed from its veins. Sex danced on its head.

'We're on,' said Daf. 'Come with us, Howard. You can stand at the back of the stage. The view's great.'

'Can I bring the tank?'

Eighty thousand people heaved and swayed while I hid in the shadows of speakers and scaffolds and while my Nepalese joint and ego simultaneously exploded.

'Now I'd like to introduce Howard Marks,' announced Gruff, the lead vocalist.

'He's going to sing his favourite Beatles song.'

The fuckers! They warned me about this. I was cornered. I could slope off, lose my street cred, and be for ever mocked and reviled in the valleys of my homeland. Or I could walk to the front of the stage and sing a Beatles song with roughly the same result. A few refrains fought each other in my mind, but

I couldn't remember how they started. Then I lost the concept of language. The tank was winking at me from the distance. I tried to grab some pre-Ecstasy reality and started counting: one, two, three, four . . . that was it. Nine. Number nine. The Beatles once wrote a song whose only lyrics were 'Number nine, number nine, number nine . . .' I'll sing that one. I grabbed the microphone, screamed 'Number nine' nine times, ambled down from the stage, and went off to the Notting Hill Carnival.

Jason Parkinson
Skateboards and Methadone – No one should be asked to handle this trip

IT WAS LATE spring, maybe early June. Night-time. It had just stopped raining. Varnish and myself were out on the orange-black wet Derby streets. We were by the hospital on Osmaston Road, looking down Keble Close that ran down the side of the hospital. There were wet, glistening cars on both sides of the road, all the way down to a dead end, a high kerb and fences with just a small alleyway to get through.

'It's a tight gap,' I said, 'but I think we can get through. Gotta mind that kerb though.'

'I don't know,' replied Varnish, 'it looks like a big kerb, and at that speed. I don't know, besides I'm not completely with it.'

Several hours earlier back at the flat we were on the nightly shift when, just before closing time, we had a late caller. I'd served her before, brought up by a good friend. The woman was probably early thirties, once good-looking, not just a worn-out shell, eaten away by heroin and a rough life. She had bleach-damaged shoulder-length hair and a cropped black leather jacket.

'I need some hash but I haven't got much money,' she told us.

I saw Varnish's face of money joy drop. He got up, sat on the couch and loaded a bong.

'Are you asking for a lay-on?' I asked, not sure what she was expecting me to say. There was no way she'd get a lay-on, she wasn't regular enough and we didn't know where she lived.

'Oh, good God no, I have these.' She pulled out a pack of ten pills. From the packaging it looked pharmaceutical.

'What are they?' Varnish jumped in, his eyes lighting up at the sight of class-A drugs.

'It's methadone,' she replied, 'ten of them. You see, it's my script but I'd rather have ten quid's worth of hash, it does a better job keeping me away from the smack, and doesn't mong me out as much.'

I turned to Varnish, 'What do you think?' After all, it was his money behind it all.

'I say go for it.' Varnish never took his eyes off the small silver packet of pills.

'Looks like you got yourself a deal,' I said. 'Ten quid's worth?'

'Yeah, if that's okay with you.'

'Believe me, it's fine with us,' I said. 'We got something to do tonight, now. Fancy a trip out on the skateboards, Varnish?'

Varnish replied but the words were lost trying to hold down the vast amount of hash he'd just inhaled through a glass bong.

I cut the hash up for the woman. As she left she warned us not to take more than four each. '. . . You'll end up puking your guts up.' With that, she left; she said she had something waiting.

We sat and ate five methadone pills each and sat smoking for a while, listening to Ween blasting out of top-range speakers with no regard for the neighbours whatsoever. *Pure Guava*, a damn fine album. Nothing happened after an hour so we cracked open a few beers; besides, it had started raining, so we figured the skateboard trip was out the question. I had gotten into skateboards and narcotics back in '91, spending most Saturday nights high on LSD skating the deserted streets of Derby, always ending up in the haunts of Markeaton Park around dawn.

No, there was nothing for it; we'd just have to sit it out in the time capsule, a ten-by-eight-foot room with a sloping roof and no windows. The floors were covered in hairy rugs, empty beer cans and bottles, and overloaded ashtrays. Varnish had two of his paintings on the non-sloping wall. One look at those and you knew he was a drug fiend. They were good too. One thing that I never understood about Varnish, he was a damn good artist, a little mutated by his intake of narcotics, but good all the same. Yet he never really used his talents to do anything, as far as I know. The last I heard he was a nightwatch security guard, on the gates of some factory or industrial estate.

But I'm being sidetracked here; I should be talking about the time-capsule room. The bottom end of the room was completely filled with Varnish's stereo equipment, laid out on a long flat coffee table. Unknown to Varnish at this point in his life was how wrecked everything in this room would get over such a short space of time. So wrecked that he would end up retreating all his belongings to the safety of his bedroom. I'd already managed to set fire to his sofa with a Zippo lighter while loading a bong. Thinking I'd snapped the lid on the Zippo lighter shut, I laid it on the sofa next to me. There it burned for several minutes until I noticed the flames lapping my leg. After that, a fat speed freak sat back on the sofa, breaking the back supports. The sofa moved to lean against the wall.

I was vegged out on the floor. At some point the methadone had kicked in real heavy, fuelled along with the beers we'd sunk earlier.

'Hey, it's stopped raining,' I said.

'I feel sick.'

'Don't worry about it, everyone gets that, it'll pass.'

'Is that normal then, to feel sick like that?'

'Well, sometimes, I guess, yeah.'

'Oh, that's fucked, that is, who would want that? Pay for a drug and it makes you sick. It's wrong, there should be a goddamn law against it.'

'Just calm down, you'll be okay in a minute, everyone gets it.'

This was the first time Varnish had taken methadone; I had failed to mention how dirty it makes you feel, or the waves of nausea that hit you. I got the feeling Varnish wasn't handling his first hit of it too well.

'Listen, it's stopped raining,' I said. 'Let's go out on the skateboards, the streets will be empty this time of night, easy skating.'

'Will it stop me feeling ill?'

'It might work, worth a try I guess.'

'Okay, let's go.'

It was late, I had no idea how long we had been stood on the top of the hill, in the middle of the road, arguing about board speeds and wet roads and what could possibly happen to you if you came off at that speed.

'I still don't know. How fast will we be when we hit the bottom?' Varnish was still uncertain about the downhill skate.

'Hell, I don't know. Look, when you get close to that kerb kick the back of your board and you'll go over the kerb.' The impatience in my voice was very apparent, well, to me anyway. I needed to be somewhere, but where that place was I wasn't too sure. Just any place but here, we stood out like sore thumbs under a bright orange street light in the middle of the junction. The police were everywhere on this street and we were carrying enough smoking implements, hash and joints to be hauled straight into a cold cell. Then they'd set on us, knowing damn well that we were on something and try to extract some piece of information before the drugs wore off.

'What's that?' Varnish was looking back up the main road into town. I could hear something too. It was coming closer. From the scrambled mess I could make out distant voices, loud, abusive, drunk.

'Come on, let's get out of here,' said Varnish.

Walking towards us were five brutish pub types, they'd seen us and were shouting something at us. I could make out, '. . . eh, skateboarder . . .' – it sounded like that looping every two seconds.

'Why?' I replied. 'We've just as much right to be here as anyone else. I'm not moving just because of them.'

'Then you stay, I'm going.'

'Well, if they want to get funny, remember we've got skateboards. Have you ever felt what it's like getting one of those in the head?' Of course he hadn't and neither had I, for that matter.

'Look, there's five of them and there's only two of us. They look really big and mean to me from here and drunk too. Fuck it, I'm going.'

Varnish scooted off down the hill, accelerating faster than I had expected. He shot down the wet road, soon reaching twenty miles per hour.

'Hey, this road may be steeper than I thought,' I shouted after him. He didn't hear but it was too late for him anyway. The five gorillas in white shirts were about fifty feet away. I could still hear them shouting 'skateboarder', but now I could also hear what Varnish must have heard: 'WANKER!'

'Oh shit.'

I stepped on the board and accelerated down the steep slope, parked cars rushing by, I felt like I was stationary and the whole world had speeded up around me, everything becoming a blurred motion, a time lapse. I could see Varnish ahead of me; he had one foot trailing on the floor, trying to decelerate his board. The drunks were somewhere at the top of the hill, we were well out of their range by now. The melodic shouted abuse had stopped. I had nearly caught up with Varnish; he brought his trailing foot back on to the board, glanced back at me, grinning insanely and hurtled towards the kerb. He kicked the tail of the board, the rear trucks clipped the kerb, but he was over. He fought to keep on the board, his arms and legs flailing everywhere.

The kerb was rushing towards me at a terrible rate; I kicked up the tail, and hurtled over the kerb. I remember thinking 'No way, you did it,' but as that thought left my mind I landed, instantly realising I had left my board back at the kerb. I landed and fell into a twenty-mile-an-hour run, my legs were trying to fold under me, I could see the broken collarbone hurtling towards me like a freight train. I kept up and even managed to slow down a bit before collapsing in a heap at the other end of the alleyway. Varnish stood under a street light, in his usual subtle manner, lighting a massive cone that could have been spotted at two hundred metres.

'Come on, let's get out of here before those geezers come after us. Where's your board?'

'I think it left me at the kerb.'

'Well, go and get it, before they come and get us.'

'Relax,' I stood up and brushed the grit and gravel off my hands. 'They're not after us, they're probably pissing up a tree somewhere by now.'

I went and got my skateboard, it was still intact. This skateboard was indestructible, one of the old wide boards. We walked awhile smoking the cone, then continued on our boards through quiet council estates and subways, ending up down on the embankment by the River Derwent. The embankment was made of concrete and stepped down to the river. Not a bad place to skate, but we were in no fit state by then to even stand on a board. The methadone hung thick in our veins. Movement seemed almost impossible. We sat by the river and smoked a couple of pipes, then I lit a joint, this time a non-conspicuous size. Water rushed over a weir nearby, creating a hypnotic sound. I don't know how long we sat there just staring off across the water watching what looked like random images and short clips of eight-millimetre film being projected on to the darkness on the other side of the river.

Something shocked me from the first peace I had felt in a long time. I looked around; everything seemed really dark and blurred. I couldn't see Varnish. My eyes began to readjust. Then there came a voice.

'Can you help me?' I looked around; it seemed to be coming from everywhere. My head started spinning. I stood up, Get a grip, goddammit, I thought, where's Varnish?

'Varnish?'

There was silence. Then: 'Yeah.'

211

'Where are you?' My vision was filling with black spots that seemed to have solidity and depth.

'I'm here having a piss. Shut up, will you, there's someone up there.' My vision began to clear; I could see a bright orange glowing stone bridge in front of me. The voice came again.

'Excuse me, please could you help me?'

I spotted a figure standing on the bridge to the left of us. He was looking straight at us. Varnish stepped out of the darkness by the river edge, zipping up his fly.

'What's up, Doc?' he said. 'Are you all right?'

'Up there,' I said. 'We've been made.'

'Excuse me, can you please help me?'

'What's the matter, man?' shouted Varnish. I instantly knew this was the wrong thing for us to do, my instincts were saying cut and run, just get the hell out of there. This was going to be bad and we were in no state to deal with it at all.

The figure walked across the bridge and down the steps towards us. 'Are you good people? Can you help me?'

Varnish said again: 'What's the matter, man?'

'It's my head, look. Look what he did to it.' By this time he was stood in front of us, he tipped his head forward, he'd been holding his head since we first saw him, but only now did it register it why. His head was split open on the top, at least ten centimetres long. It was a gaping soggy wound and he was losing quite a lot of blood from it.

'Holy shit, what the fuck happened to you?' I asked.

'This man, he hit me in the head with a tyre thing, you know a thing for the wheel.' The man looked up; he was only a boy, sixteen maybe seventeen. His face was covered in glistening thick black blood. Some had dried, he'd had this wound awhile, I remember thinking.

There was something about this boy I instantly felt uneasy about. He didn't seem right, I mean in the way he seemed to be. His general calmness after being smashed in the head with a tyre wrench. Something had put me on edge and I didn't know what.

'Holy Jesus!' I exclaimed, 'you need to go to a hospital, man.'

'Or the police,' said Varnish. 'Hell, we'll take you up there, they gotta catch this guy. You can't just go around hitting people in the head when you feel like it, there'd be anarchy. Where would we be then, eh?'

'Maybe the police wouldn't be such a good idea, Varnish,' I said.

He looked at me puzzled. I gave a you-know-why nod. He seemed to realise.

'No, I can't go to the cops,' said the boy.

'Why not?' we both asked simultaneously.

'Because I'm on a curfew. I'm supposed to be in by ten every night. If they catch me out here now they'll put me away.'

'Why are you on a curfew?' asked Varnish. 'What you done?'

'I, err . . . burgled a few houses a few years ago, when I was younger, but I've done my time, I just want the chance to get on with my own life, but they keep harassing me. They won't leave me alone and now they've put me on this curfew.'

'That's some hard shit, man,' I said.

'Don't worry, kid,' said Varnish. Oh no, please don't, but before I could finish that thought he already said it. 'We'll help you. We won't leave you out here on your own. We're good people. Honest citizens.'

Varnish put his arm around the boy and was already walking up the street.

'Varnish,' I called after him. He carried on walking, talking to the boy.

'Well, err . . . what about the skateboarding? Are we just gonna forget that then?'

There was no talking to him; he was on a mission. His mind locked on to a certain point in time where he now knew he had to be. In my experiences of the drug culture this was common practice.

'We'll take him back to the flat with us,' Varnish said as I caught up to him. We turned left and walked up St Peter's Street, past shops and travel agencies, the orange light illuminating the red brick street. The clock on the weird concrete erection in front of us said 4.47. Great, I thought, it'll be daylight soon and we can get rid of this freak. I lit a cigarette.

213

'So, tell us again, what happened to you?' asked Varnish.

The boy told us he had asked this man for the time and the guy smashed him in the head with the tyre wrench.

'So this guy was in the street when he hit you?'

'No.' The boy looked at Varnish like he was an idiot. 'He was in his house.'

Varnish looked at me full of confusion. I shrugged and dragged on the cigarette.

'What do you mean he was in his house? Were you in his house?'

'No, I just knocked on his door to ask him the time, then he hit me in the head with the wheel . . .'

I cut in. 'Tyre wrench.' This character was starting to annoy me.

'Yes, the tyre wrench. He hit me in the head here.' He pointed to his head again. Then it hit me: this boy was simple, backward.

'You knocked on someone's door to ask them the time?' asked Varnish.

'Yes.'

'Did he tell you?' I asked.

'No, he hit me in the head with a tyre wrench.' The boy scowled at me, I hopped on my board and skated off up ahead.

'Might as well get some in, seeing as we're going home,' I called back. I headed up the hill towards the concrete structure then turned it and flew back down the hill towards Varnish and the boy, lurching all over the road. As we headed home the only thing open was a massage parlour, a gigantic red-and-blue neon sign flashing on and off outside. This area of the street was constantly filled with parked Mercedes, BMWs and Jaguars.

The sky was starting to lighten by the time we got back to the flat. You could see distant clouds rolling across purple skies over the flats facing us across the square.

We went up to the top-floor flat and I made tea. Varnish and the boy went to his bedroom. I remember Varnish saying he was going to clean the boy's head. I went into the bedroom and entered a conversation I wasn't sure I was hearing. The vibrations in this room were very unusual and definitely not friendly.

'. . . Okay, I'll go and run you a bath and I'll call you when it's ready,' Varnish said. He turned to leave the room.

'What's going on?' I asked.

'His head's a right old mess. I'm gonna run him a bath so he can clean it properly.' Varnish smiled, but there was something unnerving in it. Was he keeping something from me? He turned and headed to the bathroom.

I handed the boy his tea, he said thank you. He was grinning insanely at me, I felt like I was in the 'We're gonna get ya!' scene in *The Evil Dead*, a possessed character sat cross-legged on the bed in front of me, but when would he start singing those terrible rhymes at me? I had to keep my cool; this guy was starting to get to me. Remain calm, if this kid thinks he's getting to you there is a distinct possibility he'll take advantage of the situation. It seemed like he had the mind of a ten-year-old but the deviance of a habitual criminal. He wasn't to be trusted.

I went and sat on the sofa in the left-hand corner of the room and put some music on. I heard the taps start running in the bathroom. I lay back on the sofa and drifted off into an uneasy silence. Everything I looked at looked black, even the lights. I felt like I was being swallowed into the sofa, slowly being sucked in. I could still hear the music but it seemed really far away. This sensation was familiar to me; I'd felt this type of drug many times before, sucking me in.

Varnish walked back in the room.

'Okay, the bath's ready. Come with me and I'll show you what towel to use.'

The boy got up and followed Varnish out of the room. He still had the same stupid grin on his face as he left.

I sat up and started to paste a joint together. Varnish came back into the room a few minutes later and sat down on the bed. He started to load one of the many home-made bongs that were laid around the room.

'He says he can't wash himself,' Varnish said after a minute or so.

'You what?' I couldn't believe I was hearing this.

'He says he can't wash himself. He can't even get himself undressed, I had to do it for him.' My eyes darted to Varnish in shock; he looked straight at the blank television screen not two feet in front of him, no expression in his eyes.

'Well, count me out,' I said finally. Varnish snapped out of whatever world he was in. 'No way, I'm not doing it. There's something about this character, I don't know what it is, but I don't like it. Do you really believe that story he told us about the curfew?'

'I don't know,' replied Varnish in a bilge of hash smoke. 'He's just not all there, you know, he's a bit simple. Don't worry, I wasn't asking you when I said that. I'll do it. I don't mind.'

'I don't know, that's kinda weird, you're going to give a young boy a bath you've only just met tonight, doesn't something strike you as odd here?'

'Oh God, what are you saying man?' Varnish got up and left the room, then came back in again a moment later. 'I hope you're not saying what I think you're saying, because if you are saying what I think you're saying then you're sicker than I ever thought you could be.' He stormed out making 'uck!' noises and shouting, 'That's disgusting.'

I lay on the bed smoking the joint and listened to the music, turning the volume up with my foot. What the hell was going on in there? Had I spent all this time sharing a flat with a man whose sexual orientations I had no idea of? What evil thing was manifesting itself in front of that poor unsuspecting boy, in the bathroom as we speak? That vile drug beast in the bathroom with the boy was not a man to be trusted, he enjoyed nothing more than freaking unsuspecting members of society while under the security of hard drugs. Perhaps the boy wanted it to happen, maybe he'd planned this all along, well, all except the bash in the head, but how would I know?

But good tunes at five thirty in the morning; suddenly everything is forgotten in a haze of thick grey-blue smoke and Tom Waits wailing over a king hell honky-tonky band.

I came around as the boy walked back into the room; I could feel him watching me, even without looking at him. I asked if he was okay. He said his head still hurt.

'Well, you took a pretty heavy bang in the head, I'm surprised you haven't got concussion.'

The boy returned to the exact position on the bed as he was before. Varnish came in and sat down.

We sat listening to calm sounds, smoking and drinking Ribena, thinking the vitamin C would do us some good. The sun shone into the room casting streams of yellow through the smoke-filled room. The boy asked what we were doing. I looked up from the smoking bong.

'We're smoking hash, what does it look like?'

'Can I have some?' he asked. 'It looks good.'

We pondered this for a while, maybe it would help the pain in his head, maybe it would calm him down. Maybe it would knock him out completely and we'd end up with a young boy in a coma and a big crack in his skull to explain to the police. Then when he woke he would tell the police how these two degenerate-looking men took him to their flat, bathed him and then made him smoke some drug that rendered him helpless. No, this was a bad idea, I thought. He may even just go completely uncontrollable, we'd end up with a near-fit situation, I've seen it happen before and it wasn't nice.

So we decided the hash painkiller was not a good idea. The boy began complaining that his head really hurt. Then he started to moan and rock backwards and forwards. Varnish and I decided to get him to the hospital quick, our time as Samaritans was over, we'd had enough of this creep. It was around six thirty as we stumbled to the car, my body rebounded from every step I took. I felt rubbery and I had little strength in any of my limbs. I had the boy in front of me, occasionally grabbing his jacket collar and helpfully thrusting him in the direction of the car. Varnish was in front us; he staggered around the car, pulling his keys from his jeans.

'Are you okay to drive?' I shouted.

He just about made it to the driver's door and looked up at me. 'I'm fine, we'll make it.' He looked like his head was

217

about to burst. His face had turned purple and he was struggling with the lock, muttering and swearing for a minute, then we all got in and Varnish started the battered Toyota and turned the car one-eighty out on to the main road, turning left into town. He was driving about seven miles per hour.

'Speed up, man. We're so goddamned conspicuous,' I bleated in a panic-stricken voice. I could feel the cops closing in on us right now. There were probably two of them watching us as we left the flat. They weren't there for us, hell no. Just a couple of good old-fashioned policemen having their breakfast in a quiet part of the neighbourhood after a ball-breaking eight-hour night shift. Then out stumble us two, unable to walk or even to open car doors, clamber into a car that looks like it hasn't seen an MOT certificate for five years and drive off.

'I'm speeding up now,' snapped Varnish, 'you gotta give me time.'

Something stirred in my stomach, writhing like a giant worm. The boy was still wailing, but it had got louder now.

'Arrr . . . my head, my head . . . arrr!' He was repeating this at regular intervals.

'I know your fucking head hurts,' snarled Varnish, 'we're going to the hospital, aren't we, shut up for a fucking minute, will you.' I could see he was losing control of the situation.

We made it about two hundred metres along the main road, averaging fifteen to twenty miles per hour. The churning in my stomach erupted up towards my mouth.

'Pull over, I'm going to be sick,' I shrieked.

'What?'

'Just do it!'

Varnish screeched to a halt, I opened the passenger door and threw up into the gutter. The vomit was bright purple. Varnish took one look at my sorry state of affairs and instantly threw up out of the driver's door. I looked up over the dashboard just in time to see the patrol car glide past. Everything was silent and time itself seemed to slow. I could see the judge, the scowling jury and the grey prison bars flash in front of me. Varnish sat up and closed his door.

'Oh shit,' I said, it was all I was capable of, apparently this is the most common word people say before they die.

'What?' asked Varnish.

'Cops, the cops. Oh shit, we're dead.'

'Oh fuck!' said Varnish as he saw the police car right in front of us. He dropped down in his seat, cowering and babbling. But the police car kept going and within a minute it was out of our sight. We looked at each other in amazement. How could they have not seen us? A car parked on double yellow lines at six thirty in the morning with two guys throwing up out of each door. It didn't seem possible but it had indeed happened.

'We better get going before we push our luck any more,' I said. 'Are you okay to drive?'

'I think so.'

He slammed the car into gear and sped off to the roundabout ahead of us, turning right on to the one-way system and then right again at the next roundabout. Then on to the Derbyshire Royal Infirmary Accident and Emergency car park. I was out of the car before Varnish had time to stop. I opened the rear passenger door and hauled out the kid.

'Come on, no time to waste, my lad. Let's get that head of yours seen to. How is it, your head, I mean?'

'It really hurts, I keep going dizzy.' He was whining, maybe even faking it a bit, well, that was the impression I got at the time. Varnish made it out of the car and locked it. He looked purple and swollen, ready to throw vomit on some unsuspecting doctor at any moment.

'Let's get this over with,' I said.

'Damn straight,' replied Varnish, without even looking at me; he just headed straight for the accident and emergency sign above the main set of doors in front of us.

A deathly silence hit us the moment we walked into the waiting room. There were several victims of various night-time rampages. A guy with his arm in a sling, another guy with a home-made bandage around his hand, blood seeping through and dripping on the floor. In the middle of the seating arrangement in the waiting room was an old couple in matching anoraks. They were all looking at us.

'Can I help you?' said a voice.

I swung round, trying to find the owner. I couldn't see anyone, so I improvised, just pretend you have seen them, get your bearings later.

'Err, yes. This man. He needs your help. You see, his head.' I pointed at the gaping hole in the boy's head. 'Yes, he needs your help and he's in a lot of pain, you know.'

I spotted where the sleep-deprived voice of a woman was coming from. In the wall right in front of me was a small window with a nurse in the middle, bursting out of a uniform two sizes too small for her.

'Name?' She yawned.

'Err, mine or the guy with the hole in his head?'

Varnish took the boy to sit down at the far end of the waiting room, away from any other people.

'The victim, sir,' she said. There was a severe emphasis on the 'sir', like a bad taste in the mouth. We were not liked here. This angered me, we'd spent the evening with this freak, cleaned him and looked after him most of the night, wasted the good clean drugs on taking care of someone who couldn't even bath himself.

'Look, I don't know who this guy is, we just found him in town last night with his head split open.'

'What time last night?'

'What?'

'What time last night did you find him?'

'Doesn't matter, we were out skateboarding and we found him.'

'Skateboarding?'

'Yes, skateboarding, why?' I could feel the sweat now running off my face and down my back. The conversation became more hectic, more questions, she knew I was on something and the moment I sat down she'd be on the phone to the police. Eventually she ceased questioning. I thought I was going to pass out, it felt like 105 degrees in that waiting room. No, not now, I thought, you pass out now and they're going to find you full of methadone. I could see her looking at me, but the room was rocking from left to right. I had to pull myself together.

'Well, is that it?' I asked, completely in tatters from the barrage of questions she had just hit me with. Had I told her something I shouldn't have? I couldn't remember.

'Yes, you can sit in the waiting room now, please.'

'Well, how long is this going to take?'

'You'll have to wait in line, we're short-staffed, so you'll have to wait with the others.'

I went and sat between Varnish and the boy. Varnish lay back on the chairs, his eyes were closed but I sensed he was still with us. The boy had the insane grin on his face and he had taken to rocking back and forth again. Blood had started to fill the hole in his head again.

We sat for a while in silence, the boy rocking back and forth, me staring blankly at the wall and Varnish passed out on the chairs. The methadone had calmed down now, but exhaustion was taking control. I felt sick, my stomach burned from the vomit session in the street. My arms and legs felt heavy and weak, I just sat and looked at the apple-white wall wishing I could get up and go for a coffee and cigarette, but Varnish was out of it and I couldn't leave this deranged, concussed boy on his own. Who knew what this skinny teenager was capable of doing.

'How long do we have to wait?' said the boy.

'I don't know, we're in a queue and all those people over there are before you,' I said, pointing at the other patients; only the hand victim and the old couple were left. 'And the doctors are short-staffed, so we may be here a while.'

'But my head hurts.'

'I know your head hurts, but we have to wait.' I looked at the clock, 7.45. The sun shone bright through the windows of the waiting room, burning on my tired, dilated eyes. The boy began wailing again and rocking. I turned to Varnish.

'I think this guy is losing it.'

Varnish didn't respond, he just lay over the four grey plastic chairs. This was it; I was going to have to deal with this lunatic myself. His wailing had got louder; people were starting to look round. A nurse watched from behind a mesh re-enforced window. Oh shit, I thought, he's drawing attention to us. This looks bad, two drug addicts, one passed out, the other looking like he's going to burst in a drug-crazed frenzy and a young teenage boy with a ton of blood all over his clothes and a gaping wound in his head. Any minute now the cops would walk in and that would be it.

'Ahh, my head, it really hurts. Ahh . . .'

'I know, but what can I do? Look, you're gonna have to calm it down, you're gonna get us in trouble.'

'But it hurts, I feel funny. Ahh, it hurts, it really hurts.' He was almost in tears by this point.

'I know, fucking shut up, will you.'

'I have a knife, you know.'

'What?' I looked up to the boy, his face had completely changed, there was no pain in it, no tears, just a look of insane hatred for everything in this world. I turned to Varnish but he was still gone.

'I've got a knife . . . here, in my pocket.'

My heart stopped, this was it, the end in one foul way or another, I had read about these homicidal teenage kids in several magazine articles, hell, now it was right there, sat in front of me.

'Do you? Good. And what do you plan to do with it?' I could feel my whole body swell from sweat, trying to push through dirty, clogged pores.

'I don't know. I feel funny. When I feel funny I do things.'

'Err . . . what kind of things?'

He looked straight at me. 'I hurt people.'

Sweat was pouring from my face; I had to keep control of this situation.

'Look, man, I know your fucking head hurts, okay. But we have to wait. Now, if you're not going to behave then I'm going to leave you with this worthless piece of shit here. Are we straight here, do you understand?'

He began wailing again, loud enough for everyone in the waiting room to hear.

'My head really hurts and I feel really funny. And when I feel funny, I hurt people.'

I grabbed Varnish. 'Wake up, you son of a bitch.'

'I hurt people when I feel funny, and I'm feeling funny right now. I have a knife.'

'Varnish!' I shouted. He suddenly woke.

'What . . . What is it?'

'Wake yourself up, this bastard is freaking out on me and I want nothing more to do with this. I'm going. I never wanted to help him in the first place. He's your refugee, you deal with him.'

'Did he say he had a knife?' asked a guy who had walked in ten minutes before with a bandaged leg.

'No,' I replied. 'No, he didn't. He said nothing, nothing at all. Ignore him, he's backward.'

Varnish sat up. 'What the fuck is going on?'

A doctor suddenly appeared from a blue two-tone door and called the name of the boy. Thank God, I thought, we can finally get out of here.

The boy went through the blue door but left his coat after Varnish had convinced him he wouldn't need it. Varnish searched his coat for the knife, but nothing was there.

'Right, he's no danger to these people, so let's go,' I said.

'You want to leave him here?'

'Damn straight, let's get the hell out of here before he causes us more trouble.'

'We can't leave him here. You go. I'm taking him home. I can't believe you can be so heartless, man. God, what is it with you?'

And before I could explain what had just happened he had disappeared through the blue door. I stood in the middle of the waiting room with the boy's jacket in my hand not sure whether what had just happened had really happened. Had the boy freaked out or had I imagined the whole thing in some hallucinated state. People were looking at me. Time to move I thought, but I couldn't convince myself to leave this possible psycho with Varnish so I too headed through the blue door.

Inside I found the boy and Varnish in the second cubicle. A nurse walked in with a tube of something in her hand.

'Oh, are you here again?' she said to the boy.

He grinned and said yes. The deranged mutant that had emerged earlier was nowhere to be seen, just a shy, smiling teenage boy.

'Does he come in here often?' asked Varnish.

'Oh yes, we get this one in every six weeks or so. You're not the first to bring him in.' The tube in her hand was glue. She began squirting it into his wound then squeezed the flaps of skin together telling the boy that it would sting for a minute. The boy winced.

'Where do you live?' asked Varnish. 'We'll take you home.'

He said he lived somewhere in Chaddesden, so we bundled him into the Toyota and headed at high speed up the A52 to Chaddesden and dropped him on a main street in that end of town.

'Stay out of trouble, man,' said Varnish as he left the car.

'Oh, I will. I'll be real careful from now on.' And with that he was gone.

We headed home as the warm morning sun rose over the grey Derby skyline. It was going to be a good day, I thought, shame I'm going to be spending most of it in bed.

Things between Varnish and myself deteriorated from then on. Perhaps it was that event, or the vast amounts of drugs we were caning at the time sending us into hopeless avenues of argument, or the fact that Varnish didn't have as many apprehensions to the lifestyle we were leading as I did. Or maybe I believed that what we were doing should be kept as quiet as possible. My belief was the bigger you got the more of a threat you were to the opposition. And the opposition was nasty. So I didn't want to rock the boat, we'd just slip in there and take enough to live and no more. But Varnish always wanted more. And he got it too. He flew high for a while, but the competition must have had enough of him.

One night, two large black gentlemen gained entry to Varnish's flat with the aid of an old mutual friend's brother. The two intruders stole Varnish's entire stash, roughed up his girlfriend and punched another friend in the face for only having a blim's worth of gear on him.

It's now seven years later and night covers London's south-west. Warren Zevon is blasting from the stereo and riots from Prague are on the television. It is suspected that Milosovic has fled and now two fat, grey suits sit debating the matter with Jeremy Paxman.

I look back now and can see plainly the reasons why things got as bad as they did, back then, and I wonder what happened to Varnish, was he still a nightwatch security guard, on an industrial estate somewhere in the heart of Derby. This thought fills me with two feelings, firstly immense sadness that such a great mind and a fine artist is wasting his life when he could be doing so much. And secondly that an original freak is still out there on the night shifts, drug-fuelled and ready. A one of a kind chemical monster that inadvertently keeps the world rolling while the rest of us sleep. A true wonder of nature.

'Skateboards and Methadone – No one should be asked to handle this trip', 2001

Anonymous
Confessions of a Middle-Aged Ecstasy Eater

I HAVE OCCASIONALLY been asked how I became a regular Ecstasy-eater. I was aware of its reputation as the 'love drug', had heard it described as a 'four-hour, full-body orgasm' and I found this intriguing, alluring and worthy of further investigation.

Ecstasy is delicious. Or, to put it another way, Ecstasy is delicious and I recommend highly, loudly and long that everyone whose health does not contraindicate or preclude its ingestion, ought to ingest it. Go out, I admonish you, all of you, hit the streets or collar that neighbourhood kid, drum up a contact, do a deal, repair thyselves home, soften the lights, put on some music – the best stuff – pour yourself a pitcher of ice water, perhaps two, keep a tin of Altoids handy, as well as a tube of Vicks inhalant and a couple of packs of mineral ice, make yourself comfortable, lie back and . . . swallow. An hour from now, perhaps less, you are going to experience something that shall for ever change such times as remain to you on this earth. You are going to experience something that is, every second of it, delicious – deliciously, positively, unprecedentedly w-o-n-d-e-r-f-u-l.

It is your self-anointing, and I envy you that first time. So relish it, savour it, languish it, treasure it, that sacred four hours. You have just swallowed wonder, ambrosia and mead, you have partaken of lustre and grace. Just make certain that before you swallow you know that the pill is authentic, and not some rip-off. Do that, and the rest is a piece of cake that is like no other you have ever tasted. Think of the best day of your life, or recall the sweetest, purest, most special thing along the way – person, place, moment, experience, accomplishment. Now multiply that tenfold. That does not begin to describe how impossibly delicious E is.

I am not unaware of how redolent this is of Timothy Leary's often loopy proselytising for LSD, and its 'quasi-religious' associations, but this has nothing to do with that. Ecstasy is a clarifier. It enables one to see, feel and think, if not more deeply, then certainly more clearly. The high subsides, but the lucidity lingers. In that sense, not to mention in its chemical composition, it is quite the opposite of LSD.

Ecstasy is a clarifier, but it is a personal clarifier. It is not – despite all the peace/love/unity/respect hype surrounding it – a universal one. Its lessons may be universal in their implications, but they are intended to be applied to oneself. Which is not to say that the drug does not have its social dimensions or that one ought not to do E in the company of others. Indeed I would not find it congenial to do, nor have I ever done it, alone. (As close as I ever came was on an unpeopled, night-time side street in London, and it was raining, and it was one of the memorable experiences of my life – neon, glistening, menthol, veneered in layer after thickening layer of thick honey. Lovely streets, London, and lovely, so lovely, its rain.)

But better by far to do it with those one loves, and best of all with one's one-and-only lover. And if what one takes in the broadest sense is all about human connection and empathy – E has proven highly effective in certain kinds of couples therapy – it is all the more about connecting with and feeling empathy for oneself. It is, contrary to its image as the current drug of choice among teenagers and the prevalence of its use at their 'raves', the most intimate of drugs.

I did it my first time with the woman who saved me. It was her first time as well. We were, as zero hour approached, visibly apprehensive, an attitude, I think, that is only sane. We had cleared our schedules, switched off the phones, and we were in her home, just the two of us, in our bathrobes, in the living-room, on the couch. Van was on the stereo, *Astral Weeks*, *Moondance*, *Common One*, *The Best of: Volume One*. A fire was roaring in the fireplace. The lamp was turned down low. It was mid-evening, and we had ready – as my son had taken care to instruct us – our pair of tumblers and pitchers of iced-down spring water. E increases body temperature and heart rate and elevates blood pressure, so drinking water – not beer, not liquor – is pro forma as one rolls along. And one wishes to drink because E causes dehydration – one of its most immediate side effects is a dry mouth. With much mutually nervous, serio-comic, ceremonial chit-chat, then, we each popped our pill, swallowed, waited, and – nothing. We locked eyes. We still were alive. I think we were only half amazed. I know we were relieved. Van was still belting as only Van can. It takes a while for Ecstasy to kick in – and then the world around you billows open like an eye and you are lifted and taken – coronaed, crowned, spangled and lantern-lit, your smiling face flambeaued as by a thousand chandeliers.

One of the most discernible early effects – it happened that first time, though often it does not – is what I have heard described as 'fluttery' vision. This phenomenon is as close to an hallucinatory quality as E produces, and it is so mild – and weirdly pleasant – that to label it as such is frankly inaccurate. When it happened to us, we looked at one another, smiled, and virtually in unison commented on it. Cool. Images remain intact, they just move a little, as if jagged were a verb, within the texture of their own lines. These striations are very unthreatening, and very, well, cool. And then suddenly Van was singing waaaaay over there, and then waaaaay inside the very pith of my brain, yet away outside and all around as well. And that also was. Cool.

What happened next was that everything and all at once, while clearly remaining itself, was transfigured, transmogrified, a new self, a simultaneously deeper and higher, older and newer self – smoother and softer and rounder. The world was suddenly guilt- and-worry-and wrinkle-free, palpably, beautifully buoyant – visually, texturally, aurally – transcendently right and glorious and divine. Whatever beautiful thing one can imagine, it is that much more beautiful on E. And so we looked at one another and felt one another, with our fingers and our lips and our tongues, indeed with the whole of our new-found faces, this plumbing of the new map of our bodies – new softer hair, new smoother flesh, new pinker, fresher, more fragrant, shimmering, altogether fluffier genitalia – and we smelled and tasted one another – she smelled of burst peaches and tasted as the recent salts of pearls – because sense of smell and taste is no less honed and heightened than the other senses.

We bathed in one another, each of our five senses, ten in all, because that comingling is what had taken place, its rhapsody, and humanity, and caress. And we looked to one another exactly as we felt and smelled and tasted: rapturous, heavenly, transcendent, numinous, aglow. She a resplendent, bejewelled goddess, I a radiant god. Later, I got up, walked to the bathroom – walking on E is no more difficult than walking on water or floating on air – and looked in the mirror. I wanted to see what I looked like – I am just vain enough that the thought occurred to me even in the midst of the roll – though I already had seen reflected in my lover's eyes that I looked sufficiently, there is no other word, gorgeous. (If I looked half as gorgeous as she did to me I reckoned I was in for a treat.) And the person I saw looking back at me was gorgeous, but gorgeous in a way that floored almost as much as it thrilled me.

Here, now, as I stared grinning in astonishment, I looked twenty-eight. And not some fifty-year-old version of myself at twenty-eight, but me the way I was back then. I moved closer, peered harder. I could scarcely believe it. I had recaptured myself. Dorian Gray. Fountain of Youth. Spontaneous regeneration. Somehow I had been restored, and I felt what I can only describe as an all-consuming nostalgia for the present.

And then, after helping each other off with our bathrobes, our old, nubby, cotton-twill bathrobes – suddenly spun of the finest cashmere and angelica, these clouds of talcum and down – we embraced, and kissed, and she whispered in my ear: 'We've found fucking gold.'

From: *The Guardian*, Saturday 14 July 2001

He causeth the grass to grow for the cattle, and herb for the service of man: that he may bring forth food out of the earth; and wine that maketh glad the heart of man, and oil to make his face to shine, and bread which strengtheneth man's heart
Psalm 104, verses 14 & 15

Stuart Walton
Out of It – 2

A PAIR OF dining companions scrutinizes the menu in a smart, trend-setting restaurant in a European capital city. One has opted to begin with the tempura-battered strips of calf's liver with pomegranate cream dressing, and go on to herb-crusted rack of lamb with Provençal vegetables. For the other, it will be quail terrine with redcurrant relish and rocket, and to follow, poached perch with a sauce of lemon and capers. Now for the tricky business.

That dressing on the liver might present problems for a light white wine, and without knowing precisely how sharp it will be, the choice is something of a matter of stumbling in the dark. A crisp New Zealand Sauvignon might stand up to it, and cut any residual oiliness in the batter, but then, what of the quail terrine? Surely that needs a meatier white, even a light red? The merits of a sturdy white burgundy are discussed, but the proposal is soon relinquished. An excess of oak would suit neither dish. Eventually, a compromise bottle is found. The weight and extract in a *grand cru* Gewürztraminer from Alsace will cope with the battered liver, and is a gastronomically unimpeachable match with any kind of terrine. The first bottle can safely be ordered. How, though, to find a vinous chameleon to blend with both red meat and white fish? That way, gustatory madness lies: Pinot Noir might suit a densely textured fish like tuna, but could crush the delicacy of a river fish, while lacking the tannic heft required to stand up to lamb. The richly buttery sauce with the perch will happily negotiate the fleshiness of a Barossa Valley Chardonnay, but even that wine, with its layers of oak and alcohol, is just too *white* for rare red meat. An opposite half-bottle each would be the obvious answer, were the list not so lamentably deficient in them. After much fretful chewing of bread, and flipping of pages back and forth, the issue is imperfectly resolved in favour of a bottle of *cru classe* Pauillac, the game plan being that the fish eater will be left the lion's share of the Gewürztraminer to go with the perch (which means drinking the same wine with two courses, alas), but will nonetheless be able to help finish the claret with some cheese. Now the logistics of it must be explained to the sommelier, so that he doesn't over-serve the Gewürztraminer to the lamb eater during the hors d'oeuvre.

In certain wine circles, food and wine matching has reached the status of an investigative science. A British wine periodical convokes a bunch of journalists and trade consultants to pick wines to go with a succession of dishes, the linking theme of which is strawberries. There is goat's cheese with strawberries, swordfish with strawberries, duck livers with strawberries in balsamic vinegar, and a strawberry and white-chocolate gateau. A forest of opened bottles clutters the table as the panel searches earnestly on behalf of the magazine's subscribers for the precise wine to marry with each dish. At the Fetzer winery in Mendocino County, California, there is a dedicated school devoted to this pursuit, where interested parties may enrol to spend studious days tasting and conferring. Is Sauvignon a better match than Chenin for the acid bite of sorrel, or is its upfront fruitiness more obviously suited to watercress? Then again, it depends on the dressing.

Alcohol has accrued over the millennia a rich and almost infinitely diverse set of symbolic contexts in which it may be taken, whether the aim be celebratory, consolatory, medicinal, scholastic, sacramental or gastronomic. What motivates our involvement with all intoxicants, however, is what they do to us. That may range across a spectrum from gentle tipsiness to stupefied collapse, from mild mood-heightening to gasping elation, from slight drowsiness to bare conscious narcosis, from faint dissociation to full-on hallucinogenic psychedelia.

Out of It, 2001

It was not the subtle bouquet of wine, or a lingering aftertaste of violets and raspberries that first caught the attention of our ancestors. It was, I'm afraid, its effect

Hugh Johnson

Tim Mackintosh Smith
Yemen: Travels in Dictionary Land

LUNCH AT ALI'S is not merely a matter of eating; it is the first step on the way to *kayf*. The meaning of the term has been discussed by Sir Richard Burton. One might call it, he wrote, 'the savouring of animal existence . . . the result of a lively, impressible, excitable nature, and exquisite sensibility of nerve; it argues a facility for voluptuousness unknown to northern regions'. But in the end the translator of the *Arabian Nights* admitted defeat: *kayf* is 'a word untranslatable in our mother tongue'. Lexicographers, who cannot be so realistic, have described it as a mood, humour or frame of mind. I, who chew the leaf of the qat tree, shall attempt a definition.

Ali's Restaurant is all to do with the humours. Blood, phlegm, yellow and black bile must be in balance to ensure perfect health and to enable the qat chewer to attain his goal of *kayf* since qat excites the cold and dry black bile. Prophylaxis against its ill effects means that the blood, which is hot and wet, must be stimulated. Hence the heat, the sweat, the bubbling *saltah*. Hence also the visits to the public baths before chewing qat, the insistence on keeping windows and doors shut during chewing, the elaborate precautions to avoid the dreaded *shanini* – a piercing and potentially fatal draught of cold air.

An old joke illustrates this obsession with heat. The angels, it is said, periodically visit Hell to make sure the fires are turned up. One day a group of them are detailed to check on the really wicked sinners, who spend eternity in individual ovens. Inside the first oven is a Saudi. He screams to be let out. Roasting nicely, they think, and slam the door on him. In the next oven is an Englishman; then come an American, an Egyptian and so on. All beg to be let out, but the angels show them no mercy. Eventually, they open the last door. Inside sits a Yemeni, chewing qat and apparently oblivious of the flames around him. He draws languidly on his water pipe, turns to the angels, and says: 'Hey, could you shut the door? I'll catch my death of cold.'

The other day – it might, in fact, have been almost any day – I had lunch at Ali's then bought my qat from blue-eyed Muhammad across the road. He swore I wasn't giving him what he'd paid for it (the oaths of qat sellers are notoriously unbinding). I argued. 'All right,' he said, 'take it for nothing. A present.' I folded some more notes, stuck them behind his dagger, and walked off with my purchase. Wrangling over the price is part of the business of working up a sweat. (Real *mawla'is* – that is, those 'inflamed with passion' for qat – used to run halfway up Jabal Nuqum, singing, before they chewed.) It was half past two and I was ready to start. My molar, as they say, was hot.

In a house in the centre of San'a, I climbed the stairs to another room on a roof, grander than my own. On the way up, I called 'Allah, Allah' to warn women of my presence. Perhaps I should make the point here, if it needs to be made, that this is a very male book. As a man I am excluded from the society of women, as they from that of men. Outsiders tend to see this dual, parallel system as a form of repression. The idea never occurs to most Yemeni women. They know that they wield power in many spheres, notably in the choice of marriage partners which, given an endogamous system, is a major influence on the distribution of wealth. Women play only a small role in the public domain, as they did in the West until quite recently; at least in Yemen, in contrast to Saudi Arabia, women are able to drive cars, enter Parliament, become top-ranking civil servants. But it is in the private realm of the home that the woman dominates, in practice if not in theory; men often gather to chew qat together because their homes have been taken over by visiting women.

Panting from the ascent, I slipped off my shoes and entered the room. It was rectangular, with windows on all sides which began a foot above the floor. Above them were semicircular fanlights of coloured glass. Into the tracery of the fanlights, and in the plaster of the walls and shelf brackets, were worked the names of God and the Prophet, and verses of a pious nature. It was a very legible room. Polished brass gleamed everywhere: rosewater sprinklers, incense burners, spittoons with little crocheted covers, the great circular tray with its three water pipes. Low mattresses covered with Afghan runners lined the walls. About a dozen men were sitting on them, leaning on armrests topped with little cloth off gold cushions. I greeted the chewers, interrupting their *zabj*, the rapid banter, the swordplay of insults that starts all the best qat sessions. I'd scarcely sat down when an old man opposite turned on me.

'I was in Sa'wan this morning, and I saw this Jew. And,

do you know, he looked just like you. You could have been twins!'

'But . . . but I haven't got any side-locks,' I parried feebly. Jewish Yemenis are required to advertise their religion by cultivating a pair of long corkscrew ringlets.

'Ah,' he went on, 'you know what they say: "Jewishiness is in the heart, not in the length of the side-locks." '

I made a feint to gain time: 'Tell me: exactly how many side-locks did this Jew of Sa'wan have?'

'What do you mean? Two, of course.'

'Well, it's a funny thing, but I saw a Jew in the qat market today and he looked exactly like you. You could have been twins. But he had four side-locks.'

After half an hour of this verbal fencing, the *zabj* lost its momentum and devolved into solo joke-telling.

'Once,' someone said, 'there was a blind girl. She was twenty-five years old and longing for a husband; but whenever she brought the subject up with her father he'd say, "My daughter, you are blind. No one wants you. But don't worry. You'll find a husband in Paradise." Well, one day she was up on the roof hanging out the washing when she tripped and fell, down and down, six storeys. By chance she fell into a lorry carrying bananas and she was knocked unconscious. The lorry drove on. Ten minutes later, she came to. Ah, she thought, I am dead, then, as she felt the bananas, she remembered what her father had told her and gave a little shriek: "Slowly, slowly, men of Paradise! Please take your turn."'

And many more in the same vein.

Weightier matters are discussed at qat chews, and they are a major forum for the transaction of business and for religious and political debate. Many people also chew to aid concentration on study or work, and qat is the inevitable accompaniment to all-important occasions from weddings to funerals. A funeral chew is known as *mujabarah*, a word which also means 'the setting of broken bones'. But at the classic San'ani chew, it is 'lightness of blood' – charm, amiability – that is admired, not gravitas. At a qat chew, one walks what a ninth-century poet called 'the sword-edge that separates the serious from the frivolous'.

My qat was good, a Hamdani form Tuzan. Qat is a dicotyledon known to science as *Catha edulis*. Unremarkable though it appears, chewers recognise a huge variety of types and are fascinated by its origin: when one buys qat one first establishes its pedigree. Quality is judged by region, by the district within a region, even by the field where the individual tree is grown and by the position of leaf on it. The product of a tree planted inadvertently on a grave is to be avoided – it brings sorrow. Qat can be any colour from lettuce-green to bruise-purple. It comes long or short, bound in bundles or loose, packed in plastic, alfalfa or banana leaves. In San'a, as a rule of thumb, the longer the branch, the more prestigious it is: less image-conscious chewers – and I am one of them – buy qatal, the pickings from the lower branches.

Just as in the West there are wine snobs, in Yemen there are qat snobs. I once found myself opposite one. Fastidiously, he broke the heads off his yard-long branches and wrapped them in a damp towel. It was almost an act of consecration. When he had finished, he drew on his water pipe and appraised my bag of qatal with a look that threatened to wither it. 'Everything,' he said in audible whisper, 'has pubic hair. Qatal is the pubic hair of qat. Besides, dogs cock their legs over it. He tossed me one of the tips from inside his towel. It was as thick as asparagus, its leaves edged with a delicate russet, and it tasted nutty, with the patrician bitter sweetness of an almond. There was a tactile pleasure too, like that of eating pomegranates – a slight resistance between the teeth followed by a burst of juice. I chased it with a slurp of water infused with the smoke of incense made from sandalwood, eaglewood, mastic and cloves.

Qat does not alter your perception. It simply enhances it by rooting you in one place. There is a story in the *Arabian Nights* about a prince who sat and sat in his palace. Sentient from the waist up, his lower half had been turned to porphyry. 'I used to wish the *Arabian Tales* were true,' said Cardinal Newman. They usually are, to some extent.

After the *zabj* and the jokes, conversations took place in smaller groups, then pairs, then, towards the end of the afternoon, ceased. I looked out of the windows at the city.

I find myself looking towards the place where the sun must have just disappeared. This high above sea level we are spared the more vulgar sort of sunset. The afterglow is dusty, the sky above the city like the inside of a shell. But I'm looking towards it, not at it – there's a distortion in the window pane, interesting and annoying at the same time. *A man that looks on glass, on it may stay his eye.*

It is six o'clock, or five to twelve in the Islamic day that starts with the sunset prayer. But, for a time, it is neither: the Hour of Solomon has begun, *al-Sa'ah al-Sulaymaniyyah*. *Sa'ah* has among its root meanings in the dictionary 'to be lost, to procrastinate'. At the Hour of Solomon time refracts, as if bent by a prism.

No one speaks. Introspection has replaced conviviality. Somewhere, my fingers are working at the qat, polishing, plucking. When it was still light I found a fat-horned caterpillar. A good sign – no DDT – but you don't want to chew one.

Were there a singer here, this would be his time. But the songs of the Hour of Solomon are as perilous as they are beautiful. Earlier this century in the days of Imam Yahya, singers could only perform in locked rooms, their windows stuffed with cushions. They had to hide their instruments for fear of imprisonment (fortunately, the old lute of San'a was small enough to be carried in the voluminous sleeves then worn). The Iman had banned singing with good reason: the songs are siren songs that tell of the flash of teeth beneath a veil like a silver coin in a well, of the saliva of lovers' kisses intoxicating like wine, of beauty that is cruelly ephemeral – *Lasting we thought it, yet it did not last.*

It is now quite dark. The coloured windows of neighbouring houses are lighting up, like Advent calendars.

We qat chewers, if we are to believe everything that is said about us, are at best profligates, at worst irretrievable sinners.

236

We are in the thrall of 'the curse of Yemen' and 'the greatest corrupting influence on the country' (two British ambassadors to San'a); we are in danger of 'loss of memory irritability, general weakness and constipation', and from our water pipes 'there is certainly a danger of getting a chancre on the lips' (*Handbook of Arabia*, 1917); worse, we are prone to 'anorexia' and to becoming 'emotionally unstable, irritable, hyperactive and easily provoked to anger, eventually becoming violent' (*Journal of Substance Abuse*, 5988), while in Somalia, qat has 'starved the country's children' and 'exacerbates a culture of guns and violence' (*San Francisco Chronicle*, 1993); even if we don't turn nasty, we 'doze and dribble green saliva like cretinous infants with a packet of bulls-eyes' (the English writer David Holden). In Saudi Arabia we would be punished more severely than alcohol drinkers; in Syria blue-eyed Muhammad would be swinging on the end of a rope.

In contrast to the above quasi-scientific poppycock, the only full and serious study of the effects of qat (Kennedy's – funded, it should be noted, by the US National Institute of Drug Abuse) concludes that the practice appears to have no serious physical or psychological effects. Yemenis themselves, while admitting that their habit is expensive, defend it on the grounds that it stimulates mental activity and concentration; they point out that at least the money spent on it remains within the national economy.

Qat has inspired a substantial body of literature. Compare, for example, Holden's dribbling infants with a description of a handsome chewer by the seventeenth-century poet Ibrahim al-Hindi:

> Hearts melted at his slenderness. And as he chewed, his mouth resembled Pearls which have formed on carnelian and, between them, an emerald, melting.

As well as poetry, there is a weighty corpus of scholarly literature. On the legality of qat in Islam, it has been unable to find any analogy between the effects of the leaf and those

237

of the prohibited narcotics. In the end, though, the question of its desirability and permissibility revolves around matters of politics, taste, ethnocentrism and sectarian prejudice.

I can just make out my watch. Half past seven. Time, which had melted, is resolidifying. It is now that I sometimes wonder why I am sitting here in the dark with a huge green bolus in my cheek; why I, and millions of others, spend as much time buying and chewing qat as sleeping, and more money on it than on food.

If we are to believe another major Western study of qat, we are 'making symbolic statements about the social order' and engaging in an activity that is 'individual, hierarchical, competitive'. Where you chew, and with whom, is certainly important. But to reduce it all to a neat theory – *rumino ergo sum* – is to oversimplify. It ignores the importance of the qat effect – something almost impossibly difficult to pin down, for it is as subtle and as hard to analyse as the alkaloids that cause it. It takes long practice to be able to recognise the effect consciously, and even then it sidesteps definition except in terms of metaphor, and by that untranslatable word, *kayf*.

Kayf – if you achieve it, and you will do if you choose the qat and the setting carefully – enables you to think, work and study. It enables you to be still. *Kayf* stretches the attention span, so that you can watch the same view for hours, the only change being the movement of the sun. A journey ceases to be motion through changing scenery – it is you who are stationary while the world is moved past, like a travelling-flat in an old film. Even if briefly, the chewer who reaches this *kayf* feels he is in the right place at the right time – at the pivot of a revolving pre-Copernican universe, the still point of the turning world.

One day I was buying qat when a group of tourists walked past. Blue-eyed Muhammad said to me, 'Why do people spend thousands of dollars rushing round the world, when they can chew qat?' *There is Africa and all her prodigies in us.*

I've chewed in taxis, on buses, on my motor cycle, on a truckload of firewood, in a military-transport plane, in an overturning jeep, on the 5.30 from Victoria to Sutton. In retrospect the movement was incidental. Back in the Oriental Institute, they didn't teach us the meaning of *kayf* – they couldn't have. Now, I would venture to call it a form of untravel.

In the room on the roof, sounds began to impinge: the rasp of a match, the noisy slurping of water, caged doves cooing; the snap of a twig to make a toothpick, someone buckling on his dagger. Then there was the click of the light switch. Everyone screwed up their eyes, blessed the Prophet, and went home.

There are a number of things you can do after chewing qat. You might start digging up the paving stones in your entrance hall to look for Solomon's Seal, as a neighbour of mine used to do. Or, like the Turk early this century who had not seen his wife for sixteen years and was noted for his abstemiousness, you might involuntarily ejaculate. I tend to go home, have a glass of milky tea, and do some writing. Out of the corner of my eye I used to see my pencil sharpener move very slightly, around midnight, until I stopped buying that sort of qat.

Yemen: Travels in Dictionary Land, 1999

Kevin Rushby
Eating the Flowers of Paradise – 1

CATHINONE IS A powerful psychoactive substance. And yet in Yemen qat cannot be separated from its social context – the drug is necessary, but only in the same way that frankincense has been needed at rituals for millennia. It is a prop, a token, something that symbolises more than it contains: the people have their faith in God and paradise and that He has sent them this leaf on which His name is written. Yemen, at least, would be secure form scientific 'improvements' to the flower of paradise. In AD 1543, Abdullah ibn Sharaf al-Din, son of the Imam, who first banned qat then accepted it back, wrote:

> Do you not see the pen of the Mericul One has written His name upon its pages? Eat it for what you wish to attain from this world and the next.

The West could learn a great deal from the Yemen and its elegant ability to control a drug without recourse to laws, enforcement, or scientific fiddling.

Eating the Flowers of Paradise, 1999

Jason Parkinson
Acid: The journey through living-room walls

I THINK IT was about 7 p.m. on that mentally fatal Sunday evening that we dropped the first lot of LSD. The music blasting distorted sound from the speakers positioned on the floor. The room flooded with soft, dim lights. Candles created just enough extra light for your mind to really go to work on you. We sat about, smoked and ranted, waiting for the drugs to hit.

An hour passed. Boredom and frustration set in.

'This was supposed to be strong,' I said. 'I say we do the rest, I'm just not getting anything.'

Now this statement was not entirely true, the arousal of faint double vision was there. And the copper-mouth too, lurking on the edge ready to bite you in the neck when you let your guard down.

The toilet trip was the ultimate test.

'I'm going for a shit, okay?'

'*Vale*, then we do the rest, no?'

'*Si*.'

It was uninspiring. This toilet was no good, I thought. No cheap tiles with patterns on, no stark light, just a maroon bath, chipped and flaking and me sat shitting. It came quick and fast, cleaning my insides. That's always a good sign, more with Ecstasy though. The carpet began moving, faint Aztec and geometric patterns pulsing and turning into more of the same.

Check the mirror.

All seemed well. I looked normal.

Flush chain, wash hands, leave toilet, take more acid!

Within ten minutes the living-room took on orange and red hues. Red and green neon darted over the walls, furniture and people. There are people in the room, I thought.

Guapa Morena started to dance. That would be the last I saw of her for a while, things were rising pretty damn fast. I was on the floor. Attempting to move, I crumpled into a heap on the futon managing to acquire what could have been a strewn duvet in the process. My body felt like it weighed a ton, the legs weren't going to take it. Talk was not happening either. My mouth was rebelling against me. Believe me, I tried, but it just came out the same. A strange slurping sound and foul words.

I checked the clock. It took a while to aim at it but my sight finally broke through the bubble that has formed around me.

Jesus Christ, I thought, we only dropped the second lot twenty minutes ago. We must be in trouble. The music had become drunken, I think it was Ween, but I couldn't be sure.

The TV spilled images of green and yellow women on to breathing floors. Stretched pallid skin with blue veins, spat golden sparks of ozone from ruptured warts. Wondrous squirts of stars absorbed by Arabic carvings. Pillars of gold and stone rose up to dark wooden structures. Vines and fruit clung to gazebos, high above North African buildings that framed the swirling clouds rolling high above the ceiling.

Primitive caves in terracotta stone restrained snarling Dobermanns held back by their ferocious owners on dirty ropes. Drooling froth and blood-filled mouths of twisted teeth, which lay beyond lips of broken wooden branches.

I was lying on the sofa, covered in the duvet that I had pulled up to my chin. I couldn't see Guapa but I knew she was there somewhere.

There was a massive rush, I remember images of massive freight trains hurtling towards me and then everything was green and alive.

Spanish women danced in circles of green and red, three and four arms stretching out their blue hands. Black-skinned legs covered in elastic metal, twisted and spun. Legs swapped sides and melted into thorny structures glistening like eel skin.

241

Red skies filled with green and purple swirling clouds. Foreign skies, strange planets rose just off the shore of crashing alien seas. Jesus God, a cracked Earth of plain, dried, sun-scorched yellow soil.

Green and white iced terrain spun off into space. Abandon ship, goddammit, every man for himself.

Then everything fell silent, hanging in a vast black hole pulling me into another vast universe, stars passed by at high velocity. I could see the void opening up before me, into our universe. I had seen this sky before. Dark asteroids passed on close by, smashing into discarded space junk. I wonder how long they have been there, I thought. Jesus, this place is a mess.

From behind me Earth rolled into view. Clouds clinging to its surface, hanging over North Africa casting a vast shadow down the continent.

Raining in North Africa.

It's raining.

The music had stopped. The sudden realisation of such abrupt silence rocked me. Was this the point in the movie where you see the silhouette of the killer in the kitchen doorway, your own knife in his hand? There was no one in the room, or even the house, it seemed, but me.

The rain lashed down outside. I could hear it spilling over the gutters and splashing down to the concrete patio.

Guapa Morena walked back into the room with the biggest grin on her face I had ever seen. I was lying on the sofa still. The duvet and several layers of clothing had been discarded. I was sweating heavily.

The silence was shattered by an amazing chorus of redneck jive that spiralled me off into signs of burning crosses and Nazi swastikas, fast cars and booze-fuelled rides. Down dark country lanes at high speed, the stereo cranking out Robert Mitchum's *Thunder Road*. It was around this time that the hopelessness of the situation became apparent. Then the uncontrollable laughter started. I remember babbling something like, 'This is the strongest acid I've had since the Double Dipped Red Dragon of Christmas ninety-one,' then realising what had happened that terrible night. A case of the shits had jolted me hard. What I left in the toilet I interpreted as my lower digestive system. Everywhere was splattered with blood and I had an incredibly empty feeling where my arsehole used to be. The rest of the evening became a hellish ride in a room that filled with hate and fear.

What the hell is that?

A figure stood on the mantelpiece, fat pink worms slipped around its body and over the long trench coat.

Neon, green, red, purple green, red, purple. The figure slumped to the side, catching its step. On its shoulder a crow flapped its wings frantically. The figure tried to move. It looked down. Two large nails, more like chisels, had been hammered through its feet, securing it to a large resin stand.

Undeterred, it wrenched itself free, propping itself on the Remington shotgun. It looked up at me. He's a soldier, I thought, probably First World War. Injured too.

Blood covered his bandaged face and the gun was replaced with a cheap dirty wooden crutch. He managed to limp a few steps then fell forwards. But he never hit the ground. The motion reversed, he recoiled back revealing a white skeletal face. A heavy black robe hid the rest of his body. He was sat in a great chair, in his right hand a large scythe, five foot long. The mists cleared behind him revealing a landscape that could only appear on a *Yes* album cover. Roger Dean castles surrounded by rolling hills and blue skies.

'No! I don't want that. Is this all you can give me after all these years of loyalty, fucking *Yes* album covers!'

It was then I recognised the skeletal man. The image conjured up thoughts of childhood half-dreams, in the time between you going to sleep and being asleep. And this guy was there.

'I've seen you before too . . . So don't give me that!'

There was a joint, half smoked in my hand. I fumbled around for a lighter. Smoking could be the only answer, the general feeling was getting ugly.

I was sat on the floor, now wearing shorts, a T-shirt with cut sleeves and sports sandals, black.

When did I get into these? I thought. I don't remember moving, but I must have 'cause I'm now down here.

There was a small glass bong in front of me. Had I smoked it already, or was I just planning to? I loaded the bong, smoked it and lay back on the floor. I could see the kitchen, a brown and dirty ashtray. The floor bubbled, spitting fat. It had turned into cheese and began browning under the huge ceiling grill.

It was getting hot again. I felt very light-headed. There seemed to be smoke everywhere. That copper taste was back in my mouth, a dirty old two-pence coin under the tongue.

Music began to creep in again and so did the green and red, little darts of light. The music got louder, the darts of light grew in number and ferocity.

'What music is that?'

'If you don't know now, you never will.'

Someone was laughing at me. I wanted to get up and find out who this evil person was. Who would laugh at a man in this depraved state? But before I could make my move my head filled with numbers, thousands of them. All of them, travelling downwards, almost like they were being pushed. Low-resolution images, photographs, electrical and digital diagrams.

Faster now, texts I had never seen before, in vibrant blues that turned into massive liquorice torpedo pills. Pieces of wire-frame geometry came from all sides, heading towards my central point of vision, smashing together to form some kind of weird machine. The motion got faster, pieces shot past me at a hundred miles an hour with trails of deep yellow everywhere. The thing in front of me began shaking violently, pieces still smashing into place. It better stop in a minute, I thought, or there'll be hell to pay.

Then the last piece, what looked like a fifty-foot-long toilet brush, hurtled overhead and slammed into the vibrating mass. Sparks exploded everywhere.

'My God, we're on fire, do something.'

The thing in front of me exploded, filling all my vision with white light.

'My head hurts,' I blurted. 'How do I get out of this thing, too much data, goddammit? You must have blown a fuse or something up there.'

The skeletal face appeared in front of me. Jesus, he looked pissed, I thought. Mouth open, he made a lunge for me, but I ducked.

'Just a minute, you crazy bastard,' I said. 'How the hell do I get out of here?'

The skull drove his shiny white cranium straight at me. 'Open your eyes, you arsehole!'

The room seemed stark. You could feel a vibe in the air. Something was coming. I remembered earlier in the evening Guapa Morena had said something like, 'For the coming of it all.' I didn't pay much attention at the time but now it seemed like there was something there. Did it mean something? What made me remember that earlier point of the evening? I couldn't remember anything else, just that one point in time. The more I thought about it, the more complicated it got. Heavy textured imprints spiralled across the walls that seemed to be dripping nicotine. Thick amber lung juice sliding down to the carpet, lumps dropping off.

Solid visible streams of music poured into the room, they looked like the reflections of a lake a foot above the ground. Someone else had seen this trip before, I remembered seeing it on TV. A bunch of university professors got two volunteers to take LSD so they could witness the responses the two men had.

One of the volunteers said he could see music coming out of the speaker. In my opinion this guy had done it before, he looked broken already.

Streams of this musical ribbon filled the front room.

There were four giant lizards on the wall playing cards over a crap table. They were all smoking and drinking cheap red wine. The cards were already on the table, all but the lizards at the top of the table.

He leaned forwards, laying down his hand, a royal flush. Top lizard leaned over the crap table to take his winnings. He looked up at me, grinning insanely. He wore a pair of those cheap imitation black Ray-Ban sunglasses, £2.99, as I last recall.

The other three lizards lunged for him, losing their footing.

All four tumbled out of the wall and on to the floor. As they hit, the lizards sprouted torn ears, dirty brown fur, wormlike tails and huge yellow claws.

'Jesus God! Rats all over the floor . . . nasty-looking fuckers too.'

They instantly started scampering round insanely and eating the carpet. I looked back up at the wall, unable to grasp the idea of four giant rats eating everything in this room, possibly even me. They were sure to spot me soon enough.

There was now a hole in the wall where the crap table had been. Through the hole, darkness. No, wait, I could see things moving. Eyes, no, a body, something hairy. Hundreds of huge dirty brown rats began throwing themselves out of the hole. Others clambered down the wall, widening the hole. They were everywhere, fat, foul-smelling, eating everything in sight.

I jumped up. 'Jesus jumping H Christ, this room is full of rats!'

All the rats stopped eating and turned to stare at me. They seemed unsure as to whom I was talking about.

'You better calm down, man,' came a voice. 'I'd say you lost it right about now. Look at the state of you.'

From then on things got very hazy, a resting room filled with bong and pipe smoke, music and the disjointed aspect that life takes at four in the morning when you're high on LSD, hash and marijuana.

The television was on. It spilled freaked-out Nazi dustmen, who spoke of loving children and killing any man that wronged him. On the news, the London nail bomber, David Copeland, had just been caught. A quiet and polite young man who looked like he spent a lot of time in his bedroom. A classic case, I thought, that's what happens. The good people are in their rooms building huge explosives and then there are the bad freaks like us, wrecked from an acid binge, turned to primeval jelly on a floor and being eaten by giant rats.

The revelations of the bomber's involvement in a Nazi organisation and his attempts to start a race war wouldn't be told for another year, but I think people already knew. His targets had been London's Brick Lane and Brixton, both multi-ethnic communities, and a Soho gay bar. He couldn't have been more than seventeen or eighteen. At that age I had my first joint. A late starter by all counts for this country. With no one around to teach me, I decided I'd have to dive straight in on my own.

By the end of 1993 the people, including myself, and the landscape had become very ugly. But the summer of that year was the height of my drug frenzy. Quite a good summer by British standards too.

There wasn't a drought all summer. Everything flowed through that fated top-floor flat all summer and I took my fair share. It was a time of anger, happy hate, the discovery of Ween and rejection of all that normal everyday life could offer. There was no real culture to it, just a bunch of chemically confused young mutants that took it as far as it could go, for the plain and simple reason of why not? Some of them never came back from what I heard. Others are still going.

The world is a very different place now, seven years later. Everything 'sexy', 'dynamic' and 'mobile'. A world where business and money control everything. It's economically viable to rip that person off. All the men in the office aspire to be Bret Easton Ellis's *American Psycho*, axing your work associates to death for fear that they may be just that bit better than you. Got to have the right car, the right clothes, the right woman, the right position in the office. They all seem to aspire to be this 1980s yuppie ideal. It's now hip to be in Grey business; no matter what it is, you can always ham it up when asked. Everything all your 1980s punk albums told you it would be. Is this what we are supposed to aspire to? Is this what adult life is meant to be in the twenty-first century?

If so, I want no part of it, this gig ain't for me. The only enjoyable thing in the very corporate world of the computer-game industry is watching all the other stray mutants crawling out of the woodwork. And you can spot the mutants a mile off, it's like they look at you and they know. Monsters from the dance and acid generations of the late eighties and early nineties.

I sit in that office most days and it feels like my head is

going to burst. I want to dance naked on my desk and hurl the monitor through the window into the building site below. I haven't, not yet anyway. Maybe that day will come, maybe not. But for now things were peaceful. Life was good. Guapa Morena sat next to me glaring at the TV like she wanted to kill it. We were stoned, ripped, broken, wrecked and we were more the wiser for it.

'Acid: The journey through living-room walls', 2001

All Nature wears one universal grin

Henry Fielding

J. Kelly
I Talk to Cows, You Know

DIPPING MY HEAD into the bath the other night, I was strangely reminded of an experience some years ago, when I had more sensory assaults of such intensity and ferocity in several hours than I ever had before or since. I did repeat the experience, innumerable times, but then it was just crazed, repetitive drugs-by-numbers; combined with several day-long binges, featuring far too much cheap alcohol in the style of 'King's Acre' industrial cider, and standard-issue mental collapse.

I was seventeen years of age, from a small Northern Irish town specialising in unqualified sectarianism and political bigotry; relatively sheltered from the effects of very strong hallucinogenic chemicals, but a town nonetheless. As far as I know the town is still in situ today.

That night was probably 30/31 October '88. As a virgin of serious drugs (I had, like, you know, smoked a bit of 'hash' like), it was time to ingest with the big boys; or at least in this case, a big boy who was, and as far as I can ascertain, still is, my Best-Mate-Like. It was to mean lysergic acid dyethylamide, or acid to children.

It started with a phone call.

'Hello, Stex?'

'Alright? What's up, like?'

'Are you comin' up tonight for some nonsense?'

'For your birthday? What have you got in mind?'

'Ho! Ho! Hee! Hee!'

'Right, see you around nine.'

And so it began. This was going to be a wee bit different, because he wouldn't tell me what was going to happen. But it obviously involved: a) drugs; b) huge amounts of drugs; c) high jinx.

I was left off by a mother who would gain a very different son come the next morning (and, of course, probably didn't notice); a morning when I had to go down the town and sit in the car to put off the traffic wardens, after having my mind well and truly refitted.

We must have ventured down the town before the act, because we had bought some booze (undrunk), and bizarrely, no, sadly, rented a 'blue movie' entitled *China White*, starring Ron Jeremy; a gentleman who was to cause amusement, excitement and, ultimately, confusion in the opening salvoes of the campaign. Years later, when Friend was in LA he met the said porn king, and recounted this sorry tale; the reaction of Mr Ron Jeremy was not noted. We also pathetically rented a horror film of some description, featuring a clown type, replete with comic 'afro-dazzler' wig and clownesque foldedols. I think he killed people.

By the time the porno show came on, it was time to laugh, giggle, scream, and then latterly, during the tail end of 'stage one', to meoow at the lyrics and hairy façade of Ron Jeremy: 'Oh baby, you're still the best,' (rewind that bit), sqigglywigglywigglyblurp, 'Oh baby, you're still the best.' And on it went. I still have the copy we made, or should I say remixed, possibly creating some kind of sad teenage seminal porn-acid crossover gonzo flick in the process. A rather poor start to one's first trip, I know, but I didn't have to tell you that, so stay with it.

Of course things are really getting out of hand now:

'I can't see! I can't see!' they chirruped in stereo-super-surround-o-vision-thing . . . It was time for music . . . it was time for . . . and . . . and . . . and that as well! Putitonletslistentoanddoyouwantsomecheeseontoastokayi can'tfeelthebutterthistasteslikeidon'tknowlookatyourface! montypythonmusicfuckmedidyouhearthat? DID YOU HEAR THAT! Oh shit! Hippy freak-out. Freeze-frame two mindless youths in a seventies-style kitchen holding cheese on toast at rakish angles in a late-eighties kind of way. Something outside. And outside the spectrum of things-you-want-to-hear-on-acid. But then again, how would we actually know? STOP!

The successful tripper will instinctively know at this stage to either a) ignore whatever the noise or 'thing' is and make a smart comment to the rest of the group's delight, or b) embrace it as a new experience and meet it head on and busk it without involving the 'security forces'. This experience featured a scary tattooed man with moustache, lurching disconsolately on the street looking for all the world that he has one foot nailed to the ground and doing a Shakin' Stevens, slurring wildly; drink taken: 'Seriously, Cathy, you crack me up,' reply: 'Augh, would ye ever fack aff and get back in the fackin' hoose before the neighbours see ye, ye auld fackin' hoormaster!'

It is at this point that one realises alcohol is evil, pubs are a control to keep the masses happy, and couldn't we all just understand each other that wee bit more? Yes. We are now at stage three; the I-have-more-ideas-and-revelations-than-my-drug-retarded-mouth-can-cope-with-but-I-will-try-to-communicate-in-as-deep-and-meaningless-a-way-as-possible stage. Not great, but nonetheless an important step for our young trippers, because, dear reader, we are about to discover the meaning of Jesus. Praise his holy name!

This would be about the time when we fell UP the stairs. Yes, it is possible – if LSD is not available try a couple of ten-glass bottles of good vodka. Or both! – I seem to recollect the use of tongues, possibly as some kind of steering device, but at this stage things really go into, well . . . If you are a veteran, you will know, and I can only tell you baldly what we said or did, but to really feel it, well, take a pinch of psychedelic.

Things will be getting a bit wild at this stage and you'll be really into them at this point, and you'll be really falling through the floor at this point, and you'll really be laughing like a demented hyena at this point, and at this point I love you, please, and now I'm gurning my eyes out, but it's only because I feel nothing but love! And I understand suffering. And I'm such a cunt thank you. Allluurhurheeeah! I'm swimming! Look! I can swim! Quick! Throw me a pen! Laughing. Laughing. What are you doing? 'Jee-ee-sus, say-ay-ve meeee.' What was I doing? Grapple with a pen. Why does the pen move so funny? What's so funny? I need to do something. What do I need to do? Ah! I need to do a big pish.

This gets rid of any pre-trip stuff in your system and lets the drug hit you with renewed vigour. That is, if you ever get over your first pish on acid. Better than sex? Certainly better than pissed sex. Of making an acid 'toilette' for the first time, imagine your first slash, then multiply it by an eternity encased in soft French gloving leather passed through a velvet urethra with orgasmic notes and the merest hint of loganberry toilet cleaner. The drug has now indeed hit me with a renewed vigour, so as my companion hits the lavatory, I busy myself by watching the lyrics of some song waft gently around the room, wearing the rapt expression of a Victorian moth enthusiast seeing his first really big one for the first time. I have no net, however.

This is the time of the most fantastic hallucinations. One has to appreciate the effect of all this on two idiot youths from a town where all limits are strictly defined and imposed. All gone, with one deft movement of a centimetre square on a tongue. Now we are grappling with our completely fucked minds, rather like those drunk men fighting in pubs – in slow motion and under water. We didn't expect THIS. Trying to make sense of a door, and doing so. Do we suddenly understand physics and quantum mechanics? Of course we do! We know everything. And instantly forget it.

And so on to the main event and, it must be said, most

enjoyable part of the evening, due to its lack of thinking quality: the music mong.

This involves the old, old ritual of trying to roll joints, or even one joint. To each drug is ascribed its own inherent brand of user shitness. Ask any acid eater of their joint-rolling activities and invariably it will involve long trips through darkened, insalubrious areas to fetch skins from the twenty-four-hour garage, meeting the ubiquitous madman (see above for details), and returning through the rain to a hell-hovel strewn with the last six months of your acid-brained existence, only to find that Tunnocks Tea Cakes and twenty Marboro cannot be used to fashion a joint. Still, have a fag (or 'straight' to our American pals), and be prepared to go back out. That's number-one tripper's classic. The other is the fact, the money-down cert, that when tripping furiously one's hands go into a complete funk ('Tripper's Fingers'), they suffer from an odd convulsive sweaty palsy, thus rendering joint rollage ineffectual at best and downright surreal at worst. I have seen grown men eat good hashish in resigned desperation, and these were seasoned campaigners: 'Mon, I just can't get it together, I'm so out of my mind, mon.' After several attempts with blotting paper and Sellotape we manage an ersatz spliff. It's odd how the hardest-wrought joint tastes the sweetest.

And then the song. One artiste that night stands out in particular, more for their glaring inappropriateness than anything; and also the inescapable fact that I had never heard anything quite as insanely forceful before. The song, the song. Who could forget the lovely voice of Mr David Yow, of the now sadly demised Jesus Lizard singing the lovely lines: '*Would you like to have a blockbuster up your ass? Do you think you'd like that, do ya, mutherfucker?*' Yes, indeed. This caused a minor how-do-you-do in the bedroom at the time. Cautiously a conversation emerged.

'That's fuckin' amazin',' my fellow blunderer quipped, pillow-eyed, and I, for one, had to concur, that indeed, it was, truly fucking amazing.

Stex Kelloggs and The Man With No Nickname tripped courtesy of Purple Ohms (aka Mind, Body and Soul), available from all reputable paramilitaries Province-wide.

'I Talk to Cows, You Know', 2001

Tim Southwell
Chained to a Mirror and a Razorblade

I WALKED INTO the *Loaded* office at about 10.30 a.m. The place was strangely quiet. There were a lot of people about but no one was talking. I asked Michael Holden what was going on and he informed me that James Brown had burst in a few minutes earlier and announced that the place was going to be raided by the police at any second on account of our reputation for taking lots of drugs.

'But no one brings 'em in here,' I said.

'I know,' replied Michael, 'but James is convinced there's gonna be a raid any minute.'

I started checking my drawers for unwanted contraband and then realised it was ridiculous. As far as I knew, no one at *Loaded* was stupid enough to hold up a load of drugs in their desks. I certainly knew there was none in mine and yet here I was checking the things as if I was clearing out my crack den. There was no doubt about it, cocaine paranoia had us in its fearful grip.

The mid-1990s was the era of Oasis and *Loaded*. Everyone was 'up for it', 'mad for it' and rather partial to the odd line of charles charlie charles. If Ecstasy was the drug of fancy-free acid-house ravers, cocaine was certainly the drug of the mid-1990s boy about town looking for a good time and to hell with tomorrow.

Everyone who's ever taken coke will know that it doesn't do you any good. It fills you full of confidence and Arthur Daley-speak for a couple of hours and then in the following days steals your sleep and tampers with your soul.

Yet for the Oasis/*Loaded* generation it was, Noel Gallagher famously said, 'As natural as having a cup of tea.' Well, maybe we're not all millionaire pop stars but at some stage everyone was having a go at it because there suddenly didn't seem any reason not to.

Loaded was no exception. Personally, I'd never even touched cocaine before working there. Suddenly, everyone you met was talking at breakneck speed all over each other, not listening to a single word anyone else was saying, except when they ventured 'not too bad, is it?' or 'fancy another one?'

Blimey, it was like the stuff had just been invented. For £50 you could snort up the finest mixture of baby laxative (interspersed with the odd grain of Bolivian marching powder) in the land.

In terms of performance enhancement, coke had very little to do with *Loaded*'s success. It kept you sharp and got you into 'good copy' scrapes on trips, but it was never really an office thing. For *Loaded* the drug was, as far as I know, an occasional party thing, rocket fuel for when you really wanted to cut loose and go crazy. It wasn't big and it wasn't clever but it added to the very real sense of adventure and created more than one caper.

But there's more to it than that. A couple of years prior to *Loaded*'s launch I never even knew anyone who touched cocaine. Now I don't know anyone who hasn't. And it's not just media types either. Everyone's at it. People who you'd never imagine: schoolteachers, doctors, builders, traffic wardens, shopkeepers, lollipop ladies, they're all round the back sorting themselves out.

Getting Away with It, 2001

James Hawes
Dead Long Enough

AND THEN THE guy in the bandanna asked if anyone needed sorting, and Harry said yes.

So, maybe Harry wasn't actually fucked from the day he was born. Maybe it was just the drugs. Later, when he was about to take his third line, I did my friendly duty and pointed out to Harry that he, Harry, had always said that junkies were just very unhappy people who would be addicted to something else if they were not junkies: did that not mean that he, Harry, being about to hit the booster and go finally to Escape Velocity, must logically be deeply unhappy? And if he was, at this time, for whatever reason, so deeply unhappy as to want to whack his frontal lobes through the top of his skull with charlie on top of E, maybe it would be better to knock it on the head right now and come for a walk home with me, his old and trusted friend?

He looked at me and said:—Do you want a line or not?

So maybe this is not a story of inescapable destiny but a simple morality tale whose point is that it would never have happened if not for the drugs. Or maybe that if you are going to do drugs, you should do them rather longer before your fortieth birthday, and somewhat closer to your own home turf.

So let's assume, for the time being, that we could have turned the drugs down and escaped. It would have been easy for me, at any rate. Honestly, I haven't touched drugs for years, except on Harry's False Birthdays, for three very simple reasons: (a) I don't need them, (b) I can't afford them and (c) I never come across them now. The bubble I live in never even bumps up against the bubble of the people for whom drugs are just part of Friday night. I'd never dropped an E in my life, actually. Too old to have. Or the wrong place? The wrong bubble? I mean, I had been mid-twenties, single, slim and fit, earning pretty good money, with relatively large amounts of free time and living in Zone Two . . . and I had never even bloody *heard* of the supposedly earth-shaking Summer of Love until I read about it in the papers the year afterwards. I suppose it was probably like that with most people in 1968, too.

We did coke sometimes, back then, but rarely, because it was bloody expensive. Even then I always thought charlie has only three social functions: one is to make you want to shag everyone while talking about yourself, two is to make you want more charlie and three is to make everything else seem ridiculously cheap. I mean, *why on earth not* pay hundreds of quid for some crap designer jumper, darling, if you confidently expect to put that much up your nose over the coming week or two? Why not have a Porsche? It's only a kilo, for Christ's sake. The ultimate consumer label. And since I never bought labels of any kind these days (I didn't shop any more, I went to M&S) I didn't long for this one either. Seriously, I had not even thought about drugs for years.

And yet, and yet: even as I saw Harry pay off Mr Bandanna and a palm teeny envelope and four little pink pills, even before he reached over and handed me three of them, without a word, I could feel cold waves of change rippling up and down my body in expectation, as if I was one of those kids' transforming robots. It couldn't have been physical addiction, so what was it? What was I addicted to?

All addiction is mental. No, not mental: social. It is *people* we are addicted to, hopelessly: the crap that we think we need, that carries the signs of our addiction, is just whatever particular brand of crap we associate with the people we have met and liked and now need. If they are into old cars, we will start helplessly ogling glossy magazines in order to store up facts about vintage Aston Martins we can never own; if tennis is where we found them, we shall start to obsess about racquets which are infinitely, comically better than we are; if movies are what we talk about, we shall become film buffs, just to be able to talk to them. And if they happen to be coke fiends or smackheads, or E-chicks, then we shall cultivate a semi-addiction just to make sure that when we sit with them, with these people we like to sit with, we are never short of a subject for a chat. A sure subject for a chat: that is all we want, and we will pay whatever price we have to pay to get it. Whether it is your poshy Soho cokehead club or some horrible ten-pound-bag party in a council flat that rears above the station in Sheffield, it is always the same: we do it because the people we are with do it.

So we chat, about philosophy or fitness, French lit. or soft furnishings, just to keep hearing the sound of the voices we like. We don't care what we chat about, because in the half-lit depths of our heads, all we see are their lips moving, their eyes looking, and the soft, unsynched, meaningless sound of their presence with us. Which is why people become smackheads or coke fiends: what security! When you find your smackhead or coke-fiend pals in your bar, be it marbled swankery or some dive one step up from the park bench, you know instantly what to say the moment your arse touches the still-warm seat left by whoever just got up.

And there you sit: secure as any born-again in his chapel, snug as a bug in a rug.

Dead Long Enough, 2001

Marek Kohn
Cocaine Girls in the West End

YOUNG WOMEN (THUS) reflected the immaturity ascribed to them by opinion and by electoral law. The questions of citizenship and sexuality were intertwined: the principal symbolic quality of young womanhood is nubility, which casts an interesting light on the denial of the franchise to younger women. Politically conscious women of all ages saw the restriction as demeaning, and demanded universal adult suffrage. Young women also made an unformulated demand for autonomy in the shape of a style that identified freedom with the absence of adult responsibility. Its androgynous aspect emphasised that this was the active freedom of boys, rather than the traditional sequestered passivity of girls.

Against this movement, the forces of reaction were not only weak, but arguably counter-productive. Churchill remarked that it was Joynson-Hicks who got young women the vote. And as James Laver's contemporary verse suggested, there were other ways of voting besides the ballot box:

> Mother's advice, and Father's fears,
> Alike are voted – just a bore.
> There's negro music in our ears,

The world's one huge dancing floor.
We mean to tread the Primrose Path,
In spite of Mr. Joynson-Hicks.
We're People of the Aftermath
We're girls of 1926.

In greedy haste, on pleasure bent,
We have not time to think, or feel,
What need is there for sentiment
Now we've invented Sex Appeal?
We've silken legs and scarlet lips,
We're young and hungry, wild and free,
Our waists are round about the hips
Our skirts are well above the knee

We've boyish busts and Eton crops,
We quiver to the saxophone.
Come, dance before the music stops,
And who can bear to be alone?
Come drink your gin, or sniff your 'snow',
Since Youth is brief, and Love has wings,
And time will tarnish, ere we know,
The brightness of the Bright Young Things.

Dope Girls, 1992

Aleister Crowley
Au Pays de Cocaine

I HAD NEVER been particularly keen on women. The few love
affairs which had come my way had been rather silly and
sordid. They had not revealed the possibilities of love; in
fact, I had thought it a somewhat overrated pleasure, a brief
and brutal blindness with boredom and disgust hard on its
heels.

But with cocaine, things are absolutely different.

I want to emphasise the fact that cocaine is in reality a local

258

anaesthetic. That is the actual explanation of its action. One cannot feel one's body. (As everyone knows, this is the purpose for which it is used in surgery and dentistry.)

Now don't imagine that this means that the physical pleasures of marriage are diminished, but they are utterly etherealised. The animal part of one is intensely stimulated so far as its own action is concerned; but the feeling that this passion is animal is completely transmuted.

I come of a very refined race, keenly observant and easily nauseated. The little intimate incidents inseparable from love affairs, which in normal circumstances tend to jar the delicacy of one's sensibilities, do so no longer when one's furnace is full of coke. Everything soever is transmuted as by 'heavenly alchemy' into a spiritual beatitude. One is intensely conscious of the body. But, as the Buddhists tell us, the body is in reality an instrument of pain or discomfort. We have all of us a sub-conscious intuition that this is the case; and this is annihilated by cocaine.

Let me emphasise once more the absence of any reaction. There is where the infernal subtlety of the drug comes in. If one goes on the bust in the ordinary way on alcohol, one gets what the Americans call 'the morning after the night before'. Nature warns us that we have been breaking the rules; and Nature has given us common sense enough to know that although we can borrow a bit, we have to pay back.

We have drunk alcohol since the beginning of time; and it is in our racial consciousness that although 'a hair of the dog' will put one right after a spree, it won't do to choke oneself with hair.

But with cocaine, all this caution is utterly abrogated. Nobody would be really much the worse for a night with the drug, provided that he had the sense to spend the next day in a Turkish bath, and build up with food and a double allowance of sleep. But cocaine insists upon one's living upon one's capital, and assures one that the fund is inexhaustible.

As I said, it is a local anaesthetic. It deadens any feeling which might arouse what physiologists call inhibition. One becomes absolutely reckless. One is bounding with health and bubbling with high spirits. It is a blind excitement of so sublime a character that it is impossible to worry about anything. And yet, this excitement is singularly calm and profound. There is nothing of the suggestion of coarseness which we associate with ordinary drunkenness. The very idea of coarseness or commonness is abolished. It is like the vision of Peter in the Acts of the Apostles in which he was told, 'There is nothing common or unclean.'

As Blake said, 'Everything that lives is holy.' Every act is a sacrament. Incidents which in the ordinary way would check one or annoy one, become merely material for joyous laughter. It is just as when you drop a tiny lump of sugar into champagne, it bubbles afresh.

Well, this is a digression. But that is just what cocaine does. The sober continuity of thought is broken up. One goes off at a tangent, a fresh, fierce, fantastic tangent, on the slightest excuse. One's sense of proportion is gone; and despite all the millions of miles that one cheerily goes out of one's way, one never loses sight of one's goal.

Diary of a Drug Fiend, 1970

Hans Maier
Der Kokainismus

AFTER A NIGHT of sexual prowesses, compared to which the seven labours of Hercules were a mere nothing, *I* fell asleep, only to be immediately awakened by the renewed demands of my insatiable partner. I was able to verify on myself the degree to which cocaine renders women incapable of achieving sexual relation. Orgasm follows orgasm, each one further increasing the intensity of the desire. The most sexually potent man must eventually give up the hope of satisfying such a woman. There was nothing to do but flee in self-preservation.

1926. From: *Cocaine* by Dominic Streatfield, 2001.

CHAPTER THREE

LEGALISE IT

Howard Marks
Recreational Drugs

RECREATIONAL DRUGS ARE substances consumed for purposes other than medical treatment or sustenance.

Recreational drugs are capable of changing the way we feel, think, perceive and behave. They change one's state of mind. One's state of mind may also be changed physically by making oneself dizzy, bungee jumping, parachuting, hanggliding, climbing mountains, racing cars and horses, walking tight-ropes and fasting for several days. One's state of mind may be changed spiritually. There are those who get high on Jesus, confess to priests, talk to gurus, undergo purification rituals such as baptism or *puja* and go on pilgrimages. One's state of mind may be changed psychologically. Psychiatrists practising hypnotism, psychoanalysis and time regression remove neuroses and phobias.

It seems that the activity of changing states of minds, generally, is permitted, if not approved and encouraged, by the powers that be. Authorities have no problem with my getting a high from jumping off a cliff, or getting a buzz from being zapped by a witch doctor, or being mesmerised by a hypnotist.

And one could be forgiven, perhaps, for inferring that authorities might be equally approving of changing one's state of mind by taking recreational drugs. And authorities were so approving. A hundred years ago, any respectable person could walk into a chemist in Britain and choose from a range of cannabis tinctures, hashish pastes, cocaine lozenges and opium extracts. He could immediately purchase morphine, heroin and a hypodermic syringe.

Recreational drugs exist, and some people want to take them. Authorities have attempted both to persuade people not to take recreational drugs and to rid the planet of them. The persuasion has been ineffectual and it appears that God or Nature or some equally significant entity has done a good job of furnishing the Earth with all manner of recreational drugs.

> That humanity at large will ever be able to dispense with artificial paradises seems very unlikely. Most men and women lead lives at the worst so painful, at the best so monotonous, poor and limited, that the urge to escape . . . is and has always been one of the principal appetites of the soul.
>
> – Aldous Huxley

There is no society anywhere in the world, nor at any time in history, that has not used an intoxicant.

Stewart Lee Allen
The Devil's Cup: Ladies' Lament

THE HUMBLE PETITION and Address of Several Thousand of Buxome Good-Women, Languishing in Extremity of Want . . .

SHEWETH
That since 'tis Reckon'd amongst the Glories of our native Country To be A paradise for women, it is too our unspeakable Grief we find of late that our gallants are become mere Cock-sparrows, fluttering things that come on with a world of Fury but in the very first Charge fall down Flat before us . . . all these qualities we can Attribute to nothing more than

excessive use of the most pernicious Coffee, where Nature is Enfeebled and our men left with Ammunition Wanting; peradventure they Present but cannot give Fire . . . Certainly our Countrymen's palates are become as Fanatical as their Brains. How else is it possible they should run a Whoreing to spend the money and time on a little base, black thick, nasty, Bitter, Stinking, Nauseous, Puddle-water (also known as Ninny's Broth and Turkish Gruel), so that those that have scarce twopence to buy their children bread must spend a penny each evening in this insipid stuff . . .

Wherefore we pray that drinking *COFFEE* be forbidden to all Persons under the Age of Threescore and that Lusty Nappy Beer and Cock Ale be Recommended to General Use . . . so that our Husbands may (in time) give us some other Testimonies of the being Men, besides their Beards, and that they no more shall run the hazard of being Cuckold by Dildos.

In Hopes of A Glorious Reformation, London, 1674

The Devil's Cup, 2000

And a woman is only a woman, but a good cigar is a smoke
Rudyard Kipling

King James I of England, VI of Scotland
Counterblast to Tobacco

THAT THE MANIFOLD abuses of this vile custom of tobacco taking, may the better be espied; it is fit that first you enter into confederation both of the first original thereof and likewise of the reason of the first entry thereof into this country; for certainly as such customs that have their first infiltration either from a godly, necessary, or honourable ground, and are first brought in by means of some worthy virtuous and great personage; are never, and more justly holden in great reverent estimation and account by all wise virtuous and temperate spirits; so should it by the contrary, justly bring a great disgrace into that sort of customs, which having their original base corruption and barbarity, do, in like sort, make their first entry into a country, by an inconsiderate and childish affectation of novelty, as is the true case of the first invention of tobacco taking and the first entry thereof among us . . . it rests only to inform you what sins and vanities you commit in the filthy abuse thereof:

First, are you not guilty of sinful and shameful lust (for lust may be as well in any of the senses as in feeling) that although you be troubled with no disease, but in perfect health, yet can you neither be merry at an ordinary, not lascivious in the stews, if you lack tobacco to provoke your appetite to any of those sorts of recreation lusting after it as the children of Israel did in the wilderness after quails.

Second, it is as you use, or rather abuse, it a branch of the sin of drunkenness, which is the root of all sins; for as the only delight that drunkards take in wine is in the strength of the taste, and the force of the fume thereof that mounts up to the brain, for no drunkards love any weak or sweet drink. So are not those (I mean the strong heat fume) the only qualities that make tobacco so delectable to all the lovers of it? And no man likes strong heady drink the first day (because *nenia repentefit turpissimus*) but by custom is piece and piece allured, while in the end, a drunkard will have as great a thrill to be drunk as a sober man to quench his thirst with a draught when he hath need of it. So is not this the very case of all the great takers of tobacco which therefore they themselves do attribute to a bewitching quality in it?

Have you not reason to be ashamed and to forbear this filthy novelty, so basely grounded, so foolishly received and so grossly mistaken in the right use thereof. In your abuse thereof sinning against God harming yourselves both in person and goods, and raking also thereby the marks and notes of vanity upon you by the custom thereof making yourselves to be wondered at by all foreign civil nations and by all strangers that come among you to be scorned and held in contempt; a custom loathsome to the eye, hateful to the nose, harmful to the brain, dangerous to the lungs, and in the black stinking fume thereof nearest resembling the horrible stygian smoke of the pit that is bottomless.

'Counterblast to Tobacco', 1604

For *thy sake, Tobacco, I*
Would do anything but die

Charles Lamb

Antonil
Mama Coca

AN OFFICIAL OF the Spanish Inquisition, on a mission to Quito between 1623 and 1628, described the Dominican and Augustinian monks of that city in the following terms:

'Sire, they do take coca in these two orders with the greatest abandon, a herb in which the devil has invested the most essential of his diabolic tricks, and which makes them drunk and out of their senses, so that being beside their normal selves they say and do things unworthy of Christians, and even less of ecclesiastics. I think that if the Inquisition does not use a very strong hand with such an infernal superstition, all this will be lost . . .'

Mama Coca, 1978

Mohammed El Guindy
Opium as an International Problem

The subject of Indian hemp or hashish was presented to the Second Opium Conference at its sixteenth meeting by M. El Guindy, the Egyptian delegate, in a carefully prepared address. In addition, there were circulated two documents

265

dealing with the subject. From M. El Guindy's address the
following excerpts may be given:

We must next consider the effects which are produced by the use of hashish and distinguish between (1) acute hashishism and (2) chronic hashishism.

Taken in small doses, hashish at first produces an agreeable inebriation, a sensation of well-being and a desire to smile; the mind is stimulated. A slightly stronger dose brings a feeling of oppression and of discomfort. There follows a kind of hilarious and noisy delirium in persons of a cheerful disposition, but the delirium takes a violent form in persons of violent character. It should be noted that the behaviour under the influence of the delirium is always related to the character of an individual. The state of inebriation or delirium is followed by slumber, which is usually peaceful but sometimes broken by nightmares. The awakening is not unpleasant; there is a slight feeling of fatigue, but it soon passes.

Hashish absorbed in large doses produces a furious delirium and strong physical agitation; it predisposes to acts of violence and produces a characteristic strident laugh. This condition is followed by a veritable stupor, which cannot be called sleep. Great fatigue is felt on awakening, and the feeling of depression may last for several days.

The habitual use of hashish brings on chronic hashishism. The countenance of the addict becomes gloomy, his eye is wild and the expression of his face stupid. He is silent; has no muscular power; suffers from physical ailments, heart troubles, digestive troubles, etc.; his intellectual faculties gradually weaken and the whole organism decays. The addict very frequently becomes neurasthenic and, eventually, insane.

In general, the absorption of hashish produces hallucinations, illusions as to time and place, fits of trembling and convulsions. A person under the influence of hashish presents symptoms very similar to those of hysteria.

Taken thus occasionally and in small doses, hashish perhaps does not offer much danger, but there is always the risk that once a person begins to take it, he will continue. He acquires the habit and becomes addicted to the drug, and, once this has happened, it is very difficult to escape. Notwithstanding the humiliations and penalties inflicted on addicts in Egypt, they always return to their vice. They are known as 'hashashees', which is a term of reproach in our country, and they are regarded as useless derelicts.

Chronic hashishism is extremely serious, since hashish is a toxic substance, a poison against which no effective antidote is known. It exercises a sedative and hypnotic effect.

The illicit use of hashish is the principal cause of most of the cases of insanity occurring in Egypt. In support of this contention, it may be observed that there are three times as many cases of mental alienation among men as among women, and it is an established fact that men are much more addicted to hashish than women. (In Europe, on the contrary, it is significant that a greater proportion of cases of insanity occur among women than among men.) Generally speaking, the proportion of cases of insanity caused by the use of hashish varies from 3 to 60 per cent of the total number of cases occurring in Egypt.

M. Bourgois, speaking for the French Delegation, said: 'From the medical point of view, there can be no doubt that hashish is very dangerous, and there is also no doubt that the governments wish to remove this danger. In France, hashish is treated exactly the same way as the drugs to which The Hague Convention applies. Each colony has its own regulations, based, in the first place, on local conditions and, in the second, on administrative possibilities. I would like to draw your attention to the difficulties encountered on both these points. Without going into the subject in detail, I may quote the fact that in the Congo, for example, there are several tribes of savages and even cannibals among whom the habit is very prevalent.'

From: Second International Opium Conference, 1924

Harry Anslinger
The Murderers

THOSE WHO ARE accustomed to habitual use of the drug are said eventually to develop a delirious rage after its administration, during which they are temporarily, at least, irresponsible and prone to commit violent crimes . . . a gang of boys tear the clothes from two schoolgirls and rape the screaming girls, one after the other. A sixteen-year-old kills his entire family of five in Florida; a man in Minnesota puts a bullet through the head of a stranger on the road; in Colorado a husband tries to shoot his wife, kills her grandmother instead and then kills himself. Every one of these crimes had been preceded by the smoking of one or two marijuana reefers.

The Murderers, 1961

The great masses of the people will more easily fall victims to a great lie than to a small one

Adolf Hitler

Daily Mirror
Marijuana

JUST A CIGARETTE, you'd think, but it was made from a sinister weed and an innocent girl falls victim to this TERROR! MARIHUANA.

Does that word mean anything to you? Perhaps you have heard vaguely that is a plant that is made into a drug. But do you know that in every city in this country there are addicts of this dangerous drug? In London there are thousands of them. Young girls, once beautiful, whose thin faces show the ravages of the weed they started smoking for a thrill. Young men, in the throes of a hangover from the drug, find their only relief in dragging at yet another marihuana cigarette. How do they obtain this drug – since the police are hot on the trail of all suspected traffickers? They obtain it from so many unexpected sources that as fast as one is closed by the police, so another opens up. As well as nightclubs, reputable hotels and cafés frequented by agents, they operate from the least likely places, milliners' shops, hairdressers, antique shops. But in Soho, in little lodging houses run by coloured men and women, the cigarette can be had for a secret password, and a very small sum of money. And many terrible tales are told about marihuana addicts.

One girl, just over twenty, known among her friends for her quietness and modesty, suddenly threw all caution to the winds. She began staying out late at nights; her parents became anxious when she began to walk about the house without clothes. They stopped her when she attempted to go into the street like that. At times she became violent and showed abnormal strength. Then she would flop down in a corner, weeping and crouching like an animal. Soon she left home, no trace could be found of her, but cigarettes and ends in her room were identified as marihuana.

How much does a marihuana cigarette cost? Just a shilling! Or in a 'reefer club', the low haunts where men, usually coloured, sell the cigarette, a puff can be had for sixpence. The fumes of the smoke are caressing, but they leave a somewhat acrid taste and a pungent, sickly smell. That is, to the beginner; the addict likes it, she likes it, not because of its taste or smell, but because it gives her abnormal strength and makes her indifferent to her surroundings. One day, passing a narrow street in Soho, I saw a crowd gazing at the third floor of a dingy house. A young and lovely woman, her clothes in shreds, stood perilously perched on a window ledge. Behind her was a man; he, too, was wild-looking and dishevelled; several times the girl made an effort to jump and the man feebly held her back. Soon, another man appeared. Coloured and strong, and hauled them both back. They were both marihuana addicts. As she disappeared, she could be heard screaming: 'I can fly. Well, I don't care if I die!' Unconscious of herself, or any danger, she acted on the impulse to do the impossible.

I heard of one case, a nineteen-year-old dancing girl who

was taken to a 'reefer club' by a party of friends. Soon a man was at her side, offering her a cigarette, for which he made no charge. It was a decoy. Soon she became one his best customers, spending half her salary on the weed. She sank lower and lower, her associates became criminals, drug lunatics and dope peddlers. Unlike opium, hashish and other drugs, which make their victims seek solitude, marihuana drives its victims into society, forcing them to violence, often murder. One man, in the delusion that his limbs were going to be cut off, killed his mother, father, brother and two sisters with an axe, another man would speak of people trying to corner him and hurl daggers at him. His sense of time, space and taste was distorted.

The seed is found in most hemp and birdseed. It isn't hard to make a marihuana cigarette; the plant is dried before a fire or the sun for a few days. The leaves are then chopped up and mixed with ordinary tobacco. Marihuana alone would be enough to kill the average man, and then they are loosely rolled into cigarettes, slightly shorter than the normal. For women, this menace of the cigarette is greater than for men. Here is a true story that illustrates this fact:

A girl of twenty-one was persuaded by a coloured man to elope with him. For months her father searched vainly for his daughter. One night he saw a girl. Her eyes staring wildly in front of her, her hands groping, her head leaning on a man's shoulder. He was horrified, but even more horrified when a second glance told him that this was his daughter, ravaged by neglect and ill-use. 'I am not going home. I'm going to America,' she wailed, when she saw her father. The man with her refused to give her up. The girl clung fiercely to him. There might have been a brawl but the father said 'I have a friend outside who will call the police if I'm not outside with my daughter in ten minutes.' Reluctantly his daughter went with him. In a few months she was cured of those nightmare weeks. It may happen to any man or woman. The next victim may be your best friend. A cigarette seems harmless enough but it is not so easy to check the craving. For marihuana can turn happy lives into hell.

circa 1960s *Daily Mirror*

Edward Huntingdon Williams, MD
Negro cocaine 'fiends' new Southern menace

Murder and Insanity Increasing Among Lower Class Because They Have Taken to 'Sniffing' Since Being Deprived of Whiskey by Prohibition

FOR SOME YEARS there have been rumors about the increase in drug taking in the South – vague, but always insistent rumors that the addiction to such drugs as morphine and cocaine was becoming a veritable curse to the colored race in certain regions. Some of these reports read like the wildest flights of a sensational fiction writer. Stories of cocaine orgies and 'sniffing parties' followed by wholesale murders seem like lurid journalism of the yellowest variety.

But in point of fact there was nothing 'yellow' about many of these reports. Nine men killed in Mississippi on one occasion by crazed cocaine takers, five in North Carolina, three in Tennessee – these are the facts that need no imaginative coloring. And since this gruesome evidence is supported by the printed records of the insane hospitals, courts, jails, and penitentiaries, there is no escaping the conviction drug taking has become a race menace in certain regions south of the line.

The effects of cocaine do not seem very different from those of alcohol. But in point of fact, cocaine exhilaration is much more marked and the depression far more profound and destructive to the nervous system. The victim is much more likely to have peculiar delusions and develop hallucinations of an unpleasant character. He imagines that he hears people taunting and abusing him, and this often incites homicidal attacks upon innocent and unsuspecting victims.

PROOF AGAINST BULLETS

But the drug produces several other conditions which make the 'fiend' a peculiarly dangerous criminal. One of these conditions is a temporary immunity to shock – a resistance to the knockdown effects of fatal wounds.

Bullets fired into vital parts, that would drop a sane man in his tracks, fail to check the 'fiend' – fail to stop his rush or weaken his attack. A few weeks ago Dr. Crile's method of preventing shock in anaesthetized patients by use of a cocaine preparation was described in these columns. A similar fortification against this condition seems to be produced in the cocaine-sniffing negro.

A recent experience of Chief of Police Byerly of Asheville, N.C., illustrates this particular phase of cocainism. The Chief was informed that a hitherto inoffensive negro, with whom he was well acquainted, was 'running amuck' in a cocaine frenzy, had attempted to stab a storekeeper, and was at the moment engaged in 'beating up' various members of his own household. Being fully aware of the respect that the negro has for brass buttons (and, incidentally, having a record for courage), the officer went single-handed to the negro's house for the purpose of arresting him. But when he arrived there the negro had completed the beatings and left the place. A few moments later, however, the man returned, and entered the room where the Chief was waiting for him, concealed behind a door. When the unsuspecting negro reached the middle of the room, the chief closed the door to prevent his escape and informed him quietly that he was under arrest, and asked him to come to the station. In reply the crazed negro drew a long knife, grappled with the officer, and slashed him viciously across the shoulder.

Knowing that he must kill this man or be killed himself, the Chief drew his revolver, placed the muzzle over the negro's heart, and fired – 'intending to kill him right quick,' as the officer tells it but the shot did not even stagger the man. And a second shot that pierced the arm and entered the chest had as little effect in stopping his charge or checking his attack.

Meanwhile, the Chief, out of the corner of his eye, saw infuriated negroes rushing toward the cabin from all directions. He had only three cartridges remaining in his gun, and he might need these in a minute to stop the mob. So he saved his ammunition and 'finished the man with his club.'

The following day, the Chief exchanged his revolver for one

of heavier caliber. Yet, the one with which he shot the negro was a heavy, army model, using a cartridge that Lieutenant Townsend Whelen who is an authority on such matters, recently declared was large enough to 'kill any game in America.' And many other officers in the South, who appreciate the increased vitality of the cocaine-crazed negroes, have made a similar exchange for guns of greater shocking power for the express purpose of combating the 'fiend' when he runs amok.

The list of dangerous effects produced by cocaine just described – hallucinations and delusions, increased courage, homicidal tendencies, resistance to shock – is certainly long enough. But there is still another, and a most important one. This is a temporary steadying of the nervous and muscular system, so as to increase, rather than interfere with, good marksmanship.

MAKES BETTER MARKSMEN

Many of the wholesale killings in the South may be cited as indicating that accuracy in shooting is not interfered with – is, indeed, probably improved – by cocaine. For a large proportion of such shootings have been the result of drug taking. But I believe the record of the 'cocaine nigger' near Asheville, who dropped five men dead in their tracks using only one cartridge for each, offers evidence that is sufficiently convincing. I doubt if this shooting record has been equaled in recent years: certainly not by a man under the influence of any other form of intoxicant. For the bad marksmanship of the drunken man is proverbial, while the deadly accuracy of the cocaine user has become axiomatic in Southern police circles.

WHY DO THEY DO IT?

Many of the negroes, even those who have not yet become addicted, appreciate the frightful penalty of dabbling with the drug. Why, then, do so many of them 'dabble'?

There are various facts that suggest an answer to this question, and evidence in the form of the opinions of physicians, officers and the cocaine users themselves that supports these facts. The 'fiend' when questioned, frequently gives his reason in this brief sentence: 'Cause I couldn't git nothin' else, boss.' That seems to be the crux of the whole matter.

A brief survey of conditions in the South and a bit of recent legislative history make it perfectly evident why the negro 'couldn't git nothin' else'.

In many states in the South, the negro population constitutes from 30 to 60 percent of the total population. Most of the negroes are poor, illiterate and shiftless. If we include in this class the poor whites, who are on a par with the average negro in poverty, ignorance and general lack of thrift, we may reckon the aggregate number as representing about one person in three in the entire population. Governing, or even keeping in reasonable control, such a host is an onerous task, even when most of the individuals of the host are sober. The inevitable number of alcoholics adds to that task enormously.

The simplest way to remove this added menace – it seems simple, theoretically, at least – would be to keep whiskey out of the low-class negro's hands by legislating it out of existence as far as he is concerned. And so Georgia, North Carolina, South Carolina, Mississippi, Tennessee and West Virginia passed laws intended to abolish the saloon and keep whiskey and the negro separated. These laws do not, and were not intended to, prevent the white man or the well-to-do negro getting his accustomed beverages through legitimate channels. They obliged him to forego the pleasure of leaning against a bar and 'taking his drink perpendicularly,' to be sure; but a large portion of the intelligent whites were ready to make this sacrifice if by doing so they could eliminate the drunken negro.

Of course it is nothing short of 'class legislation,' this giving to the rich and depriving the poor. But what of it, so long as the discrimination applies to whiskey? Nothing, of course – provided, always, that those discriminated against do not find some substitute worse than the original trouble maker. But unfortunately for the negro, and for his community, such a substitute was found almost immediately – a substitute that is inestimably worse even than the 'moonshine whiskey,' drugstore nostrums, or the deadly wood alcohol poison. This substitute, as I have pointed out, is cocaine; and a trail of blood and disaster has marked the progress of its substitution.

New York Times, Sunday, 8 February 1914

Antonio Escohotado
Drugs, Lust, and Satan

SOME CONSIDER THAT the medieval witch, cooking children to obtain their fat, desiring only infamy, was an invention of the inquisitors that ended up being generally believed. Others feel that they were in fact unusual beings, tending to look for artificial paradises in plants. There are also those who consider them to be representatives of the old, basically Celtic region of Western Europe. In any case, they were accused of organizing demonic rites, the so-called Sabbats, using ointments and potions. Very few people confessed to being witches until Gregory IX issued the first papal bull against them, granting the inquisitors the right to confiscate their property and belongings. Some time later, the number of sorcerers and witches had grown to grandiose proportions, and the *Roman de la Rose*, for example, declared that 'one-third of all French women' were witches.

The relationship between drugs, lust and witchcraft is exact. In 1692 the inquisitor Johannes Nider described an old woman who rubbed a certain ointment in her armpits and groin: 'After disrobing and applying this ointment she fell asleep, and with the aid of the Devil, she dreamt of the lustful Venus.'

Centuries before, in the trials of Carcasonne, the confession of an old herbalist woman read: 'In the Sabbat I found a gigantic male goat, I surrendered to him, and in return he taught me the poisonous plants.'

In 1324 a document of the Inquisition explained the belief

in flying brooms: 'While searching the attic of the lady, an ointment was found that she used to anoint a walking stick, mounted upon which she could wander and gallop through any obstacle.'

In 1470 another inquisitorial document declared 'the witches confess that on some nights they anoint a stick in order to reach a certain location, or else they rub themselves with an ointment in their armpits or in other places on the body where hair grows.'

In a woman, the other place where hair grows is that which is in contact with a broom when she rides it. The stick was used to rub or insert ointment in areas that the modesty of the inquisitor prevented him from describing, the stick serving as a sort of chemically reinforced dildo.

The same thing is suggested by a confession extracted from two women in 1540, since they 'many times, in solitude, carnally knew the Devil; and when questioned whether they had known some special delight in doing so, they repeatedly denied it, and that because of the incomparable coldness they felt in their diabolic parts.'

When inquisitors were absent, the women responded in a somewhat different manner, although the erotic might still remain. Using a certain sorcerer's ointment provided by a constable, Andres de Laguna, doctor of Charles V and Julius III, put a hysterical patient in a deep stupor. Upon her return to a normal, she addressed the doctor and her own husband, saying, 'Why did you wake me up at this time, when I was surrounded by all the pleasures of the world?' And looking at her husband, smiling, she told him: 'Stingy, I have been unfaithful to you, and with a younger and better-looking lover than you.'

[T]he use of drugs other than alcohol was punished with torture and death, regardless of whether it was religious or for enjoyment. Simultaneously, drugs were looked upon not as precise substances but rather as something riding on horse-back between an infamous aspiration and a certain ointment. 'If the accused is found with ointments on his body, subject him to torture,' says Jean Bodin in his *Instructions for Judges in the Matter of Sorcery*. This gave permission to burn people found owning an ointment for relieving pain, as long as the person appeared to be suspicious or had enemies; it was also possible that in another dwelling, the presence of very psychoactive pomades would be considered innocuous. But dealing with plants and potions seemed to authorities to be too close to abomination, and put in question the official explanation of things: namely, that the world – punished by God – was full of witches with supernatural powers, thanks to their alliance with Satan.

The drugs of the witches betrayed what was eminently forbidden, which is the desire to embrace what is *here*, as opposed to the fervor for the *beyond*. Nevertheless, the desire to again feel at home on Earth, instead of exiled in it, was what the Renaissance, the animating spirit of the modern era, was all about. Best illustrated by Faust, the new man preferred to sell his soul to the Devil rather than adore a God who is in conflict with life.

To do so he leaned of course on psychoactive substances. The formulas for ointments transmitted by Cardano and Porta contain not only hashish, female hemp flowers, opium and solanaceous plants but also ingredients of high sophistication, such as toad skins (which contain dimethyltryptamine, or DMT) or ergot-infested flour (which contains lysergic acid amide), as well as fungi and visionary mushrooms. With such a variety of drugs, and the potency derived from their admixture, a competent European sorcerer could induce various trances. He could officiate in rural ceremonies and supply the urban user, oriented toward solitary dreams and ecstasies, inaugurating an underground commerce of ointments and potions, which – under inquisitorial persecution – would become a profitable target for constables and reward hunters.

The Inquisition in the Americas started with identical premises and persecuted large numbers of natives for using their traditional drugs. It was so effective, in fact, that not until the middle of the twentieth century were many rites related to peyote, psilocybin, mushrooms and other psychoactive plants rediscovered.

The inquisitor, however, did not find in the New World the direct connection between eroticism and drugs that he saw in Europe. There were an enormous number of psychoactive substances and uses there, not to mention cults, but what was missing was the repeated scene of women in trance with things that – rubbed on broomsticks and horns – transported them to orgies demanding the attire of Eve and the ease of Venus.

The vehicles for inebriation were also different in America and in Europe. After the destruction of the ancient pharmacological knowledge, European sorcery found itself limited to the local psychoactive flora, which are solanaceous hallucinogens such as henbane, daturas, belladonna and mandrake. American sorcerers were also familiar with some solanaceous plants, but, with few exceptions, their use was and is restricted to the shaman, because they are considered 'too powerful' for others; in collective rites, visionary-type plant use based on mescaline, psilocybin and similar active principles is much more common. One might therefore say that some Europeans may have celebrated feasts with coarse drugs, very toxic and not very useful as instruments of knowledge because of the stupor, credulity and amnesia they provoke. The distance between the tumultuous medieval Sabbat and the introspective peyote rites is as long as that between a voodoo initiation and the Mysteries of Eleusis.

A Brief History of Drugs, 1999

High Archives
A Drastic Cure

CHINA PROPOSES DEATH TO DRUG ADDICTS – AFTER 1937
The Chinese Government proposes to execute all uncured drug addicts in China after 1937! This fact was revealed yesterday by Mr Victor Hoo, the Chinese delegate to the Advisory Opium Commission of the League of Nations, says Reuter. He said that 263 traffickers were executed in China last year, and figures of drug addicts and opium smokers still

run into millions. The Commission was reluctant to endorse China's drastic proposal.

From: High Archives section of *Man Bites Man: The Scrapbook of an English Eccentric George Ives*, ed. Paul Sieveking, 1981

Lester Grinspoon, MD
A brief account of my participation as a witness in the trial of Kerry Wiley

IN NOVEMBER OF 1989 Kerry Wiley, a thirty-five-year-old computer-science lecturer from Sacramento, California, was apprehended in Kuala Lumpur, Malaysia, for the possession of marijuana. He was accused of mailing himself a package containing marijuana from Thailand, and an informant tipped off the police who searched his apartment and found more marijuana. He was charged with the possession of over 500 grams of cannabis. Death by hanging is the prescribed penalty for possession of more than 200 grams (7.05 ounces) under Provision 39b of the Dangerous Drugs Act of 1983. One particularly chilling part of this law reads 'In any proceedings under this Act the provisions of this Act shall be construed and interpreted so as to give effect to the purpose of this Act without regard for ambiguities, or infirmities of language, or other defects or deficiencies therein . . .'

More than a hundred people have been hanged under this law, including eight young Hong Kong residents last summer. Bail is not allowed in such cases, and the prisoner may wait two to five years for trial. By the time Kerry came to trial he had spent over a year in the cruelly overcrowded Pudu prison, sleeping on a blanket on a cement floor in a small cell with several other prisoners, bathing in dirty water. It is not surprising that he became seriously depressed. As a twelve-year-old boy, while hiking alone in the San Jacinto mountains one winter, Kerry had slipped and fallen sixty feet down a ledge to sharp rocks below. Newspaper headlines described his survival as a 'Christmas miracle,' but he was left with

279

serious disabilities, of which the worst was painful muscle spasms in his left shoulder and arm. Like many other people, including victims of quadriplegia, paraplegia and multiple sclerosis, Kerry discovered that cannabis was far more useful for this kind of pain and had fewer side effects than any of the medicines doctors could prescribe. He began to use it regularly, and like anyone who needs a medicine, he wanted to be sure of an ample supply. There is no evidence that he ever abused cannabis or sold it.

I first heard about Kerry's plight when I received a call last February from his mother, Dr. Helen Wiley, a retired psychologist from Sacramento. Helen is a remarkable woman who, among other things, spent eight months living alone in a hotel in Kuala Lumpur to assist in her son's defence. She called me because she had read 'Medical Uses of Illicit Drugs', a chapter James B. Bakalar and I wrote for the book *Dealing With Drugs*, which she believed would be useful in the trial if I would redraft it as an affidavit. I replied that much more would be needed for her son's defense, and put her in touch with Ramsey Clark, who shortly thereafter went to Malaysia and talked with his Malaysian lawyer. Ramsey and I believed that a defense of medical necessity was the best and perhaps only hope for preventing a tragedy. Karpal Singh, the Malaysian lawyer, was understandably skeptical, since that defense had never been used in Malaysia.

By the time I testified, Kerry's defense was in the hands of another Malaysian lawyer by the name of Mohammed Shafee Abdullah. On technical grounds, he had prevented the admission of evidence concerning the cannabis Kerry allegedly mailed to himself from Thailand, but the cannabis found in his apartment (265.7 grams) would be enough to condemn him to death.

I arrived in Kuala Lumpur on Monday, December 10, 1990. I examined Kerry in Pudu prison for three hours that day, and again for two and a half hours on Wednesday, December 12. I also spent an hour with the prison psychologist who had been treating Kerry for his depression. I spent many hours with Shafee preparing the medical necessity defense, with which

Shafee had no experience. This bright and affable man arranged for me to give a lecture on the evening of Thursday, December 13, to a group of influential Malaysian physicians and lawyers. I spoke of the serious confusion embodied in the Malaysian concept of '*dadah*,' a generic term which treats opiates and cannabis as though they were identical. Most of my remarks were about the history of cannabis as a medicine. I started by pointing out that Dr. W.B. O'Shaughnessy's ground-breaking work, published in 1839, was based on his observations of the medicinal use of cannabis among Indians and Malays. Seldom have I lectured to an audience which expressed so much interest in cannabis. They seemed starved for up-to-date, reliable, realistic information about the drug.

I was called to the stand at 9 a.m. on Friday, December 14. The judge, Judge Shaik Daud Ismail, who sat without a jury, immediately expressed his irritation at my presence by asking Shafee, as he tried to introduce me, 'Why have you brought this man halfway around the globe to testify when it has been established that the defendant possessed 265.7 grams of cannabis and the punishment is prescribed?'

Shafee then introduced the notion of medical necessity and pursued the direct examination. Like so many people in the previous night's audience, the judge became increasingly interested in the medical uses of cannabis in general and Kerry Wiley's use of it in particular.

The direct examination ended at 11.50 a.m. The judge then asked the prosecutor whether the ten minutes remaining before the break for noon prayers would be enough for cross-examination. He replied, 'Oh no, my Lord! It will take two or three hours for me to get the truth out of Dr. Grinspoon.' I had heard from several sources that the prosecutor, Abdul Alim Abdullah, believed it would advance his career to convict and hang the first American under Provision 39b.

Everyone in the courtroom was surprised by the first question he put to me after the recess. He asked whether, in completing my disembarkation form for visitors to Malaysia, I had indicated that I was here for business or pleasure. I responded, 'For business.'

'And what is your business here, Dr. Grinspoon?'

'My business is to examine the patient and appear as a witness at this trial.'

He interrupted me to say, 'You mean the accused? And how many times did you examine the accused?'

'Twice.'

'How many hours did you spend examining the accused?'

'Five and a half hours.'

'Good. And now you will kindly produce for the court the written authorization from the Ministry of Health as required by law for a foreigner to medically examine a prisoner in Malaysia.'

I told him I knew nothing about this law. It was clear from their reactions that neither Shafee nor the judge knew about it either. Alim then said that he would charge and arrest me for the violation. The judge, after satisfying himself that the law existed, said, 'You are within your right to arrest this man now, but if you do, you will not be able to cross-examine him and you said that you needed two to three hours of cross-examination.' Alim then decided to put the charge on hold and cross-examine me.

He had a long list of questions, which he crossed out one by one. The more he asked, the more ground he lost. Eventually, exasperated, he said, 'Dr. Grinspoon, all that you have reported here about the capacity of cannabis to relieve suffering of one type or another comes from papers and journals. What has been your experience in observing this for yourself?'

In response I told the court how smoking cannabis had given my son, who suffered from leukaemia, extraordinarily effective relief from the pernicious nausea and vomiting caused by some cancer chemotherapies. As someone from the American Embassy later said, 'You could hear a pin drop in that courtroom.' As I spoke, the prosecutor began to shuffle and rustle papers intrusively. The judge, who was obviously deeply interested in my story, raised his voice and said, 'Mr. Alim, are you listening to Dr. Grinspoon? Are you getting this? Do you want him to start from the beginning?' Alim stopped shuffling papers. When I finished he pursued a few more questions, and abruptly stopped, although he had only asked about two-thirds of the questions on his list. He then conferred with some other government people, one of whom was in uniform. It seemed clear that they were deciding whether to arrest me. Finally he told the judge that he had concluded his cross-examination, and the court was dismissed.

We were fairly sure that, given his comments during the cross-examination, the judge would not sentence Kerry to death. We also believed that Alim had decided not to arrest me because the publicity might damage his case even further. However, as we were preparing to leave the courtroom, Allen Kong, legal counsel to the American Embassy, told Shafee and me that I was not out of danger yet, that Alim (the government) might arrest me at Subang airport that night as I left Kuala Lumpur. He gave me a telephone number where he could be reached at the time of my departure. That evening Shafee accompanied me to the airport, where he obtained an airport security badge and walked me through customs and immigration, never leaving my side until the door to the airplane was closed.

The judge issued his ruling on January 17, 1991. He said that 'on the balance of probabilities there was enough evidence adduced from the accused to show that the cannabis was for his own consumption' – specifically, 'to relieve pain from injuries he suffered in a fall off a mountain.' He was sentenced to five years in jail, of which twenty-six months remained to be served, and, as a mandatory part of the sentence, ten strokes of the rattan. The cane used in Malaysia is particularly cruel and burdens the recipient with some motion limitation and pain for the rest of his life. The sentence will be appealed, and if it fails, Ramsey Clark and I will explore the possibility of a pardon.

'A brief account of my participation as a witness in the trial of Kerry Wiley', 1991

Every nation has the government it deserves
Joseph de Maistre

United States Supreme Court
Terrell Don Hutto, Director, Virginia State Department of Corrections, et al., Petitioners, v Roger Trenton Davis

454 US 370, 70 L Ed 2d 556, 102 S Ct 703 [No. 81 – 23]

Decided January 11, 1982.

Decision: Sentence of two consecutive 20-year prison terms and two fines of $10,000 for convictions of possession and distribution of 9 ounces of marijuana, held not to constitute cruel and unusual punishment under Eighth Amendment.

Politics is perhaps the only profession for which no preparation is thought necessary

Robert Louis Stevenson

Mr. David Evans (Welwyn Hatfield):
Column 547

'We have recently heard much about the crime-fighting concept of zero tolerance. Zero tolerance cannot be applied selectively. All minor offences must be punished. Being found in possession of a quantity of drugs should be treated as a serious offence, irrespective of whether it is a small quantity or a first-time offence. If individuals fear being caught with drugs, they are less likely to purchase them, thus hitting the dealers. However, the system currently in operation does not punish possession – that is wrong. I propose a system of zero tolerance for drug abusers, which would mean that those found in possession of an illegal substance would be given an automatic gaol sentence. If I thought that it was remotely possible, I would advocate the death penalty for those in *possession* of drugs. That works in Singapore and Malaysia, so why not here?'

House of Commons Hansard Debates for January 17th, 1997

We know no spectacle so ridiculous as the British public in one of its periodical fits of morality
                                    Thomas Babington Macaulay

Garnet Brennan
Marijuana Witchhunt

MY FRIEND MELKON Melkonian was arrested and held in San Francisco County Jail, charged with sale and possession of marijuana, a year ago last January. He was having trouble raising the high bail set by the judge and had to stay in jail from January until April before friends put up the bond. I was asked to co-sign for his bond since I was a property owner in Marin County.

Several of us heard we might help his case by signing affidavits attesting to the harmless effects of marijuana and were told to meet in his lawyer's office. There were about twenty-five others waiting there when I arrived. Mrs. Molly Minudri, the lawyer, told us we could not be arrested for supplying the affidavits but that we might have to be 'cooler' about using marijuana.

Because there were so many of us, we had to take the affidavit blanks home and fill them in ourselves. I got high, wrote out the affidavit, and delivered it to Mrs. Minudri on September 27. In the affidavit I wrote:

Marijuana is not harmful to my knowledge, because I have been using it since 1949, almost daily, with only beneficial results. It has a relaxing effect when tenseness is present. My depth of perception has been increased; this carries over into times when I am not under the influence of marijuana. Teaching children is my profession. I have been a teacher for thirty years and at present am the teaching-principal of a public school. During school hours I never feel the need of using cannabis sativa; however, each recess is eagerly awaited for smoking tobacco cigarettes. I do not consider marijuana a habit-forming drug, but to me nicotine is.

I have been smoking one or two marijuana cigarettes every evening; sometimes more if school is not in session. Then I stay up later at night.

I have known some people who have become momentarily nauseated, but neither I nor anyone I have ever known has had a 'hangover' from its use.

This is a true statement.

Another of the teachers at my school, Jeff, also wrote an affidavit stating that to his knowledge marijuana is harmless, but he didn't 'cop out' – say that he had used it.

I continued teaching school and thought no more of it. I was the teaching-principal of a three-teacher public school in Marin County, in the small unincorporated village of Nicasio. In our school we have a total of forty-seven children in grades one through eight, though it is really an upgraded school – we teach the children according to what and when they can learn.

Melkon's case came up in court on October 6. Surprisingly, the attorney handed the judge forty-six affidavits from all kinds of lay and professional people. At the time it never occurred to me that my signed affidavit was anything more than a helpful gesture for Melkon.

On the afternoon of the trial a reporter from the *San Francisco Chronicle* called me at school to tell me that the trial and my affidavit were front-page news. He wanted to get all the details straight. I was rather flabbergasted. It was ten minutes before dismissal time, so I said I would go home and call back immediately. I told Jeff this and he said, 'Go home at once, this may be something big. I'll lock up for you.'

Court had dismissed after 2.00 p.m.; I was phoned before 3.00 p.m. When I called back the *Chronicle*, Mr. Raudebaugh, who covered the case at court, told me: 'This is big. Don't you know the sheriff's office has been notified, your school board has been notified. Let me come out and take pictures.' I pleaded with him to keep my school out of the papers. I didn't want the children to be disturbed by this. He asked for my address and said he'd see me in a few minutes. In near panic,

I ran out of my house, got in the car, and drove off, but after a couple of miles I turned back. This was it, I decided. I had no one to hurt, nothing to lose; come what may, I was ready.

Returning home, I got a paper bag, cleaned out drawers, ashtrays, and disposed of all the evidence.

Soon an unfamiliar car appeared. It was the local deputy sheriff, whose sister I had had in school for three years and whose nephew was in my class now. Along with him was an under-sheriff.

'I guess you know why we're here,' the deputy sheriff said.

They came into the living-room and sat grimly on the edges of their chairs. I was relaxed and very calm. They told me they had been sent by the sheriff because I had signed an affidavit saying I had used marijuana, and began asking me questions which I refused to answer, saying I would have to consult my lawyer first. Using marijuana, they said, was illegal, and then asked if they could search my house.

'I understand that a search warrant is legally necessary for this to be done, isn't it?' I asked.

'Well, yes.'

'Do you wish to search illegally?'

They seemed a bit dumbfounded, hesitated, but finally left, saying, 'Well, we'll leave it as it is.'

In the next two days they tried their best, but no judge in Marin County would sign a search warant and I've never since been annoyed by any more law enforcement officers. However, my house is 'clean.' I have had no marijuana in the house, nor have I smoked it. This way I am able to prove that marijuana is not addictive or habit-forming, any more than brushing one's teeth is habit-forming or listening to music is addictive.

Next day, Saturday, I was undecided about what to do. I didn't know whether to call my school board or just wait and see what would happen next.

I'd never been faced with a similar dilemma, so I didn't know what was expected of me. I've always had an adage to go by: 'When in doubt, don't.' So I just waited.

Soon the phone began ringing – calls from as far away as New York and Chicago. When I saw the story on the front page of the morning *Chronicle*, I understood why – my name, school district, county affidavit – it was all there in print.

The sheriff was trying to get a search warrant and my board was meeting. I just sat tight and waited. In the afternoon, a long panel truck with KPIX printed in large letters on the side came up the lane. Two men grinding cameras came across the little Japanese footbridge that leads to my house. They interviewed me on the deck of my house. It was a good interview, easy for me, because I had nothing to hide. All was truth, unadulterated and guileless. The camera continued to grind; the interviewers were kind and sympathetic, although I didn't feel I needed their sympathy.

That evening, watching the news on TV, I saw, for the first time, how things actually looked to the world.

On Sunday, after many pictures, interview after interview, and interminable calls (I completely lost track of who wanted to know what), two members of my school board arrived, looking sick at heart, sad and pale, among the cameras and newspaper people. They handed me my notice of suspension so I would be sure not to appear at school the next morning.

That evening, returning alone from an Ellington concert, I found more people waiting for me at home. Interviews by tape went on into the night; even a radio broadcast from my home by telephone for the midnight news. Things were really jumping; I still felt fine and very happy because all the country was being informed about what was happening.

On Monday, I've been told, the school was abuzz; TV equipment, parents bringing children to protect them from me in case I arrived, my school board, two members of the multitudinous county-office staff, all making sure that school would go on as usual.

Can my children understand how on Friday evening we lovingly said good night to one another and on Monday morning they had to be protected against me – all because of my telling the truth and trying to help a friend in need? Suddenly, I had become a threat to them. The children and I have been trying to be truthful, guiltless, unharmful to others and loving. Is this the way it is done?

Mrs. Minudri, now my lawyer, had been advised by Judge Karish that he would give us two weeks to get as many affidavits as we could, so I had many forms to give out. The same day I was to be interviewed by KPIX-TV and was due at 2.30 p.m. at Mrs. Minudri's office. She hadn't arrived but the cameramen and interviewers had.

We had to appear at my school for a board meeting that night so that my fate might be determined. En route we were to stop at the home of Hugh Hinchliffe, the present chairman of the Ad Hoc Committee for the Repeal of the Marijuana Laws. There we met more cameramen for more interviews. Melkon, Molly, and I were all interviewed and photographed until finally I had to call the school to say we'd be about twenty or thirty minutes late. We were followed by a TV wagon to show them the way.

At the school ground we found the space completely filled with cars, trucks, and masses of parents, hippies, sympathizers I had never met before, and the simply curious.

As we entered, giggling and hurrying into the glare of lights and more grinding cameras, a path was cleared down the center of the room and I was seated in the front row facing a long table with three grim-faced board members, their attorney and secretary. All around the edges were the cameras and the constantly moving men with the long cords and mikes.

The board meeting was already under way when we arrived. Only a few of my parents took part in the discussion, saying what a good teacher I was, how they had liked me and what I was doing, but, since I had said what I had, I had broken the law and could no longer be allowed to teach their children. Some parents, whose children I had previously taught, expressed good opinions of my teaching and begged tolerance and understanding. Several so-called hippies spoke well, some were too highly agitated to express their actual feelings. The deputy sheriff who had come to my house said, 'Why do we need this riff-raff from the city to tell us what to do? We already know what we're going to do.'

The verbal battle raged back and forth; hypocrisy was thick

in the air. I sat quietly listening, tired and cool, just waiting. Mrs. Minudri talked for me superbly. We had agreed beforehand that the final decision would be made in a closed executive session.

After some time, the board, two lawyers, the secretary, a man from the county office, and I retired to another room downstairs where they asked me if I wouldn't just resign. I couldn't bear to do this, so I refused, flatly. We talked for about an hour, very pleasantly and quietly, and decided how things were to be. The assistant county superintendent of schools, who had been there all day, said, 'I never visited a better-organized school.' The three board members moved to a corner and made their unanimous vote to dismiss me from my duties. The lawyers then discussed how to inform the full meeting upstairs of the decision, and how to cut off all further discussion by adjourning the meeting forthwith. Of course, I told them my response would be that I would appeal the case, even to the Supreme Court, if necessary. This was accepted pleasantly.

We filed back into the room with the glaring lights and grinding machines. After a stumbling reading of the prepared statement, we adjourned. All at once, I was pounced upon (like a presidential candidate who had just lost) with seventeen microphones thrust at my face, and behind each mike, a man with a question. I merely said, 'Of course, I shall appeal.' Then: 'Under the circumstances, due to the expressed feelings of the people voted for the trustees, they had no other alternative than to fire me.'

We finally maneuvered our way to the door through the downcast looks of my children's parents. I was stopped by one mother with whom I had been very friendly. She and I used to discuss freely with great understanding the problems of her three children who had been in my classes. Now she said, 'Oh, Garnet, please don't hate me!'

It was late in 1949 when I first had marijuana. I was living in Monterey and was invited to visit friends in Big Sur. After dinner, sitting around the fireplace, the man rolled a marijuana cigarette. He always rolled his own tobacco, so I thought nothing of it until he handed it first to his wife, then to me.

I had been curious about marijuana for a long time but had never made the effort to get hold of any. They taught me how to smoke it and it was at once a delight. I really felt like Alice in Wonderland – when I stood up, I kept growing, my arms became long, and I felt I might be able to fly into the Pacific when I went outside. But, of course, nothing around me was abnormal and I was aware of this. The next day was fine; everything was the same. I'm not sure what I expected, but having heard some of the myths about marijuana (which I felt to be untrue), I couldn't be sure . . .

I never used marijuana while at school, or in the morning before going to school. There was never any need for it. I did find it helpful in dealing with student problems – checking papers, making out grade cards, reports and cumulative records. I never found it necessary to write derogatory comments on files that would follow a child through life; marijuana always helped me find something good to say about the student . . .

For me, marijuana has been a fine relaxant, a beautiful cocktail before dinner, a great source of deepening perception, but I would never recommend its use for 'mixed-up' people or children. Kids are already 'turned on' if they are just allowed to be. I would never recommend its use in excess by anyone. In fact, it is difficult for most normal people to use it in excess because marijuana imposes its own limits when you have had enough. You don't need or want any more. Yet, when you will it, you can use it without the fear that it will ever become the 'Boss.'

In the meantime, I have received more than one hundred letters of support from all over the US, as well as three from boys in Vietnam. Only three letters, from retired, mis-informed, unenlightened school teachers, were critical. The Craig Biddle Interim Congressional Committee studying Criminal Procedure invited me as a witness, and I was inter-viewed by Hugh Downs on his *Today Show* in Los Angeles. I have also taken part in several college panel discussions on the subject of marijuana.

Let us hope all this will lead to changes in our laws to bring them more in line with the ideals expressed in our constitution, and strengthen the guarantees protecting the freedom of speech – for all teachers. Perhaps it will also help to open the minds of people to confront our changing world with more tolerance and thoughtfulness. May we all come to truly enjoy 'Life, Liberty and the Pursuit of Happiness.'

1967. From: *Shaman Woman, Mainline Lady: Women's Writings on the Drug Experience*, eds Cynthia Palmer and Michael Horowitz, 1982

Peter Laurie
Drugs

ONE SERIOUS-MINDED work, *Indian Hemp, a Social Menace*, was published by a barrister in 1952. He quotes as a crushing indictment of the drug and its users a series of articles from the *Sunday Graphic* – a now extinct journal. They being:

> After several weeks I have just completed exhaustive inquiries into the most insidious vice Scotland Yard has ever been called on to tackle – dope peddling.
>
> Detectives on this assignment are agreed that never have they had experience of a crime so vicious, so ruthless and unpitying and so well organised. Hemp, marihuana and hashish represent a thoroughly unsavoury trade.
>
> One of the detectives told me: 'We are dealing with the most evil men who have ever taken to the vice business.' The victims are teenage British girls, and to a lesser extent, teenage youths . . . The racketeers are 90 per cent coloured men from the West Indies and west coast of Africa. How serious the situation is, how great the danger to our social structure, may be gathered from the fact that despite increasing police attention, despite several raids,

there are more than a dozen clubs in London's West End at which drugs are peddled. As the result of my inquiries, I share the fear of detectives now on the job that there is the greatest danger of the reefer craze becoming the greatest social menace this country has known.

The other day I sat in a tawdry West End club. I was introduced by a member, a useful contact both to me and the police.

Drinks sold were nothing stronger than lukewarm black coffee, 'near beer' or orangeade.

I watched the dancing. My contact and I were two of six white men. I counted twenty-eight coloured men and some thirty white girls. None of the girls looked more than twenty-five. In a corner five coloured musicians with brows perspiring played bebop music with extraordinary fervour. Girls and coloured partners danced with an abandon – a savagery almost – which was both fascinating and embarrassing. From a doorway came a coloured man, flinging away the end of a strange cigarette. He danced peculiar convulsions on his own, then bounced to a table and held out shimmering arms to a girl. My contact indicated photographs on the walls. They were of girls in the flimsiest drapings. 'They are, or were, members,' I was told.

We went outside. I had seen enough of my first bebop club, its coloured peddlers, its half-crazed, uncaring young girls.

In their way, the pieces are small masterpieces of mass Sunday indignation; but one feels they come to the *point d'appui* only at the end of the last article:

'The day will come,' said the dusky Jesse, 'when this country will be all mixtures if we don't watch out. There will be only half castes.'

Drugs, 1967

Lester Grinspoon and James B. Bakalar
Marihuana: The Forbidden Medicine

WHEN I BEGAN to study marihuana in 1967, I had no doubt that it was a very harmful drug that was unfortunately being used by more and more foolish young people who would not listen to or could not understand the warnings about its dangers. My purpose was to define scientifically the nature and degree of those dangers. In the next three years, as I reviewed the scientific, medical and lay literature, my views began to change. I came to understand that I, like so many other people in this country, had been brainwashed. My beliefs about the dangers of marihuana had little empirical foundation. By the time I completed the research that formed the basis for a book, I had become convinced that cannabis was considerably less harmful than tobacco and alcohol, the most commonly used legal drugs. The book was published in 1971; its title, *Marihuana Reconsidered*, reflected my change in view.

At that time I naively believed that once people understood that marihuana was much less harmful than drugs that were already legal, they would come to favor legalization. In 1971, I confidently predicted that cannabis would be legalized for adults within the decade. I had not yet learned that there is something very special about illicit drugs. If they don't always make the drug user behave irrationally, they certainly cause many non-users to behave that way. Instead of making marihuana legally available to adults, we have continued to criminalize many millions of Americans. About 300,000 mostly young people are arrested on marihuana charges each year, and the political climate has now deteriorated so severely that it has become difficult to discuss marihuana openly and freely. It could almost be said that there is a climate of psychopharmacological McCarthyism.

One indication of this climate is the rise in mandatory drug testing, which is analogous to the loyalty oaths of the McCarthy era. Hardly anyone believed that forced loyalty oaths would enhance national security, but people who refused to take such oaths risked loss of their jobs and reputations. Today we are witnessing the imposition of a chemical loyalty oath. Mandatory, often random testing of urine samples for the presence of illicit drugs is increasingly demanded as a condition of employment. People who test positive may be fired or, if they wish to keep their jobs, may be involuntarily assigned to drug counseling or 'employee assistance' programs.

All this is of little use in preventing or treating drug abuse. In the case of cannabis, urine testing can easily be defeated by chemical alteration of the urine or substitution of someone else's urine. Even if the urine sample has not been altered, the available tests are far from perfect. The cheaper ones are seriously inaccurate, and even the more expensive and accurate ones are fallible because of laboratory error and passive exposure to marihuana smoke. But even an infallible test would be of little use in preventing or treating drug abuse. Marihuana 'metabolites' (breakdown products) remain in the urine for days after a single exposure and for weeks after a long-term user stops. Their presence bears no established relationship to drug effects on the brain. It tells little about when the drug was used, how much was used, or what effects it had or has. Like loyalty oaths imposed on government employees, urine testing for marihuana is useless for its ostensible purpose. It is little more than shotgun harassment designed to impose outward conformity.

Marihuana: The Forbidden Medicine, 1993

The tigers of wrath are wiser than the horses of instruction
William Blake

Stephen Jay Gould
The Forbidden Medicine

I am a member of a very small, very fortunate and very select group – the first survivors of the previously incurable cancer, abdominal mesothelioma. Our treatment involved a carefully balanced mixture of all three standard modalities – surgery, radiation and chemotherapy. Not pleasant, to be sure, but consider the alternative.

Any cancer survivor of such intensive treatment – indeed anyone who has endured aggressive medical battles against any disease – knows first-hand the enormous importance of the 'psychological factor.' Now I am an old-fashioned rationalist of the most unreconstructed sort. I brook no mysticism, no romantic southern-California nonsense about the power of mind and spirit. I assume that positive attitudes and optimism have salutary effects because mental states can feed back upon the body through the immune system. In any case, I think that everyone would grant an important role to the maintenance of spirit through adversity; when the mind gives up, the body too often follows. (And if cure is not the ultimate outcome, quality of remaining life becomes, if anything, even more important.)

Nothing is more discouraging, more destructive of the possibility of such a positive attitude – and I do speak from personal experience here – than the serious side effects induced by so many treatments. Radiation and chemotherapy are often accompanied by long periods of intense and uncontrollable nausea. The mind begins to associate the agent of potential cure with the very worst aspect of the disease – for the pain and suffering of the side effects is often worse than the distress induced by the tumor itself. Once this happens, the possibility for an essential psychological boost and comfort may disappear – for the treatment seems worse than the disease itself. In other words, I am trying to say that the control of severe and long-lasting side effects in cancer treatment is not merely a question of comfort (though Lord only knows that comfort to the suffering is enough of a rationale), but an absolutely essential ingredient in the possibility of cure.

I had surgery, followed by a month of radiation, chemotherapy, more surgery, and a subsequent year of additional chemotherapy. I found that I could control the less severe nausea of radiation by conventional medicines. But when I started intravenous chemotherapy (Adriamycin®), absolutely nothing in the available arsenal of antiemetics worked at all. I was miserable and came to dread the frequent treatments with an almost perverse intensity.

I had heard that marihuana often worked well against nausea. I was reluctant to try it because I have never smoked any substance habitually (and didn't even know how to inhale). Moreover, I had tried marihuana twice (in the usual context of growing up in the sixties) and had hated it. (I am something of a Puritan on the subject of substances that, in any way, dull or alter mental states – for I value my rational mind with an academician's over-weening arrogance. I do not drink alcohol at all, and have never used drugs in any 'recreational' sense.) But anything to avoid nausea and the perverse wish it induces for an end of treatment.

The rest of the story is short and sweet. Marihuana worked like a charm. I disliked the 'side effect' of mental blurring (the 'main effect' for recreational users), but the sheer bliss of not experiencing nausea – and then not having to fear it for all the days intervening between treatments – was the greatest boost I received in all my year of treatment, and surely had a most important effect upon my eventual cure. It is beyond my comprehension – and I fancy I am able to comprehend a lot, including such nonsense – that any humane person would withhold such a beneficial substance from people in such great need simply because others use it for different purposes.

From: *Marihuana: The Forbidden Medicine*
by Lester Grinspoon and James B. Bakalar, 1993

I, as a responsible adult human being, will never concede the power to anyone to regulate my choice of what I put into my body, or where I go with my mind. From the skin inwards is my jurisdiction, is it not? I choose what may or may not cross that border. Here I am the customs agent. I am the coast-guard. I am the sole legal and spiritual government of this territory, and only the laws I choose to enact within myself are applicable

Alexander Shulgin

Howard Marks
The Campaign Trail: British General Election, 1997

THE TWENTY-EIGHTH OF September 1996 saw the sixty-eighth anniversary of the prohibition of cannabis in the UK. I celebrated the occasion by eating and giving out cannabis cakes in Hyde Park and then turning myself in at Marylebone Police Station to confess my criminal conduct. Appointments had already been made with the Old Bill in charge. I didn't feel I was risking anything. After 3,000 days in the nick, a few more might just provide a tingle of nostalgia. True, I was breaking my United States parole conditions, but sod those bastards.

Along with about fifty supporters, and as many press, we presented ourselves, completely wrecked, to the cop at the door and explained we were distributing and consuming illegal substances. They wouldn't let me in. I skinned up and smoked. The cops refused to bust us. They didn't want to know.

Smoking spliffs, we walked back to Hyde Park, gave out more dope cakes, rented some deckchairs, and stoked up a few pipes and chillums.

Other police stations in other parts of the country were confronted with similar protests. Not all adopted the same attitude as Marylebone. A few guys were busted and were expecting to end up with the convictions of their courage. This is really nuts. Law-abiding citizens can't consume dope in police stations, but dope smugglers can.

Norwich has been a peculiarly forceful centre advancing the legalisation of cannabis. The city's 10,000 cannabis users include some long-time hardcore tokers. And they've really had enough of the bullshit. Jack Girling and Tina Smith, two of the main leading lights, asked if I would stand for Parliament in the forthcoming election on behalf of them and others like them. Jack and Tina have been smoking herbs for most of this century.

'Fuck politics,' I thought. 'They're all lying scumbags or deranged. They're the lawyers that Shakespeare wanted to kill. They don't care about anyone under thirty. They won't even put Ecstasy-testing machines in clubs where they know hundreds of kids are chancing it. Better they die than get high. It's not just a question of zero tolerance: it's one of zero understanding. No fun. I'm not jumping into bed with that lot.'

'You can make it a single issue,' said Jack Girling. 'Legalise cannabis. Everything else can wait.'

'You think just one policy is enough, Jack?'

'It's one more than the others have got. All that party stuff is silly.'

Jack was right. Party politics had certainly stuck it up England. Politicians always seemed to duck and dive real issues and encourage the electorate to vote on party preference or not at all. And they *were* a bunch of wankers. (A pity their fathers weren't.) A vote for a single-issue party, particularly one dedicated to getting stoned, would also be a vote against the current crap system, state and slime of party politics.

I have nothing but the most complete contempt and utter disgust for current drug policies. They make me puke. I have four children and cannot conceive of a love greater than that which I have for them. I don't want them dying in the streets from poisoned dope or getting sick from impurities. I don't want children handing over all their pocket money and hard-earned wages to make-believe gangsters who can't tell cannabis from plastic and don't care which they sell or how much they charge. I don't want my children to suffer multiple sclerosis, AIDS or cancers and be cruelly denied the thera-peutic benefits of natural herbs because a bunch of cock-sucking pharmaceutical companies want to sell their poisons.

I don't want my children to be callously stigmatised by society, fined and imprisoned for pursuing ancient and traditional harmless practices. I don't want any of that shite.

'All right, Jack. I'd be honoured to stand for you and that cause. What's Norwich like?'

'Come and find out.'

I had to go to Dublin first. I was doing an interview for Olaf Tyarensen of *Hot Press*, Dublin's *Time Out*, and we were then both appearing on *The Late, Late Show*, sharing the bill with the Kelly family, a professor of law, a nun, a couple of Irish stand-up comics and a few demented prohibitionists. I arrived at Heathrow well before take-off and skinned up in the Gents. The Nepalese hit during take-off as I opened my copy of *Hot Press*. There was an article by Olaf about the Coalition of Communities Against Drugs, who had taken to the city centre's streets carrying banners and placards bearing slogans like 'HANG ALL DRUG BARONS' and 'PUSHERS BEWARE'. I started feeling scared. Or was it a twinge of paranoia from the spliff? No, I was scared.

'And do you still smoke cannabis?' asked the presenter, Gay Bryne, when we were on live TV. I was still a bit unnerved by all the hostility.

'Yes,' I answered, 'as much as I can.'

'And you have it in your possession?'

'I do.'

I always carry some for luck.

A few minutes later, I walked off the set. Olaf came tearing up to me.

'The Gardai are outside asking all kinds of questions. Hide your dope, Howard. For God's sake, get rid of it.'

'Where? Where?' asked one of the comedians. 'There's nowhere to hide anything. Just throw it as far away from you as you possibly can.'

'This way,' someone shouted.

Out motley band of academics, comedians and dope dealers scrambled into the Ladies, where a TV monitor displayed an obese, non-menstruating, prohibitchionist yelling, 'He shouldn't be called Mr Nice; he should be called Mr Evil. He's a murderer.'

'Who the hell is that, Olaf?'

'That's none other than Mary Harney, leader of the Progressive Democrat Party. She was to the General what Elliot Ness was to Al Capone.'

'God, where am I?'

'How about there, Howard?'

Olaf pointed to a rubbish bin full of unsavoury garbage. I couldn't possibly put a Nepalese temple ball into that lot. The producer ran in.

'It's all right, Howard. The Gardai are not wanting to talk to you. But they do want to know at which hotel you'll be staying. You can tell me, and I'll tell them.'

I told him.

And stayed somewhere else.

The next day, I vented my anger against prohibition in a crowded room at the University of East Anglia. Almost everyone seemed to feel the same way. Why are we putting up with all this? If we want to take dope to get stoned (or healthy) and don't want adulterated poison peddled on the streets, who exactly is saying no?

'Respect, brother. You've got our vote. We'll sort out some others too.'

'How do we register? Is it too late? I never thought there'd ever be anything worth voting for.'

Jack Girling, others and I went to the Brickmakers' Arms. I had to know something about my non-dope-smoking potential constituents. I drank a few pints at the bar. Someone would recognise me soon. If not, I'd skin up.

'You're that drug pusher. Am I right? So you're trying to be a politician now, yeah?'

'Well, you're almost there,' I replied. 'But I've never had to push anything, and I've got no political aspirations whatsoever. I'm just trying to increase freedom and fun. If they made booze illegal, I'd be just as pissed off.'

'I'd be with you there. I might be with you anyway. You got any stuff with you?'

Jack came alongside.

'You all right, Howard?'

'Yeah. But I need to get off my face, Jack. I've had a hard day. Some thumping techno with the usual accompaniments would go down well. Is there life after midnight in Norwich?'

'You better talk to Luis here. His lot of DJs is actually called 'Off Yer Face'.

One look at Luis' eyes, and it was obvious he had this time of night sorted. We went to a club called Kitchen. It was so dark, I could skin up without checking if it was cool. Confetti cannons, French maids, feather dusters and rubber-clad slaves allowed ambient drum'n'bass to welcome raging hardcore, and the conflicting rhythms peacefully coexisted. Eyes were ecstatic. Nostrils were smoking.

Back in London, I called an old Oxford lawyer friend.

'Can anyone stand for Parliament, even convicted dope dealers like me?'

'Absolutely. All that's needed, Howard, is for you to be alive, not to actually be in prison, and to pay a five-hundred-pound deposit.'

'You mean ten hardcore stoners with fifty quid each to spare could get a guy into Parliament?'

'That's right. Even the potential of a few hundred votes would worry the main parties in any of the critical marginals. A few thousand could really shake them up. Single issues have been known to work. Look at the suffragette movement.'

'Can the same candidate stand for more than one constituency?'

'Of course, as precedented by Gladstone himself. If you were elected in more than one, you would have to resign in all but one of your choice. And if a person, party, or whatever, stands in more than fifty constituencies, then the government is obliged to permit a five-minute political broadcast to be screened on all channels at peak viewing time.'

Maybe I'll be part of a party. Let's hope it's non-stop. I like the connotations of the word 'party', so I formed the Legalise Cannabis Party and stood simultaneously for the four separate constituencies of Norwich North, Norwich South, Neath and Southampton West.

I can get to places that other candidates can't: squats, techno clubs, shabeens, brothels, illegal raves, prisons, recording studios, Ecstasy-safe environments, opium dens and other havens for those who wish to alter their states of minds. My election addresses have been used for everything from toilet paper to roaches. There aren't too many registered votes in these places, but they're a lot of fun. Another smoker who can get to even more places is Tricky, whose music fascinates me. His trip-hop is scary. Tricky is scary. Tricky taps that energy that the straights call gangster or superpredator, wears a dress, and tells the snitching Yankee gangsta to take it somewhere else. He was giving a concert at Norwich's University of East Anglia in a few days. I was going to be there, campaigning. We agreed to celebrate our joint presence.

At the Norwich election hustings, Labour Party candidate for Norwich South, Charles Clarke, admitted to having smoked cannabis while a young man. I asked Charles Clarke why he didn't confess to his crimes. There are no statutes of limitation in British law. He should do his bird like the rest of us. He didn't answer.

I met one of the senior administrators of the university students' union.

'Mr Marks, you can't come to the Tricky concert tonight and make political statements. It wouldn't be fair to the other candidates. There will be thousands of students there. Far more than at the hustings we hold at the Union for all political candidates. As you won't be able to campaign, it seems futile to even come here this evening.'

'That's no problem. I'm with the band.'

I met Tricky backstage.

'Tricky, can I come on stage and smoke a bong and a few joints?'

'Treat my stage as your living-room, Howard. I like this. It scares me.'

'Your fear is your strength, Tricky. Let's do it.'

The bouncers took the bong. Tricky said he couldn't go perform without his props. The bouncers said they'd bust us if we smoked from it and ringed the stage. Tricky and I got on to the music- and searchlight-swamped platform and lit joints. We rapped for a few minutes during which I made an impassioned plea for the provision of Ecstasy-testing machines. I offered to be one. I exhaled into the bong. The bouncers got ready to pounce while Tricky begged everyone to 'Vote for Howard; don't be a coward'. I threw some joints into the audience and secured a few easy votes.

The only purpose for which power can rightly be exercised over any member of a civilised community against his will is to prevent harm to others. His own good, either physical or moral, is not a sufficient warrant

J.S. Mill

Olaf Tyaransen
Fear And Loathing On The Campaign Trail

The Worst Night

'HEY – YOU! THAT'S RIGHT – YOU! THE STUPID CUNT WITH THE DARK GLASSES! I WANNA WORD WITH YOU, YOU FUCKER!'

From a distance the man looked short, squat and dumpy but, as he charged up the road towards me like some kind of crazed and bloodthirsty animal (which, in retrospect, was exactly what he was), he gradually got taller, broader and more menacing. Shit! I took a deep breath, puffed my chest out and braced myself for whatever was coming. He stopped just inches short of my nose, his ugly fifty-something face a contorted mess of undisguised redneck rage. His breath stank of something unpleasant and I nearly recoiled and stepped back, but didn't. To do so would imply weakness and that was exactly what he was looking for.

'*DID YOU PUT THIS SHITE THROUGH MY DOOR?*' he demanded with a roar, shaking a balled up piece of white paper in front of my face. It was one of my election leaflets – a folded A4 sheet detailing the reasons why cannabis should be legalised immediately. I'd had 10,000 of them printed the day before.

'*YOU'RE THAT CUNT, AREN'T YOU?*' he screamed. His nostrils flared so widely that you could have fit a fist into one of them (if it was a small fist and you wanted to put it there).

'What cunt?' I asked innocently.

'*YOU THINK YOU'RE REALLY FUCKING SMART DON'T YOU, YOU FUCKING ARSEHOLE!!*' He was screeching now, really wound up. I wondered if he was going to have a heart attack. '*WELL, LET ME TELL YOU . . .*'

He was obviously a very disturbed individual. I didn't really understand him. I mean, what kind of man gets himself so worked up about an election flyer that he feels the need to leave the safety and comfort of his own home to run down the street and pick a fight with somebody half his age? If he didn't agree with what I was saying, all he had to do was put the offending item in the bin and not vote for me. There was no need for the dramatics, no need for all this grief. I stood still and pondered this, as he continued to scream abuse in my face. Tiny specks of his spittle hit my shades, distorting his face even further. I didn't move to wipe them. I could tell that he was just waiting for an excuse. If I raised my hands from my sides he was almost definitely going to hit me. The man's son – just a kid, aged around six or seven – was standing behind him, trying to stare me out of it. An elderly couple were watching from across the street. Out of the corner of my eye, I could see curtains twitching in the windows of the house beside me.

'*. . . AND SHOVE IT UP YOUR ARSE!!!!*'

He slammed the leaflet into my hand with such angry force

that, days later, it was still bruised. I looked at him, standing there, hands on hips like Superman, waiting for me to do something, challenging me to do something. It was surreal. He seemed to personify all of the fear and loathing I had encountered over the previous six weeks – fear of radical change, loathing of anything or anyone who threatened his cosy and closeted little world. To be honest, I sort of felt sorry for him. I felt even sorrier for his son.

Despite this, I still wanted to kick the shit out of him, wanted to beat his face to a bloody watermelon pulp. He was slightly smaller than me but better built, looked like he might have boxed in his time (though maybe his ears were that shape at birth). Even so, it would have taken me less than two seconds to trip him over and slam the heel of my boot into the bridge of his nose. He wouldn't know what had hit him. After that he wouldn't stand a chance. I'd give his annoying little son a kick in the arse for good measure. Ultraviolent images flashed through my brain, pure adrenaline pumped though my veins. I was fucking furious, nearly as worked up as he was!

Fortunately, common sense took over. I visualised the headline – '*DUN LAOGHAIRE MAN ASSAULTED BY CANNABIS CANDIDATE*'. 'The election was two days away and that kind of publicity wasn't really going to help my chances (not that I had a chance in the first place). Besides, it wasn't really my style.

'You're a very rude little man,' I said. Incensed at my deliberately patronising manner, he tried to push me and I quickly caught his arm. I held it tight, but not too tight. Just firmly enough to let him know that I wasn't going to be spoken to like this. 'Go away,' I hissed.

'*YOU FUCKING WANKER,*' he screamed, going all purple in the face. '*ALL THE BRAINS IN THE COUNTRY AND THIS IS THE KIND OF SHITE WE GET! YOU FUCKING CUNT!*'

The Story of O, 2000

If people let government decide what foods they eat and what medicines they take, their bodies will soon be in a sorry state as are the souls of those who live under tyranny

Thomas Jefferson

Howard Marks
The War Against Drugs

THE FIRST PERSON to use the phrase 'war on drugs' was Richard 'Tricky Little Dick' Nixon way back in 1971. Tricky Little Dick was a fucking sharp villain who conned his way to the top. To distract the straights, he made out that the real enemy was not a yellow person with slit eyes but a plant that made you feel good. To prove his point, Tricky Little Dick played table tennis in Peking and declared war on drugs. At first, he didn't need much in the way of armed forces. After all, most plants don't carry guns. But he did need a bunch of brain-dead heavy meat-heads, so he formed the DEA, the Drug Enforcement Administration. Eventually, Tricky Little Dick got an air force and sprayed South American plants with poison.

There's never been much of a plants' civil rights move in America (most of them are vegetarians), so no one really gave a toss about Tricky Little Dick's antics until he got busted for housebreaking in the Watergate Hotel and grassed up his mates.

Peanuts then became US President. He was very nice and very clever; consequently, it didn't take long for the population to get shot of him. Americans, by now (1980), had completely lost touch with reality and only understood real slapstick, plastic popcorn and movies. The only solution was to make a cowboy actor called Ronnie into President.

No one, not even plants, wants to play war with Americans, because they cheat, lie, chew gum and talk too much. They ripped off the Red Indians and turned reggae into slavery. When Americans run out of enemies, they fight each other. There is no America without a Civil War. Now the civil

307

war is between those who take dope and those who don't.

When war is declared against a country, that country accepts the declaration and declares war back. So, American dopers, accept the declaration of war on drug consumers issued by your government and re-declare war back on the fuckers.

'Get outside those kindergartens and schools, all you American dopers. They've made you into demons. They treat you like demons. So be fucking demons. Be drug enforcers. Force them to take drugs.

'Get some Scary Sound Systems, spraying water pistols, counter-surveillance clubwear, stink bombs, lion shit (to frighten police horses and dogs), cheese, a few hookers, and maybe one rubber pointed stick full of drug-free piss, to keep next to your dick for the piss test.'

Desperate diseases require desperate remedies

Guy Fawkes

CHAPTER FOUR

COMMODIFY IT

Steven Abrams
The Oxford Scene

ONE TENDS TO be introduced to cannabis at Oxford in a casual way. Cigarettes are frequently and openly passed around at parties and small informal social gatherings. No one is urged to smoke, and it is rare to be overtly asked to join in. One takes the odd puff until finally one night one becomes properly stoned. One then tends to be "turned on" by friends and eventually introduced to the pusher of the day. Cannabis is usually smoked in a small group in congenial surroundings in rooms in college or in digs. The atmosphere is rather like that of a sherry party. A gramophone is the most essential prop. As the drug begins to take effect within a few minutes, there is usually an increase in physical activity, accompanied by great mirth. One may feel a compulsion to dance. Sensory experience of all kinds is enhanced and there is an air of conviviality. The usual 'high' is an innocuous evening spent listening to music, dancing, talking and eating. One may also venture out to a party, a colour film, or even to a pub, and during the day it is pleasant to punt on the river or visit the Ashmolean art gallery. Many persons find they are able to do intellectual or artistic work under the influence of cannabis; and I know of a case of one young man successfully sitting an examination for a fellowship when he was 'high'.

The price of cannabis in Oxford tends to be about eight or nine pounds an ounce for hashish, which is more frequently used, and a pound or so less for marijuana. This works out at about the price of a pint of bitter for the evening's entertainment. Whatever the profits may be in retailing other drugs, the margin in selling cannabis is very slim, and no one in Oxford makes a living at it. "Pushers" tend to be smokers who want to make a pound or two a week and get their smokes for free. They stay in business for a few months until they become well known and then quietly retire. The smokers take turns acting as pushers. Those who never push to make a profit are usually willing to sell small quantities of cannabis at cost to friends who have temporarily exhausted their supplies, in return for similar favours in future. One point which is clear, and indeed admitted by the authorities, is that in this country there is no organised criminal conspiracy behind the sale of cannabis. Sometimes the drug is smuggled into the country on a one shot basis by students. The major supplies are brought into the ports by merchant seamen acting for themselves and are sold to anyone who is waiting around the docks. Smaller quantities are sometimes sent through the post.

From: *The Book of Grass*, eds George Andrews & Simon Vinkenoog, 1967

Howards Marks
The Commodification of Cannabis

THE PRESENT ILLEGAL CANNABIS MARKET
Today's cannabis consumer lies at the end of a process conveniently divided into production, transportation (which often includes the crossing of international frontiers) and domestic distribution.

Production
Traditionally, cannabis seeds are planted in the spring and the herbaceous plant is harvested during the autumn. In ideal growing conditions, two crops a year may be harvested.

Harvesting entails cutting down the plants and hanging them upside down to dry in the sun. When dry, small stems, flowers, leaves and (unfortunately) seeds are combined and retained as ordinary marijuana while the largest stalks and stems are discarded.

Sinsemilla results from a variation of this method. Delta-9 tetrahydrocannabinol (THC), the primary psychoactive chemical in cannabis, occurs in unpollenated floral clusters usually referred to as buds. Sophisticated and well-researched agronomic techniques have been developed to maximise the size of these potent unpollenated floral clusters. Typically, all the male plants are eliminated during the early growth of the plant. This lack of pollination causes the female plants to enlarge their buds in order to increase their chances of acquiring whatever pollen might be around. The result of this reproductively futile process is a crop of resin-rich buds.

Hashish is produced by extracting resin from buds. Shaking, rubbing and running through densely planted cannabis crops while wearing adhesive clothing are the traditional methods of extraction. The resins are then compacted into a mass.

Most ordinary marijuana found in non-importing countries is cultivated by the indigenous population. Almost all hashish is similarly produced. Sinsemilla production is done by both cultivators in traditional source countries and home-growers in the country of consumption.

Transportation

All three transport modes of land, sea and air are employed. Individuals own and/or operate private land vehicles, yachts and planes, while loosely knit organisations and alliances also use existing commercial freight systems. Payments to police, customs, military, coastguards and other individuals in positions of authority are a common feature of these methods. The transportation of cannabis across national boundaries, excepting that of minute supplies for research and therapeutic purposes, is highly illegal and occasions the most punitive penalties. Those engaged in this trade often make huge amounts of money, and far too many of them spend several years behind bars.

Domestic distribution

With the well-known exception of the Netherlands, all countries enthusiastically prohibit the purchase of even immediately consumable amounts of cannabis. Save for a few off-the-wall counties such as Singapore, the penalties for transgression are relatively small (usually fines rather that prison sentences). Sales of bulk amounts of cannabis are universally proscribed and can attract penalties at least as severe as those for international cannabis transportation. The existence and enforcement of cannabis prohibition, coupled with the popularity of the herb, has spawned a myriad of illegal networks engaged in distribution. It's very hard for a street dealer to continue his business without being busted or, at the very least, being considered and documented as some kind of sociopath. Such casualties of cannabis prohibition have been extensively dealt with elsewhere and are not the subject of this monograph. But let's never forget them.

Cost

Today, the production, export, import, international and domestic transport and retail distribution of cannabis carry the heavy cost of surviving confiscations by the government and insuring against infiltration by law enforcement. Significant funds are used to establish information valves and blocks that afford protection to one level of distribution from the danger that might occur when an individual or organisation from another level is busted. As a result, current importation and distribution firms are inefficient both in reducing costs and preserving and transmitting useful information. Although this does have the fortunate conse-quence of supplying people with the opportunity of making a living, it also implies that costs and prices of currently illegal cannabis are inevitably greater than those that would prevail in an untaxed or moderately taxed legal market.

Maintenance

A sizeable and powerful portion of the electorate believe that the taking of all drugs (in which category they include cannabis but usually exclude alcohol, tobacco, tea and many legally prescribed pharmaceutical products) is inherently immoral and that the rest of the population should abide by this ethic even if they do not subscribe to it. Articulate and well-reasoned arguments advocating cannabis legalisation and decriminalisation have resoundingly failed to convince these anti-drug crusaders of the irrationality of their position. Unless the concerns of these moral dictators are properly addressed, one cannot expect them to do other than vigorously maintain their prohibitive stance.

The administrative agencies and bureaucracies of all countries have self-protective vested interests in maintaining the mythology of the perils of cannabis use. Many British customs officers, policemen, coastguards, solicitors, barristers, judges, probation officers, prison officers and ancillary and secretarial staff directly benefit from the current prohibition of cannabis.

Immensely powerful industrial groups such as the tobacco, alcohol, synthetic fibre, pharmaceutical and fuel industries are terrified of the competition a legal cannabis industry might provide. Cannabis gets one high, is non-addictive, is completely harmless, and it grows virtually anywhere. Neither God nor Nature wishes to sell the patent. One doesn't have to drill mines into Mother Earth nor destroy rainforests to harvest the prolific herb, so some multinationals could go broke.

Many responsible and concerned parents have pointed out to me the only argument against legalisation of cannabis with which I have any kind of sympathy, i.e., it gives their children a mode of rebellion and taboo participation that is absolutely fabulous and harmless. The parents discreetly smoke joints when the children aren't around and pretend a show of disapproval when the children behave likewise. Necessarily, such an attempt to fool the young is short-lived, and I doubt whether the parents in question would offer serious opposition to the legislation of cannabis.

313

A LEGAL CANNABIS MARKET

Advantages

There are countless advantages to legislation. It will no longer be necessary for cannabis consumers to acquire cannabis from illegal sources that force law-abiding citizens to adopt mantles of crime. Prohibition-related crime (which commonly includes murder, violence, kidnap, theft and fraud) and its pathological consequences will disappear. Sufferers of asthma, glaucoma, epilepsy, cancer, constricted bronchioles, AIDS, multiple sclerosis, migraine, pruritis and insomnia will be more likely to obtain relief. Nasty side effects caused by medically prescribed tranquillisers, sleepers, analgesics and antiemetics will be replaced by getting pleasantly stoned.

Regulation

Virtually all proposals for the legalising of cannabis share the common grounds of (1) assuming the cannabis market is irrepressible, (2) insisting that marketed cannabis carry a strictly worded, government-approved health warning, and (3) maintaining the illegality of the sale of cannabis to children. The areas of disagreement in legislation proposals tend to occur when consideration is given to the degree, if any, of government intervention.

Monopoly or near monopoly is obtained when the bulk of services is provided by one, or very few, business enterprises or government administrative agencies. Some legislation models have proposed a state monopoly of supply with all advertising illegal. Such a system more often than not leads to a relatively stable but hopelessly bureaucratised structure in which people perform routine roles as functionaries.

In an oligopoly a handful of enterprises constitute a cartel and dominate the market. This system seems equally hampered by bureaucratic paralysis.

At the other extreme, others have suggested that production and distribution be undertaken by a large number of relatively small competing private enterprises subject to government regulation.

Yet others have explicitly limited state participation to zero, or as near as possible, to punish them for having unleashed the violence and evils of prohibition on a well-meaning, peace-loving generation.

Although fettering the cannabis market is no more justified than fettering any other market, the governments that tend to exist in Great Britain and elsewhere are unlikely to consciously vote themselves out of taking, through the administrative vehicle of regulation, a hefty slice of the action.

As far as possible, regulations should be closely linked and totally dependent upon obvious and agreed failures and mistakes committed by the hitherto unregulated producers and suppliers. The government should be allowed to intervene with its cudgel of regulation only if there is good reason to believe an improvement in consumer satisfaction will be achieved.

Eventually, cannabis should be available in the same way as tea, coffee or medicinal herbs. There is a general move back to medicine based on organic compounds. This is partly due to the great dissemination of Asian herbal treatments and partly due to the public distrust of money-grabbing pharmaceutical companies that deliberately exclude the use of vegetable compounds for their own commercial gain of patenting synthetic chemicals. Agricultural products are generally exempt from legislation covering processed food. Psilocybin magic mushrooms, for example, are free from drug and excise laws. Cannabis should be equally blessed.

Unfortunately, legalised cannabis is more likely to be regulated in the same way as tobacco and alcohol. Organisations advocating legalisation have been reluctant to argue against this, probably feeling that their goals would be impossible to attain without such concession.

Who is going to do it?
Since the 1960s, there has been an almost universally prevalent belief that large tobacco companies, such as Philip Morris, in anticipation of cannabis legalisation, have registered trade names such as Acapulco Gold and Panama Red. I have known

many swear this to be true. In fact, it is not. In 1970, a group called Amorphia went through the files of the United States Patent Office and found that nobody had registered the name Acapulco Gold. Amorphia applied for the name, hoping to use it to market rolling papers. The application was refused because Acapulco gold is a generic name for a kind of marijuana, and generic names cannot be copyrighted. It doesn't really matter, of course, because Marco Polo's Bullshit will outsell Panama Red if it provides a better smoke.

This copyright mythology has helped engender the belief that tobacco companies will be the ones to market legal cannabis. Actually, there is no reason on earth to think that tobacco companies rather than other companies are more likely to get into the legalised cannabis business.

I think it appropriate for the running of legalised cannabis supply to be carried out by some of those who have already committed themselves to, or have experience in, the current illegal supplying of cannabis. Although different skills might well be required in the importation and retail distribution areas (driving ability, commercial freight expertise and shop-keeping prowess, rather than street-wisdom and deviousness), the same cannot be said to be true of the production process, where the same skills will be in demand. Nor is it true of the exportation of cannabis from most of the countries where it has been grown for millennia. From these countries, exportation of illegal commodities differs in little or no way from the exportation of legal commodities: officials are paid, and the job is done. It would be a great pity not to salvage the many honourable, trust-laden and fruitful relationships and alliances that have been established between growers (and other participants in the countries of origin) and importers resident in the destination countries.

THE TRANSITION PERIOD

Likelihood of change

There are more marijuana smokers of voting age than ever

before. Also, a greater number than ever before of non-users are now aware of what cannabis is, its harmlessness and the irrational objections to the abolition of its prohibition. Older, generally more conservative people are, albeit far too slowly, leaving the political system. Although the contributions to sanity made by the young replacements have so far been few, political leaders prepared to admit the inhaling of what they smoked are bound to eventually emerge. Meanwhile, evidence of cannabis's therapeutic qualities continues to pile up and be endorsed by respected and authoritative members of the medical profession.

It remains only for cannabis to become socially acceptable. It has been held that lower classes tend to use cannabis as a general intoxicant while upper classes use it as a stimulant. The working classes, therefore, remain criminal while the aristocrats continue to be merely decadent. As cannabis becomes more and more of a middle-class activity, the distinction between decadence and crime blurs, and legalisation is inevitable.

Mechanics of transition

The transition from the current legal market to a regular market will not happen overnight, and it will not happen smoothly. Large sections of the public will be resistant to the change and are certain to demand what they regard as protective measures before allowing legalisation to be initiated. Sales might be restricted to licensed dealers, or even qualified pharmacists. There will be coercive attempts to enforce regulation along the lines of that governing alcohol and tobacco. Drug-testing will probably skyrocket, particularly for some occupations, and there will be all sorts of penalties for driving or engaging in paid employment when traces of cannabis are detected in urine.

Although I have never known of anyone seeking medical treatment for the effects of cannabis use, some of those who oppose legalisation inexplicably envisage legal cannabis putting an additional burden on the National Health Service. Who knows what suggestions might be made from those quarters with respect to taxation and regulation.

The constant media bombardment of carefully selected phrases such as 'drug-related crime', rather than the accurate 'prohibition-caused crime', will also give rise to spurious concerns that might have to be addressed by a certain amount of transitional regulation. Some of this interim regulation will insist on informative and accurate labelling giving the cannabis's THC content, impurities, origin, date of production and other characteristics. I doubt if there will be too much in the way of objection to this from those in favour of legalisation.

There will also be resistance to legalisation from unexpected quarters. The hardened and heavy pot smoker is often convinced that should cannabis be legalised, either government or big business or both will inevitably wreck the quality and the quantity of the product available. Many consumers will continue to prefer to buy cannabis in the manner to which they are accustomed. Commercialism and other capitalistic characteristics might turn cannabis into a bland, ineffectual, designer-produced non-entity, just like non-tox beer and sliced bread. Make it legal, and then stop it from getting one high. There is no need to adopt these trappings of American Puritanism. Getting high is OK.

Everyone lives by selling something

Robert Louis Stevenson

Eleusis
The Hive Chemist

THIS IS THE tale of a character named 'eleusis.' Think of it as a work of fiction in the first person by a humble narrator, and if it seems a bit strange, remember that only the truth itself is stranger than fiction. Eleusis, for those of you unfamiliar, was the name of an ancient Greek city where the Spring Mysteries were held: a city-wide festival where consumption of mind-altering substances was the central activity in a celebration of the return of spring.

318

Organic chemistry intrigued me. It tempted me with its secret language of symbols, its demand for (nearly) blind faith in unseen collisions. MDMA intrigued me as well, with its strangely universal experience, its ability to make even the hardest soul empathic. I had tried neither organic chemistry nor MDMA, so I decided to try both. In the spring of 1994, appropriately enough, I began my chemical journey and by late winter I was already posting to a.d.c. It took so much work to learn how to make MDMA that I decided I was going to share what I learned so that others would not have to repeat my labors. However, I had serious misgivings about sharing because my quest was one for knowledge and experience while, I knew, for most others it would be for purely economic reasons. You can see my struggling in practically every post I made, the schizophrenic vacillations in tone between erudite dissertation and egomaniacal evisceration. Though I knew my posts would be put to use by those less scrupulous, I posted nonetheless, for the benefit of those who were. And now on to the experience.

I broke every rule in the book, and I did so knowingly. I ordered glassware from Aldrich with my real name and credit card. I ordered chemicals from all over with my real name and money orders. I had boxes shipped to my parents (and, later, my co-conspirators). I spent hundreds of hours in the library and posted everything I found that sounded remotely useful to the process of making MDMA. I conducted my experiments in a freakin' apartment complex, of all places, but none of these mistakes got me busted.

I did all of this in blind faith because the first time I took MDMA was my own.

Days after the reference for converting safrole to isosafrole was sent to me I made my first batch of MDMA, strictly by the book (Shulgin's, that is). Mid-November of '94, a good friend of mine and I took 110mg each from that batch and rocketed into an internal space beyond description, but not beyond comprehension. She was suitably impressed, I was ecstatic (pardon the pun), and we just happened to be doing

319

it at a friend of hers' who dealt the stuff. Needless to say, that was the beginning of a very good business relationship.

Fast forward a year, give or take a few months.

And the next question is:

So why did I leave a.d.c.?

Perhaps some of you were present back then. If so, then you probably remember a vociferous bastard named Yogi Shan who thought eleusis was about as full of shit as the Augean stables (cf. Hercules's twelve labors). Well, a couple of weeks prior to the fit hitting the Shan, so to speak, I had visited a friend in Texas and while there I bought a bunch of fairly innocuous chemicals. I packed them up in a box and went down to the local mailboxes, etc., to have them shipped back.

The box never made it.

After two weeks, I was convinced that it had been confiscated, and likely sent to either the DEA, the DOT or the BATF, so I used the ruse of Yogi's incessant criticism of 'eleusis's bad chemistry' to bid my farewell to a.d.c., as it was clearly time for me to quit the game.

This, of course, meant that ZWITTERION had to leave too, since even if he and I weren't the same person (and we were), he wouldn't have anyone to pick on anymore (didn't you notice that ZWITTERION only seemed to try out the things that eleusis posted?). As a side note, if you find it hard to swallow that ZWIT and eleusis were the same individual because of the wild difference in writing styles, keep in mind that I *am* an English major.

So what happened to 'eleusis' after that?

I packed up my lab in a blind paranoid fury. I canceled my icubed e-mail account. I encrypted and compressed every computer file, e-mail, etc., that was even remotely related to drug chemistry. I woke up every morning before 5.00 a.m., rumored to be the time the DEA would strike if they came a-knockin'. But I also knew that the paper trail was immense, that even if there wasn't anything left in my apartment when the DEA came crashing in that I would still have a lot of explaining to do. Then there was the realization that if I was under surveillance that they would already know where I put everything. I struggled to wipe my fingerprints from everything I had ever touched, but I couldn't bring myself to throw away nearly $12,000 in glassware, chemicals and equipment. I just couldn't *destroy* everything, though I *knew* that I should. Besides, how does one get rid of 11kg of safrole or 20l of THF? I'm no tree-hugger, but I'm not so environmentally unconscious that I'd pour shit like that down the drain or onto the ground.

Months went by with no sign of the DEA. Slowly but surely my co-conspirator convinced me to start up again. She used the very persuasive argument that since I had started manufacturing, no one would buy anything else (I was fanatic about quality, I never cut my MDMA, and I made sure that every dose was 100–110mg for the best possible experience). It really didn't take much convincing, though, because once you start, I don't believe you can stop until you are caught. It is too seductive, way too seductive. Viddy well, little brothers, viddy well (cf. *A Clockwork Orange*).

So I started up again, but I tried to make the lab as spartan as possible – no unrelated chemicals on the premises, no massive quantities of class-1 precursors, and definitely no product for any longer than the time it took to dry. It was futile, of course, and as I came to realize that, I took the attitude of 'fuck it'. I cranked out a 2,000-dose batch of 2-CB and gave it all away. I mustered up a 16g batch of mescaline and gave that away too. TMA, DMT, 4-Methylaminorex, et al., just to know that I could and to see what they were like.

On June 23, at around 5 p.m., the phone rang. It was Special Agent Higgins of the DEA. He was at my parents' house and wanted to ask me a few questions about all the chemicals I had purchased. I told him I would be right over, hung up, then looked at my apartment. Chemicals everywhere, glassware everywhere. There was no way to destroy enough of it to matter in the time frame allotted. I did destroy the twin 100g batches of MDP-2-P that were just starting (literally fifteen minutes prior) and dump out 500g of methylamine HCl (yes, made by decomposing hexamine), but nothing else. I just hoped that I would be able to smoothly talk my way out of the problem – at least for long enough to be able to destroy everything else.

When I arrived at my parents' house there were a dozen agents wandering around with guns, bulletproof vests, the whole enchilada. They were sorting through my old room and found maybe two documents related to chemistry and, unfortunately, a bottle of sodium in petroleum ether that I had long ago forgotten. They told me that they had all of my receipts from a certain chemical company that I used quite often and asked what I did with all of those chemicals. Well, I felt pretty confident then because I never ordered anything listed or even terribly suspicious from that company – I synthesized all of the naughty precursors myself – so I calmly answered, 'I make photographic developers with them.'

They then asked, 'Are you saying you never made crystal meth, crank, methamphetamine, whatever you want to call it, with these chemicals?' and I easily said, 'No,' followed by, 'I don't think any of those chemicals are used to make meth, otherwise how would I have been able to purchase them?'

They didn't like that one bit. No siree. Not one bit. That's when they pulled out the big guns (metaphorically) and asked if I knew anyone in Houston. The sweat started to pour. I knew what they were after. I said, 'Yes, I have a friend out there.' They asked what I thought had happened when the box I shipped never made it and I said, 'I figured UPS confiscated it for improper packaging but when I called about it they said they had no record of the shipment so then I figured it was just lost.' Then they asked the killer question, the one that made me give up because I knew I was busted.

'Do you know [blank]?'

I said, 'Yes, she's an ex-girlfriend of mine.'

'Well, we have [blank] in custody right now.'

'Oh.'

'So I'll repeat my earlier question, did you ever use this to make crystal, crank, meth, whatever?'

'No, I never made crystal meth, I think it's a horrible drug.'

'Then what did you make with it, [blank] said, "———"'
'Alright, alright. I made MDMA.'

Consent was then asked for to search my apartment, under the threat that I would be arrested if I said no and they would get a warrant anyway. I knew this would happen because of what POP-I had told me, so I signed my life away. Agents were standing by at my apartment and busted in the door as soon as my pen hit the paper. I was cuffed and taken to my apartment to identify the contents as mine (a formality) and then I was taken to DEA Holding. Apparently, seconds after I was taken away the reporters arrived. My driver's license picture was on the six o'clock news. The entire block I lived on was evacuated. Rumors started flying and all of my friends, of which only a very few knew what I did, started calling each other.

To top it all off, my ulcer started giving me a real fit (the ulcer was a by-product of living two years in intense fear of that very moment).

At DEA Holding I received the good cop/bad cop treatment. It's just like the movies, kids. Just like it. One was threatening to kick in my balls if I didn't tell the truth, the other was saying 'There, there, he's *trying* to tell the truth, give him a chance.' It was sickening. (Apparently, [blank] actually did get sick because they asked, 'You're not going to puke all over the floor like [blank], are you?')

The interrogation was rather brief, consisting only of:

1) How much x did I make? – About 800g, I said (based on quick mental calculations of what was consumed from the chemicals I knew were on the premises).
2) How often did I take it? – Three times (close enough to the truth that it doesn't matter).
3) Did I sell it? – Only to [blank].
4) She said you split the money 75–25, how much money did you make? – About eighty grand (consistent with my earlier answer of 800g).
5) How often did you make it? – About every other week.
6) How much in each batch? – 28g.

7) Who taught you how to make it? – I taught myself (true).

8) Did you get the recipe from the Internet? – No, from the library (cringe at the word 'recipe', we ain't bakin' brownies here, boys).

And that was pretty much it. I was then transported to the Orient Road Jail. On the way there I enjoyed a most memorable conversation with the agent:

'So this is pretty much the end of the road for me, eh?'

'No, Tim Allen from *Home Improvement* got busted for trafficking two keys of coke. He copped a plea, turned in a few people and look how well he's done.'

'Yeah, but Tim Allen was a dealer, and I'm a chemist. The buck pretty much stops here. I'm top of the food chain. There's no further up you can go, there's no bigger prize than busting someone like me.'

'Good point.'

'Gee, thanks.'

The worst thing about jail (so far) is it's so fucking boring that someone like me would go insane within weeks. I was so bored I counted every tile on the walls of the various rooms I was shuffled between (1,240 in the 'airblock', 2,278 in my 'pod'). Oh yes, and then there was the food – being that I am a vegetarian, it was completely inedible. Breakfast was gravy and an apple. Yes, gravy. My cellmate got a hellacious case of diarrhea from it – so bad he actually shit his britches.

The next morning I had my bond hearing in front of a federal magistrate. I was chained to two other people by the hands and feet. Reporters crowded the pews watching my every expression. My mother was there with one of her friends from work. At that moment I knew that I had truly fucked up big time; that I had let down everyone who said I was a genius that could have done anything I put my mind to. What did my clever brain get me? Shackled to a health-plan embezzler and an illegal-alien bank robber.

A private lawyer offered his services for free (my case was extremely novel – only the second MDMA manufacturer in that district of Florida). The prosecutor moved to have my bond denied and for me to be detained in Morgan Street Jail (which makes Orient Road look like a fucking resort, btw). My lawyer and I quickly consulted the federal statutes and found that what applies to methamphetamine does not apply to MDMA, so that got me out of that dire predicament. Bond was set for $75,000 and my mother put up her house to secure it. Had I not bonded out, I am quite certain I would not be alive to type this. I later received the background documentation on the DEA's 'setup' of the sting against my co-conspirators and me. What was extremely interesting to note from this was that the DEA conducted 'three trash pickups at [my parents'] residence and one trash pickup at [blank]'s.' Of course they didn't find anything because I didn't live with my parents, but I always assumed that they would be able to tell that I didn't live there. Funny thing is, they were limited to investigating 'where the chemicals were actually sent.'

Another consequence of my arrest was that most of my possessions were seized on the premise that they were either paid for with drug-manufacturing profits or they were actually used to make drugs. I could merely rattle off a list of interesting (and pricey) items that would break a materialist's heart, but the point here isn't to impress you with what I owned, rather, to illustrate that there isn't a lot of logic involved in the seizure process. Furthermore, when they do seize something you have to take them to court (in a separate civil action) to get the stuff back. This will cost you beaucoup bucks and you'll probably lose anyway (this is what my lawyer said, and he specializes in federal criminal and civil cases). Fortunately, you can sometimes 'ask' for certain things back, and if you were cooperative, they will honor the requests. Other times they will just outright give you things back. For instance, they seized about $10,000 in electronic test equipment that had absolutely nothing to do with making drugs and, besides a $3,000 digital storage oscilloscope, wasn't even paid for with drug profits. However, a 1991 Ducati 900SS motorcycle, an obvious *toy* that was paid for with drug profits, was given back to me for unknown reasons.

(They initially seized it but later said to my lawyer, and I quote, 'We want to give it back to him.' My 1988 Mazda RX-7 they ignored, saying that it was 'a piece of junk' – this was where I typically kept the 'Lonely Laptop on the Fringe' as well as a few other neat toys. Had I known that they weren't interested in 'Junky' cars (mine had some rust as well as 100k+ miles) then I would have stashed my money in it, instead of a fire safe that they naturally cracked open immediately.

Side comment: The DEA chemist said 'this is the most technologically advanced lab I have ever seen.' Well, that was something to be proud of, anyway.

A couple weeks after I was out on bond the DEA found out about the storage unit I used and which had been rented out by one of [blank]'s roommates for me. It was quite a coincidence because the day before I had told my lawyer about it and asked him what I should do. He said, 'Do nothing and see if they find it.' Well, find it they did. It took some fast talking on my part to keep [blank]'s roommate from getting arrested as well. Anyway, when they raided my apartment lab and found all of that electronic equipment they assumed I was a dangerous sonuvabitch who booby-trapped the storage unit. They called my lawyer and me to ask what was in it. I gave them very coy, circumspect answers, implying that it had been so long since I was out there that I couldn't 'exactly' remember what was in it. This was a good move on my part because it heightened their suspicion it was booby-trapped to the point that they offered me immunity for the contents as long as I told them what was there. Suddenly my memory reappeared and I rattled off about a dozen items before they decided that HazMat needed to be called in and so the circus started anew. Good thing I got immunity because inside there was a complete portable lab (I called it S.C.R.A.P. for Self-Contained Reaction APparatus), a generator, a rotary evaporator, about 400 different chemicals and some small amounts of 2-CB and mescaline.

The legal morass surrounding a manufacturing case is unbelievable. I could go on for dozens of pages about it, but instead I will summarize using the advantage of hindsight.

There are many ways one can be prosecuted for suspected drug-manufacturing, and the safest route the prosecutor can take is to just stick you with the precursors unless you were caught actually making it and/or you had product on the premises. I was caught with nothing being made and nothing on site, but the prosecutor was greedy and charged [blank] and me with 'Conspiracy to Manufacture MDMA, a Controlled Substance Analogue' anyway. I waived my right to a grand jury to be nice, and because there was no point in being formally charged since they had enough evidence to convict me of *something*. I was then offered a plea agreement that, of course, gave me nothing except taking away my right to appeal. My lawyer advised me to plead guilty, but *not* to sign the plea agreement. This is known as 'pleading open' and shows that you accept responsibility for your actions without the potentially damning loss of your right to appeal an unfavorable sentence. I don't regret this at all even though it royally pissed off the prosecutor because I still get the three-level reduction for pleading (more on this in a moment). However, my pleading open made the prosecutor so mad that he then filed a motion to have me detained prior to my sentencing (i.e. thrown back in jail). The detainment hearing was, fortunately, quite laughable because I had been complying with all of my pre-trial bond restrictions (no drugs in the urine, no arrests, I had a 'real' job and was enrolled in school), still, if the judge was in a bad mood that day it could have been a trip to nasty, razor-wire-engulfed Morgan Street for me.

I was then 'interviewed' by a federal probation officer to 'get my side of the story,' find out my background assets, etc., to make what's called a Presentence Report (PSR). Strangely enough, what I said and [blank] said pretty well matched, though she had really low-balled the estimate of MDMA I made (bless her!). Another part of the PSR is what the production capacity of the lab was according to the DEA chemist. The chemicals they considered were:

10.9kg safrole

900g isosafrole
1.8kg hexamine (equiv. To 3.5kg methylamine HCI).

This gave them a yield, based loosely on my 'notes', of between 4.8 and 6.0kg. They, of course, made some critical mistakes like not considering other necessary reagents involved, nor the fact that three moles of methylamine must be present for every one mole of MDP-2-P for the reductive amination to have a fighting chance of working. So the big argument at my sentencing, then, will be pitting my calculations against theirs. For this, I have to hire an expert witness (i.e. a chemistry professor) to do the talking for me and to lend 'credibility' to the whole deal (an expert witness is also necessary if you wish to appeal). Unfortunately, none of the professors I have attempted to contact thus far wish to speak to me (gee, what a surprise!).

Now what does all this mean, and what does it all entail?

Federal drug cases are prosecuted according to the 'level' you are at. The base offense level is determined by either:

a) the amount of drugs you made
b) the amount of drugs you could have made with the chemicals on hand
c) the amount of drugs you made + the amount of precursors you had.

We can derive a) by calculating backwards from the amount of hexamine I had consumed from the brand-new container found, which gives an amount of 766g. We can derive b) as above, which based on methylamine would be 1.8kg and based on formic acid would be 377g. The offense level for c) is then based on the amount of precursors like safrole, isosafrole and methylamine on hand plus a two-level increase for drugs actually having been made.

The base offense level for a) is 18, b) is either 21 or 16, respectively, and c), the worst, is 22. Level 22 is forty-one to fifty-one months in jail, 21 is thirty-three to forty-one, 18 is twenty-seven to thirty three and 16 is twenty-one to twenty-seven. Take three levels off for acceptance of responsibility and the possible range of time is ten months (level 13) to thirty-three months (level 19).

So that is where I am right now: somewhere between ten and thirty-three months. And what if the judge completely ignores my arguments and sentences me for the maximum quantity estimated (6kg)? Sixty-three to seventy-eight months.

My lawyer and I are not quite sure which of the above routes (a, b, or c) is appropriate because of the PSR, which only considered the amount of drugs I could have made with the chemicals on hand. I suppose I will find out when I am sentenced on Feb. 20, 1998.

What can be learned from my experience, and what are the ramifications?

Good questions, and I'll give my best guesses.

First, it is rather apparent from my interrogation and the investigation thus far that the DEA either *does not know about a.d.c.* or they 'do not care.' Yes, friends, hard as it may be to believe, outside of the 'did you get the recipe off the Internet' question, they didn't ask me jack shit about the Net.

Second, I think it is rather obvious from my tale that shipping chemicals via UPS is not a bright thing to do, but why did I do it in the first place? Because I shipped all sorts of crap through Fed-Ex all the time (what an appropriate name) so I figured because of the volume of shipments both places did that UPS wouldn't bother opening up a package unless it was leaking or stunk. Wrong.

Third, chemical supply houses *will* ask you some fairly detailed and probing questions about what you are up to. If you don't look straight-up, white-bread (not white as in race, white as in bland), Middle America then don't even *think* about showing up somewhere in person. If you want to play the 'fake company ordering chemicals' game, be aware that they will expect a company check (what, no bank account for the business? Sorry). Also be aware that should you get caught and you were using a fake business to order chemicals that can be considered 'obstruction of justice' and will merit you a two-level upward adjustment should you be found guilty. As well, don't buy all of your chemicals and glassware from one place, and never ever even *ask* about compounds that are heavily watched, scheduled or listed.

Fourth, if you are caught, try to find out what the agents know/don't know before you start spilling the beans. In my case I played very innocent with them until I found out that [blank] was arrested with fifty capsules of my product (they told her that they already had me in custody and that I said blah-blah-blah, they do that sort of thing, btw). If it does seem like they've got a pretty solid lock on you, 'be cooperative' – tell them the truth but don't get too detailed, all of the details will be debated during sentencing anyway, but being consistent from the moment you are arrested to the moment you are sentenced looks very good indeed. As well, plead guilty but don't sign the plea agreement unless you are getting a good deal out of it (and you'll only be getting something good if you turn in other people, in which case you deserve to spend eternity in Cocytus (cf. Dante's *Inferno*).

Fifth, never, I repeat, *never* throw out empty bottles, reaction by-products, documentation, etc., in the trash where you live. Take it to a dumpster far away, burn it, shred it, or whatever, but don't leave it in your trash. *I* didn't get caught because of this, but I *could have*. As well, assume your phones are tapped from day one so don't even talk 'in code' about transactions with your 'dealer[s]'. Always meet in public, and I don't mean in someone else's car, rather at a restaurant, café or bar.

Sixth, *where* you do it isn't so important as *how* you do it. I didn't get busted because my neighbors 'smelled something funny' but then again, neither did I make methylamine (or MDMA, or MDP-2-P) in the middle of the day.

Seventh, don't tell anyone you wouldn't trust with your life what you are up to. I imagine the dumbest thing one could do would be to make a whole bunch of X and then invite some 'friends' over to 'try it out' while glassware and chemicals are everywhere, but I did just that several times and no one ever made the connection. Maybe my friends were dumb, and maybe yours are too, but that's tempting fate with a little too much surety.

Eighth, make sure you have a lawyer ahead of time that is familiar with federal and state drug cases. It is unreasonable to expect to find a lawyer who has handled drug-*manufacturing* cases, but if you let them 'know' ahead of time what you are interested in, and pay the requisite (and hefty) retainer, you'll be good to go if (when) the Man comes bustin' in. Your legal expenses for defending against a DEA-levied manufacturing charge will be $15,000 plus, so keep that in mind.

Ninth, have someone else order the chemicals, if possible, but realize that they will be the ones that get the third-degree if caught. If you don't trust them with your life, and they haven't got nerves of steel, both of you will go down. Incidentally, I didn't have anyone else order the chemicals because I didn't feel I should place that sort of responsibility/burden on any of my friends (would you do that to one of yours? If so, maybe *you* aren't such a good friend).

And finally . . .

Tenth. My biggest mistake wasn't me sending that package through UPS, nor starting the product back up after it never made it, nor even deciding to make X in the first place. My mistake was not taking the time to make a huge amount quickly and then destroying everything afterwards. I should have blew out a kilogram or so then quit. One kilogram is worth up $100k and that should be enough to make anyone quite self-sufficient with proper investing and money management. Instead, I wanted to experiment with the process and find other ways of doing things as well as posting everything I found to a.d.c. I should have quit as soon as I succeeded but I couldn't resist the temptation to tweak. I can say 'should have' about a lot of things in this game, but that's the one I truly regret. The song of the Sirens is irresistible. Those who hear it and have not been tied to the mast like Odysseus will perish among the rocks (cf. *The Odyssey*).

Found on the Internet on www.lycaeum.org, 1998

Robert Bingham
Lightning on the Sun

WITH HIS FINE nine tucked between his leg and the front seat of his Lincoln, Dwayne and Julie drove up the Henry Hudson Parkway.

'I thought we were going to Brooklyn,' she said.

'How it is, before these gentlemen used to operate out of the Greenpoint area, see,' said Dwayne. 'But then one of 'em got, you know, got busted, so they moved to a different hood in Harlem. You got the stuff? 'Cause they know we're coming and if you don't got the stuff—'

'I got the stuff.'

Internally she was chanting, *the aesthetics of love, the morality of business*, over and over again. It had become her mantra. It helped calm her. She was wearing a pair of green hospital orderly pants with a pull tie, an oldie from a guy even before Asher and a black T-shirt that said CAT POWER. Between her legs was the largest handbag she could find on sale at Bloomingdale's. It held five kilos of heroin.

'How much you step on it? I hope you didn't step on it *too* much 'cause these gentlemen are the ones who do the stepping, you know what I'm saying.'

'It'll be worth their while,' she said.

The math had been very simple. She'd gone to a stupid head shop in SoHo and bought a scale. Then she'd taken Asher's three kilos and turned it into five with cornstarch. Her deal with Dwayne was 10 percent and silence. With the lights of the George Washington Bridge in sight, they turned off the highway and found themselves heading east on 157th Street. Marks of weariness, marks of woe, thought Julie. Blake. Now there was a man who understood the hallucinatory horrors of a city. Lonely black men with bagged bottles wandered the streets. The sun had set and dusk was quickly handing itself over to the night.

'So, how is this going to go down, Dwayne?'

'Very simple. I go in with the stuff. They check it out. We get the money. We leave.'

'No, that is not how it will go down. If that were to be the scenario, you'd leave and I'm left with your criminal car while you fly to Cabo.'

'What the fuck is Cabo?'

'Cabo San Lucas. You know, where O.J. Simpson used to hang out. You know O.J., right?'

Dwayne didn't say anything. He was wondering how the Haitians would take to a white lady. He looked over at her.

'So you want to come in.'

'No, I don't want to come in. I will come. See, I'm the principal in this deal.'

'Baby, you're white as milk and these gentlemen are Haitians. Like, they don't *know you*.'

'Where do they live?'

'Off St. Nicholas.'

St. Nicholas. Julie decided not to linger on the irony. She was too scared.

'Yeah, few years back, the area got busted so many times the cops, they forgot about it now. The place is old school.'

'Great. We're going to hang out with a bunch of Baby Doc Duvaliers at St. Nicholas. They better have the money.'

When she first moved to New York, she'd had an affair with a Haitian. It hadn't lasted long but he'd been a wonderful man, a bag handler for Aristide when Aristide was in New York, a great cook. She'd admired his oscillations between maudlin introspection and brutal passion. Haitians, they turned on a dime.

'Look,' she said, 'wouldn't it be better if there were two of us? You could, you know, cover me, watch my back, so to speak.'

'Okay, baby,' said Dwayne, backing into a parking space on 158th Street. 'But you better be cool.'

They got out of the car. St. Nicholas Place was a small, V-shaped concrete construct. They walked south on it for two blocks.

'Okay,' said Dwayne. 'Here it is.'

Julie breathed out and looked up at the sky. The stars were out. The stars of Harlem. Please, she said to herself, please, stars, please behave yourself tonight. They walked up a tenement stoop and Dwayne pressed an intercom button.

'It's D,' said Dwayne.

The buzzer rang.

The stairwell was not unlike many others she'd seen in the city, not unlike that of a building she'd lived in in the East Village. It was just a ratty municipal stairwell, narrow with sharp turns at each landing. As they climbed, the bag began to feel heavy and Julie light-headed. She hadn't eaten anything all day. On the fifth floor a door was cracked open and a man with dreadlocks was sticking his head out at them.

'Who is the lady, D?'

'The lady is who it is, she cool.'

'Lady, you a cop?'

'No,' said Julie. 'Not at all. Law enforcement has never been my bag.'

'Then what is your bag?'

'Weight.'

'I like that,' said the man with dreadlocks. He had terrifying whites to his eyes. 'Step on it. We been waiting on you.'

The place reeked of grass, which at once comforted and terrified her. The Hassassini; she'd once been fascinated with that particular cult of men. Eventually the H for *hashish* had been dropped. They were Middle Eastern assassins imported to Venice and elsewhere. They killed on hash. They smoked and killed in alleyways and the occasional oasis. These guys looked to be some atavistic mutation of the Assassini. There was a shotgun on a table next to what used to be referred to as a Q-P, or quarter-pound of pot. There were two other men sitting on a couch, their backs to a window with the shade drawn. Julie couldn't quite make them out. The only light was coming sideways from what looked to be a kitchen. She dropped her bag between her legs and rested her hands on the edge of the table. There was the distinct possibility she might faint.

'Brother D,' said a man from the couch. He didn't sound Haitian. 'Brother D, how you making it? That's a fine piece of ass you got riding with you. Who are you, lady? This here is my place of residence and I ain't never see you before.'

Definitely not a Haitian, she thought, more like hard-core Harlem.

'I've got five Ks of smack here. It came by way of Cambodia. It's serious shit.'

Hard-core Harlem began to laugh. The Haitian who'd opened the door squeezed her ass as he passed by and disappeared into the kitchen.

'A white lady with five Ks, now ain't that something?' said Hard-core Harlem.

The man next to him on the couch had dreadlocks and was silent. In the little light she could make out a scar running diagonally across one cheek.

'Believe me,' said Julie. 'It's something.'

'She's for real,' said Dwayne. 'She got contacts.'

'Yeah, like who?'

'A friend of mine,' said Julie, 'he knows a lot of people in Cambodia.'

'Cambodia,' said Hard-core Harlem. 'They got the fine shit, those gooks, right?'

'It moves through Cambodia,' said Julie. 'They don't grow it.'

'Yeah, well, money don't grow on my knob, neither,' he continued. 'So, D, why don't you grab that scale over there and let's see what we're fucking with.'

'She won't burn you on weight,' said the Haitian with the scar. 'She'll cut it on you.'

'You could step on this shit ten times over,' said Julie, 'and every junkie on the corner would OD.'

'Hey D, where did you find this chick, this Miss Cat Power? I like her. She got a fine set of titties and she talks real tough.'

Julie heaved the bag on to the table, unzipped one of the five zip-locked bags, and spilled about a gram onto the table.

'Here,' she said. 'Have a taste.'

The Haitian with the scar got up and came over to the table. He had a claw for a pinkie. Julie stood back. He was terrifying. The Claw took a hit off his pinkie and stood looking straight at her. Julie closed her eyes. Her compulsion to get out of the room was rampaging. It was keeping her from fainting. The Claw with the scar sniffled, and then went back and sat down on the couch. Shortly, his head kicked back. Good, thought Julie, a good sign. Then the Claw whispered something into Hard-core Harlem's ear.

'My associate is impressed. Let's see the rest of it.'

Julie took another zip-locked bag out of her purse.

'Hey,' said Dwayne. 'Like I don't mean to be speedy, but where's the money?'

'At the store, daddy. At the store,' said Hard-core Harlem.

'Well, why don't you send someone to the store.'

'I'll send someone to the store when we've verified that everything is cool.'

Hard-core Harlem got up and flipped a wall switch. An overhead light shone down on to the table. He wore tan pants and a purple rayon shirt unbuttoned so as to display his chest jewelry. Now all five bags were on the table. He opened one and worked his index finger down to the bottom, came back up, and took a hit. Then he got a scale out and began to place the bags on it.

'Okay, D, let's you, me and Miss Cat Power go down to the store. But I'm only going to give you eighty 'cause that's all I got. That fine with you, lady?'

'The deal was a hundred and ten,' said Julie.

'Like I said, eighty is all I got.'

'I'll say it again,' said Julie. 'The deal was a hundred and ten. Now I'm hearing bullshit.'

She couldn't believe it had come out of her mouth. She was role-playing an argument, the lines of which had been handed her from cinematic moments of years past.

Hard-core Harlem straightened up. A knife was dangling at his side. Now he was facing her from across the table.

'I like you,' he said. 'You got some fine titties. Later on we can party. Right now it's eighty. My mother still bakes with cornstarch.'

'I guess,' said Julie, 'I'll take it.'

'Tell you what,' said Hard-core Harlem, taking out a box

of Kool and emptying the cigarettes on the table. 'I'll make up the difference to you.'

He dipped the empty cigarette box into one of the bags and filled it with powder.

'I hope you're cutting back to less than a pack a day,' he said.

Everyone in the room laughed. Then he handed the pack to Julie.

'Now,' he said, 'let's make it down to the store.'

Lightning on the Sun, 2001

Harvey Rottenberg
Planted, Burnt, and Busted

AFTER MOVING FAR and fast for two weeks, anywhere we could cook a meal felt good, even the motel in Seattle.

The dinner dishes were done. My old lady was lounging around in a pair of sheer tights, reading. I was into a yoga pamphlet titled 'How You Can Speak With God'. The room was permeated by a feeling of well-being and peace that comes as a great home-cooked meal is digested in silent contemplation.

The door rattled. I went to check it out, putting down flashes of paranoia. 'Can't be thieves,' I thought. 'They're making too much noise.'

The door flew open. Three men in shoddy overcoats surged in, obnoxiously pushing snub-nosed revolvers before them.

The muscles of their faces were knotted by the tension of anticipation. They probably were out in the hallway for quite a while, hyping themselves to come through the narrow door. They obviously feared for their lives. But they must enjoy the feeling or they would find a less dangerous line of work.

'Police,' one ejaculated perfunctorily. But his body was still hard-on tense. And his gun jerked in tiny spasms, as he flicked his glassy eyes around the room. They were all wound like spring steel, really wired.

'Don't move,' one spat.

337

'Sit there,' his partner ordered, eyeing my chick's crotch through her tights.

'I told you not to move,' the first one menaced us, as we went to sit down.

Two more cops rushed in. We could hear them start to throw things around in the bedroom. They were gentle with the motel's property, but not very considerate of ours. Another cop appeared at the patio door, struggling with the outside lock. We were surrounded, just like in the movies. Much later, I speculated that had I been armed and violently inclined, I would have been able to kill all three of the cops who pushed through the narrow door, after the noise they made preceding their entrance, only to be shot myself trying to escape the room.

I moved to let the cop in from the patio, but stopped when one of the heaters levelled his gun at my belly. Just like in the movies, but the gun was real. It looked more solid, more real than anything else in this little drama.

'That's not where we're at,' I told him, nodding at the gun.

Apparently all the propaganda about long hair and peace and love had reached him. Or perhaps he was sensitive enough to realize that the place reeked of peaceful vibes until he and his cronies barged in.

He became embarrassed, it seemed, at having threatened me with the gun. He seemed almost surprised to follow my glance to his hand and find a hunk of deadly metal there. And, as if woken from a dream, he jerkingly holstered his weapon.

The lesson rang home. When dealing with the police, get them to holster their weapons as soon as possible. When a man holds a gun on another, he is totally captured by the idea that violent death is imminent. Even if the idea is obviously false, the gun is strong enough as a symbol to warp his perception to the point where his judgement is affected. And both the holder of the gun and the person at whom it is pointed may begin to deal with each other unaware of what the realities of the situation really are.

The tension relaxed as each of the cops came to the realization that there would be no violent resistance. There was a visible pause in the drama, as they holstered their guns and rechannelled their thoughts from the death-violence groove into relief-release-power grooves.

Some felt the release so strongly that they became manic, chatty, and started to riff with us in over-familiar terms as they rummaged through the rooms like schoolkids turned loose in an abandoned house.

When I realized how quickly the moods of these policemen changed, I re-enforced within me the determination to remain calm, as much in control of the situation as was possible. I asked if they had a warrant. They told me I'd see it later.

Let them throw our stuff around all they want, I remember thinking smugly. They may be hip to me. But the pad is clean. Everything is cool. You guys have blown a big bust by arriving a day early.

I was so sure everything would be OK that I found myself rapping about yoga to one of the cops who had caught the title of the pamphlet I still held in my hand.

One of the cops emerged from the bedroom and beckoned to the man in charge of the raid. They disappeared back into the room and I flashed on the litter of small bills. Totalling over $1,000, on the dresser top. But before I could move to protect my bread, the cop who was gleefully emptying my old lady's purse in the kitchenette squealed.

'Yours?' he asked. The tiny beaded bag looked strangely out of proportion dangling from his sausage fingers.

'It's mine,' she admitted before I could tell her to keep her mouth shut.

'This yours, too?' the cop enquired, producing a microscopic piece of hash and part of an orange tab.

She looked like a kid who had been caught at some mischief – sort of I-guess-you-caught-me-but-isn't-it-cute? But this was no indulgent parent questioning her. It was the Man.

'You are under arrest,' he told her. Blah, blah, blah, and anything you say may be used against you.

That was a drag. But she insisted on carrying, even after I warned her to cool it while I was heavy into my dealing changes. Now she knew why, I thought self-righteously.

Still, it was all cool. There was the money in the bedroom and over a thousand hits of sunshine stashed elsewhere in town. I would be able to bail her out and get a lawyer the next day. We were planning to stay in the northwest for a few seasons, anyway. My tight-assed smugness disappeared quickly. One of the detectives came out of the bedroom, pulling two lids from his coat pocket. 'We found these under the mattress,' he said sincerely, as if trying to establish the veracity of his lying words by enunciating them clearly and concisely. 'You are under arrest for violation of the Uniform Narcotics Act, etc., etc.'

I was really naive, I had really thought that a whole mob of narcs, apparently informed about my activities, were going to crash into my rooms with drawn guns, search them, and just go away if they failed to turn up any incriminating evidence. How foolish. The sight of this agent of the law, this trusted civil servant, whose word would stand against mine in any court, whipping the evidence out of his pocket in my plain view, really struck me.

Until that point I tried to project the attitude of calm, polite self-assurance that experience had taught me was the correct way to deal with petty bureaucrats and traffic cops. But the sight of this harassed little man, forced to bring along his own evidence even after being tipped to my activities by informers, was too much. I almost laughed out loud, but felt constrained to merely grin and shake my head.

He was enraged that I found his antics humorous. He rushed across the room and locked eyes with me. A mistake, since I remained calmly smiling down into his eyes, though he stuck his face as aggressively close to mine as his limited stature would allow. Considering that I stood a full head taller than he, he looked quite the fool.

'You, you, weirdo, New York ugly. What are you looking at with your buggy eyes?' he spewed. He was really trying to get me to blow my cool and swing at him, and this was the best he could come up with.

It still blows my mind that he thought his schoolgirl epithets would lure me into playing his game and maybe getting hit on or shot.

Another detective interrupted our little showdown by

crisply snapping, 'Would you like to make a statement?' The tension broke immediately to return to routine.

Suddenly, I remembered the money on the dresser. They had not mentioned that it was being held as evidence. I wanted to be sure I had it or it was accounted for when we left for jail. But again I was being naive.

'What money?' the cops who searched the bedroom chorused. The cops who had not been in the bedroom exchanged covert glances. So I announced there was over $1,000, consoled that the money would now be split so many ways that each cop, in essence, would be merely a petty thief.

Now they were anxious to move the routine along. Again, they asked if I would make a statement. Did they really expect me to cooperate, I asked, after they had planted and robbed me? I told them that if we were under arrest we would like to be booked as soon as possible, so we could start arranging for lawyers and bail.

The name-calling cop snapped back that I shouldn't tell them how to run their business. But I insisted. It's safer in a cell with a bunch of drunks than in a motel room with armed detectives. Once you're arrested, get to jail as quickly as you can.

After enough time elapsed to show me that they, not I, was making the decision to leave, they told us to move out, I had to remind them that my old lady was only half dressed though most of them had earlier made a point of ogling her ass through the transparent material of her tights. Sometimes cops will ignore the most obvious facts of your rights and comforts. They must be reminded calmly in a way that is impossible to construe as resisting arrest.

The cop who manacled us put the cuffs on loosely. 'It's the rules,' he apologized so the others would not overhear. This was the same policeman who was embarrassed at having threatened me with his gun. He also seemed very uncomfortable when his buddy flipped out and he was genuinely interested when we were rapping about yoga. It appeared that not all cops had surrendered all vestiges of their humanity when they were issued their guns. But then another cop threatened to tighten the cuffs until they cut off my circulation if I didn't shut up and stop trying to reassure my old lady that everything was going to be all right.

At the station they put us in separate glass cages and refused to allow us to use the bathroom. Instead, the brave law enforcement agents gathered around a nearby desk and made 'wee wee' jokes while playing with their guns.

Then the police led five other people I had been hanging with into the station, handcuffed. Apparently they had it in their minds that they were breaking up a big dope ring. It was not very comforting to be caught up in their hallucination. The police had come down as heavy as they could short of brutality. On the tip of an informer whom I would never face, even in court, I had been planted, burnt and busted. Half the people I knew in Seattle were also busted.

But although I wasn't certain of it, and from time to time became overcome by doubt, I knew the inequities in the system would work in my favor. The thought of those unfortunates who were caught on the wrong side of the inequalities in our system often caused concern. But I was glad to be able to take advantage of points in my favor. I cut my hair and shaved my beard, aware that my Negro cell mates could not disguise themselves so easily. But then there I was a white, middle-class, first offender with a college education. I had friends in New York and Seattle raising money for bail and lawyers.

Even though I spent two weeks in jail, and the guards liked to roust us out of bed at weird hours to inspect our cells and assholes, it was all cool.

A sweet old lady judge dropped our bail from $6,000 to less than $1,000. She was impressed that my old lady had been a teacher and social worker in Harlem and that I had been, among other things, a newspaper reporter. I got the impression that she thought the jails were too barbarous for us, but not for some other types of people. I wasn't about to argue.

Our friends sent us a beautiful, hip, young lawyer. And again, though relieved, I was disgusted because I needed an intermediary to guide me through the labyrinth of our court system. I went along, though, terribly uptight that I couldn't speak for myself and hoped to escape a jail term.

In the end the whole thing was set up before we went to court – our plea, the sentence, even the terms of our probation.

We pled guilty. The prosecutor got his conviction. In return he recommended we be put on probation for six months, after which the charges would be dropped.

The court trip had so little to do with the arrest that at times I was sure they were completely unconnected. But that's how it went down. I learned that doing time teaches lessons much more important than any I learned in college. But if you have to stand up and make a plea before a judge, a college education counts. Like Dylan sang, 'He's a clean-cut kid/And he went to college too.'

1970. From: *Getting Busted*, ed. Ross Firestone, 1972

William Burroughs
Junky – 2

IN PRACTICE, PUSHING weed is a headache. To begin with, weed is bulky. You need a full suitcase to realize any money. If the cops start kicking your door in, it's like being with a bale of alfalfa. Tea heads are not like junkies. A junky hands you the money, takes his junk and cuts. But tea heads don't do things that way. They expect the peddler to light them up and sit around talking for half an hour to sell two dollars' worth of weed. If you come right to the point, they say you are a 'bring down.' In fact, a peddler should not come right out and say he is a peddler. No; he just scores for a few good 'cats' and 'chicks' because he is viperish. Everyone knows that he himself is the connection, but it is bad form to say so. God knows why. To me, tea heads are unfathomable.

There are a lot of trade secrets in the tea business, and tea heads guard these supposed secrets with imbecilic slyness. For example, tea must be cured, or it is green and rasps the throat.

343

But ask a tea head how to cure weed and he will give you a sly, stupid look and come on with some double-talk. Perhaps weed does affect the brain with constant use, or maybe tea heads are naturally silly.

The tea I had was green so I put it in a double boiler and set the boiler in the oven until the tea got the greenish-brown look it should have. This is the secret of curing tea, or at least one way to do it. Tea heads are gregarious, they are sensitive, and they are paranoiac. If you get to be known as a 'drag' or a 'bring down,' you can't do business with them. I soon found out I couldn't get along with these characters and I was glad to find someone to take the tea off my hands at cost. I decided right then I would never push any more tea.

In 1937, weed was placed under the Harrison Narcotics Act. Narcotics authorities claim it is a habit-forming drug, that its use is injurious to mind and body, and that it causes the people who use it to commit crimes. Here are the facts: Weed is positively not habit-forming. You can smoke weed for years and you will experience no discomfort if your supply is suddenly cut off. I have seen tea heads in jail and none of them showed withdrawal symptoms. I have smoked weed myself off and on for fifteen years, and never missed it when I ran out. There is less habit to weed than there is to tobacco. Weed does not harm the general health. In fact, most users claim it gives you an appetite and acts as a tonic to the system. I do not know of any other agent that gives as definite a boot to the appetite. I can smoke a stick of tea and enjoy a glass of California sherry and a hash-house meal.

I once kicked a junk habit with weed. The second day off junk I sat down and ate a full meal. Ordinarily, I can't eat for eight days after kicking a habit.

Weed does not inspire anyone to commit crimes. I have never seen anyone get nasty under the influence of weed. Tea heads are a sociable lot. Too sociable for my liking. I cannot understand why the people who claim weed causes crimes do not follow through and demand the outlawing of alcohol. Every day, crimes are committed by drunks who would not have committed the crime sober.

There has been a lot said about the aphrodisiac effect of weed. For some reason, scientists dislike to admit that there is such a thing as an aphrodisiac, so most pharmacologists say there is 'no evidence to support the popular idea that weed possesses aphrodisiac properties.' I can say definitely that weed is an aphrodisiac and that sex is more enjoyable under the influence of weed than without it. Anyone who has used good weed will verify this statement.

You hear that people go insane from using weed. There is, in fact, a form of insanity caused by excessive use of weed. The condition is characterized by ideas of reference. The weed available in the US is evidently not strong enough to blow your top on and weed psychosis is rare in the States. In the Near East, it is said to be common. Weed psychosis corresponds more or less to delirium tremens and quickly disappears when the drug is withdrawn. Someone who smokes a few cigarettes a day is no more likely to go insane than a man who takes a few cocktails before dinner is likely to come down with the DTs.

One thing about weed. A man under the influence of weed is completely unfit to drive a car. Weed disturbs your sense of time and consequently your sense of spatial relations. Once, in New Orleans, I had to pull over to the side of a road and wait until the weed wore off. I could not tell how far away anything was or when to turn or put on the brakes for an intersection.

Junky, 1977

Howard Marks
Rizla

I WON'T GO for governments and law enforcement agencies any more; I'll go for Rizla.

I like blue Rizla papers, but I don't like the wankers that run the company. I rang their main factory and put on an American accent.

'Where are you located?'

'Llantrisant.'

'You Welsh sure have cute place names. What does it mean?'

'Llantrisant means the Church of the Three Saints. It's quite a famous place, you know. We've got the Royal Mint here.'

'The Royal Mint! Whaw! Isn't that kinda like Fort Knox?'

'No, I wouldn't say it's like a fort, exactly. They just make money there.'

'You mean it's a Federal Reserve sub-branch printing dollars?'

'No, it produces notes and coins of the realm.'

'Same odds. That's real neat. What's the real estate like there?'

'Oh, I don't know, to be honest. Can I ask who you are, sir, and why you are calling?'

'You don't recognise my voice? I'm your new boss. When I'm not working for the United States Drug Enforcement Administration as a Special Liaison Officer for the Third World Poisoning & Pulverisation Initiative, I sell tobacco to whoever the fuck buys it. To put it another way: I am Imperial Tobacco, and I've just bought your little Rizla outfit through my nominee company, Imperial Tobacco, for 185 million. I stuck three cheques together.'

'I'm awful sorry, sir. I had absolutely no idea.'

'You used to have a cute president over there called Maggie Thatcher, right? Well, she works for another nominee company of mine, Philip Morris.'

'You know Margaret Thatcher personally, then?'

'I don't see a lot of the bitch now. But I worked a lot with her and her husband, Denis, who sold us paraquat to spray the Mexican dope fields. You must remember that scam. All those junkies were trying to make out that dope was safe. We sprayed the dope plantations with poison. That took care of that argument. But that was a while back. Any ways, I think we have a Welsh vice-president, who's going to take care of marketing strategy for you guys until I get my ass over there.

He talks exactly like you. Take care of him. Show him the Royal Mint.'

'It'll be my pleasure, sir.'

Next day I rang Rizla at Llantrisant and talked in a Welsh accent, 'Hello. My boss spoke to you yesterday. Is this the hole with a mint in it?'

'This is Llantrisant, yes indeed.'

'Look, I have just one question. Do you know that king-size Rizlas are being used for making illegal joints and spliffs containing marijuana and hashish?'

'No, no, sir. That's definitely not true. We often get told this, but our surveys indicate that king-size Rizlas are bought almost exclusively by long-distance lorry drivers who like long cigarettes that last a long time on very long journeys. They don't have to stop to roll so many, you see. They save time and money this way. The idea must have really caught on. We sell loads.'

'But why are they sold in supermarkets and newsagents and not in transport cafés? Listen, I did a little survey of my own. In almost every transport café I went to, I could only buy regular-size Rizlas. In no headshop, tobacconist or news-agents that I went to did I notice a lorry driver buying a packet of king-size Rizlas. They were being purchased by all sorts of other people: kids, boozers, and even *Guardian* readers.'

'I couldn't answer that. We don't do market research down by here.'

I'm very concerned about this. I see a vast opportunity being wasted. King-size skins are being made in Wales by workers who do not know that so many millions could be sold by sensible marketing. It's not their fault; they don't know that it's heads that buy the long skins, not lorry drivers. I feel a duty to let them know. After all, it's my country, and there's a lot of unemployment there.

Jim Hogshire
Marinol, The World's Stupidest Pill

As COOL AS pills are, there are some without much value. Sometimes a pill is such a mistake it's an insult to the rest of the pill world. *The worst such pill has got to be Marinol.*

Marinol, the synthetic THC pill to stop severe, persistent nausea and vomiting, is unquestionably the stupidest pill in the world. Marinol is supposed to be marijuana in pill form. If that were only true. If such a thing existed *PAGG* (Pills-A-Go-Go) would be very impressed. But such a thing doesn't exist.

Marijuana can dramatically reduce severe nausea and loss of appetite suffered by cancer patients undergoing chemotherapy. Such a drug is essential to keep a patient in treatment to save his life. Chemotherapy is not only painful and debilitating, it makes people vomit until they are exhausted from dry heaves. Nothing stays down. Some people would literally prefer to die than endure the treatment. Patients who need every bit of strength they can get in a fight for their lives really appreciate a joint. Dope releases them from the hell of persistent nausea and pain and lets them eat. With marijuana they can keep weight on or even gain some while cancer and chemotherapy wage a literal life-and-death war within the person's body. But in California, even when medical mari-juana is voted into legality, the state shuts down the skunk stores. No one is allowed to have the drug. And cops have shown they are willing to enforce this law even against emaciated, half-dead people in wheelchairs.

A few people have fought court battles to win government permission to smoke government-grown weed in government-rolled joints. For a while it looked like the $2-a-joint federal government pot would become part of the pharmacopia. In 1992 the DEA declared any and all marijuana use illegal, even medical use. Besides, they say, there's a pill to take instead.

Marinol is the trade name for dronabinol, which,

chemically, looks exactly like one form of THC that is found in marijuana. Marijuana contains at least eleven different THC molecules and scores of other cannabinoids, but dronabinol is the 'active ingredient,' says the government.

If that were true, taking Marinol would feel like smoking marijuana . . . and it doesn't. It's also interesting that the original contender for title of 'marijuana pill' mimicked a different THC molecule altogether. They said that particular chemical was 'the active ingredient.' Then some test dogs started to die off, and the pill had to be shit-canned.

Aside from the dubious idea of giving an anti-emetic to people who retch everything they swallow, Marinol doesn't cut the pill mustard in other ways. Its effects take hours to kick in, and sometimes don't kick in at all. When Marinol does hit, however, it frequently knocks the patient into an unpleasant stupor, causes hallucinations, paranoid reactions and depression. Patient after half-dead patient prefers smoking grass.

Marinol is expensive too. Treatment with it costs between $150 to $180 a month. Marinol's hard to make. Terpene olivitol made in Germany has to be shipped to southern California, where it is tediously separated by silica gel column chromatography, and a tiny amount of nearly 'pure' (99%) product is retrieved. Then another lab takes the stuff and makes it into pills (gel caps, really), which it ships off to Ohio for redistribution. All along the way the pills are as closely watched as plutonium. Government guards who keep track of each of these stupid pills every inch of the way generate lots of paperwork, wasting who knows how much money and human effort.

If you're looking for marijuana, just grow the plant and consume it however you want.

Pills-A-Go-Go, A Fiendish Investigation into Pill Marketing, Art,
History & Consumption, 1999

Aleister Crowley
Diary of a Drug Fiend

YOU REMEMBER HOW it goes – twenty grains one penny-weight, three penny-weights one scruple – I forget how many scruples one drachm, eight drachms one ounce, twelve ounces one pound.

I got it all wrong. I could never understand English weights and measures. I have never met anyone who could. But the point is you could go on a long time on one-eighth of a grain if you have a pound of the stuff.

Well, this will put it all right for you. Fifteen grains is one gram, and a thousand grams is a kilogram, and a kilogram is two-point-two pounds. The only thing I'm not sure about is whether it's a sixteen-ounce pound or a twelve-ounce pound. But I don't see what it matters anyway, if you've got a pound of snow or H., you can go on for a long while, but apparently it's rather awkward orchestrating them.

Diary of a Drug Fiend, 1970

Robert Sabbag
A Way with the Spoon

ZACHARY SWAN'S FIRST capital investment upon his return to the United States was a laboratory gram scale. It was the one precision instrument, with the possible exception of a good automatic weapon, that was demanded by the cocaine trade. Swan selected an Ohaus, three-posted, equal-arm pharmaceutical balance with stainless-steel trays – it appealed to the professional in him. It cost $150. And it was metric. It did not know an ounce or a pound from a counterfeit Deutschmark. He was impressed.

For almost two hundred years Americans have been trying to come to grips with the metric system; refusal to adopt it, from black-market conversion tables in the elementary school arithmetic classroom to bisystematic mileposts on the nation's interstate highways, has come to be regarded as one of the unimpeachable insignias of citizenship. There is pride to be found in the embrace of a system of measurement that is unique in the world, truly one's own – different even from the British Imperial System, though few are certain exactly how it is different – and an even further glory, it seems, in not actually knowing what that system of measurement is called. The US Customary System, as it *is* called, officially and every-where, is as American as shoo-fly pie: Olympic swimming pools have confounded us for years; displacement in liters we have knowledged as having something to do with foreign automobiles and French wine; and kilometers, whatever they are, we know had something to do with extraterrestrial real estate in *The Day the Earth Stood Still* – it might as well have been cubits our alien visitor was asking for. The International System of Units – for that is what *theirs*, the one the rest of the universe uses, is called – is un-American; if it is not furlongs or fathoms it is foreign, it is something we grant chemistry teachers for their amusement. Or so one would have thought. Until recently. Only recently – and seemingly overnight – did an entire postwar generation of schoolchildren learn that the metric system was a postgraduate course.

Whatever Congress decides, and no matter how long it takes a box of Spoon Size Shredded Wheat to go from twelve ounces to 340 grams, the truth is this: the United States of America effectively converted to the metric system in, or around, 1965 – by 1970 there was not a college sophomore worth his government grant who did not know how much a gram of hash weighed. That little piece of empirical data had become a matter of pride. And, on many occasions, a matter of survival. Here was some dude, not even a chemistry major, coming on to you with mikes, grams, bricks, kilos and hundredweights; off the top of his head he could go from grams to ounces and he could tell you how many ounces he got to the kilo. He hit you with lids, caps, keys, tabs, nickel bags, blotters, buttons, spoons and everything from milli-grams to boatloads. You had to protect yourself. You had to have your weights and measures down, and the metric system

351

was where you began. Anything that came out of a pharmaceutical house or across a border . . . well, man, they just did not *know* avoirdupois weight . . . *avoir do what?* The time had come to get it together. And so today everyone over the age of twelve *knows* that there are 28.3 grams to the ounce and 35.2 ounces or 2.2 pounds to the kilogram. He may not know how *many* swimming pools to the standard football field, but he knows how to buy dope:

> Q: *And so, Johnny, if you had a pound of apples and a pound of oranges and a fifth of a pound of cherries to sell, and you needed 600 Colombian pesos to buy a second-hand bicycle, how much would you have to sell your fruit for?*
> A: *Twenty dollars a key, teach – more, of course, if I ounced it.*

There is nobody in the world, let alone at MIT or Lowell Tech, who is faster at math than a dope dealer.

Snowblind, 1998

Charlie Beer
Dave the Doorman

DAVE HAD BEEN a thoughtful and conscientious doorman for over fifteen years, he loved the job, but he decided to give it up in the blink of an eye. For the first time in his career, he had taken it personally. It turned out to be a mistake; he hoped he would live to regret it.

Dave was a big, powerful forty-five-year-old who hadn't resorted to the easy fix of steroids to gain his impressive size. He came into door work later than most; he was already thirty and needed extra cash to supplement his wages as a postman. Door work seemed like the perfect solution. His genes had gifted him with a muscular body, which had been toned through five years of hard workouts. He was social, enjoyed the nightclub scene and most of all liked helping people. Dave revelled in being one of the boys with the other doormen, even though he knew that some of them were total pricks. He had never resorted to giving punters an unnecessary slap, but he had seen plenty of beatings dished out in his time. He was a man of few words who preferred his actions to do the talking for him; there were no knuckledusters, coshes or CS gas.

The club where Dave had spent his entire door career and life was in Margate. When Dave joined the team in the mid-eighties the club was your typical provincial venue with chicken in the basket, live bands who had had one hit in the seventies that no one could remember, boys chasing girls and doormen who wore bow ties and dinner jackets. The only trouble was either drink- or girl-related, usually both. Yes, they had alcohol-induced kick-offs almost nightly but nothing they couldn't handle.

By the time the venue was taken over by a new leisure group, Dave had been promoted to head doorman. He was proud of this and enjoyed the kudos it brought; everyone wanted to be his friend. He hired and fired doormen so had rooted out all the tossers who were only working to fuck girls or totally fuck over the punters. He ran a good team; the punters and management liked them. He had long since given up working for the Post Office and couldn't imagine doing another job.

When the club was revamped, it changed to a mainstream dance venue with headlining DJs each weekend. They had extended the club, knocking into the pub next door. The punters came from London by the carload, and from Birmingham, Liverpool and Manchester by the coachload. The club was banging all weekend from when the doors opened at 10 p.m. until they kicked them all out at 5 a.m. The great thing with the new club was that there was so little trouble. Dave couldn't believe that the huge numbers of punters were so peaceful. In all ways, this was now a big club.

When the club reopened, he was a bit naive about the world of drugs. He had seen guys get huge with injections in the gym and had done the door-supervisors training that covered drug abuse. He read the papers and watched the news like everyone else so he knew about the E generation and the cokeheads. He knew that most of the clubbers were on some drug or another and as long as they stayed safe, he was OK with it. Knowing about and dealing with it are two different things. Dave soon found out how different.

The new club had only been open about two weeks when the team had caught their first dealer. One of the off-duty barmaids had been offered Es by a small-time player. The door team gripped him up, took him to the security office and searched him. They found ten Es and a couple of hundred quid on him. He seemed like a decent enough bloke so they flushed his gear down the bog, gave him the cash back and kicked him out.

Dave was used to people trying to befriend him, the punters loved to call him by his first name to impress their mates. The girls wanted to flirt with him so that they could jump the queue and hope to blag their way in. It didn't seem that odd when the large-framed guy sat opposite him in the café when he was having his regular Saturday lunchtime fried breakfast and started to chat to him. After a bare minimum of pleasantries, he tells him he knows that he is the head doorman at the club and he had a business proposition for him. Dave had already started to feel uneasy; Dave knew this guy was connected. The swallow tattoo on his neck, the Rolex watch, the ridiculously heavy gold chain, the shaved head, the true south-London accent, the Armani shirt and jeans, the tan recently acquired from Marbella were all very obvious clues. Dave had often had punters telling him they were connected to this family and that family and that he was going to get shot for throwing them out of the club; it was always bollocks, till now. The Man knew Dave had a missus, a small house, a five-year-old Ford Mondeo, the school his two kids went to, and the gym he trained at. The Man already knew too much for Dave's liking. Dave was starting to feel his heart race, his hearing was becoming affected and he could barely make out what the Man was saying, his T-shirt was getting damp with the sweat that was pouring out of him. Dave knew from years of working the door how to big himself up and front any situation. He was trying his best, he wanted to act hard, he wanted to show the man that he was not intimidated, but this was not a pissed-up punter, this was reality and it was hitting him like a baseball bat across the nose.

The business deal was simple; in exchange for cash, he was to let one of the Man's associates in to deal drugs in his club. He was to carry the gear in, so avoiding the searching on the door, and protect the dealer while he was in the club. He was to keep the other doormen away from him and his little posse of minders. The Man told him if he kept his end of the bargain, he would get two grand each and every week. Hundred grand a year tax-free is a lot of money and would ensure that his family got the best things in life. The Man didn't need to explain the flip side. The Man was not used to having people say no to him. The Man got up and walked out to his brand new black 7-series BMW parked opposite.

Dave's mobile phone rang within two minutes. It was the Man, just letting him know that they knew his number and the operation would start next week. He would be in touch. Dave had never been in a situation like this and didn't know anyone else who had or what to do. He wouldn't have dreamt of telling his missus, she would panic, he couldn't involve his family or his friends.

That night at work he was on edge, he was staring intensely at everyone trying to identify any of the Man's gang. His team knew something was wrong, as Dave was snappy with punters and the quietest he had ever been. He knew he would have to do something or else he would be in so deep he would never get out. Taking the money was never an option for Dave, it was the easy way, but that wasn't Dave. For the first part of the next week Dave thought of little else, he kept his phone with him all the time, never turned it off, waiting for the Man's call. The family was causing him more stress; he couldn't think straight and had to get them away. He shipped them off to her mother's in Suffolk. Thursday afternoon the

Man rang, he told him to meet him in a seafront car park at 8 p.m. on Saturday.

Dave hardly slept all week, he was surviving on strong coffee, and three hours' sleep a night. For the first time in years, he even went sick on the Friday night. He said he had a stomach upset but he was sick to the stomach. Saturday came and went in a blur; before he settled down, it was already time for the meet.

The car park was pretty empty when he drove in; he saw the BMW at once and parked next to it. He got in the rear seat behind the passenger. The Man was in the driver's seat, the passenger was a young guy, fairly anonymous-looking, dressed for clubbing. The Man passed him a small holdall; he unzipped it and took out two packages. The first was a large Jiffy bag that had inside it a see-through plastic bag with a self-adhesive seal at the top. It was packed with hundreds and hundreds of small pale blue round tablets, Dave could see they had the Mickey Mouse logo on them. The other package was a white envelope obviously stuffed with cash. He put both of them back in the bag. The Man told Dave to meet his guy inside by the Gents toilet at 10.15 p.m. to hand back the tablets. He made sure he knew that the dealer was going to be watched and anyone that tried to stop him dealing would be hurt. Dave nodded, picked up the bag and got out of the car.

Dave drove up to the club and parked his car; he carried the bag into the club. He put the bag in the security office and walked back out of the club. He had the cash with him; even though he hadn't counted it, he knew it would be spot on a grand. He walked across the road to the local nick. He walked into the foyer and up to the desk where a female civilian was checking the driving documents of a young lad. On the side of the counter was a metal opening, which had Kent Police Benevolent Fund on a plaque above it. Dave opened the envelope and started to feed all the £20 notes into the slot. The civvie stopped what she was doing and looked in amazement as Dave fed all the cash into the box.

He walked straight back to the club and got on with the pre-opening, all his security team turned up and the queue started to build early. Dave decided to watch proceedings from the office on the CCTV. The doors opened at 10 p.m. and within five minutes Dave had seen the dealer enter, he guessed he had seen three or four guys who were probably with him. He waited till nearly 10.30 p.m., slipped the bag of Es under his jacket and went to the loos. Although punters were coming in quickly the club was still quiet, especially near the toilets. The dealer was waiting; he was relaxed, even cocky. He knew that he was protected and connected, he knew he was untouchable by security and therefore safe from the police. The Man had set it up and it would be sweet. The dealer gave Dave grief for being late. Dave didn't reply but just walked into the toilets, they went into the cubicle on the left and locked the door. The dealer was still relaxed when Dave took the bag out, pulled it open and handed it towards the dealer with his right hand. The dealer was looking at the contents and didn't see Dave's left hand in his jacket pocket pulling a metal flask from it. By the time he saw it there was nothing he could do to stop Dave tipping its contents into the bag. The acid ate straight through the plastic bag and the contents dropped to the floor. The dealer wasn't relaxed any more, he jumped back as far as he could and watched as the acid destroyed the tablets fizzing viciously. The cubicle filled with an acrid smell that was noxious to the senses. Dave left the dealer with the ex-tablets and walked out.

Dave moved past two of the minders, who were opposite the toilets, he gave them an assured smile and went to the front of the club. He went and stood on the front door feeling a huge weight lift off his shoulders and a sense of satisfaction. The rear fire-exit alarm soon went off and he knew that it would be the dealer and his boys leaving. He expected retribution; he wasn't stupid. He also knew he was safe on the front door under the constant protection of the CCTV.

It was twenty minutes before his mobile went: it was the Man's number. He didn't answer; he didn't leave a message. The night went peacefully and the clubbers had a great time. Dave knew that the first problem time was after locking up and going back to his car. He could have left early or got some of his team to wait for him but knew that would mean more people getting hurt.

He was the last one to leave the club. He set the alarm and locked the side door. The car park at the rear of the club was empty, he had been checking the CCTV, and there hadn't been much activity out there. It looked OK, and he had already decided not to go back to home that night. He knew that he could run to his car safely even if they showed up now. Dave walked to the car and kept looking around him, no problems. He was starting to relax; he knew he was going to make the car. He stooped forwards to open the car door and his eye caught the glint of something metallic on the roof.

There are plenty of good reasons to leave Margate, and a 9mm bullet with the word DAVE etched on it and Sellotaped to his car was as good a reason he needed.

Dave the Doorman, 2001

Peter McDermott
The Immaculate Injection

THE YEAR MUST have been 1975.

I hadn't known Billy before he went to jail. He'd served a long sentence because he'd been convicted of armed robbery. He really didn't seem the type. A gentle giant, his Liverpudlian accent carried more than the faintest lilt of his Irish heritage, even though he'd been born and bred on the banks of the Mersey.

I met him through my oldest friend, Mal McGreary, who grew up in the next street to Billy in Orrell Park. I'd known Mal since my early teens. Although we had gone to different schools, we'd been drawn to each other since we were the only teenage long-haired dopers in that part of the north end of Liverpool. There might have been others who had grown their hair below the tops of their ears and attended the occasional concert, but there was nobody else with the sort of commitment that we had, with our nipple-length hair and our absolute determination to see every gig ever played in Liverpool, for free.

So Billy had just completed a long stretch and now he wanted some fun.

When the pair of them first showed up on my mother's doorstep, they wanted to know if I could cop. At that time it could be extraordinarily difficult to buy heroin in Liverpool, even though you knew everyone within a twenty-mile radius of the city who used the drug. The black market as we know it today didn't even begin to emerge until five or six years later. Virtually all opiates came from one of three places: you were registered with a drug-dependency clinic (and the one in Liverpool was notorious for its refusal to prescribe anything, though some people in one-ampoule towns like Ormskirk or on the Wirral seemed to be doing OK); you were managing to scam some GP into prescribing an opiate (but you couldn't get heroin any more – that had died out with the new laws that had led to the opening of the drug-dependency clinics); or lastly, and most likely, somebody broke into a chemist shop.

Anyway, nobody had telephones, so I went to all of the usual sources, which meant driving or taking the bus to far-flung reaches of the city: to Speke and Halewood, to Ormskirk and Toxteth. But it didn't matter where I went, there wasn't anything of interest to be had. Not heroin, not Diconal, not even as much as a Physeptone amp. Billy ended up buying half an ounce of hash and some acid from somebody, but it wasn't what he really wanted and he went home disappointed.

A few days later I got the telephone call from Mal. It was unusual because it was 8.30 in the morning, and I'd never known Mal get out of bed before lunchtime. What's more, he was extremely cryptic.

'Come on round to Billy's mother's house now,' he said. 'It will be to your advantage.'

I didn't have to be told twice. There was only one thing that excited Mal, and given how understated he was, he was obviously very excited.

It was only a ten-minute walk to Billy's house in Orrell

Park. Past my old school and across the rec. Up Hornby Road to Walton Prison, and then along the path beside the old Liverpool-to-Preston railway line, which brought you out just around the corner from his mum's. Nevertheless, I was breathless by the time I arrived.

I knocked on the front window. Billy quickly came to the door, grinning, and ushered me into his mother's front parlour. In the centre of the room there were four big cardboard boxes.

Mal was the first to speak.

'We were wondering if you could try and put a price on that?' he asked, nodding his head towards the cartons. I looked into the first, which seemed to be full of big brown bottles. The first I pulled out was titled 'Tincture of Opium' and measured two and a half litres. It was about three-quarters full. I pulled another out that was roughly the same size. Diamorphine hydrochloride, according to the label. Heroin linctus. There was even more in that one.

Then Billy spoke.

'I think that one's the box with all the shite. Take a look at the stuff in the others.'

He pushed a box over to me with his foot. When I opened it, my stomach turned over with excitement. The box was about eighteen inches wide and two feet long, and inside were scores, maybe hundreds, of little bottles and jars. Some were made of glass, some brown, some blue, some green. Others were plastic. I recognised the grey plastic cartons of Smith, Kline and French with their logo on the top. There were cardboard boxes and other bottles in the red-and-blue livery of Wellcome & Burroughs. I swear I was so excited my dick got hard.

I started pulling them out and examining the labels. Pethidine, 100 tablets. Palfium, 100 tablets. Dexedrine. Drinamyl. Valium. Nembutal. Seconal. Morphine. Heroin. My hands began to shake. There was something I needed to do before I went any further.

'Would you mind if I had a hit?' I asked.

Mal smiled, a look of total satisfaction on his face. Billy threw me a bag of works. Of course, they were all used. This was ten years before anyone had even heard of AIDS. I fished the cleanest out of the bag and went back to digging in the box until I got what I wanted.

The first bottle contained pink tablets. The second, a white, fluffy powder. My two favourite drugs. Diconal and pharmaceutical cocaine. Combined, they made the notorious 'pink speedball'. This the most dangerous, yet most intensely euphoric hit known to man or beast: just a few weeks before, I'd woken up next to a croaked Chrissy Booth, who just couldn't manage to be cautious enough with the old pink proportions. But did that bother me, or even phase me for a second? Not at all. We'd simply called the police and abandoned the apartment and went back to pounding ourselves into oblivion.

I crushed a couple of pills on a piece of cardboard using the bowl of a spoon, and when the powder was as fine as I could get it, I formed a 'V' in the card, and slid it all into the back end of a syringe, followed by a smallish pinch of coke.

I didn't want to take too much. Given the quantities available, I thought it best to do what I could to pace myself. And even though the shot was on the moderate end of the scale, it was still profoundly satisfying. The truth is, I never knew pinkies to be anything else. Until you were ready for your next, of course, and then it was as compulsive as crack.

But even though I'd been moderate in my consumption, I lost my focus, as Mal and Billy did another. Then we all did another round.

We spent the morning in a state of blissful nod, and it wasn't until the mid-afternoon that I tried to turn my attention back to the boxes.

I'd pull out a few bottles, and check them out, spend a little time in awe at both the quality and the quantity of the haul that I had before me.

There were four bottles of heroin powder in total, the largest being a blue, one-ounce bottle that was labelled 1933. As far as I could tell, there was no sign of any degradation – that heroin was as good as it had been on the day it had been manufactured. A drug fit for war heroes.

Now at that time, the price of heroin was twenty pounds a gram when you could get it. So, twenty-eight grams at twenty pounds a pop. That was over five hundred quid for that bottle alone. And there were at least three more bottles that held another five grams apiece. Not to mention the dozens of ampoules, and pills, and linctuses.

And then there was morphine. Morphine sulphate. Morphine hydrochloride. Was that heroin or not? Morphine tartrate. And every type came as several bottles of powder, as pills and as ampoules. Why the fuck had this guy kept so much stock, much of it dating back from the Second World War and before? It had only been a small corner chemist shop, but it had been in Bootle, close to the docks. Perhaps he'd stocked up in an attempt to deal with the consequences of the Blitz?

I never really made much progress in evaluating the retail and wholesale value of the stock that day. After a while, we gave up all pretence of trying to be businesslike and just settled down to a good, old-fashioned binge. At five o'clock, Billy's mum came home from work and Mal went back to his house for his tea.

Me? I was going nowhere. Not with a stash like that about. The only way that I'd leave is if I was forced to do so at gunpoint.

Billy's mother was the breadwinner of the family, a clerical officer with the tax office, and a devout Catholic. His father had some sort of serious heart condition and couldn't get about much. He could just about make it to the Windsor Castle for his lunchtime pint, and that was it. The rest of the day, he spent in the armchair in front of the TV.

Whenever we came around, the family tended to leave us alone in the front parlour, possibly believing that the pictures of the Sacred Heart and the statues of Our Lady would do an adequate job of maintaining the necessary scrutiny. Nevertheless, we pushed the boxes behind the settee, just in case she decided she needed to come in for something.

We spent that evening doing the wildest things imaginable, mixing combinations of three and four different drugs.

Speedballs that involved the use of a syringeful of coke in one arm, and a syringeful of heroin in the other, with two people shooting them in simultaneously. Billy and I matched each other shot for shot, the regular hits of coke keeping the pair of us from passing out completely.

We were just about to put together another shot when we noticed that the bottle of water we'd been using was empty. Billy didn't want to go back out into the kitchen to fill it up for fear of waking his parents, so he pondered for a moment, deciding what we should do.

Then, a smile spread across his face and he went across the room and opened a china cabinet, bringing from it a small bottle. Without saying anything, he poured enough heroin and cocaine for two more speedballs into a couple of spoons, and then opened the bottle.

'Are you up for this then?' he asked.

'Up for what? What's in the bottle?'

He didn't answer at first, just continued grinning at me.

'It's some kind of holy water, isn't it? You want to shoot up with some kind of holy water?'

'This isn't just any old holy water. This isn't your common or garden, priest-blessed tap water. This is the real deal. This stuff comes from Lourdes. This is the stuff that miracles are made of.'

Although I hadn't been brought up as a Catholic myself, I was familiar with the stories, of the stream where the Virgin Mary had appeared to a young girl and since that time, after being immersed in the waters, the lame had been healed and the blind had regained their sight. Now, it was a place where hundreds of thousands of pilgrims flocked every year in the hope that the water would work its magic on them.

'Miracle juice, huh? In that case, you'd better make mine a big one, because I'm surely in need of a miracle.'

The preparation of a fix is always a ritual in the early part of one's drug-taking career, but Billy put these two shots together with a degree of pomp and ceremony quite unlike any shot that I've done before or since. Indeed, when he presented the two filled syringes to me, so that I could choose

363

which one I wanted to do, he looked less like a junkie offering me my gun, and every bit like a priest dispensing the sacrament to a devout member of his congregation.

Rising to the occasion, I incanted a half-remembered fragment of the Catholic Mass that I'd heard once at a wedding or a funeral.

'Lamb of God that taketh away the sins of the world. Have mercy on me.'

I drove the plunger back home and waited. For what? I don't know, some sort of sign, perhaps? A bolt from the blue? To have my hit supernaturally or spiritually enhanced, somehow? Or maybe be struck down dead by a phenomenal overdose? Maybe he'd do the loaves and fishes trick with the dope.

I think what I really expected was another appearance of the Virgin who had appeared at Lourdes, declaring: 'I am the Immaculate Injection. This is what you must do with your lives.'

Instead, I got nothing. Just a normal fix in every way. I turned to Billy, who had also finished his shot, and had a beatific smile on his face. Well, he'd been brought up a Catholic. Perhaps it did work for him.

'What was it like?' I asked. 'Did anything happen?'

'Sure,' he replied. 'Just before I pushed the plunger home, I said a little prayer to the Virgin. I told her that I was going to close my eyes, and make a wish. And when I'd finished shooting the dope, I opened my eyes and my wish had come true.'

'Oh, fuck off,' I snorted. 'I don't believe you. What did you wish for?'

He smiled slyly, and then he told me.

'I wished that when I opened my eyes, I'd find myself in a room full of drugs. And praise be to God, take a look behind the couch and see what the Mother of Christ has gone and left for us . . .'

'The Immaculate Injection', 2001

364

Zoe Lund
Cul de Sac

THE SKY WENT red. Slow rivulets defined themselves, mapping the insides of her eyelids. There was a change of light.

She rubbed her eyes and looked around. Fluorescent and ugly, the place was awake. It was 4 a.m. and one could no longer sell liquor. So the people had to leave.

As her pupils adjusted, contracting even more, above her head was something she had seen before.

The *mobile des mobiles*.

Round and round they spun, all the whys and wherefores. The good reasons and the real, balanced but never content. Bobbing now, her motives were marionettes with an invisible master. She couldn't see him for there were no mirrors in the place. Subjects of torque, they twirled each on edge, off a roving axis. Prey to entropy and atrophy, empathy and apathy, they were hanged and hung as one, above her.

And faded away as the emptying club came up.

Nightclubs always look hideous at their middle-of-the-night morn. The floor was awash with alcohol, mud, drug cut and a jigger of vomit. Her footprints left brown-outlined imprints that soon would ebb away.

Like all patrons, she left quick, hand over eyes. Outside, it was night again.

She did not want to take a cab. But walk – where to?

Aha! The northwest Wind! An old joke, ever blowing her southeast. But she didn't need to cop just now. Not quite yet. Something else was driving her downtown.

At the causeway of Astor Place she stopped, questioning her direction. But thoughts were no deterrent. These streets were, as she had remembered earlier that night, vertical not merely horizontal. So she wasn't only travelling in length but also in depth. And though she could follow the map of those terrains, she had never been able to surface the guide at will. So where was she, really? She could only find out by arriving at her destination and then counting back. St. Mark's was its usual carnival and she walked swiftly, collar up, eager to slip into the anonymity of the easterly blocks where her sole identity was that of someone vaguely recognizable as another one who might know what's up.

Midway in longitude and midway in latitude, at the heart of it all, there is a dead end. In the cul-de-sac they once sold kick-ass bags, but now, as gentry forces draw lines to Avenue C, the escape route through a murky swampish backyard, complete with a sort of muddy stream, is a barren flatland. Dry and mowed into plain view, it is no cloak for your dagger. Many a time, just-copped, she had scattered herself through that mystery marshland, works poking into her thigh as she forded the sewer-brook and ran, not looking back till she was gone from the four-meter wilderness.

That land of Atlantis trees was now a nascent parking lot. The parking lot was a condo on the way.

Just a block away on Fourth Street, flat red-brick buildings had been put up, all in a row like those in down-heeled suburbia. She hadn't been here in months.

The last time her need had been clear. It was 4 a.m. and she had come to cop. The police had been busy and the heat had taken its toll. All the spots had closed down early. Long overdue for a fix, she was crying with the sickness. If she hadn't been so crazy-ill, she would never have allowed Mark, a freelance dopespot steerer whom she had never trusted, to show her where to go.

Back then, the red-brick buildings were still under construction, and to access the cul-de-sac she had to cut through the building site, passing by the silhouettes of worker-guards who gave not a shit for a passing copper. 'They won't care unless we start breaking the new windows they just installed,' said her guide. Mark was smiling too much and she didn't like it. By the occasional worker's flashlight beam, his long black face glistened in the dark. Except where his beard was. She didn't like most beards. It takes a very honest man to wear a beard for pure aesthetics. She hadn't thought anyone sold dope anymore in the cul-de-sac, but Mark had convinced her otherwise. He led her into a hallway in one of the buildings at the very dead end. A white girl of twelve or so gave her dope for good money. And she gave Mark the obligatory tip. That meant that she would have to walk home even though she could hardly stand up.

Just before the exchange she had started to cry again. 'I'm so sick, Mark,' she'd said. 'This is good, right? It's good. Right? I don't have a penny more after this. It's good, right?'

'Yeah, sure. Hey. Of course it's good,' said Mark.

Walking home with the stuff in her pants, she'd felt it burn against her belly. She tried to measure the degree of heat that the bags gave off against her skin. To perform alchemical analysis as she walked. Arriving home, she knew.

It was flour. 'Beat.'

Now she was back. Alone and with no motive. She had a scratchy, nude feeling at the nape of her neck. Like she had an unknown cunt there that she had never noticed. And autonomous, it had made a rendezvous the day that she was born. For now. To be deflowered. But her terrible lover was unknown.

To her right was the rubble-strewn plateau that had been the woodsy exit. All was now in evidence. No more dealers stood at the mouth of the forest, no more junkies scurried into the brush. It was a stage without a curtain. Naked and obscene, she felt her neck getting wet. It was then that she first heard voices. Men speaking. One was engagingly familiar, the other she recognized but it made her want to run. She understood when she heard a third voice. The squawk of a walkie-talkie.

She was clean, so she looked for the voices' dark source.

On an overlooking roof, two figures were gesticulating. She could observe their shadow-play while remaining, herself, in darkness. One, complete with regulation fat ass, was in blue. The other, diminutive and agile, was a friend. A Hispanic of considerable and evident life-competence, Joey had remained a street-life recidivist. He was certainly aware that he could 'cross over,' but she gathered he would rather die. Her friend pleaded his case while the cop registered his find in the walkie-talkie.

She moved closer to the building but remained out of sight. Knee-deep in rubble, she wondered how to help.

By the time she could climb a fire escape, the incident would be long over. If she shouted, she'd be taken for a loon. She caught words as they fell off the roof.

'This time you're out of luck cause I'm clean. But I know what you do. Every day you stake out this roof. When you see people copping, you radio their descriptions to your guys on the corner and they pick them up and take them to jail. Why do you do it, man? Yeah, you. Personally you. Why? So you can tell your wife that you put seventeen junkies in jail for buying a powder that eases their pain and hurts no one else? Do you realize that a junkie's body doesn't let him not cop? And in jail we go through cold turkey – cruel and unusual punishment for an utterly victimless act that we can't not commit. If you busted a non-junkie mass murderer and somehow put him through the symptoms of heroin withdrawal while he was awaiting arraignment, his lawyer would have an easy time throwing out the case and hanging a rap on you for torture!'

The cop had been silent through all this and did not speak even now. It was Joey whom she heard speak up again.

'What the fuck is this? I did not come up here to shoot up! The proof is that I have no works on me. You know that. You just searched me. Why are you doing this?'

'Come on, asshole,' said the cop.

'I came up here to look at the fucking sky, man. Is that a crime now too?'

The silhouettes merged for an instant, then separated again.

'Hey!' shouted the cop. 'Don't touch the evidence. That'll be another count.'

'Evidence my ass!' It was Joey. 'You just planted that shit on me! You know it and I know it!'

'And no one else,' said the cop.

She was about to yell 'I know, I know!' when the cop burst out, 'Cut it out, motherfucker, or I'll get you for assault!' Somehow she knew her friend had spat in his face. It came back to her like an instant replay. It was then that things took a wicked turn.

Only a few days before, Joey had told her that he had drugs and switchblades stashed in various places around the eastside so they wouldn't be on him but would be retrievable in case of need. She had taken it as flamboyance but realized now that this roof must have been one of those places because—

'Put it down!' shouted the cop.

'Not until you throw the dope off the roof. Get rid of your fucking "evidence".'

She cursed her monkey as he chirped, 'Wow! If it falls I'll get it!'

'Too late, asshole,' said the cop. 'Now you're really up for assault.' He paused for effect. 'Of a police officer.'

Joey was hurricane-eye calm. Each word was measured and she felt a tingle at the back of her neck. 'I don't give a fuck. At least I *am* assaulting you and you *are* a police officer.' Even more softly he added, 'Throw it over. Ditch that bullshit evidence. Now.'

Both figures were near the edge and she could see them clear against the sky. Joey whipped out of the eye and into the fury of the storm. 'Throw it over!' he screamed. 'Throw it over or I'll kill you!'

'I'll throw you over first, you fuck!'

'Then we both go.'

She lunged at their shadows as Joey made for cop and cop-gun at once. The knife, the gun, the man and the cop spiraled on the edge. She arced to a white-hot chant as her medulla vagina quaked and howled and wind tore into the chamber that could never be hymened again.

Tears welled up and blurred her vision. In that second of blindness her hearing was more acute. It seemed someone until then invisible had taken a step behind her. She turned and saw. He hadn't even screamed.

Joey lay on the ground, face up and unscathed, eyes open.

Looking at the sky. A crime.

She bent over him but heard the words, 'I'm dead.'

His knife was in his hand. Before she noticed having reached for it, his knife was in her own. She flattened herself against the building whose roof had hidden the weapon that was now hers. And she waited, knowing he would come.

It seemed like an hour before he did. Bent slightly at the ass, he walked toward the body, slow, eyes pinioned to her friend. Silent, she stood behind him. Two good yards, a long way to leap. In order for her to do it, he would have to be distracted. Her mind conjured a pigeon shitting a bullseye from on high. But that wouldn't work because the bastard wouldn't feel it. He hadn't even taken off his cap.

The cop was looking into Joey's eyes. His back radiated fear but he seemed certain he was alone. She could see that Joey's eyes bore twin tunnels through the sky. Toward something. What? Unable to resist, the cop's head made a slow tilt skyward. She felt the warmth of flower-blood at the nape of her neck.

The knife slipped through the blue cloth and deep into the cop's back. She had often heard that it takes a lot to kill with a knife, so she turned him round and face to face, in a rush of mad need to perfect the act, had him see her while she saw him. Yes, we live on after, she thought, and 'He lives' was what she said and then slit his throat.

She dropped him fast for the blood was spurting rapidly, a geyser to fill a mighty needle.

For a moment all was still and then it broke. Though city silence met the death of Joey, sirens rose to greet the cop's demise.

They'll find me. That she knew. Fast and hard.

It came to her, then. With nowhere to run, she could only stay here. Right here. Until they took her on a stretcher, herself the victim of a crime.

Her friend would be indicted post-mortem for her wound. But that didn't matter. Judges' opinions were of no consequence. Such things had not even practical import, unless you were alive. So it was a little joke between friends. A last laugh.

She thought of the fertile wound at the nape of her neck but knew that the blood that poured from that gash was only visible to the naked eye and so they wouldn't see it. She had to penetrate herself again, in the language that they knew.

The knife was dripping with the dead cop's blood. The thought flashed that she wanted to wipe it off, for that blood contained the most contagious disease of all. But there was no time. Anyhow, she knew she had the antibodies to fight off the blue plague.

She rolled up her sleeve. Now that she wasn't running, she had time, lots of it, to do things right. She took care and blessed the echo of each move.

Sleeves above her elbow, she examined her arm. Incredibly thin, it wasn't bad as arms go, etched with years of work toward the perfect design. Better I disguise all this anyway, she thought soberly. Her other arm would pass, for it confessed much less.

The blade was still red. She hoped it was sharp. By habit, she pulled her sleeve tight around the upper arm and tilted the blade so it caught the pale street light.

A smooth cut along the guidelines, at first it didn't hurt much. So she took her time. But then a locomotive rode her tracks. Her limb cried out and she knew she had to act fast before her body forbade passage.

A long cool rip hit the finish line. Straight and clean, she had left no flap to hold on to.

She backed up against the building and realized what was happening. She was bleeding. A lot. And she recognized the feeling.

Nodding. On the most illegal of drugs. She balanced her head against the building and let her eyes close over the sky.

Sirens rose, fell, rose again in the darkness of her blazing arm as her body throbbed a calliope of pain. A song sung for a marriage of will between woman and knife.

And from her new canal flowed an afterbirth of silence. Conceived at knife-injection, it was deeper than ten thousand times before. Rather than adding to the reservoir, this time the dam had burst. She was watering the sidewalks of the cul-de-sac and her fountain would rebirth the bog. Marsh vines would claim her friend and her self, and strange crabs with lanterns in their eyes would devour the remains of the officer of the law. Hard workers, these creatures would transform him in their bellies. As crustacean shit he'd be free and food again for fertile animals.

In her lidded vision, all returned.

A lido smile wrapped round her finger. Pink fingers of a black man ran through her hair. And she walked, walked, walked with her fifth column in the dream.

1997. From an unpublished collection of short stories entitled
Mobiles

William Novak
I Get Paid for Paranoia

EVERY TIME I meet a customer, I give him this sheet:

House Policies
It is hoped that these terms will be acceptable to you, and that we will develop an association of mutual trust and respect. I regard our business transaction as high-energy exchanges and look forward to enjoying a long-lasting relationship from which we will both benefit. I see myself as a person of integrity and aim to operate honestly and fairly.

Business is by appointment only. Call anytime to set up an appointment. If I'm out you will get my answering machine that will tell you when I expect to return, and will take any message you'd like to leave.

Do not discuss business on the telephone. Make an appointment and we will discuss it in person.

Do not give my name or phone number to anyone without an okay from me *beforehand*. The protocol that must be followed for introductions is as follows: Only after I feel that a stable rapport has been established between you and me will I be open to meeting your friend(s). Then I will want to talk to you about how you met them, etc., before you make the introduction.

If people are waiting for you outside, be sure they are parked or hanging out in a place where they cannot see which house you enter.

Never point out this house or anyone you meet here to anyone, ever, no matter how tempted you may be.

Don't write anyone's name or phone number on this piece of paper.

Come alone unless special arrangements have been made in advance for you to bring someone with you.

Transactions are on a cash-only basis. However, food stamps or barter may be used as a medium of exchange if arranged in advance.

You may reserve any item to be held for you for twenty-four hours.

Returns are generally discouraged. If you have any doubts, try before you buy. If you are buying for someone else and they don't like what you have selected for them, this is for you and them to resolve. In this kind of transaction you should plan in advance on taking responsibility as your friend's supplier.

The following items are not presently, and will never be, sold here: coke, speed, tranquilizers, Quaaludes, opium, barbiturates, smack, or any addicting substance – nor will any introductions be arranged involving these items.

All this is necessary. Nobody thinks he'll get busted, just like women think they won't get pregnant, that it only happens to other people. Well, it's a fact of life. They do come, and they do put you in handcuffs, and they do take you off to jail.

High Culture, 1980

Lanre Fehintola
Drugs Bust

THE FIRST THING the cops wanted to know when they burst into my house was where I'd hidden the charlie. There were six of them, four guys and two women; the women taking turns to play at good-cop/bad-cop and the guys being regular Drug Squad officers. It was a classic set-up, something like a synchronised-swimming team and almost as boring.

'I don't know what you're talking about,' I said with my arms outstretched, innocent-like. 'I live here, not Charlie.'

They laughed at that one, they thought it was funny. But the boss, let's call him 'Smith' (though that's not his real name), was not amused. Tall, thin, cropped grey hair, very pallid, he worked extra hard to distinguish himself from the others, to assert the fact that he was in charge and everything was under his control. He kept laying that on me over and over again just in case I misunderstood him the first time, like it was seriously important that I should know. I guess he wanted to show just how hip he was, that he was truly down with the scene and knew that I had ounces of the stuff stashed somewhere around the house.

He asked me again: 'Where's the charlie?'

This time laying emphasis on the cocaine angle. He was talking drugs.

'What?'

He said he wanted to give me the opportunity of coming clean before he gave orders to begin the search. I played it cool. I didn't lose my head or anything, just answered that he and his gang of burglars had arrived with the intention of searching my house anyway, so they may as well get on with it. 'And I still don't know what the fuck you're talking about. You won't find any drugs in this house!' Then, to show my indignation, I sat down and made myself comfortable. I guessed I was gonna be in for a long afternoon.

I don't think he liked that very much, it kind of undermined his authority; the other cops were smirking behind his back, anyway. I should've been trembling, I suppose; scared shitless that any minute now he was gonna find me out and I'd be for the hole. Instead I thought it was quite funny. My non-reaction to his illustrious self must've gone completely against everything they'd taught him at detective school. It was hilarious.

While his men were rummaging through the room and turning things over, he'd be standing to one side, or in a corner, just staring at me, trying to figure out the look on my face, trying to read my thoughts. And if I blinked or rubbed my eyes in any particular way he'd suddenly leap on to something in my line of vision, pick it up, then scrutinise my face again. Of course I'd simply look somewhere else, blink, rub my eyes, and he'd be off again, leaping, inspecting and scrutinising, until he got bored and changed tactics.

Then he squatted down directly in front of me, almost nose to nose, eyeball to eyeball, drilling a hole through my skull and trying to unfold my brain. I couldn't see what the others were up to with him in my face like that, so I shifted my weight to my left-hand side and peered around him. And that damn-fool-cop, interpreting any movements as shifty, dived on to whatever it was he thought I was trying not to look at.

He really was convinced I had cocaine in the house and thought he had me sussed. Every now and again he'd pick up a shoebox or a container or something, rattle it then ask me what it contained before checking it out for himself. He was so ridiculous I just couldn't be bothered with any more of his questions, they were so fuckin' mechanical and textbook-like. So I ignored him and focused my attention on the she-cop searching beneath the sofa. She was young and pretty, a slim athletic type, and had to reach far beneath the cushions to do the job right. So I've got my eyes glued to her thighs waiting for a revelation of stocking tops and perhaps an inch or so of panties.

At least that was a better prospect than the dickhead in the corner leaping around like an idiot in distress, trying to psyche me out.

I wondered to myself, why do ambitious young women like her waste themselves in the police force? I mean, she must've really believed in the job once, thought that her contribution would make a difference. I was interested and wanted to find out more, but before I could put the question to her the front door flew open and Yasmin waltzed in. She was halfway through an apology for being late then froze mid-sentence when she realised the scene she'd just walked into. Then she began to cry. I should've known better. I should never have allowed myself to be taken in by those tears, but I did. And like a fool I even tried to cover up for her, claiming that she had nothing to do with anything and had only called round to see my girlfriend.

Then suddenly it was like 'Go! Go! Go!' Two cops jumped on her like they were SAS and frogmarched her upstairs. At that moment another one of them came out of the kitchen holding up a plastic container of fluffy white powder and, 'Smith', with his épée gleaming, moved it at me, but then discovered it was only yam flower – Nigerian soul food! After a while Yasmin was dragged downstairs again, minus her Vodaphone, and with her clothes all disarrayed, and was taken off to the police station.

Something was wrong; I didn't know what exactly and there was nothing much I could do about it anyway, but I knew there was something wrong. Then, as if on cue, the other she-cop came down from the bathroom with a big grin on her face, brandishing £1,200 cash in one hand, and a bag of prime sinsemilla in the other. 'Smith' was ecstatic and almost orgasmed right there in front of us all. Okay, so he hadn't discovered any cocaine but he had got a bag of excellent ganja, and as far as he was concerned, a bust was a bust.

From: *Charlie Says . . . don't get high on your own supply: an urban memoir*, 2000

Bez
Freaky Dancin'

As THEY ENTERED the house, I could hear the panic risin' in his voice as he tried desperately to deny the crime they suspected he'd done – a gold chain an' a sovereign had been snatched from a girl's neck the night before. Why is it always at the end of some trip, when the strychnine is settin' in, an' yer skin doesn't quite seem to fit properly, that some blatherin' bastard tries to tangle yer up in his problems?

This blatherin' bastard was askin' me to vouch for his good character. I'd had Mary fuckin' Quant on my case all night, my eyes were still rollin' an' I was wearin' stupid trousers; the last thing I needed was to try an' look sincere in my opinion of his honesty. I made my excuses, grabbed my bags an' got the hell out of there as fast as I could without seemin' too shady myself. I grabbed the girl on the way, so as not to leave any debris lyin' around that I might have to go back for later.

Once out in the fresh air, the panic of the scene I'd just left began to subside; a quiet sense of relief oiled my stiff limbs an' a buoyancy came back into my step. I was thankin' God that I'd managed to escape from a potentially dangerous acquaintance without apparent incident an' was just about to vocalise this point when – *swoosh* – the CID pulled up alongside an' called me over. I handed my bags to the girl, tellin' her to take them home to my new flat, where I would meet her later. I walked over to the car an' in an instant they were upon me, grabbin' my arms an' leadin' me round to the boot. I mean, for fuck's sake, I wasn't about to be goin' anywhere, now was I? After all, I was an innocent man, or so I thought! With smug, shiny, fat smirkin' faces they opened the boot in a dramatic fashion as if they'd discovered I was a secret arms dealer or somethin'. There wavin' back at me were four puny seedlin's, the result of a stoned experiment that I'd abandoned, forgotten in the back of the kitchen. The seeds I'd thrown in the pot weren't even from a quality smoke. I was gutted; to be pulled for somethin' so stupidly small, somethin' that grows naturally in abundance all over the world, somethin' that I hadn't even intended to cultivate. Fuckin' weeds, why do they grow so easily?

To add insult to injury, the kid I'd been stayin' with was sat in the back of the car squealin' like a stuck pig about how he was prepared to take any rap but not for drugs. I couldn't believe it, all I wanted was a quiet life in the seclusion of my new pad an' now I was bein' hailed as the Percy fuckin' Thrower of cannabis land – I hate gardenin', I hate tendin' plants; why hadn't they shrivelled up an' withered with neglect like any other plant I ever owned?

Freaky Dancin', 1989

T. Coraghessan Boyle
Budding Prospects

LET ME TELL you about attrition. About dwindling expectations, human error, Mother Nature on the counteroffensive.
Let me tell you about days without end, about the oppression
of mid-afternoon, about booze and dope, horseshoes, cards,
paperbacks read and reread till their covers fall to pieces, let
me tell you about boredom and the loss of faith.

First off, Vogelsang was right. There *were* only a thousand
plants on the ground. Or to be more precise, 957. I know: I
counted them. It was the first thing I thought of when I woke
the day following my sojourn in the town jail. Early on, we'd
planted better than one thousand seedlings, and then Dowst
had managed to sprout and plant some six or seven hundred
more – at least. Or so he'd said. We were aware that we'd
fallen short of our original estimate, but we had no idea by
how much. Five percent? Ten? Fifteen? It wasn't our concern.
We were the workers, the muscle, the yeomen, and Dowst and
Vogelsang were the managers. The number of plants in the
ground and the condition of those plants was their business;
ours was to dig holes, string and mend fences, repair the
irrigation system, and see that each plant got its two and a
half gallons of H_2O per day. And so we'd never counted the
plants. Never felt a need to. There were so many, after all,
forests of them, their odor rank and sweet and overpowering,
that we simply let ourselves get caught up in the fantasy of it,
the wish that fulfills itself: of course we had two thousand
plants.

But Vogelsang never made mistakes, and now I wasn't so
sure. I lay there a moment atop my sweaty sleeping bag, a
soiled sheet twisted at my ankles, and then staggered into the
kitchen for a glass of water. It was one-thirty in the afternoon
and the house was already so hot you could have baked bread
on the counter. Phil was stretched out on the sofa behind a
tattered copy of an E. Rice Burroughs novel, perfectly inert, a
tall vodka Collins in his hand. I peered through the yellowed
window and saw that both van and Saab were gone.

'Vogelsang and Dowst leave already?' I said.

Phil snorted. 'What do you think – they'd stick around here a second more than they had to?' From above, in the insupportable heat of the loft, Gesh's snores drifted down, dry as husks.

I drank from the tap, wiped my mouth with the back of my hand. 'Last night,' I began, rummaging through the refuse on the counter for a knife, peanut butter and bread, 'Vogelsang said we've only got a thousand plants in the ground – that's crazy, isn't it?'

Phil shrugged. I was watching his face and he was watching mine. 'I don't know, seems like there's a million when you're watering.'

'Yeah,' I said, 'I know what you mean,' but fifteen minutes later I was out there in the feverish hammering heat of midday, notebook in hand, counting.

Bushes had gone brown, the grass was stiff and yellow. I trod carefully, terrified of the rattlesnakes that infested the place. (I had a deep-seated fear of snakes, of their furtiveness, their muscular phallic potency, the quickness of their thrust, and the terrible rending wound they left in the poisoned flesh. I always carried a snakebite kit with me – but of course I knew the rattler would never be so cooperative as to puncture my foot or hand, but instead would fasten onto my ear or eye or scrotum, thus negating the value of the kit – and during the cold weather, when there was no more than a chance in a million of encountering a snake of any kind, I'd worn leather gaiters. As soon as the heat had set in, and the snakes emerged, the gaiters had become too uncomfortable and I'd abandoned them.) I made a mark for every plant on the property, four across and a slash for five, and found that fewer than a thousand had survived the root rot, blight and over-and-under watering that had afflicted them. Not to mention the hundreds – thousands? – that never emerged from the tough withered husks of their seedpods or succumbed to the depredations of various creatures, from the insects in the greenhouse to the bear. Nine fifty-seven. That was the figure I came up with, and that was the figure I presented to my co-workers after dinner that evening.

The evening watering was done, and we were standing out front of the house in the long shadows, pitching horseshoes for a dollar a game. 'Vogelsang was right,' I told them, 'we've got less than a thousand plants.' It was awful to contemplate: in one fell swoop our profits had been cut in half.

'Bummer,' Gesh said, and pitched a ringer to win the game. 'That's what, thirty-six dollars you owe me now, Felix.'

But this was just the beginning of our troubles, the first clear indication that we would have to revise our expectations downward. There were more to come. A week later, we began to notice that some of our healthiest plants – chest-high already and greener than a bucket of greenback dollars – were wilting. On closer inspection we saw that a narrow band had been cut or gnawed in the stem of each plant. We were bewildered. Had deer leapt eight feet in the air to vault our fences, bend their necks low to the ground, and nibble at the hard fibrous stems of the plants rather than graze the succulent leaves? Obviously not. Something smaller was responsible, some rabbity little bounding thing with an effective range about ankle-high and the ability to crawl under a deer fence. 'Rabbits?' Phil guessed. 'Gophers?' It was then, with fear, loathing, regret and trepidation, that I remembered the dark scurrying forms I'd encountered that first day in the storage shed; a second later I made the connection with the rat traps we'd found scattered about Jones's main growing area. 'Rats,' I said.

We phoned Dowst. Rats, he informed us, live in the city: in garbage. A week later we'd lost upward of fifty plants, and we phoned him again. He looked preoccupied as he stepped out of the van, and I noticed that his skin had lost its color, as if he'd been spending a lot of time indoors, hunched over his notes on the virgin's bower or the beard lichen. We walked down to Jonestown with him, squatted like farmers socializing outside the courthouse, and showed him the ring of toothmarks that had bled a vigorous plant dry in a week's time. I watched as he ran a finger round the moist indentation and then brought it to his mouth to taste the fluid seeping from the wound. He was silent a moment, then looked up at us and announced that rabbits were decimating our crop. 'They're thirsty,' he explained, 'and here you've got a standing fountain, seventy percent water.' He rose to his feet and brushed at his trousers. 'The only thing to do is peg down the fences so they can't get in underneath.'

We pegged. Crawled on our hands and knees through the rattlesnake-, scorpion- and tarantula-infested brush, the sweat dripping from our noses, and hammered stakes into the ground, stretching our chicken wire so tight even a beetle couldn't have crawled under it. It took us a week. Dowst stayed on to supervise, to potter around the growing areas exuding expertise, and even, on occasion, to lend a hand. When we got the whole thing finished – all the fences in all the growing areas nailed down tight – I observed that we were still losing plants to the mystery gnawers, and suggested that the big bundles of twigs and downed branches we regularly came across in the woods and had as a matter of course enclosed within the confines of our now impervious fences were in fact rats' nests and that rats, not rabbits, were the culprits. Dowst demurred. But two days later, as the plants continued to wither and the toothy girdles to proliferate, he authorized Phil to drive into Santa Rosa and purchase two hundred rat traps at Friedman Brothers' Farm Supply.

By now it was early August, nearly a month since my fateful scrape with the law. We had something like 840 six-foot plants – bushes, trees – burgeoning around us. The boredom was crushing. We alternated early watering chores – two days on, one day off – so that each of us could sleep late two days a week. I almost preferred getting up early. At least you felt alive in the cool of the morning, traversing fields damp with dew, ducking through silent groves of oak and madrone, catching a glimpse of deer, fox, bobcat. We'd get back to the cabin at nine-thirty or ten, the temperature already past ninety, stuff something in our mouths and fall face forward on our worn mattresses. It would be one or two by the time we woke to the deadening heat, our nostrils parched, throats dry as dunes, and joined the late sleeper in the continuous round of drinking, pot smoking, cards and horseshoes that would put us away, dead drunk and disoriented, in the wee hours of the morning.

Each day was the same, without variation. Occasionally the pump would break down and Gesh would take it to a repairman in town and attempt to be casual about what he was doing with twenty-five-hundred gallons of water a day, or Dowst would pay a visit with magazines, newspapers, vodka and ice. But that was about it for excitement. The cards wore thin, the walls developed blisters from the intensity of our stares, we began to know the household lizards by name. 'Gollee,' Phil would say, slipping into an Atchafalaya drawl as we sat silently over our fiftieth game of pitch, 'I haven't had this much fun since the hogs ate my baby sister.'

If we saw Dowst once or twice a week, we rarely saw Vogelsang. As the plants blossomed into hard evidence, he made himself increasingly scarce, more than ever the silent partner. 'Look, I've got too much to lose,' he told us one night after he'd been summoned to repair the kick start on the surviving Kawasaki. 'I just can't take the risk of being seen up here or identified in any way with this operation. I've got business interests, property in three states, a number of other deals in the works . . .' and he waved his hand to show the futility of even trying to intimate the scope of his interests. We watched that exasperated hand in silence, thinking our own thoughts about how much he had to lose, and by extension, how little we had. To lose.

For my part, the euphoria of being allowed to stay on was quickly exhausted, and I'd come to feel as oppressed as my co-workers by the drudgery and the unvarying routine. During the long slow hours of the interminable sweltering afternoons, propped up in a chair with a tall vodka and tonic and some moronic sci-fi paperback Phil had picked up at a used-book store in Ukiah ('The *classics*, Phil,' I'd tell him, 'get me something fat by Dostoevski or Dickens or somebody'), I began to feel I was estivating, my clock wound down, brain numbed. It was then, more than ever, that I would find myself thinking of Petra.

One evening, while we stood round the horseshoe pit, winning, losing and exchanging chits, Dowst's van slid through the trees along the road and swung into the field, bouncing toward us across the brittle yellow expanse of the yard like a USO wagon come to some remote outpost. We were shirtless, bearded, dirty, our jeans sun-bleached and boots cracked with age and abuse. Behind us the sun flared in the sky, fat and red as a tangerine, and a host of turkey vultures, naked heads, glossy wings, converged on the carcass of some luckless creature struck down behind the shed. Puddles of crushed glass glinted at our feet, the sagging out-buildings eased toward the ground like derelicts bedding down for the night, and the cabin, pale as driftwood, radiated heat in scalloped waves until you had to look twice to be sure it wasn't on fire. For an instant I saw the scene from Dowst's eyes – from the eyes of an outsider, an emissary from the world of hot tubs and Cuisinarts – and realized that we must have looked like mad prospectors, like desert rats, like the sad sun-crazed remnants of Pizarro's band on the last leg of the road to Eldorado.

Dowst backed out of the van, crablike, his arms laden, and disappeared into the house. A moment later he emerged, newspaper in hand, and crossed the yard to join us. He was wearing white shorts and an alligator-emblazoned shirt, tennis shoes and pink-tinted shades. 'Hi,' he said, gangling and affable, as relaxed as a man who's just played two sets of tennis before brunch, and then held out the newspaper as if it were a new steel racket or a Frisbee. 'I thought you guys might want to see this.'

See what?

'VOGELSANG ELECTED MAYOR; POT SOARS ON COMMODITIES MARKET; JERPBAK TRANSFERRED TO JERUSALEM.'

We saw the front page of the *Chronicle*, blocks of print, a murky photograph. Puzzled, we crowded round him, scanning the headlines, passing quickly over the stories of corruption in government, poverty in the Third World and carnage in the Seychelles, until the following story leapt out from the page to seize us like the iron grip of a strangler:

WAR DECLARED ON POT GROWERS

The Drug Enforcement Administration and the State Department of Justice have formulated plans for a federally funded assault on growers of high-grade sinsemilla marijuana along the northern California coast, the *Chronicle* learned today. A federal law-enforcement grant of $400,000 has been rushed through to enable the newly formed 'Sinsemilla Strike Force' to begin operations before the fall harvest season. The strike force will coordinate federal agents and local police departments in 'sniffing out illicit growing operations,' as one source put it, in Mendocino, Del Norte and Humboldt counties. Aerial surveillance, including the use of infra-red photography, will, it is hoped, pinpoint the locations of so many of the large-scale farms, while a program of special cash rewards for turning in growers is expected to help in exposing others.

'People are tired of this sort of thing,' a source close to the strike force said, 'and they resent the outsiders that come into their community for illegal and often highly lucrative purposes. We're confident that the reward system will make it easier for local residents to help us identify and apprehend the criminals in their midst.'

Operations could begin as early as next month, the source disclosed.

Dowst was grinning sheepishly, a slight flush to his cheeks, as if he'd just told an off-color joke at a lawn party. 'Not such great news, huh?'

For some reason, the story didn't affect me as it would have a few months earlier. I was alarmed, certainly, all the vital functions thrown into high gear as I read on, but I wasn't panicked. In fact, relatively speaking, I was calm. Perhaps my run-in with Jerpbak and the little scene I'd gone through with Savoy – *everybody knows what you guys are doing up there* – had made me fatalistic. Perhaps I expected a bust. Perhaps I wanted it.

Gesh was not quite so calm. He snatched the paper from Dowst's hands, balled it up and attempted to punt it into the trees. Then he turned on him, his face splayed with anger. 'What next?' he shouted, as if Dowst were to blame. 'Christ!' he roared, and spun round to face the empty hills.

Phil was pale. He tried to laugh it off, improvising a halfhearted joke about infra-red pot and reading glasses for the eye in the sky, until his words trailed off in a little self-conscious bleat of laughter. Then, in what had almost become a reflex gesture for him, Gesh wheeled around to jab a thick admonitory finger in Dowst's face. 'Between the rats and the bears and you and Vogelsang and now the fucking federal government, there's going to be precious little of this pot to split up, you know that?'

Dowst knew it. And so did we.

But that wasn't the worst of it. The following day, after he'd made a tour of the plantation and monitored the growth of each leaf, stem and twig, Dowst announced that he'd begun sexing the plants and that within a month all the males should have emerged. 'Around the end of September, after the photoperiod begins to decline; that's when we'll get them all.'

Phil and I were playing checkers; Gesh was dozing on the couch, a newspaper spread over his face. It was mid-afternoon, and the heat was like a wasting disease. 'Huh?' I said.

'You know,' Dowst was rattling through the cans of soup in the cupboard under the sink, 'for sinsemilla pot. We've got to weed out the male plants.'

That was something we'd known all along, in the way we knew that chickens laid eggs whether there was a rooster or not, or that Pluto was the ninth planet in the solar system – it was part of our general store of knowledge. But we hadn't really stopped to think about it, to consider its ramifications or work it into our formulae for translating plants into dollars. Any fool knew that in order to get sinsemilla pot you had to identify and eliminate the male plants so that the energy of the unfertilized females would go toward pro-duction of the huge, resinous, THC-packed colas that made seedless pot the most potent, desirable and highly priced smoke on the market. Any fool. But to this point we'd conveniently managed to overlook it.

I watched Phil's face as the realization of what Dowst was saying seeped into his nervous system and gave vent to various autonomous twitches of mortification and regret. 'You mean . . . we've got to . . . to . . . throw *out some of the plants*?'

Dowst had found a can of Bon Ton lobster bisque and was applying the opener to it. 'Usually about fifty percent. It could be higher or lower. Depending.'

Phil looked like a man being strapped into the electric chair while his wife French-kisses the DA in the hallway. 'On what?'

The lobster bisque was the color of diarrhea. Dowst sloshed it into his spotless Swiss aluminum camp pot and stirred it with a spoon he'd carefully disinfected over the front burner. 'Luck,' he said finally, and he pronounced the word as if it had meaning, pronounced it like the well-washed Yankee optimist he was, a man who could trace his roots back to the redoubtable Dowsts on the *Mayflower*. Besides, he had his van, a condo in Sausalito and a monthly stipend from his trust fund. He didn't need luck.

I thought of Mendel's pea plants, x and y chromosomes, thought of all those hale and hearty many-branching glorious male plants that would be hacked down and burned – fifty percent of the crop in a single swoop and the second such swoop in a month's time. Numbers invaded my head like an alien force, a little problem in elementary arithmetic: *Take 840 pot plants and divide by 2. Divide again, allowing for one-half-pound of marketable pot per plant, to solve for the total number of pounds obtained. Multiply this figure by $1,600, the going rate per pound. Now divide by 3 to arrive at the dollar value of each share – the financier's, the expert's and the yeoman's – and finally divide by 3 again to find the miserable pittance that you yourself will receive after nine months of backbreaking labor, police terror and exile from civilization.*

Dowst was whistling. Phil gnawed at the edge of a black plastic checker, expressionless, his eyes vacant. My half-million had been reduced to $37,000. Barring seizure, blight, insect depredation and unforeseeable natural disasters, that is. It was a shock. If Jerpbak, ravenous rodents and the 'Sinsemilla Strike Force' had driven a stake through my heart, Dowst had just climbed atop the coffin to nail down the lid.

Budding Prospects, 1984

Henri de Monfried
The Farm

AFTER AN HOUR'S drive, we reached the foot of a hill covered with heather and flowering broom. A farm with tiled roofs set against it, facing the rising sun and overlooking the plains covered with orchards and wheat fields. The buildings were of granite, and seemed very ancient. They were as massively constructed as a fortress, with vaulted entrances, and the great flags which paved the courtyard had been worn away by the contact of countless generations of feet.

It was the hour when yokes of oxen returned slowly from their work in the fields, and flocks of black sheep came pouring in at the great outer gate, running in disorder towards the sheepfolds, the ewes with distended udders answering the plaintive bleatings of the hungry lambs. A warm smell of hay and the breath of trine came out to meet the chill of the falling night.

Petros went off immediately to fetch a sample of his hashish. I wondered how I was to give an intelligent opinion on it, and not betray the fact that it was the first I had ever seen. I didn't even know how the quality was indicated. I was afraid of making a fool of myself and revealing my ignorance, for after that I could be sure that all the poor stuff which had been unsaleable would be joyfully palmed off on me. I fell back on a method which is often useful. So far as possible, I would be silent. Petros came in with a fragment of brownish matter in his hand. He immediately gave me the clue to how to test the value of his merchandise, by proceeding to sniff. Then he took a piece and rolled it between his fingers into a slender cone, to which he put a match. It burned with a tiny and rather smoky flame, and when he hastily extinguished it, a heavily perfumed white smoke arose from it. In my turn I took a piece and went through exactly the same manoeuvres, only, having noticed how quickly he put out the flame, I on the contrary let it burn. Then in silence, with a cold and rather disdainful air, I held it out to him. He interpreted my silence according to his fears, and instantly exclaimed: 'Oh, but don't be afraid, I have better stuff than this. Only I thought this might perhaps interest you; it is much cheaper.'

I replied with dignity: 'I have not come such a long way to buy cheap stuff. Please show me your best at once.'

He vanished, and returned in a moment with a piece of the same matter, but less brittle and of a greenish hue. He went through the same gestures, but this time the flame was long and very smoky, and he complacently let it burn. That, thought I, is probably the sign of really good quality. Now I knew how to buy hashish. I declared myself satisfied, and we settled on the quantity I was to buy, four hundred okes (six hundred kilograms), at the price of twenty francs the oke. 'Now,' said he, 'we'll go and fetch the goods from the warehouse where they are stored.'

A servant girl brought us little wax torches, and two hefty workmen armed with huge cudgels accompanied us. Petros opened a vaulted door, behind which a stone staircase led down into the cellars. A musty smell of damp rose from this underground passage, and almost at once we came to a crypt hewn out of the living rock. In this vault, which was circular in form, sacks were piled up; this was the hashish crop of the current year. The two workmen picked out the number of sacks which corresponded to the weight I had ordered, put them in the middle of the floor, then fell upon them with their sticks, in order to break up the contents and reduce them to dust.

We must have formed a strange group. First there was

Papamanoli, the priest, in his flowing black robes, and beside him, Petros, holding in his hand a piece of white paper, into which he put a sample from each sack. Each of us held aloft a little wax taper in order to give light to the men who were beating so furiously on the bulging sacks. Our shadows danced fantastically along the vaulted roof, and the bats, panic-stricken and blinded by the light, bumped their horrid soft bodies against us, making the flames of our candles flicker. I shall never forget this scene, though the others seemed quite unconscious of its picturesque quality. Petros poured the different samples from his paper into a little bag, which he gave me as indicating the average quality of my hashish. The sacks were then carried into a barn, so that the icy cold of the night should prevent the powdered hashish from coagulating afresh.

Next morning I was awakened by a humming activity which filled the house like the murmur of a beehive. In the barn into which we had carried the sacks, a crowd of workers were going to and fro through a thick dust. In the middle of the room was a sort of table consisting of a very fine metal sieve set up on four legs. On it the hashish was being thrown in spadefuls. A big sheet was wrapped round the outside of the table legs to prevent the fine powder which fell from the sieve from blowing away. Women with their heads swathed in handkerchiefs were spreading out and sifting the powder. After this, men shovelled it into an enormous iron basin in order that it should be well mixed. Madam Petros was sitting before a sewing-machine, feverishly running up little white linen bags. These she passed to a woman who stamped an elephant on them with a rubber stamp. She in turn passed them to a third woman who filled them, weighed them with great care, and finally tied them up. They were then put in neat piles into a great press. When there were a certain number between the steel plates, a muscular workman tightened the vice and the sacks flattened out slowly until they were like square pancakes four centimetres thick. These pancakes were hard as wax; this is the form in which hashish is exported, and the elephant was Petros' trade-mark. From time to time he himself lent a hand to the brawny fellow who was working the press. I looked at the latter with interest. He was very tall; I could not see his face, as his head was covered with a towel with small eye-holes bored in it, but his eyes seemed vaguely familiar, and suddenly I realised that they were the eyes of Papamanoli. At this moment, having finished, he laughingly removed his improvised cowl, freeing his luxuriant beard and his hair, which had been rolled on top of his head. This priest seemed to take everything as a matter of course, and nobody seemed surprised to see him helping at a busy moment.

This hashish powder had gradually excited the men and women working with it, and they began to sing at the tops of their voices, and joke and laugh like mad things over nothing. I took part in this crazy gaiety like the rest, and even the plain little niece from Tripolis grew quite flirtatious. Fortunately, the work was soon completed, or I don't know how it would all have ended. Outside, a plumber soldered the zinc linings of the packing-cases in which the hashish pancakes were to be packed.

For those who are interested I shall describe briefly how the hashish comes to the state in which I had first seen it, powdered and stored in sacks in the cellar. The fields in which the hemp grows are carefully weeded and all the male plants are pulled out. The female plants which remain cannot therefore bear seeds, and the result is that the leaves become fully charged with resinous matter. The secretion of this sticky substance is further increased by breaking off the tops of the plants as they grow. When the first leaves, that is to say the lowest ones, turn yellow, the plants are carefully cut down about four inches from the ground, so as not to soil them with earth or sand. Then the crop is dried in the shade and stacked in barns. Some growers only keep the leaves, for the stems are of no value whatever. On very cold winter days, when there is a keen frost and the waxen matter secreted by the leaves has become brittle as resin, the dried plants are broken up by rubbing them between two sheets of canvas. This gives a dust made up of broken leaves and the resin which is the active part of hashish. This resin gives the powder the property of forming a sort of cake when pressed, and of softening when heated.

All the farms in this district prepared hashish; it was their chief industry. Each estate had its brand, quoted on the market, and there were good and bad years, exactly as for wines.

Hashish, 1935

Howard Marks
Ketama

CENTRED ON KETAMA (a small village a hundred miles from Tangier which once showed promise as a ski centre and hunting paradise) and on top of pine-covered crests of otherwise barren mountains lies the source of most of the world's imported hashish. The area increases every year and now covers several thousand square miles, stretching to twenty-five miles from Tangier. Almost every terraced field in the area with a water source is filled with kif plants that are planted in February and harvested in summer, when the raw plants are cut and bundled for donkey and mule transport to the homestead where they dry on hot tin roofs for up to a week. When fairly crisp, the bundles are stacked in the cool interior and stored for one to six months. The timing was excellent: they would be making hashish right now. A few well-placed phone calls to old friends soon provided an invitation to come and sample the latest produce.

I took the S302 north out of Fez. This was the Route de l'Unite, finished in 1963 and built by the recently deceased King Hassan II as the first north–south route across the Rif, which had previously uncomfortably symbolised both its own isolation and the separateness of the old Spanish and French colonial zones. All travel guides to Morocco, including the *Lonely Planet*, strongly advise giving it a miss. They warn of hooded drivers of Mercedes cars ambushing unwary visitors and press-ganging them to become dope dealers. I saw nothing like that; I must have come at the wrong time. But the road does go through Ketama.

Within hours of leaving Fez, I watched as bundles of cannabis plants were beaten with sticks over a tub covered with a sieve. At first just the good resin (destined to become the much sought-after 'double zero') got through, then eventually, after dozens of repetitions, the resin-starved powdered leaf. The sieved resinous powder was compressed and heated, binding the vegetable matter. The resin (varying in colour from light yellow brown to reddish brown) was then compressed into blocks and sealed with Cellophane or cloth.

I waited until sundown and tried the 'double zero'. A battered cassette player hung from a tree and blasted out a medley of Creedence Clearwater Revival and swing jazz. Mint tea and fruit juice flowed. Birds perched on sacks of hash. Pet monkeys played with wild cats.

Maria Golia
Nile-Eyes

> It's good to know the truth but it's better to speak of
> palm trees.
>
> – Egyptian Proverb

CAIRO'S HASHISH QUARTER, inner sanctum of the medieval portion of the city, was called 'Batneyya,' a poetic nomination since the word derives from the Arabic for 'belly' and 'nourishment.' There was a market place, a small clearing or square surrounded by cafés, shops and houses, like anywhere else in the Old City. Fellaheen herded sheep, goats nibbled piles of alfalfa, chickens squawked from their cane crates, women hawked vegetables from hemp baskets while their barefoot children played beside them. The only difference was that in the center of this rustic scene was a row of wooden tables furnished with scales and bricks of yellow and red Cellophane-wrapped hashish.

Men crowded around the tables and made their purchases in units called 'ersh,' equal to about four grams. Cigarettes were used to counterbalance the scale. Orders were placed and small chunks removed from the mother-hunk with startling precision either by tooth or knife. The going price was about a half-dollar per gram. A more elite public shopped from the relative discretion of a house just behind the square in a cul-de-sac. It had three grilled street-level windows in the façade, each one corresponding to a different grade of hashish. People lined up according to their preference for Lebanese fresh or Lebanese aged and compressed, or, for the economy-minded, Lebanese moldy, something that had suffered somewhat in the transport.

A man named Mohamed Marzouk, a fearless dealer whose exploits were the stuff of popular odes, operated this little convenience shop. At a time when the TVs and radios were spouting propagandist drivel praising Sadat in saccharine song, parodies were derived from the melodies in honor of this chubby smuggler. The fruit of his efforts was the source of what little enjoyment there was to be had by a large market segment. Mohamed Marzouk was loved and his life and freedom held sacred.

I was allowed past a long series of watchers and guards into the house. It was empty except for a few chairs and a table where the great man sat counting a thick wad of bank notes with hypnotizing dexterity. When he finished he looked up and greeted me, slapping my hand. He was somewhere between fifty and sixty years old, balding and stout, dressed Western style with a large turquoise ring set in gold. He asked me if I had completed my military service yet. This was his little joke, referring to the fact that I dressed like a boy. I had my camera and wanted very much to photograph Marzouk.

'Still working for the Israelis?' he asked amiably.

'Only on Saturdays,' I told him and he chuckled. We'd met in a nearby café operated by one of his lackeys and he'd remarked my ability to imbibe an astounding number of gozas in a single sitting. This talent attracted attention and rumors circulated to explain my frequent presence in the district. I was an Israeli or Egyptian spy. I was a whore, a lesbian, a transvestite or mad. Marzouk, an excellent student of human nature, knew that I wasn't and rewarded me with lumps of provender.

'Look, I'd like to take your picture sometime, OK?'

'Why?'

'Because you're beautiful,' I extemporized. He guffawed and slapped his thigh and called out to one of his lackeys to bring him something. His man came running and thrust a fist-sized chunk of hashish into Marzouk's hand. He admired it for a moment, turning it around and around, then bit into it like an apple and gave me a piece glistening with saliva and bearing the imprimatur of his incisors. I thanked him profusely and headed back toward the square where I saw my good friend Samy who was doing some shopping.

Latter-day dragoman, linguist and procurer, Samy was an Egyptian youth who helped me to navigate the labyrinth of Cairo. He was a trifle bug-eyed but had exemplary teeth that he habitually covered with his hand when he spoke as if to reveal their perfection would be unseemly. His father had recently died, having spent the last years of his life immersed in the Koran and making the annual pilgrimage to Saudi Arabia. In response to his death Samy started to lose hair and take tranquilizers. He was just eighteen. Flattered by my interest in his neighborhood, he led me deeper and deeper into the less accessible areas. We paused at regular intervals to visit the numerous cafés serving coffee, tea and more potent refreshment, hashish, 'fresh from the trees' as Samy said.

Samy contributed to the local economy by lightly fleecing bewildered tourists who ventured into the souk where he was born and raised. Hands in his pockets with his slouching, easy gait he made his approach: 'Hello my friend, how can I help you on this beautiful day?' He had a spiel in seven languages including Japanese and Russian. He singled out straggling, sweating victims from the mainstream of pedestrians with the precision of an Arab archer picking off sun-struck Crusaders.

He took them to a quiet courtyard that was once a silk caravansary, set them down to cool and served them mint tea.

Then he produced the articles they had seen along the way that had interested them; brass trays, cotton scarves and papery leather poufs. Samy made a show of negotiating with the tourists, implying that they were tough bargainers. When he felt they were gratified, rested and thoroughly broke, he gathered them up and returned them to their group or their bus like the most conscientious of sheep dogs. Then he pocketed a commission from the happy tourists and his friends, the local merchants, sometimes in the form of fragrant morsels of hash, this being one of the quarter's many negotiable currencies.

Samy and I took a liking to each other. We profited from our friendship by asking questions regarding our cultures. Like most Egyptians his age Samy visualized America as a combination of Disney Land, Times Square and cattle ranch peopled by eccentric Texas billionaires, hard-nosed detectives, gorgeous blondes and pistol-packing troublemakers, all of whom drove big cars and ate steaks on a regular basis. This, to him, was clear. Other aspects of daily life were less understandable. One evening as we made our way along the tangled paths to Batneyya, Samy broached a difficult subject.

'So, when they die in America,' he hazarded, hands stuffed in his pockets, 'do the women go screaming through the streets, like they do here?'

'Not exactly.' I was busy trying not to stumble while dealing with the narrow pitted streets and the hillocks of mud and sand displaced by daily hosings and endless human and animal traffic.

'And what about when they go into the hole?' Samy persisted, smoothly veering to the right to allow a man riding a bicycle balancing an immense rattan tray holding fifty kilos of flat bread on his head to pass.

'Well, they put them in a box, then they put them in a hole,' I replied, distracted by the appearance of a young girl skipping rope without the rope.

'With the box and everything?' Appalled, Samy turned to me in a rare moment when we were able to walk abreast. I did a neat hip-tuck and barely missed collision with a man exiting a doorway carrying an enormous ball of twine.

'Of course,' I answered, a trifle strident. 'What do you think, they just throw him naked into some hole, for God's sake?' Samy shook his head in distress at my tone, because that is exactly what his people do, except with a shroud, usually.

'No,' I continued self-righteously, 'they put him in a proper box first, *then* they stick him in the hole.' Samy didn't quite get it but we'd arrived at the café belonging to 'Oota' (the cat). We greeted the occupants of this vine-covered sidewalk establishment and took our places on wooden chairs whose seats were decorated with the graceful, albeit incessantly humiliated, profile of Cleopatra.

A twelve-year-old pipe boy placed a tall tin table between us and shuffled off. He returned with a tray of ten crude clay pipe bowls filled with rough-cut, molasses-soaked tobacco. Samy took a piece of hashish from its hiding place behind his ear and started biting off bits that he flattened into dime-sized disks with his gleaming teeth, placing a piece atop each of the pipe bowls.

The pipe boy returned with the pipe, or 'goza,' in one hand, and a small tea strainer full of glowing coals in the other. The goza is made from a big jar filled with water and closed with a rubber plug from which protrude two cane sticks; a short one where the clay pipe bowl fits, and another about as long as a man's arm, from which one smokes. The boy made the tiny coals glow moving the strainer in small arcs with deft twists of his wrist. It's a trick of the trade, relying on centrifugal force that makes mesmerizing ruby-red trails of light.

The pipe boy planted a pipe bowl on the short stick, spooned a few coals on top of the hashish with a worn and bent tin spoon and proffered the business end of the contraption to me. Several firm but not complete draws to get the thing going, then one long pull, straight to the bottom of the lungs, followed by a slow controlled exhalation, preferably uninterrupted by an explosive cough.

This isn't easy since the contents of the smoke include about five grams of tobacco aside from the hash. Plus, one has to make the pipe burn sufficiently because to only partially consume the hashish would be disgraceful. But I had the knack. The pipe boy winked with approval, emptied the pipe and replaced it with another for Samy. I remarked on his uncanny ability to send the smoke in two perfectly bisected jets from his nose, one flowing east, one west. Samy sensed my awe, and seized the moment to pursue our earlier conversation.

'So, is it true that in your country they put the people in the box, and then into the hole with the box and everything?' Like most Egyptians he pronounced all words that begin with a 'P' as if they began with a 'B' because 'P' does not exist in the Arabic alphabet. Hence 'but the beoble in the box.' I nodded, now engaged in the slightly easier task of attacking bipe number two.

'But what if they haven't got a box?' Samy asked reasonably, coughing a little with his mouth closed, smoke dribbling in white ribbons from his nose before exhaling the mother load.

'They buy one. I mean, maybe they can't afford a nice one so they just get a cheap one,' I answered democratically before confronting my third pipe.

Samy smiled brightly. 'Ahh, berhaps then your American government is giving sbecial boxes for the boor beoble?' He lovingly handled the long stick that he applied daintily to his mouth, taking the spoon from the boy to tamp down the coals more firmly.

'No, Samy, it's not like that. If you don't have the money for a box, you go and chop down a tree or something, but no box, no hole.'

Samy's eyes were slightly glazed as he labored to comprehension. I disposed of the fourth pipe and explained in greater detail.

'It's like this. In America and even in Europe they've got this habit of putting the people in boxes. People make a living out of making the boxes. Some of them are really nice, lined with silk cushions. Other are less comfortable and just plain. Some are even made of brass and cost lots of money, just like the pharaohs, you see?'

Samy nodded thoughtfully and polished off another pipe. I

approached my final one with a sense of achievement. Samy, too, did justice to his fifth, imagining a place where everyone has his own box, even in death. The idea of such luxury was strange to him, belonging to a world where everything is shared, even the communal bier that serves as final transport to an often common grave, and where burial (within twenty-four hours of death according to Koranic injunction) is one of the few expedients in an existence otherwise bereft of the concept of haste. 'Are you sure that they go in with the box and that the box stays there, too, for all the time?' he asked.

'Sure I'm sure.'

The café animated with men come to take their nocturnal ease, playing backgammon and drinking glasses of sugary, dark, steaming tea. One of them was dressed in an immaculate white *galabeyya*, 'King' Hussein, a Clark Gable lookalike and recent guest of one of Cairo's prison dungeons, a confirmed 'hashesh' or hash smoker. King was one of the usual suspects, a small-time hash retailer that took the rap for larger dealers during purges of the quarter. These raids were choreographed to portray Sadat as a stern disciplinarian to gratify international funding agencies and the non-smoking segment of the population. What they actually ended up doing was making local heroes out of the fall guys. Everyone knew the Sadat himself was a hashesh. We shared a round of pipes with King and Samy suggested walking to the City of the Dead to continue smoking.

Known in Arabic as the 'Toorab,' which means 'cemetery' as well as 'dust,' the City of the Dead is adjacent to the Old City, an immense desert sprawl peppered with the unmarked tombs of the populace and a community of small villa-like mausoleums that characterized the golden ages of Islam. Boulevards great and small are laid out in a sober grid with an orderliness that the living city never achieved. They are lined with walled frontage interrupted by intricate wrought-iron gates, or domed constructions. There were few cars here and considering the space, fewer people. Yet the City of the Dead was alive with people come to take residence in the tombs of their, or someone else's, forbears. Ancestors make excellent landlords.

According to Islamic custom, Fridays are set aside for visiting the cemetery and in the old days this meant a bit of a journey so the visitors would sometimes spend the night. The tombs were designed to accommodate both the living and the dead according to their divergent needs. Those of the well-to-do vary in size, materials and decor, from the modest to the marvelous. Many had courtyards, sometimes equipped with a source of water. The buildings house the remains of the deceased, moldering somewhere safely underground with perhaps a stone or marble throne-like sculpture to mark the grave. The Egyptians say, 'better misery than the cemetery.' The people living in the City of the Dead enjoyed a rare taste of both.

Adequate housing in Cairo is a thing of the past and the City of the Dead offered an attractive alternative to, some say, millions of the otherwise homeless. For Infinite Lease: quiet, spacious, luminous semi-detached and detached family tombs. Over the years the people of the Toorab organized pirating electricity and telecommunications lines from the city. They opened shops to fix radios and TVs, make mattresses and sell groceries. Laundry fluttered on clothes lines strung between tombstones. Children came home from school to the tombs and played soccer in the wide boulevards beside the decorated domes capping the crypts of forgotten Mamluk nobility. We arrived at a smoking establishment belonging to someone named Ali; a courtyard where ducks and chickens pattered about a small mud puddle beside a beautifully carved alabaster tomb marker. Our host wasted no time in calling one of his girls to serve us.

About fifteen pipes later, having admired Orion's Belt in a silence interrupted only by the chugging of the water pipe for an hour or three, we began our journey back to the living and along the way a taxi sidled up lazily beside us. Samy knew the driver and exchanged pleasantries with him and his passenger. The driver offered us a ride and I was inclined to refuse noting the care-worn condition of the car but Samy insisted they were friends and getting a taxi leaving the City of the Dead could be problematic.

The taxi was a typical black-and-white Russian-assembled Fiat wreck. I had difficulty getting the door to close, but this was not unusual. We cruised through the Dead City and I relaxed, admiring the occasional decaying monument on the way back on the main street where a roundabout is manned by motley traffic cops and today, a carful of police officers. We stopped and for some reason the police officers asked the driver for his papers. This is fairly normal. What was completely nonpareil was the driver's response. He barked something very impolite to the officer, threw the old Fiat into second gear and pulled out posthaste, shifting brusquely to pick up steam. I shared the officer's astonishment since the driver turned back towards the Toorab and was decidedly not going my way.

We were off like a slow-motion torpedo. I objected mildly to the driver's indiscretion and his choice of direction. 'What's going on?' I asked Samy. We'd covered a considerable amount of ground and were still being followed. He turned around casually to look out of the rear window and said, 'It's OK. The police are following us. We will come back later.' I nodded with drug-induced oriental acquiescence. Samy added lamely, 'Don't worry, we're in a taxi,' meaning we were innocent of whatever our conductors were running from.

Suddenly in a gut-wrenching maneuver worthy of a Hollywood stunt driver, our chauffeur pulled off the street, jumped a curb, wheeled giddily around a massive pile of garbage and onto a tomb-lined alley. We had regained the Toorab, familiar territory to our navigator. Although the police followed us in, they slowed down a moment later while we made several quick turns into the maze. Their attempt to nab us was halfhearted at best. Samy explained, 'It is forbidden,' and I supposed he referred to a religious taboo to do with the cemetery. I assumed that the City of the Dead was a holy sanctuary and off-limits to the police.

Amid much thigh-slapping and congratulations we slowed to a halt and the boys jumped out of the car. Cigarettes were exuberantly offered and lit all around. The driver opened the trunk and I discovered the reason for our getaway. I drew back as I saw what appeared to be a body in a shroud. I gathered from the irreverent conversation that I was actually looking at approximately eighty kilos of hashish. I nudged Samy, speechless. 'I told you not to worry,' he said. 'This is a very sacred place.' I said that seemed appropriate, due to the presence of the dead. 'No way,' Samy answered, 'it's because it's where they keep the hashish.'

Nile-Eyes, 2001

Charles Nicholl
The Fruit Palace – 1

'I LEARNED TO cook cocaine in Cali, '68, '69. I learned from a Chilean chemist. The Chileans were the best cooks then. He was selling his secrets. There were others like him coming into Colombia at this time.

'My first kitchen I built myself, up in the hills above the Rio Cauca, near a village called Las Animas – the Spirits. This is in the country of the Gumbianos. These are Indians that chew the coca leaf – well, a lot of them get drunk on *chicha*, but some still use the leaf. There are some *cocales* there, and plenty of coca in the markets. The Gumbianos are good, strong people. Few words, much patience. They prune the coca bush small, about a metre high. They call their bushes *ilyimera*, which in their language means little birds.

'I was the first *blanco* to set up a cocaine kitchen in this area. At first they thought I was crazy. A Gumbiano who chews the leaf perhaps uses half a pound a week. I was going into the markets and buying up four *arrobas* – 100lb of leaves at a time. In those days you could buy an *arroba* of coca for fifty pesos. With good leaves and good chemistry, 100lb of leaves will give you 1lb of cocaine.

'Later I made a deal with a grower and bought the leaves fresh from the *total*. The bright, undried leaves are the best for cooking.'

Mario spoke with slow, gruff precision. The voice was untroubled, but there was always a challenge in his eye. His beard jutted. He sent out jets of smoke through his nostrils like a cartoon bull. There are, he explained, essentially two stages in the 'cooking' of cocaine. *'De coca a pasta, y de pasta a perica.'* From coca leaf to cocaine paste or base, and from cocaine paste to crystalline cocaine. The first is a simple process of extraction, which draws out the all-important vegetable alkaloids from the leaf.

'The cocaine is hiding inside the leaf,' said Mario. 'The *cocinero* must get inside the leaf and fetch out the little bit of cocaine.' His thin hands writhed to gesture this process.

There are many alkaloids in the coca leaf, but only one of them is the psychoactive substance known to organic chemists as benzoyl-methyl-ecgonine, and to the world as cocaine. The second, more complex stage of the cooking is designed to separate the cocaine from the other alkaloids, and to crystallise it into a salt. The coca grown in Colombia and Peru, the trujillo leaf (*Erythroxylon novogranatense*), has a slightly lower proportion of cocaine to other alkaloids than the Bolivian strain, the huanaco leaf (*Erythroxylon coca*).

'To make the *pasta* out of coca leaves is very simple. You need some petrol: kerosene is best. You need a quantity of sulphuric acid, and you need an alkali. For alkali you can use lime or sodium carbonate. I used the simplest of all: *potasa*.' *Potasa*, or potash, is a crude form of potassium carbonate derived from vegetable ash. 'Most of all, you need patience,' he added.

'The first part of the operation is what we call la *salada*, the salting. Here you sprinkle and mix the potash into the leaves. If you are treating a big volume of leaves, you can do this in a pit lined with plastic sheeting. Otherwise you do it in an oil drum or plastic bucket. When you have salted the leaves you let them stand for a few hours. The potash makes them sweat. It starts to melt the alkaloids in the leaf.

'The second part is la *mojadura*, the soaking. This is when we pour the kerosene on to the leaves, drown the coca. You can also put in a bit of dilute sulphuric acid to help break the leaves down. After the soaking you must leave everything to steep for at least a day, better for thirty-six hours. While you wait, the potash is drawing out the alkaloids from the leaf. They float free in the kerosene, which holds them.

'By the end of the second day you are ready to begin *la prensa*, the pressing. If you don't have a press, you use your feet, like they do when they make *chicha*.' (*Chicha* is maize liquor, a traditional *campesino* hooch now officially outlawed in Colombia.) 'The purpose of *la prensa* is to get as much of the kerosene out of the leaves as possible. The kerosene is rich with the alkaloids. The leaves are dead now, black and rotten. You siphon off the kerosene into drums and throw away the leaves.

'The fourth stage is very delicate. This is when we take the alkaloids out of the gasolene and put them in water. This is done by pouring in water and sulphuric acid. Again you leave it, absolutely still, for a day. The acid goes in and takes the alkaloids, and they are dissolved in the water. We call this part of the process *la guaraperia*. At the end you have the kerosene on the top, and the *guarapo* underneath. The *guarapo* is a solution of cocaine and the other alkaloids.' (In ordinary circumstances, *guarapo* is the name of a drink, either a juice or a liquor, made from sugar cane.)

'Into the *guarapo* you pour more potash. This makes the alkaloids precipitate. You see the *guarapo* go milky-white. This is the first time the cocaine becomes visible. If you have some ammonia this is the best for precipitation.

'Now you are ready for the last part of the operation: *la secaderia*, the drying. This is filtering out the precipitate – you can use a sheet – and drying it in the sun or under lightbulbs. You dry it until it is like moist clay. And so you have it: *la pasta de cocaina*!'

So far, so good. You had your cocaine paste, the greenish-grey sludge that is the building block of the whole cocaine racket. This is already a valuable commodity. It can be dried off and sold as *basuko*. It is chemically stable, and can be transported through any climate without damaging its potency. How much it is worth depends on where you stand on the ladder, who you are selling to, and in what quantity.

At today's prices a pound of *pasta* can fetch anything from $500 to $2,000.

But what about the other half of the operation, the turning of *pasta* into pure cocaine, snorter's snow? This is where the real money lies. A good cook can turn that pound of *pasta* into nearly the same weight of cocaine, worth around $5,000 on the Bogota market. Here, however, I was to be disappointed. Perhaps Mario did not consider me worthy to enter this secret inner sanctum of cocaine chemistry. Perhaps I hadn't paid enough. Perhaps he was getting forgetful himself. It was eight years since he'd done any cooking. He had been nearly killed when a carboy of ether exploded in his outhouse laboratory at Las Animas. He showed me the burns on his back, marbled whorls of tissue. The fire had destroyed his materials and, worse, it had burned up most of the money he had saved. He had given up then. One of the big, Cali-based refining groups that began to emerge in the late 1970s offered to set him up with a backstreet kitchen, but he refused. He had been a cook for the love of it, he said, not the money. He was a *mano verde*, an old-style cocaine alchemist. He spat on the mafia, the faceless *peces gordos*, who ran the business now. I tried to wheedle the process out of him, but in the scrawled scraps of my notes from that night I find only broken phrases:

Potassium permanganate: knocks out the inessential alkaloids by oxidisation . . .

Organic solvents: acetone, ether, benzole, toluol. Toluol best, balsam of *tofu*, derived from Caribbean tree . . .

Gas crystals . . .

Hydrochloric acid bonds with cocaine alkaloid to form a crystalline salt. Snorter's snow is cocaine hydrochloride. Sometimes other acids used: cocaine sulphate, oxalate, hypochlorate . . .

Balance. Too much acid, coke will be *agrio*, sour. Too much carbonate, coke will be *jabonoso*, soapy . . .

To the aspiring drug chemist these might mean something. They don't mean much to me, as I'm sure Mario knew. His demeanour was getting uglier. He was tired of my questions.

He threw the information out impatiently He ran a hand over his furrowed brow. I decided it was time to give it a rest. I'd had my fifty quid's worth.

The Fruit Palace, 1985

John Hopkins
Tangier Buzzless Flies

IN THE COURTYARD of the Hotel Splendid Boujma was cutting kif. Seated on a straw hassock before a low wooden table, he began by rubbing the dry kif branches between his hands. The tiny leaves and seeds fell onto a piece of wrapping paper spread out on the table as he discarded the empty stalks one by one.

Next he shook the leaves and seeds onto a wooden cutting board, which he tilted carefully, allowing the seeds to roll down the board as he ran his hand gently over the kif. This process took some time. The seeds were placed in their own piece of wrapping paper and set aside. Now Boujma rested for a minute and took out his own supply of kif and had a smoke. Above his head the banana leaves stirred in the evening breeze. A few feet away the Sultan of Dogs lay in the hole it had dug for itself.

The hotel was quiet, with a few noises filtering in from the street. The pipe finished, Boujma resumed his work. Taking out a pocket knife, he sharpened it carefully against a stone. Separating a portion of the cleaned kif from the main pile, he pressed it firmly down on the board with his fingers and, wielding the knife like a paper cutter, commenced chopping the kif. This is a lengthy procedure, and when the kif had reached the consistency of rough powder, he poured it into a sardine can with a perforated bottom. The sardine can contained a bright Kennedy fifty-cent piece, which he shook together with the kif. The fine kif sifted onto another piece of paper, which Boujma folded over and placed beneath him on the hassock. The kif that had not passed through the perforations was dumped back onto the board to be recut with the next batch. And so, the work went on. When all of the kif had been satisfactorily chopped and sifted, Boujma reached for a wrinkled leaf of tobacco, sprinkled water on it, and began to cut and sift it as he had done the kif. This done, he brought out the kif, which had become a warm flat cake beneath his weight, mixed it with the smaller amount of tobacco, and recut and resifted it all together. The blend had a greenish-brown color, and although Boujma had chopped it very finely, each grain of tobacco and kif was separated from every other.

Now Boujma was stuffing the kif into a goat bladder, which with all the kif inside swelled to the size of a fist. The work completed, he smoothed out the wrapping papers and put them with the sardine can and knife and stone and board into a cupboard. During the whole process not one grain of kif or tobacco, not even one kif seed, had fallen to the ground, and even the barren kif stalks were wrapped carefully before being thrown away.

Tangier Buzzless Flies, 1972

CHAPTER FIVE

CRIMINALISE IT

Howard Marks
Nature Talks

A million centuries ago, plants said 'high' to animals. Roots and seeds seduced tongues and stomachs. Vine, leaf and resin interplayed with hand, heart and mind. Drinking, smelling and sucking were the order, but never the regulations, of the light and the night.

And Nature said, 'Higher.'

A pyramid here and a pyramid there. Gargling, sniffing, smoking, puking and starving for God, Siva and the Sun. Who'll have the booze? Who'll have the blow? Who'll have a line? Who gets the fun?

'I've got the dope. But stick to my brand. Use any other dope, and I'll kill you. Don't do this. Don't do that. That fruity stuff is *verboten*.'

Nature asked, 'Why?'

So pluck yew, and let's smuggle cider into the Garden of Eden. Adam's apples are shite. Eve's cool. SCAM: Some Cocaine Alcohol & Marijuana. But is the Snake in the Grass a grass? Is the slimy serpent a snitch, a snake, a chivato, a turner, a rollover, a stool-pigeon, a squealer, a rat, a traitor, a wrong 'un? Or is he the meaning of her life? Half in heaven, half in hell, half a double helix, denying his deity, demanding her DNA.

Help me, you murderous priests, you psychopathic megalomaniacs, you bloodthirsty colonialist rapists, you sadistic puritans, you non-inhalers. Help me, you manifestations of sinister and pure evil. Why have you ensured that my chemically induced changes of mind are rewarded by imprisonment and other socially acceptable forms of torture? You'll do your bird in time.

Nature said, 'Try.'

How can we get the leaves we want, the herbs we want, the grapes we want.

Nature said, 'Lie.'

And it came to pass that the world became full of scammers. Never before have so many laws been broken without a single pang of conscience. False names, forged passports, phoney driving licences, money-laundering, tax evasion, customs dodging, stolen vehicles, illegal planes, false documents, lies, lies and lots more new lies. Who cares? It's all for the cause. It's not our fault they won't let people get high. Anyway, the world of international dope dealing is fun. It's fucking great!

Beware of the weak, for the strong can take care of themselves
Kakuji Inagawa

Robert Sabbag
Smokescreen – 1

ONE OF THE distinguishing features of the marijuana business, as pursued by Americans like Allen Long – one of the attributes that distinguished the marijuana business from other fields of criminal endeavor – was a conspicuous and, to those who thought about it, rather consoling absence of gunplay. This can be explained by the fact that, for many of the industry's pioneers, the marijuana came first, in both time as well as importance. The industry was created by pot smokers, a casual brotherhood of aficionados, loosely associated, relatively young, usually stoned, united around little more than a near-religious passion for the noble weed. A characteristically (and understandably) merry band of outlaws, who pledged at least passing allegiance to the values of the counterculture to which they and their customers belonged – 'Peace and Love' being prominent among them – these people were accomplished pot smokers long before they were professional criminals. Prohibition would have gone down pretty much the same way if alcohol had been new in the roaring twenties and Al Capone had been one of a loose affiliation of drunks who had discovered bootleg whiskey in college.

The final briefing took place in a motel room in northern Virginia about ten miles from CIA headquarters. While Hathaway handed out copies of his booklets, Long read aloud from a list he had prepared. It had been decided that public relations would be well served if the Americans landed in Colombia not only carrying the money they owed, but also bearing gifts. Loaded onto the plane with the $6,000 in cash, he announced, would be Levi jeans, Nik Nik brand polyester shirts, Adidas running shoes (what seemed to Myerson to be sufficient supply to outfit the entire Indian population of the Guajira), four cases of Heineken, a case of Marlboro and a gross of Swiss Army knives.

This variation on the American CARE package, which seemed like a good idea at the time, would set a regrettable precedent, leading to ever longer lists of requests on the part of its Colombian recipients. Subsequent flights would carry patent medicines, tape players and Seiko wristwatches. On one flight down Long carried a twenty-three-hundred-dollar gold Pulsar watch to be presented to the commander of the local military garrison. A later flight arrived in Colombia carrying a seventeen-foot inflatable Zodiac with a seventy-horsepower Johnson outboard. Still another carried a brace of pedigree German-shepherd puppies.

It was flights such as these and those of other smugglers that accounted for the proliferation on the Guajira of the

Sony Trinitron as a status symbol – in homes which received no television signal and many of which enjoyed no electricity. Within three years of Long's arrival, one could visit the most humble adobe in the smallest of villages there, cut off from power and running water, and find the latest in high-end audio equipment stacked steep against a wall inside and a late model four-by-four, its high-gloss paint reflecting the sunshine, parked on the hardscrabble outside. Within that time, impoverished local Indians would come to occupy dwellings assembled with parts salvaged from out-of-commission airplanes, a wing here, part of a fuselage there, a tail number over the door. (On a trip to Perico in 1979, an elder of the nearby village reintroduced Long to his DC-3, the nose cone, complete with windshield glass, serving as a makeshift solarium on his humble sheet-metal home.) By then, with America's appetite for dope as well established as its appetite for coffee, Colombia would account for more than 70 percent of the marijuana reaching the United States from abroad, and between 30,000 and 50,000 farmers along the coast would have come to depend directly on its cultivation for their livelihood. Another 50,000 Colombians would make a living from it. Local food production would decline as tens of thousands of hectares were converted to marijuana farming, producing unprecedented prosperity and a degree of economic stability never before enjoyed on the Guajira.

The plane entered the United States in daylight, at about five in the afternoon, with all the air traffic from the Bahamas. On radar screens that were lit up like the Milky Way, it showed up as just one more aircraft, an unidentified blip. It entered US airspace not at 25,000 feet, not at 300 feet, but at 5,000 like all the others. It came in at Palm Beach, Florida, but its crew, unlike those of other flights, would not report to customs upon landing.

Coming out of the Bahamas, homing in on the Palm Beach directional beacon, Hatfield had known that within fifty miles of the Florida coast he was going to get a call from air-traffic control instructing him to switch on his radar transponder.

They had been calling for half an hour when Hatfield flew directly *over* the airport. He could not have been more conspicuous had he come in upside down.

'Unidentified aircraft, you are requested . . .'

The smugglers maintained radio silence.

'Please turn on your transponder and switch to . . .'

They did none of it. The tower ordered them to land.

'. . . execute a turn to the south, descend to twenty-one hundred feet and prepare to . . .'

They just kept flying.

'Please announce your intentions . . .'

They were overloaded, fighting a slight headwind, and Long, who spent no measurable stretch of the trip not stoned, had become fascinated by the movement of automobile traffic below. The cocaine, acting chiefly as a motor drug, did not interfere with the immaculate marijuana buzz he managed to maintain. He took note of the fact that many motorists were in fact traveling faster than he. The plane had been holding even with one red car that continued to occupy his attention until, finally overtaking the DC-3, it disappeared out of sight.

Hatfield climbed to 12,000 feet, picked up an airway, and headed northwest, pushing through central Florida. They were sucking oxygen again, and the cockpit was cold, when, over Lake Okeechobee, Long took the left seat, relieving Hatfield, who needed to rest up for the landing later that night. Exhausted now by twenty-four hours of flying, Hatfield, unlike his second officer, had not been shoveling cocaine for the past eight.

The plane was on a heading for north Georgia, where the Blue Ridge and the Great Smoky Mountains converge. The smugglers planned to disappear from radar for a while, running in and out of the valleys there, and check to see if anyone was following, before swinging around to Darlington. They were about fifty air miles north of the Everglades when in the top-left quadrant of the windshield they picked up a massive storm front coming their way.

'What do you think?' said Long.

'Hey, Frank?'

'Where are we?' said Hatfield, leaning into the cockpit.

'I think I saw Sebring back there,' McBride said.

'Give me the map.'

Moving southeast, and moving fast, the thunderstorm presented the DC-3 with fewer options than enjoyed by other aircraft. The storm was too heavy, it was carrying too much turbulence, to go through or attempt to go under, and the DC-3, with a service ceiling of about 20,000 feet, was unable by design to achieve the necessary altitude to go over it. Going east would get the smugglers safely around the formation, but constituted a collateral risk Hatfield was unwilling to take. Advancing in that direction, the storm could *very* well push them back out over the Atlantic.

'We can't gamble that kind of fuel,' he said.

And there, even with sufficient fuel, they would have to beat the US border a second time. The odds on doing so were not prohibitive, but considering that and considering what the move might cost them in fuel, Hatfield figured why go up against the percentages. To circumnavigate the storm, the smugglers took the better odds, choosing the only course left to them. They went west, into the clear sky over Tampa. And into the restricted military airspace surrounding MacDill Air Force Base.

'Cool,' said Long.

'Wake me when it's over.'

Allen Long's equanimity at this point in the trip could be explained quite conveniently by the parts-per-milliliter of dope in his blood. But viewing it that way would ignore the very elements of his personality that accounted for his being where he was in the first place. The trip was far from over, the deal was far from done. With Reed in charge of the ground crew, there was reason to be confident that the offload would go smoothly, but as source of potential danger it still could not be ignored. All that lay between Darlington and Ann Arbor, not to mention what still lay between Florida and Darlington, could be evaluated quite rationally in the light of how much could go wrong. And yet, as he sailed around the thunderstorm, Allen Long was way past worrying about anything. Whatever is gonna happen is gonna happen, he reasoned. Now he was just having fun.

If one examines the overworked principle that cops and criminals are flip sides of the same constitutional coin, one might arrive at an appreciation, if only superficial, of Long's nonchalance. The average well-adjusted individual is programmed by nature to recoil from danger, to avoid it, and, failing that, to flee. Cops are trained to run in its direction. Their fitness reports, like those of firemen and military officers, measure their ability and their eagerness to do so. Their careers thrive on confrontation and their willingness to initiate it. Allen Long and other outlaws come by this trait not by formal training, but by a combination of natural temperament and experience. Crime's rewards reinforce their antisocial behavior. The syndrome sometimes expresses itself as an addiction to action. J.D. Reed described himself as an 'adrenalin junkie,' and readily admitted that in the absence of confrontation, he felt the need to scare it up: 'I got to go wrestle a mule or have somethin' thrown at me to keep that life going.'

There is nothing particularly profound in this. It is nothing new, or even strikingly novel, and it is not unique to outlaws. The same character trait can be found in a variety of law-abiding soldiers of fortune and, to one degree or another, in the typical downhill skier. It is a quality that propels certain people to become cops and firemen in the first place. Indeed, in Allen Long's case it was one of the more innocent manifestations of a psychological profile the darker side of which revealed itself in other ways. But it helps explain why in the air over Florida, facing a constellation of negative prospects, probably the least of which was a prison stretch, Long could ignore everything but the up-side of the proposition and all the fun he was having. He was high on reefer and luxuriating in an almost unlimited supply of coke, he had an oxygen hose stuck in the left side of his mouth, a cigarette stuck in the other, he was holding a Heineken between his legs, he was flying that airplane and he was having the time of his life.

That is what makes guys like Allen Long different from you.

'Hey, what do you think those are?' he said, turning to McBride.

He directed the co-pilot's attention to four black dots, appearing like pencil points in the distance, forming a diamond in the sunlight off to the west. In the time it took Long to turn his head back, the fighter jets had closed the gap, coming in on the smugglers at about 200 knots. They made a deafening pass over the DC-3, roughing it up. Air Force F-4 Phantom jets. The cockpit shook as the tactical fighters roared by, the explosion of jet wash, hitting the fuselage, rocking in with the shock of a breaking wave.

'Hmm,' said McBride, 'were you speeding?'

The fighters came back around, and the formation pulled alongside.

'License and registration.'

A traffic stop in the wild blue yonder.

Throwing on all the brakes – gear down, flaps down, flying at a high angle of attack – the Air Force pilots were unable to slow their craft sufficiently to pace the DC-3 for more than seconds at a time. One of the fliers, hanging on the edge of the stall envelope, holding for as long as he could on the smugglers' left wing, looked Long and McBride over and checked out the cockpit. The weapons system officer, flying rear seat, tapped the edge of his helmet, over his ear, signaling Long to get on the radio.

Long raised his mike with a shrug and a series of idiotic gestures understood by international standard to mean: 'Radio's busted.'

Total platform kill. Sorry, man.

Over the cockpit radio the smugglers heard MacDill tower trying to raise them on the override frequency.

'. . . Douglas eight-six-four . . . ordered to exit military . . .'

The tower eventually gave up. And then, over their UHF receiver, the smugglers heard the F-4 reporting to MacDill.

'Looks like just another smuggler to me. And this is not our business. Tango flight is departing the area.'

No threat to national security, just some dumb, severely stoned citizens flying a planeload of drugs. The F-4 pilots raised their gear, hit the burners and were gone.

Long raised his Heineken in a farewell salute: 'God bless America.'

'The arsenal of democracy,' volunteered McBride.

'Let's have some more of that coke.'

Just before sunset, as the shadows below were lengthening and house lights were switching on, Hatfield took over. Running up the Smoky Mountain valleys, he dropped the aircraft to 1,000 feet, and disappeared from radar for a while. They were about five hours from touchdown when darkness fell, and the plane came out of the mountains dying with no lights. All three men were exhausted. It was time to shave and clean up. At some point the pilots would have to step off the plane to face the personnel of some general aviation facility. By then the plane itself would have to be cleaned up. There was still a lot of work to do.

The DC-3's extended range, thanks to the auxiliary tanks, was of significant advantage to the smugglers, enabling them as it did to land as far north as Virginia and the Carolinas. The distance between Colombia and the US border was a good piece of what put so much heat on Florida. And made Darlington such a good bet.

They were a hundred miles out when they raised J.D. Reed on the radio. He and Long, over an air-to-air frequency, gave the impression of two pilots shooting the breeze, Long transmitting not from Douglas 86459, but Cessna 4603 Zulu, on a putative flight from Hilton Head to Spartanburg.

'Yeah, we can see you over there, what are you flying?' said Long.

'This is Piper Cherokee four-six-seven-three India,' responded Reed, transmitting from the dragstrip. 'I see your lights. You at about eight-thousand?'

'I'm at eighty-six hundred, descending into Spartanburg now. Golfing was neat at Hilton Head. Are you the guy that operates the fleet of planes out of Middleburg, Virginia?'

'Affirmative,' said Reed.

'What was the weather like over Spartanburg?'

'Everything was just fine, you're going to have a fine landing, shouldn't be any problems.'

'Fine. That's an A on that then?'

'Yes,' Reed said. 'That's an A. I'd give conditions there an A.' Meaning Darlington, coded Landing Site A, was secure.

Hatfield navigated visually, carefully studying the landmarks below. As he closed in on the dragstrip, he started looking for a signal.

'I hear you. Yeah, I see your lights,' said Reed. 'I sure can. I see your lights. Can you see mine?'

The headlights on the pickup trucks flashed at the end of the dragstrip. Hatfield in response flashed the landing lights of the DC-3. Hatfield buzzed the runway, came back around to land, and Long was working the cargo doors when the airplane hit the ground. The trucks pulled up, Reed secured the hatches and Long started throwing bales. McBride, eager to be airborne, stepped back into the cargo bay and heaved bales along the fuselage, throwing them in the direction of the door. It was then, as the rhythm picked up, that one of Reed's crew, a guy named Billy, took a bale in the side of the head, momentarily knocking him cold. Reed, without missing a beat, picked the unconscious crewman up and threw him into the back of the truck along with the cargo as if he were one of the bales. 'Don't say it.' 'I wasn't going to say it.' 'Yes you were,' said Reed. 'I could tell.' 'I wasn't,' said Long. 'Yes you were.' 'Can I say it later?' 'I'll think about it.' After a quick consultation with the pilots, in which McBride confirmed that he could clear up the Visqueen by himself, Long decided that there was no need for him to go on with the airplane. The DC-3 took off without him. The plane lifted off in one direction and the trucks took off in the other. Before jumping aboard the blue Chevy Suburban in which they would follow the pot to Ann Arbor, Long and Reed, both patting themselves down for a match, looked at each other and simultaneously asked: 'Got a joint?'

EPILOGUE

There are three ways out of the dope business, the most dramatic of which will always be dying on the job. Of the other two, quitting while you are ahead or going to jail, the second is by far the more common. Those who have chosen the former – you have eaten in their restaurants, worn their sportswear, listened to music on their record labels, or maybe you have rented their real estate – are admittedly difficult to count. Those who have suffered the latter – they and their customers – have provided fifty percent of the population of the nation's prisons over the last decade.

Smokescreen by Robert Sabbag, first published in Great Britain by
Canongate Books, February 2002

But it is pretty to see what money will do
Samuel Pepys

Ed Dwyer and Robert Singer
Tom Forcade on Smuggling

THOMAS KING FORCADE died by his own hand one year ago. Although he had set aside a promising career in marijuana importing to establish and build *High Times* magazine, he never ceased to perfect his skills in the business that remained his first love. Torn between journalism and smuggling, his twin careers fertilized each other and enabled him to broaden each with an eye trained by his vast experience in the other.

In 1974, Forcade was asked whether starting *High Times* would be an alternative to smuggling dope in the never-ending struggle to turn America on.

'On the contrary,' he replied, 'it'll be a front for it.'

HILIFE: *How did you get started in smuggling?*
FORCADE: Well, I actually got started in high school. I was living in Tucson, Arizona, and I had an advantage over most people who might want to get started in smuggling: I lived fairly near the source of supply.

We all used to get high in high school, and we wanted to get '55 Chevies (this was in the mid-sixties and a '55 Chevy was the thing to have) and it soon occurred to us that we could go down to Mexico and score some dope and run it back across the border, and make some money on it. We could buy it across the border for about $30 a key in those days.

We were very careful. I think we stuffed it up underneath, between the gas tank and the trunk, and drove across with it. Very scared. They searched the whole car but they didn't find anything. So we did it again from time to time. Then we moved on to a larger scale where we would take a sack and throw it across the fence. They have a fence that runs across the border. You just drive up next to the fence, take a sack, swing it a couple of times and toss it over full of grass and pick it up on the other side. Later there was actually a spot in the fence that had a hole in it you could drive through. And then later we got into another place along the border where you could drive across with whole truckloads of marijuana.

HiLife: *What was your first big run?*
FORCADE: The first big one was when we brought a planeload across.

HiLife: *This side of the border?*
FORCADE: Yeah. What they did was, they flew over, and they dropped it out of the plane. Unfortunately, we never found part of the dope. Part of it fell on the highway; some car came along, found it, picked it up and took it in. It was in the newspaper the next day, how they found this dope. (We were very paranoid about it, that they might have found our fingerprints on the wrappers or something, but nothing ever happened.)

Later, in subsequent reenactments of this same style we lost full loads on the desert. (It may still be sitting out there, you know, 'the treasure of the Sierra Madre' or something. It might be a little dry by now.)

One time the plane landed and we were surrounded by cops. Everybody got away except one person who was nabbed and of course took the rap for everybody. It was small-scale; in retrospect it was incredibly disorganized and foolish. But that was when we got on to what I would call a professional level. That was around '68.

HiLife: *And at that point were you flying?*

FORCADE: I did fly some then, but I could usually find someone else to do it. I'm more of a professional kingpin than a technician in these things. I have other people to do the hard parts and dangerous parts. But once, this person suddenly couldn't make it. We'd already bought the weed down in Mexico, and it was my money backing the operation, so I had no choice but to do it myself.

I'd been over the route in the daytime, but I'd never flown it at night. At night you're looking for lights and the silhouettes of mountains, and you're flying by the moon, by the stars and so on, whereas by the day, you just follow the highway or the railroad tracks. Contrary to popular belief, you don't use things like compasses and stuff like that. Too complicated. We don't use them that much.

HiLife: *Do you have a pilot's license?*

FORCADE: Not only do I have a pilot's license, but I have dozens of pilot's licenses. I have about 300 hours in the air, but all the licenses that I have are phoney.

HiLife: *How much money . . .*

FORCADE: On that particular run? About $25,000. But aren't you going to ask me why it was so hair-raising? Funny you should ask me. Well, I was flying alone and got lost because, as I said, I'd never been down there at night before. They had the place lit up with bonfires and so on, so I landed, but it wasn't the smuggling place where I was supposed to be. It was some other smugglers' landing strip. They were quite upset. They had machine guns on me. They thought maybe I was a narc or something. They were expecting another type of plane and another person, and another code word and everything, and I was having quite a bit of trouble explaining myself. Also, I was out of gas.

So, what I did was, I convinced these people that, quite honestly, no one would be flying around in Mexico in the middle of the night and landing in a bonfire-lit dirt strip in the mountains unless they were also smugglers. So I parked my plane there overnight and I gave those people quite a bit of money. And their plane came in, picked up their weed, and flew out. And the next morning, I got down to a phone, called up my connection, and had him set everything for the next night, and that night I flew out to the right place and picked up the weed.

But unfortunately, on the way back up I had quite a bit of trouble because I had run the plane off into a ditch and the propeller had gotten a little bent and it was a little unbalanced, so it was making this very heavy vibration that caused the oil seal in the front of the engine to start leaking and all the oil was leaking out. By the time I got back to the United States the windshield was all covered with oil and I couldn't see, so I had to open the side windows and stick my head out of the side window and I came in that way. The engine was completely shot by then because it has two parts bolted together, and the halves of the crankcase were all vibrated to pieces. We had to put in an entirely new engine.

That type of thing is more or less typical. It seems like nothing ever goes smoothly. I don't know why it is, but there seems to be something about smuggling that causes a very high mortality rate among both the people involved and the equipment involved. You have to have incredible resources and resourcefulness.

HiLife: *Do you prefer smuggling by boat?*
FORCADE: Well, you see, one thing about the air is that they can't pull you over. I mean, there's not much they can do if they see you. On the other hand, in a plane, if your engine stops running you don't just come to a stop in the water like you do on a boat.

Out at sea your chances of getting stopped are about the same as your chances of getting stopped by the highway patrol as you're going down the highway. In other words, not very high, but it is possible, especially if you're doing something wrong or if you look suspicious. Generally, they don't stop anybody. Your chances of even seeing anybody out on the ocean are very small, the same as in the air. But if you see somebody in the air it ain't no big thing because there's not

420

much they can do about it unless they want to chase you down. In the sixties they didn't have anybody to chase you down. The ship thing required a whole different technology, but it was still technology, and I'm good at technology.

HiLife: *And freighters . . .*
FORCADE: Yeah, freighters are a very common way for dope to make it up now because the runs are getting bigger and bigger, and a two-hundred-foot freighter can obviously bring up a lot more dope than a forty-foot sailboat. They rendezvous offshore outside the twelve-mile limit. And hopefully, you meet up with them.

I must note in passing that every means I'm discussing here is very well known to the DA, and the newspapers are filled with accounts of various ways that smuggling takes place and gets busted, so I'm not blowing anything for anybody. The DA is quite aware of how dope gets in. They're also quite aware that they have almost no chance of stopping it. You rendezvous offshore with these boats in a fast speedboat.

HiLife: *Do they have the capacity to outrun a modern coast guard . . .?*
FORCADE: Well, the coast guard cutter things make about twenty-five knots or so, maybe more. And a freighter can make maybe ten or twelve knots. But a good smuggling operation usually has four or five thirty-foot boats, usually with two engines, American V-8 engines. One of these boats can make fifty or sixty miles an hour even in fairly rough weather, can outrun anything the coast guard has and can carry a ton or so. It draws maybe two and a half to three feet, and gets over waters that the coast guard can't get over, a lot of shoals and reefs and stuff down in Florida. A boat that doesn't draw very much is quite advantageous in getting near the shore and getting to the off-loading spots that would not be considered viable by the coast guard and are therefore not watched. And you've got to learn how to run these boats, be ready to outrun the coast guard if necessary. We've done it.

HiLife: *Have you ever considered smuggling with a submarine?*
FORCADE: I've heard of a couple of fairly well-documented cases of submarines being used, but it would seem to me that because of the unique noises that are given off by submarines and the fact that the US government spent billions wiring the whole ocean, supposedly to keep track of every submarine in the world, that a submarine would be the most dangerous way possible to smuggle. The minute you set out you would be being tracked by every navy electronic sonar device possible. Also, a submarine takes a lot of knowledge to run, and where do you get parts for it?

HiLife: *Does the idea of a blimp appeal to you?*
FORCADE: You know, I think if you had the ability to get together a blimp you wouldn't get into smuggling. The blimp field is so promising.

These are the kind of conversations you can get into on stoned evenings. They're a lot of fun, but they're rarely productive. The best ways are the most straightforward ways. When you're sitting around scanning these things out, all kinds of James Bondian ideas come forth, but when it gets down to the reality of it, the simplest and most straightforward way is usually the best and the way that attracts the least attention. Also, pouring gasoline on the water and lighting it like James Bond doesn't work either.

HiLife: *How do you know that?*
FORCADE: They tried it during prohibition. Being the systematic type of person that I am, I have made a thorough study of the literature of prohibition smuggling, slave smuggling, and all other types of smuggling, and they used to do it. The Italian and Irish smugglers of the twenties and thirties were about as crazy and as foolish (and in their case drunk, in our case stoned), and the fact that they would try things didn't mean that they would work.

HiLife: *What is the simplest way?*
FORCADE: I think the most common way is to pay someone off down in Colombia so you can load it up right on the dock, or

come in close at night and load it up off smaller boats. Some people are very happy to smuggle five hundred pounds hidden inside the hull of a sailboat, or load a sailboat down with five tons, and other people don't really feel like it's worth doing unless they bring in twenty-five tons on a freighter. I think twenty-five tons is a bit much to load off of small boats. At that point it becomes worthwhile and more practical to pay off someone at a dock. But if you don't know a place where you can pay off a dock, you do it at night. People who know about planes tend to plane things from Colombia.

At this end, when it gets up to twenty-five tons or so, you get to the point where you have forklift trucks and trucks with hydraulic tailgates and conveyor belts and so on and so forth. This is what we have now. We don't use this all the time, but it's available. A forklift truck is very expensive, but, like, one trip pays for it and you can just keep it in the warehouse and use it when you need it.

HiLife: *When you actually make your runs, is there any opportunity or any effort to have quality control?*
FORCADE: I think that when you get up into mass quantities it's very difficult to have much control over the quality, because it's enough to get twenty-five tons. If you know the province you get it from and the connection you get it from, you know they'll be farmers who are geographically located in a place that's producing better marijuana. I've done high-quality runs, where we were going down to specifically get the very best gold or wacky weed or something like that, but very high-quality dope is very perishable and can often become garbage by the time it gets up here.

HiLife: *About how many people are involved in your average run?*
FORCADE: We might have about twenty people or so. I mean, let's say you're unloading five tons or so; that's a lot of work. You don't want it to take hours and hours. You need five or ten people to quickly unload a boat. You don't want to have so many people that you can't keep track of them. It depends on the operation.

HiLife: *What's the scale of payment?*

FORCADE: Well, I would say it depends on the deal you have with your suppliers. If you finance it in advance, you can buy it in the field and you can get it much cheaper, but then it might get busted in the field, it might get busted on its way down, or it might get ripped off and so on. Usually, the more profit you're in a position to make, the higher risk you take, so the scale of payment varies. But I would say a captain gets like maybe $50,000 and up, a crewmember gets $25,000 and up, a handler gets a few thousand dollars. The prices are very high for the amount of work being done, but, of course, the time you're facing is quite a bit.

HiLife: *How do you get the people?*

FORCADE: First of all, you have to know them for a long time. I think five years is a good time period, the industry standard, but I would say one year is a minimum no matter how together they are. Somebody's got to have known them for one year. Somebody that you trust.

Second, they have to be cool; they have to be discreet. They can't brag to their girlfriends; they can't brag to their buddies. They can't run off at the mouth in bars because the word gets around, and they can't give interviews to magazines.

This is a real problem because anyone who's doing something desires recognition, and you seek the esteem of your friends. If you're a smuggler, people say 'What do you do?' and you don't want to say you work in a gas station. The tendency is to impress your friends. I mean, it's a very chic thing, a very glamorous thing to do, and the tendency is to tell them and ask them to keep quiet. But of course, they don't keep quiet either. You go over to their house, sit around and get high with them, and after you leave they whisper to their friends.

The other part of being cool is to have the nerve to do it, and this is a hard thing to judge. Sometimes you make a practice run somewhere and see how everybody gets along. Some people can't hack it, they don't work well together, and ego conflicts develop. When the pressure's on the ego conflicts multiply a hundredfold and everyone's armed, and you don't want people whipping out guns on each other in the midst of a heavy run because it's very disruptive and unpleasant. But usually, by the time you get to a smuggling run you've already been through some hairy things together. I mean, usually you work somebody up, you don't take them right into a run. If they do well as a lookout, or as a transporter, or as a loader or something like that, you can use them in a more critical role. But you can never really tell for sure because people who seem really together will suddenly crack, and people that you would never expect to have the moxie to keep it together turn out to be silver-star winners when the chips are down.

I think that someone running a dope operation is a sort of minor guru, or even a major guru, a charismatic figure. I think, generally, the nature of a smuggling operation is closer to that of a Far Eastern religion than it is to a corporation. There's a guru (who provides the spiritual strength) and his followers. Everyone down below is going on faith. They have to believe in the person at the top because everything you've ever been taught, everything you read in the papers, every rumour, story, anecdote and so on that comes along is a deterrent to smuggling. You have to consciously psych yourself up to think that you can make it. The paranoia in a smuggling run is extremely thick, and it's like sand in the machinery. You don't know at the time whether it's psychological warfare or real warfare. But mostly it's psychological warfare, and it's psychological warfare that's very effective.

The value of a bust is 10 percent to take those people off the set temporarily, and the other 90 percent is to scare other people out of it.

HiLife: *What makes people transcend the fear?*

FORCADE: Money motivates people to be there. But the choice to be in smuggling is not made because of the money; it's due to other factors which are social and psychological in nature. I think that people who go into smuggling are for the most part social misfits and non-conformists, antisocial people.

HiLife: *Smugglers are antisocial?*

FORCADE: They're not compliant to society's rules. They're

opposed to society, they're viruses in society. I know that this sounds something like the government's own view, but after ten years, I've concluded that this is true. I don't think it's bad. I think it's very good. I think that bringing in dope is very socially valuable, and I believe the other people who are involved in it feel the same way. The middle-class smuggler has a very keen sense of the social value of what he's doing, that it's something very worthwhile. But the money is the bottom line motivation to overcome the paranoia.

HiLife: *Can money buy protection from arrest?*

FORCADE: There are so many young people getting high in the coast guard that there are many good opportunities to buy somebody off. Sometimes they'll even do it for free. But on the other hand, some people who will tip you off on a marijuana thing can't be bought on a coke thing. It's a lot more serious. For myself, I've dabbled a little in cocaine, but the overall level of paranoia is so extremely high that I prefer to stay away from it. Once you get it in you still have to sell it, and if anybody down the line gets busted that bust is going to domino right back up to you. Everyone down the line may crack because the penalties are so great. With marijuana the penalties aren't that great, the stigma isn't great, the pressure isn't that great and it just tends to stop at the point where the person gets busted. With cocaine, the guy who gets busted with a gram may knock it all the way back to the guy who brought in ten pounds.

HiLife: *We've heard rumors of smugglers warehousing.*

FORCADE: This is an old story, and I can understand how the average American consumer with a quite legitimate paranoia about big business would be concerned about this. But the reality is that big quantities of dope have a tendency to get busted and if there's one thing a smuggler or a ton dealer wants, it's to get rid of this stuff and convert it to cash as quickly as possible. Marijuana smugglers, dealers, will stay up two or three nights just to get rid of it. I think that ton dealers and smugglers are subject to a lot of nervous breakdowns just because they're worrying about having a million dollars' worth of marijuana sitting in a garage or warehouse where a curious mailman, or a guy coming to check the water meter, or an accidental fire, or a nosy neighbour or anything like that could blow a million dollars. One would want to get rid of it as quickly as possible. Whether you're talking about the country of origin or the United States, absolutely nobody would warehouse it for a minute longer than possible, and I'd say generally the time from entry into this country to being sold to the consumers is almost always less than a month.

HiLIFE: *I've heard stories of smugglers who have gambled away much of their fortunes sitting around with their friends, snorting lots of cocaine and playing poker for days on end.*
FORCADE: I've been to a few of these gatherings, but one of the reasons I've survived is that I'm more conservative than some of these people. These people are like meteors, skyrockets; you know, they come fast and they go fast. They have short, happy lives. I'm not like that. I come in contact with people like that, but when it all comes down, it's very depressing. It's a real occupational hazard for smugglers because they have access to large amounts of very pure cocaine. Most people would never be able to develop the kind of usage patterns a wealthy smuggler could develop; they couldn't afford it; they couldn't get access to that level of quality.

HiLIFE: *Do you think doing marijuana leads to doing cocaine?*
FORCADE: No. It's two different value systems, two different worlds. There's a tendency among smugglers and marijuana dealers to stay away from it, because it's a lot of additional heat.

HiLIFE: *Do you get high when you're making a run?*
FORCADE: Yeah, you get very high. One thing about marijuana, you know, is that it's calming and it's good to smoke marijuana and keep mellow. I also think that when you're doing a run, there's a certain psychological satisfaction to smoking the dope that you're importing. It's sort of an impetus to go on with it. There's nothing more satisfying than

smoking dope that you have smuggled in yourself. Nothing gets you higher.

But sometimes you're wired so high that you can smoke a lot of marijuana and not feel much at all. The adrenalin in your blood is so extremely high it really doesn't affect you, and you smoke it more out of habit than anything else.

You know, if you're really good at smuggling you can make far more money than Mick Jagger can make. The strange thing about it is, the bigger you are, and the heavier you are, the less known you are. So it's sort of like you're the mirror image of a successful pop figure like a novelist, rock star, or sports figure. Just like a rock star gets a kick out of turning on the radio in his car and hearing one of his songs being played, a smuggler gets a kick out of going over to some friend's house and lighting up some dope and realizing that through seven hands he's now smoking the same dope that he smuggled in two months ago. You know your dope; you recognize your own dope.

HiLife: *Have you ever smoked dope with a narc?*
FORCADE: Yeah, a couple of times, unfortunately.

HiLife: *Did you enjoy getting high with him?*
FORCADE: In retrospect, no. It was extremely unpleasant to think that I had been, you know, in their presence and at ease and really conversing with them and being, as I found out later, tape-recorded by them.

HiLife: *Oh, you didn't know they were narcs at the time?*
FORCADE: Oh, no. You mean knowingly with a narc? No. I would never pal around with such people. Some people think that you can outsmart them, but I would never be chummy with them because they don't have to be smarter than you to bust you. They are also very inclined to grossly distort what you might say and do under such circumstances. It's best to stay away from them.

HiLife: *Who is the toughest lawman you ever met?*
FORCADE: I never met the toughest lawman that I ever heard of because I was a little tougher and I managed to evade him.

But I was once involved in a manhunt wherein the police were quite persistent. We had a plane which was spotted coming in and making a landing, and the police moved into the area, surrounded the plane and swooped in. We went off into the desert and hid out for about a week.

HiLife: *What's the most amount of bail you ever put up?*
FORCADE: $100,000 per person for five people.

HiLife: *Any of them jump bond?*
FORCADE: Yeah, all of them jumped bond. Occasionally that's what you have to do. I never let anybody rot in jail. Nobody's ever been abandoned in anything I've been involved with.

HiLife: *Did you ever break out of a jail?*
FORCADE: Yeah. I've broken out of jail. I've broken other people out of jail.

HiLife: *What was your most dramatic jailbreak?*
FORCADE: Some friends of mine were transporting some dope in the southwest, and they got nabbed in Texas in a small town. They got pulled over for a traffic violation, and they searched the truck and found a thousand pounds of marijuana. Naturally there was a car following the truck to make sure nothing happened. They saw the truck get busted and so an operation was mounted. There were two guys. We were able to bail one guy out because he didn't have any previous arrests, but the other person had some previous raps that he had jumped bail on, so they were holding him. He pretended to get sick and they put him in the local county hospital and chained him to the bed with handcuffs. We went in, pretending to be visitors, and sawed the chains and the handcuffs and brought him clothes and he walked out with us.

HiLife: *What was the largest bribe you ever paid?*
FORCADE: $10,000. I've also given them my own guns, my watch, my passport. In one case we gave them our plane – not voluntarily, but, you know, you give them anything they want. Once you get back to the States you can always make it back.

HiLife: *Any suggestions to someone who finds themselves in a foreign prison?*

FORCADE: Don't expect any justice, you know. Get somebody to buy out. Don't be a wise ass either. You're in serious trouble once you fall into the hands of the authorities. Proclaiming your rights and stuff is very irrelevant to these people. Buy your way out, if possible. Get to someone with political power.

HiLife: *Have you ever seen anyone tortured by DEA agents in foreign prisons?*

FORCADE: I've heard of this happening, but it's never happened to me. In smuggling circles there are stories of DEA agents shooting down planes, of planes being shot down in the course of smuggling, of people caught in the process of smuggling being executed summarily, down on the other end. They don't do it up here, but down there they feel fairly free to pull a lot of shit that they would never dream of doing inside the United States.

HiLife: *What do you think will happen to you if dope is decriminalized?*

FORCADE: Decriminalization would make my business better than ever. But legalization, I don't know. But smugglers tend to be very international by nature, and although there may be legalization in some countries there won't be in others. Marijuana use is spreading very widely. People have a greater need for psychological stimulation and mind expansion, and the worldwide appetite is growing.

If wheat was brought into this country the same way that marijuana is brought in, the price of bread would be very high. And in the future our economy won't be able to support this kind of economic waste. If 20 percent of our imports were taken out to the city dump and burned under armed guard as they do with one-fifth of the marijuana, our country would be in even worse economic shape than it is now. As our balance of payments gets worse and our dollar gets devalued, the cost of doing this is going to be more and more.

HiLife: *Have you ever flown or taken a boatload of your stuff across the Bermuda Triangle?*
FORCADE: It's a weird area, there's no question about it. You're sailing along one minute and everything is groovy, and the next minute you're upside down.

HiLife: *Do you believe in an afterlife?*
FORCADE: I hope to come back as a marijuana plant, over and over and over again.

HiLife: *Have you ever deliberately sold bad dope and made an immoral profit?*
FORCADE: I've sold a lot of bad dope, but that's because it's so hard to take it back. But I've also been involved in actually smuggling dope back across the border because it was so bad. In Mexico. You don't do this with Colombian. Although we've actually sent back boatloads of Colombian dope that was bad. It occasionally happens, but it's very rare. If you send back a boatload of Colombian right off a freight it's going to take a lot of smoothing over with the connection. But bad dope moves so much more slowly. Everyone's more dissatisfied. You may not get your money back. It leaves a bad feeling all the way along the line, whereas good dope melts away instantaneously. I've had to sell it. I felt bad about it, but it still gets you high and no one is being forced to buy it. It's a pretty open market and people apparently found it more desirable than the alternative, which is no dope at all or more expensive dope. To some extent you're measured by the quality of dope you smoke, so people are loath to have bad dope. But it still gets you high, you know, and that is what it's about, isn't it? Isn't that more important than the false ego consideration?

HiLife: *Have you had much trouble with organized marijuana-smuggling syndicates that make huge payoffs at high levels in order to bring in huge amounts of very mediocre dope?*
FORCADE: I've encountered these people's representatives down in Colombia paying bribes and I've been aware of their operations up here, but hopefully one would no more

cross these people than one would cross the police. It's sort of like the same thing. I think that on a few occasions we fell foul of these people at the other end and they fingered us. It's more a phenomenon you see at the other end than at this end, but we lost dope as a result. But it's certainly a factor. They don't like what we're doing because our dope is better and usually cheaper for its quality, so we tend to undermine the market a bit. But it's such a wide open market that it's not that much a factor. The problem is that since the government's paid off not to touch the big guys, they're then free to bust the little guys. That's the nature of government corruption.

HiLife: *Did you find it necessary to take extreme measures?*
FORCADE: I can afford to drop $10,000 on somebody and lose it. I'm not going to turn a $10,000 debt into a murder rap. I'm not into dropping bodies in the bay and stuff. Other people who are more bitter and can afford such losses less will catch up with those people soon enough and I'm always happy to pass along their address. I think that when you're in a scene like this you're protected by your circle of friends; they're your wall against the outside world. And if no one cares that you get busted you're in bad shape and if you've been so unrighteous that people want you to get busted, it won't be long before you will get busted or killed.

HiLife: *Does this mean that there's a chance a smuggler such as you might find it expedient to snitch on somebody at some time?*
FORCADE: You mean, if someone's a rat, do you drop a dime on them? Yeah, I've heard of that. I've heard of people being fingered, because they were rotten people and they had done terrible things and they betrayed the trust of everyone around them and they deserved to be taken off the set and the police were the best people to do it. But usually one avoids this because the rotten person, once they get in jail, will then turn around and finger everyone they know.

I think I've gotten this far and I've stayed out of jail this long because I try to be as honest as possible. I mean, by the standards of the industry I'm very honest. I wouldn't claim to be 100 percent honest. That would be dishonest.

HiLife: *Have you always wanted to see just how much you could get away with?*
FORCADE: In smuggling circles, to some extent one's prestige is based on the amount of marijuana that one has brought in, or is bringing in, or is involved with. But there's also a tendency to keep going and going until you get caught, until you get hit so hard that you're just knocked out real good. You get addicted to the rush of doing it. Smuggling is addictive, definitely addictive. It's more addictive than heroin. It's the heaviest game around.

HiLife: *What's the most you've ever been ripped off for?*
FORCADE: About a million and a half dollars. I got cut out of my share of a smuggling run.

HiLife: *Is it possible to net a million dollars on a score?*
FORCADE: It's common, but it's no more common than getting busted. You know, the two things can often follow each other. I think (having done it a number of times) that it takes a lot out of you. Psychologically you feel utterly and completely drained after a run. Someone who's done five or six big runs is like a seventy-year-old person. It's all combat conditions; it's all battlefield psychology. You can end up with shell shock. You can end up punchy from it. Any little incident, chance, can wipe out months of work and millions of dollars.

I don't think that most smugglers are into it full time, because I don't think most people could really take the pressure of being into it full time, and I think one of the purposes of smuggling is to make enough money to lay back for a while. I also think the nature of smuggling is an orgiastic kind of thing where you build up to it, you do it, and you know, you lay back for a while.

HiLife: *How do you feel about the sexual options that your charisma as a smuggler offers you?*
FORCADE: The nature of this business works against sexual satisfaction in that you really don't want to get involved in a

one-night stand because you can't afford to get involved with strangers. They get in the way of your activities and so on. Or maybe I'm just telling myself that.

On the other hand, long-term involvement is also difficult because you can't really promise someone you're not going to be busted or killed tomorrow. It's not the kind of life a woman wants to settle down with. What I'm really looking for is a lady smuggler to share my life with me, but I haven't found anybody like that.

HiLife: *Is smuggling pretty male-dominated?*
FORCADE: It's very male-dominated. The skills smuggling entails are taught mostly to males, but more and more women are getting into it. Women have played critical roles, of course, in coke smuggling. There's a certain type of male who psychologically gets off on the idea of using women to smuggle coke.

I have also heard of women as kingpins, or queenpins, as it were. But generally, no. It's 99 percent male. But the one thing about it is, there are plenty of openings. I'd say that in general the men in the field are more willing to work with women than the men in a lot of other fields are. It's a field that attracts very macho-type people, but everyone who's brave isn't macho. And certainly everyone who's macho isn't brave.

HiLife: *You said there are openings. Do you need any special education?*
FORCADE: I studied navigation. I actually went to a coast-guard school and studied navigation. In fact, I'm a member of the Coast Guard Auxiliary Forces. And, in the county where I live, I'm part of the sheriff's posse. It's a thin foothold into their mentality and their information, but it helps to have a few stickers on the window, you know.

HiLife: *Do you have a college degree?*
FORCADE: No, I don't have a college degree. In fact, I don't even have a high-school diploma, but I've always been a heavy reader, and I have information and knowledge which is worth far more than a college degree. The kind of education I

have can only be gained by experience, and is worth more than any college degree. I'm sure there are many people who would trade a college degree for what I know.

I'm as successful within my field as a movie star or a rock star is in their field. I'm at the top of my profession and I'm wealthy. I mean I'm potentially wealthy. Admittedly, right at the moment I'm broke, but a lot of movie stars and rock stars have had as much money go through their hands. I've done just fine.

HiLife: *Do you consider yourself a connoisseur of dope?*
FORCADE: I think almost anybody who can hoist a joint to their mouth thinks they're a connoisseur of dope. But I've had much wider experience with dope and much more access to it and I've had a variety of experiences so I might be a connoisseur.

HiLife: *What are your favorite smokes?*
FORCADE: I feel about dope the way I feel about music. I'm constantly looking for a new song, you know. Colombian is heavy, overwhelming and stupefying. I kind of like the lightness of Mexican. And the smell of Mexican. It's always very nostalgic to me, you know, because it was what I first started with. One thing I miss is the Vietnamese. You know, I once had some buddies who were involved in this Vietnamese smuggling, and it was one of my early successes in smuggling. And I really wouldn't mind getting some Vietnamese once the country gets stabilized.

HiLife: *Are there more profitable things to smuggle than dope?*
FORCADE: Well, it's interesting that you say that, because a few years ago when they had the sugar shortage some smugglers found it infinitely more profitable to be smuggling sugar across the Caribbean than dope. I've come in contact with people in Florida who are third- and fourth-generation smugglers. Marijuana is their gig now. Their fathers smuggled rum and Scotch and their grandfathers were smuggling gun-powder and slaves. It's one way for somebody who's smart,

and ambitious, to raise themselves up out of obscurity and inequality. For the hippies of today, it's like it was for the Irish and the Italians of the twenties and thirties. It's a way to get a foothold in society. Smuggling is something that's been going on for several thousand years and it attracts a certain type of mentality, in the same way that there have always been musicians and there've always been prostitutes and there've always been politicians. There's a certain segment of the population that will probably always be attracted to smuggling.

HiLife, vol. 1, no. 12 & vol. 2, no. 1, 1979

Robert Davies
Perfection She Dances

THE HASH, WHEN it arrived, was supposed to have come from a village somewhere between Sandra Kou and Asku to the north of Kashgar, but I doubted if the Germans really cared. Their relief was visible, and they could now get to work pressing and packing and preparing to leave. The hash had been sent in muslin bags, ten kilos of olive-green sticky pollen, freshly shaken from the bush and moulded by hand into balls the size of grapefruit. It smelt beautiful, but smoking it in its current state was useless.

The THC (tetrahydrocannabinol, the active constituent of marijuana) had not been activated or released and, without that, there was no getting stoned. Its pollen state also meant that it was extremely bulky, and thus difficult to conceal. To release the THC it was necessary to put it under pressure, to create an internal heat that broke down the walls which trapped the drug's potency. This process consequently reduced its volume and turned it black, making it look like the stuff everybody's familiar with.

The Germans all but disappeared from our late-night drinking sessions, preferring to use the hours of darkness to do their work. The pollen had an incredibly sweet and pungent odour that stank their room out, so it was best to be busy when there was less likelihood of the room girls barging in unannounced. Marius and Gerhard liked to press by foot. They would pack a bag with about half a kilo at a time and tie it tight. Then, while one of them sat down and turned the bag over and over and over again, the other would tread on it repeatedly, putting as much weight on it as he could. Every so often the dope was packed tighter and the bag retied. If the room was warm, about an hour of constant turning and pressing would cause the pollen to go really tacky and solid, sticking to the bag and behaving like putty. This was then turned out into a prepared tray of the size and thickness that was required which had been lined with a sheet of cling film. Another sheet was placed over the top, and it was then rolled out, using a bottle, until it was a flat, uniformly thick plaque of hash.

The Germans had each bought holdalls with removable bottoms from stiff card that gave the bags their shape. These bases were covered in a plastic which, with care, could be taken off without damage, and the board removed. A new board was made with a compartment in the centre. Hash was pressed out into the shape and size of the compartment, heat-sealed using cling film and a lighter, wrapped in tape and inserted into the space. Another piece of card was glued over the top, and the whole thing put back into the plastic. Carefully resealing it, the whole thing was then slipped back into the holdall, virtually identical to the original and unlikely to be discovered by nosy custom bods. Or at least that was the idea. It was always said that if they were intent on catching you, it didn't matter where you put it.

The problem was that these boards could only take about 250g at most, so other hiding places had to be found. Marius, Gerhard, Don and Arno had been doing this for years, and were well rehearsed in the art of concealing dope. They had been busy for a long time buying books around town – in particular, nice books with hard covers made out of thick card.

New books were much better than old ones, because it was

easier to match up new materials than old stained ones. Back at the hotel these were painstakingly taken apart, using damp cottonwool and a scalpel. The card was removed and a new one was made, capable of stashing 100g or so.

Another efficient ploy was the Campbell's soup tin method. Many a traveller would at some time or another resort to eating canned foods so it was not unusual for customs officials to see bags containing cans of sardines or cooked ham and the like. The good thing about cans was that they could hold anything from 300g up to a kilo, and were relatively quick and easy to work on. The required tools were a fine-toothed file and superglue. The lip on one end of a can is actually a tongue-and-groove joint and when the lip is filed down evenly, it eventually releases the joint and the top pops out. The contents could then either be eaten or thrown away, depending on taste, and a lump of hash put in its place, nicely sealed up in cling film. The top would then be glued back in place and sanded down to take away any residue and tell-tale marks. Nothing could be simpler.

Perfection She Dances, 2001

Charles Nicholl
The Fruit Palace – 2

SHE WAS OVERWEIGHT, tired and puff-faced, with a mouth turned down by the way things had gone. She wore glasses, and slacks that were too tight at the thighs. Somewhere behind it all you could see she had been pretty once, and the sharpness still flashed in her eyes like a zoo animal's memory of the jungle. Her eyes were sunk in sallow, mauvish shadows. She lived in a half-finished modern apartment out in Quinta Paredes, towards the airport. It smelt of plaster and oil-paint. The new doors had warped and wouldn't close properly.

I gave her the *perica*. This seemed to be my act at the moment: a notebook in one hand, a little package of powder in the other. I explained that I was writing a book about the cocaine trade. She said, 'Sure.' She followed the first stiff hit of coke with a small chaser, and by the time she was laying out the third rail the sloth had gone from her face and hands, and she wasn't slurring her words any more. She spoke fluent English in a Spanish-Yankee accent. Her voice was lovely. If you closed your eyes she was beautiful, tough and titillatingly foreign. She was Rosalita the Mule, the best in the business, who had walked cocaine through the US customs forty-three times and never got caught. Then you opened your eyes and you saw a pale faded woman in a woollen cardigan, huddled beside a single-bar electric fire. I suppose in the smuggling business that's what you call good cover.

She was from Oviedo, a small town in the Cantabrian mountains of northern Spain. Her father was a local lawyer. She had come to the States in the 1960s. A cousin had made it big in San Francisco, importing clothes from Mexico. He came back to Oviedo once a year, trailing the scent of success, bearing huge vulgar toys for the children. It had always been his promise that one day Rosalita would come and work for him in 'Frisco (as he persisted in calling it), and she would see the cable cars and bridges and deep blue bay of *la ciudad mas hermosa en el mundo*. And one day that's what happened. Cousin Bartolomeo wrote to say he could get her papers, she could come and work as an assistant in one of his Mexican boutiques. She landed in San Francisco in 1967, two days short of her seventeenth birthday. This made her in her early thirties now: she looked ten years older.

The cable cars were fine, and the Golden Gate Bridge was too, even if it was shit-brown rather than gold, but Cousin Bartolomeo did not come up to expectations. 'He was all big talk and shiny suits, but he was real mean. He wanted me because I was cheap. For a year he didn't pay me at all, only room and board. I was just cleaning, and doing odd jobs for him. He called me his *china*. He tried to get me to do other things too, you know, dirty things . . .' She raised an enquiring eye at me. My pen hovered foolishly over the notebook. 'I was pretty then,' she said, fixing me with a hard look that dared me to mumble that she still was.

She was also sharp, and it soon came to her notice that Cousin Bartolomeo had other interests besides peasant-style Mexican dresses. For one thing he was dealing in 'wetbacks', illegal Mexican immigrants, so-called because the traditional way of crossing the border was by swimming the Rio Grande. He was selling passage into the US, selling false documentation – that was probably how he'd got papers for Rosalita – and he was setting up cheap illegal labour for his business friends. The other iron, the one which really opened Rosalita's eyes, was pornography: cheap, inventive hard-core material produced in Tijuana, smuggled in along Bartolomeo's supply routes, and sold under the counter down Broadway, San Francisco's sex street. 'I've seen some things,' said Rosalita, 'but this was really filthy.' Her voice curled like a tendril round the word 'feelthy'.

'So one day I went to Bartolomeo. I said, "I want a job and a salary." And before he could say no, I said, "If you don't I tell the family back home about the porno." He couldn't believe I'd sussed him. It's like he didn't even think I had a brain.'

The following Monday morning she was behind the counter in one of Bartolomeo's Mexican clothes shops, the one up in chic Sausalito, across the Golden Gate. She got her own apartment, lived smart. She despised the pot-heads and the acid-freaks, the Haight-Ashbury flower people, the love-ins and be-ins, all the stuff which made San Francisco a byword in the late sixties. 'I kept right away from all that shit. I was so straight. Like they say, straight as a suicide falling.'

She was good at her job, and a couple of years later, when Bartolomeo was expanding his legitimate business front, he put her in charge of a new store. This was selling clothes, weavings and upmarket *tipicos* from Guatemala. From now on she travelled regularly to Guatemala City, to buy from the local shops and dealers and from the Indian markets nearby.

Up to now she was 100 per cent legitimate. 'OK, I knew the money behind the Guatemala shop was dirty, but I was clean. Everything declared, everything above board, every cent of import tax paid.'

Then, in the fall of 1970, she met Chick. Chick was a Colombian boy, a paisa from Medellin. His real name was Ernesto – 'just like Che' – but his family had always called him Chico, and he had effortlessly Americanized this into Chick. 'That was Chick all over,' she said. 'He could fit like a glove over any scene. That's why he was one hell of a smuggler.' Not that Rosalita knew anything about that when this young, handsome, dandified boy came into the shop. They got talking. He became very interested when she told him about her trips to Guatemala. He said he had very good contacts in Colombia, who could supply her with the kinds of goods she sold in the shop. The next week he came back with business cards, addresses, lists of arts and crafts shops, the whole bang shoot. He really did seem to have good connections. Rosalita was in love, Cousin Bartolomeo was agreeable, and a couple of months later she made her first trip to Bogotá. The night before she left, Chick gave her a beautiful leather travelling case. For good luck, he says, and kisses her sweetly on the cheek.

She flew down to Bogotá, met Chick's contacts, bought an impressive selection of moderately priced *ruanas*, dresses, wall-hangings, etc., and flew back into San Francisco. As usual she carried as much as possible as personal baggage, and the rest she air-freighted back. When she got back Chick plied her with questions. How had it been, getting through customs? Had there been any problems clearing the stuff she'd freighted? And so on. In fact, Rosalita said, there had been rather more questions than there were when she came back from Guatemala. This was late 1970: there was only a trickle of cocaine coming up from Colombia, but there was already a lot of marijuana, and Colombia was undoubtedly on the customs list of suspicious provenances.

But they didn't search you? Chick asked. No, of course not, said innocent Rosalita. As a matter of fact she knew the customs man quite well.

Chick danced around, and kissed her, and said, 'You're perfect, baby! You've just made us *millonarios*! He picked up the travelling case he had given her. The four little rubber studs on the bottom unscrewed, the base came away, and there was a neat little compartment inside. For a moment she thought she'd been set up. But there was nothing in it. Chick said, 'You just carried thin air into the States from Colombia. Next time, baby, you carry in $25,000.'

'You want me to carry in *money*?'

'*Plata de polvo*,' Chick laughed. Powder money.

Rosalita was shocked. She could just about handle dope: some of her upmarket friends smoked. But cocaine. That was on the outer periphery of the drug world, something she vaguely associated with junkies, blacks, jazz musicians. Chick said, 'Trust me,' and he also said, 'Try some.' Rosalita did both. Two months later she flew in from Bogotá with 3lb of Huanaco White cocaine packed in a long thin wedge in the underbelly of her travelling case. It was Rosalita's first run, and it went like a dream. 'And, you know, I'm not sure which got me higher. That first hit of *perica* Chick gave me, or that first run through customs.'

It was a very tight operation. The supplier in Bogotá was one of the clothing wholesalers Chick had introduced her to. He had a warehouse full of *ruanas* and he had a regular supply of high-grade cocaine. Rosalita wouldn't tell me anything about him: 'He's still active, you'd better not know about him.' The cocaine was packed by him, at his warehouse, in the course of their legitimate business. No money changed hands then: it was sent by Chick from San Francisco, a perfectly straight-up money draft. As soon as Rosalita brought the cargo in, Chick buffed it lightly with mannite, and laid it off as 4lb to a wholesaler in San Francisco, another Colombian, who hailed from the southern department of Huila. The 'Huila Dealer', as Chick called him, paid $8,000 a pound. Chick was buying it in Bogotá for $4,000 – a highish price in those days, but it included the packing and no-hassle facilities. 'It was nothing huge,' Rosalita said. 'We weren't greedy. It was the simple, classic run – buy, carry, sell: minimum people, maximum cover.' And it may not have been huge, but over a couple of years Rosalita did that run ten times, clearing about twenty grand each time. Overheads were zero, of course. All the expenses of the trip were picked up unwittingly by Cousin Bartolomeo. He for his part was happy with the profits from his Colombian shop, 'Andes', and on the first floor above the Guatemala shop in Sausalito.

Sometimes, for luck, she varied the run. 'Sometimes I carried in *el conejo*.' I looked up in surprise. In a rabbit? She laughed and pouted. '*Si, hombre. El conejo.* I brought the stuff in up inside me.' Of course – *conejo* is the South American equivalent of 'pussy'. She was referring to what the customs boys call 'vaginal caches'. I refrained from asking her how much she brought in on these occasions. Not, I imagine, 3lb. She also carried it sewn in ribs in her bra.

These, like the false-bottomed case, were the simplest kind of mule work there is. You just hide the stuff in the last place they'll look. If they bring out the screwdrivers and the torches your number's up, but any lesser degree of searching and questioning you can get away with. This kind of mule work is only worth it with high-density, high-profit merchandise, like precious jewels and cocaine. A pound of grass is hardly worth it, and you'd look pretty conspicuous with it stuffed up your bra.

They contemplated broadening their horizons. The other method obviously available to them was to import the cocaine in one of the crates of woollens and weavings which Rosalita air-freighted from Bogotá. The plus of this was that you could bring in much higher volume. The minus was that crates from Colombia were routinely searched before clearing customs, mainly because freight traffic was the main smuggling mode for marijuana. It was just too risky, they decided. Then the *ruana*-man in Bogotá came up with a bright idea. Impregnating the *ruanas* with a solution of cocaine. When the solution dried, the cocaine deposit nestled invisibly in the deep woollen pile of the *ruanas*. At the other end the *ruanas* were soaked once more and the cocaine recovered in solution.

But before they could put this into effect, Rosalita had her first near miss. She had the cocaine in the false-bottomed case, and she got a real going-over at customs. 'He had all my stuff out of the case, and he was pushing and prodding. Luckily we'd just put new rubber studs in the bottom, and they were real stiff. They didn't bust me, but they sure scared the shit out of me. You know, running drugs is all up here in your head, it's all good attitude. You convince yourself, you're three-quarters there to convincing the customs man. I was good, there's no doubt. I knew the ropes, I'd brought in legitimate imports for years. I felt right. When I started wearing glasses I felt even better. Not too smart, not too ragged. Just be what I am. That's the secret of smuggling, one big lie with lots of little truths around it.

'But once you see the other side – once you think: They've got my number – then you're into all sorts of problems in your head. It's all a question of what you see when you look in the mirror. Do you see a young business woman importing goods for a Sausalito boutique, or do you see a cocaine mule pissing in her pants with fright?

'I swore off it right there and then. Chick tried to persuade me. I said, "It's OK for you." Chick was always very cool. He spread everything around: different bank accounts, a couple of apartments, different phoney company names when he sent the money drafts down to Bogotá. Always have a back door open, that was Chick's motto. I said, "That's fine when you're dealing the stuff. But when you're running it," I said, "that's when there aren't any back doors. You just got to keep on going forward: one way out, no way back. I've had enough."'

Chick and Rosalita lay low for a while after that. But smuggling is like a drug itself, it gets in your blood, and after a while they were craving for action. Rosalita didn't want to do the simple Bogotá run any more. 'It's just statistics,' she said. 'No matter how good your cover, you can't keep coming in from Colombia without the customs turning you over once in a while.' She'd drawn a rum card on the last run, and got away with it. Next time not so lucky, perhaps. By the mid-seventies the heat was really on for travellers from Colombia. Dope and coke were pouring into the US. Every scam in the book was being tried by smugglers of every shape and size.

Rosalita didn't travel to Colombia any more, but she did still visit Guatemala regularly. Why not get someone else to ferry the merchandise from Bogotá to Guatemala City? she suggested. She could then relay it on from there into the States. A Guatemalan stamp in your passport was perfectly cool. There wasn't much worth smuggling out of Guatemala, nothing you could carry on your person, anyway. This time it was Chick who demurred. It meant cutting someone else in, relying on someone else's cool. 'Put another link in the pipeline,' he said, 'and at the very least you're doubling the risk of a screw-up.' It was against their hitherto so successful creed – Small is Beautiful.

Then, in the summer of '75, they found their new move. It answered both their objections: Rosalita didn't have to fly in with Colombian stamps in her passport, but Chick didn't have to lose sleep over the risks of additional mules. This was a scam that wasn't in the book. They called it the Magic Eraser move.

One day Chick brought a stranger back to their Sausalito apartment. He was an Englishman. He had blond hair scraped back and tied in a bunch, and little wire-rim spectacles. He wore an expensive suit.

'He was something like a smart hippie, something like a professor. Chick introduces him. "This is Dr Richard," he says. "Dr Richard's in plastics." Jesus, I thought – plastics, I'm really excited. But Chick *was*. He was really wired up, on to something new. He said, "Dr Richard's got something to show you, Rosalita."'

'So the guy opens up his briefcase. He takes out a piece of paper, a rubber stamp and two aerosol cans. The cans were unmarked: one plain black, one plain white. The way he put the things on the table, it was like a conjuror we used to see in Oviedo at Christmas, and that's what Dr Richard called himself. A technological conjuror.

'He took a can, the black one, and sprayed something over the paper. It smelt like new car seats. It made a sort of sheen over the paper, but after a few seconds it dried, and the paper looked just the same as before, except if you picked it up it was stiffer, perhaps, heavier. Then he inked his stamp and put a stamp on the paper. It said, "Downstream Enterprises".

That was Dr Richard's company: it did all sorts of weird clever things with plastics. Chick kept pacing around and grabbing me, and saying: "Baby, isn't it beautiful, you ain't seen nothing yet." Then Dr Richard took the other can and sprayed that over the paper. A different smell, bleachy. In a moment all the surface of the paper went a white colour, sort of frosted, like a smashed windscreen. He shook the stuff in shreds off the paper, and with a little knife he very carefully scraped the rest. When he had finished, the paper was blank. No stuff on it, and no stamp on it: it looked just like it had before he'd started.

'Dr Richard explained. It's simply a very thin, transparent film of plastic. It's something called linear low-density polyethyline laminate. He'd been doing research for years. Breaking the micron barrier, he called it. Getting down to really small molecular thicknesses. A lot of technical stuff I didn't understand. He was offering Chick the spray-cans at $5,000 a piece. I hadn't really sussed. Then Chick said, "Baby, think about it. Think what you could do with that stuff sprayed on your passport!"'

Chick and Rosalita took a long weekend and made a trial run. They motored down to Mexico with the magic eraser sprayed on the pages of their passports. They got stamped at the border, going in and coming back out. The customs also turned them over on the way out, looking for grass or heroin. They were clean, of course. This pleased Chick enormously.

Everyone has a few falls waiting for them, and this one hadn't hurt them at all. They were even more pleased when, in a motel outside El Paso, they sprayed the white can of solvent on to their passports. The plastic skin frosted up into view, they scraped it off, and – eureka! – there was absolutely no visible record left of their visit to Mexico.

This was the basic premise of the Magic Eraser runs. Rosalita was able to move in and out of Colombia without any record remaining in her passport. Passport stamps aren't everything, but a Colombian stamp undoubtedly multiplies the likelihood of getting pulled. She would fly down to Guatemala City, in the course of her legitimate business. There she would buy a round-trip ticket to Bogotá and back. She sprayed on the magic eraser before she left Guatemala City, peeled it off when she got back with the cocaine, supplied as usual by the *ruana* man. There was never any problem getting through customs when coming back into Guatemala. They were really slack. When she flew back into the States there was no evidence she'd been anywhere near Colombia. She had a bigger suitcase now: it carried 10lb. Chick had a new dealing network. The Huila Dealer had moved off to LA, and now Chick was knocking it straight out to dealers. There was a Chinaman called Jack up in North Beach, others in Berkeley and Oakland. It was more hassle, but the profits were bigger. They were making $50–60,000 a run now.

The magic eraser was cumbersome. For a start Rosalita had to spray all the pages of her passport every time – you can never be quite sure where the immigration people are going to put the stamp. There was also a slight risk because she was filling in immigration and emigration forms every time she moved between Guatemala and Colombia. She had a little side-scam on this, one of the mule's regular tricks. Every time she filled in a landing card or suchlike she made two deliberate errors. She put her first name where her family name should be, and vice versa – her family name was Amparo, which is a fairly common female Christian name. She also transposed two of the digits in her passport number. If anyone noticed on the spot, which they never did, it would be easily explained away as a mistake. It was just another bit of insurance, another spanner in the official works. If anyone started running checks, there was a chance that Amparo Rosa, passport number 1234, wouldn't get connected with the real Rosa Amparo, passport number 1324.

The magic eraser worked like a dream for half a dozen runs. But Dr Richard's invisible laminate had one major flaw: it was susceptible to heat. He had told them to keep the passports clear of any heat source, otherwise the film would crack apart, as it did when the solvent in the white can was applied.

One day in Bogotá, staying as always in the Tequendama hotel, Rosalita made one of her rare mistakes. She had to leave her room in a hurry – there'd been a change of rendezvous with the *ruana* man – and she left the passport on a window-sill. It was unseasonably hot, the window faced south, and when she returned, the passport was well and truly baked. The magic plastic film was crinkling off the pages, but not coming off neatly like it did with the solvent. The pages looked like eggs beginning to fry. She hadn't got the solvent with her, to make a proper job of it. It was back in Guatemala – the last thing she wanted to do was to remove her Colombian entry stamp *before* leaving Colombia.

She had to ditch the passport, go to the Spanish embassy – she still travelled under a Spanish passport – and get a temporary replacement. She flew back to San Francisco empty-handed, and they laid the Magic Eraser move to rest.

The Fruit Palace, 1985

Truth sits upon the lips of dying men

Matthew Arnold

John Lightfoot
The Spanish Connection

I QUICKLY LEARNT a lot about drug smuggling: who was doing what, what the risks were, how packages were wrapped and prepared for shipment to the UK and all the rumours about who had been busted. I noticed that the professional smugglers had commercial vacuum-packing machines and used vast quantities of heavy food-grade plastic bags of varying sizes, of the type in which frozen meat joints are packed in supermarkets. These were the smugglers' main weapon against the sniffer dogs.

First, two cannabis soaps are wrapped together in several layers of cling film. Then other layers are added, one of black pepper and another of coffee grains. After a final wrap of cling film the whole soap is placed in a plastic bag and sealed in a vacuum machine. The air is sucked out, and the bag shrink-wrapped around the contents in that familiar squashed-up look. The sealed bag is then cut to size and the open edge heat-sealed by the wrapping machine. The entire process takes about two or three minutes per soap for the experienced wrapper.

A consignment of a hundred kilos of cannabis contains on average four hundred soaps, and the whole lot will be wrapped and stored within a full day. Cannabis resin is a dense product and doesn't take up much room: 50kg can easily be hidden in an average family saloon such as a Ford Sierra.

The packers and wrappers are masters of misdirection and deceit. The wrapped cannabis is secreted under the back seat and in the door panels, not too much there though as the windows need room in the well of the door frame to retract when wound open.

More product is hidden within the spare wheel itself and sometimes under the front bulkhead up in the heater area. The heaters are removed, the pipes sealed off and the hot-air blower motors are taken out. At a casual glance the bulkhead looks identical to any other car, but it is only a metal and plastic shell covering. Cannabis replaces the guts of the heating system.

I have even seen cannabis placed in windscreen-washer bottles and air-filter boxes. Storing it in the engine compartment is tricky, though, because if the car breaks down then the drug could well be unearthed by a mechanic. There are the tales, jokingly passed around, of smugglers whose car engines have overheated and ignited the slow-burning resin. The resultant clouds of blue smoke have passed through the ventilation ducts and into the passenger compartment, affecting everyone in the car. Pleasantly stoned, presumably no one cared about being arrested until the next day's sober realisation of their predicament.

There are specialists who live on the Costas who professionally fix up cars just for the smugglers. The way in which they work is to obtain a vehicle, usually one on UK plates that hasn't been stolen, and doctor it. They remove the rear seats and sometimes the front ones too, the cloth facings and the padding, and fit in as much cannabis as possible into the seat frames. The padding is cut down and refitted, and then the facing material is also refitted and stitched back in place. It is a professional job, and it is hard to distinguish a cannabis-laden seat from one that has not been tampered with. If the model of car has a steel partition between the boot and the rear-seat back then that steelwork is carefully cut away. This reveals an open space, which is filled with cannabis. Later the steel is welded back into place and then resprayed in a colour match. Finally the joints are sealed with mastic that exactly replicates the manufacturer's so as to end up with a perfect-looking concealment job. Sometimes a fire extinguisher or first-aid kit is screwed on to the steelwork to add a touch of authenticity.

These cars are driven back to the UK by experienced operators who charge anything up to £10,000 per trip. The drivers apply for new papers for the car from DVLA in Swansea, take out motor insurance and buy a green card for European travel. Their documents are complete and accurate in every detail and will stand up to any check. Then they recruit passengers for the journey. There are husband-and-wife teams who, along with their children, regularly do the run between the Spanish Costas and the Channel ports.

In 1994 I heard about an English man and woman in their late fifties who were stopped and searched by French customs officers on the Hash Highway in the South of France. They had their two young grandchildren in the back of the car who were found to be sitting on forty kilos of high-quality cannabis resin. The grandparents were arrested, and the children taken into state care, until their parents travelled down from England to collect them. The grandparents are still in prison, serving a six-year sentence in addition to a massive customs fine or the option of another two years inside. I do not feel sorry for such people. They are not just naive old grannies caught up in a web of deceit but professional and experienced smugglers who carefully weigh up the risks before getting involved. They don't just walk into a bar in Spain and say, 'Hi, does anybody want me to smuggle some cannabis back to England for them?' That's an unlikely scenario. No, these people make a career of it and have probably already successfully netted thousands of pounds from previous trips.

For the experienced packer other great concealment opportunities are offered by camper vans and towed caravans. Cassette toilets are emptied, and the heavy plastic waste receptacles cut in half. They are filled with cannabis and sealed with plastic welding machines. This effectively forms a tank within a tank, after which the chemical toilet fluids are poured into the top tank. The cannabis-charged cassette unit is refitted into the caravan, and hey presto! there is both a usable toilet and a cache of hidden drugs. It's a brave customs officer who rakes around in the shit tank just for a quick look-see. The only way to be sure whether or not there are concealed drugs is to weigh the empty cassette unit and measure the depth of the cassette from the exterior as opposed to the interior. This is a nasty, smelly job that, for obvious reasons, will not be undertaken unless the authorities have a very strong suspicion that there are drugs on board the caravan.

Calor gas and propane gas bottles are also used for concealment purposes. A bottle is completely emptied of gas and carefully cut around the middle seam weld into its two component halves. The bottom half of the bottle is filled with 10kg of cannabis and then a sheet of light-gauge tin is welded over the top. Finally the two halves of the tank are welded together again and spray-painted before the gas bottle is refilled.

The usable and partly filled bottle is placed in the caravan stowage compartment and connected up to the gas supply. The bottle now functions correctly, and if a customs officer were to light the gas stove it would work. Alternatively, if the official were to disconnect the gas bottle from the small regulator and open the handwheel valve, he would get a blast of high-pressure butane gas in his face, another classic trick that is frequently used.

In touring caravans the whole of an interior wall may well

be stripped out and the interior foam and polystyrene-type insulation removed. Packets of wrapped cannabis are carefully packed inside the outer skin and secured by tapes stapled to the wooden strengthening supports. The inner wood-grain or pastel-shade veneers are refitted very carefully, and all the accessories wired back into place. Both sides of a caravan receive the same treatment so that it sits levelly on the suspension. If experienced interior fitters are used it is impossible to tell that the walls have been disturbed in any way, although there can easily be 100kg of cannabis, worth £300,000, concealed within an average family-size caravan.

Professionals don't stash cannabis in cupboards or on shelves under clothes or in biscuit tins or coffee or sugar jars. They hide the gear in such a way that no casual check could ever uncover it. These packers secrete the gear in such a fashion that damage must be done to the fabric of the storage vehicle, be it car, van or caravan, before the cannabis is revealed.

Bear in mind that the gear is wrapped so carefully no sniffer dog would discover the cache and lead his handler to a location. It is a brave customs officer, therefore, who would systematically remove the wall from a caravan or cut open a toilet cassette or remove the welded plastic fascia of a caravan fridge or the plastic panelling in a shower enclosure just on suspicion that there may be drugs stored on board. Normal border or port inspection consists of a sniffer-dog inspection of the interior while a couple of customs men open drawers and check shelves and cupboards.

A classic piece of misdirection is to secrete ten or so cartons of cigarettes in a remote, inaccessible cupboard which are invariably found during an inspection. The surprised smugglers then offer to pay duty on their uncovered tax-free haul of tobacco, while the customs men are satisfied that they have found a family bringing back some extra duty-free goods. The offenders either pay the extra duty or escape with a stern lecture about the correct use of green and red customs zones before shamefacedly driving through the inspection sheds and out to deliver the caravan full of cannabis a couple of days later to their colleagues in crime.

The customs drugs units work mainly from information from registered informants or tip-offs from the public. They can't start dismantling every vehicle going through the various Channel entry ports into the UK. Abroad in France and Spain there are temporary roadblocks set up along the Hash Highway. These often discover the cannabis hidden by amateurs in the obvious hidey-holes, but they are not equipped to start taking vehicles apart. Any contraband that will pass the sniffer dogs and is well secreted will get past them, assuming of course that the roadblocks actually stop the smugglers in the first place. Most consignments travelling up the Hash Highway are minded by babysitters at the front, who are in constant contact with the loaded vehicle. Sometimes there is another vehicle behind providing a rear security screen and acting as overwatch for the main men back in Spain. Every effort is made to ensure that nobody has any clever ideas about taking a wrong turn and making off with maybe half a million pounds' worth of easily saleable merchandise.

In 1994 and 1995 there was a growing trend to use motorbikes to carry cannabis. The ever vigilant smugglers had discovered that they were rarely stopped at border-crossing points or by roadblocks. By their very nature there cannot be any large quantities of drugs concealed on a bike, unless the gear is stowed in the side panniers or back box, but either way it would be uncovered very quickly. The smugglers quickly exploited this apparently laissez-faire policy towards motorcycles and put their carriers on to cruising bikes, thereby sending hundreds of kilos of cannabis over to the UK during the following two summers. The sight of half a dozen bikers, not long-haired yobbos but more mature, respectable citizens riding quality motorcyles such as BMWs, Yamahas, Hondas and the like, does not attract a lot of attention from police or customs officers. Furthermore, at the British entry ports bikers are the first group of travellers to be disembarked from the ferries, quickly let through immigration and customs with no more than a cursory glance at the driver's passport. There are more and more lone operators who regularly smuggle small amounts of gear for themselves. These guys and girls are usually successful because nobody is going to tip off the authorities about them. They keep their departure dates and itineraries to themselves and travel by constantly varying the routes and modes of transport. If they are caught it is usually by chance. Sniffer dogs may catch them because they don't have access to the vacuum-packing machines that are the foolproof method used by the professional gangs.

The Spanish Connection, 1992

Marijuana is for the people. Cocaine is for milking the rich
Carlos Lehder

Robert Sabbag
Smokescreen – 2

THE INDUSTRY-STANDARD wrap for bales of marijuana is threefold. The bales are first wrapped in brown paper, which is sealed with masking tape. The layer of paper is necessary because the merchandise sweats. Much like a haystack gets moist and hot in the middle, this too is organic material. And even well cured, the product needs to hold moisture if it is to maintain any level of quality. If it were wrapped in plastic alone, it would decompose as its natural juice heated up and tried to evaporate. It is wrapped in paper to absorb the moisture, then wrapped in plastic to make the bale waterproof, to protect it not only from rain and sea water, but from contamination by crude oil and bilge. The plastic is taped, and then the bale is wrapped in a burlap bag that is sewn up on the open end, making the bale easy to handle – smugglers can grab the burlap by the corners and throw the bale around.

Smokescreen by Robert Sabbag, first published in Great Britain by
Canongate Books, February 2002

Kevin Sampson
Outlaws

THAT'S WHERE I think my own operation is a step ahead. I'm not a drug dealer as such. What I'm offering is in the grand tradition of Liverpool brokers. I'm really just a frontiersman, setting a tariff, bringing goods in through the port and effecting a distribution network. My role is simple. I'm a consolidator, that's all – a consolidator. I'm at the high-risk, high-profit, zero-labour end of the market. I bring the shite in. Almost immediately, I move it on to the boys that make the real money. But I'm happy with the ratio of risk-to-gain that I deal with. I'm somewhere near the high-to-middle end of this particular chain. I deal via Bernie and mainly through Ireland. Almost all of my trade comes via the Bhoys, the Dubliners, the Irish connection. Now, these lads are fucking tasty, they are. If it weren't for the nod from Bernie I'd half have the horrors of having to deal with the cunts. Nobody's ever come out and said it's the Provos or whatever, and I'm certainly not asking no questions but let me just say they're not like most of the lads you deal with. Don't dress up. Don't make a fuss of you. Only have a laugh and joke over something horrible, and even then they only have a laugh with one another. You never really feel like you're their mate, which you're not in fairness, even though you do get them no end of tickets for the match. That's their one indulgence, the Bhoys – they love the match.

I've always left the Bhoys and Bernie to make the actual deal, the big one, the import from source. They sort it out with Turkey or Amsterdam or Colombia, depending on what the crop is, then I'll make my deal with them. And once I've dealt, I move it and fast. Mainly to firms in Kirkby, Skein or Crocky – lads I've known for years, in fairness. But I'll also supply reliable outfits from as far away as Middlesbrough and Norwich and Southampton. I'm a broker and I'll go wherever there's a sustainable and relatively docile market. One thing I'm not crazy about is stirring up the competition, by the way. Even with Bernie's say-so, I'd rather go where there's no feathers to ruff. A guardian angel can't protect you all of the time.

But I do always clear everything with Bernie. Bernie's one of our own, a very heavy hitter in London nowadays and everything I've ever done has been with his blessing. Right from the off. I as good as asked his permission when I moved in on them little places at the start. I targeted these little sleepy places where there was a population centre and that, but no cunt seemed to be taking care of business. Just because it's only Nantwich or whatever, doesn't mean the kids don't want droogs. In actual fact, it means they *double* want droogs. I put that to Bernie. I said to him, if I'm standing on anybody's toes it's only going to be some wool dealing a little bit of weed and that. I won't even zap 'em. I'll gently move them over, knowmean. That's what I put to Bernie that first time. He knew Ged'd be against it, but he stood back and took a view. He was cool-headed, not rash and emotional like our Gerrard. Bernie told us to stay well away from Windsford but he okayed Whitchurch and Northwich and a bit of Telford for YT, cleared it with the Wolverhampton mob and that's how I got started. Not kicking off. Not trying to take over. But supplementing. Having the arse to come in when others are hesitant. Securitising.

He's in business, Bernie, and that is his only criterion for decision-making. He told us that at the start, when he was talking about Cheshire and that. Does it make sense? is all he asks himself. Is it business? Not like one of them played-out Mafia things where they go on about it being, like, business and not personal and all of that baloney. The fact is that drugs IS business. Big fucking potatoes. And what I put to Bernie a couple of years ago – weird calling him Bernie after all that time, but, that's what you call him down there, that's what he likes to be called by the trade – is that there was a gap in the market. There was a demand for a sort of service industry – a well-capitalised mini-wholesaler who would supply the suppliers. Bit like selling on a debt, if we're being crude about it. It'd be a specialised field but a pretty fucking handy one. I'd have to state here and now that I did devise that whole concept, by the way, but there's a few fellas specialising in this area now. Truth is I don't mind a few people getting on the scheme, in fact it's been more help than hindrance. There's been times, quite a few of them, when Ireland has wanted me to take more than I strictly want to bring in, knowmean. But I'm adamant about the right way of bringing it into this city and the right amount to ship. One thing I do know is how the Port of Liverpool works. But there's been times when I've sensed that the Bhoys are getting a bit frustrated with old JPB, little bit impatient with my safety-first tactics, and at that point it's easy enough to bring in the fella in Ayr whose money's burning a fucking hole in his pocket. Or there's the young lad in Southampton and one or two others who're playing this particular market now. Lay some or all of the risk off against them boys. And then there's always the Boro Brothers. They don't even recognise the word risk, by the way. To them lads, it's all a case of jam today. I love them boys to death. I really do personally enjoy being around them. Their attitude to life is the same as their attitude to business. Go for it, lar. Is right. Go for it big. And while I tend to get a bit thingy about huge quantities and the possible repercussions of my name being stamped on a deal like that, the Brothers will dive all over it. As they often do, by the way.

But that's all it is that we do. It's Futures. It's just another way of playing the money markets is the way I look at it, and just look at the money market. Completely deregulated now, it is. Retired fellas playing it from their bedrooms on little PCs. People like me are, in practice, nothing more than a second wave of suppliers who serve to supplement the main guys, and only then when the need arises. It's a risk-free proposition. I don't undermine no one, I don't take from them – I fucking pay to *help* them. Get that. And it adds up. I've taken every word of Ged's teachings and turned it into big business. Big fucking business, by the way. None of his scatty-arsed heavy-duty blags for no money. I'm into big dough with all of this – and I know how it works at the other end and all too, by the way. I've got half an eye on the sell-by date. The smartest deal a real wiseguy will ever do is to get out. Not that

I madly want to get out, by the way, but it's just the law of averages. You do – you have to quit before you get quitted. Couple more jobs like this one today and I can maybe begin to think that way.

Outlaws, 2001

Roderick Kalberer
The Scam

THE CUSTOMS OFFICER taking a half-hour break at London's Heathrow Airport could never explain why some passengers aroused his suspicions. It was a question of having a nose for the job and an eye for detail. Gold watches and nylon shirts did not go together. The customs officer had been wandering around the departure check-in desks when he caught sight of the suspect. He watched the man change three large bundles of sterling into guilders and Swiss francs. Businessmen who exchanged sterling at the airport weren't exhibiting normal business acumen. Regular businessmen used gold credit cards or had their secretaries arrange their foreign exchange in advance. He watched the man deposit his baggage and then he had a word with the Home Office official on the passport desk. He waited while the suspect offered his passport for inspection, and the official memorised the name and number. Armed with the suspect's name, Samuel Tate, the officer made out a Suspicious Movement Report. He tapped the information into CEDRIC, acronym for the Customs and Excise Department Reference and Information Computer which contained over a quarter of a million suspect names. The computer referred him to the National Drugs Intelligence Unit, the joint police and customs unit at Scotland Yard, which would provide him with access to the Police National Computer. He read the information which appeared on the screen with interest. Tate had a criminal record.

The gate for the British Airways flight to Amsterdam had closed and the customs officer made his way to the departure gate to retrieve the flight coupon. The details would show where and how the ticket was bought, and whether there was a connecting flight. As he looked at the ticket details he was sure of one thing. Samuel Tate was still up to no good. He had bought the ticket for cash. That was not illegal, but businessmen usually bought tickets with credit cards or had accounts with travel agencies. Curiously, he noticed the ticket was made out to Mr Yate, and not Tate. It was probably a slip of the typist's finger, but it could also be an alias. There was also a flight connection to Geneva five days later. Cash and Switzerland suggested one thing. Dirty money. Someone, somewhere, would welcome the snippet of information about Samuel Tate.

Meanwhile, Samuel Tate sat in the aisle seat of the British Airways flight to Amsterdam, travelling business class, a *Financial Times* on his knee. Over the years he had worked hard to create the image of old money and blue blood. After all, policemen thought twice before they apprehended the upper classes. Only English gentlemen of the old school smelt a rat. His immaculate dress sense was the result of frequenting Saville Row tailors where obsequious salesmen offered advice. 'Oh no, sir. It's not done to wear a handkerchief in the top pocket of a town suit. Perhaps I could interest you in a pair of platinum cufflinks, sir? Not the gold ones in this instance, sir, if I may say so. Gold is correct for daytime use, but it's very common in the evenings.' His sartorial elegance had been an expensive exercise, but it was the details which made all the difference.

Tate's family was nouveau riche and the blood was red, but who gave a shit about all that. He certainly didn't. He peered through the porthole of the plane, watched the grey tarmac speeding past, and imagined his silver Mercedes racing along under the wing tip. He felt the sudden lurch as the plane became airborne, and he relaxed. Despite his apparent ease, airports made him nervous. There was always the fear that he might be stopped as he boarded the plane. Always the fear that he had overlooked something. Perhaps they knew he carried another identity. Perhaps he hadn't spotted their surveillance.

He was tall and slim. His dark hair was turning grey at the temples. He wore spectacles with heavy frames, which on close inspection proved to contain lenses of clear glass. They rested on a bony Roman nose. He had a high forehead from which the hairline was receding, and on which the lines of age and worry were being slowly etched. His mouth was small and straight. He was wearing a double-breasted pinstripe suit. He looked fifty, ten years older than he really was.

Tate's thoughts were broken by something unpleasant. A man had changed seats and was now sitting across the aisle from him. He was wearing a shiny blue suit which could have done with cleaning. He was somewhat greasy. Thirty years old. Why did common people always lack style when they tried to look smart? Why did they bother to dress for flights? Then Tate noticed his footwear. The socks were nylon. The shoes were well used, but they had a thick composite sole. He always looked at a person's shoes. 'You can tell a gentleman by his shoes,' his mother once told him. Gentlemen and policemen, Tate had learned.

Tate felt a flutter in his stomach. He knew why. He was paranoid. He knew all about surveillance. There were those small incongruous signs; the builder's van parked opposite his flat all day, and not a builder in sight; the dry-cleaner's van which no business could afford to leave idle; odd incidents at bars when he caught people looking at him.

The plane hit an air pocket. Tate looked up and realised the man was addressing him. 'What?' he said.

'I said, it's worrying how the wings flex in these planes.'

'They'd snap off if they were rigid,' Tate replied, curtly.

'Do you have a plane of your own?'

Some people have no idea about personal space, thought Tate. Especially the police. Again there was the little flutter in his stomach. 'No,' he replied.

'Oh! It sounded like you did. Do you often use the shuttle?'

'First time,' lied Tate. He hadn't once looked the man in the eye. He was definitely a member of the other firm. No one else would have the gall to pursue a conversation in the face of such taciturn resistance.

'It's my first time as well. I've a meeting in Amsterdam. Where are you going?'

'Amsterdam,' replied Tate, 'unless you're planning to hijack the flight.'

'Oh no. I'm going there on a business trip.' This one had absolutely no sense of humour.

'I might have guessed. You are travelling business class, after all.' Tate laboured the point.

'Yes, I'm in the textile industry. We're having a hard time in Europe. There's a lot of competition from Turkey, India and the Far East.'

Tate didn't reply. He hoped the man would shut up.

'What's your line of business, if you don't mind me asking?' The man chirped again.

Tate minded very much. 'Investment consultant,' he snapped, and wondered how to terminate the conversation. One thing was sure. He wasn't under surveillance. After all, if you could see the buggers then they weren't watching you. They'd have stopped him at the airport and asked him a question or two if they were interested. They weren't shy, but they were tenacious; and this little sod didn't look like giving up.

The flight was turning into a nightmare. He had some greaseball sitting next to him, who might or might not be a policeman. Next time he'd travel on a plane which had a first-class option. In the meantime he had to stop this conversation. He stood up and marched to the lavatory. When he returned, he opened the *Financial Times* and studied the market prices. It was hard to concentrate. He couldn't remember what was in his Swiss portfolio.

'Settling down to work?' chirped the voice.

Tate ignored him.

'I've not been to Amsterdam before, Mr Tate.'

Tate blinked. Had he introduced himself as 'Yate' or 'Tate'? He didn't know. Perhaps he'd misheard. No. He never gave the man his name. The bastard must have looked in his briefcase. Yes. He'd peered at his passport which was poking out of his briefcase. Or had he known the name before he embarked? Nasty, beady black, inquisitive eyes. 'Try the—'

he was about to say, Amstef, but remembered he had a meeting there. 'Krasnapolsky.' That would set the little shit's bank balance back a bit. He'd have a job claiming that on expenses. It would probably send the whole textile industry spiralling into a slump.

'Could you write it down for me?'

Tate looked at the hand which proffered paper and pen. If the man thought he was getting a set of fingerprints on that scrap of paper he had another thing coming. Samuel looked squarely at his fellow traveller. He stared into his eyes. He said very quietly and firmly, 'Go fuck yourself. I'm busy.' He turned back to his newspaper.

'That's nice. That's bloody charming,' commented the voice. 'It's my first time abroad and I ask some arsehole for a bit of advice . . .' He blushed. 'You're a jerk,' he finished lamely.

'What did I do?' thought Tate. 'He was only some pimply salesman and I pretended he was Pinkerton personified.' Tate had hopped in and out of taxis all over Amsterdam in case he was being followed. He had too much to lose through carelessness. 'I'm too old for this game.' It used to be fun but now it was business and he was tired of looking over his shoulder. However, a chance encounter wouldn't force him into retirement. He was at the pinnacle of his career. Even the smallest deal made a hundred thousand; and he wouldn't lift a finger for less. As the governments cracked down on drugs, the street prices soared to reflect the risks. At the same time the middlemen demanded lower prices from the producers to reflect the marketing risks. The margins widened and the profits escalated. Things had never been better. So long as he didn't take chances there was no reason why it should ever end.

It had been stupid telling an innocent stranger to fuck himself. However, it wasn't surprising if he overreacted sometimes. He was under pressure; and it wasn't helped by ill-informed drugs campaigns in England. They'd once advised the public that people with runny noses were cocaine addicts, and not suffering from flu. It was bad enough enduring inflamed sinuses half the year without that sort of insanity being broadcast. Now, depositing a grand in cash at the bank meant giving explanations in triplicate. Soon they'd be saying that anyone paying with cash was a drug pusher. It was ridiculous.

The Scam, 1995

Brian Barritt
Bust

THE BOEING HOVERS in the void above London airport, watching the tail lights of cars stream like red tracer across a revolving, neon Mondrian. It settles its long silver body on the glossy runway, opens a concave door in its side and ejects us, dazzled and disorientated, into a small square bus full of windows and reflected light – in the centre of a flawless diamond, beneath the lens of the customs. A zoom-eyed official probes our sordid belongings and retrieves two packets of Aura Vedic dysentery powder – folded like ten-bob deals of grass. He looks at this dubious yellow powder, tastes it with his forefinger, looks me straight in the eye and asks me what it is.

'Aura Vedic dysentery powder.'

'I'm sorry, sir, but I shall have to have this analysed.' BOOM! Suddenly we are associated with dope. Ravening customs hyenas run from all corners of the airport and rummage through our possessions. Solid British policemen search our emaciated bodies and find the waistcoats . . . *Fin*.

CHANCE.

GO TO JAIL

MOVE DIRECTLY TO JAIL

DO NOT PASS 'GO'

DO NOT COLLECT £200

Unknown to us, Edward and Felicity have been waiting for our arrival at the airport – the Embassy informed them, after all. Checking to see if we are on the scheduled flight, Edward is jumped on by the customs officials and a 'Welcome home' joint is discovered in his top pocket.

Felicity, seeing the arrest from the airport crowd, drives home through the manic night, trying to get to her house near Chelmsford and stash the pound of Edward's 'homegrown' before the police arrive. She drives at superspeed, crouched over certain disaster, car scuttling across the width of the road like a crab. As she takes the last bend her fanatical headlights, tunnelling through the night, are erased by the blast of electricity pouring from every window in her home. Too late . . . the 'Force', emanating malice and restrained violence, are already scavenging, carrying away the pot as if it's nitro-glycerine – without a thought for themselves.

While the fuzz are burrowing they come up with some incriminating letters from a student called Rupert, who I put up for a while in my flat in north London prior to migrating to India. Rupert has been writing letters to his friends about what good times we all had when Brian was dealing hash and distributing psychedelics. When his letters are unearthed the police hit his place as well, find a little bit of hash, make him a deal, and he promptly turns Queen's evidence.

The Road of Excess, 1998

Susan Nadler
The Butterfly Convention

ANYHOW, THE THREE of us conspirators – me doubling over in pain and tired from the debilitating heroin I had snorted last night; Andrew, trying to be cool, cool fool sitting on a hill; and Ted, wondering if his goddam ass is covered – we call Aero Cargo and discover that the package was indeed there, but we need 700 pesos or $56 to cover the taxes. For a minute I feel a huge, uncontrollable wave of paranoia overtake me and I want out – out of this bullshit riff of waiting and never knowing if we're being watched – and you know the story – if you get busted overseas, you're in for the hassle of your life – and Mexico, for all intents and purposes, is definitely overseas. And I want to run away and forget my $4,000, and my arms with track marks all over them, and the man I supposedly loved, who lived in a world of pipe dreams. But only for a minute because I knew I was in too far. So Ted scrapes together about 300 pesos and some French francs from Morocco and we all pile into the Safari and head for town to cash a check and I get the eeriest feeling that someone is watching me – but Andrew reassures me that it's only paranoia creeping up – and to keep my disease to myself because paranoia is a disease – a communicable one – you have it and to get rid of it you pass it on, brother. And on the way into town Ted explains that the so-called package is, in reality, 250 kilos of hash built into an armoire. And it should weigh 500 pounds altogether; he was a few pounds short – and he sent it out himself and there is glass in the doors and intricate carvings all over. Well – we three ain't dummies – and we know we can't haul the armoire in a Safari jeep, so we hurriedly head for José Cortezar father's mattress factory. There we find José passed out and green, nodded out under a tree. 'Hey, brother,' (brother my ass), 'we need you for a leetle while.' And Andrew and Teddy explain to José that a package has come in – they don't need to explain what it is – he nods – and a smile slips on his face – he too gets turned on by the idea of smuggling – sure, man – he will get a truck and four of his father's workers to help us unload it. Smuggling is like a drug in itself. The excitement and the fear get you as stoned, if not more so, as any drug. I always had the Mata Hari complex. Suddenly, I just don't want to be around. I want to go to the beach and swim and lie in the sun – but Ted insists that I go – just to keep it in the family . . . again, paranoia, please, brother – ol' misery sure 'nough loves its company.

So we meet José at the *casa* – me in a tiny top and cut-offs, Andrew in his hat and Ted in his pants and shirt – and we make tracks for the office of Aero Cargo in José's truck. I really don't want to be there, and I pray to whoever may be there listening to get me out of this. At Aero Cargo there is an overabundance of workers and *hombres* but we walk with our heads held high – no pun intended – I mean, we were on top of the world – temporarily, man, so temporarily. Every-one is staring so hard at us – and I know that Ted is trying to avoid being noticed – he keeps to the paneling of the office wall, leaving Andrew to pick up the package, which is in his name. Andrew pays the taxes – he is sweating so much now – and I take his hand, because I know that he is weak, and trying so hard not to show it.

And Ted is very businesslike as José and his four helpers lift up the extraordinarily heavy package and put it on the truck. Suddenly Ted panics and whispers to me, 'Susan, it's a goddam new crate it's in – I packed the armoire and it wasn't in that crate – it's brand new, I never saw it before,' as if I can come up with the answers. This debonair businessman, this big-time con artist turns absolutely beige and really, I mean this is no joke, I wish that I had a picture – his hair stands up and he really looks like a goddam chicken with his beaked nose. I say, 'Hey, man, let's pass on this deal and leave the friggin' dope here until we can figure it out.' But greed triumphs as usual as Ted decides, well, maybe the Mexicans broke the crate and had to make a new one. Because, he assures me, sweat on the backs of his hands, the package never went through the US customs, but directly from Tangier to Mexico and after all, what can we do now?

Andrew is too busy helping José to notice the newness of the crate and Ted neglects to tell him. I mean, after all, who is Andrew except the flunky who will bear all the responsibility if anything happens, because the package is in his name? And we wave goodbye to all the people at the Aero Cargo office, not realizing that about one-quarter of them are police. The drive back to the apartment is very quiet – except for José who chatters all the way, stoned and ignorant of the situation. I guess ignorance might be bliss after all. Once we return to the apartment, all the workers and José and Andrew have the unenviable task of uncrating the armoire and bringing it up the steps. Ted and I run ahead – throw out all the grass in the apartment but two joints, which I hide in *my* make-up case along with two mandrax. We stash the cocaine and household heroin in silver foil high in the closet, where I imagine it still is. Then I make fruit salad for lunch and snort the cocaine we left out. The armoire finally comes into the apartment. Four tired Mexican peons, one now definitely exhausted José Cortezar, one pooped-out Andrew and the metadirector Ted deposit one of the most beautiful pieces of furniture I have ever seen in our living-room. I give tall glasses of lemonade to all the workers and thank José, who is leaving for Ensenada in two hours. He flies out the door, and finally Andrew and I collapse in the middle of the floor with Ted pacing up and down, looking suspiciously out the window.

The armoire is a fine example of the lost art of wood-carving. It's about nine feet tall and five feet wide and the front of it is carved delicately with small figures, deer and goats. And I say to Ted, 'Where the hell is the hash?' And he smiles to himself and walks over to the armoire looking more calm and less like a scared rabbit, because he is back in his role of he-man-adventurer smuggler. We stand on a chair and I see that the whole top and bottom of the armoire are false, full of hidden shit – so to speak. Suddenly, Ted turns green again, his hair stands up like little blades of dried-out grass and he whispers, 'Someone goddam opened this, I can tell – it's not the finished color of the armoire. Now it all fits, the unfamiliar crating and the smiling Mexicans and I'm getting the fuck out of here.' Filled with fear, he thinks only of himself – and gentle Andrew, poor soul, he is cool, man, and, not to be daunted in his hour of triumph, he says, 'Hey, man, relax, we both know that the package never went through US customs, and if they had wanted to bust us we would never have received the package.' And me, free me, I have to pee fast and remember the day, two years long gone, when Ivan and I were met by the FBI and I cry because as I try to put everything in context and remember, I have the electrifying realization that soon I will only remember. I stay in the bathroom a long time, feeling myself marooned. It's June, and I feel another lousy riff coming on. And as I walk back into the other room I hear Ted droning on, '. . . and, man, I've seen too many TV shows and I know the trip get hip – if they want us, we are right now surrounded – they're only waiting for us to open up the panels and remove the hash. So let's get out of this place – maybe they'll forget our faces. Also, remember, Andrew and Susan, they can't get us for something that we didn't do, for all we know the package was a gift to Andrew from a friend in Morocco and we're cool (cool fool sitting on a hill) since we have no idea what's in the armoire.' And the chicken putters into the other room and says he wants to make reservations to leave that night – and I have the disease (paranoia) bad – I say to Andrew, 'Honey, I'm scared that they have us. Let's go to town and make reservations to leave (why the fuck aren't I at the beach?) and stay away until we feel that the vibes are okay.' And Andrew chuckles and languorously stretches out without a single doubt, like he's home free, and says to me, 'Baby, you and your paranoid buddy Ted (my buddy?), you two fly out of here tonight and I'll stay here for a few days to make sure that everything is fine – go and get your passport and visa and open tickets – we'll drive to town, make reservations, and you'll be safe in LA tonight.' I start to think, something here stinks, why wouldn't he let me go yesterday. But at this point, ladies and gents, I went to collect my papers, follow my instincts and split. I was so nervous I never even put shoes on – I took one mandrax to cool myself down – pulled my hair back, and in cut-offs and a little top (as usual) headed for the car with Andrew and Ted. The mandrax was just starting to take its effect and the three of us walked to the jeep. Ted – almost visibly shaking, got in the back, Andrew got in the driver's seat, and (did I remember to lock the door?) I was just climbing into my seat when I looked up and saw a huge Mexican, about six-two, with a mustache, a sombrero and a machine gun – and I looked at Andrew and he looked at me and I looked at him and he looked at me and I said out loud, 'Do you believe this?' And suddenly there were thirty Mexican police. It was hard to tell exactly how many since all of them were *Federales* not dressed in uniforms; and thirty machine guns and pistols and the heat, and I'm getting thrown against a car and being frisked (a little stoned by now, yelling 'Hey, man, what the fuck do you think you're doing?'), but no one understood

English and handcuffs on *Señor* Andrew – the package was in his name and someone in God's name help me – keep it cool on the outside, Susan – I mean really, what is going on? And an older man, maybe forty-five or so with a mustache and a .38 revolver asks me (Jesus – it seemed like everyone in town had gathered around our apartment building and was watching – screaming) for the key – and I don't want to go into my purse because I have grass there – keep cool – God help me to hold onto my purse – and it was like a goddam movie – the police acted like we were Bonnie and Clyde. And they break down the door – and all this Spanish talk and pandemonium and four of the big *Federales* push Ted (who has totally blown it and is hysterical by now and whispers to me 'Don't tell them a thing, cry, act innocent – ask them why are they here'), and I remember the joints in my purse; however, at this point I'm stoned on my downer and belligerent as hell – and two of the *hombres* identify themselves as American FBI men and casually say to me, 'Congratulations, girlie – you are part of the first hash bust ever in the Baja – and you're in for the longest and hottest summer of yer life.' Andrew is handcuffed and crying, 'Honey, I'm sorry, I know you've seen this movie before.' I can't cry, but as I watch the four *Federales* take hatchets and break into the armoire on the top and the bottom looking for the dope I maneuver my hand into my purse, unzip my makeup case – keeping my eyes on as many of the cops as I can – slip out the two joints and mandrax and stash the joints behind the pillows of the sofa. At least they can't grab me for possession – so I thought! And no one sees me – only Andrew and he winks at me. The sweat is pouring off his face now, and since he is handcuffed and unable to wipe it off he asks me to. As I do, the older gentleman asks me if I know what is coming out of the armoire in kilo bags (only the best hash he'll ever see) and I say no – and another man – this one older, less fluent in English, and definitely more belligerent-looking, is checking out Ted's arms for needle marks. Ted never had the guts to shoot a B-B gun, let alone dope – and I wonder if this is it for me, with enough track marks on my arms to sponsor a roller derby, but he sees only deep tan and some rather large black-and-blue marks – and a man who identifies himself, amid all the noise of hatchets and yelling, as the district prosecutor of Baja – he looks at me rather softly and says, 'Susan,' (how the hell does he know my name unless they have been watching me?), 'Susan, do you know how serious this is?' And I hostilely spit out, 'I don't know what's going on here, what is this all about?' (He's now going through my clothes – at least the house is clean of drugs.) 'I demand my rights.' And he asks me why I don't cry and I answer that I have nothing to fear, I am innocent. Meanwhile, the two American FBI motherfuckers are telling me that I have to give them the name of someone to call in the States for me because I won't be able to get near a phone, and anyway the lines are never working – and I say no – I don't need help – I'm protected, my good karma will get me out – and one says to Andrew, 'Okay, Buster, who should we call for her?' and Andrew gives them my parents' phone number and for the first time I feel fear well up because they can't possibly go through this again. The apartment is now in a shambles – the drawers are on the floor – the clothes are everywhere – the music and books all over – I can't bear the pain. The district prosecutor tells us to go to the car now – we are being taken to jail. So we are marched down the stairs and they try to handcuff me and (still hostile from my downer) I kick out – and they laugh – I see one of many police pocket my locket, given to me by my father on my sixth birthday and inscribed 'To Susan-Beth' – and I scream out at the thief but no one cares. I am just another prisoner without rights and there are hundreds of Mexicans looking for action gathered outside the house. I see Mr. Cortezar in the corner, shaking his head. Oh, the gossip now, and I wonder where Josh is, but my thoughts are interrupted by the friggin' FBI man telling me that in Mexico you are guilty until proven innocent. Andrew, Ted and I are shown into a yellow VW, I can't believe they put us together. Ted says, 'Baby, keep your mouth tight. We'll get you out of here – you just don't know a thing.' Andrew tells me not to worry, the brothers will get us out – and we do have such a good karma. This reality crashed down so quickly – goodbye, you dreamers – the realities sure do change. There is a great disparity between the dream and the fact.

The drive to the jail is short; everything is very close in La Paz. The jail, or Edificio M. Sobarzo, is an old hospital with thick walls and a lot of police hanging around outside. They take us out of the car at gunpoint, it is around four o'clock now, and I scream for Andrew to come with me. He is dragged away and the district prosecutor takes my purse and finally looks through – stops and takes out my makeup case, now empty of drugs. He then looks over my diary and I get weak in the knees – all my notes about methedrine madness and heroin. He confiscates it and I am led to a cell isolated from the rest of the jail. There are at least thirty male eyes following me – the cell they lead me to looks very small – perhaps it is a single cell for me alone. I start to panic as they open up the huge barred door and push me into a dark hole – goodbye sunlight, goodbye dark-eyed girl, you were so free so free, and the door swings shut with me wondering what in the fuck is going on.

> From: *Shaman Woman, Mainline Lady: Women's Writings and the Drug Experience*, eds Cynthia Palmer and Michael Horowitz, 1982

Poor Mexico, so far from God and so near to the United States

Porfirio Diz

Howard Marks
Disappearing Dope Dealers

SERIOUS DOPE DEALERS occasionally need to disappear, to evade the forces of law and order, to become fugitives from injustice.

Disappearance, generally, is simple: jog over a Balkan

minefield. Even if cheating mortality is neither permitted nor desired, most potential vanishers can still take the hardcore option of checking into any Third World prison under a false name. One might have to forget heterosexuality, good nosh and breathtaking vistas; but there's plenty of dope, libraries and gymnasiums. Most dope dealers, however, prefer freedom, so serious thought is necessary when determining to scarper from the Old Bill.

The two most important parameters relating to successful disappearance are where one is and what one looks like. At a location where you've never been and where no one who knows you ever visits, it doesn't matter what you look like; if you don't look like yourself, it doesn't matter where you are. Of course, if escaping the criminal injustice system, there might not be that much time available to travel elsewhere, unless on bail. And it's always a mistake to make a dash for the ports or airports. To disappear, just rent a bedsit and stay inside until your appearance is completely altered by growing (or shaving) a moustache and beard, adopting a radically new hairstyle, and varying the takeaway diet. Bedsits can be boring, so fill those idle moments by applying to the DVLC in Swansea for a few provisional driving licences. Use any names that come to mind. I once obtained one in the name of Elvis Presley. The Swansea computer didn't bat an eyelid; it didn't remember the 1950s. Get loads of junk mail in different names. Join cheesy clubs and get bits of plastic that look like credit cards. Get real. Get a life. Get a few lives.

Different clothes will be necessary but are easily acquired later, as are walking-sticks, crutches, eyepatches, scars, wigs and shades. Wheelchairs and regular glasses are a bit harder. Walk into an optician, and he'll say you need glasses. He makes money that way. The scientific community has apparently established beyond doubt that marijuana causes everything from sterility to crazed nymphomania, including long sight. So when I was on the run I smoked several more and stronger joints than usual and had my eyes tested. A special pair was made. Although they made things rather blurry (except when I was stoned), they dramatically changed my appearance from dope dealer to geography teacher.

Take a driving test with one of the provisional licences, get a Post Office savings account with the full licence as identification, then get a bank account. This can be a little difficult as bank managers are nosy bastards, but it should be possible to wing it with some bullshit about having lived abroad all one's life, or being brought up by drop-out hippie parents in the Scottish Highlands. There's nothing to lose. The bank manager is worried that he'll lose money through you, nothing else. He believes you to be the person named in the driving licence, especially if inside the plastic cover you have a photograph of the wife and kids (someone else's, of course).

One normally associates disappearing with getting false passports, and they are handy. Various ones are available in the criminal marketplace, but ideally, one wants a passport actually issued by one of the passport offices (so that it withstands today's sophisticated border checks) and one wants as few people as possible to know the name (so friends can't grass up).

Dress up as a cool clairvoyant and sit alone in a village pub reading weird colourful literature. Initiate a conversation with someone about your age and let him know you're an astrologer, palmist and numerologist, capable of telling his fortune for nothing. You'll need a few details, of course: date and place of birth, mother's maiden name, and his travels or travel plans. (Some, you'll find, will have no intention of going abroad because they don't trust foreign beer). Go to St Catherine's House, London, get the birth certificate, and fill in the passport application form. The tricky bit is getting it countersigned by someone who exists. It's much easier to get it countersigned by someone who doesn't exist. So rent another bedsit in another name and become a referee. Fill out the passport application forms in your own handwriting (immigration authorities of any country can easily and remotely check with British authorities the handwriting on the passport application form and compare it with your current handwriting). In appropriately different handwriting and ink, fill out the referee's bit on the form and on the back of the photograph. Post it to the Passport Office. The only check the Passport office is likely to make is to telephone the referee and ask if he'd countersigned the application and photograph, so just sit in the bedsit for ten days waiting for either the call or the passport. The only conceivable future worry is that the person in whose name the passport was would suddenly apply for a passport himself or mess things up in a different way. This can be overcome by using someone very trustworthy who knows you are going to use what should be his passport, will never apply for one, and will back you up in whatever way might be needed.

Your friend truthfully fills in a passport application form and takes a photograph of himself. He gets his local doctor to sign the photograph and application form as being authentic, then gives the signed form and photograph back to you. Fill in an identical application form in your own handwriting, substitute your own photograph, copy the doctor's rubber stamp and handwriting as best you can, and fill in the appropriate bits. The passport office might check with the doctor by phone, but his answers will be okay, and you don't have to rent another bedsit.

If there's enough time beforehand to plan a disappearance, some added precautions are sensible. Warn your friends of your intention of visiting somewhere remote for a long time. Then go somewhere else. If you're pretending to be killed or kidnapped, then remember to first deposit some money (not much) in a bank account and make lots of appointments. Do whatever you can indicate you had no idea what was coming.

Finally, if in a really tight spot, always remember that no one is bothered by your wearing an outrageous mask (obtainable from any kids' toyshop) unless you are actually robbing a bank at the time. Wearing an obvious disguise implies you don't need one.

James Mills
The Underground Empire

DONALD STEINBERG WAS the Henry Ford of the international marijuana industry. He had taken an idea in its infancy, tested it, refined it, reinvented it, applied daring and imagination, and ended up setting standards that would endure through the decade. Barely thirty years old, he was making more money each day than the President of the United States made in an entire four-year term, more than old-time criminals like John Dillinger and Willie Sutton made in a lifetime. In one year alone he grossed more than was taken in all armed robberies throughout the United States. He spent $2 million a year just renting jets, sometimes three at a time, to ferry his money around the country – so much cash he had time only to count the suitcases, figuring roughly a half-million dollars per Samsonite.

When it came to money, no idea was too wild, too impossible, too grand. If the human mind could dream it up, Donald Steinberg could make it work. When he was smuggling 100,000-pound loads of marijuana (worth $20 million dockside) from Colombia on other people's freighters, he asked, 'Who needs other people's freighters?' And when he had his own freighters, he asked, 'Who needs Colombia?' His executives, shippers and horticulturists branched out to Thailand, Singapore, Hong Kong, Africa, Holland, Panama, teaching everyone how to grow their product, how to fly it, ship it, sell it.

A genius of organization and logistics, Donald Steinberg was importing marijuana up and down both coasts, as many as four freighterloads a day, distributing it through a complex network spanning the North American continent, masterminding a system of procurement, importation, warehousing, shipping and wholesaling that would have been the envy of Sears Roebuck. And he was doing it all in secret, under the noses of police on four continents. He was also doing it without resorting to violence. He prided himself on that. He told himself that what he did was clean crime, hardly crime at all. But somehow, inexplicably, *unfairly*, violence pursued him. There were beatings, kidnappings, million-dollar ransoms, deaths.

Dark-haired, skinny, with soft deep-set eyes, Donald Steinberg lived the life of a rock star – private planes, limousines, groupies, weekend parties in Frank Sinatra's suite at Caesar's Palace. And he was learning some hard lessons, about himself, about his friends, about deception and dreams. Dennis Dayle hoped to continue the education.

The most remarkable thing about Donald Steinberg was not his success, extraordinary as that was, but the charismatic spell he appeared to cast over everyone who met him, and many who did not. Every cop, agent or intelligent analyst who had had even a glance at Steinberg's files came away with awe and the same compelling dream. 'What I wouldn't give for just one hour to talk to that guy.'

The Underground Empire, 1974

Shana Alexander
The Game

Thursday, October 24, 1985. The Courtroom.
A courtroom is laid out like a cathedral. Members of the public are the congregation, and they are always divided from the clergy by a railing. The jury box takes the place of the choir stalls. In this trial, the jury box is on the left, and opposite it, on the right, is another box, the soundproofed translators' booth. The raised altar at the back is the province of the judge. Or is he high priest, or grand rabbi? No matter. The question is: Who, and what, is being worshiped here?

The government calls it the biggest drug and Mafia case ever to come to trial in the United States. The press calls it the Pizza Connection. The trial about to begin here in the United States Courthouse in Manhattan will attempt to prove the existence within the nation's midst of a conspiracy to import and distribute more than one and one-half tons of pure heroin. The street value of this much heroin, the government has said, is one and two-thirds billion dollars. A small amount of the loot was discovered at the Palermo international airport in a suitcase shipped from New York City. The cash was wrapped in pizzeria aprons, which made the tabloid title almost inevitable.

The defendants are twenty-two Sicilian-born men, all of

them Mafia members or associates, and nearly all of them in the food and pizza business. They will be represented here by twenty-two trial lawyers, members of the criminal defense bar.

The man whose luck it is to be presiding here is the Honorable Pierre N. Leval. At forty-nine, just off the lengthy and difficult General Westmoreland libel case, the blond, bespectacled, deep-voiced, Roman-faced judge is a richly admired and respected jurist, a man at the height of his powers.

He indicates the chief defendant, a small, grizzled man seated in the front pew just to the right of the aisle, his back to the room. 'Gaetano Badalamenti is represented by Mr. Michael Kennedy.'

A tall, slender man with red-gold hair and gold-wire glasses stands up and tenders the jury a slight bow. 'Good morning.' A row of counsel tables has been placed in front of the first pew, just inside the altar rail, and Kennedy occupies the aisle seat, directly in front of his client.

The evidence in this massive case has taken the government five years to assemble. It includes 55,000 wiretaps, few of them in English. The Sicilian-born defendants arrived only rather recently in the United States, in the 1960s and 1970s. Earlier Sicilian immigrants refer to these newcomers as 'Zips,' not an admiring term.

All but three of the twenty-two defendants are charged with being part of a RICO (Racketeer-Influenced and Corrupt Organizations Act) conspiracy, a relatively new law that allows the government to charge that apparently unrelated criminals are in fact acting together to further the aims of an overall criminal enterprise. Organized crime itself, or the Mafia, can be deemed such an enterprise. RICO convictions carry very severe penalties.

The person chosen to deliver the government's opening statement is Department of Justice Attorney Robert Stewart, forty-nine, a man who has spent his life in law enforcement in New Jersey, and has accumulated an encyclopedic knowledge of this case. Stewart is an austere figure with pale, angular features, black-rimmed glasses, a black suit, and the voice and manner of an undertaker. He stands at a little oak podium that has been wheeled to face the jury box.

The first four front-row defendants are considered flight risks, too dangerous for bail, and the government has insisted that, for security reasons, they sit together, guarded by marshals. Gaetano Badalamenti, sixty-two, is said to be the most wanted narcotics fugitive in the world, and one time Boss of Bosses of the entire Sicilian Mafia. In short, he is the real Godfather. His elder son, Vito, twenty-eight, sits one seat away to his right. Father and son have been extradited from Madrid. Between them sits Badalamenti's Number One nephew, Vincenzo Randazzo, extradited from Zurich. The fourth jailed defendant is no relation. Salvatore Salamone, scrawny and pale, in T-shirt and rose-colored glasses, is a small-time hood who has been brought here from federal prison where he is serving a twenty-year sentence for illegal gun possession.

Normally, all the pews to the left of the aisle are reserved for reporters, sketch artists and the public. This morning the first three rows have been cleared. Alone in the front row sits a slender, muscular man, in gray suit, black tie, knees crossed. Beneath a thick mat of black hair is a face white as a Mexican sugar skull, with alert black eyes. Rudolph Giuliani, thirty-nine, is United States Attorney for the Southern District of New York. Giuliani is the composer of this entire opera. He has arranged and rehearsed this morning's rousing overture. He will be the mostly invisible maestro of the whole show to come.

Prosecutor Stewart grips the microphone tightly, runs his finger around a too-tight shirt collar, and in a flat voice, with minimal gestures, begins to tell a story. It is really a simple tale, he says: one single commodity bought, shipped, sold, replenished. But the numbers are huge. Stewart mentions 'over a ton of pure heroin worth over $333 million, a third of a billion dollars, in the space of little over a year.'

A group of individuals in the New York-New Jersey area formed a joint business venture, Stewart continues. They then got together with a friend overseas and asked: Can you provide us with this commodity? The overseas friend called his friend and said he wanted to buy a certain raw material, then manufacture it into a commodity and transport it to America, where it would be sold to customers. No checks, no bank accounts; the business was to be all cash.

'That's all that happened, ladies and gentlemen, month in and month out. But the commodity' – he pauses for as long as he can bear – 'the commodity was massive amounts of contraband. And all the individuals engaged in the enterprise were members of the Mafia, or associates of Mafia members, both in Sicily and in the United States.'

The business venture, says Stewart, came about in this fashion. After the breaking of the French Connection, in the late 1960s the Zips gradually took over heroin distribution in the United States. American Mafiosi did not touch drugs, not directly; it was too dangerous. They left that to the lean, hungry newcomers.

Mountains of cash earned from the drug trade were collected and boxed by a subsidiary group of restaurant and pizzeria owners in New Jersey. These men, also recent Sicilian immigrants, used their contacts in Italy and Switzerland to set up a money-laundering operation that moved millions of dollars into the secret Swiss bank accounts of the Sicilian Mafia warlords.

Such, according to Stewart, is the case the government will prove. The evidence, he says, has two themes. One deals with the mechanics of smuggling: how you get the drugs in, the money out. He promises that the government will show in detail how these defendants moved more than $40 million in cash to Sicily alone. This does not include money sent to Brazil, he adds with a thin smile.

'The second theme involves the dynamics of the Mafia . . . the secret criminal organization which provided the cement which held this conspiracy together.' The Mafia is extremely disciplined, Stewart explains. These men had no ability to enforce their contracts under law. But they had a secret criminal society, and Mafia discipline is so strict it enables a man to walk down a dark alley with $1 million in cash and fear no ambush.

The leader was Gaetano Badalamenti, of Cinisi, a small town west of Palermo, Sicily. He supplied the men in New York and New Jersey with heroin between 1978 and 1980, 'when he was compelled to relocate to Brazil.' Hearing this, Badalamenti worms his big head around to the left to gaze mildly upon the prosecutor and jury. He has pebbly ivory skin, a grim mouth, eyes like lumps of coal; the unreadable visage of a Pharaoh.

The Pizza Connection, 1988

CHAPTER SIX
WITH IT

James Lee
I Learn to Inject Morphia

Before commencing with my story in its proper order, I will say a few words about the drug habit generally.

During the thirty years in which I was a constant user of drugs of many kinds, various people, including some doctors and chemists, have asked me how it was that I was able to continue in the habit for so long a time, and use such large quantities of drugs, and still remain in good health.

This true story of my experiences will explain the reason, and also may show the drug habit in an entirely new aspect.

It is now many years since I gave up using all drugs, but during the thirty years with which this story deals, I have used morphia, cocaine, hash, opium, and a good many other drugs, both singly and in combination.

The doses which I became able to take, after so many years of the habit, may seem almost impossible, yet it is a fact that I have increased my dose gradually, until I could inject eighty grains of pure cocaine a day; sufficient to kill many persons, if divided among them.

At other times, when I favoured morphia, I have injected as much as ten grains per day, although the medical dose is a quarter of a grain.

My arms, shoulders and chest are a faint blue colour,

which, if magnified, reveal the marks of thousands of tiny punctures; hypodermic syringe marks.

Many years I have searched the jungles of the Far East for new drugs; testing strange plants, bulbs and roots, making extracts, and then testing them first on animals, and in some cases on myself; and I will describe later some of the strange effects produced, particularly in the case of one drug, which I will call 'The Elixir of Life'.

If some of the things I describe are horrible, they are nevertheless true. What strange sights may a man not see during seven years in a country like China, if he goes to look for them below the surface? It is a country of camouflage and hidden ways. Innocent-looking junks, quietly floating down the rivers and canals, may be really sumptuously furnished gambling dens and drug haunts, where orgies of many kinds are carried on. No European, unless he is introduced by a trusted Chinese, will ever have entry to these places.

The life of a drug taker can be a happy one, far surpassing that of any other, or it can be one of suffering and misery; it depends on the user's knowledge.

The most interesting period will only be reached after many years – and then only if perfect health has been retained – using several kinds of drugs (for one drug alone spells disaster), and increasing the doses in a carefully thought-out system, a system which was first made known to me by the Indian doctor who initiated me into the drug habit.

Waking visions will then begin to appear when under the influence of very large doses, and it is these visions which are so interesting.

I have sat up through the night taking drugs until the room has been peopled with spirits. They may be horrible, grotesque, or beautiful, according to the nature of the drugs producing them. Strange scenes have been enacted before my eyes; scenes which were very real and lifelike, and which I will describe later.

When the Dangerous Drugs Act came into force I gave up using all drugs, because the danger and risk of obtaining them was too great. The paltry quantities, about which the authorities make such a fuss, were of no use to me, and I was able to give them up without any trouble or suffering, owing to my experiments and discoveries.

This story will be as a message of hope to all drug addicts. The cure is easy, but not by the method generally adopted, that of gradually reducing the dosage: a method which will only cause intense suffering, and sometimes even death.

Underworld of the East, 2001

Alexander and Ann Shulgin
The Process of Discovery

HOW DOES ONE go about discovering the action, the nature of the effect on the central nervous system, of a chemical which has just been synthesized, but not yet put into a living organism? I start by explaining that it must be understood, first of all, that the newborn chemical is as free of pharmacological activity as a newborn babe is free of prejudice.

INTRODUCTION
At the moment of a person's conception, many fates have been sealed, from physical features to gender and intelligence. But many things have not been decided. Subtleties of personality, belief systems, countless other characteristics, are not established at birth. In the eyes of every newborn, there is a universality of innocence and godliness which changes gradually as interactions take place with parents, siblings and the environment. The adult product is shaped from repeated contacts with pains and pleasures, and what finally emerges is the fatalist, the egocentric or the rescuer. And the traveling companions of this person during his development from undefined infant to well-defined adult, all have contributed to and have been, in turn, modified by these interactions.

So it is also with a chemical. When the idea of a new substance is conceived, nothing exists but symbols, a collage of odd atoms hooked together with bonds, all scribbled out on a blackboard or a napkin at the dinner table. The structure, of course, and perhaps even some spectral characteristics and physical properties are inescapably pre-ordained. But its character in man, the nature of its pharmacological action or even the class of the action it might eventually display, can only be guessed at. These properties cannot yet be known, for at this stage they do not yet exist.

Even when the compound emerges as a new substance, tangible, palpable, weighable, it is still a *tabula rasa* in the pharmacological sense, in that nothing is known, nothing can be known, about its action in man, since it has never been in man. It is only with the development of a relationship between the thing tested and the tester himself that this aspect of character will emerge, and the tester is as much a contributor to the final definition of the drug's action as is the drug itself. The process of establishing the nature of a compound's action is synonymous with the process of developing that action.

Other researchers who taste your material will include some (most, you hope) who make separate evaluations; and it will then appear that you defined (developed) the properties accurately. Other researchers (only a few, you hope) will disagree, and they will privately tend to wonder why they failed to evaluate the material more accurately. You might call this a no-lose situation, and it is the reward for personally following all three parts of this process, namely conception, creation and definition.

But it must be kept in mind that the interaction goes both ways; the tester, as well as the compound being tested, is molded by it.

Phenethylamines and Other Things I Have Known and Loved: A Chemical Love Story, 1991

Robert Sabbag
Smokescreen – 3

REED WAS A head who, at length and unapologetically could provide poetic discourse on 'the energy, the magic, the beauty of the herb.' And mean it. He was a smoker who had started smuggling pot because he got tired of looking for it. Feeling quite emphatically that 'it should be in hand when you need it,' he was religious on the subject. Literally. Marijuana was not an article of faith, it was the Faith itself, and Reed was its Defender. All the money he made smuggling herb he reinvested in smuggling more. The millions never caught up with him, he was always working. Reed, like other smugglers, lavished disposable income on cars and boats, but only on those in which he could haul marijuana. Where another scammer might seek joy in the extravagance of a platinum Rolex, an indigo-blue Maserati or a house with eight bathrooms on the rim of Red Mountain, Reed would be quite happy, he argued, 'if I could keep enough smoke around me.'

Dope will get you through times of no money better than money will get you through times of no dope.
– Freewheelin' Franklin Fabulous Furry Freak Brothers

It was smoke, no doubt, that had led J.D. Reed to his appreciation of the transmigration of souls. Reed believed that he had been a great warrior in a previous life. 'Many lifetimes I had to be a warrior,' he reasoned – 'I got the build for it, I got the instincts' – and he took pride in the fact that, after coming of age in his present life, he had never inflicted harm on anyone. 'With my body-strength and knowledge,' he explained to Long, 'I manipulate 'em, I don't hurt 'em. That's what marijuana did for me. It turned my warrior-ness into peace.'

Reed was a warlord who had established his kingdom securely in the realm of the ethereal, and to achieve the celestial precincts thereof, he followed his very own *camino real*. The journey began with his laying hands on the highest-grade ganja any man could possibly score, and rolling a joint the size of a prairie dog. He would soak the joint in Afghani hash oil, a bottle of which he always kept handy, and hang it in the sun to dry – he would clothespin the oiler to the laundry line outside the kitchen of his ranch. Picking it at just the right moment, Reed would fire it up and smoke it until nothing but ash remained.

That was how he started his day. For anyone smoking with him, it signaled the end of the day.

Smokescreen by Robert Sabbag, first published in Great Britain by
Canongate Books, February 2002

Have you no mind to do what nobody can do for you?
                                                    Miguel Cervantes

James Lee
About Drugs

I LEARN TO INJECT MORPHIA

Beautiful places in the tropics, I have heard, are often unhealthy, and this, I found, was one of them, and it was not long before I got a touch of malaria.

Malaria causes an absolutely rotten feeling, with headache and all the rest of it, so one day when I had an attack rather worse than usual, I sent over to the hospital for the Indian doctor or 'babu', who was in charge there.

He was a fat and jolly Hindu of about forty years of age. After feeling my pulse and taking my temperature, he said, speaking through his nose like most babus do, 'Yes, sir. You have a little fever, but I will soon cure you.'

Then he called Abdul to bring a glass of water, and taking a little case out of his pocket, he opened it and took out a small glass syringe; the first hypodermic syringe I had ever seen. Withdrawing the glass plunger, he selected a tabloid from a small tube and dropped it into the syringe, replaced the plunger and drew the syringe three-quarters full of water. Placing a hollow needle on the end of the syringe, he first shook it until the tabloid was dissolved, and then injected the contents into my arm. I will never forget that first injection; the beautiful sensation of ease and comfort; the luxurious dreamy feeling of indolence and happiness which immediately ensued. Every distressing symptom of the fever had disappeared, and I only wanted to sit still in my chair. I was simply purring with content. The voice of the Dr Babu, who was a great talker, was like a gentle murmur, and I saw him through a pleasant haze.

I must have sat there for hours after he had gone, and it was growing dark, and Abdul came in with the lamp, and commenced laying the table for dinner. It was the first meal that I had really enjoyed for some days, and that night I slept well, and awakened fresh next morning.

As the day wore on, I felt not quite so well, rather tired and a little depressed, and I thought that perhaps I required a little more of the medicine the babu had given me the day before; also I felt that I would like to have another dose, so I went over to the hospital and saw the babu. He greeted me with a pleasant smile, and made no trouble about giving me another injection.

'What sort of medicine is this, Doctor?' I asked him.

'It is morphia,' he said. 'The most useful medicine in the world.'

The word morphia meant little to me then – of course I had heard about morphia addicts, but I thought I was quite capable of controlling any impulse I might have of making a habit of it, and I thought a few doses could not make such a difference; moreover, the second dose seemed to be even more potent than the first; no doubt he had given me a larger one.

I even persuaded the doctor to give me a syringe and a tube of four-grain tabloids.

After a time I found myself looking forward to the afternoon when the day's work was over, and I could take a larger dose and lie dreaming rosy dreams; meanwhile I had got in a supply of tabloids from Calcutta.

There were only daydreams, it is true, for I had not yet reached the stage where visions appear while asleep, much less that stage which extremely few drug addicts ever reach, the time when absolutely lifelike visions appear while awake. This stage can never be reached on morphia alone.

After a few months of regular indulgence in morphia I began to feel that to get the same results I had to increase my dose and also that the effect wore off more quickly.

Also, I found that my digestive system was getting out of order, and I was becoming so costive that no opening medicine had much effect. The latter symptom was causing me considerable inconvenience, and I was getting scared. I was using now about four grains a day, injected a grain at a time instead of the four-dose as at first, yet the effect was not so pleasant.

I decided that the drug habit was getting too great a hold on me, and that the time had come when I must give it up; never expecting any difficulty in doing so.

I had heard that morphia users broke themselves of the habit generally by reducing their dose a little every day, until they had given it all up.

I smile at my ignorance now, but then it seemed quite simple, so I started.

Next day I took my usual supply of morphia for the day: four grains, and mixed it in a small vial containing six syringes full of water, viz. 120 minims. I now drew up into the syringe one-tenth of the mixture (twelve minims) and threw it away replacing it by this quantity of water.

Next day I felt all right. 'Hurrah, it is easy.'

The second day I threw away twenty-four minims and added only eighteen minims of water, thus reducing the quantity of liquid per injection from twenty minims to nineteen minims; the mixture also being not so strong.

Now I did not feel so good. I found my thoughts constantly turning to morphia, and going over again the pleasant sensation I had experienced. This seemed to emphasise my present state. I really felt uncomfortable and rather irritable, and I kept thinking what a pleasure it would be to take a thumping big dose.

Pride and fear made me stick to my intention, and persevere with this so-called system, until I had reduced my consumption of morphia to two grains a day. Beyond this I could not possibly go. I was suffering terribly; I could not sleep, nor sit still, and I was on the fidget all the time. I had a horrible toothache, and I was jumpy and nervous. I could not get a wink of sleep at night, for I would be up half a dozen times walking about the room, as I had cramps in my feet and legs, which I could not keep in one position while lying in bed for more than a minute, before they began to ache again. I felt wretched in the extreme, and I think that the worst symptom of all was the horrible feeling of depression and gloom – so terrible that it defies description. Moreover, I found that every reduction of the dose increased the sufferings, not only in proportion, but probably fourfold, and I had a tolerable idea that what I was suffering then would be only a fraction of what I would suffer when I got down to the quarter of a grain.

I could not stand it any longer, and I injected a whole-grain dose.

Can anyone possibly describe the sensation of relief I felt? I think not; no words possibly could do so. It was simply Heaven, and that is all I can say. I was now thoroughly scared, because I was back on my one-grain doses, and soon I even began to feel that I would like to increase them.

I decided to see the Dr Babu, so I went over to the hospital, where I found he was attending to the outpatients.

I went into his room and waited, and began to think.

I had often noticed a peculiar look in his eyes, when I met him. Sometimes I noticed that the pupils were mere pinpoints, while at other times they were so large as to almost fill his iris. Moreover, I had noticed that sometimes he would be calm and dreamy in his manner, while again he would sometimes be full of life and energy. His moods appeared to change in many different ways.

I remembered the peculiar smile on his face when I told him that I was going to gradually reduce my dose of morphia until I had given it up.

He had enquired two or three times how I was getting on, and each time I had told him of my success he had smiled. I wondered why he had not told me how difficult morphia was to give up; so when he came in I tackled him about it.

'Sir,' he said, 'morphia is a very strange medicine, it is both Heaven, and Hell. It is very difficult to give up, but it can be done.'

Morphia should not be used by anyone for longer than a few months, he told me, because by that time it will begin to lose its pleasant effect, and it will also begin to affect the health, because the action of the drug is continually in one direction.

He told me that he used many kinds of drugs, each in turn; changing over from one to another, using them sometimes singly, and at other times in combinations, so that no one drug ever got too great a hold on him. Each time he changed over, the drug he had been using regained all its old potency and charm when commenced again.

I complained about the binding effect of the morphia.

'Yes,' he said, 'that is one of the principal reasons why the long use of morphia alone is so destructive to health. Its deadening effect on the bowels and the digestion. Although purgatives are of little use, and, moreover, are dangerous to a morphia addict, there is one sure remedy.'

Then he gave me my first dose of cocaine.

I found the effect extremely pleasant, although I only had a beginner's dose grain. It was stimulating, and exhilarating, producing a feeling of well-being, of joy and good spirits. Large doses will produce great self-confidence, and absolutely banish every feeling of self-consciousness in the most difficult situations; in fact it will make the user glory in becoming conspicuous.

Cocaine in large doses also has another effect, which I will not describe here, and this effect is considerably increased when certain other drugs are mixed with it. It is a strange fact that although cocaine, in itself, is not an opening medicine when used by any other person, the effect is immediate when taken by a morphia addict whose bowels have become inoperative.

Following the Dr Babu's instructions, I first mixed up an ounce solution containing one grain of morphia to each twenty minims of water, and another of a five per cent solution of cocaine. Starting with twenty minims of the morphia solution, injected three times a day, i.e. three grains of morphia a day, I reduced the dose by one minim each day, and added one minim of the cocaine solution, until in twenty days I was using no morphia at all, only cocaine. I experienced no inconvenience at all, or craving for morphia, only increased pleasure.

My health improved, and I became so full of life and energy and good spirits, that everyone noticed the change in me. No one suspected that I had been using morphia, they had put the change in me, from the health and spirits which I had when I first arrived to the listless and dreamy stage I had been in for some time, to malaria.

The increased brilliance of my eyes, due to the cocaine, appeared only to be an excessive state of good health and vitality.

I now experienced even greater pleasure from the indulgence in cocaine, than I had experienced when commencing to use morphia; and the fact that I had been able to give up the latter so easily filled me with pride, because in the last week or two I had read a good deal about the drug habit. I was studying a book by an Indian writer, which the babu had lent me.

It is true that I was now using cocaine, instead of morphia, but then cocaine is much easier to give up than morphia. The deprivation does not cause such distressing and terrible symptoms. I had not yet discovered the perfect cure for all drug habits, this was to come later, but just out of curiosity I tried a beginner's dose of morphia again, and I found that it had regained all the potency and effect that it had when I was first introduced to it.

Cocaine, I found, banished all desire for sleep, and as loss of proper sleep is one of the reasons why the drug quickly ruins the health, I saw the doctor about it.

I had become very friendly with him, and perhaps because I treated him differently from the way most Europeans treated the educated Indian in those days – by affecting to consider them as inferiors – he imparted to me knowledge about many strange drugs and their effects. He had devoted many years to the study of this subject, and it was due to him that I first got my great idea, with which I will deal in succeeding chapters.

He next initiated me into the art of smoking opium in the

Chinese fashion and I found that a few pipes of this, smoked just before retiring, procured me a refreshing and sound sleep, which is essential to the cocaine addict, but is so seldom obtained.

The opium is smoked in a manner which has been so often described in books that I will not say much about it here. Opium has the appearance of thick black treacle before it is cooked on a skewer, over a small spirit lamp, until it becomes the consistency of cobblers' wax. This is then rolled into a pellet the size of a large pea, and stuck on the pipe bowl with the skewer. When the latter is withdrawn there remains a small hole through the centre of the pellet.

The pipe, which is a hollow bamboo, is then held over the flame and the smoke sucked into the lungs. The effect is extremely soothing and sleep-producing, more so than any other drug, and it is a mistake to think that it produces dreams. When once the smoker is asleep, it is a sound and dreamless sleep. It is preceded by a very pleasant, dreamy state, in which the imagination is very active, and everything appears beautiful, so that even an ugly woman would appear charming.

I found that I could vary my dose of cocaine very considerably, and occasionally I would have a regular binge and then bring myself back to normal with the aid of a little morphia injected. I was again in fine health and spirits, and I was becoming more interested in my surroundings. No one suspected that I was using drugs, for there was nothing about my manner to indicate my habit, especially as during the day I used only small doses.

The Dr Babu was a jolly old soul and fond of female society, and frequently when I went over to his bungalow for an evening, I would find him entertaining some of the prettiest girls in the settlement, and sometimes he had 'Nautch Wallahs', i.e. professional dancing girls, giving an exhibition. Sometimes, also, there were other entertainers which I will not describe.

In those days I was very young and shy, and many things easily shocked me.

I found cocaine became more and more fascinating as the

doses were increasing and time went on. The small doses, such as are taken by a beginner, will produce only a remarkable increase of mental and bodily vigour, with a feeling of great strength, but without any intoxication, but if the dose is considerably increased, a kind of intoxication, which is quite different from that produced by drink, will ensue, a kind of intoxication which I will endeavour to describe later on.

Underworld of the East, 2001

Thomas Szasz
Ceremonial Chemistry

CHEMISTS, PHYSICIANS, PSYCHOLOGISTS, psychiatrists, politicians and pharmaceutical manufacturers have all searched in vain for non-addictive drugs to relieve pain, to induce sleep and to stimulate wakefulness. This search is based on the false premise that addiction is a condition caused by drugs. When a drug deadens pain, induces sleep or stimulates wakefulness, people develop an interest in using such drugs. We call drugs 'addictive' simply because people like to use them.

Our contemporary confusion regarding drug abuse and drug addiction is an integral part of our confusion regarding religion. Any idea or act that gives existence meaning and purpose is religious. Since the use and avoidance of certain substances has to do with prescriptions and prohibitions, drug addiction has two aspects: religious (legal) and scientific (medical). As some persons seek or avoid alcohol and tobacco, heroin and marijuana, so others seek or avoid kosher wine and holy water. The differences between kosher wine and non-kosher wine, holy water and ordinary water, are ceremonial, not chemical. Although it would be idiotic to look for the property of kosherness in wine, or for the property of holiness in water, this does not mean that there is no such thing as kosher wine or holy water. Kosher wine is wine that is ritually clean according to Jewish law. Holy water is blessed by a Catholic priest. This creates a certain demand for such wine and water by people who want this sort of thing. At the same time, and for precisely the same reason, such wine and water are rejected by those who do not believe in their use. Similarly, the important differences between heroin and alcohol, or marijuana and tobacco are not chemical but ceremonial. Heroin and marijuana are approached and avoided not because they are more addictive or more dangerous than alcohol and tobacco, but because they are more holy or unholy, as the case may be.

Eighteenth-century medics formed the first factories for manufacturing madmen and developed the earliest advertising campaigns for selling 'insanity' by renaming badness as madness, and then offered to dispose of it. They progressively metaphorised disagreeable conduct and forbidden desire as disease – thus creating more and more mental diseases; second, they literalised this medical metaphor, insisting that disapproved behaviour was not merely *like* a disease, but that it *was* a disease. By the twentieth century, madness was bursting through the walls of the insane asylums and was being discovered in clinics and doctors' offices, in literature and art, and in the psychopathology of everyday life. Religion and common sense lost their nerve, no longer able even to try to resist the opportunistic theories and oppressive technologies of modern behavioural science. Those who use drugs are now viewed as unable to help themselves, victims of their irresistible impulses from which they need the protection of others. This made it logical and reasonable for politicians and psychiatrists to advocate drug controls.

Presumably some persons have always 'abused' certain drugs – alcohol for millennia, opiates for centuries. However, only in the twentieth century have certain patterns of drug use been labelled as 'addictions'. Traditionally, the term 'addiction' has meant simply a strong inclination towards certain kinds of conduct, with little or no pejorative meaning attached to it. Thus, the *Oxford English Dictionary* offers such pre-twentieth-century examples of the use of this term as being addicted to 'civil affairs', to 'useful reading' – and also 'to bad habits'. Being addicted to drugs is not among the definitions listed. The term 'addiction' was understood to refer to a habit, good or bad as the case might be, actually more often the former. Although the term 'addiction' is still often used to describe habits, usually of an undesirable sort, its meaning has become so expanded and transformed that it is now used to refer to almost any kind of illegal, immoral or undesirable association with certain kinds of drugs. For example, a person who has smoked but a single marijuana cigarette, or even one who has not used any habit-forming or illegal drug at all, may be considered to be a drug addict. The noun 'addict' has lost its denotative meaning and reference to persons engaged in certain *habits*, and has become transformed into a stigmatising label, possessing only pejorative meaning referring to certain *persons*. The term 'addict' has thus been added to our lexicon of stigmatising labels – such as 'Jew', which could mean either a person professing a certain religion or a 'Christ killer' who himself should be killed; or 'Negro', which could mean either a black-skinned person or a savage who ought to be kept in actual or social slavery. More specifically still, the word 'addict' has been added to our psychiatric vocabulary of stigmatising diagnoses, taking its place alongside such terms as 'insane', 'psychotic' and 'schizophrenic'.

Ceremonial Chemistry, 1974

This extract has been paraphrased by Howard Marks.

Aleister Crowley
The True Will

King Lamus descended on me one morning, just after I had taken a dose, and was raking my brain for a reason for my action. I was alternately chewing the end of my pencil and making meaningless marks on the paper. I told him my difficulty. 'Always glad to help,' he said airily; went to a filing cabinet and produced a docket of typed manuscripts. He put it in my hand. It was headed: 'Reasons for taking it'.

1. My cough is very bad this morning. (Note: (a) Is cough really bad? (b) If so, is the body coughing because it is sick or because it wants to persuade you to give it some heroin?)
2. To buck me up.
3. I can't sleep without it.
4. I can't keep awake without it.
5. I must be at my best to do what I have to do. If I can only bring that off, I need never take it again.
6. I must show I am master of it – free to say either 'yes' or 'no'. And I must be perfectly sure by saying 'yes' at the moment. My refusal to take it at the moment shows weakness. Therefore I take it.
7. In spite of the knowledge of the disadvantages of the heroin life, I am really not sure whether it isn't better than the other life. After all, I get extraordinary things out of heroin which I should never have got otherwise.
8. It is dangerous to stop too suddenly.
9. I'd better take a small dose now rather than put it off till later; because if I do so, it will disturb my sleep.
10. It is really very bad for the mind to be constantly preoccupied with the question of the drug. It is better to take a small dose to rid myself of the obsession.
11. I am worried about the drug because of my not having any. If I were to take some, my mind would clear up immediately, and I should be able to think out good plans for stopping it.
12. The gods may be leading me to some new experience through taking it.
13. It is quite certainly a mistake putting down all little discomforts as results of taking it. Very likely, nearly all of them are illusions; the rest, due to the unwise use of it. I am simply scaring myself into saying 'no'.
14. It is bad for me morally to say 'no'. I must not be a coward about it.
15. There is no evidence at all that the reasonable use of heroin does not lengthen life. Chinese claim, and English physicians agree, that opium-smoking, within limits, is a

practice conducive to longevity. Why should it not be the same with heroin? It has been observed actually that addicts seem to be immune to most diseases which afflict ordinary people.

16. I take it because of its being prohibited. I decline being treated like a silly schoolboy when I'm a responsible man. (Note: Then don't behave like a silly schoolboy. Why let the stupidity of governments drive you into taking the drug against your will? – K.L.)

17. My friend likes me to take it with her.

18. My ability to take it shows my superiority over other people.

19. Most of us dig our graves with our teeth. Heroin has destroyed my appetite, therefore it is good for me.

20. I have got into all sorts of messes with women in the past. Heroin has destroyed my interest in them.

21. Heroin has removed my desire for liquor. If I must choose, I really think heroin is the better.

22. Man has a right to spiritual ambition. He has evolved to what he is, through making dangerous experiments. Heroin certainly helps me to obtain a new spiritual outlook on the world. I have no right to assume that the ruin of bodily health is injurious; and 'whosoever will save his life shall lose it, but whoever loseth his life for My sake shall find it'.

23. So-and-so has taken it for years, and is all right.

24. So-and-so has taken it for years, and is still taking it, and he is the most remarkable man of his century.

25. I'm feeling so very, very rotten, and a very, very little would make me feel so very, very good.

26. We can't stop while we have it – the temptation is too strong. The best way is to finish it. We probably won't be able to get any more, so we take it in order to stop taking it.

27. Claude Farrere's story of Rodolphe Hafner. Suppose I take all this pain to stop drugs and then get cancer or something right away, what a fool I shall feel!

'Help you at all?' asked Lamus.

Well, honestly, it did not. I had thought out most of those things for myself at one time or another; and I seemed to have got past them. It's a curious thing that once you've written down a reason you diminish its value. You can't go on using the same reason indefinitely. That fact tends to prove that the alleged reason is artificial and false, that it has simply been invented on the spur of the movement by oneself to excuse one's indulgences.

Diary of a Drug Fiend, 1970

There are no differences but differences of degree between different degrees of difference and no difference

William James

Robert Svoboda
Intoxicants

IN AN ORDINARY person the consumption of alcohol will lead to an enkindling of the Jathara Agni. Ayurveda recognises this and prescribes medicinal wines when there is a need to increase the appetite and promote digestion.

An Aghori, though, is not an ordinary person. Aghoris do not live to eat. An Aghori who drinks must drink not to lose his consciousness and become more enmeshed in the world's Maya, but rather to dilate certain brain cells to increase, not decrease, the awareness. Alcohol should sharpen your mind so much that a problem which might take hours to think out in the normal state can be done instantaneously. It's the same with every other type of intoxication also: if you can't control it, don't do it; you're sure to scuttle yourself.

When an Aghori takes a lot of intoxicants he feels like going to the smashan and being alone with his thoughts. He becomes more introverted; he feels like telling everyone he meets 'Leave me alone!' And if he covers himself with ashes and remains naked and shouts obscenities, no one is likely to come near, and he can be in his mood all day long. This is one of the reasons why Aghoris act the way they do. I used to do it myself.

Aghoris are thrill seekers; that's it in a nutshell. When I went to the USA in 1981, what was the thing I most enjoyed? The roller coasters! Especially 'Space Mountain' at Disney World and the old wooden roller coaster at Circusworld. I could stay on a roller coaster all day! That rush of speed, that excitement! Most people just scream and forget it, just as most people who drink get drunk and pass out, and most people who indulge in sex have an orgasm and go to sleep. But what is the use in that? That is mere bodily indulgence. To be an Aghori you must go beyond all limitations, and the biggest limitation is the limitation of the body. When we Aghoris use thrills, intoxicants and sex we use them to go beyond the body. It is the same way with music. Maybe if I use music as an example you'll understand what I mean about intoxicants and sex. Music is vibration, just like mantra. You can use it to benefit your *sadhana*. Any music will work, if it has a nice melody and a good rhythm. I love Jim Reeves because he has both melody and a good rhythm, and also pathos. I enjoy Spanish and Caribbean tunes, and I will even listen to some rock music, though much of it is too violent for my purposes. Some of our bigoted Indians say, 'Only Indian music can make your mind more meditative,' but that is all bull. It is true that our Indian rhythms are far more advanced in complexity than are the Western ones, and our tunes are much more intricate, but there is something about Western music which makes it particularly useful for getting into certain frames of mind.

Meat is also an intoxicant, by the way. It is just as intoxicating as music, alcohol, marijuana or sex. But it involves killing a sentient being, which I don't like; I am fond of animals. Besides, when you eat meat you must be in a position to ensure that the animal gets a higher rebirth, if you don't want to be stained by karma. So it is better to avoid it.

There are three important reasons why Aghoris love to take

intoxicants. First, it is a question of challenge and response. It is a contest between the Aghori and the drug: Who is stronger? Will the drug be able to overcome the Aghori's will and drown his consciousness or will the Aghori be able to control the drug's effect and bend it to his will. The exhilaration of such a duel is a sublime intoxication in itself.

Second, if the Aghori is able to master the intoxication, the force of the intoxicant magnifies the force of his concentration, since the mind is a chemical phenomenon. As the concentration is strengthened, the image of the deity which is being continually formed in the subtle body is made firmer and clearer, and this brings success at worship all the closer.

Third, Aghoris always worship Shiva, who loves intoxicants. This has a dual-purpose effect. Not only does the Aghori please Shiva by offering Him the intoxicant, but the very act of taking the intoxicant helps the Aghori self-identify with Shiva, since permanent intoxication is one facet of Shiva's personality. Shiva is intoxicated with *samadhi* consciousness: We have to work up to His level gradually.

Most people never realise that the purpose of intoxication is to sharpen the mind. They take marijuana, then eat heavily, then enjoy sex. They will enjoy penetration for one minute and think that they are copulating for years because of the drug's distortion of the sense of time. It's all such a waste.

Aghoris take all sorts of intoxicants, some much worse than these. It is a part of the *sadhana*. I used to keep a cobra and let him bite me on the tongue every hour, just for that peculiar thrill. To feed him I had to put a small hole in an egg and then forcibly pour the contents down his throat. The idea that cobras drink milk is ridiculous. I had several cobras, including one albino who had three lines on his hood: the symbol of Shiva. I kept a king cobra also. Its poison is much deadlier than that of other cobras because its diet is nothing but other cobras. I used to keep white arsenic also, and lick one of the crystals every hour or two. For my marijuana and hashish I had a special pipe made from a particular type of clay into which I had mixed arsenic, aconite, datura seeds, opium, and whatnot. It was a chillum, about a foot long. Beautiful! I used to drink twenty-four hours a day sometimes, and go through cases and cases of Scotch. I drank it neat, straight from the bottle. But after a while I began to think 'What is the use!' I have stopped most of my intoxicants, though I sometimes still drink alcohol or use bhang.

One of the big disadvantages of intoxicants is their side effects. Smoke chillum after chillum of marijuana or hashish and you are bound to develop a terrible cough, and probably chronic bronchitis. Drink bottle after bottle of whisky and your liver must suffer. Drink bhang and become chronically constipated. And long-term use of arsenic or mercury? Don't even *ask* about it. But all these substances have their own special advantages, which is why Aghoris put up with all the disadvantages.

Most people think tobacco has nothing but disadvantages. They are so wrong. Tobacco is really a marvellous plant. Nowadays it is being misused by everyone because very few know how to use it properly, and that is why there are so many side effects. Poor tobacco is blamed, instead of the stupidity of the user. If it is properly employed it can work wonders. It has a hundred important uses in Ayurveda. Do you think that the American Indians were fools to worship it? Never! They knew what it could do.

But there are even better intoxicants. The rishis used to take *soma*, which is a type of leafless creeper. Some people today think soma was the poisonous mushroom *Amanita muscaria*, but that was also merely a substitute for the real thing. Only the rishis know what the true soma is, because only they can see it. It is invisible to everyone else. Before taking the plant the rishis would worship it on an auspicious day and take its permission. If the plant refused its permission, it was left alone. If it said 'yes', if it was willing, then they would make sure the plant would take birth as an animal after its demise. Then they would gather it with the appropriate mantras. If you want to use an intoxicating plant and can't collect it yourself with mantras, you have to add a mantra afterwards if you want it to have the proper effect on you, and if you want to avoid the karma involved. Taking an intoxicant without its appropriate mantra is certain to ruin your Bhuta Agni, and your mind.

Some of my 'children' have started using alcohol or marijuana, thinking they could imitate me. But they have all landed in trouble, because you just can't fool around with these things without knowing the method. Even those of my 'children' who I allow the occasional use of intoxicants have gone beyond their limits sometimes, and I have had to be strict with them.

One boy I am very fond of started thinking he was a great Aghori because I would permit him to take intoxicants with me. I decided he should be taught a lesson for his own good to prevent him from going overboard before he was able to gain complete control. Someone had given me some charas, and this boy was anxious to try it out. You know, charas is not the same thing as hashish. Hashish is the pollen and resin of the cannabis plant. Charas is prepared by taking the fresh fleece from a slaughtered sheep, stuffing it full of this resin, and burying it in the ground for a month. The fat from the sheep and the lanolin from the fleece mix with the resin and liquify it, and the liquid drips into a little pot. After a month the pot is removed, and there you have charas.

I prepared this charas for the boy personally, mixing it with tobacco and rubbing it with my hand in a little water, and I warned him, 'Don't inhale too hard. This sort of charas gets a firm grip on your head very easily. I know you've taken plenty of intoxicants in your life, but this one is different. Beware!' But he ignored my advice, as I knew he would, and he and I started puffing away.

Within five minutes – only five – he realised he had taken too much; but it was too late. He began to lose all his body consciousness. His *prana* (vital force) collected in his throat, which prevented him from wagging his tongue. He was game for it, though, I must admit. He started to try to make the *prana* go up to the *ajna chakra* (the energy centre between the eyebrows) and then out through the *sahasrara* (the energy centre at the crown of the head) – gone for good! Had he succeeded he would have gone into *nirvikalpa samadhi*, a state in which he would have been permanently unable to self-identify with his body.

But I could not permit that to happen. After all, he still has plenty of rnanubandhanas to clear off yet, and if I prevent him from doing that, I become responsible for clearing them off myself. No thank you. So I told someone to give him some water. Drinking that glass of water kept his *prana* right there in his throat, unable to go up any farther. Of course the charas was still pushing from below. Now he was in the *trishanku* state: unable either to go up or to come down. He was neither in the world nor out of it; he lay suspended between the world – the lower five *chakras* – and the true *shunya* (state of 'spiritual vacuum') of the *ajna chakra*. So that he would not forget his lesson I permitted him to remain like that for several hours, while I went to the stables to see my racehorses. When I got back there he was, still hovering somewhere in between. When he was finally able to talk again I asked him what he had experienced. He told me, 'I felt as if I was on the threshold of forgetting everything; as if just a little farther and it would have been only Thee and Me, and from there onward only Thee – or maybe only Me.'

'Wait, wait,' I told him laughing, 'there is still time. Don't be in a hurry. To go up fast is fine, but to come down too fast is fatal.' And since that day he has always taken his intoxicants according to his capacity without permitting them to overcome his conscious mind, even by *shunya*. You must work very gradually with this intoxication business; Rome wasn't built in a day, you know.

Now, obviously, when I prepared that charas for him I added a mantra to it. Otherwise do you think the charas would have sent him into *shunya*? If that were so, all the charas addicts in the world should be enlightened by now.

One thing I always make sure to do is to take the antidote for whatever intoxicant I use. Ayurveda, our ancient Indian medical science, has provided us with methods to limit or eliminate the side effects on the body which these intoxicants cause, so that you get only the intoxication and none of the evil repercussions on your body, or almost none anyway. Even with all these precautions, however, your body will deteriorate when you take intoxicants, because your mind becomes partially free of the constraints of the body: that is the whole purpose of becoming intoxicated. Your mind works so fast that your body can't keep up with it, and it becomes flaccid, loose. The less the mind self-identifies with the body the better for your *sadhana*, but the worse for your body; your physical health will give way to improved mental health. Or at the very least you will remain healthy but you will lose weight and fitness, because you are sitting all day long without exercise or food. But then you don't care two hoots for your body because you find your mental play much more satisfactory.

Of course it is very good to possess a body when you take intoxicants; it acts as something like a sheet anchor when you want to retain your awareness. When you are ethereal you have nothing to hold on to, and other ethereal beings can play havoc with you if they catch you unaware; the possibilities are really frightening. But when you become really firm in your subtle body there is nothing to fear.

Until then, though, you need to have a strong, healthy body to withstand everything you will be going through. Don't get me wrong; I was a wrestler myself, and I appreciate the benefits of a good physique. And this is another reason I discourage people from taking intoxicants: you have to be very healthy first and have done a lot of physical and mental cultivation before you can afford to get involved in this intoxicant business. Otherwise you'll just make yourself toxic. And remember, the brain is a chemical matter, and each toxin produces a certain state of mind. So if you are not intrinsically healthy the intoxicant will not only not make your mind soar into the astral regions but it will create new brain toxins, which will overwhelm your mind with disturbing emotions, which will ruin your *sadhana*. So it is usually better to leave such things alone.

Aghoris believe in reducing sleep to the absolute minimum, because during sleep there is a possibility the mind may slip out of your control. All your careful precautions during waking will come to naught if you get caught up in a dream. Either you must suppress sleep absolutely or you must learn to control your dreams. There exists a plant for this purpose. Make a paste of it and apply it nightly to the soles of your feet. If you do it for thirty nights, or even forty nights, every night you'll get the same dream. It is a type of intoxication; the toxins from the plant are affecting the same brains cells each time in the same way. This is necessary for the *sadhana* of Svapneshvari (Goddess of Dreams). Once you get *siddhi* of Svapneshvari you can control your dreams or stop dreaming altogether. You can also control the dreams of other people, which can be very useful.

Once, one of my friends had taken Aghori Baba's stick for some work. When I asked him for it he refused to return it. I sent Svapneshvari to him. When she comes to someone she comes in a dream; her face can't be seen. She warned him to return the stick or face the consequences; he ignored the warning. This was repeated three or four nights in a row. Then Svapneshvari came to him and told him, 'This is your last warning. If you don't return it, you're heading for big trouble.' When he woke up in the morning, he found a handprint in blood on his pillow. He obstinately refused to return the stick even then. The next night Svapneshvari came to him and said, 'Now you have gone too far; take your punishment.' The next morning he and everyone in his household woke up with high fevers, which would not go down; no medicine could cure them. He returned the stick, and then the fevers subsided.

There are plenty of other uses of Svapneshvari, but any way you look at it wakefulness is better than sleep. Intoxicants can be extremely useful in *sadhanas*, or they can ruin your consciousness. It all depends on how you use them, and to use them correctly you have to die first.

Aghora, 1986

Man, being reasonable must get drunk
The best of life is but intoxication

Lord Byron

Charles Baudelaire
Be You Drunken!

ONE MUST ALWAYS be drunk. That's all there is to it; that's the only solution. In order not to feel the horrible burden of Time breaking your shoulders and bowing your head to the ground, you must be drunken without respite.

But with what? With wine, poetry or virtue, as you will. Be you drunken.

And if sometimes you awake, on the steps of a palace, in the green herbage of a ditch or in the dreary solitude of your room, then ask the wind, the waves, the stars, the birds, the clocks, ask everything that runs, that moans, that moves on wheels, everything that sings and speaks – ask them what is the time of day; and the wind, the waves, the stars, the birds and the clocks will answer you: It is time to get drunk. In order not to be the martyred slave of Time, be you drunken; be you drunken ceaselessly! With wine, poetry or virtue, as you will!

The Idler's Companion, 1997

Dreams are true while they last, and do we not live in dreams?
Alfred Lord Tennyson

Friedrich Nietzsche
Expeditions of an Untimely Man

TOWARDS A PSYCHOLOGY of the artist. For art to exist, for any sort of aesthetic society or perception to exist, a certain physiological precondition is indispensable: *intoxication*. Intoxication must first have heightened the excitability of the entire machine: no art results before that happens. All kinds of intoxication, however different their origin, have the power to do this: above all, the intoxication of sexual excitement, the oldest and most primitive form of intoxication. Likewise the intoxication which comes in the train of all great desires, all strong emotions; the intoxication of feasting, of contest, of the brave deed, of victory, of all extreme agitation; the intoxication of cruelty; intoxication in destruction; intoxication under certain meteorological influences, for example the intoxication of spring; or under the influence of narcotics; finally the intoxication of the will, the intoxication of an overloaded and distended will. The essence of intoxication is the feeling of plenitude and increased energy. From out of this feeling one gives to things, one *compels* them to take, one rapes them – one calls this procedure *idealizing*. Let us get rid of a prejudice here: idealization does *not* consist, as is commonly believed, in a subtracting or deducting of the petty and secondary. A tremendous *expulsion* of the principal features rather is the decisive thing, so that thereupon the others too disappear. In this condition one enriches everything out of one's own abundance: what one sees, what one desires, one sees swollen, pressing, strong, overladen with energy. The man in this condition transforms things until they mirror his power, until they are reflections of his perfection. This *compulsion* to transform into the perfect is – art.

Twilight of the Idols, 1889

Truth comes out in wine

Pliny the Elder

Aleister Crowley
First Aid

I FOUND THAT during the day I had fifteen sniffs of heroin. Lou had only had eleven. The reaction in my mind was this: If she can get on with eleven, why shouldn't I? Though I hadn't sufficient logic to carry on the argument to the people, millions of them, who hadn't had any at all, and seemed to be thriving.

We were both pretty tired. Just as Lamus and Lala rose to leave I took a final sniff.

'What did you do that for,' he asked, 'if you don't mind me asking?'

'Well, I think it was to go to sleep!'

'But this morning you told me you took it to wake up,' he retorted.

That was true, and it annoyed me; especially as Lou, instead of being sympathetic, gave one of her absurd little laughs. She actually seemed to take a perverse pleasure in seeing me caught out in a stupidity.

But Lamus took the matter very seriously.

'Well,' he said, 'it certainly is extraordinary stuff if it does two precisely opposite things at the will of the taker.'

He spoke sarcastically. He refrained from telling me what he told me long afterwards, that the apparently contradictory properties that I was ascribing to it were really there, that it can be used by the expert to produce a number of effects, some of which seem at first slightly mutually exclusive.

Diary of a Drug Fiend, 1970

CHAPTER SEVEN

IT

There went up a smoke out of His nostrils

II Samuel 22:9
Psalms 18:8

Howard Marks
The Story of Christmas

I'm dreaming of a stoned white Christmas, just like every other. Do I want the powdery stuff dissolving my nostrils? Or do I want to hold the icy stuff in my hands, reignite my hash hand-rolling skills, and make snowballs, the only known objects capable of indicating the difference between snowmen and snowwomen? When did it ever snow in Bethlehem?

This and other Christmas frauds was the first proof I'd encountered of my parents' ability to sacrifice their principles of honesty and say downright lies for the sake of something held by them to be more sacramental than mere truth. In their case, manifesting care for loved ones (by distributing gifts), being charitable (by helping the needy and engendering goodwill) and expressing faith (believing something despite vast evidence to the contrary) were considered higher ideals than factual accuracy. But why this deal with a saintly North Pole resident called Santa Claus upstaging infidel magic-carpet rides and, by a correct focus on hanging stockings and suspenders, making witches headfucking broomstick flights look like wanking with a piece of wood? This holy Eskimo delivers your annual dope supplies on a flying trolley operating on several reindeer power. There's no chance of being busted, even if the cops are watching: he delivers down the chimney. Cool! Then there's mince pies, trimmings, holly, King Wenceslas, crackers, fir trees, fairies, partridges, pear trees and puddings, to say nothing of loving and shagging one's neighbours under mistletoe and virgins giving birth in stables under shiny stars guiding heavily perfumed but wise Oriental despots.

At the very least, Christmas is meant to be a celebration of the birth of someone called Jesus Christ. Some say he was both God and the Son of God, born through immaculate conception provided by Himself. Logically, this renders him a motherfucker. Other unkind souls say he was a deranged faggot. Many think he was just a cool travelling dude whose dad was a carpenter and whose mum was a sweet lady called Mary. But there wasn't much love around before Jesus Christ, not in the Old Testament. A mild, peaceful and pure guy, that's for sure. Gentle as a lamb. While shepherds watched their flocks by night, Mary had a little lamb.

When the booze ran out at his mate's wedding, Jesus turned water into wine. (He'd already trodden on the water in preparation.) When he knew Judas had grassed him up, he grabbed a bottleful of red wine, swallowed it and asked to be remembered by others through their doing the same trip. He is the true vine. So let's have rivers of the Blood of Christ. Let it flow for Christ's sake. Get off your face, and see God.

The Bible indicates Christ to be a seven-days-a-week workaholic, a non-mistletoe eating Pisces (fisher of men) with an Access All Areas guest pass to all the hip, exclusive, and high places. So why make out he was a Sunday-kipping, earthbound druid born as a Capricorn in December?

The first Christian kingdom was ancient Britain under King Arthur before the English (Angles), French (Saxons) and Germans (Vikings, kind of) grabbed it. Those gallant Knights of the Round Table got well stoned and tenaciously devoted themselves to magical swords, dope-dealing Welsh wizards, shagging and the discovery of the Holy Grail, a goblet containing an inexhaustible supply of mind-bending red wine, carefully mixed with the menstrual blood of Mary Magdalene, the first holy hooker. Why are we these days expected to drink at communion, very infrequently, a mere thimbleful of sickly liquid not as potent as the average shite lager? What kind of communication is that? Even when reindeers do their trolleying thing in the sky, Rudolf is allowed to get plastered, show off his red nose, and form part of the bizarre indoctrination we suffered as kids.

Aleister Crowley
Magick in Theory and Practice

ONE OF THE simplest and most complete of Magick ceremonies is the Eucharist. Take a substance symbolic of the whole course of nature, make it God, and consume it. A Eucharist of some sort should most assuredly be consummated daily by every magician, and he should regard it as the main sustenance of his magickal life. The magician becomes filled with God, fed upon God, intoxicated with God. Little by little his body will become purified by the internal lustration of God; day by day his mortal fame, shedding its earthly elements, will become in very truth the Temple of the Holy Ghost. Day by day matter is replaced by Spirit, the human by the divine; ultimately the change will be complete; God manifest in flesh will be his name.

Majick in Theory and Practice, 1926

Jim Hogshire
The Pill as Holy Eucharist

THE UNREALISTIC VIEW of pills is possible because of what we could call the 'holy pill' syndrome. Pills are viewed by society as something holy, sort of a Eucharist.

In this analogy the pill – or host – is capable of miraculous things but only if it is treated in a certain ritualistic way. Thus, a high priest (your doctor) must first authorize its use in accordance with proper canon. It must be further consecrated by another level of priest (your pharmacist) who will place it into your outstretched hands from a counter three feet above your head.

You must not vary from the bottle's holy procedures. You must not transfer any of the pills in the bottle to another person or else something unspeakable may happen.

When pills are handled by lay people, they can become hideous things, instruments of death, sowers of discord. Drugs routinely used by psychiatrists in the USA to treat schizophrenics were the very ones used by the evil Soviets to 'torture' patients in its mental hospitals. Mom's Darvon is good for Mom only. If anyone else takes the pill consecrated for Mother's use, they are abusing it. To give anyone else one of your sleeping pills is a heretical act. To act on your need for an antibiotic without prescription is also heretical. It is also irreligious, not to mention illegal, to manufacture your own medicine without proper license – tantamount to permission from the Bishop.

Pills-A-Go-Go: A Fiendish Investigation into Pill Marketing, Art, History & Consumption, 1999

I am a mushroom
On whom the dew of heaven drops now and then

John Ford

John Allegro
The Sacred Mushroom and the Cross

THE FUNGUS RECOGNISED today as the *Amanita muscaria*, or Fly Agaric, had been known from the beginning of history. Beneath the skin of its characteristic red- and white-spotted cap, there is concealed a powerful hallucinatory poison. Its religious use among certain Siberian peoples and others has been the subject of study in recent years, and its exhilarating and depressive effects have been clinically examined. These include the stimulation of the perceptive faculties so that the subject sees objects much greater or much smaller than they really are, colours and sounds are much enhanced, and there is a general sense of power, both physical and mental, quite outside the normal range of human experience.

The mushroom has always been a thing of mystery. The ancients were puzzled by its manner of growth without seed, the speed with which it made its appearance after rain, and its equally rapid disappearance. Born from a volva or 'egg' it appears like a small penis, raising itself like the human organ sexually aroused, and when it spread wide its canopy, the old botanists saw it as a phallus bearing the 'burden' of a woman's groin. Every aspect of the mushroom's existence was fraught with sexual allusions, and in its phallic form the ancient saw a replica of the fertility god himself. It was the 'Son of God', its drug was a purer form of the god's own spermatozoa than that discoverable in any other form of living matter. It was, in fact, God himself, manifest on earth. To the mystic it was the divinely given means of entering heaven; God had come down in the flesh to show the way to himself, by himself. To pluck such a precious herb was attended at every point with peril. The time – before sunrise, the words to be uttered – the name of the guardian angel, were vital to the operation, but more was needed. Some form of substitution was necessary, to make an atonement to the earth robbed of her offspring. Yet such was the divine nature of the Holy Plant, as it was called, only the god could make the necessary sacrifice. To redeem the Son, the Father had to supply even the 'price of redemption'. These are all phrases used of the sacred mushroom, as they are of the Jesus of Christian theology.

The Sacred Mushroom and the Cross, 1970

*If a man could pass through Paradise in a dream, and have a
flower presented to him as a pledge that his soul had really
been there and if he found that flower in his hand when he
awoke – Aye, and what then?*

Samuel Taylor Coleridge

Kevin Rushby
Eating the Flowers of Paradise – 2

It was during Rasulid rule that the mystical movement of the
Sufis became a major social force, as followers of men like
Shadhili arrived with the promise of guidance for those
seeking closer understanding of God. Missionaries passed
through Mokha and Aden on their way to Africa, including
one Abu Zarbay who is credited by some Hararis with
funding their town, and by others with introducing qat to
Yemen in 1400. The name Sufi itself comes from the Arabic
word meaning wool, perhaps a reference to the simple cloth
they wore. This asceticism was one major part of the Sufi
tariqa, or path; but even more revolutionary, was their use of
stimulants to help them along to spiritual enlightenment.

Certainly, drugs seem to be able to push experiences in the
directions people are hoping and expecting to go. And for the
Sufis, like the ancient Cretans on the island of Aphrodite, that
direction was religious ecstasy. Their beliefs were varied but
centred on the idea that, by repetitive rituals of prayer and
meditation, the individual could approach God. From this
developed an idea of a secretive select group, above the laws
of man. Some took this to be licence for a life of sensuality and
luxury but most advocated simplicity and austerity. One of
these was a certain Ahmed ibn Alwan whose father was a
scribe at the thirteenth-century Rasulid court.

Ibn Alwan moved to Yufrus on the western side of Jebel Saber
where he founded a religious school and became noted for his
outspoken attacks on the kings. In legend he is credited with
using qat in his meditations and prayers, the drug lifting him and
his followers on their path to religious ecstasy. It was a time

when the 'mystic saint' was a figure of great influence and importance, and qat, with its power to work some strange alchemy of the mind, must have been a valuable tool: that mix of dreamlike unreality and sharpness of thought that bestowed instant mystical experiences – a short cut to sainthood. As ascetics too, the holy men were sympathetic towards a substance that tended to deprive users of sleep, appetite and libido.

The first coffee and qat trees to arrive in Yemen were probably planted on Saber or its neighbour, Jebel Habashi, a word from which the old name Abyssinia is derived. Initially they may have arrived in the form of powder, mixed up as teas, rather than as seeds or plants. What is clear is that both substances began to be used as part of religious ritual by Sufistic sects, knowledge of them spreading anywhere that the Sufi missionaries travelled. But the secular world was not far behind, and when qat and coffee moved out of the narrow circles of the Sufis, they became controversial almost immediately.

Eating the Flowers of Paradise, 1999

Die, my dear Doctor, that's the last thing I shall do
Viscount Palmerston

Rene Daumal
A Fundamental Experiment

MY MEMORIES OF childhood and adolescence are deeply marked by a series of attempts to experience the beyond, and those random attempts brought me to the ultimate experiment, the fundamental experience of which I speak. At about the age of six, having been taught no kind of religious belief whatsoever, I struck up against the stark problem of death. I passed some atrocious nights, feeling my stomach clawed to shreds and my breathing half throttled by the anguish of nothingness, the 'no more of anything'. One night when I was about eleven, relaxing my entire body, I calmed the terror and revulsion of my organism before the unknown, and a new feeling came alive in me: hope, and a foretaste of the imperishable. But I wanted more; I wanted a certainty. At fifteen or sixteen I began my experiments, a search without direction or system.

Finding no way to experiment directly on death – on my death – I tried to study my sleep, assuming an analogy between the two. By various devices I attempted to enter sleep in a waking state. The undertaking is not so utterly absurd as it sounds, but in certain respects it is perilous. I could not go very far with it; my own organism gave me some serious warnings of the risks I was running. One day, however, I decided to tackle the problem of death itself. I would put my body into a state approaching as close as possible that of physiological death, and still concentrate all my attention on remaining conscious and registering everything that might take place. I had in my possession some carbon tetrachloride, which I used to kill beetles for my collection. Knowing this substance belongs to the same chemical family as chloroform (it is even more toxic), I thought I could regulate its action very simply and easily: the moment I began to lose consciousness, my hand would fall from my nostrils carrying with it the handkerchief moistened with the volatile fluid. Later on I repeated the experiment in the presence of friends, who could have given me help had I needed it. The result was always exactly the same; that is, it exceeded and even overwhelmed my expectations by bursting the limits of the possible and by projecting me brutally into another world.

First came the ordinary phenomena of asphyxiation, arterial palpitation, buzzings, sounds of heavy pumping in the temples, painful repercussions from the tiniest exterior noises, flickering lights. Then, the distinct feeling, 'This is getting serious. The game is up,' followed by a swift recapitulation of my life up to that moment. If I felt any slight anxiety, it remained indistinguishable from a bodily discomfort that did not affect my mind. And my mind kept repeating to itself, 'Careful, don't doze off. This is just the time to keep your eyes open.' The luminous spots that danced in front of my eyes soon filled the whole of space, which echoed with the beat of my blood – sound and light overflowing space and fusing in a single rhythm.

By this time I was no longer capable of speech, even of interior speech; my mind travelled too rapidly to carry any words along with it. I realized, in a sudden illumination, that I still had control of the hand which held the handkerchief, that I still accurately perceived the position of my body, and that I could hear and understand words uttered nearby – but that objects, words, and meanings of words had lost any significance whatsoever. It was a little like having repeated a word over and over until it shrivels and dies in your mouth: you still know what the word 'table' means, for instance, you could use it correctly, but it no longer truly evokes its object. In the same way, everything that made up 'the world' for me in the ordinary state was still there, but I felt as if it had been drained of its substance. It was nothing more than a phantasmagoria – empty, absurd, clearly outlined and necessary all at once. This 'world' lost all reality because I had abruptly entered another world, infinitely more real, an instantaneous and intense world of eternity, a concentrated flame of reality and evidence into which I had cast myself like a butterfly drawn to a lighted candle. Then, at that moment, comes the *certainty*; speech must now be content to wheel in circles around the bare fact.

Little by little I discovered in my reading accounts of the same experience, for I now held the key to these narratives and descriptions whose relation to a single and unique reality I should not previously have suspected. William James speaks of it. O.V. de L. Milosz, in his *Letter to Storge*, gives an overwhelming account of it in terms I had been using myself. The famous circle referred to by a medieval monk, and which Pascal saw (but who first saw it and spoke of it?), ceased to be an empty allegory for me; I knew it represented a devouring vision of what I had seen also. And, beyond all this varied and partial human testimony (there is scarcely a single true poet in whose work I did not find at least a fragment of it), the

517

confessions of the great mystics and, still more advanced, the sacred texts of certain religions, brought me an affirmation of the same reality. Sometimes I found it in its most terrifying form, as perceived by an individual of limited vision who has not raised himself to the level of such perception, who, like myself, has tried to look into the infinite through the keyhole and finds himself staring into Bluebeard's cupboard. Sometimes I encountered it in the pleasing, plentifully satisfying and intensely luminous form that is the vision of beings truly transformed, who can behold that reality face to face without being destroyed by it. I have in mind the revelation of the Divine Being in the *Bhagavad-Gita*, the vision of Ezekiel and that of St John the Divine on Patmos, certain descriptions in the *Tibetan Book of the Dead (Bardo thodol)* and a passage in the *Lankdvatara-Sutra*.

Not having lost my mind then and there, I began little by little to philosophize about the memory of this experience. And I would have buried myself in a philosophy of my own if someone had not come along just in time to tell me, 'Look, the door is open – narrow and hard to reach, but a door. It is the only one for you.'

1959. From: *Artificial Paradises: A Drugs Reader*,
ed. Mike Jay, 1999

And death shall be no more; death, thou shalt die
John Donne

William James
Mysticism

NITROUS OXIDE AND ether, especially nitrous oxide, when sufficiently diluted with air, stimulate the mystical consciousness in an extraordinary degree. Depth beyond depth of truth seems revealed to the inhaler. This truth fades out, however, or escapes, at the moment of coming to; and if any worlds remain over in which it seemed to clothe itself, they prove to be the eeriest nonsense. Nevertheless, the sense of a profound meaning having been there persists; and I know more than one person who is persuaded that in the nitrous oxide trance we have a genuine metaphysical revelation.

Some years ago I myself made some observations on this aspect of nitrous oxide intoxication and reported them in print. One conclusion was forced upon my mind at that time, and my impression of its truth has ever since remained unshaken. It is that our normal waking consciousness, rational consciousness as we call it, is but one special type of consciousness, whilst all about it, parted from it by the filmiest of screens, there lie potential forms of consciousness entirely different. We may go through life without suspecting their existence; but apply the requisite stimulus, and at a touch they are there in all their completeness, definite types of mentality which probably somewhere have their field of application and adaptation. No account of the universe in its totality can be final which leaves these other forms of consciousness quite disregarded.

How to regard them is the question – for they are so discontinuous with ordinary consciousness. Yet they may determine attitudes though they cannot furnish formulas, and open a region though they fail to give a map. At any rate, they forbid a premature closing of our accounts with reality. Looking back on my own experiences, they all converge towards a kind of insight to which I cannot help ascribing some metaphysical significance. The keynote of it is invariably a reconciliation. It is as if the opposites of the world, whose contradictoriness and conflict make all our difficulties and troubles, were melted into unity. Not only do they, as contrasted species, belong to one and the same genus, but *one of the species*, the nobler and better one, *is itself the genus, and so soaks up and absorbs its opposite into itself*. This is a dark saying, I know, when thus expressed in terms of common logic, but I cannot wholly escape from its authority. I feel as if it must mean something, something like what the Hegelian philosophy means, if one could only lay hold of it more clearly. Those who have ears to hear, let them hear; to me the living sense of its reality only comes in the artificial mystic state of mind.

The Varieties of Religious Experience: A Study in Human Nature,
1902

Man does more than Milton can
To justify God's ways to man

A.E. Housman

J.M. Campbell
On the Religion of Hemp

ONE

Such holiness and such evil-scaring powers must give bhang a high place among lucky objects, that a day may be fortunate to the careful man should upon awakening look into liquid bhang. So any nightmares or evil spirits that may have entered into him during the ghost-haunted hours of the night will flee from him at the sight of bhang and free him of their binding influences during the day . . . To meet someone carrying bhang is a sure sign of success. To see in a dream the leaves, plant or water of bhang is lucky; it brings the Goddess of Wealth into the dreamer's power. To see his parents worship the bhang plant and pour Mang over Shiva's Ling will cure the dreamer of fever. A longing for bhang foretells happiness; to see bhang drunk increases riches. 'No good thing can come to a man who treads underfoot the holy bhang leaf.'

TWO

'Much of the holiness of bhang [marijuana] is due to its virtues of clearing the head and stimulating the brain to thought. Among ascetics the sect known as Atits are specially devoted to hemp. No social or religious gathering of Atits is complete without the use of the hemp plant smoked in ganja or drunk in bhang. To its devotee, bhang is no ordinary plant that became holy from its guardian and healing qualities. According to one account, when nectar was produced from the churning of the ocean, something was wanted to purify the nectar. The deity supplied the want of a nectar-cleanser by creating bhang. This bhang Mahadev made from his own body, and so it is called angai or body-born. According to another account some nectar dropped to the ground and from the ground the bhang plant sprang. It was because they used this child of nectar or of Mahadev in agreement with religious forms that the seers or Rishis became Siddha or one with the deity. He who, despite the example of the Rishis uses no bhang shall lose its happiness in this life and in the life to come. In the end he shall be cast into hell. The mere sight of bhang cleans from as much sin as a thousand horse-sacrifices or a thousand pilgrimages. He who scandalizes the user of bhang shall suffer the torments of hell so long as the sun endures. He who drinks bhang foolishly or for pleasure without religious rites is as guilty as the sinner of sins. He who drinks wisely and according to rule, be he ever so low, even though his body is smeared with human ordure and urine, is Shiva (a man of god). No god or man is as good as the religious drinker of bhang. The students of the scriptures at Benares are given bhang before they sit to study. At Benares, students of the Ujain, and other holy places, yogis, bairagis and sanyasis, take deep draughts of bhang that they may center their thoughts on the Eternal. To bring back to reason an unhinged mind the best and leanest bhang leaves should be boiled in mil, and turned to clarified butter. Salamisri, saffron and sugar should be added and the whole eaten. Besides, over the demons of madness bhang is Vijaya or victorious over the demons of hunger and thirst. By the help of bhang, ascetics pass days without food or drink. The supporting power of bhang has brought many a Hindu family safe through the miseries of famine. To forbid or even seriously to restrict the use of so gracious an herb as the hemp would cause widespread suffering and annoyance and to large bands of worshiped ascetics, deep-seated anger. It would rob the people of a solace in discomfort, of a cure in sickness, of a guardian whose gracious protection saves them from the attacks of evil influences, and whose mighty power makes the devotee of the Victorious, overcoming the demons of hunger and thirst, of panic, fear, of the glamor of Maya or matter, and of madness, able in rest to brood on the Eternal, till the Eternal, possessing him body and soul, frees him from the haunting of self and receives him into the Ocean of Being. These beliefs the Musalman devotee shares to the full. Like his Hindu brother the Musalman fakir reveres bhang as the lengthener of life; the freer from the bonds of self. Bhang brings union with the Divine Spirit. 'We drank bhang and the mystery I am He grew plain. So grand a result, so tiny a sin.'

On the Religion of Hemp, 1894

Shy traffickers, the dark Iberians come
And on the beach undid his corded bales

Matthew Arnold

Havelock Ellis
Mescal: A New Artificial Paradise

It has been known for some years that the Kiowa Indians of New Mexico are accustomed to eat, in their religious ceremonies, a certain cactus called Anhalonium Lewinii, or mescal button. Mescal – which must not be confounded with the intoxicating drink of the same name made from an agave – is found in the Mexican Valley of the Rio Grande, the ancestral home of the Kiowa Indians, as well as in Texas, and is a brown and brittle substance, nauseous and bitter to the taste, composed mainly of the blunt dried leaves of the plant.

[The] mescal rite may be said to be today the chief religion of all the tribes of the southern plains of the United States. The rite usually takes place on Saturday night; the men then sit in a circle within the tent round a large camp fire, which is kept burning brightly all the time. After prayer the leader hands each man four buttons, which are slowly chewed and swallowed, and altogether about ten or twelve buttons are consumed by each man between sundown and daybreak. Throughout the night the men sit quietly round the fire in a state of reverie – amid continual manifestations of mescal intoxication, and about noon on the following day, when the effects have passed off, they get up and go about their business, without any depression or other unpleasant after-effect.

There are five or six allied species of cacti, which the Indians also use and treat with great reverence. Thus Mr. Carl Lumholtz has found that the Tarahumari, a tribe of Mexican Indians, worship various cacti as gods, only to be approached with uncovered heads. When they wish to obtain these cacti, the Tarahumari cleanse themselves with copal incense, and with profound respect dig up the god, careful lest they should hurt him, while women and children are warned from the spot. Even Christian Indians regard Hikori, the cactus god, as coequal with their own divinity, and make the sign of the cross in its presence. At all great festivals Hikori is made into a drink and consumed by the medicine man, or certain selected Indians, who sing as they partake of it, invoking Hikori to grant a 'beautiful intoxication'; at the same time a rasping noise is made with sticks, and men and women dance a fantastic and picturesque dance – the women by themselves in white petticoats and tunics – before those who are under the influence of the god.

It would be out of place here to discuss the obscure question as to the underlying mechanism by which mescal exerts its magic powers. It is clear from the foregoing descriptions that mescal intoxication may be described as chiefly a saturnalia of the specific senses, and, above all, an orgy of vision. It reveals an optical fairyland, where all the senses now and again join the play, but the mind itself remains a self-possessed spectator. Mescal intoxication thus differs from the other artificial paradises which drugs procure. Under the influence of alcohol, for instance, as in normal dreaming, the intellect is impaired, although there may be a consciousness of unusual brilliance; hasheesh, again, produces an uncontrollable tendency to movement and bathes its victim in a sea of emotion. The mescal drinker remains calm and collected amid the sensory turmoil around him; his judgement is as clear as in the normal state; he falls into no oriental condition of vague and voluptuous reverie. The reason why mescal is of all this class of drugs the most purely intellectual in its appeal is evidently because it affects mainly the most intellectual of the senses. On this ground it is not probable that its use will easily develop into a habit. Moreover, unlike most other intoxicants, it seems to have no special affinity for a disordered and unbalanced nervous system; on the contrary, it demands organic soundness and good health for the complete manifestation of its virtues. Further, unlike the other chief substances to which it may be compared, mescal does not wholly carry us away from the actual world, or plunge us into oblivion; a large part of its charm lies in the halo of beauty which it casts around the simplest and commonest things. It is the most democratic of the plants which lead men to an artificial paradise.

If it should ever chance that the consumption of mescal becomes a habit, the favorite poet of the mescal drinker will certainly be Wordsworth. Not only the general attitude of Wordsworth, but many of his most memorable poems and phrases can not – one is almost tempted to say – be appreciated in their full significance by one who has never been under the influence of mescal. On all these grounds it may be claimed that the artificial paradise of mescal, though less seductive, is safe and dignified beyond its peers.

It may at least be claimed that for a healthy person to be once or twice admitted to the rites of mescal is not only an unforgettable delight, but an educational influence of no mean value.

The Contemporary Review, January 1898
From: *The Hashish Club: An Anthology of Drug Literature*, vol. 1, ed. Peter Haining, 1975

All are but parts of one stupendous whole
Whose body nature is, and God the Soul

Alexander Pope

Mike Jay
Blue Tide – 2

Within the low-level field of electrical conductivity which is
the medium of brain activity, messages are carried around the
brain by chemical agents known as neurotransmitters, of
which the best-known are probably dopamine and serotonin.
In 1994, the mechanism of action of cannabis was finally
understood: it's a natural analogue of a neurotransmitter
which exists in the brain, an 'endo-cannabis' in the same way
as endorphins ('endo-morphines') are our natural internal
opiates. So cannabis and opiates work by flooding the brain
with chemicals which are themselves designed to send out
waves of signals, initiating 'cascade reactions' of other
chemicals which translate these brain signals into powerful
physical reactions. In the early 1950s, it was discovered that
when the neurotransmitter serotonin was incubated in vitro in
the pineal gland tissue of mammals, it broke down into a
range of complex organic metabolites. Serotonin itself is a
tryptamine, and some of these metabolites were other
methylated tryptamines, such as dimethoxytryptamine –
DMT. What's more, these in turn broke down into beta-
carbolines harmaline, tetra-hydro-harmine and the rest.
Various mammalian and human pineal glands were then
analysed for these chemicals, and found to contain them. The
extraordinary fact was that the ayahuasca brew of harmaline
and DMT was actually present in the human brain.

Blue Tide, 2000

Where's my serpent of Old Nile?

William Shakespeare

Jeremy Narby
Biology's Blind Spot

In 1979, it was discovered that the human brain seems to secrete dimethyltryptamine – which is also one of the active ingredients of ayahuasca. This substance produces true hallucinations in which the visions replace normal reality convincingly, such as fluorescent snakes to whom one excuses oneself as one steps over them. Unfortunately, scientific research on dimethyltryptamine is rare. To this day, the clinical studies of its effect on normal human beings can be counted on the fingers of one hand.

In their visions, shamans take their consciousness down to the molecular level and gain access to information related to DNA, which they call 'animate essences' or 'spirits.' This is where they see double helixes, twisted ladders and chromosome shapes. This is how shamanic cultures have known for millennia that the vital principle is the same for all living beings and is shaped like two entwined serpents (or a vine, a rope, a ladder . . .). DNA is the source of their astonishing botanical and medicinal knowledge, which can be attained only in defocalized and 'nonrational' states of consciousness, though its results are empirically verifiable. The myths of these cultures are filled with biological imagery.

Shamans say the correct way to talk about spirits is in metaphors. Biologists confirm this notion by using a precise array of anthropocentric and technological metaphors to describe DNA, proteins, and enzymes. DNA is a *text*, or a program, or *data*, containing *information*, which is *read* and *transcribed* into *messenger*-RNAs. The latter feed into ribosomes, which are molecular *computers* that *translate the instructions* according to the genetic *code*. They *build* the rest of the cell's *machinery*, *namely* the proteins and enzymes, which are *miniaturized robots* that construct and maintain the cell.

The Cosmic Serpent, 1995

It has, I believe, been often remarked, that a hen is only an egg's way of making another egg

Samuel Butler

Peter Matthiessen
At Play in the Fields of the Lord

A DOG TURNED in its circle and lay down in the shade, and a vulture swung up and down in a short arc above the jungle, as if suspended from a string. In the heat of the siesta, the street below was hollow as a bone.

He took the cork out of the bottle, and holding his breath to kill the bitterness, drank off half the brown fluid in a series of short gulps, gargling harshly when he was finished and spitting the residue into the street. The aftertaste made him gag. He sat down on the window sill and in a little while the nausea receded, leaving only a thick woody taste and a slight vagueness.

A half-hour passed. Maybe the Indian had watered the infusion. A voice in the salon below sounded remote to him, and he nodded; he was on his way. A little more ayahuasca, Mr. Moon? He took up the bottle and drank off another quarter of it, then set it down very slowly. You've made a bad mistake, he thought; already he knew he did not need it. The effects were carving very suddenly, and he stood up and stalked the room. In *overdose*, he had read somewhere, *the extract of* Banisteriopsis caapi *is quite poisonous and may bring on convulsions, shock and even death.*

How silent it was – the whole world was in siesta. He glanced quickly out the window, to take time by surprise; the dog slept soundly, and the vulture still swung up and down its bit of sky, dark as a pendulum. From the far end of the street, a solitary figure was moving toward him, down the center of the street – the last man on earth. There you are, he thought, I have been waiting for you all my life. Now he was seized with vertigo and apprehension; his heart began to pound and his breath was short. He went to his bed and lay down on his back. He felt a closure of the throat and a tension in his chest, a metal bar from chin to navel to which the skin of his chest was sewn. Breathing became still more difficult, and a slight pain in the back of his head became a general, diffused headache. He turned cold and his teeth chattered; the hands pressed to his face were limp and clammy.

I am flying all apart, he thought; at the same time his chest constricted ever more tightly. *Let go*, he told himself aloud. *Let* go.

He rolled over on his side and blinked at the other bed. The man on the bed retreated from his vision, shrinking and shrinking until he was no bigger than a fetus.

Color: the room billowed with it; the room breathed. When he closed his eyes, the color dazzled him; he soared. But there was trouble in his lungs again, and his heart thumped so, in heavy spasmodic leaps, that it must surely stall and die. He broke into a sweat, and his hands turned cold as small bags of wet sand . . .

He sat up, aching, in a foreign room. He could breathe again, although his heart still hurled itself unmercifully against his chest: how thin a man's poor chest was, after all; it was as thin as paper, surrounding a hollow oval space of wind and bitterness. *Thump, thump-ump, um-thump*; it would crash through at any minute, and what then? Do I greet it? Introduce myself? How long can a man sit holding his heart in his hands?

He keeled from the bed and drifted to the window, but the figure coming down the street was gone; again he had missed some unknown chance. The street was void, a void, avoid. Dog, heat, a vulture, nothing more. A dog, a vulture, nothing more, and thus we parted, sang Lenore.

Singing. Somewhere, somewhere there was singing. His whole body shimmered with the chords, the fountainhead of music, overflowing. The chords were multicolored, vaulting like rockets across his consciousness; he could break off pieces of the music like pieces of meringue.

You're sleeping your life away, he told the dog.

Do you hear me? I said, Do you hear me?

*

528

Meri-wether, Sheriff Guzman said. *That's some name for a red nigger, ain't it? You're the smart one, ain't you, kid? Ain't you supposed to be the smart Cheyenne? Done good in the war, and now they gone to send they little pet Christ-lovin Cheyenne to college, ain't that right, kid? Well, kid, if you're a real smart Injun, you won't even go and look at me that way, you'll keep your Injun nose clear, kid.*

Oh, to be an Indian! (Now that spring is here.) Big Irma: *Be a good boy, Lewis. Do not fight so much. You come back and see us now.* Alas, too late – the world is dead, you sleepyhead. The Inn of the Dog and the Vulture. There are voices, you see, then singing voices, then strange voices, then strange musics, hollowed out, as if drifted through a wind tunnel, these followed by a huge void of bleak silence suggesting DEATH.

The Story of my Life, by Lewis Moon

Now . . . something has happened, was happening, is happening. BUT WILL NOT HAPPEN. Do you hear me? I said, DO YOU HEAR ME?

A softer tone, please.

To begin at the beginning: my name is Meriwether Lewis Moon. Or is that the end? Again: I was named Meriwether Lewis Moon, after Meriwether Lewis, who with Lieutenant William Clark crossed North America without killing a single Indian. So said my father; my father is Alvin Moon 'Joe Redcloud,' who lived up on North Mountain. Alvin Moon still traps and hunts, and in World War I, when still a despised non-citizen, exempt from service, joined those 16,999 other Indians as insane as himself who volunteered to serve in World War I. Alvin Moon is half-Cheyenne; he went down South when he came home and took up with a Creole Choctaw woman named Big Irma and brought her back up to his mountain. The worst mistake that Alvin Moon ever made was trying to educate himself; his information about Lewis and Clark was the only piece of education he ever obtained, and it was wrong. He used to joke that he couldn't educate himself unless he learned to read, and how could he learn to read if he didn't educate himself? So he left off hunting and trapping and came down off his mountain and took work near the reservation to keep his children in the mission school, to give them a better chance in life.

Again: my name is Lewis Moon, and I am lying on a bed (deathbed?) in a strange country, and I hear eerie voices and a crack is appearing on the wall, wider and wider, and the bulb in the ceiling is growing more and more bulbous, and will surely explode – a crack (of doom?) of lightning down the walls.

The extract of B. caapi is a powerful narcotic and hallucinogen containing phenol alkaloids related to those found in lysergic acid, and whether or not it finds a respectable place in the pharmaceutica of man, it has held for unknown centuries an important place in the culture of Indian tribes of the Amazon basin.

At the time of my experiment I was lying in a narrow room with a corpse in the next bed, with god, a vulture and a dog as witnesses and wishing that Marguerite was here. Marguerite. I wish to tell Marguerite that the reason I did not make love to her that time in Hong Kong was not because I did not want her but because I had reason to believe that in the late, low hours of the week before, I had contracted a low infestation. I did not know Marguerite well enough to give her crabs – you understand? Marguerite had alabaster skin, triumphant hair and an unmuddied soul, and a swinging little ass into the bargain.

I have opened my eyes again, to shut off all that blue. Color can threaten, overwhelm, whirling like that – an ant in a kaleidoscope might sense the problem. But out here the bed shudders, the chair sneaks; the bureau budges; they back and fill, about to charge. From above, the bulb socket descends like a falling spider, leaving the bulb behind.

B. caapi, which is named for the caapi *of certain Brazilian Indians, is also the* camorampi *of the Camps, the* natema *of the Jivaro, the* ayahuasca *or* haya-huasca *of the Quechua-speaking peoples, the* yage *of Ecuador, the* soga de muerte *of most*

Spanish South Americans, names variously translated at 'Vine of the Devil,' 'Vine of the Soul,' 'Vine of Death': the Spanish term means literally 'vine rope of death,' the soga referring to the jungle lianas used commonly as canoe lines, lashings, ropes, etc. In addition to certain medical properties, the vine can induce visions, telepathic states, metaphysical contemplation and transmigration; these conditions are used by the Indians for the reception of warnings, prophecies and good counsel. Among many tribes one purpose of the dream state is identi-fication of an unknown enemy, and the use of it is thus related to the Jivaro practice of taking tsantsas, *or shrunken heads . . .*

I am cut off, I feel both silly and depressed; it is the solitude, not solitude but isolation . . . Death is the final isolation, but from what, from what?

I am trying to reach out to you, but I do not know who you are, I cannot see you. I only feel your presence in this room. Perhaps . . . I wonder . . . are you inside me? And if so . . . Now listen carefully: there is a lost reality, a reality lost long ago. Are you in touch with it: can you tell me – did you see? – the man with the blue arrow –

Or are you the figure in the center of the street? So you came here, after all! Can you hear me? I said, CAN YOU HEAR ME? CAN-YOU-HEAR-ME!

I cannot reach him through the sound and silence, distant sound and deepest silence, like a thick glass barrier between the world of the living and myself, as if I were wandering on an earth which had suddenly died, or in a Purgatory, myself already dead.

There is something that you have to understand.

Now look what's happening – can you see? It's Him, the Dead Man. Resurrection. Rising out of bed. Not suspecting that I am already dead, he will attempt to kill me.

He stops: *StopshoutinforChristsake!*

Here he comes, intent on the kill. He has broken the glass wall. He drags me across the room. He has a costume, he is all dressed up like a soldier of fortune, he is very hip; but see the rosy cheeks behind that beard? An enormous child!

'You are an Enormous Child!'

Nevermindmejustlookinthemirra! Whatareyousomekindof-addictorwhat? Gowanlookatyaself!

See the pale face in the glass! The face is rigid, and the eyes are dark and huge. Over the left eye drifts a dark shadow, like a hand. There you are, I see you now, and the bearded man, your warder. He knew his lucidity could not last, and because he had taken too much, he dreaded going under again, and he started to ask Wolfie for help. 'Hey,' he said. But he could not ask, he had never asked in all his life, and even if he asked, what could poor Wolfie do? There were no sedatives in Madre de Dios; sedation was superfluous in a graveyard. He pushed away and tottered toward the window, where he fell across the sill. The dog and the vulture were gone. The light was tightening in the way it always did before the sudden jungle night, and down the center of the street a solitary figure walked away. The bottle stood open upon the sill; he drank it to the bottom.

He crouched beside the window sill, his back to the world without, and far away he heard them coming, the marching of huge nameless armies coming toward him, and once again his hands turned cold. He felt very cold. On the wall of the room, over the door, he saw a huge moth with a large white spot on each wing. It palpitated gently; he could hear the palpitations, and the spots were growing. And there was a voice, a hollow voice, very loud and very far away, calling through glass, and there were hands on him and he was shaken violently. The voice rose and crashed in waves, rolling around his ears; it was getting dark.

NowlistenI'mgonnatellGuzmanzweflytomorrowawright? AwrightLewis? IsaidAWRIGHTLEWIS?

He looked at the man and the man's head, fringed with hair; the head shrank before his eyes and became a *tsantsa*. He could not look, and turned away. A figure crossed his line of vision, moving toward the door. The door opened and light came in. The voice said *Thisisnowheremanl'vehadenough*.

Don't go . . . I need . . . Don't go. I need . . . But he could not hear his own voice, and he could not have said just what he needed. From over the man's head the large white eyes of the moth observed him; they pinned him, like incoming beams. The music crashed, the wave . . . The door was dark again. He pushed himself to his feet and stared out of the window. The dark was rolling from the forest all around, and the sky was so wild as the sun set that it hurt his eyes. He reeled and fell, then thrashed to his feet and fell again, across the bed, and was sacked down into the darkness as the music burnt the walls and overwhelmed him.

His body diffused and drifted through cathedral vaults of color, whirling and shimmering and bursting forth, drifting high among the arches, down the clerestories, shadowed by explosions of stained glass. In the dark chapels of the church was a stair to windy dungeons, to colors rich and somber, now, and shapes emerging; the shapes lowered, rose in threat and fell away again. Fiends, demons, dancing spiders with fine webs of silver chain. A maniac snarled and slavered, and rain of blood beat down upon his face. Teeth, teeth grinding in taut rage, teeth tearing lean sinew from gnarled bone. Idiocy danced hand in hand with lunacy and hate, rage and revenge; the dungeon clanked and quaked with ominous sounds, and he kept on going, down into the darkness.

He opened his eyes, gasping for breath; he drifted downward. Once the abyss opened out into air and sunlight but there were papier-mâché angels, and again he broke off chords of music from the air like bits of cake: the Paradise was false and he went on. A spider appeared, reared high over his head, then seized, shredded and consumed him. Voided, he lay inert in a great trough, with molten metal rising all about him in a blinding light. SO THIS WAS BRIMSTONE. The missionary's pasty face peered down at him over the rim: *This is a proud day for the mission, Lewis, and a proud day for your people. We all count on you.*

Eyes. Eyes. He struggled to free himself, but the stake held in his heart, the hole in his heart; even breathing hurt him, even breathing. He clawed at his own chest to ease it. If only he could get that pain out, then his heart would bleed his life away, but gently.

A roar of trapped insects, flies and bees, and he among them: mad drone and bugging and brush of hairy, viscous legs scraping toward remote slits of air and light, of acrid insect smell, of flat inconscient insect eyes, unblinking, bright as jewels, too mindless to know fear, oh Christ, how mindless. Humans . . . A human mob, pounding its way into the bar, in search of – what? It did not know. It had no idea what it was hunting, but was hunting out of instinct, with myriad flat insect eyes, trampling everything underfoot; he shook with fear. Like a rat he was; a famine rat of broken cities, a quaking gut-shrunk rat, scurrying through the wainscoting of falling houses. His skeleton flew apart, reassembled in rat's skeleton; his spine arched, his tiny forefeet and long furtive hand, the loose-skinned gassy belly; he poised, alert, hunched on his knees upon the bed, hands dangling at his navel; long nose twitching. In the mirror across the room he saw the hair sprout on his face and the face protrude.

He found his way across the room and stared so closely into the glass that his nose touched it; he watched the face wrinkle and turn old; he saw his own raw skull again and groaned. Then another mask, a new expression, hard and sly and cold. As he watched, it softened and turned young and wide-eyed, gentle; the muscles in his stomach eased, and he recognized the self of boyhood mornings. He was touched by this last face and grinned at it in embarrassment; but just as he grinned, self-consciousness returned to poison him; and the boyish face turned hard again and mean, and the lips drew back upon sharp teeth and the eyes glittered, and the whole body tensed with an anger of such murderous black violence that he recoiled from his own hate, falling back again across the bed. A huge dead dog had its teeth locked in his throat; and the metal bar dragged at his chest again, and when he closed his eyes the Rage descended, a huge and multilimbed galoot in hobnailed boots and spurs, eyes bulging, teeth grinding, cigars exploding in its mouth and flames shooting from its ears, bearing a club spiked with rusty nails, wearing brass knuckles and outsize six-guns; in its blind snot-flying rage, it blew its own head off by mistake: This thing came stomping down out of his mind, and he gasped, Look at that guy, that guy is so mad, he blew his own head off by mistake! His body relaxed and he howled with laughter, lying now with his back on the floor and his feet on the bed, and as he laughed, the gnawed and painful stake which had pierced his chest as long as he could remember cracked and opened like an ancient husk and turned to dust, and he could breathe again.

Here was Rage again, exploded now, hung up like an old scarecrow, like a big broken toy with one loose eye and loose old parts and springs and stuffing every whichy-way-all hung up on itself, poor critter. Rage danced somewhat sheepishly to guitar and wind, as if to say: Well, just because I'm *angry* doesn't mean I don't enjoy a dance or two . . .

Lucidity. He sighed. He lay there all laughed out and loose, loose as a dead snake slung on a rail, lay there drunk with gentleness and pleasure. *Be a good boy, Lewis, do not hate so much.*

Oh good old Wolfie, Wolfie would die laughing. The thought of the Old Wolf laughing, *dying* of *laughing*, set him off again, but this time, even as he laughed, an apprehension came.

He crawled to the corner of the room, where he crouched low, watching both door and window. The noises were surrounding him, there was something happening to him, something *happening* and he felt too tired now to deal with it. If he could only stop his laughing, but he could not; his laughter grew louder and louder, and when he tried to stop he could not close his mouth. It stretched wider and wider, until he swallowed the ceiling light, the room, the window and the night; the world rushed down into the cavernous void inside him, leaving him alone in space, pinwheeling wildly like a jagged fragment spun out from a planet.

A terrific wind blew, and his ears rang with the bells of blueblack space; the wind sealed his throat, his flesh turned cold, his screams were but squeaks snapped out and away by the passage of night spheres. Nor could he hear, there was no one to hear, there was no one where he had gone – what's *happening, what-is-happening* . . .

He had flung himself away from life, from the very last ties, had strayed to the cold windy reaches of insanity. This perception was so clear and final that he moaned; he would not find his way back. You've gone too far this time, you've *gone* too far . . .

As he whirled into oblivion, his body cooled and became numb; inert, like a log seized up and borne out skyward by a cyclone; he struggled to reach out, catch hold, grasp, grip, hang on, but he could not. He could not, he was made of wood, and there was nothing to hang on to, not even his own thought – thought shredding, drifting out of reach, like blowing spiderwebs. He was gone, g-o-n-e, *gone*, G-O-N-E, gone – and around again. The howling was in his head, and all about lay depthless silence. His screaming was ripped away before it left his mouth, and the mouth itself was far away, a huge papered hoop blown through and tattered by the gales. The air rushed past, too fast to breathe; his lungs sucked tight, shriveled like prunes, collapsed. He died.

Death came as a huge bounteous quiet, in the bosom of a high white cloud. The wood of his body softened, the knots loosened; he opened up, lay back, exhausted, mouth slack, eyes wide like the bald eyes of a corpse. He glimpsed a hard light lucid region of his mind like a lone comet, wandering far out across the long night of the universe.

At the end of his long night of uproar and hallucinations, Lewis Moon had a dream. He dreamed that he walked homeward up the bed of an empty river and out onto a blasted land of rusted earth and bones and blackened stumps and stunted metal, a countryside of war. In the sky of a far distance he saw a bird appear and vanish; but no matter how far he walked, the world was one mighty industrial ruin, a maze of gutted factories and poisoned ground under the gray sky. He came finally to a signpost, and the signpost had caught a fragile ray of rising sun. He ran toward it, stumbled, fell and ran again. The signpost pointed eastward, back toward the sun, and it read: NOWHERE.

Very tired, he turned back along his road, crossing the dead prairie. Though he had not noticed them on his outward journey, he now passed a series of signs all pointing eastward. Each was illuminated by a ray of sun, and each bore the same inscription: NOWHERE.

The terrible silence of the world made him move faster, and soon he saw, on the eastern horizon, the dark blur of a forest. He ran and trotted weakly, bewildered by the crashing of his feet upon the cinders. Another sign, and then another, pointed toward the wood.

As he drew near, the wood became a jungle, a maelstrom of pale boles and thickened fleshy leaves, shining and rubbery, of high, dark passages, and hanging forms, of parasites and strangler figs and obscene fruited shapes. But even here there was no sound, no sign of movement, not even a wind to stir the heavy leaves, sway the lianas; there was only the mighty hush of a dead universe.

He started forward, stopped, started again. Too frightened to go on, he turned around and saw what lay behind him; then he sat down on the road, and this time he wept.

When at last he lifted his eyes, he saw a signpost at the jungle edge; it was obscured by weeds and leaves and the tentacles of a liana, and at first he thought that its inscription was identical to all the rest. But this sign did not point anywhere, and as he drew near and stared at it he saw that its inscription was quite different. It read: NOW HERE.

Astonished, he ventured on into the darkness of the jungle. Soon he came to a kind of clearing cut off from the sky by a canopy of trees, a soft round space like an amphitheater, diffused with sepia light. Everything was soft and brownish, and the ground itself quaked beneath his feet, giving off a smell of fungus and decay. In the center of the clearing he strayed into a quagmire; very quickly he sank, too tired to struggle. But as he passed into the earth and the warm smells of its darkness, he was still breathing without effort, and soon he dropped gently into a kind of earthen vault. Though closed off from the sky, this cave was suffused by the same soft brownish light as in the clearing far above. Here was a second sign, which read: NOW HERE.

The passage through the soil had cleaned him of his clothes, and he was naked; as he stood there, small black spots appeared in pairs upon his skin. He pressed at them and discovered to his horror that the black spots were the tips of snail horns; at each touch a naked snail slid out through his skin and dropped to the cave floor. His hands flew wildly about his body, and the snails slid out and fell, until finally the earth at his bare feet was strewn with slimy writhings. Now, from the darkness near the wall, numbers of salamanders crept forward; each salamander grasped a snail behind its head and writhed in silent struggle with it, the soft bodies twitching back and forth in rhythm.

He backed toward one side of the room and fell into a tunnel. He ran along the tunnel, no longer afraid, for there was light ahead. He ran like a boy.

The tunnel emerged like a swallow's nest from the side of a high bank. Far below he saw a jungle clearing in a huge sunlight of the world's first morning, and in the clearing the Indians awaited him. Naked, he leaped into the radiant air, and fell toward them.

At Play in the Fields of the Lord, 1991

ACKNOWLEDGEMENTS

I would like to thank Vintage, in particular Susan Sandon for first suggesting I work on an anthology, Caroline Michel for having the faith that I would do so, and Arzu Tahsin for patiently enduring my demands and idiosyncrasies. Much of my own writing has relied on my columns for *Loaded*, and I am grateful for their permission to do this. I would also like to thank Crofton Black, Caroline Brown, Jamie Byng, Mike Jay, and Golly Marks for invaluable assistance in research, editing, and proofreading; Joe McNally, Paul Sieveking, James Oliver, Andy McConnell, The British Library, New York Public Library, Drugscope, Fitzhugh Ludlow Hypertext Collection, Schaffer Library for Drug Policy, Erowid Vaults and Lycaeum.org for the tracking down and loan of rare books. My greatest thanks have to be reserved for Mary Carson, the finest, most tenacious, and best researcher any writer could wish to have.

* * *

The editors and publishers gratefully acknowledge permission from the following to reprint stories or extracts from works in copyright. Every effort has been made to obtain necessary permissions with reference to copyright material. We apologise if inadvertently any sources remain unacknowledged.

STEVEN ABRAMS: from *The Book of Grass: An Anthology on Indian Hemp*, edited by George Andrews and Simon Vinkenoog (Peter Owen, 1967), reprinted by permission of Peter Owen Ltd, London; **M. AGEYEV :** from *Novel With Cocaine* (Penguin Classics, 1999); **LOUISA MAY ALCOTT:**

from 'Perilous Play' in *Tales of Hashish* by Andrew C. Kimmens (William Morrow, 1977); **SHANA ALEXANDER:** from *The Pizza Connection* (Weidenfeld & Nicolson, 1988); **NELSON ALGREN:** from *The Man With The Golden Arm* (Doubleday, 1949), reprinted by permission of Donadio & Olson, Literary Representatives; **JOHN ALLEGRO:** from *The Sacred Mushroom and the Cross* (Abacus, 1970); **STEWART LEE ALLEN:** from *The Devil's Cup* (Canongate Books, 2000), reprinted by permission of Canongate Books and Soho Press Inc.; **ANONYMOUS:** 'Beware my friend . . .' (poem found on the wall of a Jamaican café in Shepherd's Bush, London); 'Confessions of a middle-aged Ecstasy eater' from *The Guardian* (14 July 2001); 'The African Fang Legends' from *White Rabbit: A Psychedelic Reader*, edited by John Miller and Randall Koral (Chronicle Books, 1995); **HARRY ANSLINGER:** from *The Murderers* (Farrar, Straus & Cudahy, 1961); **ANTONIL:** from *Mama Coca* (Hassle Free Press, 1978); **HARRY ASHER:** 'They Split my Personality' from *Saturday Review* (1 June 1963); **BRIAN BARRITT:** from *The Road of Excess* (PSI Publishing, 1998), reprinted by permission of the author and the publisher; **WILLIAM BARTON:** from 'From A Dissertation on the Chymical Properties and Exhilarating Effects of Nitrous Oxide Gas' in *Mindscapes: An Anthology of Drug Writings*, edited by Antonio Melechi (Mono, 1998); **CHARLES BAUDELAIRE:** 'Be You Drunken!' from *The Idler's Companion* (1869); 'The Playground of the Seraphim', translated by Aleister Crowley, from *The Equinox*, Number 3 (1910); **JACK BEECHING:** from *The Chinese Opium Wars* (Harcourt Trade Publishers, 1977); **CHARLIE BEER:** 'Dave the Doorman', published by permission of the author; **BEZ:** from *Freaky Dancin'* (Pan Books, 1989); **ROBERT BINGHAM:** from *Lightning on the Sun* (Canongate Books, 2001), reprinted by permission of the publisher; **VICTOR BORCKIS:** from *With William Burroughs* (Fourth Estate, 1997); **JOHN G. BOURKE:** from *Scatological Rites of All Nations* (1891), reprinted in *Artificial Paradises: A Drugs Reader*, edited by Mike Jay (Penguin Books, 1999); **T.**

CORAGHESSAN BOYLE: from *Budding Prospects* (Granta Books, 1984); **GARNETT BRENNAN:** 'Marijuana Witchhunt' from *Shaman Woman, Mainline Lady: Women's Writings on the Drug Experience*, edited by Cynthia Palmer and Michael Horowitz (Quill Books, 1982), © Evergreen Review, 1967; **WILLIAM BURROUGHS:** from *Junky* (Penguin Books, 1977), and *The Naked Lunch* (Grove Press, 1959); **JAMES M. CAMPBELL:** from 'On the Religion of Hemp' (Indian Hemp Drugs Commission, 1893–4); **MORDECAI COOKE:** from *The Seven Sisters of Sleep* (James Blackwood, 1860); **ALEISTER CROWLEY:** from *Diary of a Drug Fiend* (Samuel Weiser, 1970), and *Magick: Part III: Magick in Theory and Practice* (Samuel Weiser, 1991); **GEZA CSATH:** 'The Surgeon' (1910) from *The Magician's Garden and Other Stories*, translated by Jascha Kessler and Charlotte Rogers (Columbia University Press, 1980); **DAILY MIRROR:** an article on marihuana; **RENE DAUMAL:** from *A Fundamental Experiment*, translated by Roger Shattuck (Hanuman Books, 1991); **ROBERT DAVIES:** from *Perfection She Dances* (Mainstream Publishing, 2001), reprinted by permission of the publisher; **MILES DAVIS:** from *The Autobiography* (Simon & Schuster, 1989); **HENRI DE MONFRIED:** from *Hashish* (Penguin Books, 1946); **CHARLES DICKENS:** from *The Mystery of Edwin Drood* (1870, unfinished); **ALEXANDRE DUMAS:** from *The Count of Monte Cristo* (1846), in *Tales of Hashish* by Andrew C. Kimmens (William Morrow, 1976); **ISABELLE EBERHARDT:** from *The Oblivion Seekers* (City Lights Books, 1972); **JOHNNY EDGECOMBE:** from *Calypso Train*, published by permission of the author; **MOHAMMED EL GUINDY:** 'Opium as an International Problem', an address given at the *Second International Opium Conference* (1924), from Schaffer Library for Drug Policy, California; **HAVELOCK ELLIS:** from 'Mescal: A New Artificial Paradise' (1898), reprinted in *The Hashish Club: An Anthology of Drug Literature* (Volume 1), edited by Peter Haining (Peter Owen, 1975), reprinted by permission of Peter Owen Ltd, London; **THE EQUINOX:** 'Testing Cannabis on

Dogs' from *The Equinox: The Review of Scientific Illuminism*, Volume 1, Number 1 (1909); **ANTONIO ESCOHOTADO**: from *A Brief History of Drugs* (Park Street Press, 1999), reprinted by permission of the publisher; **DAVID EVANS**: a speech in the House of Commons on drugs, from *Hansard* (17 January 1997); **LANRE FEHINTOLA**: from *Charlie Says . . . don't get high on your own supply: an urban memoir* (Scribner Books, 2000); **MARIA GOLIA**: from *Nile-Eyes*, © Maria Golia, 2000, published by permission of the author; **STEPHEN JAY GOULD**: from *Marihuana: The Forbidden Medicine* by Lester Grinspoon and James Bakalar. Revised & Expanded Edition (Yale University Press, 1997), reprinted by permission of the publisher; **NIALL GRIFFITHS**: from *Sheepshagger* (Jonathan Cape, 2001), reprinted by permission of the author; **LESTER GRINSPOON**: from *The Trial of Kerry Wiley* (Harvard Medical School); (with James B. Bakalar) from *Marihuana: The Forbidden Medicine*. Revised & Expanded Edition (Yale University Press, 1997), © 1997 by Yale University Press, reprinted by permission of the publisher; **CHARLIE HALL**: 'The Box' from *Disco Biscuits*, edited by Sarah Champion (Sceptre, 1997); **JAMES HAWES**: from *Dead Long Enough* (Vintage, 2001), reprinted by permission of The Random House Group Ltd; **SADEGH HEDAYAT**: from *The Blind Owl* (Canongate Books, 1997), reprinted by permission of the publisher; **HIGH ARCHIVES**: 'China Proposes Death to Drug Addicts – After 1937' from *Man Bites Man: The Scrapbook of an English Eccentric GEORGE IVES*, edited by Paul Sieveking (Penguin Books, 1981), © Jay Landesman, reprinted by permission of Jay Landesman; **JIM HOGSHIRE**: from *Pills-A-Go-Go: A Fiendish Investigation into Pill Marketing, Art, History and Consumption* (Feral House, 1999); **MICHAEL HOLLINGS-HEAD**: from *The Man who Turned on the World* (Blond & Briggs/New English Library, 1973); **JOHN HOPKINS**: from *Tangier Buzzless Flies* (Atheneum, 1972); **HASSAN MOHAMMED IBN-CHIRAZI**: from 'A Treatise on Hemp' (1300), reprinted in *Tales of Hashish* by Andrew C. Kimmens

(William Morrow, 1976); **JAMES GREY JACKSON**: from *An Account of the Empire of Marocco* (Frank Cass, 1968); **KING JAMES I**: from *Counterblast to Tobacco* (1604); **WILLIAM JAMES**: from *The Varieties of Religious Experience: A Study in Human Nature* (1902); **MIKE JAY**: from *Blue Tide: The Search for Soma* (Autonomedia, 1999), reprinted by permission of the author; **PHILIP JENKINS**: from *Synthetic Panics: The Symbolic Politics of Designer Drugs* (New York University Press, 1999) reprinted by permission of the publisher; **RODERICK KALBERER**: from *The Scam* (Coronet, 1995), reprinted by permission of the author and Hodder Headline Plc; **H. H. KANE**: from *The Curious Adventures of an Individual Who Indulged in a Few Pipefuls of the Narcotic Hemp* (1888), from Fitz Hugh Ludlow Memorial Library Hypertext Collection, San Francisco; **JULIAN KEELING**: from *Drugstore Cowboy* (The Idler, 1996), reprinted by permission of the publisher; **JONATHAN KELLY**: 'I Talk To Cows, You Know', published by permission of the author; **CARL KERENYI**: from *Dionysos* (Princeton University Press, 1976), © 1967 by Princeton University Press, reprinted by permission of the publisher; **MAREK KOHN**: from *Dope Girls: The Birth of the British Drug Underground* (Lawrence & Wishart, 1992); **GEORGE LANE**: from *Early Mongol Rule in 13th century Iran: a Persian Renaissance* (Curzon Press; forthcoming late 2002) reprinted by permission of the publisher; **PETER LAURIE**: from *Drugs* (Pelican Books, 1967); **JAMES LEE**: from *Underworld of the East* (Sampson, Low, Marston & Company, 1935); **MRS FRANK LESLIE**: from 'California: A Pleasure Trip from Gotham to the Golden Gate' (April, May, June 1877), from Fitz Hugh Ludlow Memorial Library Hypertext Collection; **JOHN LIGHTFOOT**: from *The Spanish Connection* (Blake Publishing, 1992), reprinted by permission of the publisher; **MEDLAR LUCAN & DURIAN GRAY**: from *The Decadent Gardener* (Dedalus Books, 1998), reprinted by permission of the publisher; **ROBERT LUND**: 'Mikey's Tale' (10 September 1997), reprinted by permission of the author; **ZOE LUND**: 'Cul de sac' from

Mobiles reprinted by permission of Robert Lund; **PETER MCDERMOTT**: 'Immaculate Injection', published by permission of the author; **TERENCE MCKENNA**: from *Food of the Gods* (Rider Books, 1992); **HANS MAIER**: from *Der Kokainismus* (1926), reprinted in *Cocaine* by Dominic Streatfield (Virgin Books, 2001); **PETER MATTHIESSEN**: from *At Play in the Fields of the Lord*, © 1966, reprinted by permission of Random House, Inc.; **CHRISTOPHER MAYHEW**: 'An Excursion out of Time' from *The Observer* (28 October 1956), reprinted by permission of the publisher; **JAMES MILLS**: from *The Underground Empire* (Doubleday, 1974); **SUSAN NADLER**: from 'The Butterfly Convention' in *Shaman Woman, Mainline Lady: Women's Writings and the Drug Experience*, edited by Cynthia Palmer and Michael Horowitz (Quill Books, 1982), © 1976 by Susan Nadler; **JEREMY NARBY**: from *The Cosmic Serpent: DNA and the Origins of Knowledge* (Gollancz, 1998); **R. K. NEWMAN**: 'Opium Smoking in Late Imperial China: A Reconsideration' from *Modern Asian Sudies*, 29:4 (1995), © Cambridge University Press, reprinted by permission of the publisher; **CHARLES NICHOLL**: from *The Fruit Palace* (Heinemann, 1985), reprinted by permission of David Higham Associates; **FRIEDRICH NIETZSCHE**: from *Twilight of the Idols*, translated by R. J. Hollingdale (Penguin Classics, 1990); **WILLIAM NOVAK**: from *High Culture* (Alfred A. Knopf, 1980), © 1980 by William Novak, reprinted by permission of Alfred A. Knopf, a division of Random House Inc; **BRIDGET O'CONNOR**: 'Heavy Petting' from *Intoxication: An Anthology of Stimulant-based writing*, edited by Toni Davidson (Serpent's Tail, 1998); **JASON PARKINSON**: 'Acid. The Journey through Living Room Walls', and 'Skateboards and Methadone', published by permission of the author; **JOHN BAPTISTA PORTA**: from 'Women are Made to cast Off Their Clothes and Go Naked' in *Wildest Dreams: An Anthology of Drug-Related Literature*, edited by Richard Rudgley (Little, Brown & Company, 1999) reprinted by permission of Richard Rudgley; **DAWN F. ROONEY**: from *Betel Chewing Traditions in South-East Asia* (Oxford

ACKNOWLEDGEMENTS

University Press, 1993); **HARVEY ROTTENBERG:** from 'Planted, Burnt, and Busted' from *Getting Busted*, edited by Ross Firestone (Penguin Books, 1972); **KEVIN RUSHBY:** from *Eating the Flowers of Paradise* (Flamingo, 1999); **ROBERT SABBAG:** from *Smokescreen* (Canongate Books; forthcoming February 2002), and *Snowblind* (Canongate Books, 1998), reprinted by permission of the publisher; **KEVIN SAMPSON:** from *Outlaws* (Jonathan Cape, 2001), reprinted by permission of The Random House Group Ltd and Peters Fraser & Dunlop Group Ltd on behalf of the author; **R. E. SCHULTES & R. RAFFAUF:** from *Vine of the Soul* (Synergetic Press, 1992); **ALEXANDER & ANN SHULGIN:** from *Pihkal: A Chemical Love Story* (Transform Press, 1991), and *Tihkal: The Continuation* (Transform Press, 1997), reprinted by permission of the authors; **RONALD K. SIEGEL:** from *Intoxication: Life in Pursuit of Artificial Paradise* (E. P. Dutton, 1989); **TIM MACKINTOSH SMITH:** from *Yemen: Travels in Dictionary Land* (Picador, 1999); **TIM SOUTHWELL:** from *Getting Away With It* (Ebury Press, 2001), reprinted by permission of The Random House Group Ltd; **ROBERT LOUIS STEVENSON:** from *The Strange Case of Dr Jekyll and Mr Hyde* (1886); **DOMINIC STREATFIELD:** from *Cocaine* (Virgin Books, 2001), reprinted by permission of the publisher; **ROBERT SVOBODA:** from *Aghora, At the Left Hand of God* (Brotherhood of Life, 1986), reprinted by permission of the publisher; **THOMAS SZASZ:** from *Ceremonial Chemistry* (Anchor/Doubleday, 1974); **BAYARD TAYLOR:** from 'Hasheesh' in *White Rabbit: A Psychedelic Reader*, edited by John Miller and Randall Koral (Chronicle Books, 1995); **DEREK TAYLOR:** from *It Was Twenty Years Ago Today* (Simon & Schuster, 1987) reprinted by permission of Transworld publishers; **HUNTER S. THOMPSON:** from *Fear and Loathing in Las Vegas* (Paladin, 1972); **OLAF TYARANSEN:** from *The Story of O* (Hot Press Books, 2000), reprinted by permission of the publisher; **UNITED STATES SUPREME COURT:** Decision in the Case of Terrell Don Hutto v Roger Trenton Davis (11

January 1982); **STUART WALTON:** from *Out Of It* (Hamish Hamilton, 2001); **EDWARD HUNTINGTON WILLIAMS:** 'Negro Cocaine "Fiends" New Southern Menace' in *New York Times* (8 February 1914), from Schaffer Library of Drug Policy, California; **ELIZABETH WURTZEL:** from *Prozac Nation* (Quartet Books, 1996), reprinted by permission of the publisher.

INDEX

HOWARD MARKS

MR NICE

An Autobiography

**'A folk legend . . . Howard Marks has huge charisma. He
sounds like Richard Burton and looks like a Rolling Stone'**
Daily Mail

During the mid-1080s Howard Marks had forty-three aliases,
eighty-nine phone lines and owned twenty-five companies
trading throughout the world.

At the height of his career he was smuggling consignments of up
to thirty tons of marijuana, and had contact with organisations
as diverse as MI6, the CIA, the IRA and the Mafia. Following a
worldwide operation by the Drug Enforcement Agency, he was
busted and sentenced to twenty-five years in prison at Terre
Haute Penitentiary, Indiana. He was released in April 1995 after
serving seven years of his sentence. Told with humour, charm
and candour, *Mr Nice* is his own extraordinary story.

'Frequently hilarious, occasionally sad, and often surreal' *GQ*

'A man who makes Peter Pan look like a geriatric with sleeping
sickness' *Loaded*

'Marks weaves a fascinating story spiced with brilliant details,
far stranger than fiction' *FHM Magazine*

VINTAGE